Library of
Davidson College

An Anthology
of Chancery English

AN **Anthology** OF **Chancery English**

JOHN H. FISHER

MALCOLM RICHARDSON

JANE L. FISHER

The University of Tennessee Press

Knoxville

Copyright © 1984
by The University of Tennessee Press / Knoxville.
Manufactured in the United States of America.
All Rights Reserved.

The paper in this book meets the guidelines for permanence and durability of the Committee on Production Guidelines for Longevity of the Council on Library Resources. Binding materials have been chosen for durability.

Library of Congress Cataloging in Publication Data

Fisher, John H.
An anthology of Chancery English.
Includes bibliographical references and index.
1. English language—Middle English, 1100-1500—Texts. 2. English language—Middle English, 1100-1500—Grammar. 3. Great Britain—History—Henry V, 1413-1422—Sources. 4. Great Britain—Politics and government—1399-1485. 5. Great Britain—Court and courtiers—Language. I. Richardson, Malcolm, 1947-
II. Fisher, Jane L. III. Title.
PE505.F5 1984 427'.02 84-3516
ISBN 0-87049-433-3 (alk. paper)

Contents

Preface ix
Introduction xi
The Chancery Hand.. 3
The Signet Letters of Henry V (Documents 1-105) 5
Later Signet and Privy Seal Papers (Documents 106-160) 17
Proceedings of Parliament (Documents 161-232) 20
Indentures (Documents 233-241) 25
Orthography 26
    Phonetic Spellings 29
    Variation of Unaccented e/i/o/u 31
    Prefixes... 33
    Suffixes... 34
    French Words and Spellings........................... 34
    Dialectal Spellings 35
Vocabulary... 36
Morphology... 38
    Articles... 38
    Nouns—Plurals.. 39
    Nouns—Genitive/Possessive 40
    Adjectives... 41
    Pronouns 42
    Verbs.. 45
    Adverbs 49
    Prepositions and Conjunctions 49
    Negation... 50

Notes 52
Collations of Original Petitions with Enrollments 63
List of Documents 67

The Documents 77
    Editorial Principles and Works Cited 79
    The Signet Letters of Henry V (Documents 1-105) 84
    Later Signet and Privy Seal Papers (Documents 106-160) 147
    Proceedings of Parliament (Documents 161-232) 194
    Indentures (Documents 233-241) 294

Glossary of Forms 305
Index of Names 404

Plates

Plate I. Letter of Charles V, 22 October 1366. *following page xvii*
Arch. nat., K49, no. 14.
Plate II. Document 1. Exemplar (from the Signet of
Henry V?). PRO C81/1326/36.
Plate III. Document 57. Signet letter of Henry V
by Shiryngton. B.L. Cotton Galba B.I, fol. 157.
Plate IV. Document 46. Signet letter of Henry V
in Toly's hand. B.L. Cotton Julius B.VI, fol. 97 (35)
Plate V. Document 70. Autograph draft by Henry V?
B.L. Cotton Vespasian F.III, fol. 8.
Plate VI. Document 201. Petition concerning the rape
of Isabell Boteler. PRO SC8/27/1305.

Preface

This book has been an adventure in autography. It has been composed to the stage of camera copy in the study of John and Jane Fisher, with the pains and pleasures attendant upon such total control. In 1975-76 John and Jane Fisher spent the winter turning over the velums in the Public Record Office and securing photocopies of the earliest Chancery records in English. They returned to Knoxville and began transcribing them in the summer of 1976. That fall Malcolm Richardson began a dissertation on the influence of Henry V on the development of the official language, and in the summer of 1977 he travelled to the PRO to continue collecting copies of the Signet letters of Henry V, which he transcribed in 1977-78. As these materials were transcribed, Jane Fisher entered them in the DECsystem 10 at the University of Tennessee, and John Fisher, with the assistance of Charles Reese, printed them out through paper tape on a Compugraphic ACM 9000.

In the winter of 1980 the Fishers returned to London where, with the assistance of a professional record searcher, they read the printout against the original manuscripts. During the summer of 1981, with the assistance of Charles Boyd of the University of Tennessee Computer Center, the 70,000 words of text were sorted into a concordance. This massive pile of paper was conveyed to Malcolm Richardson to be converted into the glossary of forms and the index of names, while John Fisher brooded over the text and wrote the introduction. In 1982-83 Jane Fisher keyboarded the glossary and the introduction. In the meanwhile the Graphic Arts Service of the University of Tennessee had graduated from the paper tape ACM 9000 to the electronic MCS 20/22. Vivien Goff of the Computer Center and Pandora Riggs of Graphic Arts worked out new programs to allow the computer to set type on the new Compugraphic via an Osborne word processor. The result by the fall of 1983 was camera copy for the University of Tennessee Press. The cooperation of the staffs of the University of Tennessee Computer Center, the Graphic Arts Service, and the University Press has been beyond the call of duty. Jim Billingsley, Design and Production Director of the Press, to whom this material has come in bits and pieces over the years, has demonstrated unfailing sympathy and forbearance. To all concerned, we express our heartfelt thanks.

Without much encouragement and support the project would never have come to fruition. In the early stages, John Fisher consulted with Norman Davis, Angus McIntosh, and Michael Samuels about materials to be searched and methods of presentation. Norman Davis was kind enough to read the text proper after it was printed out the first time and made many helpful suggestions. Thomas Cable read the entire manuscript for the University of Tennessee Press and likewise caught errors and made useful suggestions. Chadwick Hilton and Rose Norman helped with the proof-reading. But the final responsibility rests upon the Fishers and Malcolm Richardson. We have checked and proofed to exhaustion; still no one could be more conscious than we of the imperfections in the final product.

The Fishers' initial collection of material in 1975-76 was supported by a fellowship from the National Endowment for the Humanities. Their trip back to read proof was supported by a travel grant from the John C. Hodges Better English Fund of the English Department of the University of Tennessee. Malcolm Richardson's first trip to collect the Signet letters was likewise supported by a Hodges travel grant, while two subsequent trips to collect further materials and to read proof were funded by stipends from the National Endowment for the Humanities (1979) and from the American Council of Learned Societies (1982). All of the computer costs were borne by the Hodges Better English Fund. Joseph Trahern, Department Head, and Wanda Giles, Office Supervisor, have been constantly supportive in handling the administrative detail.

Transcripts of documents 14, 43, 46, 57, 69, 70, 112, 116, 122, and 159, and reproductions of the originals of 46, 57, and 70 appear by permission of the Keeper of Manuscripts and Head of the Photographic Services of the British Library. Transcripts of all the other documents and reproductions of the originals of 1 and 201 appear by permission of the Controller of H. M. Stationary Office.

J. H. F.
M. R.
J. L. F.

22 September 1983

Introduction

This anthology is a collection of examples of the earliest use of English for official writing, transcribed from the original membranes in the Public Record Office and the British Library. The first item is an exemplar, perhaps from the Signet of Henry V. Items 2-105 are correspondence from the Signet Office of Henry V from the time he embarked for France in August 1417 until his death in August 1422. Items 106-109 are later Signet letters, 1434-1455. Items 110-160 are Privy Seal and related correspondence, 1408-1455. Items 161-232 are petitions to the King, Parliament, and Chancery, and actions on these petitions, 1388-1455. Items 233-241 are non-Chancery indentures, 1384-1462, printed for comparison.

The collection is intended to complement R. W. Chambers and Marjorie Daunt's *A Book of London English, 1384-1425* (1931). Chambers and Daunt recognized that their records were local: "We hope that this collection of seventy-five documents, though it will doubtless be subsequently enlarged, affords in the meantime good evidence as to what was current London English between 1384 and 1425." But, they added, "this is, of course, only part of a much bigger question—the question of what was recognized as standard English in the later Middle Ages. What is wanted is a collection of all the official documents in the English tongue, from the time of the Conqueror to that of Henry VI." This anthology is intended as a first step toward providing such a collection.[1]

The materials are deliberately random since, like those in Chambers and Daunt, they are intended to illustrate the general drift of the written language toward uniformity rather than the practice of individual scribes. Only in the Signet of Henry V has individual usage been distinguished, and even there it reveals more about the uniformity of the office practice than about the individuality of the scribes. Of the

103 Signet letters of Henry V, 91 are here printed for the first time.[2] Of the 50 Privy Seal documents, 46 are printed for the first time.[3] Of the 72 Parliamentary and Chancery documents, 20 are printed for the first time.[4] None of the nine indentures has been printed before. Although the earlier transcriptions of those documents that have been printed are in the main accurate, they have always been recapitalized and repunctuated, and there has been some normalization of spelling, as i/j, u/v, z/ȝ and so forth. For purposes of linguistic study, our transcriptions have followed the originals as closely as our typography would allow. The features we have not been able to reproduce are the crossed letters, ꝉ, ħ, ꝑ, etc., and the final flourishes, ñ, ğ, etc., which are preserved in the typography of Chambers and Daunt. Where such marks represent abbreviations, they have been expanded in italics, but in the documents we have examined many of the marks appear to be totally without function. The glossary lists all forms of each word in the corpus by office, date, and frequency.

We follow M. L. Samuels in calling the official written English of the first half of the 15th century "Chancery English"[5] although it emanated from at least four offices, Signet, Privy Seal, Parliament, and the emerging Court of Chancery itself. The generalized term is valid in an historical sense. By the end of the 15th century the term "Chancery" had come to be restricted to the royal courts of law, but until the departmentalization of the national bureaucracy into various offices, which began in the reign of Henry VII, Chancery comprised virtually all of the national bureaucracy except for the closely allied Exchequer. Thomas Frederick Tout, who made a life-time study of the workings of Chancery and its affiliated offices, begins his *Chapters in The Administrative History of Mediaeval England* by quoting Palgrave's observation that "Chancery was the Secretariat of State in all departments of late medieval government."[6]

As Tout and others have pointed out, all medieval administration grew out of the household of the King.[7] The ruler entrusted the administration of his dominions to his household servants. Chancery grew out of the little office connected with the chancel, or chapel, where the chaplains of the court occupied themselves between divine services in writing the King's letters. In an age when writing was a rare art with laymen—even with kings—executives did not authenticate their letters by signing them, but by affixing their seals. So the most responsible of the chaplains was entrusted with the King's seal and inevitably came to be trusted with the responsibility for composing and authenticating the royal correspondence. As the royal administration grew more complex, the confidential clerk who handled the King's correspondence became the most trusted of his ministers, in effect prime minister, and to discharge his work he had to gather about him a staff of skilled assistants. These, in turn, would look to the Chancellor rather than to the King as their master, and so the household of the Chancellor would begin to separate itself from the royal household at large. As the tasks of the Chancellor's clerks became more technical, the clerks became more indispensable. Orderly functioning of government services could be maintained only by a continuing staff which carried on its activities little affected by the fluctuations of kings and ministers. Hence, the household of the Chancellor would become what it was by the middle of the 13th century, the household of Chancery, where the continuity of the office was emphasized rather than the importance of the person ruling over it at any given time.

Until the 14th century there was little association between Chancery and Westminster. Like the rest of his household, Chancery followed the King in his peregrinations about the country, and correspondence up to this time may be dated from York, Winchester, Hereford, or wherever the court happened to pause (as the King's personal correspondence—the Signet correspondence—continued to be throughout the 15th century). It is important to observe that in its movement about the country, the court as a whole must have reinforced the impression of an official class dialect, in contrast to the regional dialects with which it came in contact. For two centuries this court dialect was spoken French and written Latin; after 1300 it gradually became spoken English and written French. The English spoken in court then and for a long time afterward was quite varied in pronunciation and structure. But written Latin had been standardized in classical times, and by the 13th century written French had begun to be standardized in form and to achieve the lucid idiom that English prose was not to achieve until the 16th century. Increasingly as the 14th century progressed, this Latin and French was written by clerks whose first language was English. Latin was the essential subject in school, but the acquisition of French was more informal, and by the end of the century we have Chaucer's satire on the French of the Prioress, Gower's apologies for his own (quite acceptable) French, and the errors in legal briefs which betoken Englishmen trying to compose in a foreign language.[8] By 1400 the use of English in speaking and Latin and French in administrative writing had established a clear dichotomy between colloquial speech and the official written language, which must have made it easier to create an artificial written standard independent of the spoken dialects when the royal clerks began to use English for their official writing after 1417.

The Hundred Years War between England and France influenced

the evolution of Chancery and the process by which Chancery English began to be standardized. When Edward III was absent from the realm, Chancery was localized in Westminster. By 1345 the recognized "place" of Chancery was "the south-west angle of Westminster Hall where said Chancellor commonly sits at the marble table among the clerks of Chancery discharging the duties of his office."[9] The last full-scale removal from Westminster was at the time of Richard II's quarrel with London in 1392-93. When Chancery returned from York to Westminster in 1393, it was spared the inconvenience of working in one corner of Westminster Hall while the two benches were sitting in the other corners of the same hall. It was now assigned "a place newly appointed in the white hall of Westminster for the office and session of the chancellor and the clerks of chancery."[10]

This move represented the beginning of the division between the administrative and judicial functions of Chancery. A second recognition of the division occurred about the same time. In 1232 Henry III had assigned 70 marks a year for the support of a *domus conversorum*, a house for converted Jews, to be created in what is now Chancery Lane. Never in great demand, this house fell into almost complete desuetude after the Jews were banished from England in 1290. So the Chancellor began to use it as a residence for the Chancery clerks when the court was in Westminster. The rolls were stored for safekeeping in the Tower of London, but during the 14th century the *domus conversorum* became the place in and near which the clerks lived and copied the new rolls. Several Keepers of the Rolls during the 14th century were also named keepers of the *domus conversorum*, and finally in 1377 the *domus* was officially deeded to the Keeper of the Rolls. Henceforward the *domus* was the recognized center of Chancery business, called the Rolls Chapel and (with the adjacent buildings) the Rolls House until the Public Record Office was built on the same site between 1845 and 1895.[11]

In addition to offices separate from the royal household, the 14th and 15th centuries saw the expansion of the work of government into several offices. From the time of the Magna Carta onwards, the rivalry between the king and the barons for the control of government had modified the character of the chancellorship so that by the 14th century the Chancellor had become nearly as much an agent of the magnates as the chief minister of the crown. From this time on we have the history of kings attempting to create new personal offices for administration, and these offices being absorbed one after another into the official bureaucracy. The Chancellor and the Great Seal were the King's personal instruments until they were formalized during the bad reigns of King John and Henry III. The Wardrobe and Privy Seal were then created as personal offices and so continued until Privy Seal began to be used as the secretariat for the King's Council in the bad rule of Edward II. Then the Signet was devised as the King's personal secretariat until it declined in importance during the infancy of Henry VI. The King's Secretary was a personal officer until he, too, was formalized into Secretary of State in the time of Henry VIII. Although these were separate offices, there was movement of clerks from one office to another.[12] V. H. Galbraith has remarked that Chancery, Privy Seal, and Signet "form a single, great administrative machine for the discharge of routine business [although] the precise way in which this complicated system worked is imperfectly known."[13]

It would appear that the Signet office of Henry V was most influential in establishing the conventions of Chancery Standard. There is some evidence of the emergence of linguistic nationalism before this time in the argument repeatedly used to whip up Parliamentary support for the continuing war with France, that a French victory would annihilate the English language. This argument appears in the Latin account of the opening address to Parliament in 1295, and in the French accounts of opening addresses in 1344, 1346, and 1376.[14] In 1362 the clerks admit for the first time that Parliament was addressed in English.[15] This may be because this was the Parliament that enacted the statute that all court proceedings must be conducted in English because the litigants could not understand French.[16] Although this statute was not enforced, and the common law courts continued to plead in French down to 1731, the court of Chancery from its inception in 1394 conducted most of its proceedings in English. The *Rotuli Parliamentorum* report that the parliaments of 1363, 1364, and 1381 were opened in English. How many in between or afterwards were addressed in English we do not know because the clerks did not trouble to include the phrase "dit en Engleis."[17]

But until the death of Henry V there was no concerted movement towards the adoption of English for government or business. Before 1422 there are some seventy English entries in the London civic documents, printed in Chambers and Daunt and elsewhere, and nineteen in the *Rotuli Parliamentorum*. These show little uniformity in orthography or morphology and many continue to exhibit features of regional dialect.[18] The earliest group of official documents in English in uniform style and language are the English Signet letters of Henry V. Until his second invasion of France in August 1417, Henry's correspondence had been in French, but from August 1417 until his death in August 1422 nearly all of it is in English. The reasons for the change can only be inferred. No document has come to light expressing his views or prescribing the use of English, but there is evidence of his sensitivity to linguistic nationalism. One of the first acts of his reign was an assent, in English, to a petition by the Commons that statutes be made without altering the words of the petitions on which they were based.[19] In treating with the French and Burgundians, his ambassadors insisted on using Latin rather than French. At the Council of Constance, Henry's ambassadors demanded to know "whether nation be understood as a people marked off from others by blood relationships and habit of unity or by peculiarities of language (the most sure and positive sign and essence of a nation in divine and human law)." Hence, it may be inferred that upon his invasion of France in 1417, he found it expedient to adopt English to secure popular support for his military expedition.[20]

Immediately after Henry's death, English entries in the *Rotuli Parliamentorum* become more frequent, and by 1450 they are the rule.[21] From the year of Henry's death (1422) comes the familiar statement by the Brewer's Guild as to why they were changing their record-keeping to English:

> Whereas our mother-tongue, to wit the English tongue, hath in modern days begun to be honorably enlarged and adorned, for that our most excellent lord, King Henry V, hath in his letters missive and divers affairs touching his own person, more willingly chosen to declare the secrets of his will, and for the better understanding of his people, hath with a diligent mind procured the common idiom (setting aside others) to be commended by the exercise of writing: and there are many of our craft of Brewers who have the knowledge of writing and reading in the said English idiom, but in others, to wit, the Latin and French, before these times used, they do not in any wise understand. For which causes with many others, it being considered how that the greater part of the Lords and trusty Commons have begun to make their matters to be noted down in our mother tongue, so we also in our craft, following in some manner their steps, have decreed to commit to memory the needful things which concern us. . . .

The original of this statement by William Porland, the Brewers' clerk, is in Latin; the translation is from the Brewers' Abstract Book. The passage nicely illustrates the complementary roles of Signet and Chancery. "Letters missive" refers to the Signet letters of Henry V; the "matters" of the Lords and trusty Commons refers to the proceedings of Parliament and of Chancery.[22]

Over the next quarter of a century the King's Council, Parliament,

Chancery, municipalities, guilds, and private individuals turned to writing in English.[23] It remains to trace the relationship between the written language of Signet and Chancery, and the written language of the corporations and guilds, the scriveners, and the early printers. But such a study cannot be made without a basis for comparison. This collection of texts is intended to provide the materials for such a comparison.[24]

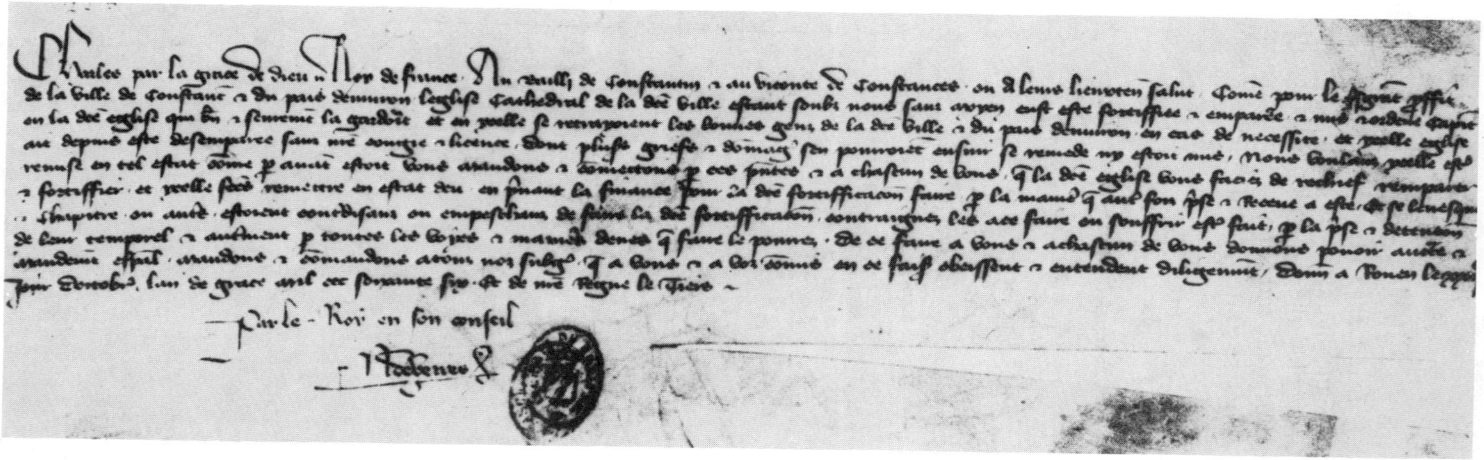

Plate I. Letter of Charles V, 22 October 1366. Arch. nat., K49, no. 14/. (90%)

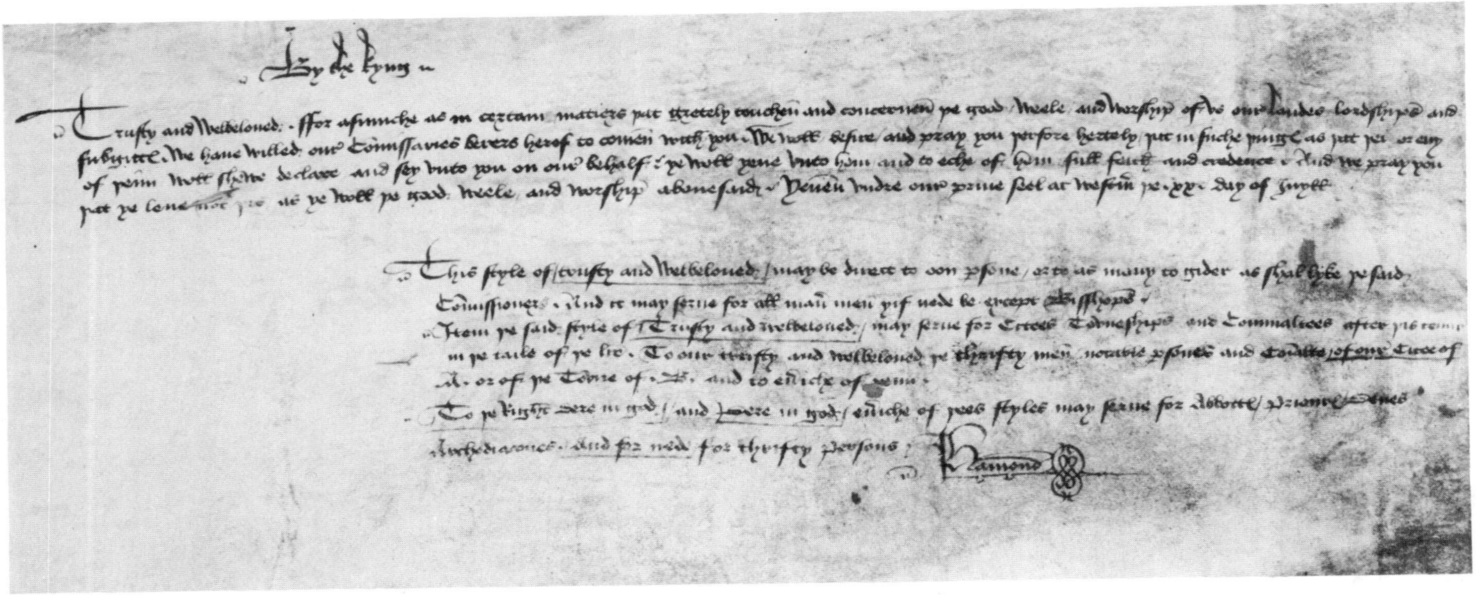
By þe kyng

Trusty and welbeloued. ffor asmuche as in certain maters þat gretely touchen and concernen þe good weele and worship of vs our landes lordships and subgittes. We haue willed our Commissaries berers herof to comen with you. We wol desire and pray you þerfore hertely þat in suche þinges as þat þei or any of þeim wol shewe declare and sey vnto you on our behalf ye wol yeue vnto hem and to eche of hem full feith and credence. And we pray you þat ye leue not [illegible] as ye wol þe good weele and worship abouesaid. Yeuen vnder our priue seel at Westm' þe .xx. day of Juyll

This style of trusty and welbeloued may be direct to oon persone or to as many togider as shal like þe said Commissioners. And it may serue for all man men yif nede be except Bisshopes.

Item þe said style of Trusty and welbeloued may serue for Citees Townships and Communaltees after þis forme in þe taile of þe lre. To our trusty and welbeloued þe thrifty men notable persones and Comunaltee of our Citee of M. or of þe Towne of .B. and to eche of hem.

To þe right dere in god and dere in god eche of þees styles may serue for Abbottes Priours Denes Archediacones. And for nede for thrifty persons.

Hamond

Plate II. Document 1. Exemplar (from the Signet of Henry V?). PRO C81/1326/36. (79%)

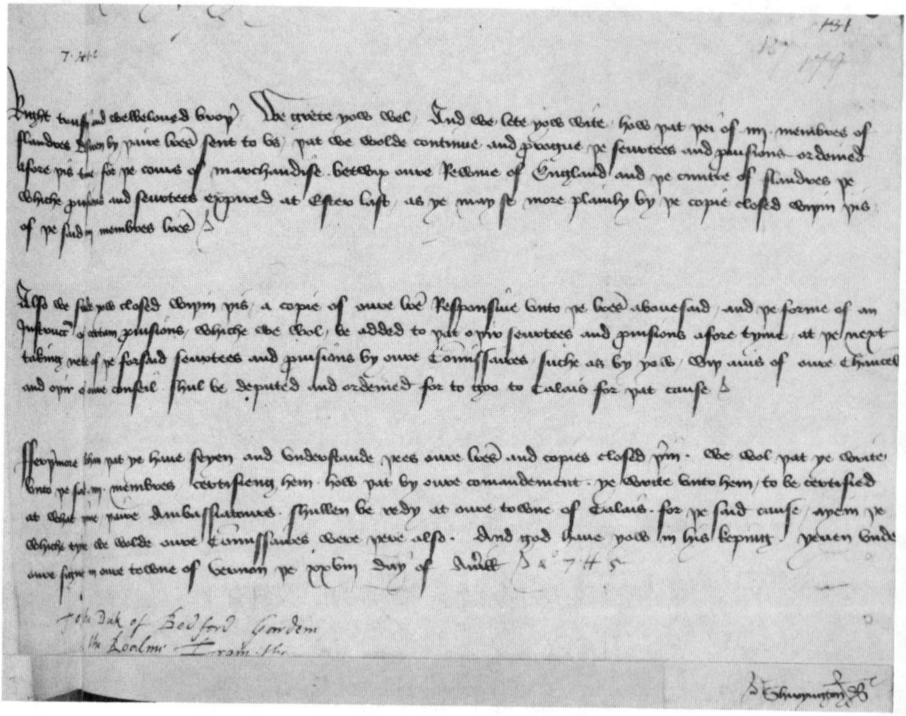

Right trusty and welbeloved brother We grete yow wel And we lete yow wite how þat þe iiij membres of
Flandres whiche by thaire lettres sent to us þat we wolde continue and prolongue þe sewrtees and pensions ordeined
afore þis tyme for þe cours of marchandise bitwix oure Reaume of England and þe contree of Flandres þe
whiche pensions and sewrtees expired at Ester last as ye may se more plainly by þe copie closed withyn þis
of þe said iiij membres lettres

Also we sende yow closed withyn þis a copie of oure lettre Responsive unto þe lettre abovesaid and þe forme of an
Instrument of certain pensions whiche we wol be added to þat oþer sewrtees and pensions afore tyme at þe next
taking veue of þe forsaid sewrtees and pensions by oure Commissaires suche as by yow brother and of oure chauncel
and oþer of oure conseil shul be deputed and ordeined for to goo to Calais for þat cause

ffurthermore whan þat ye have seyen and understande thees oure lettres and copies closed þerin we wol þat ye write
unto þe said iiij membres certifieng hem how þat by oure comandement ye write unto hem to be certified
at what tyme thaire Ambassiatours shullen be redy at oure towne of Calais for þe said cause ayein þe
whiche tyme we wolde oure Commissaires were þere also And god have yow in his keping Yeven under
oure signet in oure towne of Vernon þe xxvij day of Averill

To the Duk of Bedford Gardein

S Shiryngton

Plate III. Document 57. Signet letter of Henry V by Shiryngton. B.L. Cotton Galba B.I, fol. 157. (89%)

Hen. R.   Br[other] kyng   Britannia:

Right trusty and welbeloued Brother, We write now asel And as we suppose It is not out of yo[ur]
Remembrance in what wyse and sorte We haue shewed yow by oure last p[er] good and hasty reparacon and restitucion
were ordened and made at al tymes If suche attemptates be suyned be made by other p[ar]ties amonge
ye treuwes taken betwene us and oure Brother ye Duc of Britaigne, And not withstanding oure said last
swete complaynte made and sent vnto us be no faulte of reparaon and restitucion If suche attemptates
as be made by certain of oure subiettes and liege[s], as ye may understande by a supplicacon sent to us be oure said
Suc[cesso]r, whose supplicacon we send to you also by bring pr[e]sent bere he to haue ye more plume knowlache
of ye mat[ter]e There for we eest and charge yow yat ye wille to passe ovur thaunce[ll] to haue knowlache of ye
same supplicacon, and yat yow we shal yat ye do tende to us in al hast at yo[ur] p[er]sonnete y[a]t ben oure
trusty counseiller in ye supplicacon abouesaid And yat als in alle other knaulegid make ye do ordeyne
so hasty and iuste Remede reparacon and regracon upon such attemptates don by oure subiettes in coroborarion
of oure treuwes yat womun haue cause hireafter to complayne in suche wyse as thai soun for defaute of
right doyng into the cause to write to yow alwayes as don for suche cause, confidez ye gret
occupacon yat we haue otherwyse And we haue yow in his keping wryten und[er] oure signet in oure hoste
afor Roan ye xvije day of Novembre

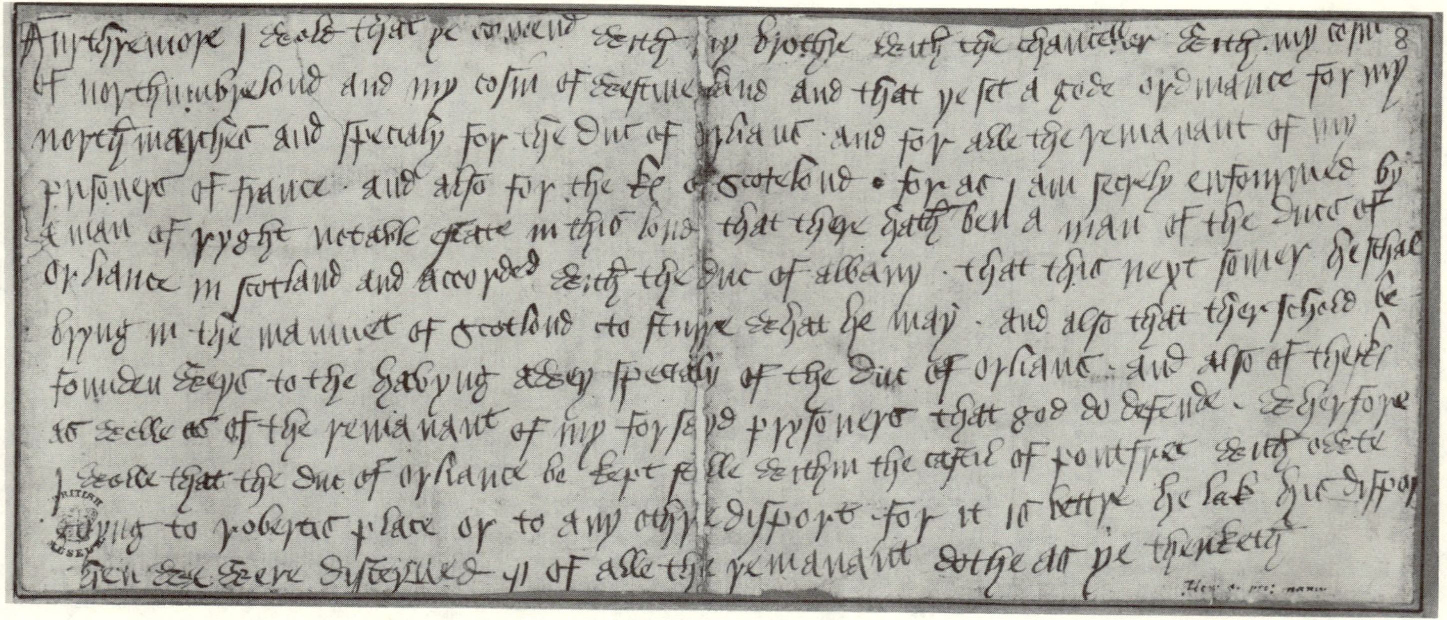

Furthermore I wolde that ye comend with my brother, with the chanceller, with my cosin 8
of northumbrelond and my cosin of westmerland and that ye set a gode ordinance for my
north marches and specialy for the duc of orliance and for alle the remanant of my
prisoners of france and also for the K. of scotelond. for as I am secrely enfourmed by
a man of ryght notable estate in this lond that there hath ben a man of the duc of
orliance in scotland and accorded with the duc of albany that this next somer he shal
bryng in the mawmet of scotlond to sturre what he may. and also that ther scholde be
foundon weyes to the havyng awey specialy of the duc of orliance and also of the K.
as welle as of the remanant of my forsayd prisoners that god do defende. wherfore
I wolde that the duc of orliance be kept stille withyn the castil of pontfret with owte
goyng to robertis place or to any other disport for it is better he lak his disport
then we were disceyved. of alle the remanant dothe as ye thenketh

Plate V. Document 70. Autograph draft by Henry V? B.L. Cotton Vespasian F.III, fol. 8. (95%)

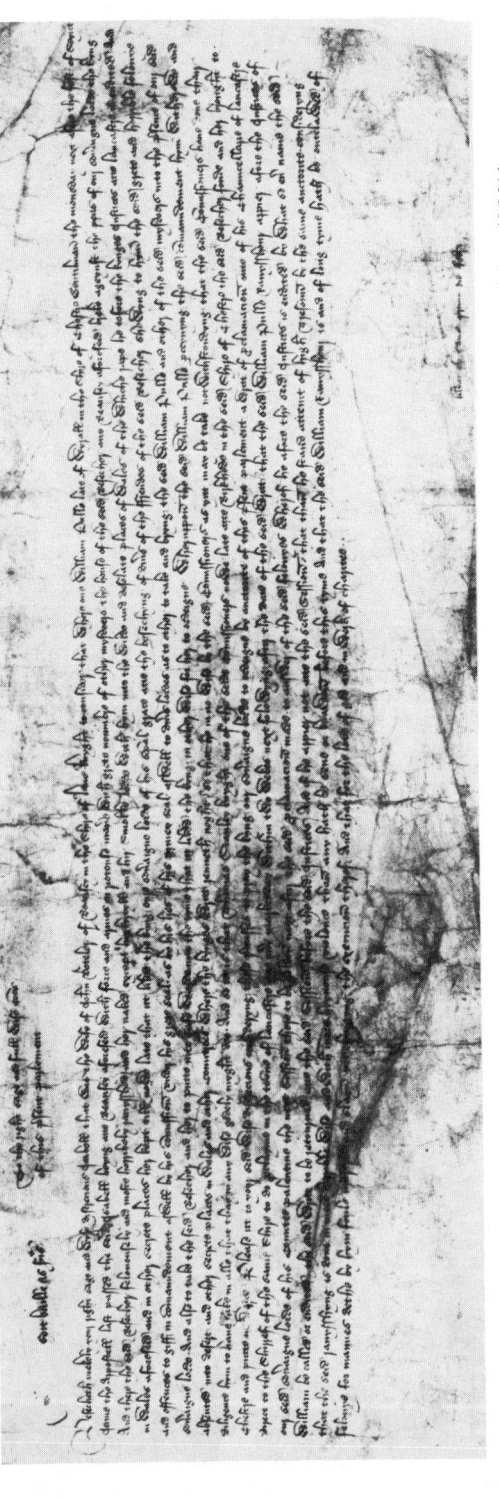

Plate VI. Document 201. Petition concerning the rape of Isabell Boteler. PRO SC8/27/1305. (88%)

An Anthology
of Chancery English

THE CHANCERY HAND

The Chancery hand in which most of the documents in this anthology are written is a form of an international business hand originating in the Italian chancelleries in the 13th century, spreading to France early in the 14th, and to England after 1350. It has been suggested that it was imported by the English scribes of the Privy Seal Office of the Black Prince. In England, it merged with the business script that had developed in the 13th century.[1] This native cursive has usually been called "court hand" after the guild of "scriptores litere curiales" first mentioned in London in 1357.[2] As L. C. Hector points out, the term "court hand" meant merely the cursive script, characterized by much ligation of letters, used to write business transactions, in contrast to the formal book hand (textura) in which the strokes were executed separately. Court hand embraces but is not restricted to scripts written in the courts of justice. This hand, which M. B. Parkes has renamed anglicana,[3] is characterized by a two-compartment *a* with an upper lobe rising above the line, a two-compartment *g*, long *r* with a stem descending below the line, and a short *s* in which the larger lower loop often descends slightly below the line. The duct of the script is vertical, with little contrast between broad and narrow strokes.

In the second half of the 14th century this court or anglicana hand was modified by the continental business hand. As Parkes observes, the most important difference between the new script, which he calls secretary but which we shall refer to as Chancery, and the traditional court hand is that the duct of Chancery hand is more fluent, tending to slant towards the right, with sharp contrast between broad and fine strokes caused by a different way of cutting and holding the pen. The smooth curves of court hand tend to be replaced by angular, broken strokes, and some letters in Chancery hand are formed differently: *a* with a single compartment, *g* with a tail, *r* shaped like 2, and *s* with its modern proportions. The more fluent duct and the simpler forms of some of the letters made Chancery somewhat easier to write than court hand.[4]

The indebtedness of the English Chancery hand to the French may be seen by comparing the 1366 letter by Charles V (Plate I)[5] with the exemplar by Hammond (Plate II; item no. 1 in this anthology), the signed letter by Henry's Signet clerk Robert Shiryngton (Plate III, no. 57), and the one probably by William Toly (Plate IV, no. 46). The contrast between these set professional hands and a non-professional hand may be seen in the draft possibly by Henry himself (Plate V, no. 70). Plate VI (much reduced) shows the Chancery hand in a 1437 petition to Parliament (no. 201). Plate IV (to take the clearest example) shows the continental forms of *a, g, r,* and *s,* and the slanted contrastive duct. These are all features of the French text of Plate I. The large capitals beginning the first lines of Plates II, III, and IV are somewhat like those of Plate I, but there are much closer parallels in some of the other manuscripts. By contrast, the non-Chancery script of Plate V shows a less fluent duct than the professional pieces, along with the anglicana forms of *a, g, r,* and *s* (as in *Scotland, accorded,* line 4).

Mastery of the official hand was one of the qualifications for professional employment as a Chancery clerk. No records of examinations survive from the 15th century, but the Cursitors Admission Roll, PRO C220/15/8, extending from 1578 to 1661, contains records of examinations whose form varies hardly at all over the 83 years. First a problem is set by the applicant in Chancery cursive, then a Latin writ is made in a more formal bastard secretary or engrossing hand covering the same transaction. These are followed by the recommendation:

> To Lord Chancellor. Our duties in most humble wise considered may it please your honour to be advertized that according to the accustomed manner heretofore in that behalf used wee whose names are here under written have examined Richard Crosse one of the Clerks of John Symond Esq one of the Cursitors of the high court of Chauncery who hath served vnder the said John Symond as his clerke in his office of a cursitere by the space of eleven yeares, who as well for his honest character as for his skill in the course of common practisse and also for his faire writing now find to be sufficient & fit person to be admitted to execute the office of a cursiter if it may stand with youre Honourable pleasure to admit him thereonto.

The recommendation is attested by from three to six signatures. Finally comes the Chancellor's paragraph of admission, sometimes in Latin and sometimes in English.[6]

In this collection, all of the Signet letters of Henry V are in Chancery hand. Forty-one of the 51 Privy Seal documents are in Chancery hand (80%), and 48 of the 72 Chancery documents (66%). The distribution of documents over the decades reveals a gradual increase in the number of documents in Chancery hand which parallels the extension of Chancery usage.

Presumably the petitions not in Chancery hand were the original bills submitted to the King or to Parliament and Chancery. The extent to which these were re-written by the Chancery clerks is moot, but there can be little doubt that they were produced under the influence of Chancery models.[7] It is our contention that the conventions of the of-

Privy Seal	Before 1420	1421-30	1431-40	1441-50	After 1451	Total
Chancery hand	5	11	21	3	1	41
Non-chancery hand	0	1	8	1	0	10
Chancery Proceedings						
Chancery hand	1	4	23	7	13	48
Non-Chancery hand	5	8	7	3	1	24

ficial languages (orthography, morphology, syntax, and idiom, in Latin, French, and English) were learned along with the hand both by Chancery clerks and by their imitators, and that Chancery usage thus led the way towards the standardization of the written language.

THE SIGNET LETTERS OF HENRY V (DOCUMENTS 2-105)

Nearly all of the documents in this anthology are epistolary in form, either letters of instruction by the King or some other official, or petitions by individuals or institutions to the King, the Lord Chancellor, the Council, or Parliament. Standardization in style and language can be seen in the process of development in the Signet letters of Henry V. To some degree, this regularization appears to reflect Henry's personal style and usage. The *Calendar of Signet Letters of Henry IV and Henry V,* edited by J. L. Kirby, describes 156 letters by Henry V.[1] The first 45, written in England, are in French. The last two of these (Kirby 806, 807) are dated aboard ship at Portsmouth. From the time Henry reached France in August 1417 until his death in August 1422, nearly all of his Signet letters are in English.[2] The 103 English letters here printed are what Florence Harmer in *Anglo-Saxon Writs* calls "administrative instruments," and Hubert Hall in his *Formula Book of English Historical Documents* "warrants for issue."[3] That is, they are letters addressed to the Lord Chancellor or other officials requesting issuance of documents under the Great or Privy Seal, or other appropriate action. Usually these letters were written in response to petitions to the King. Many merely ratify the original letters of petition that accompany them (see nos. 39, 40 in this anthology), like the "letters of credence" with which envoys had been provided in earlier times when they conveyed their messages orally.[4]

The Signet letters here printed represent only part, and perhaps the linguistically less influential part of Henry's English correspondence. Letters from him in English are preserved in Rymer's *Foedera*, the Letter Books of the London Corporation, and the chartularies of other English civic and ecclesiastical institutions. It was letters like these that led guilds and corporations to change their own language of record from Latin and French to English, as reflected in the 1422 statement by the Brewers Guild. However, all of these civic letters are preserved in copies by others of the originals written by Henry's secretariat.[5] Only the 103 Signet letters preserve the original work of his personal clerks. Our collection has been restricted to these and to other primary documents.

The English letters of Henry V put the stamp of authority on the conventions of style and language employed by letters in the vernacular. These conventions had long been established in Latin and French. James J. Murphy traces their origin to the *Dictaminum radii* of Alberic of Monte Cassino, written about 1087.[6] Within a few decades the movement shifted to Bologna, where the formulae of the *ars dictaminis* were standardized in a form that was to remain constant for the next three hundred years. The "parts" of a standard *ars dictaminis* letter were established as 1. *salutatio,* 2. *benevolentiae captatio,* 3. *narratio,* 4. *petitio,* 5. *conclusio.* It is worth noting that the *petitio* was the heart of the letter—either a request for something (a petition) or a request that something be done (an instruction). Murphy traces the migration of the *ars dictaminis* into France, Germany, and Spain. England was generally an importer not a producer of *dictamin* theory. Peter of Blois, a transplanted Frenchman, about 1187 produced *De arte dictandi rethorice,* which promulgated the Bolognese tradition along with more general instruction in prose composition. It lists five genres of prose composition—*epistola, historia, testamentum, invectiva, et expositio qua glosa dicitur*—but devotes most of its attention to the five parts of a standard letter. Gervase de Melkley (c.1200), John of Garland (c.1250), John de Briggis (c.1350), Thomas Sampson (c.1380), and Thomas Merke (c.1400) are influential names in the history of *dictamin* in England.[7] Clearly the tradition was known and practiced in the royal and episcopal chancelleries. All of the theoretical treatises and formularies so far discovered are in Latin and French, but the influence of *dictamin* may be seen in the earliest English vernacular letters.[8]

The five parts of the standard *ars dictaminis* letter are represented in the English correspondence of Henry V as follows:

Letter no. 60
  1. *Author* By þe king

2. *Salutation* Worshipful fader yn god oure right trusty and welbeloued
3. *Greeting* We grete yow wel /
4. *Exposition* And for asmuche as we haue ordeined oure trusty and welbeloued knyght Iohn of Radclif. to be oure Conestable of Bourdeux And also to be Captaine of oure Castel of fronsac for þe grete trust þat we haue to his trewthe and discrecion.
5. *Disposition* we wol and charge yow þat by þauis of oure broþer of Bedford and oþer of oure conseil þere in Englande. ye trete and accorde wiþ þe said Iohn for his abidyng þere. And so þat he may do vs good seruice. as hit semeþ best to youre discrecions for oure auantage and proffit of þe cuntree And þat ye spede him in al þe haste þat ye may. And se þat he tarye not þere: as oure trust is to yow
6. *Valediction* And god haue yow in his keping
7. *Attestation* Yeuen vnder oure signet in oure Castel of Rouen þe [xvi day of May]
8. *Signature of the clerk* Shiryngton

As we shall see, in petitions part 5 is a plea instead of a command. Alberic's early treatise followed classical tradition in placing special emphasis upon the *exordium* and *salutatio*. The traditional formula is *x to y salutem*.[9] In formal Latin charters intended as public confirmations of royal actions *x* and *y* could be spelled out in great detail, e.g.: "Edwardus, Dei gratia Rex Anglie, Dominus Hibernie, et Dux Aquitanie, archiepiscopis, episcopis, abbatibus, prioribus, comitibus, baronibus, justiciariis, vicecomitibus, prepositis, ministris, et omnibus ballvis et fidelibus suis, salutem . . ."[10] But in letters used as administrative instruments the formula was simplified, e.g.: "De par le Roy. Reverent pere en Dieu. Nous vous chargeons . . ."[11] Item no. 1 in the anthology reflects the importance of the salutation in the Signet letters.[12] All but seven of Henry's English letters are headed "By the king." Of the seven which lack the heading, five have the relevant portion torn off; no. 51 appears to be a draft; no. 81 appears to be taken from a roll. None of these letters has the formal third-person opening of a royal charter, although no. 81 provides the wording for such an opening in all three languages.

The first three letters (2, 3, 4) are addressed to "Worshipful fader in god"—i.e., Henry Beaufort, Bishop of Winchester, Chancellor 1413-1417; or Thomas Longley, Bishop of Durham, Chancellor after 23 July 1417. In letter 6 (25 September 1417), the salutation is extended to "Worshipful fader in god / right trusty and welbeloued." As indicated by the exemplar (no. 1), this address might be directed to one person or many.

It derives from the longer formula "archiepiscopis . . . fidelibus suis" (above) which had been simplified in French letters to "trescher et bien ame."[13] In Henry's letters, the simple salutation alternates with the extended salutation until letter 20 (April 1418) after which the simple form never occurs. Beginning with 52 (February 1419) the extended salutation is further augmented to "Worshipful fader in god *oure* trusty and welbeloued." The regularity of this evolution appears to be deliberate. Seven letters (10, 16, 46, 57, 66, 73, 87) are addressed "Trusty and welbeloued broþer"—i.e., John, Duke of Bedford, regent during Henry's absence, and later Humphrey, Duke of Gloucester. Two letters (77, 81) are to "Right trusty and welbeloued broþer Riʒt worshipful and worshipful faders in god." Five others are merely to "Trusty and welbeloued."

The formulae of the greeting and valediction show more variation than the address. The phrase "We grete yow wel" renders the *salutem* of the *x* to *y* formula. Virtually all of the Anglo-Saxon writs printed by Florence Harmer begin with the formula "Eadward kyng gret Aylmer bisscop," which translates "Ego Eadwardus rex saluto Aylmerum episcopum."[14] Most of the Anglo-Saxon writs end with some form of "God seo eow alre freond" or "God eow geheold," which in turn translates "Deus vos omnis conseruet."[15] The greeting and the valediction come through the Latin and French into Henry V's English, e.g., "By the kyng   Worshipful fader in god Right trusty and Welbeloued. We grete yow ofte tymes Wel . . . And the holy goost haue yow in his keping" (9). Both greeting and valediction appear in early letters in Toly's hand (9, 10). Letter 20, also in his hand, has the greeting only. Toly, Hethe, Caud—, and hand y include the greeting in most letters after 20, but only Caud— (37), Toly (46, 50), and an unidentified hand (48) include the valediction until we come to Shiryngton (54). From 54 through 67 (excepting 59) Shiryngton, Toly, and Caud— regularly include both greeting and valediction. With 68 this usage comes to a halt. Only two of the remaining letters (unidentified hand 71, Toly 89) have both greeting and valediction; 10 letters have either one or the other; 26 letters have neither. Since many of these final letters were written by Shiryngton and Toly, one wonders what caused the change in style.

The attestation and dating of Henry's letters translate a formula developed in the 13th century in Privy Seal, "Datum sub privato sigillo nostre apud N," followed by the day, month, and regnal year.[16] As the Signet came to replace the Privy Seal for the King's personal correspondence, the same wording was used without the regnal year, e.g., "Donne desouz nostre Signet, a nostre manoir de Wodestoke, le xxvj jour de Januar."[17] Most of Henry V's English letters are "yeuen vnder oure signet in—" followed by place, day, and month, but not the year.

Item 6 is "wreten" not "given." Nos. 90, 91, 93, 94 are given under "oure signet of þeegle in absence of our oothir." Nos. 69 and 70 are incomplete.

The expositions usually begin with one of three set phrases: "We do you to wite," "And for asmuche," or "We sende yow closed wiþin þis lettre." The first of these echoes an earlier formula. Anglo-Saxon writs begin in the third person, "Eadward kynge gret Alfwold .b.," and immediately switch to the first person singular, "ic ciþe eow," which translates "sciatis" or "significamus vobis."[18] Until 1189 English kings used the first person singular to refer to themselves in all documents, but after the coronation of Richard I the royal chancery adopted the practice current in European chancelleries and English episcopal chancelleries of using the plural of majesty.[19] Although in his autograph letters, Henry used "I" (see below), his dictated letters nearly always begin "we wol" which echoes the "quare volo" of the Latin charters.[20] *Wol / wolle* occurs 129 times in the 103 short letters of Henry V compared to only 24 times in the other 135 documents in this collection. In contrast *will* as a verb occurs only once in Henry's letters (11 times as a noun—"oure will") whereas *will* both as verb (23 times) and noun (18 times) is the common form in the later documents. This is one instance in which the royal formula did not carry over into Chancery practice.

The style and language of the Signet letters of Henry V emanated from the hands of six scribes whose names are signed, and perhaps as many as thirteen others whose hands can be distinguished. Otway-Ruthven observes that the 15th-century Signet office consisted of four or more clerks.[21] Only Robert Shiryngton and William Toly served through the whole course of Henry's expedition, 1417-22. John Hethe served next longest, and the others for shorter periods. The purpose of the signatures found in the lower right hand corners of some of the letters is not clear. Otway-Ruthven says that this is a practice that began in the time of Richard II, was discontinued under Henry IV, and recommenced toward the end of the reign of Henry V.[22] In the English letters, the signature is always that of the scribe, which is difficult to explain because the scribe would not usually be the secretary entrusted with authenticating the letter. Furthermore, the appearance of the signatures is too erratic to indicate any system of validation. In the list that follows, the inclusive dates are those of the first and last letters signed by, or in the hand of, an identified clerk.

Robert or *Walter Shiryngton* (first letter 12 August 1417, last May 1422). There is uncertainty as to the identity of this scribe. The signature is only "Shiryngton," and Otway-Ruthven identifies two of Henry V's Signet clerks by that name, Robert and Walter.[23] All of the letters signed

"Shiryngton" are in the same hand. Signet letter no. 8 mandates a grant to "Robert Shiryngton," so presumably this scribe is Robert who became controller of the King's works from 1423 to his death in 1452. Evidently both he and Walter served as chancellors of the Duchy of Lancaster and Walter succeeded Robert in at least three prebends. There are 19 signed letters (55s, 56s, 57, 59s, 60, 61s, 62s, 64s, 68s, 73s, 75, 76s, 83, 91s, 92s, 98s, 99, 102, 104). The *s* represents the decorative flourish by which Shiryngton identified many, but not all, of his letters (it appears after "King" in the heading, at the end of each paragraph, and before the signature in Plate III); seven letters probably in the same hand (41, 54, 65s, 72, 77, 78s, 79s); and four early letters possibly in the same hand (2s, 6s, 39, 44s)—total 30. Shiryngton's style and spelling are very regular. His heading is usually *By the kyng,* but seven times spelled *king.* The first letter (2) has neither greeting nor valediction, and the second has a uniquely worded valediction (6.7). Five others have only the greeting (39, 41, 44, 59, 68). Nine of the next 11 have both greeting and valediction (54, 55, 56, 57, 60, 61, 62, 64, 65). His last 15 letters have neither greeting nor valediction. After the greeting, all but eight letters introduce the exposition with one of the three set phrases, *And lat yow wite* (57, 78, 79). *We sende yow closed* (always *yow* except 102.1), *And for asmuche.* There are only a few non-standard forms: *þey, þaire, þeym,* but *hem* (2.3, 57.10, 64.10); usually *nat,* but *not* (60.7, 72.4); *furst; right,* but *riȝt* (77.1, 98.1); *knight,* but *myȝt, knyȝt* (6.2, 77.3); always *þow / þoo* for though; *halde* (104.2), and two non-standard negatives, *ner no manere* (64.8), *þat ye ne couthe not* (72.4).

William Toly (first letter 22 September 1417, last 18 June 1422), master of St. Mary's Hospital, Norwich, in 1419 secretary to Cardinal Beaufort, and in 1443 secretary to Henry VI: 15 signed letters (47, 49, 50, 66, 67, 82, 84, 85, 86, 89, 93, 97, 101, 103, 105); eight probable (4, 9, 10, 11, 20, 30, 46, 58); and one possible (22)—total 24. Toly's hand is similar to Shiryngton's (see Plates III and IV) and his style and orthography nearly identical. The first seven letters are *By the kyng;* after that regularly *king.* Like the first two by Shiryngton, his first two letters have neither greeting nor valediction (4, 11); no. 9 has a more extravagant valediction than usual; 30, 47, 49 have only the greeting; 82, 84, 85, 86 have only the valediction; and eight have both greeting and valediction (9, 10, 46, 50, 58, 66, 67, 89). The last five, like the last of Shiryngton's, lack both phrases. Thirteen of the 24 letters introduce the exposition with *We send yow closed* (always *yow*), *for asmuche* (always with *u*), *And doo you to wite* (in 49 only). There are a few non-standard forms: letter 4 has *worshepful, schul, tovn* which indicate either that it is not by Toly or that his style had not yet stabilized; *right, might, knight* are usual except *riȝt* (20.1, in another unsigned letter); *þay, þaim, þaire*, but *hem* (50.4, 58.5); *we han* (11.2), but usually *haue; furst; knowelache* (66.3, 93.2) vs Shiryngton's *knowlege* (79.4).

John Hethe (first letter 20 July 1418, last 18 June 1420), identified by Otway-Ruthven as really a clerk of Privy Seal:[24] two signed letters (87, 88); eight probable (13, 29, 32, 33, 34, 36, 38, 42); seven possible (15, 18, 25, 28, 31, 35, 45)—total 17. *By the kyng* always with *y*. None of Hethe's letters has the valediction; only nine have the greeting (29, 32, 33, 34, 38, 42, 45, 87, 88). All but three introduce the exposition with one of the three set phrases. Pronouns *þey, þaire*, but only *hem* (13.3); *han* (13.1, 28.4); *nat* (18.4, 45.1); *lychwyse* (32.13): *knawe; knowlech*.

Thomas Andrew (Andrieu) (first letter 28 February 1419, last 16 September 1420), of whom Otway-Ruthven records only that he was granted a pension of Hereford in 1420:[25] two signed letters (52, 80); two probable (53, 74)—total 4. All *by the king*, with *i*. None of Andrew's letters has either greeting or valediction. Nos. 53 and 80 begin the exposition *for asmuche*. The forms are quite regular: *þaire, þayme* in the postscript to 53, not in Andrew's hand; *not* (74, 80) vs Shiryngton's and Hethe's *nat*.

John Depeden (first letter 7 March 1421, last 31 July 1421), master of the free chapel of St. Giles, Little Maldon, 1425; four signed letters (90, 94, 95, 96). *By the kyng* always with *y*. None of the letters has the greeting; 90 and 95 have the valediction; 94 and 96 follow the salutation directly with *for as muche*. Depeden has several non-standard forms: *her* (90.2, 96.6) but *their* (96.8); *swich* (90.3) but *such* (90.6); *youen* (90.7) but *yeuen* elsewhere; *Wurshipful* (94.1); *whech* (95.2); *ar comen* (96.3).

Caud— (first letter 20 May 1418, last 23 June 1419), perhaps Richard Caudray, King's secretary in 1420. Only part of his signature is visible on 63. Caudray was of noble birth, a notary, and in 1446 Warden of King's College, Cambridge: one signed letter (63); two probable (26, 37)—total 3. *By the king* (26), *kyng* (37, 63); *right trusty* (26), *riȝt* (37, 63); *þe saide supplicacion seyen* (26.5), *seen* (37.4); 26 has no greeting or valediction; 37 and 63 have both. Exposition begins *We sende (to) yow closed* (26, 37), *And for asmuche* (63).

None of the letters in other hands is signed. It is possible that a study of the files might make it possible to assign some of the hands to William Hayton or Thomas Tibbay, listed by Otway-Ruthven as Signet clerks between 1417 and 1422. However, the variety of hands in the remaining letters makes it nearly certain that more clerks were involved than are listed by Otway-Ruthven.

Hand x: letters 3 and 7 (5, 30 September 1417), in similar hands and concluding with the same flourish, are probably by the same scribe. Both begin *By the kyng.* Neither has the greeting or valediction. The forms are quite regular.

Hand y: letters 8, 17, 21, 23, 24, and 43 (2 November 1417 to 21 October 1418) appear to be by the same hand. All begin *By the kyng.* Eight and 17 lack both greeting and valediction; 21, 23 have the greeting only; 43 has both. *And for asmuche* (23, 24); *And wol ye wite* (43); *right* (21, 43), *riȝt* (17, 23, 24); *brawt* (24.5); *halde* (43.3); *last* for *lost* (24.12); *þei, þaire, þaim* but *hem* (43.4); *knoweleche* (43.9). Letter 8 mandates a grant to Robert Shiryngton *en due form* (8.2). The same phrase occurs also in 2.6, a letter probably in Shiryngton's own hand. Did he provide a draft for 8?

Hand z: letters 19 and 27 (4 April, 27 May 1418) appear to be in the same hand, and both end with the same sort of convoluted, verbose instructions, unlike the direct style of most of the letters. *By the kyng* (19), *king* (27); *We sende you closed* (19, 27); *hem* (19.3, 27.3). Neither has greeting or valediction.

Unique hands: the scripts of 5, 12, 14, 16, 40, 48, 51, 69, 70, 71, 81 cannot be easily identified with any of the above. Their style and forms are quite standard although 51 and 69 in quite different hands use *y* for *þ* throughout. The petition from St. Mary Graces (40) that accompanies 39 is not in Chancery hand but except for an archaic negative, *we ne haue* (40.10), its forms are standard.

Letter 70 is of particular interest because it has been identified by Kirby and others as being possibly in Henry V's own handwriting.[26] The script is firm and practiced, but not that of a professional scribe (see Plate V). Trying to determine the extent to which Henry's own practice influenced the style of his Signet clerks must begin with this exemplar. Its grammar and spelling are remarkably close to MnE. This is the only Signet document which uses first person "I." The letter to Tiptoft printed below does the same. The spelling shows some predilection for *re* rather than *er: Furthremore, northumbrelond, brothre* (all 70.1); *othre, bettre* (70.8); but alongside these, *chanceller* (70.1), *somer* (70.5). The only other non-standard forms are *scold, be founden,* and *secrely* (70.3 for secretly). The tone is direct and businesslike, with no ceremonial salutations. The main and subordinate clauses flow logically: "I wole . . . that ye set a gode ordinance . . . for I am secrely enfourmed . . . that this next somer he shal bryng . . . and also that . . . wherfore I wolle that . . . for it is bettre he lak desport than we were disceyued. of alle the remanant doth as ye thenketh." This shows greater consistency of construction than is usual in 15th-century letters. The series in the first clause (70.1) is well formed. That in the second clause

(70.2-3) connected by a series of *ands* is more colloquial. In the next clause (70.4), MnE would use *who* for *and* (as I am secrely enfourmed . . . that there has . . . who accorded). "To the havyng awey" is not a MnE idiom for "taking away" or "rescuing."

Henry's direct, sinewy style is revealed even more clearly in the famous "secret" letter of 1417 about his negotiations with his French prisoners, printed in Rymer's *Foedera* IX.327-30. The original has been lost.

Tiptoft, I Charge yow, by the Feith that ye owe to me, that ye kepe this Matere, her after Writen, from al Men secre save from my Brother Th'Emperor owne Persone; that never Creature have Wittyng thereof, withowt my especial Commandement, of myn owne Mouthe, or els Writen with myn owne Hand, and Seely'd with my Signet:

Kepeth this Charge, as ye will Kepe al that Ye may forfet to Me.

Also, I wol that Ye say to my Brother, atte begynnyng, or ye Open the Matere, that the grete Trust and Love, that I have to hym (as he proeveth me grete cause) maketh me to let hym have Knowyng of oon of the secreest things that Touchis me, to that Entent that I wol nothyng do but that he shall have ful Knowyng therof: And also that I trust so muche yn his Secreces, that this, that ye shal sey hym, shall be secret, as for hym, from al erthly Cretures; And so I require hym that hit may be, as my Trust is yn hym.

And, when he wil say that he will kepe her yn Secre, ye shal sey hym,

FURST how that the Lords, that been my Prisoners, han often, as ye Tiptoft herde or ye went, spoken to me of Tretees of Pees; but when hit came to the Conclusion, it was to noone other Ende but allonely for thaire Deliverance: to the whiche I wolde not have Assent; ne to suche Thyngs as they spaken of as for Tretee, for hit was but for Delay of my Voyage, to the which I wolde not Assent as ye know Tiptoft.

And then they asked me, and Desired that I wolde aske of hem what I wolde Desire; and they wolde yeve me by Avys, such an Awnswer (savyng thaire Worshipps) as should gre Me,

And then I askyd hem that they shoulde knowe me (as of right hem ought) for thaire Soveraigne Lord; And of that hit was saide, by the Duc of Orliens, in Name of Thaym al, that therto [th]ay[27] myght ne cowth non Answer;

And so Departes as then.

And aftir the duc de Burbon desired to speak with me; and so he dyd: And thees weren hys Words yn Substance that Folowen; savyng he spak French.

My Lord, Seth God sent us ynto your Hands, ther hath been many Wayes Meved And for the most Partie, at all Tyme, ye have Desiryd that we shuld know yow for Ryght wise Kyng of France, seyng that yowre Ryght is grete; wherfor many of us, or this, han sent ynto France, to sech and to have more ful Knowyng of your Ryght then any of us hadde before our takyng: And, of Trowth, herof we had more Knowyng then we had ever before; And, for my self, I dare wel say, for I knowe more than ever I dyd of youre Right.

Also, My Lorde, I have herde yow Desire to have certayn Lordeshippes and Londs &c. as spoken by yow and by youre Subzgitz; And, yf ye myght have thoo, that, atte reverence of God, &c. And for the Goode of Pees, ye wolde freely of youre Wil Renons the right, ye have now in the Corone of France, to hym that now occupieth hit, and to his Heris, as Forme moste be made on both the Sydes: The which I, Duc of Burbon, thenketh as for your Partie, a grete and resonable Profre; that ought not to be Denyed by hym, that he Name youre Adversary.

And Tiptoft, ye shal understande that the Landes been, named by hym also, moche as is Comprehendyd withyn the Grete Pees, yn the Forme as they be thereyn Comprehendyd And Harefleu, with as much of Normandie that lithe next to it, as I wol agree me; And al holden yn the Forme as the Pees maketh mention.

Wherfor, the foresaide Duc desired of me that I wolde yeve him leve, upon such Seurtee as I wolde seme resonable, to go ynto France yn Name of all his Felawes, whereto he saide he supposeth to bryng hem: And so he hath; For they al have desired that he may go for hem al, to meve myn Adversary, desire him and require hym, that he deliver me the Lands that I ask, and yn the same wise as I aske hem; saying hym that, as his Trewe Men, hem thenketh, that he oght to do hit.

And these wer the Words that the Duc behyght me,

If hit be full graunted at my next Commyng ynto France this Yere, with Godds Grace, to resceive hem;

And, if hit were Denyed by myn Adversarie, Then said the Duc thus,

My Lorde, If this be denyed by Youre Adversaire we have acquit us, And yn especial I Duc of Bourbon, And then I shal haste me to yow, so that I shall kepe the 5 Day by Yer set; seteyn yn the meen Tyme all my Castels and Strenghes yn such Governance, as I shal be sure to have hem when me lust; and I comen ynto youre Presence, as with Godds Grace I wol not fayle, I behete yow, by the Trewth of my Body, to do yow Homage as to my Soveraign Lorde rightwise Kyng of France; And I shal shew youre Right so clere to al Men that hit shall wel be knowen that I do but as me oght; and that he, that doeth not the same as I shal, doth ayeins his Worship; Beseechyng yow (My Lorde) that this be kept secree to my Commyng ayein, for else hit were to me, ther beyng, to grete a Peril.

Whereupon I have Grantyd hym Leve to go, yn the Wise as ys before Writen, for al his Felawes that been my prisoners, not wittyng to noon of hem of this Matere, save to the Duc hymself; nor also ther ne is no Personne, yn this Lande, save Derham and I that is knowyng herof.

And ye shal say to my Brother, that me thoght this Profre so resonable, that I oght in no wise have Denyed hit hym; And also he told me, that he supposed, that mo, that been here, wol do the same, But that I knowe not of certaine.

As of the Tyme of the Ducs goyng, hit shal be al sone as his Seurte is redy Commen, which Seurte I sende to yow, and to all youre Felawes, Writen, as ye may see more pleynly; but of his Commyng ther nys as yit no Day set; when ther is I shal sende my Brother Worde, And how I procede yn this Matere and yn all other.

Also, ye shal pray my Brother that he suppose not that for any Tretee, that they wol make, that I wol leve my Voyage, with Godds Grace; for sekirly, with his Mercy, I shall not faile, but fully holde such Purpos, And yn the same Wise as I have sent hym Word by yow.

Also thanketh hym of the Frendely Letter that he sent, one among all other by Diprant; whereby that I have Conceyved the Brothers Assistence, that I trust to have of Hym.

And, Tiptoft, as touching this Matere of the Duc of Burbon, if ye thenke that ye kan not say this redely to Th'Emperor, I wol that ye take Maistre Phelip a Letter that ys Closyd heryn, And is of Credence; by the which Credence I wol that ye make Maistre Phelip to swere on a Booke, and in verbo Sacerdotis, that he shal never discover this Matere, withowte my special Leve; as ys above Writen of youre self.

And, for any thyng, Pray hertly my Brother that, yn no wise, he discover not this, no more to any of myn owne Men, then to any other Man.

Also I wol, that and hit happen that ye be departed from my Brother Th'Emperor or this Com to yow, that yow go ayein to hym; yn alwise sendyng to me by Hartank, if ther be any thyng that asketh haste; And yn especial, whedir my Brother is accorded to that Matere, that ye went for, or no?

And, for the secrenes of this Matere, I have writen this Instruction wyth myn owne Hande, and seled hit with my Signet of th'Egle, the 25 Day of Januar, that is the Day of Conversion of St. Paule.

The peremptory address "Tiptoft" is in contrast to the courteous formulas of address and greeting in the scribal letters. The lucidity of the prose and effectiveness of the rhetoric are impressive. "Kepeth this Charge, as ye will Kepe al that Ye may forfet to Me" expresses the power of royalty about as succinctly as it could be expressed. The instructions as to how to reassure the emperor (paragraph 2), the direct address to Tiptoft throughout, the dramatic recreation of Bourbon's language, and the urgency of the tone reveal the strong personality underlying Henry's reputation as a soldier and as a diplomat.[28]

The reference to the letter of credence for Master Philip is interesting since so many of Henry's Signet letters are warrants attesting the validity of accompanying petitions. The spellings *secre* and *secrest* in the printed letter are the same as in the holograph (70.3), but note *secret* in the second paragraph. There is no instance in the printed letter of *re* for *er*. The spelling *Furst* is that used by Shiryngton and Toly, and we find other non-standard forms found also in the Signet letters: *they, thaire, thaym* but more often *hem; or* for *ere; is* for the *es* inflection (cf. *robertis place,* 70.8); *han; sech* for *seek; moche; thoo; ther ne is no person, there nys as yit.*[29]

The holograph and the secret letter suggest that Henry may sometimes have written drafts for his clerks, but many of the Signet letters appear to be the products of dictation, and the short warrants are formulaic. Henry's imperious personal voice is heard in "Chanceller there is oon Thomas walweynes wyf which hath maad a greuous compleynt . . ." (93.1); "we han vnderstande þat Slake is deed . . ." (13.1); "oon þat hyght Colchestre" (28.2); "It is not out of youre Remembrance in what wise and how ofte we haue charged yow by oure lettres . . . And not withstanding oure saide lettres diuers compleintes be maad and sent vnto vs" (46.1, 4); "And for asmuche as we haue a maner of dowte / whether kynwolmersh occupie clerely and wiþowte scrupule / þospital of saint Antony" (62.2). The confidential tone reappears in 43: "And for as muche as ye knowe better þanne we doo . . . In asmuche as ye knowe better þanne we . . ." Unlike the clear subordination and logical structuring of the holograph and secret letter, 81 shows evidence of hasty dictation: *and* in lines 4, 6, 7, 8; *also* in 11; *ferthermore,* 12; with a postscript following the conclusion (81.19). The same sort of incremental dictation is revealed by the postscripts of 6.9, 30.5, and 53.4, and by the run-on style of 57. There are at least 27 letters with enough of a personal voice to have been drafted or dictated by the King. Twenty-six are formulaic warrants accompanying letters forwarded to the Chancellor for action, and 49 are routine requests for action. At most, Henry would have indicated what the action should be, leaving it to the clerk to patch together the standard phrases.[30]

LATER SIGNET AND PRIVY SEAL PAPERS
(DOCUMENTS 106-160)

During the minority of Henry VI, the Signet office declined in importance—an infant had no need for a personal secretariat. The later Signet letters (106, 107, 108, 109, 117, 130, 132, 133, 134, 135, 136, 137, 148, 150, 151, 152, 154, 155, 156, 157) are written in the name of the King by secretaries or members of the Council. As such, they fall in with the materials classified as Privy Seal. The Privy Seal papers are letters by the nobility and senior officials, petitions to the Council, and Council minutes. Our selection from these materials makes no pretense at completeness. It is fuller before 1430 when there was relatively little material in English and grows progressively more selective from 1430 to 1455. Nevertheless, the items printed provide a chronicle of the movement towards regularization of the written language within the inner circle of government. Before 1436 several documents bear the signatures of the members of the Council, who were acting in behalf of the King.[1] After 1436 several are initialed by the King.[2] Unlike the Signet letters of Henry V, which from the beginning are in regular hand and language, until 1440 there are Privy Seal papers in non-Chancery hands, showing non-Chancery forms, but after 1440 these papers grow increasingly regular. In 1450 a set of Council minutes in non-Chancery hand (158) contains a few non-Chancery forms (*euerich, thof*), and Thomas Haseley, Clerk of the Crown, used northern *g* instead of Chancery *y* in words like *giftes* and *ageyn* (159). These examples remind us that the King's secretaries were not always members of the clerical cadre who were responsible for the fair copies of writs and letters that were sent abroad. Many of the secretaries were university graduates; some had been educated abroad. They were men of learning, proficient in Latin, who tended to end up as deans and bishops.[3] Such rising magnates had not been subjected to the rigorous training in the households of Chancery and did not necessarily write in the official hand and language. It was documents by the professional clerks—what we today might call the typing pool—that circulated throughout the country and helped to establish the model for official English.

Of the letters written in the name of the infant King, only 137, 148, 150, 151, and 156 are not in the epistolary formulas of the *ars dictaminis*. These five are royal indentures in contractual language. No. 156, an indenture with William Pyrton for manning the castle of Guysnes, is a model of lucid exposition, precise vocabulary, and exact reference.

These royal missives have few non-standard forms and spellings. In the moving report by the infant King to his uncle John of Bedford (1423, no. 117) *hem* alternates with *þayme,* and we find *swiche* and *we knowin* (117.18, 22). No. 130 has *hem axeth;* 137 has *mych* in a superior insert in a different hand—no doubt by some untrained superior! The items written by Adam Moleyns (148, 150) are completely standard. No. 151 with a note by William Bekynton has *Archebusshop* (151.2) but *Bisshop* (151.2, etc.). No. 154 has several French spellings: *paix* (154.2), *displeasire* (154.3), *Paloys* (154.6). But the noteworthy characteristic of these missives is their uniformity. Nos. 130, 132, 133, 134, 154, and 155 are addressed to groups of recipients and would have gone out in many copies, showing how the royal style could serve as the model for correct usage.

The differences in the three versions of summons to arms (132, 133, 134) show the sorts of variations that could occur in multiple copies of a single exemplar. No. 134 would appear to be the earliest since its postscript is in a different hand; 132 is written throughout in much the same hand as 134. The changes in wording make the meaning more exact: *in all þe hast ye may* and *on Mary Magdelan next* (134.8, 9) have been expanded to *in alle þe haste þat ye maye, on mary Maughdelenes day next* (132.8, 9); *ayenst oure seide rebell. and enemye* (134.17) has become *and enemyes* (132.16). No. 133 (much damaged) is written throughout in another hand. It shows both misunderstanding and differences in spelling: *in wise as at this tyme* (132.7, 134.7) becomes *in wise & as at this tyme* (133.4), which makes no sense; *seconde day of Iuyll* (132.14, 134.14) is changed to *secund day of þe moneth* (133.7).

The early letters by the Bishops of Durham and Winchester to Henry V (112, 113) show that the standardization in Signet was in advance of that in the episcopal chancelleries. The 1417 letter by Thomas Longley, Bishop of Durham, has *t* for inflectional *d* throughout and the north midland dialectal forms *kirk* and *has* (112.7, 9). The 1420 letter by Henry Beaufort, Bishop of Winchester, regularly represents final *th* by *ht* (*knowyht, wyht, comyht,* etc.), and uses the proclitic negative *I nolde* (113.12) and the phonetic spelling *hynesse* (113.17). In contrast Beaufort's 1432 letter is very regular; *han halden* (127.5) is its only non-standard form. The 1420 letter, a fascinating exercise in self-exoneration, might well have been written by the archbishop himself, whereas the 1432 letter is certainly by a secretary. Although these letters observe the decorum of the *ars dictaminis,* they are more fulsome in their salutations.

The letters by other members of the court, Gloucester 1432 (125), York after 1423 (126) and 1435 (129), and Tiptoft 1438 (144), are very regular. Only Tiptoft's has forms like *her* (144.4, but *their* 144.6, 17) and *hynesse* (144.15). Gloucester's and York's letters use the epistolary conventions of the Signet letters. The bishops' and Tiptoft's missives are petitions.

The forms and language of the letters by the royal clerks (110, 111, 128, 138, 140, 141, 143, 159, 160) show more non-standard forms than when the clerks are writing in the name of the king or some other important official. Robert Frye in an early letter (1408, no. 110) is quite regular except for *Worsshupfull* (110.1, 2). William Soper (1415, no. 111) has *liche* and *nane* (111.5, 6—curiously representing different dialects). Richard Selby (1432, no. 128) has *wyche/wiche, hour* for our (128.5), and *ought* for out (128.17). John Croke (1438, no. 143) has *wich*. Thomas Haseley (1450, no. 159) foreshadows changes to come about in the next century, spelling *gift, ageyn, geten,* and *gyuen* with *g* instead of *y*. Richard Sturgeon (1454, no. 160) uses archaic *hure* for *their*. These forms occur so seldom in the royal and ducal correspondence that their appearance in the letters by the clerks marks the style as a shade less formal than that of the official missives.

The Privy Seal memoranda and working papers (115, 116, 122, 131, 158) are very regular, with spellings like *eny* and *betwix* that are found in many of the royal missives. *Hem* is found occasionally, but usually *them*. Other non-standard forms are *knowlich* (115.25); *wich* (116.2); *furst* (131.7); *euerich; thof* for though (158.22, 30). These documents are in competent but uninspired prose.

The petitions by private individuals in this section all deal with official business. Many have an authentic personal voice. In no. 114 John Cappe pleads for supplies and assistance in his defense of the Castle of Banelyngham "for I am a olde man and haue be hurte and maymed and loste my good in ȝowre werrys be ȝowre ennemyes / so that I haue not where with to do to ȝowre castell as I desyre" (114.5). The petition about the ship Maryknight is a fascinating and well-told story, whose orthography suggests that it was not by an official scribe. Many of its *wh* words are spelled *w* (*wiche, wan* 145.2, 15, etc.). The scribe was aware that these should have *h,* as indicated by his correction of *w(h)ile* (145.9). The petition by William Byngham on behalf of Clarehall, Cambridge, is interesting evidence of the educational responsibilities of parish priests and the provisions made for their training. The style is more awkward and inverted than in most correspondence—"stande þe dores shet" (146.8), "ben voide .lx. scoles" (146.10)—and there are other differences, like *there* for *their* and the archaic *ycalled* (146.5, 15). On the other hand, 147, concerning the mistaken identity of an Oxford scholar, is in typical Chancery hand and language.

Two of the petitions by the three nurses of the infant Henry VI are in one hand (119, 120) and the third in another (121). The dates indicate that 121 is the original. It would appear that 119 was adapted from that, and 120 from 119. The progressive tightening of the style is instructive.

"Lyke vn to þe hyghe and to þe descrete councell" (121.2) becomes "Lyke vn to þe hygh and discrete councell" (119.2, 120.2); "to be paied yn what place þat þe said discrete councell woll assign" (121.4, 119.4) becomes "to be paid yn what place þat þei will Assign" (120.4), etc. There is some drift towards more modern forms, as when *kynges* (121.2, 119.2) gives way to *kyng* (120.2), and *woll assign* (121.4) becomes *will Assign* (119.4, 120.4). The *s* inflection for the third person singular *lykis* (119.3, 120.4) looks to the future, but is not the standard Chancery form. In all versions, *hygh* (line 1) contrasts with *hye* (line 7 or 8). But *sho* in the derivative versions is more archaic than *sheo* in the original (121.7).

The 1437 deposition signed by Adam Moleyns (142) is one of the most interesting pieces in the collection. It describes a dramatic confrontation, using the words of the participants. Lord Faunhope utters the only *þu* (142.26) in the anthology, addressing a social inferior. At one point there is a genitive without *s*, perhaps a mistake, *lord ffaunhop fete* (142.76). Moleyns' style is compact and sophisticated, with only a trace of archaism.

PROCEEDINGS OF PARLIAMENT AND CHANCERY (DOCUMENTS 161-232)

The Ancient Petitions to Parliament (SC8) and Parliamentary Proceedings (C49) are petitions presented to the Parliament and actions upon these petitions. As Sir Francis Palgrave observed, Parliament was originally called not for the purpose of making laws or levying taxes but to hear the complaints of individuals and the commonwealth. It was the King's great and extraordinary court of justice.[1] During the reigns of Henry IV, V, and VI, most petitions came to be addressed to Parliament instead of to the King and Council. The movement of this activity from French and Latin into English has been chronicled above.[2]

The Early Proceedings (C1) are petitions and depositions concerned with Chancery as a court of law. According to the Preface to the printed Calendars (1827),[3] these proceedings commenced in 1394 (17 Richard II) when the Chancellor and his clerks began to hear petitions directly, at the behest of the Council and during the interims between parliaments. The questioning of witnesses appears at first to have been oral, but by 1422 (1 Henry VI) all Chancery judicial procedures had been reduced to writing. All of the materials preserved from the reign of Richard II are French. None have been preserved from the reign of Henry IV. The few from Henry V are mostly French and Latin. But from the beginning of the reign of Henry VI, the proceedings of the court of Chancery appear to have been preserved more systematically, and nearly all of them are in English. The Chancery hand appears less regularly in these than in the Privy Seal documents. A study of the files reveals the reason. The non-Chancery petitions appear to be the originals of complaints submitted to Chancery, which had then to be copied over by the Chancery clerks before being presented officially.[4] There is one instance in the anthology of the original in non-Chancery hand along with its more regular copy (nos. 219, 220), and there are other examples in the Public Record Office of Latin redactions of non-Chancery originals.[5] The important observation here, to hark back to the table of hands at the end of the Introduction, is the way in which the non-Chancery hands were progressively replaced by Chancery hand. Until 1430 documents in non-Chancery hands predominate; after 1430, those in Chancery hand. This, again, parallels the drift towards Chancery spelling and morphology.

The petitions follow the same general format as the royal missives except that they typically have five parts instead of seven:

Petition no. 170

 A. *Address* To the kyng our souerayn lord & to my lordes of his counseil.
 B. *Identification of the Petitioner* Besechet humebely your most obeisant subget Thomas Burton knyght
 C. *Exposition* how that the saide Thomas hath accompted in your Escheqer for the kepyng of the Erle of Ewe. Arture of Britayne & Bursegand that was Marchal of ffraunce And ouer CCCli released & lv li xvj s viij d disalowed ther ys clerly founden due to the saide Thomas . . .
 D. *Petition* That hit like to your benigne grace be auise of my said lordes of your said counseil to consider the long labour and heuy and dredeful charge of the said Thomas & the seide sommes above relesed and disalowed and in discharge of the soule of the kyng your noble fader that was. whom god assoil ordaigne swyche paiement or agrement for the said Thomas of the sommes aforsaid as thinketh to your saide benigne grace be auis of my said lordes of your counseil
 E. *Valediction* for the love of god and dede of charitee.

The parts of the Signet letter omitted from the Parliamentary and Chancery petitions are (2) the greeting, (6) the attestation, and (7) the signature of the clerk. Instead of the heading (1) *By the King,* there is (B) the name of the plaintiff. The disposition of the Signet letter (4) becomes a request for action (D).

Many of the petitions provide dramatic vignettes of 15th-century life. The earliest (161), by the Mercers of London, describes the rough- and-tumble politics of Chaucer's London. John Newport on the Isle of Wight (218) evidently used the same sort of tactics as Nicholas Brembre. The threats on the life of Willyam Midylton (173) and of the members of Parliament (195) and the detailed list of belongings stolen from John Bredhill (197) read like entries from a modern police blotter, as do the murders of Isabell Carpenter (194) and Isabell Bakeler (212) and the rapes of Anne Appleton (189) and Isabell Boteler (201). The petitions of Commons concerning regulation of the stews of Southwark (192, 193) and the curious petition (213) to "acquite all and euery prest aswell religiouse as seculer of all maner feloniez. of rape done by fore the first day of Iune next comynge And also to pardon and relese . . . all and euerich prest Seculer stipendiar annuell . . . by cause of takyng excessious selarie contrarie to the statutes theruppon made . . ." (213.5-9) open vistas on other kinds of civic problems. The vicissitudes of trade and manufacture are revealed in the fates of the servant of William Warwyk (196) and of the ship Seynt Auton (211), and by the complaint of Gieffrey Qwyncy, chandler of Norwich (190), and the weavers of Oxford (203, 204), and against importers of spices (208). More personal is the petition of the Commons that they be excused from kissing the King because of the plague (207). At their best, as in the petitions of the Bishop of Bath (185) and of John Frebarn (225), the narrative prose of the petitions is a lively forerunner of the cony-catching pamphlets of Robert Greene and the verisimilitude of Defoe and Swift.

None of these are intended as self-conscious or belletristic, but they do reveal the emergence and spread of standard prose. Like the hands and physical disposition of the texts, the style and language are so uniform as to suggest the work of a group of clerks trained and working in the same environment. Not all of these petitions are in Chancery hand and language. The petition of Willyam Midylton (173) is in a non-Chancery hand (although the notation at the end is in good Chancery) and full of northern dialectical forms which would have been eliminated by a Chancery clerk. Although the petition for the speedy trial of Lollards (174) purports to be by Commons, it is in non-Chancery hand and contains such non-Chancery forms as *her* for their, *mych, havyn, hye,* and awkward expressions, e.g., "they lye long tyme other while a yeer or two [in Prison]" (174.5). The petition of Baltazar Vivald (175), signed by members of the Council, is in non-Chancery hand and full of non-Chancery forms (*Besekeþ, browʒth, accordit*, etc.). The petition from the inhabitants of Uchayron Percell in Wales (178) in non-Chancery hand is more nearly standard, but still has *yhold, ymade, hynesse, hose* for whose, etc. The original form of the Parliamentary assent to peace negotiations with France is in non-Chancery hand with such forms as *it nys noʒt, swych menys* (182.11, 21). The petition by the citizens of Lymerick (198), in non-Chancery hand, has non-Chancery forms. The non-Chancery forms in the later petition about cleaning up the stews of Southwark in non-Chancery hand, *hye, stablet, refret, han, convycte* for convicted (193), may be compared with the lack of such forms in the earlier petition in Chancery hand (192).

Of a particular interest is the petition of Thomas Bodyn which exists both in an original form in non-Chancery script (219) and in a copy in Chancery script (220). The salutation has been corrected in the chancery version—John Kempe was not "Cardinall of yorke"—and there are other refinements: "Besechyth mekely yowre" is expanded to "Sheweth mekely to yowre gracious lordship"; the numbers in 220 have *th* suffixes; unnecessary "thenne nexte sewyng" (219.12) is omitted (220.12); "a certeyn peyn" (219.18) is strengthened to "a notable payne" (220.18); "of that as where accorde and couenaunt was made" (219.2) is changed to "that where accord and covenaunt was made" (220.2); "prentice with" (219.4) to the more modern "prentice to" (220.5); "nexte sewyng" (219.6) to "next comyng" (220.6); "twoo yer" (219.8) to "two yeres" (220.8); most interestingly "halfe a yer" (219.8) to "half-a-yer"—the only appearance of hyphens in these selections; "to lerne" (219.8) to "for to lerne" (220.8); *fro* (219.11) to *from* (220.12). No. 220 sometimes obscures the meaning by hasty copying, as when "ther ffrendeʒ" (219.4) is reduced to "the frendeʒ" (220.4), "wythyn the age" (219.4) to "with in age" (220.4). The spelling of 220 is more modern: regularly *said* (219 regularly *seid*), *at (att), by (bi), his (hys), in (yn), one (on), this (thys), write (wryte), Allhalowen (all halowen), Please (Plese)*. In some cases 219 is the more modern: *do* (220 *doo*), *owene (awen), the ende (the yende*—but see 219.15 / 220.16), *gracious (graciouce), it (hit), these (thise)*. Nevertheless, the overall effect of the Chancery version is both more modern and more polished.

Even when they are in Chancery script, documents in less disciplined hands are likely to contain most non-standard forms: in 168, 3rd person *has, appiers;* in 169, 3rd person *encreses and growes,* conj. *liche;* in 171, *myche, wyche, wale;* in 176, *yshutte, hare dorys;* in 177, *oure aller moder, aller fader, swich;* in 183, *Besechuth, whuch, resonabull;*

in 184 (from Lincolnshire), *has ben and ʒit are;* in 185 (in a very colloquial passage), *he seies, sich, mych*. From 1440 onwards, the documents in Chancery script have fewer and fewer non-standard forms no matter what the recorded residence of the plaintiff. Only the 1450 petition from the Isle of Wight (218) is consistently non-standard although written in fluent Chancery script: *her(e)* for their, *wos* for whose, *pure* for poor, *thorw, y rulyd, aller, hye,* and the unaccented vowel often *u—hus, pepul, sensabul, furst, aftur, trobul.*

The drift towards standardization can also be seen in the process of enrollment. Many of the parliamentary petitions that were acted upon favorably were later copied onto the Rolls of Parliament (PRO C65) which serve as the basis for the published volumes of the *Rotuli Parliamentorum*. These rolls were copied in a handsome engrossing hand (very much like that which M.B. Parkes designates bastard secretary). The principle was, obviously, to represent the original exactly. The substantive words are seldom changed, no matter how eccentric the spelling (cf. 207 whose spellings of *bien, ffisisseanes, grettest, thair,* etc. are copied exactly). It is therefore interesting to see how much unconscious normalization there was of inflectional endings and form words. The full collations of 16 texts appear as an appendix to this essay (p. 63), but, in summary, eight of the 16 texts reveal the following drift towards modern standard:

Item no.	No. of more modern forms in enrollment	No. of less modern forms in enrollment
174	15	2
192	61	14
194	12	6
201	9	6
202	52	26
208	6	0
210	21	5
217	16	12

Seven of the texts reveal a drift toward non-standard forms:

177	2	5
195	1	6
206	1	3
212	29	39
213	5	7
224	9	25
228	2	4

No. 207, referred to above, is copied almost exactly. The evidence of the second list is less impressive than that of the first. In some cases there are really too few changes to indicate a drift. In item 212, 21 of the 39 changes to less standard are the enrolling scribe's predilection for changing *said* to *seid*. In item 224, six of the 25 changes to less standard are *i* to y, and eight are *i* to *e*. In spite of the mixed evidence, the conclusion to be drawn is that when the clerks were engaged in their most formal and meticulous task of enrolling the acts of Parliament for posterity, their hands were more careful and their forms more nearly like modern written standard.

As the 15th century proceeded, official documents grew more and more regular. The Signet Office of Henry V was closely controlled and highly disciplined in its forms and language. The early documents of Privy Seal and Chancery are less uniform, but as time passes the uniformity increases. We observed above that the early letters of the archbishops (112, 113) are less standard than Beaufort's letter of 1432 (127). Similarly, the petitions to Parliament by the Mercers of London (1388, no. 161) and Thomas Paunfeld (1414, no. 163) have more non-standard forms than the earliest English memoranda of Council business (1421, no. 115; 1424, no. 122), and these, in turn, have more non-standard forms than official correspondence and memoranda of later decades (cf. 156, 157, 158). From 1435 onwards (items 199-232), the private petitions have as few non-standard forms as the Signet letters of Henry V.

THE INDENTURES (DOCUMENTS 233-41)

The nine indentures printed at the end of the collection bear out the generalization that the most regular forms appear in documents in Chancery script. Nos. 234 (1426), 236 (1428), and 240 (1456) show both Chancery hand and, in the main, Chancery language. Nos. 233 (1384), 235 (1427), and 241—the latest document in the collection (1462)—are not written in Chancery hand and contain many non-Chancery forms. Nos. 237 and 238 (both 1445) are not in Chancery hand, but are essentially in Chancery language. And no. 239 (1453), although in Chancery hand, contains several non-Chancery forms, e.g., *liggyng* (line 4), *graunten* (plural *en,* line 9), *mo* (line 13), *euerych* (line 19), *her* (for their, line 22).

ORTHOGRAPHY

Most discussion of 15th century orthography has been directed towards ascertaining the sound changes between Chaucer and Shakespeare. There has been little recognition of the fact that the most important development of the century was the emergence of writing as a system coordinate with, but independent from, speech.[1] It is characteristic of all official languages—Chinese, Sanskrit, Latin, Arabic, or any other—that they are written in the same way, no matter how they are pronounced (with the result that eventually the "correctness" of the spoken language comes to mean the extent to which it reflects the orthography, morphology, syntax, and lexicon of the official written language). From 1066 to 1400, while Latin and French were the official written languages in England, there was no official English standard.[2] English writing was regional and individual. During the 15th century an official standard began to emerge. That this was a written standard is obscured by the treatments of the historians. For example, in their excellent *History of the English Language* (1978), A. C. Baugh and Thomas Cable remark that Sir Walter Raleigh spoke with a broad Devonshire accent, but conclude, "However, subject to the variability characteristic of a language not yet completely settled, written English in the latter part of the sixteenth century is fully entitled to be called a standard speech."[3] Chambers and Daunt in the first sentence of their Preface speak of "the importance of London English in the history of the development of standard English speech" and then go ahead to suggest that the characteristics of "standard English" be identified by collecting official documents. Now speech is not writing. Standardization of writing proceeded faster—and has proceeded further—than standardization of speech. H.C. Wyld spoke of a 15th century "scribal tradition" the "deviations from which" throw light on pronunciations. He remarks on a description of the funeral of Henry VI:"Its meaning is clear and unambiguous and its style perfectly businesslike. It is an admirable example of an official document and of the type of London English in which these were written. The phonology [read "orthography"] and accidence are curiously like our own. . . ."[4]

Wyld's statement could stand as an epitome of this anthology. Magdalene Weale in her appendix to Chambers and Daunt speaks of one document as representing the "state dialect."[5] E. J. Dobson has presented evidence that by the 16th century there had come into existence the notion of a correct pronunciation for standard English.[6] This pronunciation was identified with the speech of well-bred, well-

Orthography 27

educated people in London and the Home counties. According to the testimony of the orthoepists and grammarians, it appears to have been a conservative language, which closely paralleled the conventional spellings, resisting the simplification of consonant clusters like *wr, kn, gn,* and the loss of spirant *gh*. But it is not clear to what extent the statements by Cheke, Hart, Coote, and other contemporary authorities are based upon spelling pronunciations of the sort that restored the initial *h* to many French borrowings *(habit, heritage, host, humor)* and etymologized pronunciations for *absolve (assoil), captive (caitif), corps (cors), throne (trone),* and the like.[7]

The Chancery clerks fairly consistently preferred the spellings which have since become standard. The documents in this anthology show the clerks trying to eliminate the kind of orthographic eccentricity found in the Privy Seal minutes, the petitions passed on to them for entering in the rolls, and most of the documents printed by Chambers and Daunt. At the very least, we can say that they were trying to limit choices among spellings, and that by the 1440's and 1450's they had achieved a comparative regularization. The listings in the glossary indicate the frequency of the various forms. For example, *such* is the preferred Chancery spelling, with other forms in a distinct minority. *Such(e)* appears 185 times throughout. *Sich* appears in one document (221, four instances), *sych* in two (208.4, 233.16, 19), and *seche* once (161.43). Variants of *swich* appear eight times (three times in 177), *sweche* twice (in 237). *Muche* appears 16 times, *moch(e)* 19 times, while *mych(e)* is used five times, only once after the 1430's (221.17). Similarly, *which(e)* appears 93 times, not counting *whych(e),* etc. *Wich* forms occur 21 times and *wech* 13. *Not* is a distinct Chancery preference. *Nat* is found only eleven times in the Chancery documents, as opposed to 89 incidences of *not*. However, some Chancery clerks preferred the more elaborate *gh* spellings *(noght,* etc.) more than did clerks in other offices (see below under "Phonetic Spellings").

The auxiliary verbs *can, could, shall, should, would,* and *ought* are regularly written in at least an approximation of their modern spelling. *Kan* is found only once (208.10), while *can* is usual. *Coude* appears twice (159.9, 225.8) and *couthe* appears in its place in four Chancery documents (72.4, 218.26, 223.24, and 230.3). *Shal(l)* is quite regular, however, with variants of *shull* in seven Chancery documents. Both *shuld(e)* and *shold(e)* variants are found in early Chancery documents, but after the 1430's *shold(e)* drops out entirely. *Shoulde* is found in only one document (204, four instances). Modern *would* is regularly *wold(e)* (55 times), the only notable exception being *wald* (in 171.6). *Ought* is the usual form (sometimes with ȝ), while *aught* appears twice in Signet letters (67.7 and 82.5).

Words with *and* in MnE show more of a tendency to be spelled with *ond* as the period progresses, although *and* is still frequent. *Hand* / *handes* are the regular forms. *Hond* singular does not appear in Chancery documents after 1420, although the plural in *ond* appears in documents until the 1450's (40.13, 191.7, 196.14, 210.17, 30, and 218.5). Throughout the 1440's and 1450's *ond* is the preferred spelling in *lond, Englond, stond,* and (less frequently) *notwithstonding*. For example, *land(e), landes,* etc., appear 16 times in documents after 1440, while *lond(d), londes,* etc., appear 23 times. *England* is found twice, *Englond* 12 times. Variants of *stand* are never found after 1440, while variants of *stond* appear eight times. *Nothwithstanding* is complicated by the large number of variant spellings, but appears to show the same tendency.

Chancery clerks preferred *many* and *any* to their numerous variants. *Many* is found 21 times from the earliest documents, while *meny* is used only three times. *Any* is used 89 times, as against 68 of *eny. Ony* never appears after the 1430's. Conjunctions are likewise regularized to their modern forms. *But* appears 70 times, *bot* only twice in early Chancery documents (168.9 and 171.6). *And* is never *ond, ant,* etc., while *because* is spelled with *au* throughout all 241 documents. *If / yf* is standard after the 1430's in all but one instance (217.25), although variants appear in earlier documents: *yif* (4), *yef* (4), and *ȝef* (in 164 only, five instances).

Several authoritative observations about Chancery Standard are not confirmed in the documents printed below. The increasing use of *ea* in words like *reason* and *measure* noted by Scragg[8] is not at all apparent in any series of government documents. Words like modern *appear, appearance, ease, east, feast, lease, mean,* and *reason,* are nearly always found as *appere, ese,* etc. Occurrences of the *ea* in words like *reasonably* and *treasons* are exceptions. Likewise, the preference of *gaf* for modern *gave,* mentioned by Samuels,[9] is not apparent here, *gaf* appearing only once (in a Privy Seal document, 153.7). Variants of *yeven* are found 128 times in the Signet letters in the formulaic attestation, e.g., "yeven at our castle of Dover"; *g* forms appear three times in non-Chancery items. *Yift* appears 17 times with *y,* eight with *g; ayenst* 75 times with *y,* four with *g,* but *again* 22 times with *g* and eight with *y.*

In words like *chancellor* and *grant,* Chancery clerks normally preferred *au* to simple *a,* whereas the Signet Office most frequently used the more modern form. All but two of the 53 usages of noun and verb forms of *grant,* for example, are found in Signet letters, while the Chancery uses forms of *graunt* 85 times, with no instances of *grant.*

Chancerye, chancellerie, chanceller, etc., are spellings restricted to Privy Seal and (especially) Signet documents, with the sole exception of *chanceller* in a petition from the earlier 1420's (172.1). *Chaunceller, chauncellerie,* etc., are in documents from all offices, but are much more numerous in Chancery documents. Variants of *chauncerye* appear 12 times in Chancery sources, only two times elsewhere. Variants of *chaunceller* appear 20 times in Chancery sources, 16 times elsewhere. Similarly, variants of *fraunchise(s)* are standard in Chancery usage, except in 204 (where both the *au* and *a* spellings appear) and 185. Other words for which the Chancery distinctly preferred the *au* spelling include *commaund, governaunce,* and *suppliaunt.*

Naturally, some words were highly unstable in spelling, even by 15th-century standards. The full variety is displayed in the glossary. MnE *realm* and ME *reame* are minority forms beside variants of *roialme, reaume,* etc. The numerous variants of MnE *poor* and *people* make it clear that these words were very far from being standardized, and the same can be said to a slightly lesser extent of common administrative words like *bailiff* and *sheriff.* Furthermore, different spellings within a single document show how little orthographic variations tell us about pronunciation. Thus, document 240 uses *chambres* four times and *chambers* twice; 159 uses *serviteur* twice, *servitour* once; 203 has *work, werk,* and *wirkith;* 142 has both *countenance* and *countenaunce;* 224 varies *successors* and *successours;* 190 has singular *weighte* but also *wighte* and *wightes;* and the list could be extended. Yet a comparison with literary documents of the same period would probably reveal that government documents were more regular in their spellings than literary works.

Phonetic Spellings

Distinctly phonetic spellings are hard to identify in the Chancery documents. Scribes were inclined to use spellings that did not take account of the new pronunciations developing around them. This appears particularly in the case of the native palatal *g/gh,* which continues as the dominant form, but with enough exceptions to indicate that the drift towards vocalization was under way. *High,* for example, appears 47 times with *gh* (*heygh, heigh,* etc.) and 18 with *i/y* (*hie, hye,* etc.). Frequently both spellings occur in the same document (e.g., 120. 2/8, 174.8/9, 193.1/19). *Nigh* is always *gh; knight* is always *gh* except twice with *ʒ* (*knyʒt); night* is *gh* except once *niht; ought* once *ouʒt; right* three times *riʒt* and once *ryth* (218.30). There is variation between noun forms *nought* and *nowht;* the negative *nat / not* (186 times) has *gh* forms (33) and *ȝ* forms (12). *Through* has *gh* forms (13) and *ow* (7); *though, gh* (2), *ow* (3), and once *thof* (158.30); *thought, gh* (8), *ow* (1). The uncertainty about the *gh* spelling leads to such hypercorrections as *withought* (usual form *without), felaughes* (usually *felawes), hough* (usually *how / hou).*

In contrast to the continued use of *gh* spellings, *ig* is the minority form in French words: *soverein,* 130 times; *sovereign* 113; *atteint* seven times, *atteignted* three; *apparteyn* ten times, *apperteigne* three; *capitaine* five times, *capitaign* three all in 167; *certain* 91 times, *certaigne* three; *foreyn* appears three times never with *ig; arained, mentayne, remayne* have occasional *ig* forms; *atteigne* appears three times always *ig; parteigneyng* appears only once, in this form.

There is similar uncertainty about the French *is: ile* 26 times (all in 218), *isle* once (187.3); *dimes* once, *dismes* 19 times; *elit* twice (9), *eslit* once (24.13); and the incipient Latinisms *appoincte* twice (115.5, 7) for *appoint* eight times, and *appunctuament* (126.4). *Verdite* (202.6) is the only form. It is interesting to see French *assaut ou affray* rendered first into English *assaute or affray* (195.1), and later *assault or affray* (195.7, 11).

The documents also show the usual alteration between *d* and *th* in words like *whether* and *thither,* an ambiguity not resolved until the 16th century or later. All of the documents clearly favor the *d* form. *Murder* is always *d; dethe* (death) and *further* are nearly evenly distributed with *dede, furder.* In only one instance where MnE requires *d* do we find *th, hundreth* (143.3). Otherwise, the *d* form prevails, most often in the variants of *fader,* but also in variants of *moder, togeder, thider, gadre, gaderers.* To what extent these spellings reflect pronunciation remains a question.

The documents are more conventional in their inclusion of *h* in French words like *host,* where it was probably not pronounced. There are six instances of *oost/ost,* as opposed to 28 of *hoost.* Since all 34 instances are from Henry V's Signet, the sojourn of the Signet clerks with Henry in France might have contributed to their scrupulousness. Variants of *heir* are found 40 times with *h* and only three times *eyres* (164.6, 233.3, 6). Other French words, such as *homage, honour,* and *horrible* usually take *h,* even though it was almost certainly not pronounced. Cases of hypercorrection creep in, *horatour* (205.2), *habundant* (167.19, and five other instances), *habade / habyde* (173.7, 13), *vssher / huissher* (73.2). Besides *oost / ost,* the only incidences of dropped aspirates are in *ospital* (five times in Signet letters) and *owres* (hours, 222.18).

Variation of Unaccented e/i/o/u

Before surveying prefixes, suffixes, and inflections some account must be taken of the variation in the spelling of vowels in unaccented syllables. In the Chancery documents, alternation between e, i, o, and u in unaccented syllables does not indicate dialect but merely the obscurity of the vowel in this position. The drift towards standardization is indicated by the increasing tendency to spell this vowel e. In the following examples, the variations between i and y and between u and w have been normalized under the most frequent form since these must be accounted as more nearly graphemic than orthographic variations (like the variations between u and v, i and j).

Noun plurals
costis	4 times	costes	6 times		
goodis	6 times	goodes	41 times	goodus	2 times
prestis	2 times	prestes	7 times		
yerys	1 time	yeres	18 times		

Noun possessives
goddis	7 times	goddes	17 times
kyngis	14 times	kynges	82 times
popis	1 time	popes	1 time

Verb 3rd person
askith	2 times	asketh	5 times
besechith	10 times	besecheth	17 times
longyth	2 times	longeth	25 times
requerith	1 time	requereth	9 times

Verb past tense and past participles
grantid	14 times	granted	71 times
lykid	2 times	liked	10 times
passid	9 times	passed	38 times
paiid	2 times	payed	24 times

Verbs with en suffix
boryn	1 time	born(e)	3 times
boundyn	1 time	bounden	7 times
comyn	3 times	comen	5 times
knowyn	2 times	knowen	10 times

Other unaccented syllables

broþir	4 times	broþer	27 times			
fadir/ fadris	14 times	fader/ers/res	154 times	fadur	1 time	
noþir	2 times	noþer	10 times			
pepil	7 times	people	45 times	pepul	4 times	

O and *u* tend to appear more frequently in non-Chancery documents. Isolated instances appear in at least seven Chancery items: *viergerschup* (118.2); *ellus* (122.9, see *ellys* 122.14); *writon* (126.11); *whuche* (133.2); *sonnor* (sooner, 134.15); *lorshupes* (lordships, 185.1); *huld* (held, 222.16); *hur* (her, 222.5). Sometimes Chancery scribes used *o/u* forms alongside *e/i*. For example, a 1430-31 petition of a merchant from Ghent in good Chancery hand has *Besechuth* (183.1), *aftur* (183.23) alongside *besecher* (183.25), *brother* (183.4); *arerode* (183.31), *payode* (183.31), *rehersode* (183.29), *conteignode* (183.22) beside *conteigned* (183.20), *passed* (183.9 etc.), *onswered* (183.12); *goodus* (183.29) beside *wolles* (183.4 etc.); *resonabull* (183.24 etc.) beside *semblable* (183.32); and *whuche* (183.9, 14) beside *whiche* (183.5 etc.).

A 1449 petition, in non-Chancery hand, by Commons that priests be pardoned for rape has *vexud* (213.2), *rerud* (213.11) beside *troubled* (213.2), *grauntid* (213.19). This late petition has other non-standard forms: *euerich* (213.7 etc.), *your influent grace* (213.4), *lordes . . . graunten* (213.10).

A 1450 petition by Commons, again in non-Chancery hand, has *pepull* (217.12) beside *noble* (217.2), *temporell* (217.30); *wurkying* (217.20 etc.) beside *wer* for were (217.40), *makers* (217.10); and *yut* (217.29) beside *kepte* (217.3).

A 1450 petition from the Isle of Wight in Chancery hand has *aftur* (218.9 etc.), *furst* (218.31), *oþur* (218.9), *ondurtake* (218.39) beside *vndirtake* (218.4), *oþer* (218.26), *nombre* (218.7); *constabul* (218.41), *sensabul* (218.7 etc.), *trobul* (218.49), *pepul* (218.7) beside *peple* (8 times) and *pepil* (twice), *castel* (218.15), *honourable* (218.29). This manuscript, although in Chancery hand, contains other non-Chancery forms: *hus* 15 times for his; *hud* for hid (218.50); [they] *courson* for cursen (218.27); *her / ham* beside *ther / þem; your aller wisdoms* (218.16); *thorw, mygh, ryth, hynesse* for through, might, right, highness; *y rulyd, silf, strenthe, anherited*.

A 1427 Winchester indenture in non-Chancery hand has *fadur* (235.3) and *tendurly* (235.15) beside *clerk* and *oþer; kyngus* (235.10) beside *lettres, werres; þryftyust* (235.9) beside *aprest, by twext;* and *Bysshup*

(235.3), *wytennssuth* (235.2), *lyuuth* (235.15), and *buþ* (235.11 etc.). It also has other non-Chancery forms like *y sende, yhadde, en* for an, and *hy, hem, here* for they, them, their.

We may conclude that the movement in Chancery documents was towards the *es, ed, eth, est* spellings, but that *i* forms continued to be used through 1460. Frequently the two forms appeared side by side: *endented and ensealid* (222.7); *clensyd, garbaled* (208.4) but *garbelyd, clensyd* (208.8); *reumys* (182.4), *reumes* (182.11); *purchasyd* (192.8), *purchased* (192.9). In non-Chancery items there are more *u/o* spellings for unaccented items than in Chancery documents.

In detailing the forms in the discussions that follow, these *e/i/o/u* spellings have been normalized under the most common form. These variations, as well as *i/y, u/w,* and *u/v* are ignored in calculations of frequency.

Prefixes

Since prefixes were unaccented, they were subject to the same kinds of irregularities and inconsistencies as the inflectional endings. Adding to the confusion was the lack of standardization of often competing Latin- and French-derived prefixes such as *in, im, en,* and *em.*

Many words with prefixes beginning in *in/im* in MnE were written with *en/em* prefixes in Chancery documents. One explanation for this is the continuing French influence; another is the drift towards *e* as the regular vowel in unaccented syllables, noted above. But the relative strength of each explanation is difficult to determine. In any case, *en* prefixes where MnE requires *in* are sometimes preferred in Chancery writing. There are, for example, 33 instances of *entent(e)* as opposed to one of *intent,* and that in an ecclesiastical petition (153.8) where the Latin *in* would be expected. Likewise we have *endenture* and its plurals 25 times and *indenture / indentures* only six times, five of them in non-Chancery items (238 and 239). *Informed* is found once (as a past participle, 146.9), while variants of the infinitive *enforme* are the clear preference, with 27 listings. Other cases where the *en* form is preferred include *enheritaunce* and *endented*. Prefixes beginning with *im* in MnE show the same kind of variation, with preferences for *empechment* and *enprisoned*.

Assimilation of *n* to *m* before *p* is irregular. *Empechement* and its variants appear four times to one of *inpechement* (196.29), but variants of *enprisonement* appear six times to one of *imprisonment* (230.18), variants of *enprisoned* (including *inprisoned*) five times to two of *imprisoned*, while *enprowe* (115.3 improve) and *enpouerisshing* (232.27

impoverishing) are found only in *en* forms, once each. *Employment* is found twice, *enploiement* once (158.41).

The *un/vn* prefixes sometimes appear as *on*. Most notable is MnE *unless*, which appears only as *onlasse* (62.4), *olasse* (69.20), and *oolesse* (122.10, 14). Also found are *oncurteise* (142.28 uncourteous), *ondurtake* (218.39 undertake), and *ontrouth* (142.6 untruth).

Prefixes which appear in MnE with Latin *ad* still usually appear in their French form *a*. The MnE noun *advice* is 32 times *a (avis,* etc.) and 19 times *ad*; the MnE verb *advise* is six times *a* and five times *ad*. *Adnullacion* and *adnulling* appear once each alongside *annullen* once. Hypercorrection appears when an official hand notes on the dorse of a petition "he hath be resumed to þe kynges advayle [avail]" (227.20).

All of this having been said, we should not overlook the fact, evident in the glossary, that the preponderance of prefixes already have their modern forms in both Chancery and non-Chancery documents. Furthermore, most of the words noted in this section are legal or administrative locutions or parts of formulaic phrases ("as we ben enfourmed," etc.) and would be the kinds of words clerks might prefer to keep close to their law-French forms.

Suffixes

Inflectional endings will be treated under morphology. Other kinds of suffixes are usually in their modern form. The only notable exception is *tion,* which usually appears as *(c)cion,* its OF form. The only exceptions are *action, confirmation, consolation, distruction, jurisdiction, petition,* and *reformation.* Yet even in this list the *tion* spellings are the exception: only for *iurisdiction* do the *tion* spellings outnumber the alternates (four to two), and *tion* endings are found only once each among the variants of *confirmation, consolation, distruction,* and *reformation.* Even these may not be *t* since the formation of the letters sometimes makes it difficult to distinguish *t* from *c* in this context.

French suffixes also appear, although infrequently. *Gracieux* is the most common, although *odieux* and *victorieux* also occur. The French suffix *eur* is found only in *seruiteur* and *suyteurs,* each appearing only once.

French Words and Spellings

As might be expected, scribes, whose primary training was in French and Latin and who moved easily from one language to the other, frequently dropped French words, idioms, and spellings into the middle of English sentences. The use of plural adjectives, mentioned above, seems particularly jarring, although the actual number of plural adjectives is not large, and most appear in formulaic phrases: *seculers, severalx, subtiles, temporalx, wyseʒ, certains, diuerses, espiritualx,* and *excoutories.* For a very few words, scribes preferred the French spelling to the English one. *Manoir* and its variants appear 11 times for MnE manor, while the English *manours* appears only once (210.19). *Maistre* appears 67 times, and *master* only three (all in 181). Purely French spellings like *paix, proef, reproef, boef, grocier,* and *oncle* can be found occasionally. *Moue/meue* forms appear five times each, *moeue* forms four times.

But these documents indicate that the period of the greatest influx of French spelling into English was over. Except in the cases noted above, most French-derived words are consistently found in anglicized and/or modern forms.

Dialectal Spellings

Although non-standard dialectal spellings naturally catch the trained eye, the actual number in these documents is fewer than might appear at first reading. Most of them occur in either early or non-Chancery documents, or appear to have been copied by the Chancery clerks from other sources. Distinct Southernisms, for example, are virtually nonexistent outside of the rare adverbial *-lich* (see below under Morphology).

The relative absence of Northernisms which otherwise failed to find their way into London or MnE is more surprising than the lack of Southernisms since so many masters in Chancery were apparently from the north, particularly Yorkshire and Lincoln. The most dialectal document is item 173, a Yorkshire petition which found its way into the records with little or no Chancery editing. In it we find the only incidences of the Northern *qu/qw* for *wh*, "to qwhylk of yam forsayde" and "Qwharfore lyke it to yhour gracious lordeschip" (173.11, 14); *kirke(e)*, which otherwise appears only in 112; *lang* for long; and *knowan*. No. 112, the 1417 letter by the Bishop of Durham, discussed above, contains other Northernisms, but has *kirk* alternating with *church* (112.3, 7). Privy Seal items 117, 123, 139, 169 also contain scattered Northernisms, but Northernisms are rare either in the Signet letters (e.g. *knawe* 16.2, 45.2, 69.3) or Chancery (e.g., *lang, amanges* 169.2, 4).

VOCABULARY

As might be expected in legal and administrative documents, the vocabulary is limited. There are about 3,000 separate entries in the glossary for some 70,000 words of text in 241 documents. By and large, it is a modern vocabulary. There are only 138 obsolete and archaic forms and meanings. The meanings and citations for these words are given in the glossary. In the following lists, the words tagged [1] are variant forms, [2] are variant meanings of familiar forms, [3] are archaic or dialectal. Those in italics are actually obsolete—34 in all. At the time this comparison was made, the *MED* ended with *preven*; the words marked * are from the part of the *MED* not yet published.

Not in *OED* or *MED* (11)
afferyng arterie[1] asferforth[1] beselered[1] deanee[1] desclaunderouse[1] esker[1] *munyeles* plesament[1] poentot[1] *tressecloth*

In *MED* but not in *OED* (9)
abitted apeched[1] arrysers[2] *broggid* disheredacon[1] *enblaied* iakes[1] laborenis[1] *maynour*

In *OED* but not in *MED* (18)
appunctuament[1] contendentes[1] countermark[1] *fuage* *prouowr[1]
*reddicioun refet[1] *revigeryng[1] *risers[2] *sanappes *semble[1] *stre[1]
*suynte[1] *sysors[2] *thraves[3] *vaillable[1] *vineres[1] *vpberers[1]

In both *OED* and *MED* (100)
acusement[1] adnullacion[1] adradde[1] *afferant* affiance[1] affray[1] *agreggeable* aiel algates[3] als[1] alssone[1] ambassiat[1] *amenusyd* ammocion[3] amobre[3] amoeve[1] anenst[3] *anientisched* apaide[3] apeiryd[1] apert[3] *apportes appreste* arere[1] arted[2] artitulerly[2] assise[2] assoil[3] *attemptates* aulmosner[1] *avaled* avoutoures[1] awaite[2] balyngers[3] *bonchef* bordell[1] brandards[1] brocage[1] busshementes[3] *bynome* carrakes[3] cassen[1] caterye[2] cheker[1] *chevised* closed[2] comenceour[2] cominalte[1] contentacion[1] costage[1] *costereres* cosynage[1] covyne[1] custumably[1] custumer[2] demure[2] denture[1] deuoir[2] *dimmissoun* disassent[1] dorser dortour eftsones[2] emboldishing[1] empleted[3] *encheson* endosed[1] *entremet* fortalice[3] *garbaled* garnisons[1] glebe[3] gouernaille[1] gree[3] *grucching hanaper* hyght[3] *iewys* intendaunce[1] las[1] leuacion[1] mainprise[3] *maumet* maundement[1] mavlers[1] mene[3] merque[3] mois[3] mortisment[1] mow[1] nonsuyd[1] ne[3] o/oo[3] *oeps* otteraunce[1] paroche[1] *pelyd* pight[1] portinaunce[1] *portouse*

Several usages are worth commenting on:

1. Variants of *anientishen* are found six times in these documents, in all cases referring to a loss or diminution of revenue or income. The relative frequency of this word supports the impression one gets from the *MED* that it is primarily a legal and ecclesiastical term, rarely used in literary works. Significantly, Chaucer uses it only in the moralistic *Tale of Melibee*. Although it seems to have been a rather common word, at least in the written language, the *OED* indicates that it failed to survive the early Renaissance.

2. *Attemptates,* referring to violations of a truce or treaty, reflects a desire on the part of the legal and diplomatic profession to introduce a new word into the language for a limited purpose. Apparently the word was sufficiently bland to be preferable to *violation, attack,* or a similar English word, and was consequently adopted from French to fill the need for diplomatic obfuscation. It is not recorded before the time of Henry V (the *MED* cites document 46.5) and only appears in legal documents until the Renaissance, when it became a synonym for *attempt*. It was always an inkhorn term, however, for the *OED* records Puttenham's 1587 citation of it as an aureate borrowing, and soon after that it was apparently dropped from use.

3. *Broggid,* meaning "to suborn a juror," is one of the rarest words in this collection, since its claim to a place in the language is based solely on its appearance in 189.18 (cited by *MED*). The writer of this petition may well have invented the word, since, to judge from the petition, he had more literary flair than the usual petition-writer. Certainly the phrase in which it appears—where he claims that one William Aleyn "broggid, hyred, and embrasid to hym" some jurors—is more vivid and rhythmical than we usually meet in these petitions. In any case, the *MED*'s supposition that it is related to *broggour,* a factor, agent, or go-between, is logical enough.

4. The same writer also included the first recorded English appearance of *defesable* (189.26), although it appears in *RP* in a French entry over a hundred years earlier. Unlike *broggid,* however, *defesable* has remained in the language (as *defeasible*) although it is by no means common. It is a natural formation from other legal terms such as *defeasance* (OF *defesance*) and *defease,* and we might well suspect that its failure to appear in other medieval English-language documents is purely accidental.

5. *Depauparte* (226.6) is another inkhorn term used by the Latinate Yorkshire abbot given to spinning out phrases like "amynused, dycresed, depauparte, and anyentysed." The entry here antedates the

OED/MED citation (from Capgrave, c 1464) by about ten years.

6. Both the *OED* and *MED* cite *marchantlich* (MnE merchantlike) in 172.6 as the sole recorded medieval occurrence of this word, although it must also have been used in everyday speech and in documents now lost. The *MED* definition—"by way of barter, in trade"—is surely only partially correct. The context, stating that a man "receyved the verray value marchantlich in wolles," implies rather that it means "according to the fair value of trade and according to the highest standards of honesty within the business community."

7. Along the same line, *mainprise,* a very common term in medieval law shown in both the *OED* and *MED* only as a transitive verb, can be found at least once as intransitive: "and so I meinprised to go at large" (162.8). Since the writer of this otherwise regular petition must have had some training in legal usage, this is probably another case where a normal usage has not found its way into the dictionaries.

Several petitions are notable for their extensive lists of everyday objects. The petition (197) of the unfortunate John Bredhill is particularly valuable since he inventories nearly all of the effects in his household which, he claims, were stolen from his parsonage in Staffordshire. His exhaustive catalogue is of considerable interest for social historians, although the more practically minded may well wonder how five men could carry off such a huge load, including a mare, two colts, sixteen hogs, and ten pigs. Also worth noting are the lists of building materials found in the indentures 233 and 238, where some of the technical terms seem slightly at variance with the definitions found in the *OED* and *MED*.

MORPHOLOGY

Articles

The article before consonants is nearly always *a*. There are two manifest mistakes in early writs: "a olde man" (114.5), "a answer" (162.12). Twice *a* stands before *h*: "a hole ȝere" (205.5), "a hode" (212.10), but *h* is usually regarded as a vowel. Semivowel *y* is always treated as a consonant: "a yere" (56.3, 148.7, etc.). Usually *a* precedes numbers: "a hundredth shillyngis" (143.3), "a .C. li" (164.21, 180.37, etc.), "he answered . . . with a sexti" (142.12, in the record of an oral deposition).

An is the article before vowels. Usually *h* is treated as a vowel: "an hool aduis" (130.4), "an hurte" (132.5), "an hors" (147.6), etc. Three times *an* stands before numerals: "an C li" (189.16, 33), "an hundred pound" (239.23). The spelling *ane* occurs four times. Three times in one petition full of Northern forms it means either *an* or *one*: "woulde haf slayn me with ane polle axe," "lygand still in ane awayte," "for ane worde I spak" (173.6, 9, 12). The fourth time it is merely a variant spelling of *an*: "ane accion of couenaunt" (221.5).

The is used as a noun marker much as in MnE. However, it is often used as a marker with pronouns of reference: "The said (abovesaid)," "the which." This use is treated below in connection with adjectives.

Occasionally *a* and *the* are omitted: "as cruell . . . child" (222.14), "abide vnto tyme" (202.11), "at bygynnyng" (69.16), but this use is not frequent enough to suggest a pattern.

Nouns — Plurals

The inflections of nouns are much like those in MnE. There are no inflections for nominative, dative, or objective. Plurals are usually indicated by *es/eʒ, is/iʒ*. Five times we find *n*: in a 1433 inventory of stolen goods, "viij ellon . . . of cloth" (197.18); in a 1456 non-Chancery indenture from Northampton "the Brithirn and sustern" (240.22); *brethern* (145.8) and *bretheryn* (153.17).

In French ʒ was an abbreviation for *es*, on the way to becoming silent. It was used most often for verbs and modifiers: *assembleʒ, desireʒ, tennuʒ, gardeʒ, noʒ* (nous), *toʒ* (toutes), *desouʒ, ditʒ*. Only after *t* was ʒ commonly used for the plural: *enhabitauntʒ, suppliauntʒ, tenentʒ*. There was a distinct preference for *s* as the sign of the plural for nouns: *voʒ sageʒ discrecions, toutʒ Quinʒismes, les ditʒ Commissioners, toutʒ les libertees, franchises, profites, commoditees, emolumentes, autres appertenances* (all these from *RP* IV.160—where ʒ is, however, transcribed *z*). In Chancery English ʒ is frequently used as an abbreviation for *es*, most often after *t*. It is used this way in 22 words from *accomtʒ* to *tenementʒ*. All except the following five have *s/es* variants: *emprisonmentʒ, entendauntʒ, inhabitauntʒ, lieutenantʒ, profittʒ / proffiteʒ*. The ʒ is also used as substitute for *es/s* after *t: detteʒ, herteʒ*—eight words; after *d: ffrendeʒ, londeʒ*—four words; after *g: wageʒ, chargieʒ, kingeʒ*—five words; after *l: castelleʒ*; after *m: sommeʒ, dismeʒ*—four words; after *n: nonneʒ, personeʒ, towneʒ*; after *p: lordschippeʒ*; after *r: honoureʒ, heireʒ*—four words; after *s/c: braseʒ, iusticeʒ*—six words; after *ch: marcheʒ*; after *u: reueneuʒ, issueʒ*; and after *e/i/y: feofeeʒ, baillieʒ*—seven words. Only two of this group do not have *es/s* variants: *bushelʒ* where ʒ stands for *es*, and *braseʒ*. All of this last group now end with voiced *z*, but the prevalence of the *tʒ* spelling indicates that the ȝ in this context was not a phonetic symbol but merely an abbreviation or graphemic variant for *es* or *s*.

Z and ȝ (yogh) are represented by the same grapheme. There is no instance of a short *z* in the records here analyzed. It is possible that the scribes sometimes lifted the pen on the tail of the consonant, but the tail is always present.

The frequency of the *s*/ȝ plural without *e* reveals a drift towards the contracted pronunciation of the plural. However, the historical *es* predominates in spelling. For example, *reuenus* two times, *reuenuȝ* five times, *reuenues* seven times, *reuenueȝ* twice in one entry; *seruantȝ* eight times, *seruantes* ten, *seruanteȝ* two; *patentȝ* 23 times, *patentes* 67, *patenteȝ* five; *profits* one time, *proffitȝ* five, *profites* 19, *profiteȝ* three. Syncope is most frequent after *n* and *r*: *pensions, peticions, porcions, fermours, freeholdes, gouernours,* and *scholers* have no *es* variants. But in the same item as *scholers* (146), we find *scholes* three times. In other records *heirs* five times, *heires* 21; *maters* nine, *materes* 25; *lords*/ȝ twice (215.17, 227.9), *lordes/eȝ* 74 times. In a few instances, the contracted ending is spelled with French *x* when it appears after *l*: *vesselx* (51.2, 187.9, etc.), *sealx* (156.20, 36), *Ioialx* (131.22, 23), but the *x* plural occurs more frequently in modifiers (see below). The only mutated plurals noted in these passages are *men* and *women*. The only unchanged plural is *hors*, singular 147.6, plural 96.1, 3; 145.11.

Nouns — Genitive / Possessive

The majority of the genitives in these passages are genitives of association formed with *of*, e.g., *writtes of liberate* (21.3), *of Seint Osewoldes of Gloucestre* (33.3), *in the tyme of kyng Harry Aiel of kyng Iohn* (203.4), *þe maister of þe said youre suppliaunt* (205.4). At least once the *of* is omitted, creating an appositive: *þe saide estatȝ gentilmen and communes* (71.5). With *manner* the *of* is always omitted: *all maner men* 37 times, *all maner revenuȝ* 34 times. At 197.11 we find *i paire bedes*. Quantifiers like *pair, dozen, score, brace,* evidently did not require *of*.

The *es* possessive is always personal and seldom contracted (but see *the kyngs pees,* 186.4). In this respect it is more conservative than the plural. There is no instance in these documents where the *es* genitive is represented by *his*. The nearest are *þat worthy prince ys Sowle* (165.7) and *my modir is dywte* (241.10, 13) where the *is/ys* is graphemically separate. The usual form is *the kyngis counsaillours* (142.4), *oure Cousin Courrenays landes* (49.3), *mannys sugestion* (127.4), *to my said lord Cardinales handes* (131.18), *oure liege lordes Custumes* (187.7), *þe popes court* (91.2), *wiþ goddes grace* (30.3).

Adjectives

Except in formulae adapted from the French, adjectives are not usually inflected in the Chancery documents. *Aller* is found four times in two documents: *oure aller moder þe cherche of Canterbury, oure aller good fader* (177.5, 7); *your aller wisdoms* (218.16, 33). (Item 177, a 1427 petition on behalf of the Archbishop of Canterbury, has other non-Chancery forms: *we han, swich, to cassen and annullen.)* Item 218 is the 1450 petition from the Isle of Wight whose non-Chancery characteristics have already been noted.

Adjectives inflected for number usually appear in the French order, following their head words: *possessions Aliens* (151.7, etc.), *marchauntes artificers* (231.5), *marchaunt3 denis3eins* (180.19), *writtes . . . suffisant3* (213.9), *lieutenant3 generalx* (156.30), *letteres patentes* 91 times—only once *lettres patente* (6.12)—*lordes spirituelx and temporellx*, 10 times; *spirituell and temporelx* once; *spirituelles and temporelles* once—*lordes spirituel and temporel* 11 times. *Gracieux* is a variant spelling for *gracious(e)*. Three times out of 15 it appears to agree in number with a following plural noun, but the remaining instances appear to indicate that this *x* is not inflectional.

Adjectives in the English order are sometimes inflected: *certeins endenturs* (168.7, 171.3), but 26 times this *certein(e)* is uninflected; *diuerse3 partie3* (213.1 and six times more, but 51 times uninflected); *seueralx warrentes* (148.4—at 195.4 we find the French idiom *jours severalx*); *3our wyse3 discrecions* (168.9). This last represents the collocation of an English modifier and a French headword. Normally the plural adjectives, whether preceding or following the headwords, are French. But it should be pointed out that the common pattern in Chancery English is that of MnE—the adjective precedes the noun it modifies and is not inflected for number when the noun is plural.

The positive *mo / moo* appears seven times, the comparative *mor(e) / moore* 96 times. Twice *mo* is a modifier: *about moo the whiche thynges* (159.44), *more land or mo tenementes* (239.13). Five times it is used as a free form: e.g., *.lx. scoles and mo* (146.10, and see 188.3), *Iohn Tyrell and othor mo* (164.11, 39), *some yonge poure scolers and moo* (146.16). But *more* is the usual form for adjective, pronoun, and adverb: *þere be no more compleinte* (44.7), *o lasse yenne more may be geten* (69.20), *se moore cleerly* (15.3), and the formula *vij 3er and more* (163.50 and ten times more).

One of the most characteristic locutions in the Chancery documents is the determinative *said / abovesaid / aforesaid / beforesaid*. *Said* alone is used either as a verb or as a modifier. As modifier it always precedes its headword: *þe said commissioners* (1.7), *the said William* (156.2). *Said* is never used as a substitute. The same is generally true of *foresaid* although four times it follows its headword: e.g., *þe Pryour of Neustede foresaid* (143.6), *oþir godes and herneys foresaid* (211.29), and one time it is used as a substitute: *that the forseyd pleyne hym* (164.27). The other forms are never used as substitutes and follow their headwords except in three instances: *the aforseid besechers* (178.15), *the aboue seid somme* (183.6, 188.8). The usual order is *the Dettes abousaide* (84.6), *the auctorite aforesaide* (180.34), *in this fourme before seid* (202.28). The customary orders—*said* preceding the head word, the other forms following the headword—follow French usage: *des ditȝ Suppliauntȝ par les enchesons suisditȝ* (RP IV.160.6). The French, in turn, follows the Latin: *quod dictus Johanes habet, pervenient de manibus de Kynefare infra forestam predictam* (Nicholas, Proceedings IV.197).

Late is used 37 times as an adjective meaning former or deceased: *the reign of yowr late souereign* (178.8), *the seide late Shirreves* (190.9), *in late dayes begonne* (192.2), *wyth. diuerse late pestylenceȝ* (235.9). Seventy times *late* is used as an adverb meaning lately.

The demonstratives and relatives are taken up in connection with pronouns.

Pronouns

The first person singular nominative pronoun is always *I*, five times spelled *y*. The possessive is usually *my* before consonants and *myn(e)* before vowels and *h*. There are a few exceptions which look like errors: *myne generall Attorneys* (126.9) where the vowel of *Attorneys* may have influenced the choice of the pronoun; *myne neyghebores* (163.18); *my entent, my absens* (126.8, 10); *my owne, my entent, my Executors* in a non-Chancery indenture (241.10, 14, 15); *my officers* (185.3).

The objective *me* is 41 times out of 55 the indirect object of a verb or the direct object of a verb or preposition. The other 14 instances are idioms no longer used. *I recomaunde me* occurs eight times (111.1, 112.1, etc.) where MnE would use the reflexive *myself*. *I haue demenid me* (113.15) is the only instance of the untranslatable "ethical dative." MnE might use adjectival *my costs* for *in costes of me & myne* (173.14) and *my assent* for *withoute assent of me or of my officers* (185.3), although the compound object of the preposition makes both of these instances problematical. *As me thoughte* (163.19) and *how me owȝt noȝt* (185.7) are impersonals. *Ye declared me* (110.1) is an ambiguous dative object which MnE would render *to me*.

Morphology—Pronouns

Nominative plural *we* is regular. Plural possessive *our(e) / owr(e)* is regular as the bound form; *oures* is regular as the free form. There is only one intensive: *to the same matere oureself wittyng* (89.9). Objective *us* is used as the indirect object of the verb or the direct object of a verb or preposition 195 out of 207 times. There is at least stylistic significance in the fact that 140 of the 207 occurrences of *us* are in the correspondence of Henry V (which comprises less than one fourth of the total text in the anthology), and 10 of the 18 non-MnE uses. Seven times in the Signet letters of Henry V and twice elsewhere, *us* is reflexive: e.g., *we hald vs wel agreed* (9.2), *we Recommaund vs vn to your lordship* (211.1). Eight times *us* is in what would be in MnE unidiomatic positions: e.g., *We your owne pore prestes vs recommande to your high and gracieux Lordship* (40.1), *ffor certayne materes vs moeuyng* (106.1, 155.1). Three times in Henry V and once later, *us* is used with the impersonal: *whan vs likeþ* (62.6), *at begynnyng vs yenkey* (69.16), *vs semeth* (81.19), *vs nedeth* (109.2).

Second person nominative singular *þu* occurs only once (142.26), in the transcription of an oral deposition; *thee* does not occur at all. *Ye* is used regularly as the nominative for both singular and plural, *you(e) / yow(e)* as the objective, *your(e) / yowr(e)* as the possessive. The free form *yours* appears only in one signature: *Robert ffrye youres* (110.4). *You* is used with the impersonal: *as yow þenkeþ* (55.4, 93.7), and there are 13 instances of *if it like / list / plese yow* (115.5, 111.1, etc.). *Yourself* occurs once as the intensive object: *in propir personeȝ to com by for yhour self* (173.17).

He / his / him and *she / her / her* are regular. *She* is spelled *scho / sheo* in three parallel petitions in different hands (119.7, 120.7, 121.7), revealing how faithful copyists could be to their originals. The form *her* may be the oblique of *she*, the plural possessive *their*, or the adverb *here*; *here* may be any of these or the verb *hear*. *His* appears once as a free form: *man of his* (142.40); *hers* does not so appear in these selections. *Himself* appears twice as an intensive, 13 times as a reflexive, but the usual reflexive is still *him / hym*—38 times. It is worth noting that reflexive *hym self* occurs only once in Henry V (65.5) and once in Privy Seal (156.5). The other 11 occurrences are in Chancery petitions, indicating that this form was a later, popular development. *Herself* occurs only once, as an intensive (18.3). The reflexive is *her*, e.g., *kepte her a goode womman* (212.6). *It / hit* is regular, often used as the impersonal subject: e.g., *And hit ys oure wille* (73.2); *like it vnto youre mageste* (123.11). *His* never appears in these documents as the possessive of *it*.

Except in one 1427 non-Chancery indenture, the nominative plural is always *they;* no. 235 has all the archaic plurals, *hy, here, hem,* as well as other non-Chancery forms. *Her(e) / har(e) / harre / heer* is used 63 times for the possessive plural alongside *their* (57 times), *thair* (11), *þeire* (25), *þaire* (17), *ther* (9), *þar* (3), *þer(e)* (2), *theyre* (2)—total 126. On the other hand, *hem* appears 148 times (11 times spelled *ham(e)*, alongside *them* 120 times, spelled *them* (21 times), *theym* (32), *þeim* (16), *þaim* (13), *þaym(e)* (9), *thaym(e)* (4), *theim* (9), *þeym* (11), *þem* (3), *þam* (1), *thethm* (1). Clearly *hem* was very much alive—as it is in colloquial 'em today—while plural possessive *her* was on the way out. *Hem / ham self* occurs as the reflexive eight times, *thaym self* once (193.15).

That is used as a demonstrative or a relative 1711 times. In the first 200 instances in the Signet letters of Henry V, it is used as a demonstrative six times; in the first 200 in Privy Seal, 16 times; in the first 200 in Chancery 27 times. On the other hand, in the first 200 instances in Henry V, *þat* is used as an auxiliary with conjunctions and adverbs six times (*as þat, because þat, for þat, how þat, if þat, while þat*) and 58 times with *wol* (*we wol þat*—once in MnE idiom, *hit is oure wille þat*, 59.8). This usage occurs less often in Privy Seal and Chancery. In the first 200 instances in Privy Seal there are three uses as auxiliaries and one *wol þat;* in the first 200 instances in Chancery, 11 are auxiliaries (*how that* seven times, *by cause that* two times, *after that, whether that*) and *wol þat* not at all.

The plural of *that* is *tho / thoo / þoo,* found 16 times. Twice we find *those* (146.4, 226.15). *This / þis* is always a demonstrative; plural *thes / these / thise / þes / þese / þise.* One time *þis* is used before a plural (158.15).

Which is found as a simple relative (A) 105 times: e.g., *xx Marc which we haue granted* (52.3), *my laste wille which apperith* (241.17), and (B) 104 times with *þe:* e.g., *þe whiche we sende you* (63.7), *for þe which he is bounde* (106.3). It is used (C) 13 times where MnE would use *who:* e.g., *Slake is deed Which was dean* (13.1), *Thomas walweynes wyf which hath maad a greuous compleynt* (93.1). (D) Nine times this *which* usage takes *þe:* e.g., *þerl . . . þe whiche dooþ* (12.2), *your seid besecher the which of tendre age* (232.15). *Which* is used as determinative (E) 51 times: e.g., *at whiche tyme* (64.9), *which wyne* (211.20); this usage with *þe* (F) 77 times: e.g., *þe which borde* (142.36), *the whiche Traitour* (159.14). The relative with *the* was modeled on the French form "lequel." In this case, the Signet of Henry V was somewhat more idiomatic than either Privy Seal or Chancery. For AB the total for all entries is 50% with *the;* for Henry V only 42% with *the.* For CD the total is 41% with *the;* for Henry V 37% with *the.* For EF the total is 60% with

Morphology—Verbs

the; for Henry V 59% with *the.* But Henry V twice uses *which þat* for *who* (34.2, 38.1), a form not found in the later documents.

Who is never used as an interrogative in these selections and only twice as a relative, once in the 1388 petition of the Mercers where it stands for whoever, *for who reproued such an officer* (161.23), and in a 1430 petition, *no mencion made . . . who shuld distreigne* (181.19). *Whose* and *whom* are used frequently as in MnE. There is one error of the ear: *on who sowle* (141.3).

What is used 15 times as whatever: e.g., *in what wise* (43.4), 17 times as a relative, and three times as an interrogative.

Verbs

In verb forms, the most evident difference from MnE is the use of *eth/eþ* as the ending for the 3rd person singular and for the imperative. It will be interesting eventually to trace the process by which this characteristic of Chancery Standard gave way to the *es/s* ending for the 3rd person and the zero ending for the imperative. Third person with *s* is never found in the Signet letters of Henry V, and we have noted it in only eight of the other 136 documents: in a 1417 letter from Thomas Longley, Bishop of Durham, which contains several non-Chancery forms, *has* occurs beside *apperteneth* (112.5, 9); in 1423 parallel petitions by the nurses of the infant Henry VI *as long as þam lykis* (119.3) and *as long as þe said descrete councell lykys* (120.4) appear beside *hath;* the 1423 petition by Thomas Rokeby begins with the conventional *Besecheth,* but all the other 3rd person endings are colloquial: *has, appiers, askys* (168.2, etc.); the 1423 draft of a Privy Seal letter setting forth payments to soldiers uses *encreses and growes* (169.10)—it would be interesting to know whether this was changed in the final draft; a 1429 petition from a retainer living in Windsor Castle begins *Biseches full lowelich and mekelich* (123.1); a 1430 petition from Lincolnshire uses *has ben* and *has bee* along with *are* (184.2, 4, 11); a lively 1432 letter from the Bishop of Bath lapses into *And he come to me in is owen persone þis daie & seies he wole noȝgt* (185.6); and a non-Chancery indenture has a downright solecism, *Iohn & william has putte yeir seles* (238.19). The contexts indicate that these are lapses from what must have been regarded as the formal *eth* ending for the 3rd person. The only ending for the imperative that we noted is likewise *eþ: we pray yow spekeþ vnto þarchebisshop* (26.10). The usual subjunctive 3rd person has zero inflection, as in MnE, e.g., *ȝef he go* (164.40).

The Midland *en* inflection for the plural verb is more common than

Northern *s* for the 3rd person singular—*en* being a conservative tendency and *s* a radical tendency. The *en* plural occurs in 13 of the 104 Signet letters of Henry V; 3 of 54 Privy Seal documents; 18 of 71 Chancery documents; three of the nine non-Chancery indentures. The percentages may reveal the drift more clearly than the actual numbers: *en* appears in 12% of Henry's letters and 6% of the Privy Seal, all of which are by Chancery clerks, versus 25% of the Chancery documents, many of which are not by Chancery clerks, and 33% of the indentures, none of which are by Chancery clerks. Nearly all of the occurrences of *en* are sporadic, in the midst of plural verbs with zero inflection: e.g., *merchantes . . . asken, Ianevoys maken, yay . . . desire, subgitȝ shuld* (69.10, 11, 13, 18); *there they leyn and communyd* (145.7); *they purchace and taken the matere . . . and cariene hit a way* (203.18). The two documents that use *en* most consistently are two of the earliest, the 1388 petition of the Mercers (161) and the 1414 petition of Thomas Paunfeld (163). *Besechen* and *prayen* are sometimes formulaic introductions in petitions which contain no other *en* plurals (cf. 202, 212, 217, 222, 227, 231). *Weren* occurs nine times compared to *wer(e)* 123 times. Clearly the *en* plural was on the way out although it persisted in set phrases and non-standard documents until after 1460.

The *en* ending was likewise a minority form for infinitives and past participles. The infinitive with *en* never occurs in the Signet letters of Henry V. It is found in one Privy Seal and four Chancery documents and in three of the nine indentures. These are sporadic usages, sometimes linked closely with non-*en* infinitives, e.g., *myȝte take and resseyuen* (198.8). There is an *en* infinitive in the exemplar (1.2), but the document with the most inflected infinitives is the 1414 petition by Paunfeld (163). The inflected infinitive is not found in the Mercers' petition (161), which, along with Paunfeld, uses the most *en* plurals (see above). But it is found in other London documents: twice in Chancery (179.8, 10) and three times in London indentures (233.14, 234.4, 237.19). The other appearances are in the non-standard petition for the Archbishop of Canterbury (177.20) and a petition from Limerick (198.8).

The *en* inflection was added to the past participles of several verbs which do not take it in MnE, and omitted from some that do: *hath abiden* (89.6); *in late dayes bygonnen* (193.2) beside *in late dayes begonne* (192.2); *bee / ben comen, ar comen* (74.5, 207.8, 96.3) beside eight uses of *come* as past participle; *be /hath bounden* (69.23, 131.8, etc.); *haþ founden* (24.3, 202.14—8 times) beside *hath found(e)* 11 times; *is holden* 17 times—never *is held*; *haue leten* (240.3)—never *have let; the saiden* (211 three times, evidently an individual aberration); *is witholden* (156.2). *Understanden* occurs nine times as a past participle; *stood / stode* occurs as the past tense of *stand* but never as a past participle. Past participles lacking *en* are *most be take awey* (40.11 and nine times more); *was take* (211.23) but *to be taken* eight times; *was broke* (199.42), *was broken* five times; *hath spoke* (98.2); *þey be chose* (87.5), *chosen* five times; *haue / be / do* (142.44 and nine times more, but none in Henry V).

The past tense and past participle are nearly always indicated by *ed*. Voiceless *t* occurs in petitions from the Earl of Ormond, *to be arrest* (124.4), and the Chamberlain of North Wales, *comprehendet* (191.3). The non-standard 1417 petition from the Bishop of Durham regularly spells the preterit with *t*: *passet, receyuet, liket,* etc. (112). *Wont* (three times) is *wonede* at 203.8, 14. *Went* (145.2), *wentte* (113.21) is *wende* at 194.6.

Another minority verb form is the past participle with *y* prefix. This occurs in 13 documents, none of which originated in Chancery, although some were copied over by Chancery clerks. One instance each is found in ten items: the 1388 Mercers' petition, *ydo* (161.3); 1438 Cambridge, *ycalled* (146.15); 1427 Southampton, *yshutte* (176.7); 1432 Hampshire, *y paied* (187.7); 1432 Somerset, *y nemnyd* (188.7); 1434 Limerick, *ywrete* (198.18); 1437 Bristol, *y callid* (202.36); 1439 presumably London, *yfound* (208.9); 1450 Isle of Wight, *y rulyd* (218.30); 1462 Devonshire, *y knowe* (241.1). A 1427 Winchester indenture has four instances: *y.sende, y.hadde* twice, *y. left* (235.5, 7, 8, 10); a 1429 petition from Wales, *yhold, ymade* (178.8, 10); a 1435 petition from Bristol, *ymade, yholde, y certified* (199.3, 28, 40).

The usual inflection for the present participle is *ing/yng*, occasionally *eng* (114.4, 129.3, etc.). In a 1440 petition by the Abbot of Bury St. Edmunds, a dialectal *end* creeps in: *and serue god prayend deuoutly* (153.9).

The verbs *to be* and *to do* show some differences from MnE. *Are* occurs in eight documents, only one from Henry V's Signet, *men þat ar comen* (96.3), and two others from Chancery (206.6, 210.18). The others are in various petitions ranging from Thomas Paunfeld (1414) to the Earl of Wiltshire (1454) (163.32, 184.11, 204.31, 223.13, 224.8). No document has more than one instance of *are*; the usual Chancery form is *be / ben / been*. So much of Chancery style is conditional that it is hard to tell whether the prevalence of *be* is purely stylistic or sometimes morphological: e.g., *if it so be* (5.7 and often elsewhere), *yif it be not oþerwise* (142.32); but *be / been* are used where MnE would certainly use *are*: e.g., *ffor asmuche as we be fully auysed* (28.1), *We be gladde* (137.1), *we been enformed* (51.1), *whiche ben vnder arest*

(145.23). *Be* is used for *been*: e.g., *it hath be vsed* (5.2), *Iohn Hull haath long tyme be* (14.1). *Been* is used for infinitive *be*: e.g., *to ben vsed* (161.47), *to been arered* (179.8). *Been* is used for *has / have*: e.g., *whiche by the deces of Robert . . . been descended* (89.4), *for asmoche as we and our counsail . . . been acertained* (117.4). *Beyng(e)* is used regularly in Henry's Signet letters to mean remaining: e.g., *oure greet seel beynge in youre kepynge* (15.5); *Robert haburgeham Sqwyer beynge heere in our seruice* (31.2). This usage occurs 22 times in the letters of Henry V and only twice (188.11 and 215.28) in the other documents. In the non-Signet items, *beyng* usually means state of being: e.g., *my lordys þere beyng present* (122.41), *he ther of not beyng gilty* (147.7).

Another feature of the Signet letters of Henry V is the use of *do / doo* as an auxiliary verb. There are three uses of *do*: (A) as a main verb, e.g., *þat ye do þis þing* (32.14); (B) *do* meaning "cause to be done," e.g., *we do you to wite* (87.1); (C) *do* as a vaguely causative auxiliary, e.g., *we wol ye do make a patent* (i.e., cause a patent to be made, 62.5). In the Signet letters (nos. 2-105) the A usage appears 23 times, B 12 times, and C 45 times. Of these last 45, 20 are the verb phrase *do make*, and the others similar collocations (e.g., *do write, do ordeyne, do kepe*). This usage is less frequent in Privy Seal and Chancery: Privy Seal (nos. 110-160) A 19 times, B 3, C 7; Chancery (nos. 161-232) A 20, B 2, C 5. However, the indentures (nos. 233-241) again make heavy use of C: A 2, B 1, C 6—*do byld* (233.18, 20), *do make* (237.9, 14), *do to make* (239.6), *do bryng* (238.16). It would appear that the causative auxiliary did not catch on in the Chancery offices generally, and MnE has followed the Chancery usage.

The use of *wol(e) / woll(e)* is likewise more frequent in the Signet letters of Henry V than in the later documents, but this is probably stylistic. Of the 137 uses in the Signet letters all but 13 are in the collocation *we wol* introducing the King's commands (see above p. 9). Of the other 13, 11 are simple futures: e.g., *as many shippes as wol suffice* (30.2). In the non-Signet documents, *wol* appears 11 times as a command, *The kyng wol. by þauis of his counsail* (131.8), and 20 times as a simple future, e.g., *I biseche yow þat ye wole consider þis matier* (185.10). All of the *wold(e)* forms in Henry V are in *we wolde* collocations of command. The *wold* forms in the other documents are all conditionals: e.g., *sche wold not assent* (212.5), *the seid Iohanne wolde haue departid* (222.16). *Wil(le)* is only twice used as a command, in a Signet letter, *We wil þat ye do make* (3.2), and in a 1440 Signet draft: *Wherefore we wille and pray yow* (107.4). In the same 1440 item it is a simple future, *ye wille putte* (107.6). Otherwise *will* is always a noun in the Signet letters (eight instances), but a simple future in the other documents, 24 instances. Evidently *wol* was disappearing and *will* was coming in both as a sign of the future and as a verb of desire or command.

We have noted only one instance of a proto-progressive verb form: *Thambassatours . . . haue be sumwhat taryed . . . Neuerthelees þei beth in comyng* (135.4).

Adverbs

The mark of the adverb in the Chancery documents is regularly *ly*. The earliest document in the anthology, the London indenture of 1384, has only this form (233.7, 25 *li*; 233.16, 23, 29 *ly*), but the 1388 petition of the Mercers, has *lich* twelve times (161.6, 11, 13, 29, 33, 35, 47, 54, 60, 67, 69, 71) and *ly* twice (161.29, 47). The 1429 petition of William Pope, the royal retainer living at Windsor Castle, begins *Biseches full lowelich and mekelich,* thoroughly mixing the dialects, and has *fully* later on (123.1, 9). A 1424 petition from Darbyshire has *marchantlich* (172.6). A 1433 petition from Salisbury begins *Shewith lowely* but has *hastylych* in an insert (196.1, 23). *Euerych(e)* appears in the Signet clerk Toly's last letter for Henry V (105.5), and twelve times in later documents, but *euery* appears 44 times, *mekely* eight times, and *oonly* twice. Clearly *lich* was a dialectal form that continued to be used but was disappearing from Chancery Standard.

Than(ne) is used 34 times as MnE then (adv.) and 13 times as than (conj.). *Then* is always adverbial except at 69.20, and 211.35. The form *alwey* occurs nine times alongside *allways* three times (like MnE toward / towards, forward / forwards).

Prepositions and Conjunctions

Prepositions had not been sorted out in Chancery English to the extent that they have been in MnE. There is indecision about the use of *at, in,* and *on: at oure Abbaye of Beekhelwyn* (30.7), *in oure Abbaye of Beekhelwyn* (31.7), *in point of deth* (196.13), *on al wise* (151.13), *on the same* (158.6), *sommes of moneye rennyng on hem* (26.4). Twice *in* is rendered by the French *en, en due forme* (2.6, 8.2). The most frequently used preposition is *of:* = about, *in dowte of his lyff* (164.40), *be agreed of the areragez* (168.12); = at, *men of Armes* (156.4); = by, *yerely of owre grante* (2.3), *he aught to haue of right* (82.5); = for, *of long tyme* (201.30), *Biseche ȝou of helpe* (162.12); = from, *ye cesse of al suche* (5.7); = in / on, *of tyme passed* (5.2), *xl fote of lengyth* (233.19), *entred of record* (122.27). *To* is used for *at: go to large*

(164.40); *by* for *for*: *by so long tyme* (210.16, etc.). *Before* refers 41 times to time and 36 times to place: *beforn* always refers to place; *behinde* always to time. The abstract use of *after* can be broader than in MnE: *be reuled after þaduise* (122.35 and four times more). *Als* occurs 17 times, always in documents with other non-Chancery forms (e.g., 112, 161, 168 etc.), but only once in the Signet letters (6.4). *As* is the favorite form throughout (811 times).

Betwix appears to have been favored by the Signet of Henry V and Privy Seal and in the non-Chancery indentures. *Betwene* is the favored form in the Chancery documents. *Betwix* appears nine times, *betwene* three in Henry V; *betwix* ten, *betwene* two in Privy Seal; *betwix* five, *betwene* two in the indentures; but *betwix* nine, *betwene* 23 in the Chancery petitions.

The subjunct infinitive is 85 times connected by *for*: *we write . . . vnto þe quenes conseil for to deliuere* (18.5), *it shal be leful to the seid Robert . . . for to distreyne* (237.20). But more frequently *for* is lacking.

Some verbs take completive prepositions found in MnE colloquial idiom: *þe day he deyed on* (63.4), *make hym out oure lettres* (80.5).

Negation

The proclitic negative is seldom found in these selections. The MnE negative, auxiliary + not + main verb, is the usual form, but a common variant is main verb + not.

There are 13 proclitic negatives, two from the Signet letters of Henry V: *we ne haue but litil comfort* (40.10), *ye ne couthe not ymagyn* (72.4)—the latter resulting in a typical double negative. Six more are found in Privy Seal and Chancery documents dating before 1430 (* = *nys*; ** = *nolde*) 113.24; 117.8, 12; 163.8; 176.10; *172.8; four from documents between 1430 and 1440, **113.12; *181.19; *182.11; 190.17; and one from a Privy Seal draft of c1440, *that ye ne do neither soeffre* (154.5).

This diminishing usage was replaced by the verb + not: *ye leue not þis* (1.5), *there men dorst nought trauailleden* (161.43), and forms more like MnE: *þe barons . . . wol not discharge hem* (26.4), *þer can not be arered vj li* (223.15). The verb + not occurs 37 times in comparison to auxiliary + not + verb 174 times: *he come not* (183.13), *the . . . shirreves ordeyned not* (190.9), in contrast to *haþ not brawt* (24.5), *wolle not appere* (183.14). *Not*, spelled also *nat, notte, noht, nogt, naght, noght, noȝt, nogth, naught, nought, niouȝt, nowht,* is always a negative particle except twice: *he hadde nowht for reparacion* (16.6), *go to noght* (189.34).

Some 86 times the negative is formed with *no / noo:* e.g., *they schul paye . . . no custume* (4.3), *I kan no nothir write* (112.11), *i dar kepe þaim no lenggre* (185.11). Three or four times this locution, which is acceptable MnE, is replaced by the not + any form: *thaym self nought sufferyng any englisshman* (193.15), *Shiref be not vexed by any astate* (223.35). *No wise* is used ten times, *no manere* nine times: *þe possessions þat Longeth þerto yn no wyse* (39.4), *noo maner of paiements be made to no maner persone* (115.24). The indefinite *no one* is always (13 times) expressed by *no man: suffreth no man to doo hym wrong* (82.5).

No / noo almost always appears before consonants, *non / noon / noun* usually before vowels and h; exceptions are *noon liueree be made* (40.16), *tourneth to noon neer ende* (69.15). Sometimes *none* is a pronoun: *if þere noon bee* (67.7), *non suche that haue so duellyd* (192.24). *Nor* is sometimes rendered *ne* or *ner*. *Neither* (11 times) is rendered *neþer* (three times) and *nother* (five times). At 183.15 *noþer* means *nor* and it appears twice in double negatives, *no nother* (112.11, 199.11).

NOTES

Introduction

[1] Ernst Dolle, *Zur Sprache Londons vor Chaucer,* Halle: Niemeyer, 1913, analyzed the language of seven charters in English, two by William the Conqueror and the other five before 1160, and the 1258 proclamation of Henry III, but these are remnants of the Anglo-Saxon tradition rather than precursors of the modern.

[2] 103 Signet letters because no. 40 is a petition to the King from St. Mary Graces which accompanied no. 39. Signet letters previously printed: 6, 43, 46, 57, 58, 67, 69, 70, 71, 81, 82, 98.

[3] Privy Seal documents previously printed: 116, 117, 122, 159.

[4] Parliamentary and Chancery documents not previously printed: 162, 168, 169, 170, 175, 176, 178, 185, 186, 191, 198, 200, 203, 204, 205, 209, 211, 219, 220, 221.

[5] M. L. Samuels, "Some Applications of Middle English Dialectology," *English Studies* 44 (1963), 81-94, rptd. Roger Lass ed., *Approaches to English Historical Linguistics,* New York: Holt, 1969, pp. 404-18. See also Samuels, *Linguistic Evolution,* Cambridge: Cambridge Univ. Press, 1972, pp. 165-70.

[6] T.F. Tout, *Chapters in The Administrative History of Mediaeval England,* 6 vols., Manchester: Univ. of Manchester Press, 1920-33, I.3. F. Palgrave, *An Essay Upon the Original Authority of the King's Council,* London, 1834.

[7] Discussion of the origin of Chancery is found in Tout, *Chapters in Administrative History,* passim, but esp. Vol. I; Tout, "The English Civil Service in the Fourteenth Century," *Bulletin of the John Rylands Library* 3 (1916-17), 185-214; Tout, "The Household of Chancery and Its Disintegration," *Essays in History Presented to R. L. Poole,* ed. H. W. C. Davis, Oxford: Oxford Univ. Press, 1927, pp. 46-85; H. C. Maxwell-Lyte, *Historical Notes on the Use of the Great Seal of England,* London: H. M. Stationery Office, 1926, pp. 1 ff. A bibliographical survey is to be found in Malcolm Richardson, *The Influence of Henry V on the Development of Chancery English,* Diss. Univ. of Tennessee, 1978.

[8] Gower's apology is in *The Complete Works of John Gower,* ed. G. C. Macaulay, 4 vols., Oxford: Clarendon, 1899-1901, I.391, Balade XVIII.4. Examples of bad law French are quoted by F. W. Maitland, *The Year Books of Edward III,* Selden Society 17(1903), I.xli ff.

[9] Tout, "Household of Chancery," pp. 58-59, drawing upon Rymer's *Foedera,* III,53-62.

[10] "Household," p. 60.

[11] The fullest history of the Rolls House is by H.C. Maxwell-Lyte, *Fifty-Seventh Report of the Deputy Keeper of Public Records* (1896). In *Historical Notes on the Use of the Great Seal,* p. 4, Maxwell-Lyte observes that the separation of the household of the chancellor from the household of the king began in 1260 when Henry III granted Nicholas, Archdeacon of Ely, then Chancellor, 400 marks a year for the maintenance of himself and the clerks of Chancery. See also W. Holdsworth, *A History of English Law,* 17 vols., London: Methuen, 1903-12, I.419 ff.; B. Wilkinson, *The Chancery under Edward III,* Manchester:

Univ. of Manchester Press, 1929, pp. 57-59; and V. H. Galbraith, *An Introduction to the Use of the Public Records,* 2nd ed., Oxford: Oxford Univ. Press, 1949, pp. 1 ff.

[12]For example, see the Signet clerks of Henry V discussed below. In addition to their service in the Signet Office, Robert Shiryngton was controller of the king's works and eventually chancellor of the Duchy of Lancaster; William Toly was secretary to Cardinal Beaufort and eventually to Henry VI; John Hethe was a clerk in Privy Seal; and Richard Caudray became secretary to Henry V in 1420.

[13]Galbraith, *Introduction to the Use of the Public Records,* p. 28. See also Tout, *Chapters in Administrative History* I.16, II.305; Wilkinson, *Chancery under Edward III,* Chap. 2, esp. pp.24-25; J. F. Baldwin, *The King's Council in England During the Middle Ages,* Oxford: Clarendon, 1913, pp. 236 et passim; A. J. Otway-Ruthven, *The King's Secretary and the Signet Office in the Fifteenth Century,* Cambridge: Cambridge Univ. Press, 1939; Florence M. G. Hingham, "A Note on the Pre-Tudor Secretary," in *Essays in History Presented to T. F. Tout,* ed. A. G. Little and F. M. Powicke, Manchester, 1925, pp. 361-62; L. B. Dibden, "Secretaries in the Thirteenth and Fourteenth Centuries," *EHR* 25 (1910), 438.

[14]1295: "[Rex Franciae] linguam Anglicam, si conceptae iniquitatis proposito detestabili potestas correspondeat, quod Deus avertat, omnino de terra delerre proponit," W. Stubbs, *Select Charters,* 9th ed., London, 1913, p. 480. 1344: "& coment son dit Adversaire [the French King] s'afforce tant come il poet a destruire nostre . . . dit Terres & Lieux, & la Lange d'Engleterre," *RP* II.150b. 1346: "Et sur ce fu monstre une Ordenance faite par le dit Adversaire, & ascuns Grantz de France & de Normandie, a destruire & anientier tote la Nation & la Lange Engleys," *RP* II. 158b. 1376: "son dit Adversaire . . . s'afforce par toutes les voies q'il poet . . . a destruire nostre Seigneur le Roy & son Roialme d'Engleterre, & d'ouster de tout la Lange Engleys, que Dieu ne veulle," *RP* II. 362b.

Linguistic nationalism was likewise makings its appearance in France. Ferdinand Brunot, *Histoire de la Langue Française de Origins a nos Jours,* 1900-10, 12 vols., Paris: Colin, 1966, I. 369-70, lists a series of French royal orders about the use of French—all expressed, of course, in Latin: by Philip the Fair (1285-1314), letters were to be written to "bonis villis gallicanis in gallico, et occitanis in latino"; by John the Good (1350-64), royal ordinances were to be transmitted "in lingua materna" [it is interesting though probably not significant that Henry IV challenged the crown "in lingua materna," *RP* III. 422.53]; by Charles the Mad (1380-1422), royal proclamations were to be disseminated "in romanico sive romana lingua." The reluctance of the inhabitants in the south of France in the 14th century to accept Parisian French as an offical language led to the persistence of Latin in this region, as in England. The ordinance of John the Good could have provided a model for the English statute of 1362; the ordinance of Charles could have provided a model for the action of Henry V.

[15]1362: "Primierement feust crie fait en la Sale de Westminster par . . . du Chanceller par cause que plousours Prelatz, Seigneurs & Communes, qui duissent venir a cest Parlement ne sont pas . . . preschein a venir. Au quel jour,

esteantz nostre Seigneur le Roi, Prelatz, Countes, Barons, & les Communes en la Chambre de Peinte . . . monstre en Englois par . . . de Grene, Chief Justice le Roi, les Causes des Somons du Parlement," *RP* II. 268; the omissions are illegible in the original Roll, C65/20/1. That the records were not kept in the language of the oral discussion is clearly indicated by Statute I.C.15, 36 Edward III, which directs that despite the use of English for oral pleading, court records are to be enrolled in Latin: see F. Pollock and F.W. Maitland, *The History of English Law*, 2 vols., Cambridge: Cambridge Univ. Press, 1898, I.83, note 3, and note 21 below.

[16]1362: "Et apres le Chanceller dit, coment les Prelatz, Ducs, Contes, Barons, & toute la Commune, avoient monstrez au Roi les grantz Meschiefs que sont avenuz as pluseurs du Roialme, de ce que les Leies, Custumes, & Estatutz de dit Roialme ne sont pas conuz comunement en ycel, par cause q'ils sont pledez, monstrez, & juggez en la lange Franceois, q'est trop desconu en la dit Roialme, issint que les gentz qui pledent, ou sont empledez, en les Courtz le Roi & les Courtz d'autries, n'ont entendement ne conissance de ce q'est dit pur eux ne contre eux par lour Sergeantz & autres Pledours.

"Et par cela cause & pluseurs autres le Roi desirrant le bon government & tranquillite de son poeple, & de ouster les Meschiefs que sont & purront avenir cele partie, de l'assent des ditz Prelatz, Ducs, Contes, Barons, & Commune en cest present Parlement assemblez, voet que toutes Plees que serront a pleder en ses Courtz quelconques, devant quelconques ses Justices, ou en ses autres Places, ou devant ses autres Ministres quelconques, ou en les Courtz & Places des autres Seigneurs quelconques deinz son Roialme, soient pledez & monstrez en la lange Engleise . . .," *RP* II.273b. As may be seen, this statute is broader than the law courts. It requires all the King's ministers, i.e., all departments of government, to conduct their oral inquisitions and discussions in English.

[17]*RP* II.275a, II.283a, III.98a. In 1377 the Archbishop of York, then Chancellor, specifies "j'ay dist sont tant a dire en Franceys" (*RP* III.3a). In 1384 and 1385 (*RP* III.184, III.203) the opening of Parliament is recorded in Latin instead of the customary French; see note 21 below.

[18]Of the 75 documents printed by Chambers and Daunt, eight are missives from Henry V (i.e., Signet) and two others are from the Dukes of Clarence and Bedford (i.e., Privy Seal). Sixty-five may be classed as civic documents. Susan Hughes in *English in the Letter-Books and Plea and Memoranda Rolls of the Corporation of London, 1377-1422, in Comparison with Contemporaneous Chancery English: Their Possible Roles in the Evolution of Chancery Standard and Modern English,* Diss. Univ. of Tennessee, 1978, and in the summary of her conclusions in "Guildhall and Chancery English 1377-1422," *Guildhall Studies in London History* 4 (1980), 53-62, added five printed civic items to the 75 in Chambers and Daunt, one from *Guildhall Letter Book H* and four from the *Plea and Memoranda Rolls*. In her study Hughes concluded that the Guildhall scribes picked up the usages of Henry's Signet letters even more rapidly than did the scribes who wrote the pre-1422 entries in the *Rotuli Parliamentorum*. In this connection, see also J. H. Fisher, "Chancery and the Emergence of Standard Written English in the Fifteenth Century," *Speculum* 52 (1977), esp. pp. 896-98. The nineteen pre-1422 *Rotuli Parliamentorum* entries are as follows: 1) 1388 Petition of the Mercers (III.222); 2) 1397 Address

of Judge Rikhill on the impeachment of Gloucester (III.378); 3) 1399 Henry IV's claim to the throne (III.422.53); 4) 1399 Henry IV's general amnesty (III.423.56); 5) 1399 Justice Thyrnyng's address to Richard II (III.424.59); 6) 1399 Account of Richard II's response (III.424.60); 7) 1399 Sentence delivered by Justice Thyrnyng (III.451.9); 8) 1403 Petition of Northumberland (III.524.11); 9) 1404 Henry IV's answer to petition from Commons asking him to "leve upon his owne" (III.549.20); 10) 1405 Appointment of Henry Percy (III.605.8); 11) 1411 Ordinance between Lord Roos and Robert Tirwhit (III.650.13); 12) 1411 Same as 11 (III.650.14); 13) 1414 Petition from Commons asking that laws not change the language of petitions (IV.22.22); 14) 1414 King's assent (IV.22.22); 15) 1414 Petition of Paunfield (IV.57); 16) 1415 One English sentence in a French petition of Meryng (IV.73.17); 17) 1421 Decree on taxation (IV.151.10); 18) 1421 Petition from the Physicians (IV.158); 19) 1421 Petition from the Soldiers (IV.159).

Of these we located the originals and have printed nos. 1 and 15 (documents 161, 163). In addition, we have printed three English petitions from the Early Chancery Proceedings of the reign of Henry V: no. 164 in Chancery hand and language, 165 and 166 in non-Chancery hand and language.

[19] The petition and assent are nos. 13 and 14 in the previous list. The English of the petition is somewhat less standard than that of the assent: *axe, axed,* vs. *askynge; hie* (high), *of lasse than they* (unless they). Both entries have *lust* with the dative: (13) *as theym lust,* (14) *as him lust.*

[20] On Henry's encouragement of English see Richardson, *Henry V,* pp. 71-72 and "Henry V, the English Chancery, and Chancery English," *Speculum* 55(1980),726-50; Otway-Ruthven, pp. 28-29, 46; K. B. McFarlane, *Lancastrian Kings and Lollard Knights,* Oxford: Clarendon, 1972, p. 119; Margaret Wade Labarge, *Henry V: The Cautious Conqueror,* London: Secker and Warburg, 1975, pp. 53, 145. The statement of the ambassadors at Constance is from C. H. Lawrence, *The English Church and the Papacy in the Middle Ages,* London: Burnes and Oates, 1965, p. 211.

[21] In *RP* 1422 there are English 6 entries, French 35 entries, Latin 5 entries, out of a total of 46 entries; 1423: Eng. 10, Fr. 43, Lat. 7, total 60; 1425: Eng. 13, Fr. 25, Lat. 19, total 51; 1426: Eng. 9, Fr. 20, Lat. 19, total 38; 1427: Eng. 6, Fr. 34, Lat. 13, total 46; 1429: Eng. 18, Fr. 33, Lat. 26, total 70; 1430-31: Eng. 7, Fr. 32, Lat. 14, total 46; 1432: Eng. 9, Fr. 33, Lat. 19, total 52; 1433: Eng. 18, Fr. 34, Lat. 23, total 69; 1435: Eng. 8, Fr. 14, Lat. 10, total 29; 1436-37: Eng. 15, Fr. 15, Lat. 11. total 38; 1439: Eng. 29, Fr. 27, Lat. 12, total 63: 1441-42: Eng. 21, Fr. 16, Lat. 9, total, 39; 1444: Eng. 34, Fr. 8, Lat. 13, total 51; 1447: Eng. 12, Fr. 7, Lat. 8, total 25; 1449: Eng. 15, Fr. 6, Lat. 10, total 25. The individual entries come to more than the total because when they are in two or three languages, they have been counted two or three times. After 1450 the only French entries are the lists of receivers and triers of petitions, which continued in French until at least 1503 (the end of the printed *RP* volumes) except that in 1491 and 1495 these lists are in Latin. Beginning in 1425, the opening of Parliament, which had been customarily recorded in French, began to be recorded in Latin; Latin was used for the opening, for descriptive headings, and for a few entries at least until 1503. Some of the entries during the early part of the century reveal again that the discussion was in English. For exam-

ple, no. 16 of 1426 (*RP* IV.298) has the exposition in Latin, but the lines spoken by the witnesses are in English. In no. 19 of 1432 (*RP* IV.393), the clerks of the Royal Chapel present a petition in Latin, but the introductory appeal to Parliament is in English. The transition from French to English in the Statutes of the Realm came when the statutes began to be incorporated in the Rolls of Parliament during the reign of Richard III, see Pollock and Maitland, *The History of English Law,* I. 86 note.

[22]Quoted here from Chambers and Daunt, *Book of London English,* p. 139. The statement is quoted by A. C. Baugh and Thomas Cable, *A History of the English Language,* 3rd ed., New York: Prentice-Hall, 1978, p. 153, with "lords" and "commons" lower case, which conceals the reference to Parliament. In the *Drapers' Company Transcripts of the Earliest Records in the Possession of the Company,* London: Chiswick Press, 1910, the records are in French (with an increasing number of interlarded English words and phrases) until 1441. In that year, without explanation, the records begin, "Thys accompt y made the ix day of Nouembre the xixthe yer of kyng Harry the vjthe by John Gedney maist*er* John Wotton John Derby Robert Bertyn & Thomas Cook Wardeynes of the craft of draperes for the yer last past ffurst rewceyued by the accompt of the olde Wardeynes in the box" (p. 64), and thereafter the records are all in English. It is interesting to observe in an entry as late as 1441 the non-Chancery form *y made.*

[23]The largest group of Council proceedings are in B. M. Cotton Cleopatra F.III and IV and Cotton Vespasian F.VII. These, supplemented from manuscripts in the PRO E28 files, have been edited by Sir Harris Nicolas, *Proceedings and Ordinances of the Privy Council of England,* 7 vols., London, 1834-37. Nicolas begins with 1389-90. The first English entry, instructions to an English diplomat, is 1410 (1:323-27); the second, advice from the peers on the French succession, is 1414 (2:140-42); in 1417, there is a letter in English from the bishops to the King (2:236), and the first Council minutes in English (2:237-39). Throughout the rest of Henry V, the English is mostly letters, although two discussion papers (2:350-58, 2:363-67) suggest that the business of the Council was being carried on in English. Beginning with the conciliar rule in the name of the infant Henry VI, Council minutes in English begin to grow more frequent. In 1437, the year in which Henry VI assumed rule in his own name, the proceedings become nearly all English. We may observe in passing that Rymer's *Foedera* gives a quite erroneous impression of the rate at which English penetrated the administration, first because Rymer concentrated on foreign relations and charters and grants, where French and Latin persisted longest, but also because of his own linguistic prejudices. Rymer included an English document only when he could not find one in French or Latin that told the same story.

The typewritten list of Ancient Petitions in English in the PRO (SC8) gives an indication of the movement of Parliamentary and Chancery proceedings from French and Latin into English. Before 1400, there are only two petitions in English; 1401-10 none; 1411-20 eight; 1421-30 sixty-three; 1431-40 one hundred and thirty-two; 1441-50 one hundred and thirty-five; 1451-60 one hundred and forty-two. But after 1455 the collection begins to peter out as the judicial functions of Chancery become more independent of Parliament (between 1451-55 there are one hundred and twenty-six English petitions; 1456-60 only sixteen).

The earliest notable collections of private papers are the Stonor Letters and Papers (1290-1483, the first English letter in 1420), the Paston Papers (1440-86), the Cely Letters (1472-88), the Plumpton Correspondence (1461-1551), and the Trevelyan Papers (1446-1643). Norman Davis, "The Language of the Pastons," *Proceedings of the British Academy* 40 (1955 for 1954), pp. 119-44, shows the drift in the usage of John II and John III towards Chancery after 1460. Mary Patricia Relihan, *The Langage of the English Stonor Letters, 1420-1483*, Diss. Univ. of Tennesse, 1977, finds lack of standardization and non-Chancery forms even in the latest letters. The greatest regularity appears to be in letters from individuals who might be presumed to have had formal training in the law or to employ professional clerks. She concludes that neither location nor date of composition appears to make much difference; training in writing the standard language appears to be the significant factor.

[24] The best summary to date is Chaps. 2-4 in D. G. Scragg, *A History of English Spelling*, Manchester: Manchester Univ.Press, 1974. Scragg acknowledges the influence of Chancery and gives a good general summary of its orthographic conventions. N. F. Blake has treated the language of Caxton and the early printers in a series of articles: "English Versions of *Reynard the Fox* in the Fifteenth and Sixteenth Centuries," *SP* 62 (1965), 63-77; "Caxton's Language," *NM* 67 (1966), 122-32; *Caxton and His World*, London: Deutsch, 1969, pp. 173 ff. Blake holds that the early printers impeded the process of standardization since they lacked the training of the scribes and set type from manuscripts employing different conventions.

Chancery Hand

[1] On the origin and development of the English business cursive (court or anglicana) hand see M. B. Parkes, *English Cursive Book Hands 1250-1500*, London: Scholar, 1979, p. xx, etc; L. C. Hector, *The Handwriting of English Documents*, London: Arnold, 1958, p. 54, etc. On the possible influence of the scribes of the Black Prince, Pierre Chaplais, *English Royal Documents 1199-1461*, Oxford: Clarendon, 1971, p. 52.

[2] H. T. Riley, *Memorials of London*, London: Longmans, 1868, p. 295. On the broad meaning of the term court hand, Hector, p. 54; Hilary Jenkinson, *English Court Hand, A.D. 1066-1500*, 2 vols., Oxford: Clarendon, 1915, I. 5.

[3] Parkes, *English Cursive Book Hands*, pp. xiv-xvi.

[4] On the characteristics of the 14th century reform, Parkes, p. xix; Hector, pp. 52-54; Chaplais, p. 52.

[5] Plate I is from Georges Tessier, *Diplomatique royale française*, Paris: Picard, 1962, Plate IX, p. 232.

[6] The letter incorporating the Guild of Cursitors, 4 September 1573 (PRO 220/15/4) is calendared in *CPR, Eliz. I*, no. 416, p. 96. PRO 220/15/7 begins with the oath of office in a lovely book hand and continues with regulations for the cursitors' activities. PRO 220/15/8 contains the records of admission. On the history of the guild see the *First Report of the Committee on Public Records* (1800, in the PRO), pp. 233ff; H. C. Maxwell-Lyte, *Historical Notes*

on the Use of the Great Seal, p. 15.

[7] See Proceedings of Parliament note 5 below and D. 220 for examples of originals re-written by Chancery scribes, and p. 24 above for the tendency of enrolling scribes to standardize the spelling of the original petitions. James F. Baldwin, *The King's Council During the Middle Ages*, pp. 238ff, and even more emphatically A.R. Myers, "Parliamentary Petitions in the Fifteenth Century," *EHR* 52 (1937), 385-404, 590-613, argue that the original petitions to Parliament were not drawn by the Chancery clerks but by scriveners and other non-professional scribes. However, Maxwell-Lyte, *Historical Notes*, pp. 155, 265; Wilkinson, *Chancery Under Edward III*, pp. 78-80; C.H. McIlwain, *The High Court of Parliament and Its Supremacy*, 1910, rptd. New Haven: Yale Univ. Press, 1934, p. 210; and W. Baildon, *Select Cases in Chancery 1364-1471*, Selden Society 10 (1896), p. xii, all agree that the similarity in style, form, and appearance indicates that the Ancient Petitions in the PRO (SC8) were drawn up by the Chancery clerks. The decreasing number of documents in non-Chancery hand is evidence of the growing monopoly of the Chancery clerks. This monopoly came to be concentrated in the office of the "Six Clerks," whose control of the inflow and outflow from Chancery became a scandal by the 18th century, and was not terminated until 1842; see Holdsworth, *History of English Law*, I. 421-23, and T.W. Braithwaite's more sympathetic view, *The Six Clerks of Chancery: Their Successors in Office, and the Houses They Lived In—A Reminiscence*, London, 1879.

N. Denholm-Young, *Handwriting in England and Wales*, Cardiff: Univ. of Wales Press, 1954, p. 35, observes that "the special set Chancery hand became stereotyped in the reign of Henry VI." H. F. Jenkinson, *English Court Hand*, I.15, says "No doubt [this standardization] was at first unconscious, due to the recruiting of clerks in different departments by the system of apprenticeship." Apropos the larger question of the influence of Chancery, Jenkinson, "Elizabethan Handwriting," *Library* 3 (1922-23), 3-4, remarks that the "fashions" in business hands "were largely set by the royal courts and other departments of public administration, and in developments which occurred in public administration from the 13th century downwards we find a very close connexion with those of writing, means of authentication of executive documents, and the conventional form of these documents, the departments or functionaries which controlled and issued them, and even the language in which they were written—all these went through a series of changes closely parallel to each other and those of handwriting." M. T. Clanchey, *From Memory to Written Record*, London: Arnold, 1979, pp. 50-57, discusses the way in which the practice of producing authenticated documents spread from the royal Chancery and Exchequer to episcopal sees and civic guilds and corporations. The earliest bishops to inaugurate registers both had been Chancery officials.

Signet Letters of Henry V

[1] J. L. Kirby, *Calendar of Signet Letters of Henry IV and Henry V, 1399-1422*, London: H. M. Stationery Office, 1978.

²Five letters to his subjects in France are in French, Kirby, 877, 878, 879, 882, 884. But Henry did not always communicate with his English subjects in English. Jules Delpit, *Collection général des documents Française*, 1847, rptd. Geneva: Slatkine Reprints, 1971, pp. 216-19, has an example of a letter to the Londoners in French and a reply in French to one of the King's English letters.

³Florence E. Harmer, *Anglo-Saxon Writs*, Manchester: Manchester Univ. Press, 1952, p. 24. Hubert Hall, *A Formula Book of English Historical Documents*, 2 vols., Cambridge: Cambridge Univ. Press, 1908-09, I. 100ff.

⁴Pierre Chaplais, "English Diplomatic to the End of Edward III's Reign," in *The Study of Medieval Records: Essays in Honour of Kathleen Major*, ed. D. A. Bullough and R. L. Storey, Oxford: Clarendon, 1971, pp. 34-35.

⁵Kirby has calendared all of the MS Signet letters of Henry V, and we here print all of the English, but the copies of his letters in other collections have not been listed or collected. The beginnings of such a collection are in Malcolm Richardson, *The Influence of Henry V on the Development of Chancery English*, pp. 21, 49, and Appendix A.

⁶James J. Murphy, *Rhetoric in the Middle Ages*, Berkeley: Univ. of California Press, 1974, pp. 203ff.

⁷Murphy, p. 239. Martin Camargo has in hand editions of the works of the English writing masters.

⁸The conventions of early English letters are discussed by C. L. Kingsford *English Historical Literature in the Fifteenth Century*, Oxford: Clarendon, 1913, and *Prejudice and Promise in XVth-Century England*, Oxford: Clarendon, 1925; by Norman Davis, "The *Litera Troili* and English Letters," *RES* 16 (1965), 233-44, and "Style and Stereotype in Early English Letters," *Leeds Studies in English* 1 (1967), 7-17. The only English letter so far discovered in a dictaminal formulary is printed and discussed by Linda Ehrsam Voigts, "A Letter from a Middle English Dictaminal Formulary in Harvard Law Library MS. 43," *Speculum* 56 (1981), 575-81.

⁹Harmer, pp. 24-26.

¹⁰Hall, *Formula Book*, I. 32.22.

¹¹Hall, *Formula Book*, I. 109.20. "De par le Roy" could sometimes come at the end, cf. Chaplais, *Royal Documents*, Plate 5c, 10c. Chaplais, pp. 28-29, speaks of the more formal salutations as characteristic of "administrative writs" and the less formal apostrophe as characteristic of informal, friendly letters. However, the Signet letters of Henry V must be construed as administrative instruments.

¹²Hall, *Formula Book*, I.98, dates this exemplar c 1483, but it is in the same sort of hand as that of the Signet clerks of Henry V and is in the same C81 collection in the PRO. The double S decoration after Hammond's signature (see Plate II) is similar to that used by Shiryngton from no. 68 onwards, replacing the simpler S decoration of his earlier letters (see after "king" in the heading and just before the signature in Plate III).

¹³Hall, *Formula Book*, I.105.110; 111.124.

¹⁴Harmer, p. 160.18.

¹⁵Harmer, p. 165.25; 199.38, 220.45, etc.

¹⁶Chaplais, *Royal Documents*, p. 27.

[17] Hall, *Formula Book*, I.105.110.
[18] Harmer, pp. 120.1, 121.2, etc.
[19] Chaplais, *Royal Documents*, p. 13.
[20] T. A. M. Bishop, *Scriptores Regis*, Oxford: Clarendon, 1960, p. 20.
[21] A. J. Otway-Ruthven, *The King's Secretary and the Signet Office in the Fifteenth Century*, p. 111. Otway-Ruthven summarizes the careers of the Signet clerks, pp. 180ff.
[22] Otway-Ruthven, pp. 26-27.
[23] Otway-Ruthven, pp. 182-84.
[24] Otway-Ruthven, p. 157, note 12, cites no. 88, but not no. 87. Otway-Ruthven does not find the appearance of Hethe's signature on 88 "conclusive" evidence that he was a Signet clerk; but, one may ask, what would a Privy Seal clerk be doing signing two letters dated from Meleun, not to mention the 15 other letters that appear to be in the same hand? A. L. Brown, "The Privy Seal Clerks in the Fifteenth Century," in *Essays in Honour of Kathleen Major*, ed. D.A. Bullough and R. L. Storey, lists Hethe in Privy Seal ante 1398 and post 1422 (p. 262, n.2).
[25] Otway-Ruthven, p. 185.
[26] Kirby 881 and references.
[27] Rymer has *may*.
[28] On the reflection of Henry's personality in his epistolary style, K. B. MacFarlane, *Lancastrian Kings and Lollard Knights*, p. 117; C. L. Kingsford, *Henry V*, 2nd ed., New York: Putnam's, 1923, p. 82. On Henry's education, see Richardson, *Henry V*, Chap. II.
[29] A third example of Henry V's own prose that might be considered is his will, printed by J. Nicolas, *A Collection of All the Wills of the Kings and Queens of England*, 1780, rptd. New York: Kraus, 1969, pp. 236-43. However, this was not written either by Henry himself or by any of his Signet clerks, but by a scribe with several North Midland characteristics: the preterit is usually (but not always) *t*, and we find *agayn, ar, kan, yngland, erchbisshop*. Beside these Midland forms, we find *symplich*, and *hir* beside *yaire* (in Nicolas þ is always rendered *y*).
[20] Letters possibly drafted or dictated: 5, 6, 16, 18, 24, 28, 30, 32, 43, 46, 51, 53, 57, 60, 62, 64, 67, 69, 70, 71, 72, 77, 81, 93, 96, 98, 104—total 27. Letters requesting action: 3, 7, 8, 9, 10, 11, 12, 13, 14, 17, 20, 21, 23, 25, 29, 31, 34, 35, 36, 38, 41, 45, 48, 49, 50, 52, 59, 63, 68, 74, 75, 76, 78, 79, 80, 83, 85, 86, 87, 88, 89, 90, 91, 94, 97, 99, 101, 103, 105—total 49. Letters approving requests in accompanying petitions: 2, 15, 19, 22, 26, 27, 33, 37, 39, 42, 44, 47, 54, 55, 56, 58, 61, 65, 66, 73, 82, 84, 92, 95, 100, 102—total 26.

Later Signet and Privy Seal Papers

[1] Items signed by the Council: 124, 131, 175, 191.
[2] Items initialed by Henry VI: 106, 108, 138, 140, 143, 149, 151, 153, 158.
[3] Otway-Ruthven, *The King's Secretary*, pp. 76, 87, etc.; L. B. Dibden, "Secretaries in the Thirteenth and Fourteenth Centuries," *EHR* 25 (1910), 430-44.

Proceedings of Parliament

[1] Palgrave, *Essay Upon the King's Council,* p. 21; McIlwain, *The High Court of Parliament.*

[2] See Introduction, note 21. A broad topic which we cannot here pursue is the political ambience for the revival of English as the language of government: the weakness of Henry IV as a usurper, which strengthened Parliament; the need of Henry V for the support of Parliament in his French wars; the ineffectuality of Henry VI throughout his long, nominal reign; the culminating civil war between factions of the nobility. All of these contributed to the decline of the Anglo-Norman aristocracy and the rise of the native population. It seems no accident that the term and concept "gentleman" emerged during the same period that government and business were adopting English for official use: see B. Wilkinson, *Constitutional History of the Fifteenth Century* (London, 1964), Chap. 1; T. B. Pugh, "The Magnates, Knights, and Gentry," *Fifteenth Century England,* ed. Chrimes, Ross, and Griffiths, Manchester: Manchester Univ. Press, England, 1972, pp. 86-128.

[3] *Proceedings in Chancery in the Reign of Queen Elizabeth, with earlier examples,* Vol. I, Record Commission, 1827, Preface.

[4] See Chancery Hand, note 7.

[5] For example, PRO/C1/6/318 and 321 are depositions concerning the divorce of Lady Margery of Langford in a non-Chancery legal hand whose most noticeable characteristic is its spelling of the preterit *t* (*asket, assemblet, anoydet*). Items C1/6/319 and 320 are Latin redactions of these English depositions in neat Chancery hand.

Orthography

[1] Richard Venezky, *The Structure of English Orthography,* The Hague: Mouton, 1970, pp. 25-29, reviews the development in this century from the view that writing exists merely to represent speech to the view that writing is a coordinate, independent system. In *The Structure of American English,* New York: Ronald Press, 1958, Nelson Francis observes, "The English writing system tends to employ a single combination of graphemes to represent a given morpheme, disregarding for the most part all except the grossest phonemic differences between allomorphs. As a consequence of this general principle, we may note two qualities of our writing system: (1) the morphemic relations between words are usually more apparent in the written form of the language than in speech; (2) the pronunciations of words are not all clearly represented in writing" (pp. 468-69).

[2] Angus McIntosh has argued that the regional orthographies of Middle English were conventional rather than phonetic, but the study of Middle English texts must, nevertheless, begin by examining the orthographic—often graphic—idiosyncrasies of the individual scribe. See McIntosh, "The Analysis of Written Middle English," *Transactions of the Philological Society,* 1956, pp. 26-55; "A New Approach to Middle English Dialectology," *English Studies* 44 (1963), 1-11. D. G. Scragg, *A History of English Spelling,* traces the collapse of the

OE Standard and the re-formation of the MnE Standard. On pp. 35ff., he treats the influence of Chancery. J. Berry, "The Making of Alphabets," in *Readings in the Sociology of Language*, ed. J. A. Fishman, The Hague: Mouton, 1972, p. 378, gives a bibliography of works advancing the view of writings as a primary system.

[3] Baugh and Cable, *A History of the English Language*, p. 250.

[4] H. C. Wyld, *A History of Modern Colloquial English*, London: Unwin, 1920, pp. 65, 89.

[5] Weale, in Chambers and Daunt, p. 293, no. 47.

[6] E. J. Dobson, "Early Modern Standard English," *Transactions of the Philological Society*, 1955, pp. 25-54; rptd., *Approaches to English Historical Linguistics*, ed. Roger Lass, New York: Holt, 1969, pp. 419-39.

[7] On spelling pronunciations, Scragg, *History of English Spelling*, pp. 41 n., 54; on disparagement of the evidence of orthoepical evidence, Wyld, *History of Colloquial English*, p. 115; on defense of orthoepists, E. J. Dobson, *English Pronunciation 1500-1700*, 2 vols., Oxford: Clarendon, 1969, I. Chap. ii, esp. pp. 190-98.

[8] Scragg, *History of English Spelling*, pp. 48-49.

[9] Samuels, "Some Applications of Dialectology," p. 418.

COLLATIONS OF ORIGINAL PETITIONS
WITH ENROLLMENTS (See p. 24)

* More modern form
   No. 174   SC8/24/1197 (line 2) hygh] C65/86/46 *high   *divers] diuerses   (line 3) havyn] *hauen   acusyd] *acused   (line 4) counceyll] *counseill   othir] *other   (line 5) eny] *any   (line 8) shul] *shall   commyttid] *committed   eny] *any   (line 9) eny] *any   (line 10) *temporall] temporell   caas] *cas   askith] *asketh   delyverd] *deliuered   ellis] *elles   (line 11) iewys] ewes that   deservid] *deserued
Original more modern, 2; enrollment more modern, 15.

   No. 177 SC8/25/1222 (line 1) greet] C65/88/18 *gret   (line 2) *vnskilfully] onskilfully   (line 3) *sholde] schulde   (line 8) *shul] schul   (line 9) *write] whrite   hooly] *holi   (line 19) *specially] speciali   (line 20) to be] be to
Original more modern, 5; enrollment more modern, 2.

   No. 192 SC8/277/13830 (line 1) dyscrecion] C65/92/42 *discrecion   worschipfull] *worshipfull   parlement] *parliament   (line 2) consyder] *consider   peple] *poeple   (line 3) Stwys] *Stewys   (line 4) *In] inne   ryght] *right   (line 5) *withein] with inne   *dwellynge] duellyng   sayd] *said   (line 6) selff] *self   (line 7) *pitye] peti trowthe] *trouth   pryvile logyd] preuyle logid   (line 8) *gret] grett   (line 9) sufficyaunt] sufficeaunt   bene] *been   *returned] retourned (line 10) Bayllefs] *Baillifs   felonyes] *felonies   trespases] *trespasses   (line 11) pleys] *plees   *diuerse] diuerses   *Iuges] Iugges   hys] *his   (line 12) marchall] *marshall   hys] *his   dysherytaunces] disheretaunces   (line 13) *true] trwe   lyege] *liege   souerayne] *souereigne   ben] *been   (line 14) ben] *been   morderyes] *murderyes   robberyes] *robberies   vnponischyd] *vnponishid   (line 15) sayd] *said   peple] *poeple   hostryes] *hostries   sayd] *said   (line 16) deden] *diden   atte] *at   sayd] *said   (line 17) *like] lyke   dyscrecions] *discrecions   consydered] *considered   peple] *poeple   (line 19) ryght] *right   ys] *is   (line 20) parlement] *parliament   (line 21) retorned] retourned   shereff] sheref   baylef] *Baillif   mynisterys] *ministres   souerayne] *souereigne   sayd] *said   (line 22) ony] *any   mynister] *minister   stuarde] *steward   marchall] *Marshall   (line 23) partye] partie   partye] partie   (line 24) atte] *at   sayd] seid   (line 25) sufferyd] sufferid   *withe in] with inne   sayd] *said   Sutwerk] *Suthwerke   (line 26) *only] onely   sayd] *said   Stwys] *Stewys   estcheuyng] *escheuyng   murdereris] murdererys   robberyes] *robberies   been] *been   lykly] *likly   (line 27) sayd] *said   (line 28) tauernis] *tauernes   ben] *been   *enprisonyng] inprysonyng   (line 29) bodyes] *bodies   *after] aftre   dyscrecion] *discrecion   sayd] *said
Original more modern, 14; enrollment more modern, 61.

   No. 194 A stain on the enrollment renders part of each line illegible. SC8/26/1281 (line 1) souerain] C65/92/43 *souereign   (line 2) husbundman]

husbondman (line 3) wijff] *wyff (line 4) *had] hadde *him] hym *go] goo (line 5) Brydham] *Bridham (line 6) wijff] *wyff (line 8) slitte] slytte fro] *from (line 9) horrebely] *horrybly (line 10) mourdure] *murdire thoursday] *thursday *Bishop] bisshop bi] *by *said] seid (line 11) *said] seid endyteth] *endited bi for] *befor (line 12) forsaid] *foresaid (line 15) mourdur] *murdure
Original more modern, 6; enrollment more modern, 12.

No. 195 C49/26/4 (line 5) *parliament] C65/97/41 parlement (line 6) *said] seid *parliament] parlement (line 7) *said] seid (line 11) burgeys] burgeis *þe] thio (line 12) *parliament] parlement (line 14) aforne] *afore
Original more modern, 6; enrollment more modern, 1.

No. 201 SC8/27/1305 (line 2) wyse] C65/94/14 *wise (line 4) atte] *at (line 5) *numbre] noumbre (line 6) soueraigne] *souereigne (line 7) *wilde] wylde (line 9) *other] othre *special] speciall (line 18) godely] *goodly *is] ys (line 19) atte] *at (line 23) writt] *writ seid] *said (line 25) *palentine] palentyne aftir] *after (line 27) writt] *writ appier] appere
Original more modern, 6; enrollment more modern, 9.

No. 202 SC8/27/1308 (line 1) *right] C65/94/38 ryght (line 2) *executors] executours (line 3) please] like (line 5) *trespasses] tresppases *falshedes] falshotes disceites] *desceites atte] *at suyte] *suite (line 6) gylty] gilty by] *be (line 7) wheruppon] wheruppon seid] *said (line 8) ayens] *ayenst seid] *said (line 9) seid] *om. by cause] *be cause seid] *said trespaces] *trespasses *falshedes] falshotes *deceites] diseites (line 10) atte barre] *at the barre by fore] *be fore (line 11) comytted] *committed that] om. (line 13) *by] be suyte] *suite (line 14) *therupon] þeruppon *in] yn was founden] *was founde be] *by seid] *said seid] *said (line 15) *Wherupon] Wheruppon seid] *said (line 16) atteynt] *atteint (line 17) greet] grete for the same] om. (line 19) *purposing] purposyng (line 20) godds] *goods bodyes] *bodies greet] grete *ymagined] ymagyned (line 21) trespases] *trespasses ayens] *ayenst (line 24) And in Southrey] and in the shire of Suthrey (line 26) beten] betten *enprisoned] emprisouned hym] *him (line 27) trespaces] *trespasses supposid] *supposed *to be doon] to be doo trespaces] *trespas supposid] *supposed somm] *some (line 28) *before] bifore (line 29) by cause] *be cause (line 30) *þerupon] ther uppon *will] wolle sute] *suite (line 32) labore] laboure sutes] *suites (line 33) *enformed] enfourmed greet] grete (line 34) hym] *him peple] *poeple dyuers] *diuers (line 35) callid] ycalled (line 36) callid] *called be] *by *sueth] suyth seid] *said (line 37) remyttid] *remitted (line 39) enfourmour] *enfourmer be] *by (line 40) seid] *said (line 41) peple] *poeple *discrecions] discrecions (line 42) *diuers] diuerses seid] *said greet] grete ben] *been (line 43) *therupon] þeruppon *king] kyng (line 44) aucorite] auctoritee the same] this present ordeyne] *ordeine (line 45) establie] estable (line 46) wardeine] wardeyne hym]

Collations 65

*him (line 47) *kynges] kyngges *or] othire seid] *said (line 48) war-
deyn] *wardein thynges] *thinges seid] *said (line 49) determyned] *determined (line 50) marc] marck (line 51) in wey] in the wey
Original more modern, 26; enrollment more modern, 52.

No. 206 C49/23/14 (line 2) *certein] C65/95/39 certeyn (line 3) *deliuered]
delyuered (line 4) Cite] Citee (line 6) *receit] recette (line 7) Escheker]
Escheqer wyse] *wise
Original more modern, 3; enrollment more modern, 1.

No. 208 SC8/27/1328 (line 3) Spyceres] C65/95/60 *Spyceries (line 4) Spyceryes] *Spiceries ne] *nor (line 6) temporeles] *temporels (line 8) sayd]
*said (line 12) sayd] *said
Original more modern, 0; enrollment more modern, 6.

No. 210 C49/25/7 (line 3) assoyle] C65/96/29 *assoil (line 9) wiche]
*whiche (line 13) be] *by (line 14) profiteȝ] *profitȝ (line 15) *honoureȝ]
honureȝ (line 16) fraunchyseȝ] *fraunchiseȝ (line 18) wiche] *whiche vndirstond] *vnderstond consciens] *conscience (line 23) wiche]
*whiche (line 25) yowe] *you thei] *they (line 27) myht] *myght (line
28) *landeȝ] londeȝ (line 29) thei] *they (line 30) thenne] *thanne (line
33) thei] *they (line 34) suffise] *suffice (line 39) thei] *they (line 45)
*reigne] regne (line 47) wiche] *whiche (line 51) thei] *they (line 53)
wiche] *whiche (line 54) wiche] *whiche (line 56) *said] seid *considered] considerid
Original more modern, 5; enrollment more modern, 21.

No. 212 C49/26/5 (line 1) please] C65/97/42 om. benygne] *benigne (line
3) tiuesday] *tuesday *Saynt] seynt (line 4) rauesshed] *rauisshed sche]
sho (line 5) *him] hym *clothes] clothis (line 6) *goode] gode (line 7)
*at] atte noghte] *not *at] atte (line 8) twyes] twies twyes]
twies stikked] *stiked sche] *she (line 9) all so] *also *at] atte plase]
*place *said] seid *said] seid hit] *it (line 10) keyes] *keys *goods]
goodes catells] catels (line 11) *clothes] clothis *said] seid vppon]
*vpon (line 12) *forsaide] seid ys] *is (line 13) *remayneth] re-
meyneth *tenur] tenour (line 17) yow] *you (line 18) vppon] *upon ordeigne] *ordeine (line 19) *saide] seid hit ys] *it is *forsaid] forseid *by] be (line 20) putte] *put *said] seid (line 21) murdre of the]
om. *said] seide *any] eny ys] *is (line 22) *any] eny (line 23) *said]
seid all so] *also (line 24) *any] eny yf] *if be founden] *be
founde *saide] seid (line 25) vppon] *vpon schuld] *shuld (line 27)
*said] seid *saide] seid (line 28) all so] *also *said] seide (line 30)
*said] seide *goodly] goodely *said] seide (line 31) *said] seide (line
32) *saide] seid *saide] seid (line 33) *saide] seid *saide] seid *they]
thei *said] seid (line 34) *forsaid] forseid yf] *if (line 35) sche]
*she wolle] *wille (line 36) *any] eny yn] *in
Original more modern, 39; enrollment more modern, 29.

No. 213 C49/27/14 (line 2) *troubled] C65/99/25 trobbled   (line 5) *all] al   (line 6) *parliament] parlement   euerich] euerych   (line 7) *stipendiar] Stipendarie   forfature] *forfeiture   (line 8) by cause] *because   (line 9) may haue writtes here vppon suffisantʒ for theire discharge withouten eny Chartre suynte] may haue Chartres of pardons withoute any fine or feę here vppon suffisantʒ for theire discharge   (line 11) soueraigne] *souereigne   (line 13) Seynt] Seint   (line 15) preestes] prestes   (line 16) *Stipendiaries] Stipendaries   preestes] prests   committid] *committed   (line 17) by cause] *because   (line 20) *said] seide   *saide] seid   (line 21) payng] paiyng
Original more modern, 7; enrollment more modern, 5.

No. 217 SC8/2/52 (line 2) *proclaimed] C65/100/57 proclamed   (line 3) published] publisshed   *ʒeland] ʒgelend   (line 4) *wise] wyse   forfetur] *forfeiture   (line 5) ys] *is   (line 6) subgiettes] subgeetes   (line 7) bifore] byfore   (line 8) requisitore] requisitorie   (line 10) wete] *wite   (line 12) noon] *non   oþer] om.   (line 15) yf] *if   *continuell] contynuell   (line 16) seid] *said   *holland] holand   (line 17) *all maner] almaner   (line 18) eny] *any   (line 20) schuld] *shuld   (line 21) for] om.   *halfe] halue   (line 22) *halfe] halue   þer of] om.   (line 23) and that] that om.   (line 25) eny] *any   (line 27) noon] *non   *unto] ynto   (line 29) premysses] *premisses   (line 30) avise] avyse   *temporell] temporelx   (line 33) comeyng] *comyng   yf] *if   (line 34) *all maner] almaner   (line 38) forfaitur] *forfeiture   (line 41) *if] yf   (line 43) noon] *non   indur] *endure
Original more modern, 12; enrollment more modern, 16.

No. 224 SC8/28/1358 (line 2) *wisdoms] C65/102/57 wysdoms   (line 3) *Maner] manour   (line 4) litill] lytill   (line 5) *fader] fadir   (line 6) blissed] *blessed   Seint] seynt   (line 7) *worship] wurship   *glorious] glorius   *Archebisshop] Archebysshop   *whos] whoos   (line 8) *many] mony   lyneally] *lineally   *descended] discendid   *glorious] glorius   *moder] modir   (line 9) sette] *set   seint] seynt   beryed] beried   (line 13) *heirs] heires   *premisses] premysses   (line 17) dayly] *daily   souerain] *soueraigne   (line 18) souerain] *soueraigne   souerain] souerayn   (line 19) *fader] fadir   (line 21) *oþer] othir   (line 22) *wyfe] wiffe   (line 23) *disposicion] dispocicion   (line 24) *it] hit   (line 25) souerain] souerayn   (line 26) auctoritee] auctorite   (line 27) *establissh] establyssh   (line 31) *heirs] heires   *any] eny   *oþer] othir   (line 33) rehersid] *rehersed   *oþer] othir   (line 35) onely] *only   (line 36) *oþer] othir   (line 37) thouowson] *thauowson   aforseid] *aforeseid   (line 38) charitee] charite
Original more modern, 25; enrollment more modern, 9.

No. 228 SC8/28/1373 (line 10) resumpsion] C65/103/47 *resumpcion   (line 12) *other] othir   *commodites] commoditees   (line 14) *effectuall] effectuell   hym] *him   (line 15) *standyng] stondyng
Original more modern, 4; enrollment more modern 2.

LIST OF DOCUMENTS

Plates are in italic.

The Signet Letters of Henry V

1. *The exemplar C81/1326/36*
2. Henry V, Shiryngton's hand?, 12 August 1417   C81/1364/34
3. Henry V, x hand, 5 September 1417   C81/1364/36
4. Henry V, Toly's hand, 22 September 1417   C81/1364/37
5. Henry V, unique hand, 23 September 1417   SC1/43/157
6. Henry V, Shiryngton's hand?, 25 September 1417   C81/1364/38
7. Henry V, x hand, 30 September 1417   C81/1364/39
8. Henry V, y hand, 2 November 1417   C81/ 1364/40
9. Henry V, Toly's hand, 17 December 1417   C81/1364/41
10. Henry V, Toly's hand, 17 December 1417   C81/1542/9
11. Henry V, Toly's hand, 18 January 1418   C81/1364/42
12. Henry V, unique hand, 19 January 1418   C81/1364/43
13. Henry V, Hethe's hand, 20 January 1418   C81/1364/44
14. Henry V, unique hand, 10 February 1418   Cotton Vesp. C. XII, fol. 155
15. Henry V, Hethe's hand?, 28 February 1418   C81/1364/45
16. Henry V, unique hand, 17 March 1418   SC1/43/158
17. Henry V, y hand, 22 March 1418   C81/1364/47
18. Henry V, Hethe's hand?, March 1418   C81/1364/46
19. Henry V, z hand, 4 April 1418   C81/1364/48
20. Henry V, Toly's hand, 6 April 1418   C81/1364/49
21. Henry V, y hand, 28 April 1418   C81/1364/50
22. Henry V, Toly's hand?, 1 May 1418   C81/1364/51
23. Henry V, y hand, 15 May 1418   C81/1364/52
24. Henry V, y hand, 15 May 1418   C81/1364/53
25. Henry V, Hethe's hand?, 19 May 1418   C81/1364/54
26. Henry V, Caud— hand?, 20 May 1418   C81/1364/55
27. Henry V, z hand, 27 May 1418   C81/1364/56
28. Henry V, Hethe's hand?, 2 June 1418   C81/1364/58
29. Henry V, Hethe's hand, 2 June 1418   C81/1364/57
30. Henry V, Toly's hand (signed Stone in another hand), 3 June 1418   C81/1364/59
31. Henry V, Hethe's hand?, 5 June 1418   C81/1364/60
32. Henry V, Hethe's hand, 8 June 1418   C81/1364/61
33. Henry V, Hethe's hand, 22 June 1418   C81/1364/62
34. Henry V, Hethe's hand, 26 June 1418   C81/1364/63

35. Henry V, Hethe's hand?, 10 July 1418   C81/1364/64
36. Henry V, Hethe's hand, 9 August 1418   C81/1364/65
37. Henry V, Caud— hand? 30 August 1418   C81/1364/66
38. Henry V, Hethe's hand, 13 September 1418   C81/1364/67
39. Henry V, Shiryngton's hand?, 21 September 1418   C81/1364/68
40. Petition from St. Mary Graces, accompanying D.39, non-Chancery hand, 4 September 1418   C81/1364/69
41. Henry V, Shiryngton's hand, September 1418   C81/1364/70
42. Henry V, Hethe's hand, 5 October 1418   C81/1364/71
43. Henry V, y hand, 21 October 1418   Cotton Galba B.I, fol. 164
44. Henry V, Shiryngton's hand?, 23 October 1418   C81/1364/72
45. Henry V, Hethe's hand?, 27 October 1418   C81/1364/73
46. *Henry V, Toly's hand, 29 November 1418   Cotton Julius B.VI, fol. 97*
47. Henry V, Toly signed, 28 January 1419   C81/1366/8
48. Henry V, unique hand, 30 January 1419   C81/1364/74
49. Henry V, Toly signed, 30 January 1419   C81/1366/10
50. Henry V, Toly signed, 11 February 1419   C81/1366/5
51. Henry V, unique hand, 12 February 1419   SC1/43/162
52. Henry V, Andrieu signed, 28 February 1419   C81/1366/9
53. Henry V, Andrieu's hand?, 2 March 1419   C81/1366/15
54. Henry V, Shiryngton's hand, 17 March 1419   C81/1366/6
55. Henry V, Shiryngton signed, 6 April 1419   C81/1365/1
56. Henry V, Shiryngton signed, 20 April 1419   C81/1365/2
57. *Henry V, Shiryngton signed, 28 April 1419   Cotton Galba B.I. fol. 157*
58. Henry V, Toly's hand, 28 April 1419   C81/1365/4
59. Henry V, Shiryngton signed, 28 April 1419   C81/1365/3
60. Henry V, Shiryngton signed, date torn off   C81/1366/13
61. Henry V, Shiryngton signed, 19 June 1419   C81/1365/5
62. Henry V, Shiryngton signed, 20 June 1419   C81/1365/6
63. Henry V, Caud— signed, 23 June 1419   C81/1365/7
64. Henry V, Shiryngton signed, 7 July 1419   C81/1365/8
65. Henry V, Shiryngton's hand, 11 July 1419   C81/1365/9
66. Henry V, Toly signed, 12 July 1419   E28/33/5
67. Henry V, Toly signed, 22 July 1419   C81/1365/10
68. Henry V, Shiryngton signed, 25 July 1419   C81/1365/11
69. Henry V, unique hand, not dated   Cotton Vesp. F.I. fol. 104
70. *Henry V, Henry's own hand?, not dated   Cotton Vesp. F.III, fol. 8*
71. Henry V, unique hand, 11 October 1419   E28/33/13
72. Henry V, Shiryngton's hand, 1 November 1419   C81/1365/12

List of Documents

73. Henry V, Shiryngton signed, 5 January 1420   SC1/43/160
74. Henry V, Andrieu's hand?, 21 January 1420   C81/1365/13
75. Henry V, Shiryngton signed, 10 February 1420   C81/1366/1
76. Henry V, Shiryngton signed, 28 March 1420   C81/1365/15
77. Henry V, Shiryngton's hand, 30 March 1420   SC1/43/161
78. Henry V, Shiryngton's hand, 10 April 1420   C81/1365/16
79. Henry V, Shiryngton's hand, 14 April 1420   C81/1365/17
80. Henry V, Andrieu signed, 25 April 1420   C81/1365/18
81. Henry V, unique hand, 22 May 1420   C54/270/m17d
82. Henry V, Toly signed, 4 July 1420   C81/1365/19
83. Henry V, Shiryngton signed, 20 July 1420   C81/1365/20
84. Henry V, Toly signed, 16 September 1420   C81/1365/21
85. Henry V, Toly signed, 22 September 1420   C81/1365/22
86. Henry V, Toly signed, 30 September 1420   C81/1365/23
87. Henry V, Hethe signed, 8 October 1420   C81/1543/21
88. Henry V, Hethe signed, 8 October 1420   C81/1365/24
89. Henry V, Toly signed, 5 November 1420   C81/1365/26
90. Henry V, Depeden signed, 7 March 1421   C81/1365/28
91. Henry V, Shiryngton signed, 11 March 1421   C81/1365/29
92. Henry V, Shiryngton signed, 9 May 1421   C81/1365/30
93. Henry V, Toly signed, 22 May 1421   SC1/43/159
94. Henry V, Depeden signed, 8 June 1421   C81/1365/31
95. Henry V, Depeden signed, 18 July 1421   C81/1365/32
96. Henry V, Depeden signed, 31 July 1421   E101/188/10/2
97. Henry V, Toly signed, 13 October 1421   C81/1365/33
98. Henry V, Shiryngton signed, 29 October 1421   C81/1365/25
99. Henry V, Shiryngton signed, 14 November 1421   C81/1365/27
100. Henry V, Shiryngton's hand?, 15 February 1422   C81/1365/34
101. Henry V, Toly signed, 8 March 1422   C81/1365/35
102. Henry V, Shiryngton signed, 28 March 1422   C81/1365/36
103. Henry V, Toly signed, 30 April 1422   C81/1365/37
104. Henry V, Shiryngton signed, May 1422   E101/188/10/1
105. Henry V, Toly signed, 18 June 1422   C81/1366/12

Later Signet and Privy Seal Papers

106. Henry VI, initialed Rh, Chancery hand, 1 February 1434   E28/55/1
107. Henry VI, non-Chancery hand, 13 April 1440   E28/63/5
108. Henry VI, initialed Rh, Chancery hand, 26 August 1452   SC1/43/184
109. Henry VI, Chancery hand, 5 June 1455   SC1/43/182

110. Letter of Robert Fry, Clerk of the Privy Seal, 18 June 1408?, Chancery hand, fairly regular forms   E28/29
111. Letter of William Soper, Clerk of the Exchequer, to the Chancellor, 11 December, after 1415, Chancery hand, non-Chancery forms (see 139)   E28/37/105
112. Letter of Thomas Longley, Bishop of Durham, Chancellor, possibly to Henry V, after 1417, Chancery hand, north Midland forms   Cotton Vesp. F.XIII, fol. 71
113. Letter, possibly by Henry Beaufort, Bishop of Winchester, to Henry V concerning his marriage, 6 June 1420, non-professional hand, non-Chancery forms   SC1/43/192
114. Petition of John Cappe, 11 November 1420, Chancery hand, fairly regular forms   SC1/51/118
115. Memorandum from Council to the King, 1421, two Chancery hands, the second with some non-Chancery forms   E28/35/13-14
116. Privy Council minute book, 1422, Chancery hand, irregular forms and style   Cotton Cleo. F.IV, fol. 3
117. Privy Seal letter on behalf of King to John, Duke of Bedford, 15 May 1423, Chancery hand and forms   E28/41/75 (105)
118. Petition of Janyn Cassons, 3 March 1423, non-Chancery hand but regular forms   E28/39
119. Petition of Maud Fosbroke, drynurse to the infant Henry VI, 28 April 1423, Chancery hand, non-Chancery forms   E28/40/18
120. Petition of Margaret Brothnam, chamberer to the infant King, 1423, hand and forms like 119   E28/40/19
121. Petition of Joan Asteley, nurse to the King, 27 April 1423, different Chancery hand, forms somewhat more regular   E28/40/20
122. Privy Council minute book, 1424, Chancery hand and language   Cotton Cleo. F.IV. fol. 17v-18r
123. Petition of William Pope, royal retainer, 1429, Council signatures, Chancery hand but non-Chancery forms   E28/50/9
124. Petition on behalf of the retainers of the Earl of Ormond, 1430, Council signatures, Chancery hand and language   E28/51/69
125. Letter of Humphrey, Duke of Gloucester, to the Chancellor, 16 June, between 1432 and 36, Chancery hand and language   SC1/44/8
126. Letter of Richard, Duke of York, to the Chancellor, 5 June, after 1423, Chancery hand and language   C81/1715/39
127. Letter of Henry Beaufort, Bishop of Winchester, to the Chancellor, 29 April, after 1432, Chancery hand and language   SC1/44/12
128. Petition of Richard Selby, possibly Clerk of Chancery, after 1432,

Chancery hand, some non-Chancery forms   C1/12/179
129. Letter of Richard, Duke of York, possibly to John Frank, Master of the Rolls, 17 May 1435, Chancery hand and language   SC1/44/45
130. Draft of a summons to Parliament, 28 September 1435, language regular, text in non-Chancery hand, addresses in Chancery hand   E28/56/1
131. Memorandum of Council business, 20 February 1436, Council signatures, Chancery language, non-Chancery hand   E28/56/28
132. Summons to arms, first version, 1436, Chancery hand and language   E28/57A
133. Summons to arms, second version, 1436, Chancery hand and language   E28/57B
134. Summons to arms, third version, 1436, Chancery hand and language   E28/57C
135. Draft of instructions to Sir John Stokes and other ambassadors, 7 March 1436, Chancery language, non-Chancery hand   E28/56/40
136. Corrected draft of commission to Richard, Duke of York, 12 May 1436, Chancery hand and forms (þ sometimes y)   E28/57D/23
137. Corrected confirmation of a commission, 22 May 1436, non-Chancery hand, Chancery forms (except y for þ, "mych" in correction)   E28/57/28
138. Petition of John Stok, royal retainer, initialed Rh, 5 November 1436, Chancery hand and language   E28/58/15
139. Petition of William Soper, Clerk of the Exchequer, 1437, Chancery hand, non-Chancery forms (see 111)   E28/58/62
140. Petition of Thomas Frank, Clerk of the Privy Seal, initialed Rh, 20 February 1437, Chancery hand and language   E28/59/21
141. Petition of William Walysby, Treasurer to Queen Katherine, 8 November 1437, Chancery hand and language   E28/58/4
142. Deposition on Lord Faunhop written by Adam Moleyns, 10 February 1437, non-Chancery hand, Chancery forms   C49/22/18
143. Petition of John Croke, Clerk of the Exchequer, initialed Rh, 1438, Chancery hand, some non-Chancery forms, Latin notation by Adam Moleyns   E28/62/10
144. Petition of John Tiptoft, 1438, Chancery hand, some non-Chancery forms, notation by Adam Moleyns   E28/60/59
145. Petition concerning the ship Maryknýght, 1438, Chancery hand, some non-Chancery forms, notation by Adam Moleyns   E28/60/47
146. Petition of Clarehall, Cambridge, 1438, Chancery hand and forms (except "ycalled")   E28/62/10/40
147. Petition of Thomas Colland, Oxford scholar, 23 June 1438, Chan-

cery hand and language   E28/61C
148. Royal warrant written by Adam Moleyns, initialed Rh, 2 June 1438, non-Chancery hand, Chancery language   E28/61/3
149. Petition of Richard, Earl of Salisbury, initialed Rh, 1439, non-Chancery hand, Chancery forms (except "liche")   E28/63/42
150. Royal warrant written by Adam Moleyns, 27 April 1439, non-Chancery hand, Chancery language   E28/59/74
151. Royal grant, initialed Rh, 4 November 1440, Chancery hand and language, notation by Thomas Bekynton   E28/65/27(4)
152. Summons to Court of Chancery, 23 July 1440?, signed Brewester, Chancery hand and language   SC1/61/59
153. Petition of William, Abbot of Bury St. Edmunds, initialed Rh, 1440, Chancery hand, some non-Chancery forms   E28/64/27
154. Draft of summons to appear before the Privy Council, c 1440, addresses attached, Chancery hand, some French forms   E28/27/71(124)
155. Summons to the Court of Chancery, c 1440, Chancery hand and language   SC1/61/60
156. Royal indentures between the King and William Pyrton, 10 February 1441, Chancery hand and forms   E28/66/34
157. Letter from the Signet of Queen Margaret, 8 January 1446, Chancery hand and forms   SC1/44/13
158. Council minutes, initialed Rh, 1450, non-Chancery hand, Chancery forms (except "euerich," "thof")   C49/26/18
159. Petition of Thomas Haseley, Clerk of the Crown, c 1450, Chancery hand and forms (except "giftes," "ageyn," "geten")   Cotton Cleo. F.IV. fol. 126
160. Petition of Richard Sturgeon, Clerk of the Crown, 1454-55, Chancery hand and forms (except "hure" for their)   C1/24/79

Proceedings of Parliament and Chancery

161. Petition of the Mercers of London, 1388, Textura / Chancery hand, non-Chancery language   SC8/20/997
162. Petition of Cecily Tikell of London, before 1413   Chancery hand, non-Chancery forms   E28/29/69
163. Petition of Thomas Paunfeld of Cambridgeshire, 1414, non-Chancery hand and forms   SC8/23/1143A
164. Petition of Rauf atte Ree of Lancashire, between 1416 and 1421, Chancery hand, non-Chancery forms   C1/1/21
165. Petition of William Dodde, royal retainer, after 1417, non-Chancery hand and forms   C1/1/14

List of Documents 73

166. Petition of Roger Wodehill of Strete, Devon, before 1421, non-Chancery hand, some non-Chancery forms   C1/1/18
167. Petition of soldiers in Calais, 1421, Chancery hand, some non-Chancery forms   SC8/24/1168
168. Petition of Thomas Rokeby, royal retainer, 18 May 1423, non-Chancery hand and language   E28/41/76
169. Draft of letter accompanying payment to soldiers, 1423, Chancery hand, non-Chancery forms   E28/41/103
170. Petition of Thomas Burton concerning prisoners in France, 1424, Chancery hand, non-Chancery forms   E28/43/58(35)
171. Petition of John Staverne of Canterbury, 1424-26, non-Chancery hand and language   C1/1/25
172. Petition of Johan Kymburley of Derby, 1424-26, non-Chancery hand, some non-Chancery forms   C1/1/26
173. Petition of Willyam Midylton of Holderness, Yorks, 1424-26, non-Chancery hand, north Midland forms   C1/1/27
174. Petition by Commons for speedy trial of Lollards, 1425, non-Chancery hand, some non-Chancery forms (e.g., "mych," "havyn," "her")   SC8/24/1197
175. Petition of Baltazar Vivald of Genoa, Council signatures, 1426, non-Chancery hand and language   E28/47/83
176. Petition of the mayor and citizens of Southampton, 1427, non-Chancery hand and language   E28/48/19(4)
177. Petition on behalf of the Archbishop of Canterbury, 1427-28, Chancery hand, some non-Chancery forms   SC8/25/1222
178. Petition of the residents of Uchayron Percell, Wales, 1429, non-Chancery hand and language   E28/51/A6
179. Conditions of payment of a parliamentary subsidy, 1430-31, non-Chancery hand, Chancery language   C49/20/1
180. Conditions of payment of a parliamentary subsidy, 1430-31, non-Chancery hand, Chancery language   C49/20/2
181. Petition concerning payments to Newgate prisoners, 1430-31, Chancery hand and language   SC8/25/1235
182. Parliamentary assent to peace negotiations with France, 1430-31, non-Chancery hand and forms in the main text, Chancery hand and language in the codicil   C49/19/27
183. Petition of Levin le Clerc of Ghent, 1430-31, Chancery hand, some non-Chancery forms   SC8/25/1238
184. Petition of the residents of Marblethorp, Lincolnshire, 1430-31, Chancery hand, north Midland forms   SC8/25/1245
185. Petition of the Bishop of Bath, 1432, Chancery hand, some non-Chancery forms   SC1/43/166

186. Petition of Jeynkyn Stanlay, royal retainer, 1431, Chancery hand and language   E28/51/53
187. Petition of the citizens of Lymington and Newport, Hampshire, 1432, Chancery hand, some non-Chancery forms   SC8/26/1271
188. Petition of Robert Coker of Somerset, 1432-39, Chancery hand and language (except "y nemnyd")   SC1/57/121
189. Petition of Thomas Appleton of Dartford, Kent, after 1432, non-Chancery hand, Chancery forms   C1/1/41
190. Petition of Gieffrey Qwyncy of Norwich, after 1432, Chancery hand and language   C1/1/42
191. Petition of Thomas Walton, Chamberlain of North Wales, Council signatures, 1433, Chancery hand, some non-Chancery forms   E28/54/42
192. Petition of Commons concerning the stews of Southwark, 1433, Chancery hand and language   SC8/277/13830
193. Petition of Commons concerning the stews of Southwark, 1436, non-Chancery hand, Chancery forms   SC8/27/1309
194. Petition concerning the murder of Isabell by her husband John Carpenter of Sussex, 1433, Chancery hand and forms SC8/26/1281
195. Proclamations and petition concerning the safety of members of Parliament, 1433-34, Chancery hands and forms   C49/21/14 and C49/26/4
196. Petition of Wylliam Warwyk of Salisbury, 1433, Chancery hand and language (except "þoo," "hastylych")   SC8/27/1303
197. Petition of John Bredhill, retainer of John Bate, Clerk of Chancery, after 1433, Chancery hand and language   C1/2/18(21)
198. Petition of the mayor and citizens of Limerick, Council signatures, 1434, non-Chancery hand, Chancery forms (except "ywrete")   E28/54/43
199. Petition of Thomas Norton of Bristol, 1435, Chancery hand and forms (except "Beseketh," "y made," "y holde") (see 202)   SC8/27/1307
200. Petition of William Norton of Wales, 1436, Chancery hand and forms   E28/58/56
201. *Petition concerning the rape of Isabell, wife of John Boteler of Lancashire, 1437, Chancery hand and forms   SC8/27/1305*
202. Petition concerning the estate of Thomas Norton of Bristol, 1437, Chancery hand and forms (see 199)   SC8/27/1308
203. Petition of the weavers of Oxford, initialed Rh., 1438, Chancery hand and language   E28/62/36
204. Warrant transmitting the petition of the weavers of Oxford, 1438, Chancery hand and forms (see 203)   E28/62/35

List of Documents 75

205. Petition of John Loveyn of Normandy, 1438, non-Chancery hand and forms   E28/61/11
206. Royal proclamation appointing tax collectors, 1439, Chancery hand and forms   C49/23/14
207. Petition of Commons to be excused from kissing the King's hand because of the plague, 1439, Chancery hand and language (except "euerich")   SC8/27/1327
208. Petition of Commons concerning the spice trade, 1439, Chancery hand and forms   SC8/27/1328
209. Assignment of power-of-attorney by Richard Wydevyll, 1441, non-Chancery hand, Chancery language   SC1/44/11
210. Petition concerning administration of royal holdings, 1442, Chancery hand and forms   C49/25/7
211. Petition concerning Fernand Dalueys and his ship Seynt Auton, 1443, Chancery hand and forms   SC1/57/89(65)
212. Petition concerning the murder of Isabell, wife of Roger Bakeler, by John Bolton, 1444, Chancery hand and forms   C49/26/5
213. Petition of Commons that priests be pardoned for accusations of rape, 1449, Chancery hand and forms (except "euerich")   C49/27/14
214. Bill seeking to regularize the collection of customs, 1449, Chancery hand and forms   C49/27/17
215. Petition of John Talbot to be named Chancellor of Ireland, 1449, text in non-Chancery hand, response in Chancery hand, language mostly Chancery   SC8/27/1345A
216. Petition of Thomas Parr of Cumberland, 1449, Chancery hand and language   SC8/27/1347
217. Petition of Commons concerning trade with Braband, 1450, non-Chancery hand, Chancery language   SC8/2/52
218. Petition of the inhabitants of the Isle of Wight, 1450, Chancery hand, non-Chancery forms   SC8/28/1352
219. Petition of Thomas Bodyn (original version), 1450-54, non-Chancery hand and forms   C1/19/491
220. Petition of Thomas Bodyn (Chancery copy), 1450-54, Chancery hand and forms   C1/19/492
221. Answer of Robert Chirch to petition of Thomas Bodyn, 1450-54, Chancery hand and forms (except "ane," "sich," "mych")   C1/19/493
222. Petition of Thomas FitzHarry and his wife, 1453, Chancery hand and language   C1/1/70
223. Petition of Thomas de la More, Sheriff of Cumberland, 1453-54, Chancery hand and language (except "arn")   SC8/29/1446

224. Petition of James, Earl of Wiltshire, 1454, Chancery hand and language (except "are")   SC8/28/1358
225. Petition of John Frebarn of London, lighterman, 1454, Chancery hand and language   C1/2/36(53)
226. Petition of the abbot and convent of Seynt Germayne, Yorks, 1455, Chancery hand and language   SC8/28/1363
227. Petition of William Neel and William Laweshull that their grants not be resumed, 1455, Chancery hand and language   SC8/28/1369
228. Petition of Thomas Scargill that his grant not be resumed, 1455, Chancery hand and language   SC8/28/1373
229. Petition of John Heron to be made Constable of the Castle of Bameburgh, 1455, text in Chancery hand and language (except "beseketh"), annex in non-Chancery hand with some non-Chancery forms   SC8/28/1380A
230. Petition of Thomas Yong for restitution after his arrest for speaking out in Parliament, 1455, Chancery hand and language   SC8/28/1387
231. Petition of the citizens of Oxford, 1455, Chancery hand and language   SC8/28/1388
232. Petition of Richard Ford, Clerk of the Exchequer, 1455, Chancery hand and language   SC8/28/1393

Indentures

233. London indenture, 1384, non-Chancery hand, language surprisingly like Chancery   E40/A1779
234. Stonor indenture, London, 1426, Chancery hand and language   C146/C1223
235. Winchester indenture, 1427, non-Chancery hand and language   E28/48/18
236. Bristol deposition, 1428, Chancery hand, some non-Chancery forms   C49/22/19
237. London indenture, 1445, non-Chancery hand, Chancery language   C146/C3584
238. Lincoln indenture, 1445, non-Chancery hand, Chancery language (except "has")   E101/504/19
239. London indenture, 1453, Chancery hand, some non-Chancery forms   E40/A2495
240. Northampton indenture, 1456, Chancery hand and language   E40/A7651
241. Devonshire indenture, 1462, non-Chancery hand and language   C146/C273

The Documents

EDITORIAL PRINCIPALS AND LIST OF WORKS CITED

The purpose of this edition is to represent as exactly as feasible in computer composition the texture of written English in official documents between c 1417 and c 1455. Plates II-VI indicate the physical appearance of the documents transcribed. Nearly all are on parchment. The transcriptions are diplomatic. Errors have not been corrected but painstakingly preserved (e.g., Thokynge 162.3, wirtte 171.8, wronfully 197.4, etc.) since they reveal the degree of care and standardization in a given document or office. Capitalization follows the original. Only W offers a problem. In Chancery hand, W is always a large character, and few scribes clearly distinguish W from w. All have been treated as lower case except where a distinction could be inferred. Paragraphing, virgules, and periods likewise follow the originals except that in the manuscripts most periods are elevated to the middle of the line. Other marks of punctuation—usually the inverted semicolon or more elaborate flourishes—have been indicated by colons. The colon itself never appears in the manuscripts.

All expansions have been italicized. Superscripts (like t or r in $þ^t þ^r$ or l and x in numbers $M^l c^x$) have been treated as expansions (þat, þer, Ml, cx). Long z and yogh have both been rendered ȝ since they are indistinguishable in the originals. It may be that the tail of z is sometimes lighter than the tail of yogh, but that is a matter of judgment; the tail is always present. The computer cannot render the flourishes at the ends of words or the crossed l and h preserved in the record type of Chambers and Daunt. These marks have been ignored except for final er/re (October, Westminstre). In instances where there is no such expansion (e.g., Octobr 130.2, 221.27) it is because there is no flourish. Every expanded e has been italicized but not every flourish has been expanded into final e. The reader may assume that final g, m, n, and r usually end with a flourish, and that final h and l are often crossed. To study these marks, one would have to return to the originals.

Several corrected drafts are included among the selections to study whether the corrections are merely substantive or sometimes linguistic (only occasionally are they linguistic). Superscript insertions, corrections over erasures, inferences from damaged copy, and other additions and emendations in the text have been enclosed in parentheses with notes explaining the nature of the correction. Cancelled passages have been printed (when they could be read) enclosed in square brackets. All parentheses and brackets are editorial. In order to refer to specific words in the text, it was necessary to number the lines. Since the Compugraphic typesetter does its own justifying, it was imposible to make these line numbers come regularly in the margins. They have therefore been inserted in parentheses in the body of the text. Although this makes the page less attractive, it makes citation in the introduction and glossary convenient (i.e., Sqwyer 31.2 refers to the word in the second line in document 31).

The printed works cited in the notes to the documents are as follows:

Samuel Bentley, *Excerpta Historica, or Illustrations of English History*. London, 1883.

A. L. Brown, "The Privy Seal Clerks in the Early Fifteenth Century," in *The Study of Medieval Records: Essays in Honour of Kathleen Major*, ed. D. A. Bullough and R. L. Storey. Oxford: Clarendon, 1971, pp. 260-81.

Calendar of Close Rolls (CCR).

Calendar of Patent Rolls (CPR).

R. W. Chambers and Marjorie Daunt, *A Book of London English, 1384-1425*. Oxford: Clarendon, 1931 (CD).

Henry Ellis, *Original Letters Illustrative of English History*, Series I, II, III. London, 1824-46.

O. F. Emerson, *A Middle English Reader*. New York: Macmillan, 1905.

Forty-first Report of the Deputy Keeper of Public Records. London: The Public Record Office, 1880.

Hubert Hall, *Formula Book of English Historical Documents*, 2 vols. Cambridge: Cambridge University Press, 1908-09.

J. O. Halliwell-Phillipps, *Letters of the Kings of England*, 2 vols. London: H. Colburn, 1848.

J. L. Kirby, *Calendar of the Signet Letters of Henry IV and Henry V (1399-1422)*. London: H. M. Stationery Office, 1978.

Friedrich Kluge, *Mittelenglisches Lesebuch*. Halle: Niemeyer, 1912.

John Le Neve, ed., *Fasti Ecclesiae Anglicanae, 1300-1541*, 3 vols. Oxford: Oxford University Press, 1854 (Vol. 2, Diocese of Chichester, compiled by J. M. Horn).

T. Livius, *Vita Henrici Quinti*, ed. Thomas Hearne. London, 1716.

H. C. Maxwell-Lyte, *Historical Notes on the Use of the Great Seal of England*. London: H. M. Stationery Office, 1926.

Lorenze Morsbach, *Uber den Ursprung der Neuenenglischen Schriftsprache*. Heilbronn: Henninger, 1888.

H. N. Nicolas, *Proceedings and Ordinances of the Privy Council of England*, 7 vols. Records Commission, 1834-37.

Proceedings in Chancery in the Reign of Queen Elizabeth, 3 vols. Records Commission, 1827-32 (*PC*).

Rotuli Parliamentorum, 6 vols. London, c 1783 (*RP*).

Somerset Record Society Publications, Vol. 33.
Thomas Rymer et al., *Foedera, Conventionis, Literae, etc.*, 3rd ed. reprinted, 20 vols. in 10. Farnborough: Gregg, 1967.
Victoria Histories of the Counties of England. London, 2 vols. comp. William Page, London: Constable, 1909.

THE SIGNET LETTERS OF HENRY V

1

Early Date?   C81/1326/36   Signet of Henry V? (exemplar)
(1) By the Kyng
Trusty and welbeloued. ffor asmuche as in certain matiers þat gretely touchen and concernen þe good / (2) weele / and worship of vs our Landes lordships and subgittes We haue willed our Comissaries berers herof to commen with you: We (3) woll / desire / and pray you þerfore hertely / þat in suche þinges as þat þei or eny of þeim (4) woll shewe declare / and sey vnto you on our behalf: ye woll yeue vnto hem / and to eche of hem full feith and credence: And we pray you (5) þat ye leue not þis as ye woll þe good weele / and worship abouesaid: Yeuen vndre our priue seel at westminstre (6) þe .xx. day of Iuyll

This style of trusty and welbeloued may be direct to oon persone / or to as many (7) to gider as shal lyke þe said Commissioners: And it may serue for all maner men yif nede be except Bisshops:

Item (8) þe said style of Trusty and welbeloued may serue for Citees Tovneships and Cominaltees after þis tennour in (9) þe taile of þe lettre: To our trusty and welbeloued þe thrifty men notable persones and Cominalte (10) of our Citee of .A. or of the Tovne of .B. and to eueriche of þeim.

To þe Right Dere in (11) god / and Dere in god eueriche of þees styles may serue for Abbottes / Prioures / Denes Archediacones. (12) And for nede for thrifty Persons

Hamond
Hammond's hand
Printed Hall, *Formula Book*, I.98

2

1417   C81/1364/34   Signet of Henry V
(1) By þe kyng: S
Worshipful fader yn god. We sende yow closed wiþin þis lettre a cedule contenyng þe (2) names of certein maistres / for owr owne grete shippes Carrakes Barges and Balyngers to þe whiche maistres we haue granted (3) annuitees / suche as is appointed vpon eche of hem: in þe same cedule / to take yerely of owre grante while þat vs (4) lust: at owr Eschequer of westminstre / atte þe termes of Michelmasse and Ester by Euen porcions. Wherfore we wol and (5) charge yow þat vnto eche of þe said maistres / ye do make / vnder owr grete seel beyng in yowre

warde owr le*tt*res (6) patentes sauerales en due forme after þeffect and pourport of owr said (grant)e¹. yeuen vnder owr signet (7) atte owr Castel of Touque þe xij. day of Aoust:

Hand possibly Shiryngton's
Calendared Kirby 808. Printed Ellis, 3rd ser., I.72-74. Grants recorded 12 Aug. 1417, *CPR 1416-22*, pp. 120-21.

¹ torn and stained

3

1417   C81/1364/36   Signet of Henry V
(1) By þe kyng
Worshipful fader in god. ffor as muche as We haue ordeined and assigned our Welbeloued seruant Robert Rodyngton. (2) to be surueour of þe makyng of our toures at Portesmouth. We wil þat ye do make vnder our greet seel (3) a Co*mm*ission to þe same Robert. suche as ye þenke resonable and necessarie for þe goode and hastie spede. (4) of our werkes forsaid. during while vs lust. Yeuen in oure Towne of Caen þe .ve. day of Septembre vnder our signet

Hand x
Calendared Kirby 809. Appointment recorded 5 Sept. 1417, *CPR 1416-22*, p. 122.

4

1417   C81/1364/37   Signet of Henry V (damaged)
(1) By the Kyng:
Worshepful fader in god we wyl that ye doo make writtes of p*ro*clamac*io*n in to alle oure portes of (2) Englond . . .¹ al maner men that wil bryng vitailles vn to oure tovn of Caen for the Refresshing of vs and of our hoost in our (3) Duchie of Normandie that they schul paye therfor no custume / so that they fynde sufficeant seurte. (4) that they shal brynge the sayd vitailles vn to our said tovn of Caen for the refress . . . ¹of our seyd hoost / yeuen vnder our (5) signet in our Castel of Caen the .xxij. day of Septembre

Toly's hand
Calendared Kirby 810. Orders recorded 18 Oct. 1417, *CCR 1413-19*, pp. 838-39.

¹ torn

5

1417   SC1/43/157   Signet of Henry V
(1) By þe Kyng:
Trusty and Welbeloued. By a supplicacion of greuouse compleinte. putte vnto vs yn name of þe Priour and (2) Couent of oure cathedrale chirche of Bathe. We haue vnderstande how albeit þat of tyme passed mynde it hath be vsed and (3) acustumed þat ye of þe Cite of Bathe. shulde ryng no belle / no day (in þe week)[1] til þey of (4) þe s(aid chirch)e[2] hadden first rong þair belles. Neither at night aftir þe tyme þat þey (5) had rong / yit . . .[1] aȝeinstonding þe long continuance of þe same vsag and custume. ye of late tyme haue do (6) þe contrary and wilfully do fro day to day. yn greet disese and preiudice of þe forseide Priour and Couent. but if (7) remede couenable be ordeined þer vppon. Wharfor we wol if it so be. and charge you expressely þat ye cesse of (8) al suche manere newe and wilfulle gouernance yn þe matire forsaide. and conforme yn to þe gode (9) custume of olde tyme vsed and continued here a fore. vnto oure comyng with þe grace of god ynto our Realme (10) of Englond. þat we may haue ful knowloche of þe matire and to ordeine suche remede þer vppon (11) as we shal be þan auised. by wey of trouthe and of right. Yeuen vnder our signet at oure towne of Caen þe xxiij. day of Septembre
    Chancery hand
    Calendared Chambers and Daunt, p. 259, no. 38; Kirby 811. See no. 33 below. This letter is quoted in a French petition from the convent, SC8/176/8781.
        [1] rubbed and stained   [2] torn

6

1417   C81/1364/38   Signet of Henry V
(1) By þe Kyng   S
Worshipful fader in god / ryght trusty and welbeloued / yf þer be eny trewes to be taken now þis (2) wynter / betwene vs and þe Scottes. We Wold þat owr vncle of Excetre myȝt come to vs wiþ his good heelp (3) and pray yow / þat after yowre good auis and discrecion / ye ordeyne for þis in þe best wise / þat ye can / for (4) þat doon. we wold / owr said vncle were wiþ us wiþ his good heelp als sone as he miȝt þow hit were yitte wiþ (5) the fewer meyne. Also we send a lettre to owr cosin þe Bysshop of Excetre for maistre Iohn Copthorn to com(e to)[1] (6) vs / and a noþer to þe Bysshop of Lincoln / for maistre Thomas Brounce in þe same wise the whiche lettres (7) we pray yow / þat þey

be redely send forþe. and þat in al haast / as we trust to you / And þe holy Trinite (8) haue yow alwey in his kepyng. Wreten vnder owr signet atte owr Towne of Caen þe xxv day of Septembre. fferþermore (9) we wol þat to þe chirche of hambury þat is voide by maistre William Corff / þat is passed to god. as hit is said (10) and longeþ to owr yifte / be presented (in)² owr name Iohn woborne oon of þe prestes of owr Chapelle þat soiourneth (11) at wyndesore by owr lettres . . .³ þerof to be maad . . .³ in due forme: Also þat ye do (12) make lettres patente vnto maistre Richard holme to be maistre of owr College of Cambrigg / as maistre Ricard Derham was. (13) Also we haue yeuen to Will. hayton þempension of Saresbury þat whan tyme is ye do him haue suche lettres þer (14) upon / as þe cas asketh   G G

    Hand possibly Shiryngton's
    Calendared Kirby 812. Printed Ellis, 3rd ser., I.74; Maxwell-Lyte, *Great Seal*, p. 119. Presentation recorded 3 Oct. 1417, *CPR 1416-22*, p. 123.
    ¹ torn   ² superior insert   ³ cancel

7

1417   C81/1364/39   Signet of Henry V
(1) By þe Kyng
Worshipful fader in god. ffor as moche as we haue granted to our welbeloued clerc of þoffice of our signet (2) Robert Shiryngton. þe prebende whiche maistre Richard Derham had yn þe chirche of Chichestre. And is now voide by þe (3) deces of þe same maistre Richard. as it is said. and longeth to oure gifte by reson of þe temporaltees of þe saide (4) chirche beyng yn oure handes. by cause of þe voidance þer of: we wol þat þeruppon. ye do haue to þe (5) forsaid Robert. our lettres patentes vnder our greet seel beyng yn youre Warde. Yeuen vnder our signet at oure towne of Caen þe laste day of Septembre.
    Hand x
    Calendared Kirby 813. On the Seaford prebend, see Le Neve, *Chichester Diocese*, p. 38.

8

1417   C81/1364/40   Signet of Henry V
(1) By þe kyng
Worshipful fader yn god We wol þat to oure clerc Robert Shiryngton

ye do haue our le*tt*res (2) patentes vnder owr grete seal en due forme / of þe p*re*bende þat was maistre Richard Derehams in þe chirche of (3) Chichestre / þe whiche is voide by his deeþ and longeʒ to owr yifte be cause of þe temp*or*altees of þe (4) bisshoprich of Chichestre / of whiche mat*er*e we haue writen to yow afore þis tyme / yeuen vnder oure signet at oure Chastel (5) of Alencon þe second day of Nouembre
    Hand y
    Calendared Kirby 814. Confirms no. 7 above. See *CPR 1416-22*, p. 132.

9

1417   C81/1364/41   Signet of Henry V
(1) By the kyng
Worshipful fader in god Right trusty and Welbeloued. We grete yow ofte tymes Wel. And for as muche as we haue vnderstande (2) that maistre Iohan Chaundeler that was Deen of Salesbury is chosen bisshop of the same chirche / Wherof we hald vs wel agreed / and (3) therto we yeue our assent Roial and we wol wel / that after the Consecrac*ion* of the said Elit he haue liu*er*ee of his (4) temp*or*altees / And the holy goost haue yow in his keping: yeuen vnder our signet in our hoost afor ffaloise. the .xvij. day of Decembre
    Toly's hand
    Calendared Kirby 815. See no. 10 below.

10

1417   C81/1542/9   Signet of Henry V
(1) By the kyng
Right trusty and Welbeloued brother / We grete yow often tymes Wel / And for as moche as We haue vnderstande that (2) maistre Iohan Chaundeler that was Deen of Salesbury is chosen Bisshop of the same chirche. Wher of we hald vs wel agreed / and therto we (3) yeue oure assent Roial / and we wol wel that after the consecracion of the said Elit / he haue liueree of his temp*or*altees / (4) And the holy gost haue yow in his keping / yeuen vnder our signet in oure hoost afor ffaloise / the .xvij. day of Decembre /
(Assent of Council, in French, follows in a different hand.)
    Toly's hand
    Calendared and French printed, Kirby 816. Assent recorded 22 Nov. 1417, *CPR 1416-22*, p. 126. Livery recorded 8 Jan. 1418, *CPR 1416-22*, p. 131.

11

1418   C81/1364/42   Signet of Henry V (right side torn off)
(1) By the kyng.
Worschipful fader in god / We wol and we charge yow / that vp on theffect and the teneure of oure le*tt*res (2) patentes . . . we han granted and assigned to oure welbeloued Richard Whytyngdon and Richard harowedon monk of Westmins. . . (3) V^c mark yeerly vp on the issues of the hanaper of oure chancellerie for the byldynge of oure chirche of Westmins. . . (4) ye doo maake writt*es* of liberate with the clause that folweth her after / Preferramento dece*m* miliu*m* librarum Regi in parliamento suo nup*er* fac*to* non obstante / (5) yeuen vnder oure signet in our hoost beside oure toun of ffaloise the xviij day of Januer
   Toly's hand
   Calendared Kirby 817. Grant recorded 14 Dec. 1413, *CPR 1413-16*, pp.145-46.

12

1418   C81/1364/43   Signet of Henry V (damaged)
(1) . . . kyng. /
Worshipful f . . . usty and welbeloued. We Wol þat ye calle vnto you our Iustices and ordeine þat our Riȝt trusty (2) . . . ed cousin þerl of huntyngdon þe whiche dooþ us good seruice / on þis side þe see . . . es and tenem*ent*ȝ as reson and lawe wollen Yeuen (3) vnder our signet in our hoost biside . . . vne of faloiȝe þe xix. day of Ianuier:
   Chancery hand
   Calendared Kirby 818, who suggests that it is related to no. 39 below.

13

1418   C81/1364/44   Signet of Henry V (left side missing)
(1) By þe Kyng:
(Worshipful fa)¹der in god. ffor as moche as we han vnderstande þat Slake is deed Which (2) was dean of oure Chapelle . . . wol þat Sir Iohan Prentys of oure Chapelle haue þe said deannee. but þat he departe not out of . . . (3) Yeven vnder oure signet in oure hoost at oure town of Faleyse þe .xx. day of Ianuer: . . . make oure Clerkes of oure Chapelle haste hem vnto vs al þat þey may. so (4) þat þey faile not with . . . wiþ vs atte begynnynge of lentyn in any wyse: S S

Hethe's hand
Calendared Kirby 819. Grant recorded 28 Jan. 1418, *CPR 1416-22*, p. 132.
¹ torn off

14

1418   Cotton Vesp. C. XII. fol. 155   Signet of Henry V
(1) Worshipful fader in god / Right trusty and Welbeloued / ffor as moche as oure welbeloued squier Iohn Hull haath long tyme be in oure (2) ambassiat and seruice in the parties of Spaigne for the whiche as he haath compleined to vs he is endaungerd gretly (3) / and certein goodys of his leyd to wedde / Wherfor we wol / that ye see / that theer be taaken dewe accomptes of the said Iohn. how many (4) dayes he haath stande in oure said ambassiat and seruice / and thervpon that he be contented and agreed in the best wyse as (5) longeth vn to hym in this cas. yeuen vnder oure Signet in oure hoost beside oure toun of ffaloise: the: x. day of ffeuerer
(Latin note follows)
   Chancery hand
   Calendared with explanation, Kirby 820. Printed Ellis, 3rd ser., I.64; Nicolas II.239.

15

1418   C81/1364/45   Signet of Henry V
(1) By þe Kyng
W(or)shipful¹ fader in god Ryht trusty and wel beloued. For as moche as we haue granted of oure grace (2) speciale to o(ure)¹ welbeloued Esquier Piers Gerueys þe londes and tenementes þat weren hugh ffastolfs (3) knyght as ye may se moore cleerly by þe supplicacion whiche þe saide Piers putte vnto vs closed wiþinne (4) þis lettre: We wole þat ye (do)² make vpon þe same supplicacion by vs graunted. lettres patentes vnto (5) þe said Piers Garueys vnder oure greet seel beynge in youre kepynge in due forme. Yeven vnder oure signet in oure Castel of Caen (6) þe xxviij. day of ffeuerer:
   Hand possibly Hethe's
   Calendared Kirby 821. See no 55 below. Grant recorded 28 Feb. 1418, *CPR 1416-22*, p. 134.
¹ torn   ² superior insert

16

1418   SC1/43/158   Signet of Henry V
(1) By þe kyng
Riʒt trusty and welbeloued broþer / We haue resceyued youre le*tt*res / by þe whiche ye desire (2) to knawe our entent as touching þe deliuerance of þe temporeltees of saint dauid / vnto Benet Bisshop of þe (3) same chirche of saint dauid / þat was of Bangore / In þe whiche matere we wol þat þe said Benet haue þe (4) Issues of þe said temporeltees / from þe deces of his p*re*decessour / þat was our Confessour / so þat ye / (5) and our Chanceller trete wiþ him / in suche wyse / þat seurtee taaken / as yow semeþ after youre discrecion he aske (6) ne taake for no rep*a*racion of our said Confessour / con(sid)eryng[1] þat he hadde nowht for rep*a*racion / whanne he (7) was maad bisshop þere / And elles it were our entent / þat our said Confessour shuld haue þe prouffitʒ of þe (8) forsaid temporaltees vnto þe date of þees le*tt*res / And if ye may nat wel trete þe said Benet þer to / (9) spekeþ effectuelly vnto þarchebishop / þat he do his deuoire / as touching þe forsaid rep*a*racion / þat (10) he agree resonably þe said Benet / Consideryng þat þarchebishop maade noon vnto our Confessour abouesaid / Yeuen (11) vnder our signet at oure Cite of Baieux þe .xvij. day of marche

Chancery hand
Calendared with explanations, Kirby 822. See no. 23 below. Grant recorded 1 June 1418, *CPR 1416-22*, pp. 151-52.
[1] torn

17

1418   C81/1364/47   Signet of Henry V
(1) By þe kyng:
Worshipful fad(er in)[1] god / riʒt trusty and welbeloued / We wol / þat to s*i*r (2) Nichol Wynbush clerc of our petit bagge / ye do haue / oure le*tt*res of collacion Vnder oure grete seel in due forme / (3) of a prebende in Chichestre / þat voided now late and longeþ vnto ou(r)e[1] yifte / by cause of þe (4) temporaltees of þe bishopriche of Chichestre / in like wise as oure Chamberlain wrote vnto yow now late fro faloiʒe / (5) for þe said s*i*r Nichol / vnto þe p*re*bende a forsaid / Yeuen vnder our signet in oure Cite of Baieux þe xxij. day of Marche.

Hand y
Calendared Kirby 823. Grant recorded 22 March 1418, *CPR 1416-22*, p.150.
[1] torn

18

1418   C81/1364/46   Signet of Henry V   (Right side missing)
(1) By þe kyng
Worsh(ipfu)l[1] fader yn god riȝt trusty and welbeloued. For asmoche as we yaf now . . . (2) Robert Chicheley Aldermen of london wiþ oþer / in an annuitee of xx.marc . . . Recluse of Berkyng. by cause she (3) miȝt nat haue þannuitee her self: for . . . of london. as in oure lettres patentes / it is more clerly contened / (4) we wol . . . of liberate courrant & allocate dormant / natwiþstandyng any preferreme(nt)[1] . . . we write (5) at þis tyme vnto þe quenes conseil / for to deliuere (6) certain endentures vn . . . Syon at Shene / touching certain money þat is due to her / of þe ferme of saint . . . endowed vnto oure said howse: So we pray yow . . .[2] þat ye be helpyng to þat matere . . . deliuerance of þendentures aforsaid / yeuen vnder oure signet in oure Cite of Baieux . . . day of M(arche)[1]

Hand possibly Hethe's
Calendared with explanations, Kirby 824. Grant recorded 12 May 1417, *CPR 1416-22*, p. 102.
[1] torn   [2] cancel

19

1418   C81/1364/48   Signet of Henry V
(1) By þe Kyng:
Worshipful fader in god. We sende you closed herewiþynne. two supplicacions taken vnto vs þetoone yn name of (2) Thomas Brounflet knight Robert Wiclyff clerc / and Iohn Ellerker / and þe toþer in name of Robert Wiclyff person of þe (3) chirche of Rudby and William Reson chaplein. to þat eende / þat we wolde yeue hem licence to enfeffe (4) Iohn hohom knight / william ake and Robert Constable Escuier yn þe Manoirs of Baynton. Birdsale. Doncastre. Rosyngton & (5) Bramham in yorkshire with þappertenances so þat þey beyng in possession / þerof might enfeffe (6) Maude somtyme wife (of)[1] Pierres Mauley knight yn þe forme more fully specifie(d)[1] with in (7) þe supplicacions aforsaide. Þe whiche we haue granted: Whar fore we wol þat vppon þe teneur of þe same (8) supplicacions ye doo mak(e)[1] oure lettres patentes. Vnder our greet seel of oure saide licence after þe cours (9) and forme of oure Chancellerie vsed in like cas afore þis tyme. Yeuen vnder our signet at Baieux þe .iiij. day of Auril

Hand z
Calendared Kirby 825. Licences granted 12 Feb. 1419, 4 April 1421, *CPR 1416-22*, pp. 179, 263.
¹ torn

20

1418   C81/1364/49   Signet of Henry V
(1) By þe Kyng
Worshipful fader yn god riȝt trusty and welbeloued / We grete yow wel / And for as muche as we haue (2) vnderstande / þat þe prebende of Swerdys yn oure chirche of Deuelyn ys voyde yn lawe / and longeþ to oure (3) collac*i*on we have yeue to oure trusty and welbeloued clerc maister Thomas Bolton bringer of þis þe same prebende / (4) wherfor we wol þat ye maake le*tt*res of oure collac*i*on of þe saide prebende vnder oure greet seel to oure said clerc (5) yn due fourme / yeuen vnder oure signet yn oure cite of Baieux þe .vj. day of Au*er*ill
Toly's hand
Calendared Kirby 826. Grant recorded 6 April 1418, *CPR 1416-22*, p. 149.

21

1418   C81/1364/50   Signet of Henry V (right margin missing)
(1) By þe kyng:
Worshipful fader yn god right trusty and welbeloued. We grete yow wel And albe it / þat . . . (2) parlement by þe whiche we haue a preferrement .x.ml. li. as ye knowe: yitte we wol: þat . . . in yowre warde ye do make (3) writt*es* of liberate and allocate vnto oure welbeloued squier Iohn . . . is due vnto him. of suche annuitees as he hath of (4) oure grante Yeven vnder oure signet in . . . Caen þe xxviij. day of Au*er*ill
Hand y
Calendared Kirby 827. Confirmation of annuity recorded 7 Nov. 1413, *CPR 1416-22*, p. 119.

22

1418   C81/1364/51   Signet of Henry V
(1) By þe kyng
W(orshipful)¹ fader yn god right trusty and Welbeloued / We sende

yow closed wiþ ynne þees a (2) supplicacion put vnto vs yn þe nam of oure welbeloued Roger Waltham / by þe whiche he haþ prayd vs for (3) certein causes contened yn þe saide supplicacion / we wold graunte hym to be oon of þe barons of oure Eschequer / yn (4) þe stede of Robert Sandford þat is god betaght / Considering þat he might be of power to doo vs þe better (5) seruice yn oþer occupacion as we haue sette hym ynne for oure prouffit / as ye may be more clerly enfourmed (6) by þe saide supplicacion / So we wol þat ye see and vnderstande clerely al þe matere contened þer (7) ynne / and þervpon ordeine suche prouision as hit semeþ best to youre Discrecion for oure prouffit and auantage (8) yn þis cas: yeuen vnder oure signet yn oure Castel of Caen þe furst day of May /

Hand possibly Toly's

Calendared Kirby 828. Petition SC8/185/9223. Appointment recorded 15 July 1418, *CPR 1416-22*, p. 170.

¹ torn

23

1418 C81/1364/52   Signet of Henry V
(1) By þe kyng

Worshipful fader yn god riʒt trusty and welbeloued We grete yow wel / And for asmuche as we haue Receyued (2) a bulle direct vnto vs / whiche we sende yow closed vnder oure signet by þe bringer of þis / touching þe promocion of (3) maistre William Barowe to þe bisshopriche of Bangore: we wol þat he haue liueree of þe temporaltees (4) of þe said bisshopriche of Bangore / and do his feaulte in suche cas duely accustumed / Yeuen vnder oure signet in oure Castel of Caen þe xv. day of May

Hand y

Calendared Kirby 829. Livery recorded 5 June 1418, *CPR 1416-22*, p. 167.

24

1418 C81/1364/53   Signet of Henry V
(1) By the kyng:

Worshipful fader yn god. riʒt trusty and welbeloued. we grete yow wel / And for asmuche as we haue vnderstande (2) by yowre lettre wreten in oure Cite of London þe iiij. day of May / how þat þe bisshop of saint Dauid haþ (3) founden seurte in oure Chancellerie / þat he shal neuer vexe ne inquiete þexecutours of þe testament of his last (4) predecessour / þat was our Confessour þe whiche god assoille / but for asmuche as þe said bisshop of saint Dauid haþ (5) (not)¹ brawt into oure said Chancellerie þe bulles of his translacion dirett vnto vs / þat þees bulles þer seen (6) he mighte make certein renunciacion in suche cas accustumed in conseruacion of oure Regalie / þe deliuerance of his temporaltees (7) as yit been deferret. wherfore we sende yow by þe berer of þis þe said bulle / and wol þat þe (8) said bisshop haue lyueree of his temporaltees / and do his fewte / as hit haþ been vsed duely in suche cas afore þis tyme. (9) and god haue yow in his kepyng / fferþermore / for asmuche as we haue granted to oure clerc Robert Shiryngton þe prebende (10) whiche sir Laurence haukyn þat is god betaght hadde now late in oure Chirche of Chichestre. we wol þat ye do (11) make vnto þe said Robert oure lettres patentes vnder oure grete seel beyng in yowre warde in due forme. Considering (12) þat he lost by oure comandement. a noþer prebende in þe same chirche / to þe vse of oure trusty (13) and welbeloued clerc maistre henry ware / keper of oure priue seel and eslit of oure chirche abouesaid / yeuen vnder oure signet in oure (14) Castel of Caen þe xv day of May abouesaid: Also we do yow to witte þat we haue granted vnto oure welbeloued clerc William (15) Toly þe pension of þe abbot of Bataille. wher vpon we wol þat oure said clerc haue suche lettres vnder oure (16) grete (seel)¹ as þe cas askeþ

Hand y

Calendared with explanations, Kirby 830. See no. 15 above and 31 below. Livery recorded 1 June 1418, *CPR 1416-22*, pp. 151-52.

¹ superior insert

25

1418   C81/1364/54   Signet of Henry V

(1) By þe Kyng:

Worshipful fader in god. Ryght trusty and Welbeloued: For as moche as we haue granted to our wel beloued (2) Chapellain Maistre Iohan Cruche Comenceour and licenced in diuinitee: þe prebende of west wythryng in þe Cathedrale chirche (3) of Chichestre þat is voide. be þe deþ of maistre Richard Alkeryngton and belongynge to oure collacion / be (4) reson of þe temporalitees. of þe Bysshopriche of Chichestre. now beynge in oure handes. to haue it wiþ alle þe ryghtes (5) and appurtennances þerof: and also þat we haue granted to Thomas ffeltewell preest: presentacion to þe (6) chirche parochiele of Rademeld voide and belongynge also to our yefte be þe reson abouesaid: We wol þat vnto þe saide (7) persones: ye do make her vpon oure *lettres* seuerall vnder oure greet seal beynge in your warde in due forme. Yeven vnder (8) oure signet in oure Castel of Caen þe xix. day of May:

    Hand possibly Hethe's
    Calendared Kirby 831. Presentations recorded 1 June 1418, *CPR 1416-22*, pp. 154, 168.

26

1418   C81/1364/55   Signet of Henry V
(1) By þe king

    Worshipful fader yn god. right trusty and welbeloued / We sende to yow closed wiþynne þees oure (2) *lettres* a supplica*cion* putte vnto vs yn þe name of þe priour and Conuent of oure house of Ihe*su* of Bethleem (3) at Shene of þordre of Chartuse makyng men*cion* how þat þe barons of oure Eschequer at Westm*instre* wol (4) not discharge hem of certeine so*m*mes of moneye rennyng on hem at oure saide Eschequer for diue*r*ses dimes and quinȝimes (5) granted vnto vs by þe clergie and comunes of oure Reaume of Englond. we wol þat þe saide supplica*cion* seyen / (6) and vnderstanden by yow / and oure *lettres* paten*tes* m(ade)[1] vnto hem þerevpon / ye doo ordeine and see / (7) þat þai be discharged of þe saide dymes and quinȝimes after þeffect of oure saide *lettres* (8) paten*tes* and if þat þe said *p*riour and couent may not be discharged by þe vertue of oure same *lettres* (9) patentes þanne we wol / þat ye ordeine yn þe best wyse þat ye can / þat þai be discharged as for þis (10) tyme of þe dymes and quinȝimes abouesaid / Also we pray yow / spekeþ vnto þarchebisshop of Canterbury (11) / þat oure *lettres* patentes made vnto þe saide priour and Conuent touching þe discharge of þe saide (12) dymes and quinȝimes be entred in his Registre / if ye þinke hit goodly to be doon / yeuen under oure signet yn oure Castel of Caen þe xx. day of May:

    Hand possibly Caud—
    Calendared Kirby 832.
    [1] rubbed

27

1418   C81/1364/56   Signet of Henry V
(1) By þe king:

Worshipful fader in god and right trusty and welbeloued. We sende you closed wiþynne þis / a sup*plicaci*on (2) putte vnto vs. by william holand of Glatton. by þe whiche he hath besoght vs to foryeue vnto him. and to Margerie his wife (3) þe suite of oure pees þat to vs longeþ ayeins hem for þe causes specified in þe saide sup*plicaci*on. (4) as it is more fully contened þerynne and in acopie of þenditement take þervppon. closed in þe same sup*plicaci*on (5) / and forto grante vnto hem also al her goodis and catels. to vs for þe same cause forfait and beyng in oure handes. Wherfore we wol (6) þat seene by you and vnderstande þe saide sup*plicaci*on. Whiche of oure grace especiale. We haue fully granted. after (7) þeffect þer of: ye do haue to þe saide william and Margerie þer vppon. oure *lettres* patentes vnder oure (8) greet seel. in due forme. yeuen vnder oure signet at oure Cite of Lisieux þe xxvij. day of May

Hand z

Calendared Kirby 833. Pardon recorded 12 June 1418. *CPR 1416-22*, p.168.

28

1418   C81/1364/58   Signet of Henry V

(1) By þe kyng

Worshipful fader yn god right trusty and welbeloued. ffor asmuche as we be fully auysed to make oure maistre (2) mason as maistre (S)teven[1] was: oon þat hyght Colchestre / whiche is maistre mason boþe of þe Chirche of york (3) / and of westm*instre* (we w)ol[1] þat ye sende for þe said Colchestre / and þat ye yeue him his charge / (4) and do make him a patent vnder oure grete seel / suche as han been accustumed afore þis tyme in þat caas / Yeuen vnder oure (5) signet in oure Town of Barnay in Normandie þe second day of Iuyn:

Hand possibly Hethe's

Calendared Kirby 834. Appointment recorded 6 July 1418, *CPR 1416-22*, p. 170.

[1] torn and rubbed

29

1418   C81/1364/57   Signet of Henry V

(1) By þe Kyng

Worshipful fader in god ryht trusty and wel be loued. We grete you wel. And for as moche as our trusty and wel beloued (2) knyght. william Bowys þat is of Retenue of our Ryht trusty and entierly wel beloued broþer þe Duke of Clarence. is (3) continuelly abydynge here in oure seruice. We wol and charge you. þat vpon oure le*tt*res patentes of confirmac*io*n (4) maad vnto þe said william of þe grantes of certaine annuitees granted vnto hym afore þis tyme. ye do make our writtes of (5) liberate and allocate necessaires vpon our saide le*tt*res patentes. Notwithstondynge þe preferrement of x*ml*. li. (6) granted vnto vs afore þis tyme (as ye knowe)¹. Yeven vnder oure signet at oure Town of Bernay þe second day of Iuyn

    Hethe's hand
    Calendared with explanations, Kirby 835. Confirmation recorded 4 Aug. 1413, *CPR 1416-22*, p.98.
    ¹ superior insert

30

1418   C81/1364/59   Signet of Henry V
(1) By þe kyng.
    Worshipful fader yn god / right trusty and welbeloued We grete yow wel / And we wol þat yn al haste possible (2) ye doo ordeyne / þat out of oure port of Bristowe be sent to Wa*te*rford in Irland as many shippes as wol suffice for þe (3) shippyng of þe priour of Kylmaynan / wiþ .CC. horsmen and .CCC. footemen to come to vs yn al hast wiþ goddes grace / And þat (4) þis be not left yn no wyse / as oure trust ys to yow / Yeuen vnder oure signet / at oure town of Bernay / þe. iije. (5) day. of Iuyn: (Another hand) fferþermore we wol and prey yow þat for any þing ye haste þe said shipping (6) for þe same Priour and þey þat shal come to vs wiþ him taryen for noon oþir but for lacke of shipping / (7) yeuen vnder oure signet at oure Abbaye of Beekhelwyn þe iiiþe day of þe said moneþ
    (Signed) Stone
(Order for shipping, in French, follows in the second hand.)
    Toly's hand. Signature in a different hand.
    Calendared and French order printed, Kirby 836. Commission recorded 27 Oct. 1418, *CPR 1416-22*, p. 202.

31

1418   C81/1364/60   Signet of Henry V
(1) By þe Kyng
    Worshipful fader in god. ryht trusty and wel beloued / ffor as moche

as we haue vnderstande by a supplicacion (2) put vnto vs. þat Robert haburgeham Sqwyer beynge heere in our seruice on þis syde of þe See in þe (3) compaignie of our trusty and wel beloued þe lord ffiȝhugh oure Chamberlein. is pursued and empleted in our Royaume (4) of Engeland in certaine cause personneles. whiles þat he is heere in our said seruice. wher by he haþ lost and (5) is in poynt to leese many of his goodes fro day to day. We wol þat ye do ordeyne vn to þe said Robert oure lettres (6) of protection in þe commune forme. whiche may be soufficeante and vaillable vnto hym duringe þe (7) tyme þat he is in our said seruice on þis syde of þe See. Yeven vnder oure signet in oure Abbaye of Beekhelwyn. þe .v. day of Iuyn:

   Hand possibly Hethe's
   Calendared and letters of protection cited, Kirby 837.

32

1418   C81/1364/61   Signet of Henry V
(1) By þe kyng:
Worshipf(ul)¹ fader in god Ryht trusty and welbeloued we grete yow wel And sende you closed wiþinne (2) þees lettres. a copie of certaine lettres sent vnto vs from oure Broþer þe Duc of Bretaigne. for to haue (3) Restitucion of certaine goodes of Hamon Martyn breton and oþere of his sougittes of Bretaigne specified in þe (4) same lettres whiche shulde haue be taken vpon þe See by certaine of our sougettes. of Cornewaille. as ye may se moore (5) cleerly by þe saide copie. þe whiche. seen and vnderstanden and hauynge ful knowleche wheþer þe sugestion comprehended (6) in þe same lettres be trewe. we wol and charge you. þat ye se and ordeyne þat hasty restitucion of (7) þe forsaide goodes be maad and þat ye do compelle our saide sougettes to make restitucion abouesaid in obseruynge (8) duely for our partie þe trewes taken betwix vs and our said Broþer of Bretaigne/. And knoweþ wel þat our wil (9) and desire is þat þe saide trieues be kept as Iustly for oure partie. as we wolde þat þey wer kept towardes vs for his partie (10) and in suche wyse þat nouther he ne his saide sougettes haue no cause raisounable to compleyne vnto vs her after for þis (11) cause ne for non oþer semblable for defaute of Ryght as we haue write to our Ryht trusty and welbeloued broþer of Bedeford (12) by oure oþere lettres. And also in wyse as we wol þat restitucion be maad of þe forsaide goodes. yn (13) lychwyse / we wol þat deliuerance of þe Barge and persones specified in þe saide copie be maad wiþ þe (14) saide goodes. so þat

no defaute be founde on our partie. And we wol þat ye do þis þyng by þauys (15) of our said broþer. to whom we write semblablely at þis tyme for þe same matire. Yeven vnder our signet in our hoost afore Louiers þe viij. day of Iuyn.
(Subsequent orders, in French, follow in a different hand.)
Hethe's hand
Calendared with explanations and French printed, Kirby 838.
¹ torn

33

1418   C81/1364/62   Signet of Henry V
(1) By þe Kyng.
Worshipful fader in god Ryht trusty and wel beloued. We grete you wel. And do you to wite þat we (2) haue seen a supplicacion directe vnto vs þe whiche was closed in your lettre and sent vnto oure ryht trusty and (3) wel beloued Clerc maister henri Ware for þe Priour and þe Couent of þe Priorie of Seint Osewoldes of Gloucestre touchinge (4) þappropriacion of þe Chirche of Mynstreworth in our Shire of Gloucestre / and þe whiche supplicacion we (5) sende to you closed wiþinne þes our lettres. and haue granted it fully vpon þis condicion: þat (6) þe saide Priour and Couent. do appropre þe forsaide Chirche wiþinne a yeer next folwynge after þe date of (7) þes lettres. So we wol þat vpon þe contenue of þe same supplicacion / ye do maake vnto þe (8) said Priour and Couent our lettres patentes vnder oure greet seel. beynge in youre warde in due forme. Yeven vnder our signet (9) in our hoost afore Louiers. þe xxij. day of Iuyn:
Hethe's hand
Calendared Kirby 839. Licence recorded 1 July 1418, *CPR 1416-22*, p. 169.

34

1418   C81/1364/63   Signet of Henry V
(1) By þe kyng
Worshipful fader in god Ryht trusty and wel beloued: We grete you wel. And we wol þat vnto oure wel beloued (2) Sqwyer Ianico Dartas. which þat is abydyng wiþ vs in oure seruice heer in þes parties: ye do make vpon þe (3) lettres patentes by þe whiche he takeþ of vs a certaine annuitee durynge his lyf of þe issues of our (4) Citee of london: our writtes of liberate and allocate vnder oure greet seel for þe terme

of Pascqu*es* last passed. notwithstondynge (5) þe preferrement of xml.
li. granted vnto vs afore this tyme Yeven vnder our signet at oure town
of Louiers. þe .xxvj. day of Iuyn:

Hethe's hand
Calendared Kirby 840. Confirmations recorded 20 July 1418, *CPR 1416-22*,
p. 170.

35

1418   C81/1364/64   Signet of Henry V
(1) By þe kyng
Worshipful fader in god. Ryght trusty and wel beloued. ffor as muche
as oure ryht trusty and welbeloued Clerc (2) . . .¹ maistre henri ware.
Elit to þe Bysshopriche of Chichestre haþ deliuered to vs þe bulles of
(3) prouision maad vnto hym by oure holy fader þe pope of þe said
Byssho(pri)²che. and þe same Elit haþ maad (4) renunciac*i*on of alle
þe wordes contened in þe said bulles of prouision þat myghte be
preiudiciel (5) vnto vs and to oure corowne: And also maad his feawte.
vnto vs for þe temporalitees. þat longen to þe forsaid bysshopriche.
(6) We wol þat by oure le*tt*res to be maad in due forme vnder oure
greet seel: ye do make to þe said Elit restituc*i*on (7) and liueree of þe
temporalitees þat longen to þe same Bysshopriche: oure saide le*tt*res
vnder oure (8) greet seal beringe þe date of þe .xiij. day of þe moneþ
of May last passed. Yeuen vnder oure signet in oure (9) hoost beside
our town of Pont de larche. þe .x. day of Iuill:

Hand possibly Hethe's
Calendared Kirby 841. See no.23 above. Livery recorded 13 May 1418, *CPR
1416-22*, p. 171.
¹ cancel   ² torn

36

1418   C81/1364/65   Signet of Henry V (rubbed)
(1) By þe kyng
Worshipful . . .¹ We grete you wel And for as muche as þe trewes
taken b(etwen)e¹ vs and (2) oure broþer þe Duc of B(re)taigne¹: been
proroged vnto halowmesse next coming. we wol þat þ(er)¹ (3) vpon ye
ordeine that þer be proclamac*i*on maade in alle oure portes and in suche
places as hit haþ been (4) vsed and accustumed to be doon in like caas
afore þis time / And god haue yow in his keping yeuen vnder oure signet

in oure hoost before Roan þe ix. day of Aust.
Hethe's hand
Calendared Kirby 842. Prerogation of the truce, Rymer, *Foedera* IX.613-14.
[1] badly rubbed and/or torn

37

1418   C81/1364/66   Signet of Henry V
(1) By þe kyng
W(or)shipful[1] fadre yn god / riȝt trusty and welbeloued / We grete yow wel / And we sende yow closed wyþinne (2) þees oure le*tt*res a supplicacion (pu)t[1] vn to vs yn the name of oure welbeloued yn god (3) þe Prieur and Couent of oure Cathedrale chirche of Bathe the whiche supplicacion vs semeþ resonable / So we wol þat (4) þe same supplicacion seen / and þe mat*er*e þerinne contened pleinly vnderstanden by yow / ye do ful execucion (5) of right vpon þe same supplicacion / aftre youre discrecion / And god haue yow yn his keping yeuen vnder oure signet yn (6) oure hoost afore Roan þe xxx day of Aougst
Hand possibly Caud—
Calendared Kirby 843. See no. 5 above. Commission of inquiry recorded 30 Aug. 1418, *CPR 1416-22*, p. 205.
[1] torn

38

1418   C81/1364/67   Signet of Henry V
(1) By þe kyng
Worshipful fader in god. Ryht trusty and wel beloued We grete you wel. And for asmoche as Thomas Toky which (2) þat haþ an annuitee of x li. to take yeerly by þe handes of þe fermours of þe subside and aulnage of saale (3) cloþes. of our Citee of York: is heer wiþ vs in our duchie of Normandie abydynge continuelly in our s*er*uice: We wol þat (4) vnto þe same Thomas vpon his le*tt*res patentes maad vnto hym of þe same annuitee: ye do maake our writtes of (5) liberate and allocate vnder our greet seal beynge in your warde in due forme: wiþ þis clause / notwiþstandynge þe (6) preferreme*n*t of .xml. li. granted vn to vs in oure parleme*n*t Yeven vnder our signet in oure hoost afore Roan þe xiij. day of Septembre:
Hethe's hand
Calendared Kirby 844. Confirmation recorded 16 June 1413, *CPR 1413-16*, p. 66.

39

1418 C81/1364/68 Signet of Henry V
(1) By þe king
Worshipful fader yn god right trusty and welbeloued. We grete yow wel / And we sende yow closed wiþin (2) þis / a copie of a Lettre sent now late vnto vs by þabbot and Conuent of oure hows of Graces beside oure towre (3) of London / So we wol þ(at)¹ ye shewe al þe fauour and ese þat may be don by lawe and conscience vnto (4) oure said hows so þat hit be nat spoilled of noon of þe possessions þat Longeth þerto yn no wyse / Vnto þat (5) we nowe ordeyne at oure comyng hoom wiþ goddes grace / to put hit yn Reste and quiete / yn asmuche as hit is of oure fundaccion (6) / for whiche cause we haue hit moche þe more yn chierte as reson is / Yeuen vnder oure signet yn oure hoost afore Roan þe xxj day of Septembre

Hand possibly Shiryngton's
Calendared with explanation, Kirby 845. Letter follows, no.40 below. For more on the dispute see *CPR 1399-1401*, pp.274-75; *RP* IV.110; *VCH London* I.462.

¹ torn

40

1418 C81/1364/69 Petition from St. Mary Graces
(1) Most excellent and noble prince and our most gracieux souerain Liege Lord We your owne pore prestes vs recommande to (2) your high and gracieux Lordship Preying both day and night for your good estat and good spede as wele as for the hele (3) of your . . .¹ personne the whiche we preserue and mayntene thurgh his grace longe tyme to his plesament (4) and to confort to al your lieges Most excellent and noble prince & our most gracieux liege lord plese to you for to . . .¹ (5) þat your pore hous the whiche we occupie vnder your gracieux lordship is so villed and empored fro day to day bi the (6) plee that hath be and (þat)¹ continueth (betwix)¹ our (worthi)¹ lord the Erle Huntyngton and vs: and we be there bi (7) so vexed and (unquieted)¹ that we may not thus endure withoute your gracieux help and socour the whiche at al tymes (8) haue put your noble hand as a cristen prince . . .¹ deliuerance of holichirche fro daunger of tribulacions.and diseses Wherefore we (9) beseche you our souerain lord as mekely & deuoutely . . .¹ that with your yen of pitee and mercy like you to consider (10) how that now late in your absence we ne haue but litil comfort and in cas that . . .¹

beyng now in plee the whiche is the (11) most substance of our lyuelode be take awey fro your seide hous & shuld not be of power for to bere the charges of diuin seruice (12) and of other werkes of pitee and de(uoci)on[1] as it was founded and ordeyned bi your most noble progenitours And þerfore (13) vouche ye saaf of your high goodnesse for to take this matere in to your gracieux hondes vntil your comyng home the whiche god (14) graunte sone for to be with as moche worship and prosperite as euer hadde any prince and than for to (r)ule[1] it after the (15) high discreccion of you and of your conseil or els for to send your gracieux lettres to your Chanceller of England (16) that noon liueree be made of the same land withou(t)[1] a Scire facias like as it was ordened and granted in your (17) parlement bifore your departyng In whiche thing our souerain liege lord and most gracieux (king)[1] ye may (18) sette (vs)[1] your pore bedemen in grete ese of hert for to bisie vs the better in diuin seruice as we be bounde to do (19) Vnderstondyng (howeuer)[1] our most gracieux lord that your deuout Chapellain Sir Roger Grenway now late our Abbot & gouernour (20) is passed to god to our grete discomfort and heuynesse and as we suppose the grete thought and bisinesse that he toke for to susteyne (21) the charges of the plee was grete cause of his infirmite as your humble liege man the berer of this lettre can declare to your (22) excellence if it like you for to here him to whom we bieseche your gracieux audience and ful credence in this bihalf Most excellent and (23) noble prince and our most gracieux souerain liege Lord we bieseche the holy trinitee that he you haue euermore in his holy (24) kepyng both body and soule Written at London vnder our commoun seel the iiij day of September

Non-Chancery italic hand
Calendared Kirby 845.
[1] rubbed

41

1418   C81/1364/70   Signet of Henry V
(1) By þe kyng
Worshipful fader in god right trusty and welbeloued / We grete yow wel / And for asmuche as we haue comanded (2) oure welbeloued seruant and squier. maistre Robert Bonsergeant: to go hoom at þis time / Considering þat he is so biset (3) wiþ sekenesse / þat he may do vs no seruice on þis side þe see / we wol þat of suche annuitees (4) as he haþ of oure grante for terme of his lyf. ye ordeine þat he haue oure

writte*s* of liberate and allocate / (5) fro te*r*me to te*r*me as hit shal nede / by þe whiche he may be redely paid at eche te*r*me of his annuitees (6) aforsaid / Yeuen vnder oure signet in oure hoost afore Roan þe . . .¹ day of Septembre:
    Hand possibly Shiryngton's
    Calendared Kirby 846. Confirmations recorded 12 June, 18 Dec. 1413, *CPR 1413-16, pp. 95, 144.*
    ¹ space left for date

42

1418   C81/1364/71   Signet of Henry V
(1) By þe kyng
Worshipful fader in god. Ryht trusty and welbeloued We grete you wel. And we sende you closed wiþinne (2) þes Le*tt*res a supplicac*i*on put vnto vs. by our beloued se*r*uant William Cursun. by þe whiche he desireþ þat (3) we should write vnto you for a certaine matire þat is contened in þe said supplicac*i*on as ye may se more plainly by (4) þe same. So we wol þat þe same supplicac*i*on seyen. and þe matire contened þer in. wel vnderstanden by (5) you. þat ye do ordeyne so þer vpon by your good avys. þat our said se*r*uant haue non hindrynge þerof (6) now in his absence. but þ*at* ye se þe more tendrely þerto be cause þat he is heer continuelly abydinge wiþ (7) vs in our se*r*uice. Yeuen vnder our signet in oure hoost afore Roan þe .v day of Octobre:
    Hethe's hand
    Calendared Kirby 847.

43

1418   Cotton Galba B.I. fol. 164   Signet of Henry V
(1) By þe kyng
Right worshipful and worshipful faders yn god / right trusty and welbeloued / We grete yow wel / And wol ye wite / þ*at* þambassiatours (2) of oure broþir þe Duc of Baire / bringe*rs* of þis / haue been here wiþ vs / and doon þeire ambassiat (3) in suche wyse / as we halde vs wel apaide / And among oþir þinge*s* declared vnto vs / þei haue desired to (4) knowe / how it standeth bitwix vs / and þe princes of Duchelond and in what wise þei goue*r*ne hem towarde*s* vs / and in (5) especial how Duc Iohan of Baire su*m*tyme Elit of Lieges goue*r*neþ him anenst vs

/ for as þei sey / þereafter (6) wol oure broþir of Baire gouerne him / to þe same Iohan / And for asmuche as ye knowe better þanne we doo / how (7) þe said Duc Iohan gouerneþ him towardes vs / and oure Rewme of Englande / and oure suggettes. we remitte hem to (8) haue ful declaracion and verrai knaweleche of you in þat matere. Wherefore we wol þat ye comune wiþ þaim of þis (9) matere / latyng hem haue knoweleche þerof / and how yow þenke þat oure brothir of Baiere shulde (10) gouerne him anenst þe same Duc Iohan / for ye mowe trustely anogh comun wiþ þaim of suche materes / as vs (11) þenkeþ by þe gouernance þat þei haue shewed to vs / Moreouer þei haue desired of vs / to be (12) counseilled be what weye / þai might best and most seurly Retourne hoom ayen into þaire cuntre / owt of oure Rewme of (13) Englande. Consideryng þat þe trewes whiche were bitwix vs / and þe Duc of Bourgoine. expired at Mighelmasse (14) last passed / wherfore In asmuche as ye knowe better þanne we / how þai of fflandres and also of hollande gouerne (15) þaim towardes vs / and oure soubgettes. we desiryng in al wise þe sauf Retournyng hoom of þe said Ambassiatours / (16) wol þat ye counseille and aduise hem in þe best wyse þat ye can for þe seurete of þaire Retournyng (17) / And whiles þai tarie yn oure land / we wol þat þere be shewed vnto hem / al þe fee fauor and chere / þat may (18) be doon yn goodly wyse. And also þat ye oure Chanceller doo make vnto þaim / soufficeant writtes of passage. In suche (19) wyse as þai may haue redy passage owt of oure land / from what port þai come too / vnto what port þayme is Leuest to (20) drawe to by yowre aduis / And almighty god haue yow in his kepyng. yeven vnder oure signet in oure hoost afore Roan the xxj day of Octobre
    Hand y
Calendared with explanation, Kirby 848. Printed Ellis, 3rd ser., I.61-63.

44

1418   C81/1364/72   Signet of Henry V
   S   (1) Worshipful fader yn god right trusty and welbeloued. We grete yow wel. And sende yow closed wiþin þees / a supplicacion (2) dir(ect)[1] vnto yow / and by þe whiche. oon Marke william of Bristow merchant. desireth to haue remedie of (3) certain wrong(es)[1] and iniuries doon to him / aswel as to þospital of þe trinite beside Bristow / touching (4) þe manoir of Ruggewey by Rober(t)[1] Russell maire of Bristow / and william Burgh / as ye may haue more pleine knawleche

(5) by þe said supplicacion. So we wol þat ye se þe said supplicacion. and if þe matere contened (6) þerin oughte to be examined by oure conseil hit be do / and þervpon ye ordeine þat Right be doon / as Lawe and (7) conscience wollen / þat þere be no more compleinte ne poursuite maad vnto vs on þis side þe see / touching (8) þat matere. Yeuen vnder oure signet in oure hoost afore Roan þe xxiij day of Octobr(e)[1]

    Hand possibly Shiryngton's
    Calendared Kirby 849. Recognisance recorded 16 Feb. 1419, *CPR 1413-19*, p. 524.
    [1] torn

45

1418   C81/1364/73   Signet of Henry V

(1) Worshipful fader yn god / oure right trusty and welbeloued We grete yow wel / And we wol / þat nat wiþstandyng þe (2) preferrement þat we haue of .x. ml. li as ye knawe wel / ye ordeyne þat oure welbeloued squier Iohan Ascow: (haue)[1] (3) oure (writ)tes[2] of Liberate and allocate vnder oure grete seal in due forme. by þe vertue of þe (4) whiche: he may haue paiement of þat / þat is due vnto him of suche annuitees as he haaþ of oure grante by oure lettres (5) patentes And þat ye se þe better to him / by cause he is here wiþ vs continuely in oure seruice / Yeuen (6) vnder oure signet . . . [3] in oure hoost afore Roan þe xxvij day of Octobre:

    Hand possibly Hethe's
    Calendared with explanations Kirby 850. Confirmation recorded 20 June, 17 July 1413, *CPR 1413-16*, pp. 66, 69.
    [1] rubbed   [2] torn   [3] cancel

46

1418   Cotton Julius B.VI. fol. 97(35)   Signet of Henry V

(1) By þe king[1]

Right trusty and welbeloued / brother / We grete yow wel / And as we suppose / It is not out of youre Remembrance in what wise and (2) how ofte we haue charged yow by oure lettres / þat good and hasty reparacion and restitucion were ordeined and (3) maade at altymes of suche attemptates as hapned to be made by oure sugettes / ayenst þe trewes taken betwix vs (4) and oure brother þe duc of Bretaigne / And

not withstanding oure saide le*tt*res diuers compleint*es* be maad and sent vnto vs (5) / for defaulte of rep*a*racion and restitu*cio*n of suche attemptat*es* as be made by certein of oure subgett*es* (6) and lieg*es* as ye may vnderstand by a supplica*cio*n sent to vs by þe said duc / whiche supplica*cio*n we sende to yow (7) closed wiþ ynne þees le*tt*res for to haue þe more pleine knoweleche of þe trouthe / wherfor we wol and (8) charge yow / þat ye calle to yow oure Chancell*er* to haue knowelache of þe same supplica*cio*n: and þat doon / we (9) wol / þat ye doo sende to vs in al hast al þoo personnes / þat been oure sugettes contened in þe supplica*cio*n (10) abouesaid / And þat also in alle other semblable mat*er*es / ye doo ordeine so hasty and Iuste Remede / restitu*cio*n / and rep*a*racion (11) vpon suche attemptat*es* doon by oure sugett*es* in co*n*seruac*io*n of oure trewes / þat noman haue (12) cause hereafter to compleine in suche wyse as thai doon for defaute of right doyng / ner we cause to write to yow alweys as we doon (13) for suche causes / Considered þe gret occupac*io*n þat we haue otherwyse / And god haue yow in his keping / yeuen vnder oure (14) signet in oure hoost afor Roan. þe.xxix. day of Nouembre
   Toly's hand
   Calendared Kirby 851. Printed Nicolas II.243.
   [1] on a detached slip, different paper(?)

47

1419   C81/1366/8   Signet of Henry V
(1) By þe king
Worshipful fader i(n g)[1]od / right trusty and welbeloued / We grete yow wel / And we sende yow closed (2) wiþ ynne þis a (s)upplicacion[1] put vnto vs in þe names of william ffowler of þe contee of Buk*ingham*shire (3) gentil(man)[1] william Buktoft / and Richart Brount / þe whiche supplica*cio*n seen and vnderstanden (4) by yow / wiþ þe circumstances / yif ye can be trewely enfourmed þat þe suggestion be trewe þat is contened in (5) þe said supplica*cio*n / we wol þ*at* þe same william: william: and Richard haue pardon in due fourme / of þe (6) so*m*me specified in þe saide supplica*cio*n / yeuen vnder oure signet / in oure town of Rouen / þe .xxviij. day of Ianuer /
   (Signed) Toly
   Toly's hand
   Calendared Kirby 852. Pardon recorded 29 March 1419, *CPR 1416-22*, p. 216.
   [1] torn

48

1419   C81/1364/74   Signet of Henry V
(1) By þe king
Worshipful fader in god / right trusty and welbeloued / we grete yow wel / And for asmuche as þe trewes (2) bitwix vs / and ou(r)e¹ broþir þe duc of Bretaigne been proroged vnto þe feste of alhalowmesse (3) next comyng / and for . . .¹ wekes after / in þe same fourme as þei were taken þe last yere at Alencon / (4) we wol þat in al hast ye do proclame in due fourme þe said prorogacion in al places nedeful and accustumed (5) in suche cas / And god haue yow in his keping Yeuen vnder oure signet in oure Castel of Rouen þe xxx day of Ianuer

Chancery hand
Calendared with explanations, Kirby 853. Prorogation recorded 12 Jan. 1419, Rymer, *Foedera* IX.663.

¹ torn

49

1419   C/81/1366/10   Signet of Henry V
(1) By þe king.
Worshipful fader in god right trusty and welbeloued / We grete yow wel / And doo yow to wite þat (2) we haue yeuen vnder oure greet seel here / þe chirche of Morton / whiche as we were enfourmed voyded be þe deces (3) of oon maister Richard Penelles and longed to oure yift / be cause of þe beyng of oure Cousin Courrenays landes (4) yn oure handes / the whiche oure yift we signiffie vnto yow to þat ende / þat ye witt / we wol hit take (5) effect / yeuen vnder oure signet / in. oure town of Rouen. þe .xxx. day of Ianuer

(Signed) Toly

Toly's hand
Calendared Kirby 854. Presentation confirmed C64/10/36; Deputy Keeper's Report no. 41, p.727.

50

1419   C81/1366/5   Signet of Henry V
(1) By þe king.
Worshipful fader in god. right trusty and welbeloued / We grete yow

wel / And we wol / þat ye doo make / (2) vnto Thomas Cochare of oure town of Douorre / whiche haþ doon vs seruice here on þis side þe see / writtes of (3) liberate and Allocate / in due fourme / for þat þat is behynde and due vnto hym. of .iiij. d (þe day)¹ granted vnto (4) hym by certein lettres patentes / confermed by vs / to Receiue hem of þe fee ferme of oure Cite of Canterbury. (5) by þe handes of oure baillifs of þe same place / Not wiþstandyng þe preferrement of .x.m*l*. pound. (6) graunted vnto vs / by parlement as ye knowe / And god haue yow in his keping / yeuen vnder oure signet / in (7) oure Castel of Rouen / þe .xj. day of ffeuerer

(Signed) Toly

Toly's hand

Calendared Kirby 855. Grant recorded 1 Dec. 1399, *CPR 1399-1401*, p. 138; confirmation recorded 7 June 1413, *CPR 1413-16*, p. 25.

¹ superior insert

51

1419   SC1/43/162   Signet of Henry V

(1) Worshipful fader in god right trusti and welbeloued we grete you wel And witeth yat we been enformed yat ye kyng of Castel maketh (2) a grete armee of vesselx whiche shuld be redy / in short tyme as is sayde for to doo ye harme ayeinst vs and oures yat yay (3) may / whiche god defende. and in especiale yat yaire purpos is to doo yaire powaire for to brynne and destrue oure shippes and ye (4) nauie of oure lande and namely oure shippes at Hampton And also yaire ordinance is to lande in our(e)¹ Reaume for to (5) doo thannoye yat yay may / Wherefore we wol and charge you / yat by yauys of oure brothre of Bedford and of othir suche as semeth to (6) youre discrecion: ye ordenne in alle haste for ye gouernance of oure lande And for ye saufwarde of seurkepyng of oure saide (7) vesselx at Hampton and in othir places where as eure yay bee And yat yay of ye portes and of ye see coost al abowte be warned (8) here of in alle haste and charged to be wel awaytyng and redy at al tymes if any suche thyng happen: yeuen vnder oure signet in (9) oure Castel of Rouen ye xij day of ffeuerer

Non-Chancery hand

Calendared Kirby 856. Commissions of array recorded 5 March 1419, *CPR 1416-22*, pp. 209-12; Rymer, *Foedera* IX.702.

¹ torn

52

1419   C81/1366/9   Signet of Henry V
(1) By the King:
Worshipful fader in god oure trusty and welbeloued / We wol and charge yow þat vnto oure Welbeloued clerc Iohn Hethe (2) / ye doo make out writt*es* of Liberate and Allocate / from te*r*me to te*r*me / wiþ the clause / non obstante / (3) þe prefer(re)ment¹ / of þa*n*nuite of xx Marc / which we haue granted hym by oure le*tt*res patent*es* (4) / of the fee ferme / of oure town of Iarnemouthe / to take hit by þe handes of oure baillifs of the saide toun f(or)² (5) the tyme beyng / And seeþ þat þis be doon / notwiþstandyng / any co*m*mandement / yeuen vnto yow / to þe contrary (6) here afore / Yeuen vnder oure signet / at oure town of Rouen þe xxviij*e* day of ffeuerer
(Signed) Andrieu

Andrieu's hand
Calendared Kirby 857. Confirmation recorded 12 June 1413, *CPR 1413-16*, p. 70.
¹ torn   ² rubbed

53

1419   C81/1366/15   Signet of Henry V (Right corner missing, approximately one fifth of the first four lines)
(1) By the King:
(Wor)shipful fader in god / oure trusty and welbeloued / for asmuch . . . a (2) Patente closed vnder oure signet / and ensealled with oure grete sea . . . Syon / þe whiche Patente / fore haste myȝht not be (3) enrolled here . . . enrolled in England. Not wiþstanding / þe two names rased . . . Yeuen vnder oure signet / at (4) oure town of Rouen / þe ij*e* day of March /
(Another hand) The two names aforesaide been þerles of Arundell and of (5) warrewik þe whiche wer Rased / because þey wer myssette And for asmuche as oure saide patent is of a þyng perpetuel: (6) we wol þat ye do write hit ayein of a more substancial hande / and seel hit vndre oure seel beyng yn youre warde. And now (7) þat we haue satisfied to þe desire of þayme of Syon as towardes þaire profession. we wolde (8) þat for any thyng þe profession wer hasted. wherto we pray yow to stere and to help þat ye may.

Hand possibly Andrieu's
Calendared Kirby 858.

54

1419   C81/1366/6   Signet of Henry V
(1) By þe king:
Worshipful fader yn god. oure right trusty and welbeloued. We grete yow wel. And we wol. þat vpon þe (2) contenue of þe supplicac*ion*. whiche we sende yow closed here wiþin: ye ordeine suche writt*es* of liberate and (3) allocate vnto oure welbeloued knight william Cromewell. as haue be maade to oþ*er* afore þis tyme in like cas. Notwiþstanding (4) þe p*re*ferrement of .x. m*l*. li. And god haue yow in his keping. Yeuen vnder oure signet in oure Castel of Rouen þe xvij. day of Marche:
   Shiryngton's hand
   Calendared with explanation, Kirby 859. Confirmation of grant recorded 1 Oct. 1414, *CPR 1413-16*, p. 240.

55

1419   C81/1365/1   Signet of Henry V
(1) By þe king   S
Wor(ship)ful[1] fader yn god / oure right trusty and welbeloued. We grete yow wel / And we wol þat seyen and (2) vnderstande by yow þe mat*ere* contened in þe sup*plicacion* / whiche we sende yow closed here wiþin (3) / touching certain þing*es* granted vnto oure welbeloued squier. Ianico dartasse: as ye may se more pleinly. by þe (4) saide sup*plicacion*: ye doo ordeine þat he haue suche writt*es* as may Lawefully be hadde / and suche as yow þenkeþ (5) resounable in þe cas. And god haue yow in his keping. Yeuen vnd*er* oure signet in oure town of vernon þe vj. day of Au*er*il   S
   (Signed) Shiryngton
   Shiryngton's hand
   Calendared with explanation, Kirby 860.
   [1] torn

56

1419   C81/1365/2   Signet of Henry V
S   (1) By þe king   S
Worshipful fader in god / oure Right trusty and welbeloued. We grete yow wel / And we wol þat after þe (2) teneur of a sup*plicacion*. whiche

we sende yow closed wiþ ynne þis / ye do make oure le*tt*res of saufconduit. vnder (3) oure grete seel in due forme / duryng for a yere / And god haue yow in his keping / Yeuen vnder oure signet in oure towne of vernon þe xx*the*. day of Auril   S
  (Signed) Shiryngton
  Shiryngton's hand
  Calendared Kirby 861.

57

1419   Cotton Galba B.I fol. 157   Signet of Henry V
(1) By þe king S
  Right trusty and welbeloued broþer / We grete yow wel / And we lete yow wite / how þat þei of .iiij. membres of (2) flandres desiren by þaire le*tt*res sent to vs / þat we wolde continue and prorogue þe seurtees and prouisions (3) ordeined afore þis time for þe cours of marchandise. betwix oure Rewme of England and þe cuntre of flandres þe (4) whiche prouisions and seurtees expired at Ester last / as ye may se more plainly by þe copie closed wiþin þis of (5) þe said iiij. membres le*tt*res S
  Also we send yow closed wiþin þis / a copie of oure le*tt*re Responsiue (6) vnto þe le*tt*res abouesaid / and þe forme of an Instrucci*on* of certain prouisions / whiche we wol / be added to (7) þat oþir seurtees and prouisions afore tyme / at þe next taking newe of þe forsaid seurtees and prouisions (8) by oure Co*m*missaires / suche as by yow / wiþ avis of oure Chancell(or)¹ and oþir of oure conseil shul be deputed (9) and ordeined for to goo to Calais for þat cause S
  fferþermore whan þat ye haue seyen and vnderstande (10) þees oure le*tt*res and copies closed þerin. we wol þat ye write vnto þe said .iiij. membres / certifieng hem. (11) how þat by oure comandement. ye write vnto hem / to be certified at what tyme þaire Ambassiatours. shullen be redy at oure (12) towne of Calais. for þe said cause / ayein þe whiche tyme / we wolde oure Co*m*missaires were þere also. And god haue (13) yow in his keping. Yeuen vnder oure signet in oure towne of vernon þe xxviij day of Auerill   S
  (Signed) Shiryngton
  Shiryngton's hand
  Calendared with explanations, Kirby 862. Printed, with the letter from Bruges and the King's reply, Nicolas II.250-54. See no. 65 below.
    ¹ torn off

58

1419   C81/1365/4   Signet of Henry V
(1) By þe king.
Worshipful fader yn god oure right trusty and welbeloued / We grete yow wel / And we sende yow closed wiþ (2) ynne þees oure le*tt*res. a supplicacion of greuous compleynt / put vnto vs by. *sir* Rogier wodehill person of (3) Strete / as ye may see more clerely by þe same supplicacion / wherfor we wol þat þe forsaide supplica*c*ion wel (4) vnderstanden and considered by yow / ye doo calle before yow bothe parties speciffied in þe same supplicacion / and þaire (5) causes herd / þat ye doo vnto hem boothe / right and equite / and in especial þat ye see þat þe porer (6) partye suffre no wrong / but þat ye make suche an ende in þis matiere / þ*at* (we)¹ be nomore vexed hereafter (7) wiþ taire complainte*s* / And god haue yow in his keping / yeuen vnder oure signet / at oure town of Vernon þe .xxviij. (8) day of Aue*r*ill
  Toly's hand
  Calendered Kirby 863. Printed *PC* I.xvi.
  ¹ superior insert

59

1419   C81/1365/3   Signet of Henry V
(1) By þe king   S
Worshipful fader yn god oure right trusty and welbeloued. We grete yow wel And for asmuche as we be enfourmed / (2) þat oure le*tt*res patentes by þe whiche we haue granted vnto oure welbeloued squier Pierres Garueys. þe (3) warde of þe landes and tenement*ȝ* þat were hugh ffastolfs knight þat is godbetaght: be nat vaillable. by (4) cause. þe value is nat expressed. in oure saide le*tt*res / and also. for suche wardes been assigned for þe despenses (5) of oure howsholde. we wol. þat ye do make vnto oure said squier oure le*tt*res patentes vnder oure grete seel in due (6) forme / of þe said warde beryng þe date of oure furst grante. nat wiþstanding þat mencion is nat maade of þe (7) verraye value yerly / and also natwiþstandyng þat suche wardes been assigned for þe despenses of oure howshold. (8) for hit is oure wille þat he (haue)¹ suche le*tt*res patentes as may be vaillable (and resonabe)¹ to him in þis caas. (9) Yeuen vnder oure signet in oure towne of vernon þe xxviij day of Aue*r*ill   S
  (Signed) Shiryngton
  Shiryngton's hand

Calendared Kirby 864. See no.14 above. Grant recorded 28 Feb.1418, *CPR 1416-22*, p. 134.
¹ superior insert

60

1419   C81/1366/13   Signet of Henry V
(1) By þe king
Worshipful fader yn god oure right trusty and welbeloued. We grete yow wel / And for asmuche as we haue ordeined (2) oure trusty and welbeloued knyght Iohn of Radclif. to be oure Conestable of Bourdeux And also to be Cap*taine* of oure Castel (3) of fronsac for þe grete trust þat we haue to his trewthe and discrecion. we wol and charge yow þat by þauis of (4) oure broþer of Bedford and oþer of oure conseil þere in Englande. ye trete and accorde wiþ þe said (5) Iohn for his abidyng þere. And so þat he may do vs good seruice. as hit semeþ best to youre discrecions for oure (6) auantage and proffit of þe cuntree And þat ye spede him in al þe haste þat ye may. And se þat he tarye (7) not þere: as oure trust is to yow And god ha(ue yo)w¹ in his keping Yeuen vnder oure signet in oure Castel of Rouen þe . . .¹

(Signed) Shir(yngton)¹
Shiryngton's hand
Calendared with other references Kirby 865.
¹ torn off

61

1419   C81/1365/5   Signet of Henry V
(1) Worshipful fader yn god / oure right trusty and welbeloued. We grete yow wel And we wol þat vpon þe contenu of þe sup*plicacion* (2) closed wiþin þis / ye do make vnto oure welbeloued seruant Piers Logge / yeman of oure Cha*m*bre oure (3) writtes of liberate and allocate vnder oure grete seal in due fourme / by vertue of þe whiche / he may haue paiement of al (4) þat is behinde and due vnto him of vj.d a day / by þe handes of þe visconte of Wilto*n*. not wiþstanding (5) þe preferrement of x.m*l*. li. þat we haue as ye knowe wel / And god haue yow in his keping. yeuen vnder (6) oure signet in oure towne of Mante þe xix. day of Iuyn   S

(Signed) Shiryngton
Shiryngton's hand
Calendared with references, Kirby 866. Grant recorded 26 Aug. 1416, *CPR 1416-22*, p. 56.

62

1419   C81/1365/6   Signet of Henry V
(1) By þe king
Worshipful fader yn god: oure right trusty and welbeloued / We grete yow wel / And for asmuche as we haue a manere (2) of dowte / whether kynwolmersh occupie clerely and wiþowte scrupule / þospital of saint Antony by oure yifte or noo / (3) for to eschewe þe peril yn conscience / þat myght be vnto vs by þe yeuyng / and to hym (by)[1] þe (4) resceyuyng of þe said hospital / þat god defende / on lasse þan þe title wher clere yn lawe and conscience. We wol (5) ye do make a patent vnder oure greet seel vnto þe said kynwolmersh of þe Deanee of saint martin(es)[1] grande (6) yn London. Takyng furst of him souffissante seurtee þat he shal be redy al tymes to resigne þe said hospital / whan vs likeþ (7) to commande hym / And yf hit be foun(d)[1] þat noo scrupule be yn oure yifte. þat we made vnto hym of þe (8) said hospital / wherof we wolde ye sent vs worde yn al goodely haste. þan we wol þat kynwolmersh chese to kepe / stille (9) whether hym haþ leuer þe forsaid De(anee)[1] or hospital / And If hym haþ leuer þe Deanee / and to leue (10) þospital we holde vs content / but þan hit is oure wille / þat þow he kepe stille þospital wiþ te Deanee (11) for a tyme / to þat we haue disposed þerfore / þat he dispende not þe Reuenues and comoditees of þe said (12) hospital / but kepe þaym stille hooly vnto oure comyng hoom with goddes grace. And If he wol perauanture holde (13) stille þospital if hit stande clere. we wol he fynde semblable seurte to resigne þe Deanee ayein into oure handes And (14) god haue yow in his keping. Yeuen vnder oure signet in oure town of Mante þe xx. day of Iuyn   S
 (Signed) (Shir)yngton[1]
Shiryngton's hand
Calendared Kirby 867. Grant of deanery to Kynwolmersh 1 July 1419, *CPR 1416-22*, p. 218.
[1] stained

63

1419   C81/1365/7   Signet of Henry V
(1) By þe kyng
Worshipful fadre in god / and oure Riȝt trusty and welbeloued : We grete you wel / And for asmuche as by þexpresse (2) and especiale avyse and consent of oure Riȝt trusty and welbeloued vncle þe Duc of Excestre / to whome we had granted (3) by oure lettres patentes þe keping

of alle þe landes þat shul longe by heritage vnto oure trusty and welbeloued (4) Cousin Iohn son and heire to william Roos of hamelak þat helde of vs in chief þe day he deyed on / durynge þe non age (5) of þe said Iohn: we of oure special grace haue granted vnto oure said Cousin plein lyuere of alle þe (6) landes þat longen / or may longe vnto him by heritage wyþynne oure Reaume of Engeland / or elleswhere aftre þe fourme (7) of a copie of a patent annexed to a supplicacion take to vs: þe whiche we sende you closed wyþynne þees oure (8) lettres: we wol and charge you þat in al þe goodely hast þat ye may ye make vpon oure said grant to oure said Cousin (9) oure lettres patentes aftre þe fourme of þe said copie þat we sende you and also suche wryttes of lyuere / (10) and yn suche fourme and nombre as is necessarie and vaylable for him wiþ al þe h . . .[1] and fauour þat ye may. (11) So þat þis be not take to non euel example: notwyþstandyng þat of oure grace we wol hit An(d)[1] (12) god haue you in his keping: Yeuen vnder oure signet at oure towne of Mant þe xxiij. day of Iuyne

(Signed) Caud . . .

Hand Caud—

Calendared Kirby 868. The petition is SC8/182/9061. Grant to Exeter recorded 22 Sept. 1414, *CPR 1413-16*, pp. 235-36; to John Roos 8 July 1419, *CPR 1416-22*, p. 263.

[1] torn off

64

1419 C81/1365/8 Signet of Henry V

(1) By þe kyng   S

Worshipful fader yn god / oure right trusty and welbeloued / We grete yow wel And forasmuche / as we lete sende (2) for maistre Richard garsedale oon of þe contendentes of þe prouoste of þe Oriell to þat ende (3) þat for his partie / shulde no thyng be poursuyd neither at þe Courte of Rome ne elles (where)[1] but þat / (4) þat controuersie shulde be put in Respit vnto oure comyng hoom wiþ goddes grace / for oure occupacion (5) is suche þat we mow nat wel entende to suche materes here / Wherefore we wol þat ye make booþe þe (6) said garsdale whiche comeþ now hoom be oure leue / and also Lentwardyn / com afore yow / and þat ye take seurte soufficeant (7) of bothe þe parties / þat neither of hem shal make ferþer poursuyt of appelle at Courte of Rome / ner no (8) manere of poursuyt þere or elles where / as touching þe said contrauersie vnto oure comyng as before / at (9) whiche tyme oure entent ys / to put þe same controuersie to a goode and rightwyse conclusion and þe said partie (10) yn Rest. And yf any of hem haue þe saide poursuyt of apelle hangyng yn Court þat þey abate hit / and sende to Revoke (11) hit yn al haste / and þat þay make al suche as been þaire attornes or doers yn Court spirituel or temporel to (12) surcesse. And we wol ferþermore as touching oure said College of þoriell / þat ye put hit yn suche gouernance / (13) as semeth to yowre Discrecion for to doo vnto oure Comyng. And god haue yow yn his keping / Yeuen vnder oure signet in oure town of Mante þe vij day of Iuill   S

  (Signed) Shiryngton
  Shiryngton's hand
  Calendared with explanation, Kirby 869.
  [1] superior insert

65

1419   C81/1365/9   Signet of Henry V
(1) By þe kyng
  Worshipful fader yn god / oure right trusty and welbeloued / We grete yow wel / And we sende yow closed wiþ yn (2) þees / (a)[1] supplicacion put vnto vs / by oure poure ligeman Iohan Bone. vpon whiche supplicacion / we wol (3) þat ye doo hym haue þat that right and lawe wollen yn þe cas / but þat oþersyde beeth wel avysed or to (4) grete duresse be shewed vnto hym / or to any of oure suggettes yn persone or yn goodes / for þe suggestions or appechementes (5) of (him)[2] þat calleth hym self person of wortham. vnto þe tyme þe verray trowþe be clerely (6) examined and knowen / of his accusacions / oþer elles þoo þat he accuseth. han be noted afore tyme of suche defaultes. (7) for þe forsaid person is holden to besy in suche maters / And god haue yow in his keping / Yeuen vnder oure (8) signet in oure town of Mante þe xj. day of Iuill   S

  Shiryngton's hand
  Calendared Kirby 870. The petition is SC8/179/8940. See *CCR 1419-22*, p. 5.
  [1] torn   [2] superior insert

66

1419   E28/33/5   Signet of Henry V
(1) By þe king.
  Right trusty and welbeloued broþer / We grete yow wel / And we

sende yow closed wiþ ynne þees (2) oure le*tt*res / a supplicacion putte vnto vs / on þe behalue of will Godard and Agneis his wyf / Wolnyng / (3) þ*at* knowelache hadde of þe trouthe of þe mat*er*e contened in þe same supplicacion / ye calle (4) vnto yow oure Iustices / And by þaire aduis / ordeineth þat bothe parties nempned in þe forsaide supplicacon (5) haue right / soo þat nouther of þaim haue cause to compleine hereafter for defaute of Iustice / And god haue yow in (6) his keping / yeuen vnder oure signet at oure toun of Mante .þe .xij. day of Iuill:

(Signed) Toly

Toly's hand

Calendared with explanations and other references, Kirby 871.

67

1419   C81/1365/10   Signet of Henry V

(1) By þe king

Worshipful fader in god / oure right trusty and welbeloued / We grete yow wel / And we wol ye wyte / þat þe (2) priour of oure hows of saint Bartholomew / in Westsmythfeld of London haaþ poursued vnto vs here on þis side þe (3) see / for confirmacion of alle þe yiftes grantes / priuileges / franchises and libertees graunted vnto oure saide hows by oure (4) progenitours and predecessours / And for asmuche: as ye might by vertue of youre office haue doo maad hym oure le*tt*res of (5) confirmac*i*on wiþoute þat hym shulde haue neded to poursue ferther vnto vs / we suppose þere bee sum cause (6) resounable / why ye haue not doo hit / in cas þat he haue poursued vnto yow þerfor / wherfor if ye knowe any suche cause why (7) ye aught not to make hym oure forsaide le*tt*res / we wol þat ye certiffie vs what hit is And if þere noon bee / þat (8) þanne ye doo maake vnto þe forsaide priour and to þe conuent of oure saide hows of seint Bertho*lo*mew / (9) oure lettres paten*tes* of confirmac*i*on vnder oure greet seel in due fourme of alle þe yiftes / grantes / priuileges (10) / franchises and libertes / whiche þay haue / as is abouesaid of þe yifte or grant of oure progenitours and predecessours (11) / leuyng out þe clause licet / And god haue yow in his keping / yeuen vnder oure signet / at oure town of Mante. þe (12) .xxij. Day of Iuyll

(Signed) Toly

Toly's hand

Calendared Kirby 872. Printed Maxwell-Lyte, *Great Seal*, pp. 119-20. Confirmation recorded 27 Sept. 1419, *CPR 1416-22*, pp. 239-46.

68

1419   C81/1365/11   Signet of Henry V
(1) By þe kyng   S
Worshipful fader yn god / oure Right trusty and welbeloued / we (2) grete yow wel / And for asmuche as we haue granted vnto oure welbeloued clerc of oure Chapelle / Thomas Gyles / þe prebende (3) whiche / Iohn Cooke late clerc of oure saide Chapelle / hadde wiþin oure free Chapelle of hastynges. We wol þat (4) þervpon ye do make oure lettres patentes in due fourme. vnder oure grete seel / as þe cas asketh / Yeuen vnder (5) oure signet in oure town of Mante þe xxv. Day of Iuill   S
(Signed) Shiryngton
Shiryngton's hand
Calendared Kirby 873. Confirmation recorded 25 July 1419, *CPR 1416-22*, p. 219.

69

1419   Cotton Vesp. F.I. fol. 104   Signet of Henry V
(1)Worshipful fader in god oure right trusty and welbeloued. We grete yow wel / And wol ye wete / yat we haue Receiued youre lettres (2) whiche ye sent vs last by hugh of oure chambre / by whiche we conceive / yat among other yinges whiche ye write vn to vs (3) of / ye desire to knawe oure entent touchyng ye trewes taken vn to Alhalwen tyde betwix vs and flaundres / of whiche trewes writtes (4) of proclamacion been passed vnder oure grete seel. whervpon we wol ye wete / yat we hald vs agreed of ye proclamacion / (5) after as in ye writtes be contened / And in cas yat yay of flaundres wol here after desire prorogacion of ye said trewes / (6) we wolde yay were halden in hand wiy tretee / vn to ye tyme ye haue certiffied vs yerof / and knowe oure entent ayeinward / (7) And of o thing we wold ye were wel aduised / yat in any trewes takyng (with hem)[1] hereafter yere were put yn / alle oure suggettes (8) as wel of oure duchie of Normandie / and of oure other lordshippes / as of oure Reaume of Englond

And as touchyng ye tretee wiy (9) yembassiatours of Gene / of whiche ye haue send vs a cedule / sent vn to yowe be Escourt / In whiche cedule the merchantes of (10) oure Reaume of England asken after ye vttermast estimacion of yayre godes yat were taken be ye Ianeuoys .x ml.li. And (11) ye same Ianevoys maken estimacion of ye same goodes at vii.

m*l*. Cxxiiij. li. wolnyng for to stand in oure goode (12) grace et beniuolence paye wiy oute any excepcion / iiij. m*l*. li. at Resonable termes / oure subgettes and oure merchandes (13) of oure land hauyng hereaftre fre commyng and goyng to Gene / as yay of Gene desire to haue in to oure Reaume of England / (14) witteth yat consideryng ye vnese yat ye merque of hem of Gene haay / doon: as wel in strengthyng of oure ennemys / as in hindryng of (15) ye cours of marchandise betwix oure Reaume and yaym / and tourneth to noon neer ende for hom yat han ye merque. yan hit did / at (16) bygynnyng / vs yenkey[2] and we wold / yat such somme as yay profer were accepted / yf no gretter myght be haad in short tyme / (17) wiy ye condicion yat we vnderstond / yay profre / yat is / yat oure sugettes of Englond etcetera: may be fre in alle yaire portes (18) (to which we wold were put yat oure subgitʒ shuld be free in alle yaire portes)[1] as wel as to passe by hem to what other portes (19) yaim lust by waye of marchandise / if this myght be haad. And alle this we committe to yow and to ye Remenant of oure counseil to (20) be wroght after youre discrecions and comun aduis / for as (of)[1] ye somme al ying considered / we halde hit Resounable o lasse yenne more (21) may be geten / wiy oute taryeng of yaccord / And if yis matere myght be concluded in oure Reaume of England before yow / hit were (22) oure entent / And ellis if yat may not bee / we wol wel yat yeende be maade at Calais wyt a goode Instruccion And yat it be seyn (23) / yat yay be wel bounden / not to [holde][3] (helpe)[1] nor suffre non of yaires to helpe noon of oure ennemys ayeines vs ner noon of oures / nouther be (24) land ner water / And yat in ye best wise yat may be haade.

Also as touchyng yat now late ye saide Ambassiatours of Gene haue writen vn (25) to oure Ambassiatours sharpely / yat [Awe][3] (al be)[1] hit / yat yaire vessell and marchandes haan been late taken be oure suggettes (26) / ye tretee of pees so nigh concluded / neuer ye later yay wol a byde an answar after as was accorded whiche haad from vs / (27) yay wol send to Gene / Not wolnyng other wise yanne as before trete ner conclude / but yf yay haue other in commandement from yaire (28) souueraines / The answar may be wel maad yat til yai be ful thorogh wiy vs / yat yay shal no thyng haue but werre / And yerfor desire (29) of hem to make ye sonner ende / for in oure partie / and yay wol be Resounable hit shal not halde / but yat good Rest and frensship shal be /

Chancery hand except y for þ
Calendared Kirby 874. Printed Nicolas II. 255-57. See no. 53 above. Order to proclaim truce recorded 14 July 1419. *CCR 1419-22*, p. 47; Rymer, *Foedera* IX.784.

[1] superior insert [2] i.e., þenkeþ [3] cancelled

70

1419(?)   Cotton Vesp. F. III. fol. 8.   Autograph draft by Henry V?

(1) Furthremore I wole that ye comend with my brothre with the chanceller with my cosin of northumbrelond and my cosin of (2) Westme(r)land[1] and that ye set a gode ordinance for my north marches and specialy for the Duc of (O)rlians[1]. (3) and for alle the remanant of my prisoners of France. and also for the king of Scotelond. for as I am secrely enfourmed by (4) a man of ryght notable estate in this lond that there hath ben a man of the Ducs of Orliance in scotland and accorded with the (5) Duc of albany. that this next somer he shal bryng in the maumet of Scotland to sturre what he may. and also that ther schold be (6) founden weys to the havyng awey specialy of the Duc of Orlians. and also of the king as welle as of the remanant of my (7) forsayd prysoners that god do defende. wherfore I wolle that the Duc of Orliance be kept st(i)lle[1] withyn the castil (8) of pontfret with owte goyng to robertis place or to any othre disport. for it is bettre he lak his dispor(t)[1] (9) (t)hen[1] we were disceyued. of alle the remanant dothe as ye thenketh

Non-Chancery hand; Henry V's own hand ?

Calendared Kirby 881. Printed Ellis, 1st ser., I.1-2; Halliwell I.92; T. Livius, *Vita Henrici Quinti*, pp.99-100.

[1] torn

71

1419   E28/33/13   Signet of Henry V

(1) By the king

Trusty and welbeloued We grete you wel. And as touching youre credence to declare to þe Lordes esperituel (2) and temporel and also to al þe gentilmen and comunes of oure contree of guyenne aftre þat ye haue presented to ham (3) oure Lettre the copie of þe whiche we sende vnto you closed in þees to þat ende þat þer vpon ye may (4) grounde youre saide credence þe better to oure entencion and desir / the whiche been þees þat for the seuretee and (5) conseruacion of oure saide contree we wol and desire þat þe saide estatz gentilmen and communes by general (6) assent grante vs a fuage þorow oute al oure forsaide contree and þat aswel vpon esperituel persones as temporel (7) for þe sauuacion of oure contree and harmyng of oure enemis And also if nede be þat more be granted þan þe (8) same fuage we wol þat by þe good auys

of oure trusty and welbeloued þerle of Longuille Captal de buch and þat (9) ye see also in youre good auys and discrecion what þat yow semeth best and þat ye laboure it by þe best (10) deliberacion and diligence þat ye can and may as oure trust is to you and as ye desire oure lordship God haue (you in)[1] his kepyng yeuen vnder (11) oure signet at oure toune of Mante þe xj day of Octobre
    Chancery hand
    Calendared Kirby 883. Printed Nicolas II.265.
[1] stained

72

1419   C81/1365/12   Signet of Henry V
(1) By þe king
Worshipful fader in god oure right trusty and welbeloued We wol þat ye sende hedir vnto vs sir Thomas (2) Suthwell preste / in al resonable haste. And ferþermore we wol and also charge you þat ye ordeyne þat þat (3) be effectuelly doon in dede. þat we wrote vnto you as touching þe Duc of Orliens as oure trust is to you. for the (4) cas is so grete þat ye ne couthe not ymagyn hit gretter. And as touching þe chirche of Lughtbourgh in contie of (5) Lercestre longyng to oure yift: we wol wel þat oure welbeloued clerc Robert ffry remembred to vs by youre lettres (6) haue þe saide chirche / So þat he be preste or atte leste infra sacros wiþ yn þis yere aftre þe (7) tenour of þe comun lawe Yeuen vnder oure signet at oure toune of Mante þe first day of Nouember.
    Shiryngton's hand
    Calendered Kirby 885. Presentation recorded 10 May 1419, *CPR 1416-22*, p.249.

73

1420-21   SC1/43/160   Signet of Henry V
(1) By þe kyng
Right trusty and Welbeloued broþer. We sende yow closed (2) wiþ ynne þees / a supplicacion put vnto vs: by William Mynours. yeman huissher of oure Chambre. And hit ys oure wille: (3) þat ye be as fauorable to him yn þis matere: as ye may resounably: And þat al þe fauour be doon vnto (4) him / bothe afore oure chief Iustice of oure benche / and also afore oure Chaunceller : that may be doon / by Lawe

conscience and reson. (5) And broþer see ye þerto. Consideryng his beyng here in oure seruice. yn wyse as ye wote. Yeuen vnder oure signet (6) in oure towne of Rouen þe .v. day of Ianuier   S
(Signed) Shiryngton
Shiryngton's hand
Calendared Kirby 886.

74

1420   C81/1365/13   Signet of Henry V
(1) By the King
Worshipful fader in god oure right trusty and welbeloued. We wol þat ye doo al the fauour and ese þat (2) ye may lawfully vnto Iohan Spendeloue bringer of þees touchyng þe bille whiche we sende vnto yow closed wiþynne (3) þees oure le*tt*res. And if ye may lawfully doo al þat þe same bille conteneth / we wolde ye dide hit. And we wol þat (4) ye doo delyu*ere* vnto maistre Roger Whelpdale Elit of Karlell þe temporaltees of þe bisshopriche / as sone as his (5) bulles bee comen / not withstandyng þ*at* he hath not made homage þerfore to vs / Yeuen vnder oure signet at oure town of Rouen þe xxj day of Ianuer:
Hand possibly Andrieu's
Calendared Kirby 887. Commission of inquiry for Spendelove recorded 1 July 1420, *CPR 1416-22*, p.320; livery to Whelpdale recorded 17 March 1420. *CPR 1416-22*, p. 264.

75

1420   C81/1366/1   Signet of Henry V
(1) By the Kyng
Worshipful fader yn god / oure Right trusty and Welbeloued / ffor asmuche as oure seruant Iohn Bayll barbour hauyng (2) of oure confirmac*i*on .x. marc yerly for terme of his lif at oure Eschequer: ys behinde and vnpaide þerof .vj. yere at (3) Ester next comyng as he sayth: We wol / þat ye ordeine / þat he haue oure writt*es* of liberate and allocate / by þe (4) whiche he may be paide of þe saide annuitee / Notwiþstandyng þe p*re*ferrement þat we haue as ye knowe / (5) Yeuen vnder oure signet yn oure towne of Rouen þe x day of ffeue*r*er /
(Signed) Shiryngton
Shiryngton's hand
Calendared Kirby 888. Confirmation recorded 1 Oct. 1413, *CPR 1413-16*, p. 101.

76

1420 C81/1365/15 Signet of Henry V
(1) S By the Kyng.
Worshipful fader in god / oure Right trusty and welbeloued / We wol þat ye doo make vnto oure welbeloued (2) knyȝt Iohn saint Iohn oure writt*es* of liberate and allocate / by vertue of þe whiche he may be paide of þat (3) / that is due vnto hym of þannuite þat he takeþ at oure Eschequer by oure le*ttr*es patentes / Natwiþstandyng (4) þe preferre(ment)¹ þat we haue / as ye knowe / Yeuen vnder oure signet in oure town of Rouen þe xxviij day of Marche /
(Signed) Shiryngton

Shiryngton's hand
Calendared Kirby 889. Grant recorded 17 July 1414, *CPR 1413-16*, p.234.
¹ rubbed.

77

1420 SC1/43/161 Signet of Henry V
(1) By þe kyng
Right trusty and welbeloued broþ*er* Riȝt worshipful and worshipful faders in god / and trusty (2) and welbeloued we sende vnto yow wiþ þees oure le*ttr*es a Rolle vnder oure signet contenyng certain articles aduised by oure (3) welbeloued knyȝt Iohn Tiptoft Sen*eschal* of oure duchie of guyenne / for þe gou*er*nance of oure said duchie And (4) þansweres yeuen by oure conseil here / vpon þe same ar*ticles*. Wherfore we wol þat ye execute þe said answeres (5) as fer as to yow may apparteyne And þat þis be doon in suche wyse / þat oure said Sen*eschal* and maire of Bourdeux / (6) be nat taried yn oure Rewme of England / but hasted al þat is possible as oure truste is to yow / for hit is grete necessite / (7) þat þaire goyng be hasted al þat may be doon / Yeuen vnder oure signet in oure Town of Rouen þe xxx. day of Marche.

Shiryngton's hand
Calendared Kirby 890.

78

1420 C81/1365/16 Signet of Henry V
(1) By the kyng
Worshipful fader in god oure Right trusty and welbeloued. We late

yow wite lyke as we haue doo or þis þat (2) we haue granted (vnto)¹ oure welbeloued clerc Iohn Stopyndon þempension þat longeþ to oure nominacion (3) by þe vacacion of oure chirche Cathedrale of Excestre. þe whiche oure grant / we wol take effect / Albe hit: (4) þat sithe we wroote last vnto yow (þerof)² haue falle a new vacacion of oure saide chirche / by þe deces of hym/ (5) þat was before of Chestre for elles shulde oure said clerc beer no proffit by oure furst graunt / And semblably we wol / þat (6) oure welbeloued clerc William Toly haue þe pension of þe bisshopriche of Chestre. notwiþstanding þe chaunge &c as ye (7) wote. And thridly we haue granted vnto oure clerc of oure signet Thomas Andrew / þempension þat longeth to oure nominacion (8) by þauoidance of oure chirche cathedrale (9) of hereford. Wherfore we wol / þat as soone as due tyme Requireth: ye doo make oure writtes in due fourme vpon oure (10) said grantes: Yeuen vnder oure signet in oure town of Rouen þe x. Day of Auerill   S
  Shiryngton's hand
  Calendared with explanation, Kirby 891. Stopyndon, Toly, and Andrew (Andrieu) were all Signet clerks.
  ¹ torn   ² superior insert.

79

1420   C81/1365/17   Signet of Henry V
(1) By þe kyng
  S   Worshipful fader in god oure Right trusty and welbeloued / And lat yow wite / þat þe worshipful fader yn god þe (2) bisshop of wircestre / haþ doon his feaultee to vs here / as for þe temporaltees þat longen vnto his bisshopriche. (3) and also maade Renunciacion aftir þe fourme þat ye sent vs. whiche we signiffie vnto yow: to þat ende þat ye haue (4) knowlege þerof wolnyng þat ye shewe him and his proctours al þese and fauour þat ye may goodely: and (5) þe more specialy by cause of his beyng here in our seruice: Yeuen vnder oure signet in oure town of Rouen þe (6) xiiij day of Auerill /
  Shiryngton's hand
  Calendared Kirby 892. Livery recorded 18 Oct. 1419, *CPR 1416-22*, p. 246.

80

1420   C81/1365/18   Signet of Henry V
(1) By the king
Worshipful fader in god right trusty and welbeloued / For asmuche

as of oure special grace we haue granted (2) to þelit of Chestre late
Abbot of saint Albons / to haue þe temporalitees of þe bisshopriche
of Chestre not withstanding (3) þat he is not yit sacred bisshop þere
We wol and charge yow / þat in al goodly haste after þe Recepcion
(4) of þees oure lettres ye ordeyne þat deliuerance bee maad vnto þe
said elit of þe said (5) temporalitees and that ye make hym out oure
lettres patentes þere vppon / such as þe cas Requireth. (6) Yeuen vnder
oure signet at oure town of Rouen þe .xv. day of Aueril
(Signed) Andrieu
Andrieu's hand
Calendared Kirby 893. Livery recorded 15 April 1420, *CPR 1416-22*, p. 276.

81

1420   C54/270/m17d   Signet of Henry V

(1) Riʒt trusty and welbeloued broþer Riʒt worschipfull and worschipfull faders in god and trusty and welbeloued ffor as muche (2) as we
wote wele þat youre desire were to here Ioyfull tydinges of oure goode
spede touching þe conclusion of pees betwix (3) þe two Rewmes et cetera
we signiffie vnto yow þat worschipped be oure lorde þat of oure labour
haþ sent vs a goode (4) conclusion vpon moneday þe xx day of þis present moneþ of May we arriued in þis town of Troyes / And on þe moro
(5) we haddeyn a conuencion betwix oure moder þe quene of ffrance
and oure brother þe duc of Burgoigne as Commissairs of þe king (6)
of france oure fader for his partie / and vs in oure (owne)[1] personne
for oure partie / and þaccorde of þe said pees perpetuelle (7) was þere
sworne (by)[2] boþe þe saide Commissaires / yn name of oure forsaide
fader / And semblably by vs in oure owne name / (8) And þe lettres
(þervpon)[2] forwiþ enseled vnder þe grete seel of oure saide fader to
vs warde / and vnder oures to hym warde þe (9) copie of whiche lettres
we sende you closed yn þees to þat ende: þat ye doo þe saide accorde
to be proclamed yn (10) oure Citee of london / and þorowe al oure
Rewme þat al oure pueple may haue verray knowlege þerof for þare
consolacion / as wel as (11) kepe hit aftir as longeþ vnto þayme Also
at þe saide conuencion was mariage betrowthed betwix vs and oure wyf
doghter of oure forsaid (12) fader þe kyng of france / And ferþermore
for asmuch as we must by vertue of þe saide accorde vse a newe stile
duryng þe lyf (13) of oure saide fader / we sende yow in a cedule wiþin
þees oure stille þat we wol vse herafter boþe in latine in (14) englyssh
and in ffrenssh. Chargeyng yow þat in al thing þat passeþ duryng the
tyme aforesaide aswel vnder oure grete seel as (15) al oure oþer seeles

wher euer hit bee and in proclamacions ye ordeyne þat oure stille be vsed after þe (16) conteneu of þe saide cedule And þat þe scripture of all oure seeles be amended þerafter yn al haste / And so (17) chargeþ by oure writtes all oure officers / þat þis may long vnto aswel yn England as yn Irlande and yn guyenne for so wol (18) we ordeyne þat shalbe doon heere / yeuen vnder oure signet in þe saide Town of Troyes þe xxij day of May abouesaide / And as (19) touching þe scripture of þe seeles vs semeth / þat þis worde Regent may be owte wel ynogh

To oure Right trusty and welbeloued (20) brother þe duc of Gloucestre wardein in oure Rewme of Englande and to all þe remanent of oure conseil þere

(21) henricus dei gracia Rex Angliae heres & Regens regni ffranciae & Dominus hiberniae

(22) henry by þe grace of god kyng of England heire and Regent of þe Rewme of ffrance and lorde of Irlande

henry par la grace de (23) dieu Roy dengleterre heritier & Regent du Royaume de ffrance & seigneur dirlande

Et memorandum quod promissa (24) sunt irrotulata virtute litteris de priuato sigillo domini Regis Cancellar Angliae directi & infilactis

Cancellar (25) in primis domini Regis de hoc anno residentis

Chancery hand

Calendared with explanation, Kirby 894. Calendared *CCR 1419-22*, p. 108. Printed Halliwell I.102-03; Rymer, *Foedera* IX.906-07.

[1] superior insert   [2] rubbed

82

1420   C81/1365/19   Signet of Henry V
(1) By the king

Worshipful fader in god right trusty and welbeloued / We sende yow closed wiþ ynne thees a supplicacion putte (2) vnto vs by a poure tenant of oures / Rauf atte Ree. which compleineth hym of certain grete wronges and griefs doon vnto hym (3) as ye may more clerely parceiue by the same supplicacion / Wherfor we wol and charge yow / þat the saide supplicacion seen (4) and wel understanden by yow / and had pleine Informacion of the trouthe of þat þat is contened therein / ye see and ordeyne (5) þat oure saide tenant haue al þat he aught to haue of right in this partie / and suffreth no man to doo hym wron(g)[1] (6) in no w(yse)[2] touching the matere contened in his saide supplicacion asmuche as ye may lette hit / ner þat he (7) be not wrongf(ully ouerlad)[2] by maintenance of lordship ner other wyse / for as we been enfourmed beside þat (8) þat is contened in the saide supplicacion / the personnes whiche he compleineth hym vpon / be gretely maintened ayenst hym / (9) And therfor we wol that ye take hede / the more tenderly to his matere And so þat he haue no cause for lak of right (10) to Retourne hider ayein vnto vs compleyning / And god haue yow in his keping yeuen vnder oure signet at Monsirtan ou Sault yonne the .iiije. day of Iuill

(Signed) Toly

Toly's hand
Calendared with explanations, Kirby 895. Printed PC, p.xviii.
[1] torn off   [2] rubbed and torn

83

1420   C81/1365/20   Signet of Henry V

(1) By þe kyng

Worshipful fader in god oure Right trusty and welbeloued. For asmuche as we bee enfourmed þat þabot (2) of Gloucestre is passed to god: we haue granted vnto oure welbeloued clerc william Toly þempension. whiche longeþ vnto (3) oure yifte: by cause of þe creacion of hym þat shal be next Abbot of þe same place: wollyng þat ye doo make (4) þervpon oure lettres vnder oure gret seel in due fourme as þe cas Requireth. Yeuen vnder oure signet at þe (5) siege before Meleun þe .xx. day of Iuill

(Signed) Shiryngton

Shiryngton's hand
Calendared Kirby 896.

84

1420   C81/1365/21   Signet of Henry V

(1) By the king

Worshipful fader in god / right trusty and welbeloued / We sende yow closed wiþ ynne þees a supplicacion putte (2) v(n)to[1] vs by Thomas Gray / grocier and marchant of oure Cite of London making mencion of certain dettes whiche the lord Talbot / (3) þat is god betaught shuld owe to hym and to his wyf as is more pleinely contened in the same supplicacion / Wherefor we wol and (4) charge yow / þat þees oure lettres with the saide supplicacion seen by yow / ye doo comme tofore yow / the enfeffours / (5) þat þe same supplicacion maketh mencion

of / and seeth / þat þay contente þe forsaide Thomas: (6) of al that thay been bounde by right and Reson to contente hym of touching the Dettes abouesaide / And god haue yow in his (7) kepyng yeuen vnder oure signet in oure hoost afore Meleun: the .xvj. day of Septembre
  (Signed) Toly
Toly's hand
Calendared Kirby 897.
[1] torn.

85

1420   C81/1365/22   Signet of Henry V
(1) By the king
Worshipful fader in god: oure right trusty and welbeloued / for asmuche as we haue granted vnto oure welbeloued (2) clerc Robert Rolleston oure warderober the chirche of warton in oure Conte of Lancastre / whiche standeth voide in lawe / as we (3) been enfourmed / and longeth to oure yift / we wol and charge yow / þat ye doo make vnto oure saide clerc / oure lettres (4) of collacion of þe saide chirche / in due fourme / And god haue yow in his kepyng / Yeuen vnder oure signet in oure hoost / afore Meleun / the / xxij. day of Septembre /
  (Signed) Toly
Toly's hand
Calendared Kirby 898. Presentation recorded 2 Sept. 1420. 9 July 1421, *CPR 1416-22*, pp.299, 374.

86

1420   C81/1365/23   Signet of Henry V
(1) By the king
Worshipful fader in god / right trusty and welbeloued / For asmuche as hit is doon vs to vnderstande that the vicaire general of (2) the bisshop of Chestre that last was / before hym that now is / maad collacion of the prebende of hondesacre in oure Cathedral chirche (3) of Lichefeld whiche voided by the deces of Iohn aullforth / vnto Robert ffitȝhugh soon vnto the lord ffitȝhugh oure (4) Chamberlain / And hit is soo / that before that the saide Robert was put in possession of the saide prebende as hit is saide / oure saide (5) chirche fel voide and so be cause of the temporaltees thereof beyng in oure handes the disposicion of the saide prebende (6) longeth clerely vnto vs / we wol and charge yow

/ þat ye doo make oure le*tt*res of Ratifficacion vpon his title and possession (7) that he hath now / or elles of newe / if nede bee / doo make hym oure le*tt*res of collac*i*on of the same prebende in due (8) fourme / so that he may haue the same benefice by oure title / in caas ye haue maad collac*i*on to noon other / for oure entente is / (9) that he haue hit / If there bee no thing passed oure seel of the contraire / And god haue yow in his keping / yeuen vnder oure signet / (10) in oure hoost afore meleun / the last day of Septembre /
(Signed) Toly
Toly's hand
Calendared Kirby 899. Grant recorded 4 Nov. 1420, *CPR 1416-22*, p. 303.

87

1420   C81/1543/21   Signet of Henry V
(1) By þe kyng
R(yht trusty)[1] and welbeloued broþer. We grete you wel. and we do you to wite þat it (2) is oure wil and entente þat ye d(eclar)e[1] a parlement to be holde monday þe second day of (3) Decembre (next)[2] for certaine causes þe whiche we wol do you to haue knowlech of in al haste. And also (we)[2] wol and charge you (4) þat ye se þ*at* Iustices of pees. Shereues. Eschetours. Coroners and suche officers as shul be maad. be suche p*er*sones (5) as ben able & worthy þerto & þ*at* ben no troublers in þaire contrees. and þat þey be chose wiþoute (6) brocage or fauour of p*er*sones or any oþere vnleeful. meenes. after þ*e* statut & ordennances maad þ*er*vpon. (7) Yeuen vnder oure signet in oure hoost afore Meleun þe viij day of Octobre:
(Signed) I hethe
(Consent of the Council follows in Latin in different hand and ink.)
Hethe's hand
Calendared and Latin printed, Kirby 900. Writs recorded 21 Oct. 1420, *CCR 1419-22*, pp. 124-25.
[1] torn   [2] superior insert

88

1420   C81/1365/24   Signet of Henry V
(1) By þe Kyng
Worshipful fader in god Ryht trusty and Welbeloued. we grete you wel. And we wol and charge you þat as soone (2) as ye ben certain þat

þe bulles of oure holy fader þe pope: ben come for þe translacion of þe Bysshop (3) of hereford vnto þe chirche of Excestre: þat be oure le*tt*res to be maad vnder oure greet seal: ye do make Restituc*i*on (4) of þe temporalitees of þe said Bysshopriche of Excestre. vnto þe said Bysshop in forme as þaym oughte (5) to be wiþoute taryinge. Yeven vnder oure signet in oure hoost afore Meleun þe viij. day of Octobre:
   (Signed) 1. hethe
Hethe's hand
Calendared Kirby 901. Livery recorded 31 Oct. 1420, *CPR 1416-22*, p. 303.

89

1420   C81/1365/26   Signet of Henry V
(1) By the king
Worshipful fader in god Right trusty and welbeloued. We grete (2) yow wel / And for asmuche as oure se*r*uant Iohan H(er)tishille[1] hath shewed vnto vs by supplicacion / that s*ir* Richard Stanhapp (3) knight / letteth and destourbeth hym and his attourne / wrongfully / and ayenst lawe and conscience / to Reioisse and occupie (3) a place with certaine Rentes / with ynne the toun of Claworth in the Conte of Notyngham / whiche by the deces of Robert (4) hertishil his Cousin / been descended vnto oure saide se*r*uant by waye of heritage as to the Right heire of the saide place and (5) Rente*s* Of whiche thing If hit soo bee / we be no thing wel plesed / we wol and charge yow / considering þat oure saide (6) se*r*uant hath continuelly abiden in oure se*r*uice sith oure commyng in to this land / þat ye see and ordenne / (7) þat he haue no wrong by the said Stanhapp / ner by noon other / in his absence / but that he may pesibly Reioisse and occupie his (8) saide heritage / and his Attourne Receiue the proffitȝ thereof to his vse / and (algates)[2] vnto oure commyng hoom with godde*s* (9) grace in to oure Reaume of England so þat we may / If nede bee. doo entende to the same mat*er*e oureself / (10) wittyng þat we write semblably vnto oure brother of Gloucestre / vpon this same mat*er*e / And god haue yow in his keping / (11) Yeuen vnder oure signet / in oure oost afore Meleun / the v. Day of Nouembre
   (Signed) Toly
Toly's hand
Calendared Kirby 902.
   [1] rubbed and torn   [2] superior insert

90

1421   C81/1365/28   Signet of Henry V   (right side torn)
(1) Be the kyng
Worshipful fader in god our trusty and welbeloued / ffor certein causes of science mevyng vs wee haue taake þe (2) Priour . . . kermerdyn which is of our patronage / and alle her men. seruans. possessions. goodes and katell & cetera (3) in to our sauf proteccion . . . þat yee do maake hem a proteccion in due fourme as swich cas requereth for (4) to endure two yeer: ffurthermore we wol . . . and keepynge of all our forseid Priourie and of all þyng longyng ther to be committed (5) to þe Priour of Lanthony (beside Gloucestre)[1] and to Iohan Ru . . . Sauf to keepe and gouerne to þe proffyt of our (6) said hous of kermerdyn. duryng þe forsaid tyme after þe best fourme of proteccions maad in such cas. And god haue yow in (7) his kepynge. youen vnder our signet of þeegle in absence of our oothir at Webley þe vij day of March.

(Signed) Depeden

Depeden's hand
Calendared Kirby 903. Commitment and protection of the priory recorded 28 April 1421, *CPR 1416-22*, p.338.

[1] superior insert

91

1421   C81/1365/29   Signet of Henry V   (right margin torn)
(1) By þe kyng   S
Worshipful fader in god / Right trusty and welbeloued. we consideryng þe goode and agreable seruice / þat (2) þe worshipful fade(r)[1] in god þe bisshop of hereford oure proctour in þe popes court / haþ doon (3) to vs / and yit dooþ dayly as ye knowe: haue of our special grace Respited his hommage / þat he shulde make vnto vs / by (4) cause of his bisshopriche: vnto his comyng hoom from cour(t)[1] wolnyng þat vpon þis oure grante ye doo make vnto (5) hym / or to his proctours in his name. suche lettres as þe cas axeth vnd(er)[1] oure grete seel in due (6) fourme. Yeuen vnder oure signet of þegle in absence of oure oþer. at oure towne of Shrouesbur(y)[1] þe xj. day of Marche:

(Signed) Shiryngton

Shiryngton's hand
Calendared Kirby 904. Livery recorded 9 Nov.1420, *CPR 1416-22*, p. 304.

[1] torn

92

1421   C81/1365/30   Signet of Henry V   (top torn)
(1) Worship(f)ul[1] fader in god / oure Right trusty and welbeloued we sende yow closed wiþin thees. a supplicacion (2) put vnto vs by Mar(ger)ye[1] Deye / touching certain extorcions and harmes doon vnto hir howsbond and hir / by maistre (3) Iohn Armesby Notarye of Leycestre / as in þe same supplicacion hit is more clerely contened. So we we wol þat ye doo (4) sende for þe saide maistre Iohn by writte / And examineth þe matere / And þervpon ordeyneth þat Right (5) be doon to þe partie compleignant. wiþowte any long delaye / And þe more fauorably. consideryng þe pourete (6) of þe saide Margerye: Yeuen vnder oure signet at Lambhithe the .ix. day of May   S

(Signed) Shiryngton
Shiryngton's hand
Calendared Kirby 905.
[1] torn and rubbed

93

1421   SC1/43/159   Signet of Henry V
(1) By the king
Chanceller there is oon Thomas walweynes wyf which hath maad a greuous compleynt vnto vs vpon sir Iohn (2) Skydmore And for asmuche as we had ordenned bothe parties for to bee before vs or oure conseil for to (haue)[1] had knowlache (3) of the matere þat þay stande in debat fore / and for to haue made an ende þereof / And hit is soo (4) now / þat we may nat g(oo)dly[2] ende þere to at this tyme / as ye wot considered oure hasty departyng hens / we w(ol n)at[2] (5) nat wiþstandyng / þat we suppose she standeth not in the right / be cause s(he is)[1] sumwhat a descl(aunder)ouse[2] (6) womman / and also þat we kepe nomore to be wexed wiþ hir encombrous poursuites / þat ye doo sende (7) for bothe the saide parties to comme before yow at suche day as yow semeth Resounable / for to here the saide matere of controuersie / (8) and make an ende therein / as we shal telle yow to morwe more pleinly by mouthe But algates / yeueth hem to morwe here day / whanne thay (9) shal be with yow / yeuen vnder oure signet of the Egle at lambehith / this day / þe .xxij. day of may

(Signed) Toly
Toly's hand
Calendared with explanations, Kirby 906.
[1] torn   [2] rubbed

94

1421   C81/1365/31   Signet of Henry V
(1) By the kyng
Wurshipful fader in god our right trusty and welbeloued / ffor as muche as we be enfourmed þat þe (2) Corrodie of our abbeye of hyde in hamptshire. is voide now by the deth of Thomas Meweys þat last occupied and hadde hit / which (3) corrodie of our speciale grace we haue yiuen to our welbeloued Clerc of our Chapele Iohan hunte / We wol and charge yow. þat (4) yee do maake oure *lettres* patentes in due fourme vn to our said Clerc of þe corrodie forsaid / yeuen vnder our signet of (5) þe egle in absence of our oothir at our town of Douorre þe .viij. day of Iuyn:
(Signed) Depeden
Depeden's hand
Calendared Kirby 907.

95

1421   C81/1365/32   Signet of Henry V
(1) By the kyng
Worshipful f(ader in)¹ god our trusty and welbeloued / We haue receyued a supplicacion put (2) vn to vs be our trusty and welbeloued knyght henry Brounflete that is with vs in our seruice (in)¹ þees parties / to whech (3) supplicacion we haue take but litel heed / Neueretheles we wol and charge yow / þat þe said supplicacion be (4) yow seen / and þe matere þerinne comprised discretly considered / ye do hym þe ese þat yee may (5) as ferfoorth as right and lawe wol / So that by cause of his beynge heere in our said seruice he be not wrongfully hyndred ne (6) harmed in no wyse / And god haue yow in hys keepinge / yeuen vnder our signet in our hoost at seint Denys of Moronval beside Dreux. the .xviij day of Iuyll.
(Signed) Depeden
Depeden's hand
Calendared with explanation, Kirby 908. The petition, in Latin, is SC8/175/8713.

¹ torn and rubbed

96

1421   E101/188/10/2   Signet of Henry V
(1) By the kyng
Trusty and welbeloued: ffor as muche as we be enfourmed / Thomas de la Croix hath sent hors and certain (2) Armerers and hernois for vs vn to our town of Caleys We wol and charge yow expresly þat ye ordeine þat þe (3) saide hors and þe men þat ar comen wiþ hem come to vs in al seur haste / and send sum trusty man for to go wiþ (4) hem / þat may haue þe ouersighte and gouernance of hem alle / And þat be seurly and saufly conduyed fro (5) thens to Seintomere / and so to Arras / And fro thens to Amyas / there abiding vn to þe tyme they haue seur conduyt from our (6) brothir of Burgoigne or fro sir Iohan de Luxemburgh. to þe whiche we haue writen for her sauf passage fro thens to Aubiualle (7) fro whens our garnisons wiþ goddes grace shullen conduit hem to Parys where we wol they abyde til þey haue woord of (8) our wille / And þey comen to Parys we wol he þat shal come fro yow with hem / sende vs woord of their comyng thider. yeuen (9) vnder our signet in our Oost at seint Denys de Moronval beside Dreux the laste day of Iuyll:
(Signed) Depeden
Depeden's hand
Calendared Kirby 909.

97

1421   C81/1365/33   Signet of Henry V
(1) By the king
Worshipful fader in god / oure right trusty and welbeloued / For asmuche as hit is doon vs to vnderstande that (2) the bisshop of London is passed to god / we lat yow wite / that we haue granted vnto oure welbeloued seruant Iohan Hanham. (3) clerc of oure Caterye the pension of hym that shal be next bisshop of the same place wol(nyng)[1] & chargyng yow / that there (4) vpon whanne tyme commeth ye doo make hym oure lettres vnder ou(re gree)t[1] seel in due fourme / Yeuen vnder oure signet in oure oost (5) at Laigny sur marne / the xiij. day of Octobre
(Signed) Toly
Toly's hand
Calendared Kirby 910.
[1] torn

98

1421   C81/1365/25   Signet of Henry V
(1) By the king
Worshipful fader in (god)¹ / oure Riȝt trusty and welbeloued ffor asmuche as we haue vnderstande by youre le*tt*res late (2) sent vnto vs þat oure wyf þe quene hath spoke vnto yow. and desireth þat hir phisicien myght haue sum benefice (3) wiþowte cure of oure collacion / in þe whiche mate*r*e ye desire to haue knowlege of oure wil we signiffie vnto yow / (4) þat hit is wel oure entent whanne any suche benefice voydeth of oure yifte þat ye make collac*i*on (5) to him þerof / And after certiffieth vs what hit is þat he haþ Yeuen vnder oure signet in oure oost beside Meaulx þe xxix. day of Octobre:
(Signed) Shiryngton
Shiryngton's hand
Calendared Kirby 911. Printed Ellis, 3rd ser., I.71.
¹ torn and rubbed

99

1421   C81/1365/27   Signet of Henry V
(1) By the kyng
Worshipful fader in god / oure Right trusty and welbeloued We wol and charge yow. that at what tyme / oure welbeloued (2) knight Iohan Cornewaille / bringeth vnto yow / oon called Mareschal Des Rues. for to swere þe pees that is made betw(een ou)re¹ (3) fader of france and vs: ye take his ooth and lat him swere tofore yow þe same pees / after þe fo(urme)² of (4) þe copie whiche we sende yow closed wiþin thees / Yeuen vnder oure signet in oure hoost at Ruthueil besi(de)² Meaulx þe xiiij. day of Nouembre.
(Signed) Shiryngton
Shiryngton's hand
Calendared Kirby 912.
¹ torn and rubbed   ² torn off

100

1422   C81/1365/34   Signet of Henry V   (torn)
(1) By the kyng
... in god Right trusty and welbeloued We sende yow closed wyþyn

thees: a supplicacion put vnto vs (2) / by Thomas . . . (co)mpleinyng him / how þat he beyng here in oure seruice oon Robert Roklee Squier haþ (3) dissesed him of þe manoi(r) . . . with þappourtenances in york shire / as in þe same supplicacion hit is (4) more clerely contened / Wherfore we wol þat . . . (e)uidences of bothe parties ordeine so for þat matere þat (5) his beyng here in oure saide seruice be nat harmeful nor . . . but þat he stande in as goode condicion as he did at (6) his comyng owt wiþ vs Yeuen vnder oure signet . . . saint faron beside Meaulx þe xv day of ffeuerer

    Hand possibly Shiryngton's
    Calendared Kirby 913.

101

    1422   C81/1365/35   Signet of Henry V
    (1) By the king
    Worshipful fader in god / oure right trusty and welbeloued / for asmuche as we be enfourmed that maister William (2) Kentwode is elite to the deanee of oure chriche of london / the whiche eleccion / he assentyng / is confermed and by the same (3) confirmacion / the Archedeaknee of london in oure saide Chirche / the which the saide maister william last (4) occupied / is voide / and longeth clerely to oure yifte / the temporaltees of the bisshopriche beyng at this tyme in oure handes (5) / We haue yeuen the saide Archedeaknee / to oure welbeloued clerc / sir Iohn / Snell oure Aulmosner Wherfore we wol and charge yow / that (6) ye doo make (hym)¹ oure lettres necessaire therevpon / in fourme accoustumd And god haue yow in his keping / yeuen vnder oure (7) signet in oure oost at Seintfaron / beside Meaulx the .viij. day of Marche
    (Signed) Toly
    Toly's hand
    Calendared Kirby 914. Grant recorded 16 March 1422, *CPR 1416-22*, p. 414.
    ¹ superior insert

102

    1422   C81/1365/36   Signet of Henry V
    (1) By the kyng
    Worshipful fader in god / oure Right trusty and welbeloued / We sende you closed wiþin thees oure lettres (2) a supplicacion put vnto

vs by marchantes of Paris / Rouen / Troyes / and Brugees / as ye may see þerby / And wol and (3) charge yow / þat ye enfourmed of þe matere contened in þe same supplicacion / ordeineth that Right be doon vnto (4) þe saide marchantes after þe lawes and coustumes of oure Rewme of England / wiþowte any long delay /(5) Yeuen vnder oure signet in oure ost at þe toun of Meaulx. þe xxviij. day of Marche /

(Signed) Shiryngton

Shiryngton's hand
Calendared with references, Kirby 915. Commission of inquiry recorded 22 April 1422, *CPR 1416-22*, p.443.

103

1422 C81/1365/37   Signet of Henry V
(1) By the king
Worshipful fader in god oure right trusty and welbeloued For asmuche as we haue yeuen and granted vnto maister Iames Cole / (2) proctour vnto oure hous of Syon at Shene / the prebende whiche is voyde in oure chirche of London by the deces of maister (3) Iohn Maluern / and longeth vnto oure yifte and disposicion at this tyme / be cause of the temporaltees of the bisshopriche (4) of London beyng in oure handes by waye of the voidance of the same chirche / we wol / that there vpon ye doo make vnto the saide (5) maister Iames Cole oure lettres patentes vnder oure gree(t)[1] seel in dew fourme / yeuen vnder oure signet / at (6) Meaulx / the. last day of Aueril /

(Signed) Toly

Toly's hand
Calendared Kirby 916. Grant recorded 10 June 1422, *CPR 1416-22*, p.438.
[1] torn off

104

1422 E101/188/10/1   Signet of Henry V
(1) By the kyng
Trusty and welbeloued / we haue Receiued youre Lettres whiche ye sent vnto vs last / And as tou(chyng þe)[1] (2) bargayne of Brekstone contened in þe same / we halde vs wel appaide / And as to þe prisonners of Crotey (3) whiche ye hau(e in)[2] keping / hit is o(u)re[1] wil þat ye kepe hem forth as straitely as ye can (sauyng þair lyues)[3] to (4) tyme þat we be oþerwyse aduised / fferþermore as touching ou(r) . . .[2] hurt

/ we wol þat ye ordeine (5) þat he be sent into þe north cuntre to Robert of waterton. to whom we . . .² for to Receiue him and to putte him to renne (6) in sum of oure parcs þere: yeuen vnder oure signet at m . . .² of May:
  (Signed) Shiryngton
  Shiryngton's hand
  Calendared with explanations, Kirby 917.
  ¹ faded   ² torn   ³ superior insert

105

1422   C81/1366/12   Signet of Henry V
By the king
  (1) Worshipful fader in god / oure right trusty and welbeloued / We wol and charge yow / that ye make oute oure writtes to oure (2) viconte of hamptshire / for to make Proclamacion in oure saide vicontee / in alle place accoustumed / that alle manere (3) men that haue any grond or land with ynne oure toun of Portesmouth / with ynne suche a certein day as ye shal li(mit)¹ (4) by youre discrecion / comme and chalenge / eche man his owen grond / So that hit may be knowen sekirly what g(ron)d¹ (5) is longing to euerych of hem / And that grond that is not chalenged / with ynne the saide day limited / we wol ye ordeine / (6) that hit be saised in to oure handes / yeuen vnder oure signet / at Saint liȝ the .xviij. day of Iuyn /
  (Signed) Toly
  Toly's hand
  Calendared Kirby 918. Order recorded 21 July 1422, *CCR 1419-22*, p. 263.
  ¹ torn and rubbed

LATER SIGNET AND PRIVY SEAL PAPERS

106

1434 E28/55/1 Signet
(Initialed) R h

(1) Henri &c To þe Tresorer and Barons of oure Eschequir gretyng ffor certayne materes vs moeuyng we wol and (2) charge you þat vnto oure welbeloued Squier Iohn Ardern hauyng þe kepyng to ferme of oure manoyrs of Shene Petresham (3) and hame with þeir apperte-naunces / for þe which he is bounde to paye yerly for þe saide ferme to vs at our (4) Eschequir xxiiij. li. as it is conteyned in oure le*tt*res patentes / We wol and charge you þat ye allowe vnto þe (5) saide Iohn Ardern .vij. li. v. s. v. d yerly or elles discharge him yerly of. vij. li. v. s. v. d in the payment of his saide ferme / That (6) is to wite fro þe feest of Seynt Michell. the yere of oure Regne xv*the*. Also longe as he shall haue And occupie þe (7) said kepyng or ferme at all tymes. yeuen &c

  Dat' apud Westm*onasterium* p*ri*mo ffebruarii anno &c xii*o*
Chancery hand

107

1440 E28/63/5 Signet or Privy Seal (draft)
(1) By þe kyng

Trusty and welbeloued &c ffor asmoche as (we haue ordeyned)¹ oure welbeloued [sir w]² sire. (2) w. (Moreton)¹ [n] to entende and ouersee [oure] þe rep*ar*acion (as well)³ of oure towne of Caleys as of þe (3) wateris þere. the whiche we truste shal do vs [right] good and behouful se*r*uice. and þe better if by your (4) good assistens. Wherefore [y] we wille and pray yow. þat at suche tyme [as þe] as [ony] (5) vrgent case & necessite askyth [to] ayde of more peple [þant] þan be þere of workemen or laborenis (6) þat ye wille putte to youre good helpyng hand like as we [vn] be enformed ye haue do herebefore for whiche we (7) can yow right good thanke.

 (Another hand) yeuen at Westm*instre* þe xiij day of Auerell A*o* xviij Rh. vj
 (8) To the Lieutenant and Soudeours of the Towne of Calays
 (9) To þe Mair of the Staple of oure Towne of Calays and his felship marchant*es* ther
 (10) To the mair of the towne of Calays and burgeys of the same
Non-Chancery hand
 ¹ superior insert ² matter in square brackets cancelled ³ marginal insert

108

1452 SC1/43/184 Signet
(Initialed) R h
(1) By the king
Trusty and welbeloued. we grete you wel. And albe it that oon Thomas Beneste (2) of Solihille taylour. for certain greete offenses crimes and treasons by him doon ayeinst our Royal personne. was after the due (3) processe of our lawe endited and therupon arained and atteint / and Iugement yeuen. which Iugement as ye knowe wel (4) shuld be putte in execucion as to morwe. in the town of warrewyk / yet natheles we stured of pite and mercy by our own (5) mocion / haue graunted and yeuen him grace of thexecucion of the said Iugement / and ouer þat (6) haue pardonned him alle his trespaces and crimes & treasons of which he was endited trusting þat he [ne]¹ (7) neuer wol offende ayeinst our Royal maieste herafter / wherfore we charge you þat Immediatly after the (8) receyuing herof ye cesse vtterly of eny execucion doing vpon him by occasion of the premisses. And þat ye faile (9) not to obserue þis our commandement / as ye wol ansuere vnto vs / Yeuen vnder our signet at our Castel of kenelworth the xxvj day of Aoust

Chancery hand
¹ cancelled

109

1455 SC1/43/182 Signet (right margin torn off)
(1) By the king
Trusty and welbeloued. we greet you wel. and for asmoche as we be occupied and laboured as ye knowe wel. with (2) sikeness . . . whiche. to be deliuered and cured by the grace of oure lord. vs nedeth. the helpe. entendance and laboure of suche (3) expert . . . in the crafte of medicines as ye be in (Relem)¹ amonges alle other. oure affeccion and desire. right especially. (4) is sette. we des(ire)² you that ye be with vs at oure castel of wyndesore the .xij. Day of this moneth and entende vpon oure (5) persone for the . . . ye faille not as oure singuler trust is on you and as ye desire. and tendre of oure helth and (6) welfare yeuen vndre . . . the v Day of Iuyn.

(Another hand) To maistre Gilbert of Salesbury
Chancery hand
Printed Rymer, *Foedera* XI.366
¹ rubbed ² torn off

110

c1408   E28/29   Letter of Robert Fry, Clerk of the Privy Seal (right side torn off)

(1) Worsshupfull Sire and frend: Upon the matire whiche ye declared me now Late at London touchyng the . . . I haue comuned with my (2) Lord the Chaunceller of Engeland. opon whiche matire as y vnderstand he hath . . . worsshupfull Lady of wilton: in the whiche matire y (3) praie yow. that ye be effectuel and trusty frend as . . . yow parfit affiance: I write in haste at London: the: xviij day of (4) Iuyn: And with the grace of . . . deserue hit ayenst yow. in such wyse that ye shulleth holde yow content:

(Signed) Robert ffrye youres
Chancery hand
Described by A. L. Brown in *The Study of Medieval Records,* ed. Bullough and Story, pp.260ff.

111

After 1415   E28/37/105   Letter of William Soper, Clerk of the Exchequer, to the Chancellor

(1) Ryght worshipfull lorde I recomaunde me to youre gude lordship as yowre seruant And plese it yowe to haue in knowlage (2) that I am enfourmed that ther is a saue condit graunted to be prolonged for a Ship of Spayn called the Mare of Bilbawe (3) wher of is Maistre petre de Dariega & that ye desire to haue in knowlage what profite it hathe bene to the kyng or may (4) turne (h)eraftre[1] Please it yowe to wit that the sayd shipp aryved late (here)[1] in this porte & the kyng answerd of Custum & (5) s(u)bsidie[1] inward & outeward in that viage the sum of xlix li & is liche to haue as moche more at his next comyng / And in this (6) to my simple conceit the kyng may take avail & the Contre & no man hurt And as tithynges here bene nane as yit And god haue yowe in (7) kepyng written at Suthampton xj day of Decembre

(Signed) your seruant William Soper
Chancery hand
[1] torn

112

After 1417   Cotton Vesp. F.XIII. fol.71   Letter of Thomas Longley, Bishop of Durham, Chancellor, possibly to Henry V

Later Signet and Privy Seal Papers

(1) Souereyn lord with als meke & entier hert as I kan or may I recomande me to your Roial maieste to ye whiche plaise it to wite yat (2) on monday at nyght last passet I haue receyuet youre fulworschipfull le*tt*res by ye tenure of ye whiche it hath liket yow to let me (3) wite how ye be enforme(d)[1] y*at* with Inne youre churche of duresme vnder ye warde of two monkes of ye churche & ye last priour (4) ya*t* ded. is & of [on][2] a man y*at* is clepet mydelton y*er* shuld be c*er*tein thyng y*at* to yowe (5) app*er*teneth as (it)[3] is more sp*ecia*ly writen in youre said le*tt*res.

(6) Ye whiche youre le*tt*res by me receyuet & vnderstanden ye said monday atte nyht. I haue on tysday in ye morning ordeynet a sufficient (7) p*er*sone yat with youre message & ye enform*acio*n yat come with hym is goen in al godely hast to your said kirk of duresme (8) y*er* to charge on youre behalue ye priour yat now is yat out of ye said chirche ne priory be not remwet ne delyu*er*et no kist no (9) othir Instrument yat may cotene gold syluer or [Iuillo][2] Iuell chartre muniment or othir euydences y*at* y*er* has (10) (bene)[4] left to kepe: til ye forsaid prio*ur* & I may speke to gedir and more to yat matire haue I noght mow do as yet but als sone (11) as I (may)[4] more do ye shal haue wityng y*er* of /. as of [othir][2] tythyngs I kan no nothir write but suche as by (12) myn othir le*tt*res I send yow by ye berer of yes Souerein lord ye holy gost haue yow in his kepyng   Writen att pontfreu yis thoresday in ye morning
    youre humble preest of duresme
(In a later hand) To our souerainge lorde ye Kynge.
Chancery hand
[1] trimmed off   [2] cancelled   [3] rubbed   [4] superscript insert

113

1420 SC1/43/192 Letter, possibly of Henry Beaufort, Bishop of Winchester, to Henry V

(1) In all wyse my souereyne lord I recomandde me to ʒowr moste noble grace wyht all the lowlinesse (2) that any subgit kan þenkke or deuise And at ʒow luste my souereyne lord to lete me ʒowr (3) moste humble liege man to haue knowleche be ʒowr gracious. lettris. of the pees and mariage ocludid. the whyche (4) godde knowyht I haue desirid. as. herttyly. as euer dide any poor creature. and that for goddis worshyp and ʒowr moste (5) noble herttis. ese. And also for the souereyne gladnesse and comfortes that we ʒowr trwe pepil. haue and. (6) wyht goddis mercy. shall haue In the lyklynesse of succession of ʒowr bodily heyrys. þat. lord þankke (7) ʒow. þat. is verray pees. and wyht all

the humblesse that any subgit kan þankke hys souereyne. (8) lord I
þankke ȝow. my moste gracious. souereyne lord And there as. hyt
lykyd. ȝowr hynesse to wryte In (9) ȝowr forseide gracious lettris þat
ȝe purpose the time of ȝowr mariage. as. sone aftir the feste of the
(10) trinite as couenable time comyht In the beste tyme of the ȝer I
beseche godde. And trwly my souereyne lord but if (11) ȝowr hynesse
hadd comanddid me the contrarie if I myht haue be to goddis. wrshyp
and ȝowrys at that (12) blessid. gladde mariage I nolde for no thyng
be thennys but godde blissid mote he be wlle not þat I haue In thys
worde (13) þat. þat I moste desired. of the whyche to see þat Ioyfull
day of ȝowr mariage haht ben. on. Besechyng (14) ȝow my souereyne
lord to haue In ȝowr noble remembrauncte wyht what Conclusion of
(15) reste I departid laste owte of ȝowr graciouse presence and aftir
þat I haue demenid me syht I (16) kam. In to thys ȝowr reaume and
wyht goddis grace shall to my lyuys. ende lyk as I truste to godde ȝowr
humble (17) lyge man my. Cousin. Chaucer. haht pleinly. enformid
ȝowr hynesse or thys time. Also my souereyne lord (18) whanne I was
on the grette see I made awowe þat aftir time I were onys. In ȝowr
reaume of Engeland I sholde no see (19) passe. saue on pilgrimage vn
to I hadde be at Senct Iamys and for þat cause. whanne I was at ȝowr
toun (20) of Calays. for the grete desir I hadde. to see the prosperite
of ȝowr moste dredde and noble persone I. (21) wentte streht fro thennys. to ȝowr moste gracious presence. for if I hadde goone In to ȝowr
reaume of Engeland I (22) myht not haue come In to Normandie to
my pilgrimage hadde be doo. And therefore my souereyne lord. wyht
all the humblesse (23) þat any. subgit kan þenkke or deuise I beseche
ȝowr hynesse to take not to displesaunsse (24) mi nowht comyng. for
godde knowht I ne feyne not ne no colour seke Besechyng godde In
all wyse my souereyne lord to saue (25) and kepe ȝow body and sowle
and sendde ȝow. In thys blissid sacrament of mariage Ioye prosperite
longe (26) to endur wyht heyrys of ȝowr body. to hys. blissid wrshyp
and ȝowrys In singuler comfortes of all ȝowr (27) trwe pepyll of the
whyche I am. on. and euer shall be. wrytyn at waltham. the vj day of
Iuin.
(28) ȝowr humble subgit and trwe liege man. H W.
Chancery hand but unprofessional format. A holograph?

114

1420   SC1/51/118   Petition of John Cappe
(1) Ryght hye prynce and soueraigne graciouse lorde I recomaunde

me to ȝow And for as myche as my mayster Sir Roger (2) Saluayn is passyd owte of this worlde whoes soule god assoile I shalle do ȝowre comaundement to abyde vpon the saue garde (3) of ȝowre castell at Banelyngham with alle my myght and alle my power be the grace of god tylle ȝe sende other (4) charge or comaundement Prayenge ȝow to dyrecte ȝowre gracious letters to ȝowre vetyllere of Caleis to delyuer (5) suffissaunt vetaille for the sustentacion of ȝowre castell / for I am a olde man and haue be hurte and maymed and loste my (6) good in ȝowre werrys be ȝowre ennemyes / so that I haue not where with to do to ȝowre castell as I desyre / (7) but euere I pray ȝow to be my good and gracious lorde. and assigne sum refresshement to ȝowre powre soudeours that wille (8) abyde vapon the saue garde of ȝowre castell tylle ȝe sende other ordenaunce. Ryght hye prynce and soueraigne graciouse (9) lorde the holy blessyd trynyte haue ȝow in his kepynge. wreten atte castell of Banelyngham the xj day of Nouember

(10) Be ȝowre powre liege Iohn Cappe

Chancery hand

115

1421   E28/35/13-14   Privy Seal: Council Business

(1) To þe kyng. oure souuereigne Lorde:

Primerment. þat it like yow to graunte lettres vndre (2) youre priue seell directed to all youre Capitaines Lieutenantȝ and bailliez of youre towne & marchez of Caleis chargyng (3) þaim to supporte youre Tresourier. and his deputees to enprowe. and to sette to fferme all youre landes Rentes tenementȝ with (4) all oþer commoditez of youre towne. and marches afoersaide to þe moste prouffit. in confermacon of (5) youre worship and right as þey desire to stande in youre good lordshippe.

Item þat it like yow. to appoincte what (6) gouuernance þat youre Castell of Guisnes shall be putte Inne. and what persone shall haue þe kepyng. and (7) saufegarde therof.

Item þat it like yow to appoincte what gouuernance that youre Castell of Baunelingham shall (8) be putte Inne. And what persone shall haue þe kepyng and saufegarde þerof.

Item þat it like yow. þat (9) youre priue Seell be charged to make warant soufficeant for youre Tresourier to be allowed in his accompte of all manere Stuffe (10) and ordonnance. deliured and pourveied by youre Commandement as it pereth by endenture deliured vn to þe clerke of þe (11) ordonnance atte þis tyme.

Item þat hit like yowe to Charge yowre priue Seell to make a warant soufficeant / to youre (12) Tresourier of Caleis þat he may occupie youre Seell þe which he hath In kepyng. as oþer Tresouriers haue vsed befoer (13) tyme In letyng oute youre landes and tenementȝ te which will tourne yow to greete prouffit. for defaute þat it hath notte (14) be vsed. ye haue hadde greete losse.

(Second sheet and hand) Item that it like yow soueraign Lord to consider the grete mischief (15) and poentot of youre said towns And marches of Caleys And þervpon appointe sufficeaunt assignement for the paiement And saufgard of the (16) said towne and marches.

Item for as muche soueraigne lord as thexceketeurs of sir Roger Salwyn natcompteht no (17) ferther but to the iiij. daie of ffeuerer last passed the daie of his discharge. þerfore that it like that your priue seal be charged (18) to make warantȝ sufficiaunte for your seid Tresorer he fro the seid .iiij. daie of ffeuerer to Resceyve al maner of Reuenuȝ (19) and recepts and proufits longing to the seid office in to the first daie of his Charge after the tenor of his patent with the wages and (21) fees longing to the seid office And also that he Accompte þerfore deuhely and bi the sa(ide)¹ warrant to haue therof deuhe allouance vpon his (22) accompt:

Item sith it list yow that he have the seid office of Tresourier and the charges wiþ all like it your (23) hiȝnes that wiþ oute his aduis noon officers be made in þoo partes but such as he schall Ansuere fore to yow (24) siþ he schall Rekene And accompt for hem wiþ this if it like that noo maner of paiements be made to no maner (25) persone of the Reuenuȝ. neiþer of thentres ne of thissues þeer but by þespeciall knowlich and hand (26) of your said Tresourer siþ he schall accompte þerfore.

Chancery hand
¹ torn

116

1422   Cleopatra F. IV. fol.3   Privy Council Minute Book

(1) My lord of Gloucestre   The Archbishop of Canterbury   The Bisshopes of London Wynchestre Norwych & wircestre The Duc of Excetr   Therl of March   Warrewyk   Marchal   Northumberland   Westmorland   The Lord ffitȝ hugh   Sir Rauf Cromwell   sir walter hungerford   sir Iohn Tiptoft   sir walter Beauchamp

(2) The wich Lordys a boue said ben condescended to take hit vpon

hem in þe manere (3) and fourme þat sueth. ffirst foras muche as execuc*i*on of lawe and keping of pees stant muche in Iustices of pees Shirrefs (4) and Eschetours / the proffitȝ of the kyng and þe Reuenues of þe Roiaume ben gretly encresced or anientisched (5) by Coustumers Countrollours porsours serch(ers)¹ and all such oþer officers. Therfore þe same Lordys wol and desireth þat (6) such offices and all oþer be maade by aduis and denominac*i*on of þe said Lordys. Saued always and reserued to my (7) Lordes of Bedford and of Gloucester alle þat longeþ vnto hem by a special act maad in parlement And to þe (8) Bischop of Wynchestre. that þat he hath graunted him by our souerain lord þat last was of whos soule god haue mercy / and by auctoritee of parlement confermed . . . (Text changes without a break to French.)

Chancery hand
Printed Nicolas III.16-17.
¹ trimmed off

117

1423 E28/41/75(105)   Privy Seal: for the King, to John, Duke of Bedford

(1) Right trusti and most beloued vncle / We grete yow wel wiþ al our herte / And signifie vn to yow as for your consolation (2) (þat)¹ at þe tyme of þe writing of þese þankid be god we wer in perfite hele (3) of persone / tristing to our lord þat (as we desire)¹ in semblable wise ye so be And for asmoche as we and (4) our counsail hier been acertained as wel be þe effecte and euidence of your werkes as be þe credible (5) reportes and writinges maad vn to vs and to our said counsail fro tyme to tyme of þe singulier diligence & (6) þe fulnotable [and laborious]² seruice þat ye doon vn to vs In gouuernaunce of oure Reaume of ffraunce (7) as wel as of our Duchie of Normandie we þanke our lord þer of and yow as hertily as we kan willing & (also)¹ (8) praing yow alwey so to continue (euyr fro wel to better as)¹ we ne [doute]² doute in no wise wiþ te grace of oure (9) lord but þat ye so wol. / And considering þat in acomplishing of your desir. we send now vn to yow the B. of l.³ / also our (10) dier and welbeloued cosin þeril Marshal / and þe lord Wilby / wiþ notable puissaunce of þis our (11) Reaume of Englond. We (desire &)¹ pray yow þat at þair comyng vn to yow ye Receyue & demene hem & also ordeine hem to be (12) tretid and demenyd benyngly and fauorably so þat þiey ne haue no resonable cause of grucching greue nor complaint (13) but þat þay and þair feleship haue cause to reioise hem and contente hem of þair comyng vn to yow

(14) In our seruise & þat as wel þay as oþer of our sugites hier take þer be occasion (corage)¹ (15) & [to]² wille to goon þiþer at al tymes when our behoof shal asshid [& hit shal be . . . of þaym]² / And as towardes (16) our bel vncle of Excester whoom our lord now late visitid wiþ seknesse blessid mote god be he is rekiueryd (17) & wiþ his grace shal be wiþ yow in al goodly haste whoom and oþer þat we send [þat]² now vn to yow (18) to assiste yow as for þe tyme in counsail / We pray yow goodly & effectuelly to hier in swiche þinges as þay (19) shal auise yow of fro tyme to tyme for (þe worship of god þe)¹ [þe]² goode of vs (& of yow)¹ & of [boþe]² our (20) Reaumes & Duchie abouesaid willing also þat ye yeue (faiþ &)¹ credence to þat þat þe said bisshop of (21) london &c shal say on to yow on our behalue And almyghty god &c

(Different hand) yeuen at Westmynstre þe. xv day of May (22)
(After three lines skipped, the first hand) Right trusti and welbeloued cosin. for asmoche as we knowin þat ye desire to be acertained fro (23) tyme to tyme of our prosperite & welfar we lete yow wite þat þankid be our lord at þe tyme of þe (24) writing of þese we werin in perfite hele of persone & so plesit vn to hym þat ye be / And ouer þis (25) witiþ þat we sende vn to our fultrusty & most beloued vncle of Bedford. A. &c to þe whiche we wol þat (26) ye yeue faiþ and credence In þat þat þay shal say vn to yow on our behalue And Almyghty &c
(Second hand) don come dessus.
Chancery hand
Printed Nicholas III.86-88; Ellis, 2nd ser., I.99-100.
¹ superior insert   ² cancelled   ³ Bishop of London

118

1423   E28/39   Petition of Janyn Cassons
(1) To the kyng oure souuerein lord
Bisecheth lowly youre pore Ianyn Cassons squyer of my lord of Wynchestre. that sith the Office (2) of Viergerschup in the kynges Chapelle of Wyndesore is . . .¹ voide by the deth of Iohan Clifford of whom god haue mercy. (3) like youre highnes by thaduis of my redoubted lord of Gloucestre and of al youre noble . . .¹ graunt your saide (4) bisecher the same office of vierger with al the fees and appurtenances that longeth ther to in wise like as the said (5) Iohan . . .¹ terme of life for goddes sake. and as he shal euer praie for youre hight estat and for al your noble lignie

(Another hand) Dat' ap*ud* West*m*o*n*asterium terc*i*o die Marcii A*n*-no &c p*r*imo
Non-Chancery hand
¹ washed out

119

1423   E28/40/18   Petition of Maud Fosbroke, drynurse (first of three versions)

(1) To þe hygh and myghty Prynce þe Duc of Glouc*ester* and oþere of þe councell of our souueraign (2) lord þe kyng

Lyke vn to þe hygh and discrete councell of oure souueraign lord þe kynges to gr*a*unt (3) vn to Mald ffosbroke drynorysse vn to oure said souueraigne lord þe kyng x li by yere for as long as þam lykis and (4) to be paid yn whatt plasse þ*at* þe said discrete councell will Assign for þe goode s*er*uyse and entendauntȝ þ*at* (5) þe said drynorysse hath don fro þe day of þe berth of our souueraign lord vn to þis day consideryng (6) þ*at* þe said Mauld hath noþer reward As fee by for grauntede of our said lord for þe wach and laboure (7) þ*at* scho hath had fro þe day as yit es a boven rehersid vn to þis day wherfor and yit lyke þe said hye and (8) discrete councell to gr*a*unte þe said Mauld þe said x li yn þe way of Charitee and Almouse

(Another hand) Donee a West*m*i*n*stre le xxviij jo*ur* Daurill Lan p*r*im*i*er
Chancery hand

120

1423   E28/40/19   Petition of Margaret Brothnam (second version)

(1) To þe hygh and myghty Prynce þe Duc of Glouc*ester* and oþer of þe councell of our souueraign lord (2) þe kyng

Lyke vn to þe high and discrete councell of oure souueraign lord þe kyng to gr*a*unt to (3) Morgrete Brothnam Chambrer and Wesher of oure said souueraign lord þe kyng C s for as long as þe said descrete (4) councell lykys and to be paid yn what place þ*at* þei will Assign for þe goode s*er*uice and entendantȝ (5) þ*at* þe said Chambrer hath don fro þe day of þe birth of oure soueraign lord vn to þis day consideryng (6) þ*at* þe said Morgrete hath noþer reward nor fee be for gr*a*unted of oure said lord for þe wach (7) and labor þ*at* scho hath had fro þe

day as yit es aboven rehersid vn to þis day wherfor and yit like þe (8) said hye & discrete councell to graunt þe said Morgrete Brothnam þe said C s in þe wey of Charite and Almous.
Chancery hand

121

1423   E28/40/20   Petition of Joan Asteley (third version)
(1) To þe hyghe and myghty Prynce þe duc of Gloucester and other of þe councell of oure souueraigne lord (2) þe kyngeȝ
Lyke vn to þe hyghe and to þe descrete councell of oure souueraigne lord þe kynges (3) to graunte vnto Ioan Asteley norysse of oure said souueraign lord þe kyng xx li by yere at þe terme of here lyve (4) to be paied yn what place þat þe said discrete councell woll assign for þe goode seruyse and entendauntȝ þat (5) þe said norysse hathe doen fro þe day of þe berthe of oure said souueraign lord vn to þis day consideryng (6) þat þe said Ioan hath neyther reward ne fee by fore graunted of oure said lord for þe wache and labour (7) þat sheo hath had fro þe day as hit is a boven rehersed vn to þis day. Where fore and hit lyke þe said (8) hye and discrete councell to graunte þe said Ioan Asteley þe said xx li for þe terme as hit is a boven wreton yn (9) þe wey of charite
(Another hand) Donee a Westminster le xxvij jour (dauerill)[1] Lan &c primier
Chancery hand
[1] rubbed

122

1424   Cleopatra F.IV. fol. 17v-18r   Privy Council Minute Book
(1) Thise ben certain prouisions for þe good of þe gouernance of this land that þe lordes which ben of (2) þe kinges. counseil desireth
First that my Lord of Gloucestre ne noon other man of þe counsail in no (3) suyte þat shal be maad vnto hem. schal no fauour graunte neithr in billes of right. ne of office / ne of benefice. (4) that loongeth to þe counsail / but oonly to ansuere that the bille shall be seen by all the counsail and the partie suynge so (5) to haue ansuer:
Item. that all the billes. that shull be putt vnto the counseil. shul be onys in the woke / at the lest / that (6) is to saye on þe Wednesday redd bifore þe counsail / And their ansueres endoced by þe same counsail / And on þe (7) friday next folewinge declared to þe partie suyng:

Item / that alle the billes that comprehende materes terminable (8) at the commune lawe that semeth nought feyned be remited there to be determined. but if so be that þe discrecion of the counsail feele to (9) greet might on that oo syde and vnmyght oo that other: (or ellus oþer cause Resonable þat shul moeue hem.) [1]

Item. (10) if so be that eny matere suyd in the counseil falle in to diuerse opinions: that oo lesse than the more partie of the counseil. (11) beyng present in the tyme of discord falle to that oo part: that be nought enacted as assented And the namys of the bothe (12) parties enact by the Clerc of the counseil with here assent or disassent:

Item. that in alle suytes that be maad to the (13) counsail in materes Whois determinacion Loongeth Vnto the counsail. but if it so be that thei touche the weel of þe king. (14) oure souerain lord. or of his Roiaume hastely to be spedd. ellys that they be nought enact doon by the counseil. oo lesse than to (15) the nombre. of vj [or iiij][2] att the leeste of the counsail with the Officiers that ben present be of oon assent / And att alle tyme (16) the names of þassenteurs to be writen of their owen hand in the sa(me)[3] bille:

Item. for asmuche as it is to greet (17) a schame / that in to Strange countrees oure souuerain lord shal write his lettres by þaduise of his counsail. for such materes (18) and persones as the counsail writeth in his name. And singuler persones of þe counsail. to write the contrarie: that it be (19) ordeynned. that noman of þe counsail presume to doo it on peyne of shame and reproef:

Item. that the Clerc of the counseil (20) be sworn. that euery. day. that the counseil sitteth on eny billes bitwix partie and partie. that he shal as ferr as he can. aspye. which (21) is the porest suyteurs bille / and that first to be redd / And ansuered/ And the kynges Sergeantes to be sworin trewly and plainly. (22) to yeue the poore man that for such is accept to þe counsail / assistence and trewe counsail in his matere so to be suyd with oute (23) eny good takyng of hym: on peyne of discharge of þeir offices:

Item. for asmuche as it is lykly. that many materes (24) shul be treted a fore the counsail. the which toucheth the kinges prerogatifes and freehold o that oo partie. (25) and othr of his sougets o. þat othr: in the which matires the counsail is not lerned. to kepe the. kinges. rightes. (26) and þe parties bothe. withoute thaduise of the kinges Iustices which ben lerned. both in his prerogatifs. and in his comune (27) lawe. That in alle such materes his Iuges be called therto and their aduise with their namys also to be entred of record. what (28) and how they determyne and aduise therinne

ffor the good keping of pees & reste in þis Reaume in the which stont (29) þe prosperitee and welfare of oure souerain Lord and of alle þestatys of þis land. hit is aduised (30) assented and assured by my Lord of Gloucestre and by all my lordys spirituel and temporel þat yf any (31) matere be now or haue bee not yit decided or schal be hereafter bitwyx lord & lord by þe sturyng of which (32) matere þe good Reste and pees of þis land myght in any wise be letted or troubled: þat in all suche materes (33) þe partie þat hit toucheth shal open to my forsaid Lord of Gloucestre and to þe Remenant (34) of my Lordys of þe Consail suche matere or materes as toucheth him with þe circumstances þerof and þerynne (35) be reuled after þaduis of my forsaid Lord and lordes and in non oþer wise. and suche Rule as þe Conseil (36) ordeyneth þe parties to obeie. And so like as þei doo in materes þat toucheth hem selfes: þei (37) shal doo in alle oþer materes þat touchen or mowe touche them or theirs by weye of feoffement (38) or in ony other wyse. And þat my forsaid lord of Gloucestre. and all myn other Lordes assure diligently truly & (39) indifferently in suche materes to hem opened to procede with outen ony parcialtee or fauour:

This ordenance (40) abouesaid to kepe my Lord of Gloucestre openly assured in his persone to all þe remenant of my lordys þere (41) beyng present and þey ayenward assured him the same by here trouthe in his hand. First.   My Lord of Canterbury   Wyncestre (42)   Norwych   Worcestre   Roucestre   Duresme   Karlill   þerl Mareschall   þerl of Stafford (43)   þe Lord Cromwell   Scroop   Hungerford   Tiptoft   þe Treseror   þe Priue Seal

Chancery hand
Printed Nicolas III.148-52.
[1] added in the same hand   [2] cancelled   [3] superior insert

123

1429   E28/50/9   Petition of William Pope, royal retainer (right side faded)

(1) Vnto þe kynge oure full souerain lorde

Bisechis full lowelich and mekelich youre humble seruant (2) and Squyer William Pope: That where as howe Iohn Cassons Squyer of youre graciouse graunte hath þe Office of (3) vergiershippe or Ostiarshippe of þe compaignye of þe Gartier withynne þe . . . Wyndesore togider with þe (4) mansion vnto þe same withynne þe saide Castell pertenynge: And also for to bere þe Rodde tofore yowe and youre (5) heires In procession in festiuall dayes with þe wages of xij. d þe day for to betake of þe Reuercions issues and (6) . . . Manoir of kenyngton oþerwise callidde Coldkenyngton in þe Shire of Middilsex by þe handes of þe (7) ffermours Resceiuours Baillifs Prouostes or Gaderers of þe same Manoir for þe tyme beeng as by youre gratious (8) lettres patentʒ to hym þerof . . . Shewe the which youre gratious (9) lettres patentʒ þe saide Iohn Cassons is in full wille and is fully assentede and accorded to restore in to youre (10) Chauncerie þere to be cancellede: to þe effect entent and purpos þat þe saide William þe . . . (11) mansion and wages and alle oþer mare profites and appurtenantʒ may haue: Where apon like it (12) vnto youre mageste roiale of youre grace especiale to graunte vnto þe saide William þe saide Office with þe (13) saide mansion and wa . . . commoditees and appurtenantʒ þerto longyng or pertenyng in þe same (14) manere and fourme as þe saide Iohn Cassons it hath hadde and occupiede durynge youre gratiouse wille And he shall praye god for yowe:

(Signatures in different hands) H. gloucestre   H Cantuar
I Ebor   Canc   W london   P Elien   I huntyngton
Chancery hand

124

1430   E28/51/69   Petition on behalf of the retainers of the Earl of Ormond (right side torn off)

1) Pleese it vn to the King oure souerayn Lord to graunt / lettres of his prive seel to your Lieutenant or (2) . . . in Irland þat thay graunt licences of absence with out fin / to all þaym þat shal come out (3) . . . in ffrance in þe feloweship of Iames le Botiller Erill of Ormond til þe fest of Sey . . . comyng a twolfmonth (4) And to charg þe said lieutenant or depute & Counsell . . . (as)[1] to be arrest at your prese to (5) serue þe said Erilles retenu out of Irland in to Engl. . .

(Signatures in different hands) H Gloucestre   H. Cantuar
I Ebor   Canc   W london   P Elien   I . . .   I huntyngton
Chancery hand
[1] rubbed

125

1432-36   SC1/44/8   Letter of Humphrey, Duke of Gloucester, to the Chancellor

(1) By the Duc of Gloucestre & Constable of the Castel of Douor wardein & Admiral of þe .V. Portes

Worshipful (2) fader in god. oure right trusty and right welbeloued we grete you wel. And for asmuche as we ben enfourmed þat oure trusty (3) and welbeloued knight sir Iohan fastolf hath take a suyt ayeinst certein personnes of hastynge & Brithelmeston in (4) þadmiral court of England for a trespasse supposed to be doon apon þe high see ayeinst a place callid þe hors (5) Shoo þe which personnes be come afore you. in my lordis chancerye by vertue of his writtes. We praye (6) you hertly in asmuch as þe said high see ys withinne þe Iurisdiccion of our Admiraltee of þe said portȝ: (7) þat þe said matier be not Remitted to þe said Admiral Court of England In eschuyng þe hurt þat (8) perauenture mighte inconueniently falle to our said admiraltee of þe saide portȝ be þat meene. (9) as we trust you. And our lord haue you in his keping. Yeuen vndir our signet at Sandewych þe xvj day of Iuyng

Chancery hand

126

1423-50   C81/1715/39   Letter of Richard, Duke of York, to the Chancellor

(1) Right worshipfull and reuerent fadir yn god / and my right entierly welbelouyd cosyn I recommaund me vnto yow (2) as hertly as I can / thankyng yow of youre goode cosynage shewyd vnto me. yn especiall the tyme of my beyng yn the seruice (3) of oure soueraigne lord the kyng. yn his Reaume of ffraunce and Duchery of Normandie   And forasmoch as I haue and shall be absent (4) certaigne yerys after the appunctuament of oure saide soueraigne lord yn his saide Reaume of ffraunce and Duchery of Normandie. (5) hit is vnder your fauore and goode wille expedient vnto me. forto haue generall Attorneys to pursue noȝt only matiers (6) and causes longgyng to me / buȝt also forto defend all causes and matiers mouyed aȝenst me / yn my saide absens: Wherfore (7) I pray hertly yow / forto do make letters patentȝ vnder the grete seale of oure saide soueraigne lord Recordyng and affirmyng (8) that my entent is and I woll / And by this writyng I make ordeigne and depute. my right trusty and welbelouyd sir Nicholl (9) Dixon one of my. Councellours yn the Reaume of Englond. and my right welbelouyd seruaunt Iohan Wyggemore myne generall Attorneys / (10) forto pursue and to defend all matiers & causes with me and aȝenst me yn the tyme of my absens byforesaide / to whom and all other of my (11) partye yn such matiers. I pray yow to be goode lord. Writon

at Rone the .v*the* daye of Iuyn
Youre trew cosyn and frend
Richard Duc of york
Chancery hand

127

After 1432   SC1/44/12   Letter of Henry Beaufort, Bishop of Winchester, to the Chancellor

(1) Worschipful fadr*e* in god (and Right)[1] trusty and Welbeloued Brothre and frend: I. grete yow Right hertely wel And sende yow (2) herinne encloosed a bille of [a tennant of myn of farnham called][2] Thomas Gode. which as he saith now dwelleth atte (3) Colcestre and of tyme passed hadd pourchaced and dwelled atte Stowemarkett in Suffolok. And as ye may see by the saide poeu*ere* (4) mannys su(ges)t*ion*[1]. two men of Stowemarkett þat is to saye Thomas Sengelton & Iohan Ady whom þe saide poeu*ere* (5) man hadd enfeoffed of trust. han halden hym oute of his hous and lifloode as he sayeth .v. yeer & mor. And forasmoche as the open (6) wroong þat is doon hym in þat partie yif hit bee soo. is full odieux and agreggeable. In example of othr mysdoers in cas (7) semblable. I wolde pray yow worshipful fadr*e* in god. my Right trusty & welbeloued Brothr & frend for to doo be sent for. by writtes (8) sub pena the saide Sengelton and Ady. And thay bothe vpon the saide suggestion which is a mat*ere* of conscience (a forn yow)[3] (9) to be examined atte such a day as ye wol assigne. And to be Reuled & iustified in þat partie As good faith trouthe and conscience (10) sholde Requere aftre your good discrecion As I truste yow And worshipful fadr*e* in god my Right trusty and welbeloued brothr (11) and frend Our blessed lord god haue yow eu*ere* in his gracioux protection and keping   Writen atte merton the xxix day of Auerill

Chancery hand
[1] rubbed   [2] cancelled   [3] superscript insert

128

After 1432   C1/12/179   Petition of Richard Selby, possibly Clerk of Chancery

(1) To the ful reuerent fader in god Bysshop of Bathe & of welles Chaunceller of Englonde

(2) Besechith meekly your poer Chapelyn Richard Selby clerk that

wher as he was late vicare of the chirche of Seint stephns in the Town (3) of Seint Albons in the Shir of hertford by the presentacion of on Iohn Abbot of Seint Albons by vertu of wyche presentacion (4) he was admitte & Institute in the seyd Chirche wyche ys of the value of xxv mark be yer And wher the xxti day of August (5) the yer of hour (lord the kyng that now is the xx at Iseldon in the Shir of Middlesex on william Rachedale preest come to the (6) seid besecher seieng & affermyng)[1] that he was person of the Chirche of Northwodebernyngham in the shire of Norfolk (7) wiche is of the Value of xxviij mark be yer atthe presentacion of oon Iohn Palton of the seyd Shire of Norfolk wher as the seyd william (8) was neuer person of that Chirche nor of non other Chirche in the same Shire of Norfolk nor neuer was noon suche Iohn (9) Palton patron of the seyd Chirche of Northwodebernyngham And ther Accorde toke by twene the seyd bysecher & william that (10) iche of them shuld haue others Chirche And iche of them gete other A presentacion from his patron by vertu of wiche Accorde (11) the seyd bysecher Accordyng to this couenant resigned & gate A presentacion of the seyd abbot to the same william (12) by vertu of wyche presentacion the seyd william was inducte institute in the same vikerage & the forseyd william (13) deliuered to the seyd bysecher A presentacion of the seyd Chirche of Northwodebernyngham forged & feyned in (14) the name of the seyd Iohn Palton ther As the seyd Iohn was neuer patron of the seyd Chirche of Northwodebernyngham nor (15) the seyd william was neuer person of the same Chirche of Northwodebernyngham nor or noon other chirche in the (16) seyd shire of Norfolk And so the seyd william is vikary of the seyd chirche of seintstephens And your seyd bysecher withoute (17) Any Chirche to his finall vndoyng & destruccion with ought youre gracious helpe in this matier please it your (18) gracious lordshipp to concidre thes premisses and theruppon to graunte a writte sub pena directe to the (19) same william Rachedale to apper by fore you Att A certeyn day be you to be lemytedd ther to be examined vppon thes premisses (20) as good feithe & concience requireth for the loue of god & way of charte

    Plegium de prosecutio Radnus Clerk   Iohanes Bernewell
    Chancery hand
    [1] over erasure

129

1435   SC1/44/45   Letter of Richard, Duke of York, possibly to John Frank, Master of Rolls

(1) Right trusty & entierly welbeloued frende / I grete you often tymes wel / And thanke you with al myn hert of þe grete (2) gentilesse and kyndenesse þe whiche hit hath liked vnto you / to shewe herebefore aswel vnto me / as vnto myn officers & (3) seruantes atte reuerence of me / Prayeng you hertily of good continuance / And for asmuche / as for suche materes (4) and þinges as I shal haue adoo and to poursue in oure souuerain lordes courtes in Irlande / hit is right nedeful (5) for me to haue certaine personnes þere and to haue auctorite and power of þe kyng oure saide souuerain (6) lord forto bee myn attournees / I pray you with al myn hert / þat hit like you / forto doo make lettres patentes (7) vnder þe kyng oure saide souuerain lordes seel in deue fourme / forto endure iiij. yere namyng in thayme Robert (8) Doudale and Iames water forto bee my saide attournees / as my singulier trust is vnto yow / Right trusty and entierly (9) welbeloued frende. oure lord haue you in his keping writen vnder my signet at westmynster þe xvij day of May.

(10) The Duc of york Erle of þe marche & of vluestre

Chancery hand

130

1435   E28/56/1   Privy Seal: Summons to Parliament (draft with addresses attached)

(1) By the kyng

Riȝt worshipful fadre in god / for as muche as sithe þe tyme þat we wrote vnto you last by (2) oure writtes vndre oure greet seel to be with vs in oure parlement at oure paleis of Westminster þe x day of Octobr (3) next commynge as ye knowe wel / ther be fallen vpon vs so grete materes of weght and charge concernyng þe (4) weel of vs and þis oure Reaume / þat þe purueance of þe Remedie for hem axeth of uerraie necessite an hool (5) aduis and consail of alle þestates of oure parlement / we desire and charge you as ye loue vs þat alle (6) excusacions cessinge ye be with vs and þe Remenant of þe lordes of oure parlement at oure said paleis (7) (þe)[1] said day contened in oure writ sent vnto you there to yeue your assent and aduis vpon þe saide Remedies / (8) wetinge for certeine þat at þis tyme we neyþer may ne wol haue your persones commynge vnto oure (9) said parlement excused in eny manere / yeuen &c xxviij day of September Ao xiiijo

To þe Arche bisshopes
To &c alle þe lordes semble

(Followed by a full list of addressees on the next vellum)
Text in non-Chancery hand, addresses in Chancery hand
[1] superior insert

131

1436 E28/56/28 Privy Seal: Memorandum of Council Business
(1) The xx day of ffeuerer. þe xiiij. yere &c at Westminster / The kyng consideryng þe good herte and kyndenesses. (2) þat his greet Oncle þe Cardinal hath at alle tymes in his necessitees shewed vnto him and specially now at þis tyme. in (3) his greet necessitee. for þe settyng forth of his greet armee into his Reume of ffraunce and Duchee of Normandie for þe (4) sauue gard and defense of þe same ffor þe settyng forth of þe which armee: the said Cardinal graunteth to lene vnto þe (5) kyng at þis tyme. with oþer sommes. by him lent before. for þe kynges saide necessitees þe somme of . . .[1] þabouesaid (6) sommes soo before. by him lent. accounted vndre þe same somme of xxml. li: vpon such seuretees as foloweth:

(7) Furst as for þe somme of xml. marc. late by þe said Cardinal lent vnto þe kyng for his greet necessitees: (8) ffor þe repaiement of þe which somme. he hath diuers lordes bounden vnto him by seuerall obliga(cions)[1] The kyng wol. by þauis of (9) his counsail þat þe saide obligacions remaigne in his said Oncles handes by the same auctoritee as þei were deliuered (10) vnto him:

Item and for þe somme of Ml marc. by þe said Cardinal. also lent vnto þe kyng for his greet (11) necessitees. for þe seuretee of þe which. he hath tailles. of þe iijde: partie of þe dysm committed vnto þe kyng. by his (12) Clergie þe xij yere of his regne. paiable at Martynmasse next comyng: The kyng by þauis of his said counsail. wol (13) þat þe said tailles remaigne vnto his said Oncle as þei were appointed at þe tyme of þe deliueryng of hem: And ouer (14) þat þat he haue for þe seuretee of þe same Ml marc such weddes. as he hath of þe kyng at þis tyme of þe value of Ml marc (15) til þat he be contented of þe somme of Ml marc. soo by hym lent. as aboue:

Also þe kyng wol by þauis (16) &c þat my said lord þe Cardinal haue sufficeant assignement for seuretee of repaiement for þe somme (17) of xjml. marc. now by hym lent of þe first partee of þe xv. graunted vnto þe kyng in his last parlement. paiable at Witsontyde next comyng. whereupon he (18) shal haue tailles. and lettres patentes such as he wol agree hym vnto and yf þe same paiement of þe xv. come not to my said lord Cardinales handes (19) by mydsomer day. next folowyng. þat þenne þe Tresorer of England. shal content þe said Cardinal in prest paiement of þat þat he (20) shal lene of gold in gold l & of þat þat he shal lene in siluer in l siluer. of þe somme þat is (21) to him due:

Also and for þe somme of viijm marc. reest of þe saide somme. of xxm. li. Whereof þe said Cardinal (22) hath non assignement: The kyng wol. þat þer be deliuered vnto hym Ioialx to the value of þe somme of xiijml marc. like as it may be accorded (23) betwix þe said Cardinal and þe Tresorer of England. with powere of Sale. of þe said Ioialx so to be engaged for defaute of paiement at the xvme (24) of Martynmasse next comyng. and þe oþer half of þe saide somme of viijml marc at Witsontyde after (25) þat Martynmasse (þen)[2] next folowyng

And þe kyng by þauis of his said counsail wol þat vpon þees (26) Articles: in eueri of hem: the Chaunceller of England and þe keper of þe kinges priue seel for þe tyme beyng make suche & as many lettres & warrantȝ (27) vndre þe kynges greet & p(riue seele)s[3] as for execucion of þe same Articles as the caas shal requir (28) . . . [1] Cardinal shal duely be demaunded.

(Signatures in different hands) H gloucestre   I. Ebor
H Northumbyrlonde

Non-Chancery hand
[1] water stained   [2] superior insert   [3] torn

132

1436   E28/57A   Privy Seal: Summons to Arms (first of three versions)

(1) By þe kynge

Trusty and welbelouyd ffor asmoche as he þat calleth him Duc of Bourgoigne oure rebell with his puissaunce (2) of fflemmenges Picardes Bourgoignons and oþer is come ouer þe water of Grauelyng and hath pighte his tentes (3) with Inne oure Pale of þe marches þere willyng and disposyng him to gete oure Toune of Caleys and alle oure strengthes (4) in þe marches þere þe whiche if so were þat god defende shulde be vn to vs you oure Reamme and subgittȝ (5) to grete an hurte and a perpetuelle shame we þerfore willyng to resiste þe malice of (þe)[1] saide callyng him Duc dispose (6) vs in persone for to go to oure Citee of Caunterbury for þe rescous to oure said Toune and marches Wherfore we (7) desire and praye you hertely as oure feod man in wise as at þis tyme we desire and praye oure oþer feod men þat (8) in alle þe haste þat ye maye ye make you redy and alle þe defensable people þat ye can and maye and (9) drawe you þeder to ward vs So þat ye be þere at þe ferþest on mary Maughdelenes day next redy in (10) your beste arraye for þe said rescous with oþer of oure feod men and trewe subgittȝ to whom we write sembly for (11) þe good of vs you oure Reaume and subgittȝ of þe same And in no wise faylleth her of as oure singuler truste ys in yowe: (12) yeuen vnder oure priue sealle at Westm*inster* þe laste day of Iuyn

And trusty and welbeloued after the writyng of thise le*tt*res (13) come to vs tithynges that the seide callyng hym Duk hath take our fortalice of Oye and slayn all our souldiours ther Inne And that (14) the seconde day of Iuyll next co*m*myng purposith hym redyly to be before oure seide Town of Caleys for the sonner rescous of (þe)¹ (15) which oure beall vncle of Gloucestre Capitayn of the seide Town and Marches. hath desired of vs to go thedir in p*er*sone so that he (16) may be compaign-ed with a notable retenue accordyng to his estate And of myght to make a feld ayeinste our seide rebell and enemyes Wherefore (17) we pray yow as aboue that ye faille not to be with your retenue with oure saide vncle at Sandwych the seide Mary Magdeleyn day redy (18) there to awayte on oure seide Vncle and take the passage to ward Caleys at far-thest

Chancery hand
¹ superior insert

133

1436   E28/57B   Privy Seal: Summons to Arms (second version, badly damaged, in a smaller hand than A)

(1) . . . Duk of Burgoyne oure rebell with his puissans of ffleming . . . water of Gravelyng and . . . willyng and disposyng (2) hym to gete oure toun of Caley . . . þere the whuche if so were . . . to grete an hurte and p*er*petuell shame. We (3) therfore willyng to resiste the malice of the said callyng hym Duk dispose . . . rescous to oure said toun and marches. Wherefore (4) we desire and pray you hertly as oure feod man in wise & as at this tyme . . . make you redy and al the . . . poeple that ye (5) can and may and drawe you theder toward . . . best array for the seid . . . oure foed men and true subgitts to whom we . . . yeven (6) vnder oure priue seal (at Westm*instre*)¹ the last day of . . .

. . . callyng hym Duk hath take oure fortalys (7) Of Oye and slayn all our sowdyours þerinne And . . . þe secund day of þe moneth . . . sonner rescous of (8) þe whiche our beal Vncle of Gloucestre . . . and

marches hath desirid of vs to go thider . . . and of myght to make a (9) feld ayenst our seid rebell and enemys wherfore we pray yow . . . þat ye faille not to be wyth . . . redy þer to (10) awayte on our seid vncle and take þe passage toward Caleys atte ferthest:
  Chancery hand
  [1] superior insert

134

1436   E28/57C   Privy Seal: Summons to Arms (third version)
(1) By the kyng
Trusty and welbeloued for asmoche as he þat calleth hym Duc of Bourgoine oure rebell wyth his (2) puissance of fflemynges picardes Bourgoignons and oþer is come ouer the water of Gravelyng and (3) hath pight his tentes with Inne oure pale of the marches there willyng and disposyng hym to gete oure tovne of Caleys (4) and all oure Strengthes in þe marches þere. the which if so were þat god defende shuld be vnto vs (5) yowe oure roialme and subgettes to grete an hurte and perpetuell shame: we þerfore willyng to resiste the malice of (6) the said callyng hym Duc. dispose vs in persone for to goo vnto oure Citee of Caunterbury for the rescous to owre seid (7) tovne and marches. wherfore we (desire)[1] and pray yowe hertly as oure feod man in wise as at this tyme we desire and pray oure (8) oþer feod men. þat in all þe hast ye may ye make yowe redy And all the defensable poeple þat ye can and may (9) And drawe yowe thider toward vs Soo þat ye be there at the ferthest on Mary Magdelan next redy yn youre best array for the (10) seid rescous with oþer of oure feod men and trewe subgettes to whom we write semblably for the good of vs you (11) oure reaume and subgettȝ of the same and yn no wise faileth here of as oure singuler trust ys yn you yeuen vnder oure (12) priue seal at Westminstre the last day of Iuyn

  (Another hand) And trusty and welbeloued after the writyng of (13) thise lettres come vnto vs tithinges that the seide callyng hym Duk hath take oure fortalice of Oye and slayn (14) all oure soudiours ther Inne and that the seconde day of Iuyll next commyng purposeth hym redely to be before (15) oure . . .[2] of Caleys for the sonnor . . .[2] of whiche oure beall vncle Gloucestre Captayn of the seide Tovn (16) and Marches hath desired of vs to go thedir in persone so that he may be compaigned with anotable retenue accordyng (17) to his estats and of myght to make a feld ayenst oure seide rebell. and enemye wherfor we pray

you as aboue that ye (18) faille not to be with your retenue withe oure seide vncle at Sandwiche the seide Mary Magdeleyn day redy there to awayte (19) on oure seid vncle and take the passage toward Caleys at fartherst
Chancery hand
[1] over erasure   [2] rubbed

135

1436   E28/56/40   Privy Seal: Instructions to Sir John Stokes and other Ambassadors (draft)
(1) By the kyng
Trusty & welbeloued ffor asmoch as we be credebly enfourmed þat (how it be þat)[1] Thambassatours. of (2) þe heres of Spruce & of þe [cees of þ][2] Citees of þe hansere haue be sumwhat taryed in (3) þier comyng for to haue mete with you for þe materes þat we sende you for Neuerthelees. þei (4) beth in comyng: [We][2] and as we vndrstonde wol come down to Bruges (wher for)[1] we wol & charge you þat ye abyde stylle at (5) Caleys [without þat ye departe fro þens][2] vnto þe tyme þat ye haue redy word fro þe sayd Ambassatours (6) [þat þei beth come to bruges][2] & (wher)[1] þat ye (& þei)[1] shal meete [with hem þer or at Caleys abouesaid][2] (7) for þe speed of þe matteres wherfor ye be sent. Yeuen at westminstre (8) þe vij day of March Anno xiij
To maistre Iohn Stokes & oþer our Ambassatours ioyned with (9) him beyng at Caleys
Non-Chancery hand
[1] interlinear insertion   [2] cancelled

136

1436   E28/57D/23   Privy Seal: Commission to Richard, Duke of York (corrected draft)
(1) By the kyng:
Ryght trusty and right welbeloued Cosin. We sende to yow at þis tyme oure lettres of poiar and (2) Commission as for youre Lieutenancie and gouernaille in oure behalue in oure Reume of ffrance and Duchie of Normandie / (3) and with hem we sende to yow oure answeres yeuen to certein articles late ministred by yow to vs and oure conseil with oþer (4) articles of Instruccion auised by vs and oure seid conseil / þe whiche we wole þat ye obserue in þe office (5) committed vnto yow. prayeng

yow þat considering þe greet [iooardie]¹ (jupardie)². þat þe said (6) cuntrees standen in and þenterprise þat dayly fallen þere by oure ennemyes (and also ye grete hurt and losse þat (7) (daylye)² renneth upon vs as wele for your longe abode / as for ye costes of shyppes which [fro day to day]¹ (8) (as it noht vnknowen to you)² standen vs to grete charge / with outen lenger delaye.)³ [in all þe haste possible]¹ ye (9) with your retenue take youre passage into oure said Reume and Duchie to þe consolacion and comfort of oure trewe (10) subgettes. þere. And right trusty and right welbeloued Cosin for asmuche as oure welbeloued Secretarie Maister Laurence (11) Calot disposeth hym at þis tyme for to passe with yow into oure said Duchie þere for to abide and for to do to vs (12) and to yow such seruice. as he can in his best wyse as he oweth to doo. we praye yow þat ye haue hym specially recommended (13) aswel to som lyflode. as to his wages partiegnyng to his office / after þeffect of a cedule. which we sende to yow closed withynne (14) þese. And god haue yow in his keping. yeuen vnder oure priue seel at Westminstre þe xij day of May:

(15) ⁴To oure right trusty and right welbeloued Cosin Richard Duc of york oure Lieutenant of oure Reume of ffrance and Duchie of Normandie

Chancery hand
¹ cancelled   ² superior insert   ³ addition in a finer secretary hand marked for insertion after ennemyes   ⁴ a third hand

137

1436   E28/57/28   Privy Seal: Confirmation of a Commission (corrected)

(1) Trusty & wele be louyd. We be gladde (for as mych)¹ þat we her [your]² at dyuerse tymes of your. gode demeynyng (2) (and manly gouernaunce)¹ as touchyng ye safe guarde of our toune & castell of Crotey wher of we thank you (hertlye)¹ prayng (3) you so (to)¹ continue (at all tymes)¹ [Trustyng fully]² Noght dowtyng but þat at þe comyng of our counseil next (4) to gedrs þe which shall be In ye octaues of ye trynite (next commyng)¹ Such purveaunce shal be made for you and ye continance (5) of your abode (yere)¹ as wele of money fo³ your wages as oþer wise. yat vp o⁴ (6) reson ye shall holde you (wele)¹ contente. youen &c xxij day of May Anno xiiijo

Non-Chancery hand
¹ superior insert   ² cancelled   ³ fo *sic*   ⁴ o *sic*

138

1436 E28/58/15 Petition of John Stok, royal retainer
(Initialed) R h nous avons graunte
(1) Please hit the kyng oure souerain lorde graunt vnto youre contynuell seruant Iohn Stok (2) sergeant porter in youre worshipfull houshold the Corrodie in thabbey of Peterburgh the whiche is in youre gracious gifte (3) in like maner and fourme that oon Iohn Swan now late passed vnto god had. with the arrerages sithen the day of his deth vnto now (4) this day at / the reuerence of god and in wey of charite

(Another hand) lettre ent feust faite a Westmonstieur le quint iour de Nouembre. lan &c xve.
Chancery hand

139

1437 E28/58/62 Privy Seal: Petition of William Soper, Clerk of the Exchequer
(1) To the kyng oure souerain lord
Right mekely besecheth to your souerain lordship youre pore seruant William Soper (2) Clerk of your Shippes that for as moche as he hath stonde charged with right greet and combrous occupacions in the seid (3) Office as well in the tyme of your gracious ffader late oure souerain lord whom god assoil As in all your gracious (4) regne and yit doth. but it stondeth so right souerain lord that your forseid besecher hath made a vowe to do certein (5) Pilgrymages beyonde the see. the whiche he may not do whiles he stondeth thus charged with the seid Office Wherfor plese hit vnto (6) your souerain lordship. that the seid Beseker may be discharged of the seid Office. And that som other man with the same (7) office myght be charged. resceyvyng alle manere thinges perteynyng vnto the same Office that may be founde due (8) be accompt in your Escheker in suche manere and fourme as it hath ben accustomed before this tyme in caas semblable (9) to thentent that the seid Beseker with your graciouse licence may do the Pilgrymages be him so promised / And of your noble grace (10) hym to graunte your graciouse lettres patententʒ for his tuicion and fauour in all parties duryng his seid (11) pilgrimage in manere as before thys tyme hath ben graunted to your oder seruantʒ in cas semblable. And of (12) your more haboundant grace to graunte that the seid Beseker may haue xx sakes of wolle for his despenses vnto the parties (13) of lumbardye paiyng

the custumes and other deuairs as langeth to your Staple at Caleys for the loue of god and for charitee. Consideryng (14) graciouse lord that the seid Pilgrymage was avowed and promysed for the greet periles and combrous occupacions (15) that be liklynesse at diuerse tymes myght haue falle in the Office aboueseid. Consideryng also that the seid Beseker (16) groweth into such age that if the seid Pylgrymage be not don in right short tyme. it may neuere be don be hym:

Chancery hand

140

1437   E28/59/21   Petition of Thomas Frank, Clerk of the Privy Seal

(Initialed) R h

(1) To the kyng oure souerain Lorde:

Shewieth moost lowely youre full humble and continuel seruant Thomas (2) ffrank. Keper and filacer of youre Recordes in thoffice of youre priue seal. Howe þat duryng þe tyme of .viij. yere (3) nowe passed his fader William ffrank of Richemond and he. haue been fermours of þe Priorie Alien of Begger at Richemond in þe (4) Countee of York paiyng þerfore .vij li. vj s viij d by yere to Quene Iehanne whome god assoille and she to bere þe grete (5) Reparacion of þe same þe which reparacion and oþer charge were suche yerely duryng þe forsaide tyme / (6) þat all þe proufit of þe saide priorie passed not yerely to þoeps of þe saide Quene þe somme of .v. li. (7) Please it vnto youre moost benigne grace to consider þe dayly seruice þat þe said Thomas ha(th)[1] doon aswell vnto þe (8) moost cristen Prince late oure souerain Lorde youre fader on whoome god haue mercy as to you our souerain lorde during (9) þe space of .xxe. yere. þe seruice also þat by goddes mercy. he shal do vnto youre hieghnesse in tyme to come. (10) And þervpon of youre moost hiegh and habundante grace / to graunt vnto þe saide Thomas the forsaide[2] Priorie (11) of Begger Alien in þe Countee of york with milnes dysmes landes tenementes & possessions what þei be of olde tyme þe (12) said Priorie longyng & eny (manere)[3] fro þe decesse of þe saide Quene duryng his lyfe. withouten eny thyng þerfore (13) yeldyng to you (or to your herys)[2] (In Recompensacion of the saide seruices)[2] Purueied allway þat þe same Thomas. (14) bere reparacion and all manere of oþer charges þerto necessarie due or accustumed: Not withstondyng þat (15) mencion is not made of oþer grantʒ and yiftes by youre saide hieghnesse here afore made to þe same Thomas. (16) ne of þe verraie value yerely of þe saide Priorie after þe statutes or ordinaunce made to þe contrarie (17) And þe saide Thomas shal dayly pray for you as he is moost þerto bounden: And þat wythouten eny fee of (18) (youre grete)² seel for þe loue of god and in way of charitee:

Lettre ent feust faite a wyndesore Le xxme. jour de ffeuerer lan &c xvjme

Chancery hand
Grant recorded *CPR 1436-41*, p. 197.
¹ torn   ² over erasure   ³ superior insert

141

1437   E28/58/4   Petition of William Walysby, Treasurer to Queen Katherine

(Initialed) R h nous auouns graunte

(1) Please it to the Kyng oure souerain Lord of youre Benigne grace to (2) graunte to youre humble seruant and Oratoure sir William Walysby Tresorer with the Quene youre (3) moder the denerye of hastynges in the dyose of Chichester the whiche Prestewyke Clerke of youre parlement late had on who (4) sowle god assoile And youre saide Oratour shal pray god for yow.

(Another hand) lettre ent feust faite a Westministre le [xv]¹ viije. jeur de November. lan &c xve.

Chancery hand
¹ cancelled

142

1437   C49/22/18   Deposition signed by Adam Moleyns

(1) The xe day of ffeuerer the vije yere of the kyng at Westmynstre in the Sterre Chambre beyng þanne present þe (2) high and myghti Prince Duc of Gloucestre the Bisshops of Bath Chanceller and of seint dauid þerlis of Saresbury (3) and Northumbr the lord Cromwell Tresorer of England William lyndewode keper of þe kyngis priue seal and Robert (4) Rolleston Warderober the kyngis counsaillours examined þe person(s)¹ whoos namis here on folow vpon þe ryot (5) (that)² was doon at Bedford. þe xije. day of Ianuer þe yere aboue said. AND FIRST. was called before þe (6) seid (counsale)³ Thomas wawton and sworn vpon a bok to sey the playn trouth and nouȝt to mene it with eny ontrouth for (7) hate or euel will neiþer for loue ner fauour but plainly report as it was in dede nouȝt sparing for no persone ne for no (8) þing

and he seid plainly he wolde seye þe trouth in such þingis as shulde be demaunded of him .FIRST. it was (9) asked him yif he hadde sette his seel vnto þe certificat þat was yeue and put vp to þe kyng vpon þe lord (10) ffaunhop as touching þe seid mater of Bedford / and he answered ye. And forthwith asked yif he knewe þe mater content in the (11) said certificatt and he answered ye HE WAS asked with what pepil þe lord ffaunhop come to þe Toune of Bedford at þat tyme (12) and in what array he answered as to þe nombr of persones with a sexti and as to (þe)ire[1] array with pikk doublettis (13) and swerdis and bokelers and þus arraied some of þeime come in to þe halle / and as too of þeime within þe (14) barre IT WAS asked yif þe seid lord ffaunhop at oþer cessions a fore þat tyme was wont to come in like array he (15) answered ye. HE WAS asked wheder he cam to þe halle before þe lord ffaunhop / and hou many of þe iustices were (16) þere to giders ar þe lord ffaunhop cam he answered þat he and Iohn Enderby / Iohn ffitȝ and harry Etwell cam (17) to þe halle before þe lord ffaunhop / HE WAS asked yif þei all knewe wel þat þe lord ffaunhop was in þe (18) towne of Bedford and yif þei hadde eny spech of him amonges þeime iiije. and to all þis he aunswered ye. HE WAS (19) demaunded yif he sent to þe lord ffaunhop eny word of þeire beyng þere to geders or warned him þat þei wolde (20) procede in þe cessions or ellis þat þei taried vnto his comyng to euerich of þis he answered nay / but þei (21) iiije. sat downe and proceded not to þe cessions but commoned to geders HE WAS. asked yif he and his felaws such time as þe (22) lord ffaunhop come to þeime dede him eny reuerence or what countenance þei made (he seid)[3] þat his þre felaws stode (23) vp and he sitting stille a valed his hode. HE WAS asked hou þe lord ffaunhop demened him after his comyng to þeime / And he (24) answered þat he sat him (doune)[1] and callid to him Iohn ffitȝ and william Pek and willed þeime to sitte downe by (25) him and þe seid ffitȝ aduised þe lord ffaunhop to take vnto him wawton (and)[1] and Enderby for þei were (26) a boue þe seid ffitȝ in þe commission / and þe seid lord ffaunhop aunswered (þeim nay)[2] come and þu (27) will þe (toon)[2] shal be wolcome þe toþer may chese and þis communicacion had þei sat downe (28) to (gideris)[1] HE WAS. asked hou þe rumor and noyse fill amonges þeime / he answered by oncurteise langage be twene (29) Iohn ffitȝ Geffray and a seruant of þe lord ffaunhops þe which þe seid lord ffaunhop bad to answere to þat (30) þe which was seid vnto him and þe same seruant forthwith sauyng þe reuerence of his lord seid it was fals and so lyued (31) þe said Iohn fitȝ Geffray and forth with wawton seith þat he seid to þe lord ffaunhop it is þe vnruliest (32) cession þat I haue euer sey in Bedford and yif it be not oþerwise reuled I wol complaine vnto þe kinges (33) counseill to þe which þe lord ffaunhop shulde haue seid complaine (34) as þo wole y defie þi menasing and all þine euel will wawton seide he answered I sette litil of þi defiance and (35) with þis þere was rumor and noyse in þe halle and soo þei rose vp boþe þe lord ffaunhop wawton (36) Enderby and all þe remenant / and þe lord ffaunhop stode vpon þe Cheker borde þe which borde stode a fore þe (37) benche HE WAS asked yif he sye þe lord ffaunhop drawe eny dagger he seid forsoth nay he was asked wheþer he sawe (38) eny dagger in his hande and he seid ye. furþermore he was asked in what wise he helde þe dagger in his hande þe point (39) forth riȝt foynyng / or ellis þe point towardes his elbowe downward / and to þis he said he wist nat / HE WAS also (40) asked yif he sawe þe lord ffaunhop (or any man of his)[4] smite eny man or made eny likly countenaunce to smyte he said nay / HE WAS (41) also asked wheþer þe lord ffaunhop such tyme as he stode vpon þe borde labored to þe cessing of þe (42) rumor and debat or ellis þat he stured and moued þe pepil to rumor / and he answered þat he labored to cesse þe noyse (43) and þe rumor þat was in þe halle He was asked wheder he labored effectuelly or ellis faintly and vnder colour of (44) his labore soffred harme to be doo / he answered þat to his vnderstandyng he labored to þe keping of pees / and to stynte þe noyse and Rumor (45) þat was in þe halle and alsoo diligently as euer he sawe man. HE WAS asked what the seid lord ffaunhop dide such tyme as (46) the noyse was cessed / he answered þat he went vnto his ynne. and with his owne seruantȝ lete feleshipped þe seid (47) wawton / and oþer of his felaws / vnto þeire logginges for þeire more seuretee and þe lord ffaunhop willed (48) wawton to haue come dronken with him as he hadde Enderby seyeng to wawton þat he sholde be welcome for he yaf him drink which (49) he hadde lesse cause to loue þanne (him)[1] menyng be Enderby: IOHN Enderby called before þe counsail in fourme as it (50) is reherced of Thomas wawton in like wise swore vpon a bok to (sey)[2] þe trouth in þe mater a boue said & þe which he promissed to do &c. (51) EXAMINED vpon þe first article he seide at þe tyme of makyng of þe certificat þe which was sent vnto (52) þe kyng his felawe and he were in d(i)fference[3] and discorde not forþanne he sette his seal þerto. AS TO þe secunde to (53) þe þridde to þe fourthe to þe fifte to þe vje. and to þe vije. articles he accorded in all (54) his deposicion and answere with Thomas wawton: AS TO þe viije. he seide þat þei stode vp all such tyme as (55) þe lord ffaunhop come to þeime. AS TO þe ixe. and þe xe. article he accorded in substance with (56) þe seid wawton confessing alsoo þat he him self drewe out his owne dagger / and in þe tyme of þe rumor his man brought (57) him a swerd and in what wise he departid from his dagger he can not sey. AS TO þe xje article he seith þat he sawe (58) not þe lord ffaunhop to drawe eny dagger / neiþer þat he hadde eny in his hande: EXAMINED vpon þe xije. (59) and þe xiije articles he accorded with Thomas wawton no þing varyeng in substance. IOHN ffitʒ in like (60) wise as wawton and Enderby sworn vpon a bok and examined answereth as it folowith: IN THE first and þe secunde Article (61) he accorded with wawton: IN THE þridde þe iiije and þe ve. and þe sexte Articles he accorded in his (62) deposicion with wawton and Enderby: AS TO þe vij article he accorded with Enderby and not with wawton: AS TO (63) þe viij article he accorded alsoo AS TO þe ix article he accordith with wawton. IN þe. xe article he (64) accordith with Enderby boþe þat he sawe þe lord ffaunhop to drawe no dagger neiþer þat he hadde eny in (65) his hande In the xje and xij articles he accordeth with wawton and Enderby AND ALSO in þe xiije article noþing (66) chaungyng in substance. HARRY Etwell examined and sworn vpon a bok to sey trouth In þe first article he accordith with his (67) felaws: IN THE secunde article he accorded also with his felaws saue he va(ri)ed[5] in nombre seyng þat þe lord ffaunhop come (68) to Bedford with xl. or l. persons / IN THE iije þe iiij þe v. and þe vje. articles he accordid with (69) his felaws IN þe vij and þe viij. articles he accorded with Enderby (IN þe ixe)[3] and þe xe. (70) articles he accordith with wawton IN þe (xie. xij and xiije)[3] articles he accordith with his felaws: THE xxiiij (71) day of ffeuerer þe yere a boue seid at westmynstre Thomas Stratton vnder shereue of Bedford in þe (presence)[1] of the high and myʒti prince þe (72) Duc of Gloucestre the Bisshop of Bath Chaunceller of England þerle of Saresbury lord Cromwel tresorer of Englonde: þe lord hungerford William (73) lyndewode keper of þe kinges priue seal þe kinges counsaillours / swere vpon a bok to make trewe and iuste (74) answere in þat shulde be demanded him of þe Ryot doon at Bedford: FIRST he was demanded yif he was priue of þe (75) certificat þat was made vnto þe kyng by wawton Enderby ffitʒ and Etwell and he seid ye: MORE OUER he was (76) demanded where he sat at þe cession tyme. and he answered at þe lord ffaunhop fete inasmoche as he was clerc of þe (77) cessions: HE WAS asked hou þe rumor be gan / and he þerein accorded with þe (seye)ng[1] of wawton and soo he dede in all (78) his deposicions sauyng in þe xj Article he varied from all seyeng / þat þe lord ffanhop (su)ch[1] tyme (79) as he stode vpon þe Cheker borde he made (countenance)[1] towardes Enderby as he wolde haue smete him / but he seith he smote him not

Adam Moleyns

Moleyn's non-Chancery hand
[1] rubbed   [2] over erasure   [3] torn   [4] superior insert   [5] crease

143

1438   E28/62/10   Petition of John Croke, Clerk of the Exchequer
(Initialed) R h
(1) To The kyng our souerain Lorde
Besechith humbly to your highnesse your humble (2) seruant Iohn Croke oon of þe Clerkis of your Eschequyer þat hit please to your high & noble (3) grace to graunte vnto your said seruant þannuel pension of a hundreth shillyngis be yere wich (4) þat the Pryour of Neustede vpon Acolm in the countye of lyncoln oweth and is bounden to geve & bere yerly to (you)¹ (5) And lyeth in your graciouse gifte / to haue and to resceyve þe said pension yerle duryng his (6) lyfe be the handes of þe Pryour of Neustede foresaid þat now is or for the tyme shal be And he shal pray god for you
   (Latin notation of grant by Adam Moleyns)
   Chancery hand
   Grant recorded *CPR 1436-41*, p. 306.
   ¹ superior insert

144

1438   E28/60/59   Petition of John Tiptoft. Adam Moleyns' note at the end.
(1) To the kyng oure souereigne lorde
Besechith mekely youre humble Seruant Iohn lord Tiptot and of Powys where as ye (2) beyng in youre gret councell at þe Hospitall of Seint Iohn of Ierusalem be side london xiijthe. day of (3) Nouembre the yere of youre full nobill Reigne the xvjthe concideryng the gret laboures costes and diligence which haue fallen (4) and shull fallen to your Councellours of youre seid Councell In recompence of her seid labours costes and diligenceȝ don & (5) to be don graunted to Serteyn lordes of youre seid Councell to eche of them a certeyn Somme of money yerly to be taken for (6) terme of their lyves that is to sey to youre seid besecher as on of youre seid councell a mong oder C. marc for terme of his lyve (7) as in an Acte ther uppon made in youre seid Councell the day and place aforseide more openly it apperith Please to youre hynesse (8) concidering þe long seruice that youre seid besecher hath don to you and the full nobill and gracious prince kyng (9) Henry the fourthe youre Aiell And to the full nobill and gracious prince kyng Henry þe fifte your fader whos soules god (10) assoile. to graunte to youre seid besecher Iohn lorde Tiptot and of Powys. be your gracious

*let*tres patentis in forme youen (11) the day and place a fore seide. youre Manoir of Bassyngbourn and þe baillywyk of Badburham of the honour of Richemond in (12) the Counte of Cantebrige with all the londys tene*m*entis medis pastures mylles wateres vineres ffysshynges Rentes Seruices bailles (13) hundredes Tournes Courtes letys libertes Castellwarde Gide of Richemond Custumes ffraunchieȝ retornes of writtes and other (14) youre *p*receptis and execucions of þe same vnto the seid Manoir and bailliwyk longyng or *p*erteynyng in recompens of the seid (15) hundred marc as it is conteyned in a Sedule annexed to this peticion more ouer please it vnto youre hynesse to graunte youre gracious (16) *let*tres vnder youre pryvy Seall directe vnto youre Tresorer and barouns of your Eschequer comaundyng them to discharge all (17) other fermers of all maner fermys rentis and charges of and for the seid Manoir bailliwyk londys tene*m*entis and Rentis with all their (18) apportenance fro the seid xiij. day of Nouembre duryng þe lyfe of youre seid besecher And he shall prey to god for you

(19) (Moleyns' autograph postscript) Þe kyng at his maner of kenyngaton þe v*the* day of maij þe xvij yere of his regne (20) bi þadvise of his consail graunted þis bille And þat þe besecher haue þe mane*r* þat he here (21) asketh so þat þe ouerpluse of þe saide maner a bove C marc valew by þe yer he paye vnto þe (22) kyng And þat þe keper of þe p*r*iuay seall do make Suffisaunt warant vn to þe Chaunceler (23) þat he hereupon do make le*t*tres pat*entes* in forme of þe cedule annexed here to soo þat hit a corde (24) with þis endocement Beyng p*re*sent yn tyme of þis graunte þe duc of Glouce*ster* þe Cardynal (25) and þe thre Officers
Adam moleyns
Also þat he make suffisaunt warant vn to þe Tresorer (26) and þe Barons of þeschequyr to make discharge vn to þe ffermers (&c)¹ yn maner as hit is a bove desired
Chancery hand
¹ superior insert

145

1438   E28/60/47   Petition to the Council concerning the Ship Maryknight. Moleyns' notation at the end.

(1) Vnto the kyng oure souuerayn lord and his most discrete and sage Counsell

Be yt remembred that how a ship called (2) Maryknyght of Amsterdam in Holand of wiche the Maister ys called Petre Van ley went with certein Merchaundiseʒ ynto Iseland (3) and there was lade with stokfissh and other merchaundiseʒ and the Merchantʒ ther yn cleped Copeman Iohn William (4) Sale and Heyn Rosen with other of Amsterdam and Clays Williamsone Van Herlam. And so yt happed the seid ship Maister and Merchauntʒ (5) to mete with a Ship of Hull with xl men ther yn vnder the costes of Irland at the feste of Michelmasse last passed At (6) whiche tyme the seid shippes with the persones of bothe the seid parties were Sworn togedir to be either others frende with (7) oon assent and promisse And so as frendes they sailed togedir to Crakfarwes in Irland and there they leyn and communyd togedir (8) as brethern eche of theym cheryng other duryng iij wokes and fro thennes they sailed togedir to Dalkesound in Irland and there they (9) came ynne on seynt lukes Even last passid And the sonday folwyng they herd masse and ete and drank togedir in Develyn And w(h)ile¹ the (10) seid Maister and Merchauntes of the seid ship called Maryknyght were at diner the said persones of the Ship of Hull (11) hyred theym hors priuely and rode downe to the seid shippes And there the same sonday they toke the said ship cleped Maryknyght (12) lade thanne with Stokfyssh oyle and lynnencloth and other Merchaundises to the value of xvC li And thanne come Englissh folk (13) to the seid Merchauntʒ of the Maryknyght and bad theym beware whom they had lefte yn their Ship sayng that yt was likely be (14) taken And there vppon the seid persones of the ship of Hull goyng to do the said wrong / yaf to oon henry wales Gentilman duellyng (15) abowte the coste of Develyn x marcʒ to lette and arreste the seid Maister and Merchauntʒ wan they come downe toward (16) their Ship cleped Maryknyght And so they were met and sonderly prisoned yn dyuerse prisons that they myght not Reskewe (17) their owne ship And thanne the Maier and Merchauntes of Develyn / seyng the seid Maister and Merchauntʒ of the sayd (18) Maryknyght hauyng the said wrong and vntrue enprisonement with theire strengthth and poiar had theym out of prison and lete (19) theym walke at large At wiche tyme the seid mysdoers of the ship of Hull were goon forth and sailed away with bothe the seid Shippes (20) to Portile in Northwales And there the seid William Sale Merchaunt of the seid ship cleped Maryknyght happed come to (21) Portile And there he Aspied iij of the seid Misdoers that toke the said Maryknyght whiche iij ben called Thomas Crathorn Merchaunt (22) of york William Cokeram Merchaunt of Beuerle and William Abbot Merchaunt of lynne And there the same William Sale (23) did to be arrestid the seid iij mysdoers and bothe the said Shippes and godes the whiche ben vnder arest and kepyng of (24) Henry Noreys depute to the Chamberleyn there And thanne tho iij Mysdoers seiden wan they were so arestid that they were not (25) gylty of the seid wrongfull takyng of the seid ship cleped Maryknyght with the said Merchandiʒes And the same William Sale seid to (26) theym that he wold fyght with the seid iij Mysdoers that they were at the said mysdede doyng And thanne seid oon of the same mysdoers (27) that ys called Thomas Crathorne that he wold fight with the said William Sale that yt was contrarie that the same William (28) saide And there vppon they cast eche to other their gloves whiche were taken vp and ensealed by Henry Noreys Depute of the Chamberleyn (29) of Northwales And so the same Depute arrested bothe the seid iij Mysdoers and also the said William Sale to be kept til (30) the said mater be tried byfore you gracious lord and your noble counsell Werfore Iames Rose Sederyk Iohnsone and Copeman Iohn (31) Merchauntʒ of the said ship cleped Maryknyght besechith you of your speciall grace to considre this premisseʒ and by (32) the avise of your worthy and noble counsell ther vppon to sende your letters of priuat seale directid to the said Henry (33) Noreys comaundyng hym by the same to come (hym self aswel as to bryng)³ te said William Sale as the said Thomas (34) Crathorn William Cokeram and Williamm Abbot to appere byfore you and your seid counsell (at Westmynstre)³ yn þe (35) quynʒisme of Trinite terme next comyng and furder more to answere and receve that ye and your counsell wol awarde in this (36) partie And more ouer yeuyng yn charge to the said henry to kepe sauely and suerly the said shippes and Merchaundiseʒ til he haue other (37) comaundement of you vppon peyne of CC li for the loue of God and yn way of Charite

(Moleyns' endorsement) þe kyng bi þaduise (38) of his conseil graunted þis bille at Westminster þe xvj day of maij þe xvij yer and willed þe keper (39) of his priay² seal to do wryte lettres after þat þe case requyreth and as hit is desired here (40) aboue Beyng present þe Chauncele þe Erle of Saresberi and þe keper of þe priuay seal

.A.moleyns

Chancery hand

See *CPR 1436-41*, pp. 270, 501, for the fate of the unfortunate Maryknight.

¹ h superior insert   ² priay for priuay   ³ over erasure

146

1438   E28/62/10/40   Petition for Clarehall, Cambridge, to take over Godshouse Grammar School (right end water damaged)

(1) Please it vnto you our souerain lord graciously for to conceyve how þat with in this your Reamme of Ingelond / (2) is ful grete heuynesse and anyentisment of Clergie and of mayntenance of diuine seruice also

with in short tyme (3) like for to faile . . . defaute of Scolemaistres
of Gramer / where of as now ben almost none in the vniuersitees of
(4) Oxenford and Cambrigge ouer those þat most nedes teche and abide
stille there / suffisant to enforme yonge persones (5) in there Gramer
. . . which in this your Reamme / vndrestondyng of latyn / to the edify-
ing of cristen Soules makyng of euidences / to (6) rule Spirituel and
temporall necessarie / nor communicacion with Straungers and Alientʒ
amonge your (7) pleople may not well be hade / And also how that
thurgh defaute of such maistres of Gramer þe moste part of Gramer
Scoles in (8) this land in Contrees where as the presenter here of hath
ben conuersaunt and riden stande þe dores shet in Somoch (9) that as
he knoweth and credibly is informed on the Est partie of the wey /
ledyng from Hampton to Couentre / and (10) so forth no ferther North
than Rypton / ben voide .lx. scoles. and mo / beside all other Countres
of this your lond the which haue (11) ben occupied all at ones with
in this .l. yere. wherfore your continuel bedeman and Prest william
Byngham person of (12) Seint Iohn ʒacharie of london the presenter
of this matere consideryng how that in Cambrigge a ryght devoute (13)
fader called maister Richard kendale / þat there somtyme taught Gramer
set a ful spedy wey there toward / by a tretyce þat he (14) labored /
And also your seid bedeman and preest hertly desiryng þat a remedie
might be devysed ageyn the seid mischief / yf (15) it were in his power
/ hath so labored þat there is made / a poure loggyng ycalled Goddeshous fast by Clarehalle in Cambrigge / (16) where in poure Children
shull haue free herbergage for thre . . . foloweth here bynethe / where
in ben some yonge poure scolers and moo (17) shull be as god sendeth
sustinance for theim / that by goddes grace shull be drawen forth there
/ for to comense in Gramer (18) and also be ordered preestes and than
ordeyned in to diuerse Contrees of this land there to porveye theim annuels and seruices (19) and to teche Gramer in places / where Scoles
ben voide and stande now desolat thurgh the seid defaute Of the which
seid scolers (20) And of other as your seid Preest hath done / afore
this tyme / withouten supportacion and helpe / no lenger he may (21)
continue / the which to him is ful hevy / and therfore he hath labored
vnto diuerse notable persones of your people (22) in tyme comyng /
so that he trusteth þurgh the Suffraunce of god and by your gracious
licence of a mortisment / þat (23) there shall be lyflode ordeyned for
to fynde and sustene with all perpetuelly and continuelly scolers to
gouerne (24) theim / Consideryng most gracious lord / how þat for
Maistres and Scolers of all other liberall Sciences / vsed in your seid
(25) vniuersitee / liflode is ordeyned and endowed / savyng onely for
Scolers of Gramer which . . . and grounde of all þe seid (26) facultees

And there vpon graciously for to graunte licence to the Maistre and Scolers of Clarehalle in the vniuersite (27) of Cambrigge for to resceyue þe forseid Mansion and other lyflode of þe value of . . . by yere wiþouten fyn or fee of such as is nat holden (28) of you by knyght Ceruice immediatly / in fortheryng of the same entent / after þe fourme of a Cedule to this (29) bille annexed in quiknyng and reviguryng of the said faculte of Gramer that as now is bothe seek and febyll / þurgh the seid (30) defaute / in all parties of this your Reamme of Inglond / by the which said lyflode / from hennes forward / socour may be (31) ordeyned for drawyng forth of Maisters of Gramer in Goddeshous aforseid / after þe fourme rules and statutes / as is (32) contened in the seid Cedule hereto annexed / So þat by the ferveure and swetnesse of your high deuocion hertly fixed in god (33) and by the labours of your seid poure Prest this so nedefull and meritorious work / may come to gode effecte / for the loue of (34) god and in wey of Charitee.

Chancery hand

147

1438   E28/61C   Petition of Thomas Colland, Oxford Scholar

(1) (Superscript notation of grant; non-Chancery secretary hand) My lord hath grantid this bille

To the kyng oure souerain (2) lord

Humbly bisecheth Thomas Colland of Oxinford in Oxinford shire Scoler. that where he is endited the Monday next befor the (3) feste of Seint George the yere of your regne the xv at Oxinford before William Brampton maier of the same Toun William herberfeld (4) Thomas Daggevile and Iohn North Aldermen Robert Tretherf and Robert Walford Baillifes of the same at the vieu (5) of frankplegge there holden that the forseid monday the seid Thomas Colland by the name of Thomas Colland of Oxinford (in Oxinford Shire)[1] Scoler in the feste (6) of translacion of seint Thomas the martir last then passed at Oxinford an hors of hug Gerard price of xv s. felonousely (7) shuld haue stolen. the whiche enditement was to hym purposid maliciousely he ther of not beyng gilty as all the cuntre (8) knoweth. Wherfore please to yow souerain lord of your merciable grace. considering that your seid pouere oratour (9) is not gilty of the seid felonie ne is not of power to sue his deliueraunce in no manere wise. and that he was the (10) tyme that the seid felonie was supposed and longe before at london in the seruice of the Bisshop of Bangore. to graunte (11) your lettres of pardon to him of the seid felonie. for the loue of god and in the wey of charitee.

(Same hand as superior notation) H chambellan of Ingland
(Another hand) Lettre ent feust faite a Westminstre le xxiij Iour de Iuyn Lan &c xvije.
Chancery hand
¹ superior insert

148

1438   E28/61/3   Royal Warrant, written by Adam Moleyns
(Initialed) R h
(1) The king commandeth the keper of his priue seal to make suffisant warrant to þe Chaunceller of England that he by (2) lettres patentȝ yeue licence vnto such lordes as shal be atte tretee of peas at Caleys &c to haue stuff with (3) þeim of gold siluer coyned & in plate & al oþer þinges such as is behoueful to euch of þeim (4) after þair estat: & þat þe same (keper of)¹ our priue seal make heruupon such seueralx warrentes (5) As þe clerc of þe counseil can declare him after þe kinges entent / And also þat þe said keper of (6) our priue seal / make a warrant to þe Tresorer of England & to þe Chamberlains to paie Robert whitingham (7) such wages for þe viage of Caleys abouesaid (for a quarter of a yere)¹ as so apperteineþ to a Squier to take (8) / And also a noþer warrant to þe said Tresorer & Chaumberleins to put in gage such Iewelx as (9) he hath in keping of þe kinges for money to be emploied in second paiement for þarme into Normadie (10) at þis time: yeven² at Wyndesore þe secunde day of [Iul]³ Iuin. þe . xvij yer of þe kyng
Adam Moleyns
Moleyn's non-Chancery hand
¹ superior insert   ² smaller, more legible hand   ³ cancelled

149

1439   E28/63/42   Petition of Richard, Earl of Salisbury
(Initialed) R h
(1) To þe kyng our souerain lorde
Bisecheth humbly Richard Erl of Salisbury of your grace especial (2) to graunt hym þe keping of your towne & Castel of Carlele & of þe West march toward Scotland to haue fro (3) þe ende of þe terme þat þe bisshop of Carlele in theym now hath / to þende of ten yeres þen (4) next filowyng in such fourme as þe said bisshop þe saide kep-

ing hath Takyng þe said Erl for þe same keping (5) euery yere during þe same x yeres M*l* li in such manere fourme & places & with such surties & preferrementʒ (6) of & to Paiementʒ of þe somme aforsaide / as þe said bisshop hath for þe keping of þe said towne Castel & (7) march by (indentures and)¹ your lettres patentʒ þervpon to be made in due fourme / to þe said Erl / (8) And if it happen þe said bisshop. in eny wise to leve þe keping of þe towne Castel & march aforsaide. afore þende (9) of his saide terme. þat þen þe said Erl. may haue þe keping of þe same towne Castel & march for x (10) yeres next filowyng after þat levyng / takyng þe said Erl for þe same keping euery yer of þe same x yeres (11) M*l* li in such manere fourme place & wyth such surties & preferrementʒ to hym by your lettres (12) patentʒ to be made / as It is abouesaid. And þe said Erl shal within iiij yeres next after (his)² entree / to þe said (13) keping do repair þe dungeon of þe said Castel. so þat he yerly haue during þe same iiij yeres l. li to be (14) taken of þissuʒ profitʒ & Reuenuʒ commyng of þe shir of Cumberland / by þe handes of (15) þe shirif þere for þe tyme beeyng by your lettres patentʒ aforsaide of graunt also þerof (16) to hym to be made. consideryng þat if þe said dungeon wherof (partie be)³ downefallen: hooly fal downe / as It is liche (17) to do but if hasty reparacion þerof be made / wol cost yow M*l* li & more / for . . .³ And þat (ye)¹ yif nowe . . .⁴ (18) for þe said keping. l li yerely more. þen þe said Erl desireth to haue (of yow)¹ for þe said keping And (he shal pra)y³ god for yow

Non-Chancery hand
¹ superior insert   ² blotted   ³ washed   ⁴ erasure

150

1439   E28/59/74   Royal Warrant written by Adam Moleyns

(1) þe xxviij day of April þe xvij ye¹ of þe kyng he biþaduise of his consail at Westmi*n*stre (2) charged þe keper of his priuay seal to do make warent suffisaunt vn to þe Tresorer of Englond and þe Chamberlayns (3) to paye by wey of Reward to Iohn lowyngbargh & henri munke (maysters of þe gunnys)² for them and for þer (4) iiij seruantes xxvj marc v s ij d. Beyng present þarchebischopp of Canterbury þe Bischoppes of (5) Bath and Lincoln þe Erlis of Stafford Saresbury and Suffolk the Tresorer and þe keper of þe priuay seal Adam moleyn

Moleyn's non-Chancery hand
¹ ye sic   ² superior insert

151

1440 E28/65/27(4) Privy Seal: Royal Grant. Note by Thomas Bekynton.

(Initialed) R h

(1) Right trusty and welbeloued For asmuch as the xij. day of September last passid we haue enfeffid by oure (2) Le*tt*res paten*tes* the worshipfull fadres in god Henry the Archebusshop of Canterbury. Iohn Bisshop of Bathe and of Welles. (3) Iohn Bisshop of Saint Asse*ph*. William Bisshop of Salesbury and oure trusty and welbeloued Cousyn William Erl of Suff*olk* (4) and also oure welbeloued Iohn Som*er*seth Thomas Bekynton Richard Andrewe. Adam Moleyns Clerk. Iohn hampton. Iames ffenys (5) Squiers and William Tresham in alle the Priouries Manoirs Landes tenemen*tes* Rentes se*r*uices pensions por*c*ions apportes (6) and possessions withynne oure Royavme of England and Wales and the Marches of Wales whiche ben callid Priouries and possessions (7) Aliens than being in oure handes. And also the Rentes and fermes whiche any p*er*sonne than was bounde to yelde vnto vs for (8) suche Priouries and possessions to haue and to holde with the Reuersions aswel of the same Priouries and possessions whan (9) they shal falle as of any other Priouries and possessions whiche (10) any p*er*sone holdith hath or occupieth for t*er*me of lif by the lawe of England in dower terme of yeres or any other (11) wyse to the seid Archebusshop Bisshops Erl Iohn Thomas Richard Adam Iohn Iames and William and to their heires and Assignes (12) from the fest of Pasche last passid for eu*er*e As in oure seid le*tt*res theruppon made hit is conteyned more at large (13) We wol therfore and charge yow that on al wise alle the Assignemen*tes* of the seid Priouries and possessions Rentes and (14) fermes or of any of theym made to any persone or persones sithen the seid fest of Pasche last passed ye doo theym to be callid (15) again and that ye chaunge alle suche assignemen*tes* So that the hool Reuenuȝ of the same Priouries possessions Rentes and (16) fermes from the same fest forthward may be hadde and receyued by the seid feoffes withoute any interrup*c*ion aftre theffecte (17) of oure seid g*r*aunte And thes oure le*tt*res shal be vnto yow suffisant warant. Yoven vndre oure priuee seel &c.

(Note in Bekynton's hand) (18) The k*i*ng hath co*m*maunded le*tt*res after this forme to passe vnder his (19) p*ri*ue seal. At Wyndesor þe iiij day of November. A*n*no &c xix. Bekynton

To þe Tres*ur*er of Engla*n*d

Chancery hand

152

1440(?)   SC1/61/59   Privy Seal: Summons to the Court of Chancery
(1) By þe kyng.
Trusty and welbeloued: Sith we be enformed þat ye in þe Contree þere (2) as ye be. haue committed dyvers riottes and attempted dyvers thynges contrarie to oure lawes and pees: we (3) wolle and charge you: þat ye all excusaions ceessyng be afore vs in oure Chauncellarye wheresoeuer it be þe (4) .xvij. day of Augst next commyng þere to aunswere to þe matieres abouesaid: and such othr as shalbe declared vnto (5) you at youre commyng And we wolle ye leue not this in anywise Yeuen vnder oure priue seal at Westminstre. þe .xxiij. Day of Iuyl
Brewester
Chancery hand

153

1440   E28/64/27   Petition of William, Abbot of Bury St. Edmunds
(Initialed) R h
(1) To the right heigh and myghty prince most Christien kyng oure althir souerayn (2) lord
Mekely besechith youre humble and trewe chapeleyn Willyam Abbot of youre Monasterye at Bury to whiche Monasterye (3) youre noble progenitoures whos soulys god reste as to the place of (theire)[1] deuout fundacion han grauntyd at reuerence (4) of the blissed kyng and martir seynt Edmond there incorrupte bodyly in shryne restyng notable ffraunchise and ful (5) special pruilegijs as in the chartris of there graunt it is clerly specified whiche fraunchise be youre chartre is at this (6) day graciously confermyd And for the defence and sauyng of the right of the seid fraunchise Abbotis of the seid Monasterye (7) chapeleynes vn to youre noble progenitoures gaf out of there lyflode before tyme of mende to a styward certeyn (8) maneres to the intent that the seid chapeleynes and alle there successoures shuld not be trobled for the seid fraunchise but (9) quietly preyse and serue god prayend deuoutly for there foundoures as religious and contemplatif personys shulde (10) But sithe it is so that now of late tyme dyuers mysdoerys coveryng them vndir lordchipe dayly make resistence and interrupte (11) the fraunchise ayens all good reule of the lawe of youre rewme and wil suffre no lawe to be executyd ther yn of the (12) whiche to gret

inco*n*uenyence myght falle ffor as moche that the styward of the fraunchise whiche be inheritaunce ocupieth (13) the maneres tho were youyn oute for defence and conseruyng of the seid fraunchise is duellyng and abydyng in a foreyn chyre (14) wherfore youre seid chapeleyn may not in tyme of nede haue redy recurs vn to hym And the Erl of Suf*f*o*lk is (15) a gret lord in the cuntre and goodly to youre seid Monasterye to whom youre seid chapeleyn many tymes may haue redy recurs Lyke it vn to (16) youre heighnesse and good g*r*ace to yeve hym in comaundement vndir youre grete seal to supporte maynteigne and defende youre (17) seid Monasterye youre seid chapeleyn and alle your p*r*estys his bretheryn wyth alle othir thynges tho of right longyn vn to (18) them And correcte suyche p*er*sonys as be there mysdoerys and opp*r*esseres so that alle youre prestys be occasion therof (19) may here aftir more quietly preyse and serue god and pray to hym for the wel and bonchef of youre heighnesse wythoute troble of opp*r*essioun (20) yn honour of oure lord and of charite.

(Latin note by Adam Moleyns follows)
Chancery hand
[1] superior insert

154

c 1440   E28/27/71(124)   Privy Seal: Summons to appear before the Privy Council (draft with addresses)

(1) By the king

Trusty and Welbeloued: We be credebly enfourmed that what by you and other of youre affinitee and . . .[1] in the (2) Countrees where as ye be wherethurgh oure paix is gretely troubled and broken to the greet hurt . . .[1] poeple dwellyng in the Contree (3) there to oure Right greete displeasire: Wherfor we woll and charge you strang(ly)[1] that ye may forfaite vnto vs and (to)[2] ren into oure (4) greuous indingnac*i*on / that fromhensforward ye cesse and do be cessed . . .[1] affinitees and alliaunces alle suche (riotous)[2] reules (5) and goue*r*naunces and that ye ne do neither soeffre to be doo . . .[1] affinitees any thing that myght be to the trouble or breche (6) of oure saide paix or in any wyse sarue therto . . .[1] persone afore vs and oure Counsaill at oure Paloys of Westm*i*nster in the (7) .xv*me*. of saint Michell next commy(ng)[1] to answere to suche matiers as that shall thanne be shewed and declared vnto you at youre (8) comyng / And . . .[1] priue seal at Westm*i*nstre the .viij. day of Iuyl:

(Addresses) lord of Wesperlande   Robert Ogle Knyght   lorde Clyfford Robert Ogle Squier Baron of Graystok Roger Thornton Iohn Neuil knyght Mair of Neucastell Thomas Neuil knyght The Sherief of Neucastell Thomas Percy Robert Rodys³ Rauf Percy

Chancery hand

¹ washed and torn   ² washed   ³ different hand

155

c 1440   SC1/61/60   Privy Seal: Summons to the Court of Chancery

(1) By the kyng

Trusty and Welbeloued. ffor certaine causes and consideracions / vs and oure counsaile specially (2) moeuyng We woll be þauis and assent of oure saide counsaile and straitely comaunde you that ye do bring þe body of (3) Laurence de bona villa late Priour of þe hous of Marie Mawdeleyn of Golclyff in Wales before vs in oure Chauncellarie / (4) where so euere it shall be withynne þis oure Royaume of Englande / at þe quinszeme of saint Michel next (5) commyng And þat ye leue not þis in enny maniere / Vpon þe peyne of .VC. li. Yeuen vndre oure priue seal at Westmonstier þe .xj. day of September.

Chancery hand

156

1441   E28/66/34   Royal Indenture

(1) THIS ENDENTURE MADE bytwix the Kyng oure souuerain Lorde on þat one part and William Pyrton Squier on þat other (2) part. Wittenesseth / that the said William is witholden with þe kyng lieutenant of his Castell of Guysnes / fro þe .ix. day of (3) Ianuer last passed duryng þe terme of vj. yere þenne next folowing / And the said william shall haue continuelly with him (4) abidyng vpon þe saufgarde of þe said Castell duryng þe saide tyme .l. men of Armes on foote himself accompted (5) onely on horsbak and .l. Archiers on foote / takyng for him self .ij s. on þe day for euerich of þe saide men of Armes (6) .viij. d. and for euerich of þe saide Archiers on fote. vj d a day duryng þe werre Of þe which wages þe (7) saide william shall be paied for him and his saide Retenue for a quarter in hand at þe makyng of þees endentures & so (8) fro quarter to quarter at the beginnyng of euery quarter

duryng þe (tyme)¹ aforesaide by þe handes of þe Tresourer of (9) Caleys for the tyme being Of þe which paiement the said william shall receiue for him and his saide Retenue / þe thrid peny in (10) vitailles couenables and at suche price as þey be worth at Caleys þe tyme of þe deliueryng of hem by þe (11) handes of þe said Tresourer / and yf þe said Tresorer may not performe þe thrid peny in vitailles as afore (12) it is saide. he shall performe in monoye to the same william all þat that he shall lak duryng þe tyme (13) aforesaide / And yf it fortune that þe kynges Aduersairs be of suche myght þat by liklinesse þe saide Castell (14) be put in grete perill of enny sodeine aduenture by trewe espiall. withouten þat it were stuffed with greter nombre of (15) men of Armes & Archiers that þen þe said william shall aduertise þe kyng and his counsaile þerof and þey (16) to pourueye him in all hast possible oute of þe Royaume of Englande or oute of þe towne of Caleys vnto þe nombre (17) of .CC. persones men of Armes & Archiers or within after þe discrecion of þe kynges counsaile and as þe cas. requireth (18) Also yf þe kyng for enny cause moeuyng him and his counsaile woll resume into his handes his saide Castell within þe saide (19) tyme / the forsaide william shall haue warnyng þerof half a yere afore þe day of his discharge of þe said (20) Castell by lettres vnder þe kynges grete or priue sealx and in lyke wyse þe saide william shall yeue (21) warnyng vnto þe kyng or his counsaile by an half yere / that if he for sekenesse lak of paiement or other cause resonable may not (22) occupie þe saide lieutenancie So þat the kyng may purueye a newe lieutenant þer and þe said william (23) to stande discharged ayenst þe kyng withouten enny empeschement in tyme commyng / And the kyng oure souuerain lorde shall (24) haue aswell þe thrid partie of wynnynges of werre / of þe saide william as þe thridde of þe thriddes / (25) whereof þe persones of his saide Retenue shall be answeryng vnto him of þeire wynnynges of werre / be þey prisoners (26) prayes or other þinges taken by werre and all droitȝ of werre accustumed / Of þe which thriddes and thridde (27) of thriddes / and also droitȝ þe said william shall by his othe or by þe othe of his executour or executours of his (28) testament trewely answere to þe kyng oure saide souuerain lorde in his Eschequier at Caleys / And also þe said william (29) and þo of his saide Retenue shall haue all maniere prisoners þat shall be taken by hem. duryng þe said tyme except (30) princes and sones of Princes / mareschalx & lieutenantȝ generalx and þo þat bere þe armes of ffraunce except also (31) him þat calleth him Duc of Bourgoigne and all his mareschalx and lieutenantȝ generalx / the which shall remayne and be (32) prisoners vnto þe kyng oure said souuerain / lorde and for þe which he shall make resonable agreement to him or to hem þat (33) so shall take þeime And þe saide

william hath vndertake sauely to kepe the saide Castell to þe worship and proufit of (34) oure said souuerain lorde the kyng duryng þe tyme aforesaide and not to deliuere þe saide Castell to enny persone bot to (35) our souerain lorde þe kyng abouesaide / or to his heirs kynges of Englande or at þeire commaundement by þeire (36) lettres of grete or priue sealx In wittenesse of which þing to þe partie of þis endenture (37) remaignyng with þe kyng oure saide souuerain Lorde þe saide william hath putte his seal. Yeuen at westminstre þe (38) x day of feuerer þe yere of þe Regne of the kyng oure said souuerain lord xixe.
   Chancery hand
   [1] torn

157

1446   SC1/44/13   Signet of Queen Margaret: Letter concerning a case in Chancery

(1) By the Quene

Right worshipful fader in god / our Right trusty and right welbeloued / We grete you wele. And for asmuche (2) as the proctours of our seruant Bawdewyn Saheny of Spynall marchant / haue doon vs to be enfourmed that the action & plee (3) hanging / bitwix the said Bawdewin & oon william Bowes of york marchant / touching certeine money whiche hath be delaied on (4) þe part of the said william / this viij yere or more / as It is said / is nowe broughte lawfully vnto the point of (5) sentence / to be yeuen in the Courte of Chauncellerie: We therfore pray you hertly sith that ye haue be at al times for our sake (6) vnto þe said Bawdewin good and especial lord in his Right: ye wil now in his absence conclude your (7) tendernesse & faueur vnto his proctours / and In as goodly hast / as ye may by lawe trouth & gode conscience to procede / to (8) Iuggement shewing herein suche expedicion and beniuolence / as ye haue doo hiderto / As the cas hath Required / whereof we (9) thanke you hertly: In whiche thing ye shul mowe not oonly doon vs grete pleasance / but also vnto our Right entierly bestbeloued (10) fader the king of Sicile / in ministring thexpedicion of Iustice: Right worshipful fader in god / our (11) Right trusty and Right welbeloued. Our lord haue you in his blessed keping Yeuen vnder our signet at my lordes (12) Castel of Windesore the viij day of Ianuer

   Chancery hand
   Commission recorded *CPR 1441-46*, p. 30; deposition *CCR 1441-46*, pp. 444-45.

158

1450   C49/26/18   Minutes of Council Action
(Initialed) R h

(1) Memorandum that the kyng by thaduise of his counseil hath ordeined graunted & appointed that al maner assignementʒ (2) by tailles rered or made vnto sir Iohn Stourton Tresorier of the kinges house for thexpensis of the same house the xviij. day (3) of Iuyl last passed on certein (C)ollectours[1] of Custumes & subsidies in diuers portes in this lande fro the first day of (4) October last passed vnto the first day of October next commyng. to be made & rered a mountyng to the somme of xij Ml li for (5) thexpensis forsaide vnto the said Tresorier of household shal specially be preferred & paide asferforth as good wil (6) growe. wherof they may be contente afore al other assignementʒ made. or to be made on the same be it by tailles grauntes. patentʒ. (7) or writtes vnder the grete seal or lettres vnder the priue seal or secret signet or in eny other wise to what (8) persone so euer hit. be. by the discrecion of þe Tresorier of England. eny act graunte ordenance or (9) appointement into the contrarie made. natwithstandyng / And that writtes excoutories. vnder the Kinges grete seal (10) be direct to the custumers for payement of the same assignementʒ. as often tymes as the case shal requere / by (11) þaduise of the saide tresorier of England. And how be it þat to somme conceites. it wol be thought þe (12) appointement made for preferrement of þe household shuld be into þe delaye & hurt of oþer (13) mennys paiementʒ yit neuertheles þe king willing aswel þastate & honour of his household to be (14) perfourmed & kept in al þing as it ought as þe gode & sure contentacion of his dettes to his poeple[2] (15) hath graunted & ordeined þis appointement for his household to be kept for þis yeer / (16) and wil by þe lordes of his counseil it be commaunde & seen how in þe meane tyme þe moost conuenient (17) waies & meanes of remedie may be had for þe good prouision & contenting of his astate aswel of his (18) household as in al oþer wise and for þe sure & good paiement. of his dettes. trusting with þe (19) mercy of god þerappon to conclude such remedies be þe yeer finisshed as may be to his worship and for (20) þe wele of his peple.

Also by the same aduise it is ordeined graunted & appointed. that special charge & commaundement (21) be yeven by the. king. in writing to the Chaunceller of Englande. and to þe keper of the priue (22) seal. þat thof by importune labour & pursute made. vnto the kinge it happen. eny thing of graunte to passe (23) his highnes. which might lette hindre or disapoint þappointement made for his household. they & euerich. of theym. (24) to whom hit. appertenith shal differre & put in suspence þexploit &. execucion. of al such. grauntes. to the tyme (25) the Tresorier of Englonde be commynde with therof. & his aduise. &. agrement be had therin as the case shal requere (26) for the proffit of the king. and for. the wele & good of his household.

And also semblably that this wryting may be. warrant (27) & a commaundement vnto your said Chaunceller. þat he in no wise suffre no maner of patentʒ ner (28) chartres passe seled without þe ful payement for the ffyne & fee. & for the seal of þe same as þe case requerith. (29) be it with the clause. saunʒ fyne ou ffee. or eny other wise.

And semblably by thaduise forsaid it is ordeined (30) þat thof by importunite. of sute or for lak of iust informacion ther passe the. king. his Chaunceller. or priue (31) seal. eny thing which might be preiudicial to þappointement forsaid ther be special charge & commaundement. (32) yeven to the tresorier of England þat for eny commaundement or writing vnder the. grete seal priue seal. or secret (33) signet to be direct. vnto hym. he dyffer þexecucion þerof. to the tyme he here the kinges commaundement & (34) wil therin by his mouthe. and that special charge &. commaundement be made vnto the Barons. of þescheker (35) in wryting. that they in al wise. differ þexecucion & allowans. þerof be it for pardon. special licens (36) or eny other graunte. be it neuer so special vnder the grete seal. priue seal. secret signet. or in eny other fourme. (37) to the tyme. they. haue taken. aduise. therof. of the Tresorier of England. and þat he yeve his assent þerto.

(38) And if so be that the said Tresorier of England be ouer ruled. or charged contrarie. to thente of the premises wherthrow (39) the reuenuʒ of the portʒ. wardes mariages vacacions. of Bisshopriches & of. Abbeyes priories or eny oth house of Rligion (40) forfaitures. casueltees. or other reuenus whatsom euir they be. may not com to his handes because of eny graunt warrant or (41) commaundement fro hens forth to be made for thenploiement of theym. to othir vse þan for the said household or elles if (42) ther be no shipping of wolles. by al the said tyme. þat then the said tresorier of Englonde be hold for excused & stande (43) discharged of his promise. made for the. household & bere no blame ner put in eny defaute thof. the appointement made (44) for the household be not kept aftir the forme it is ordeined for. and þat al the premises. be to hy(m)[1] exemplified. (45) articulerly vnder the grete seal.

And that for the good & sure accomplisshment of al the said. premises. the Chaunceller (46) of England and the Priue Seal. shal do make fro tyme. to tyme. as many & as large wryting*es* vnder the king*is* grete seal & priue (47) seal as to the. tresorier of England. shal bethought. behoful & necessarie in that behalf.

Non-Chancery hand
[1] torn   [2] 1-inch cancel line covering erasure

159

c 1450   Cotton Cleopatra F.IV. fol.126-27   Petition of Thomas Haseley, Clerk of the Crown

(1) Besecheth and ful humbly preieth youre pouere se*r*uiteur Thomas Haseley on of þe Clerkes of youre Corone graciously (2) to considere howe in the absense of that victorieux prince youre blessed ffader whom god assoile hym beyng in his sharp werris and (3) g*r*acious conquest of ffraunce and Normandie youre seide se*r*uitour be the co*m*maunde-ment of youre most g*r*acieux (4) vncle the duc of Bedford on whom god haue me*r*cy that tyme Regent of þis youre noble Roialme and aduys of alle the grete (5) counseill her a commission was assigned to take and areste Thomas Payn of Glamorganshire Walsshman that brak þe Tour of (6) London nowe beyng in Neugate su*m*tyme Clerk and chief conseillour to s*i*r Iohn Oldecastell Traitour atteint to your seid g*r*acious (7) ffader the whiche Thomas Payn as Traitour was in the feld armed a geins your seid fa(der)[1] with þe llollardes be side (8) seint Iames next Charyngcrosse and eschaped vn hurt or taken til your seid besecher aaccompanied atte his cost and all maner expenses (9) (with)[1] notable poiar be the space of v daies and vj nyghtes lay for hym in the most secrete wyse that þei coude: and so (10) with help and g*r*ace of most almyghty god youre seid se*r*uiteur toke hym and arested hym atte myd-nyght in a place beside your (11) Castell of Wyndesore where atte that tyme was þe Kyng of Scottes kept as prisoner to your seid ffader and that same nyght (12) this seid Traitour shulde haue broken the seid Castell be treson and goon with þe seid Kyng toward Scotland in proef wher of I (13) founde in þe Traitours purs a cedule wreten of alle places of giftes and loggynges appointed to hem fro Wyndesore vn to Edyn-bourgh (14) in Scotland and so he confessed the whiche Traitour and cedule I delyu*e*red to þe Bisshop of Duresme thanne Chaunceller (15) and William kynwolmerssh thanne Tresorer of þis your seide (n)oble[2] roialme and þe seid Traitour þanne was (16) her committed to prison til þe comyng a geyn of your seid most gracious fader into þis roialme from your seid (17) duchie of Normandie and þanne in his nexte parle-ment here in þe counseil chambre of þe seid parlement a fore your (18)

seid rightwys fader and alle his lordes present þere þe seid Traitour was brought and þe cedule aforeseid (19) and your seid suppliant in that presence examined of alle matiers abouesaid and othre circumstaunces and incidentʒ (20) and þe maner of takyng of hym atte whiche tyme your seide moste noble ffader declared and seide a fore all his lordes that (21) takyng plesid hym more þanne I hadde geten or Gyuen hym x. *ml* li for þe grete inconueniences that weren like to (22) falle in his longe absense oute of þis roialme and so committe(d)¹ this Traitour to þe Tour of London þere (23) saufly to be kept and þanne immediatly of his oune roiale largesse and bounteuous grace with outen axing of your seid (24) suppliant or eny man for hym graunted to hym xl. li a yere to take terme of his lif in what place in Inglond of hys that I (25) wold sauyng his oune demesne demesne³ landes and þe duchie of lancastre and commaunded þe seid Regent (26) Chaunceler and Tresorer gif your seid suppliant were not sped a fore his departyng oute of Inglond to spede hym in his absence in recompense (27) of his costes (expenses trewe diligentʒ acquitaill and labour a foreseid)⁴ a fore whiche spede youre seide fader was dede and (28) so his graunt void.

Item to considere howe your seid suppliant be þe commaundement and ordinance of your seid (29) ffader at his first parlement holden atte leycestre was sent fore to leycestre to appere a fore your seid blessed fader where he of his (30) oune mocion appointed assigned and ordeigned the seide suppliant seconde Clerk of his parlement with sir Iohn Frank (31) nowe Clerk of youre rolles that tyme chosen chief Clerk of þe parlement þat hadde and toke xl li yerely þerfore (32) while he occupied / and youre seide suppliant shuld hadde x li yerely as other men toke to fore hym the whiche office he occupied fro (33) þat tyme into youre þredde parlement hens holden atte westmynstre atte whiche he myght not be for grete sikenesse (34) and so departed and neuere com in þe parlement sithe that tyme and neuere hadde peny of alle his tyme of þe (35) seide .x. li. ne of þe seide xl. li ne non othre regard in no manere wyse

Item howe youre seide suppliant in the (36) tenthe yeere of youre roialme aspied and toke in youre ryver of Thamise tweye shippes fretted with wolle cloth and othre merchaundise (37) to a notable value and weren seiled and departed and no custume ne othre deuoirs to you souerain lord þerof due paied (38) wherefore alle was forfaited and be þe seid suppliant to his grete perell and labour taken and to you answered as it appereth of (39) record in youre escheker þe whiche coste the seide suppliant more thanne .xx. li whereof he sholde haue had half after the fourme (40) of statuyt and hadde no thyng

Item howe youre seid suppliant this same yeer of youre regne hath taken and arested (41) diuerse men empesched of high treson ymagined a geyns youre persone and mageste roiale and destruccion of youre land and (42) lawes the which he sent be youre roile commandement to youre presence be your Squyer Gilbert Parre the which were taken alle (43) atte his cost and many othre grete þinges doon to your highnesse and plesirs whiche were to longe to expresse here and nowe is (44) aboute moo /

The whiche thynges be youre seid highnesse conteined plese it to youre most benigne and abondant grace to considere (45) the longe and continuel seruice don be the seide suppliant to youre graunde fader and fader kynges of Inglond and to you (46) soueraign lord as it is a fore expressed and þe grete age of youre seid suppliant and in recompense of alle his costages (47) expenses and labours and diligences a foreseid of youre seide grace graunten to youre seide suppliant an annuitee terme of his (48) lif in manere and fourme conteined in the cedule to þis bill annexed / and youre writtes and allocate currant and dormant (49) for allowance of payement of the same withoute payement of eny fee for the seales of the same writtes

Chancery hand
Printed in Bentley, *Excerpta Historica*, pp.144-48.
[1] trimmed off   [2] rubbed   [3] demesne repeated at the beginning of the next line   [4] crease

160

1454-55   C1/24/79   Petition of Richard Sturgeon, Clerk of the Crown

(1) To the right noble and gracious lord the Erle of Salesbury Chaunceler of Englond

(2) Mekely bisech Richard Sturgeon that where he and on William hall were sesed in hure demene as in fee symple yn a certayn (3) parcell of lond yn the parych of Tottenham Called Sokettis lond and the saide Richard and William so sesed. the same (ha)ll[1] (4) by hure dede yaf to on Iohn lurchon and Nicholas Baly and to hure heires yn fee. to that entente that when they were required they (5) shulde make a st(at)e[2] ayen of the same parcell to the saide Richard and to his heires and his assignes yn fee for euermore. (6) And how be it that þe saide Iohn diuers tymes hath ben required by the same Richard to make to hym astate of the (7) sa(id)e[1] parcell accordyng to thentent of his feffement of the same parcell. that to doo the saide Iohn hath refused and yet doth to (8) make any such astate to the saide Richard. but kepeth still thesstate

to hym in this party made as ys a fore saide. to grete hurte to the (9) saide Richard / Wherfor like it to youre goode lordship to graunte seuerall. writtis sub pena directe to the saide Iohn as Well (10) as to þe saide Nicholas to a pere before you yn the Chauncery and there to be examyned vppon the content of this bill (11) and to doo as r(ight an)d² concience asketh and requireth for the loue of god and yn way of charite

(Latin notation of securities follows.)
Chancery hand
¹ torn   ² rubbed

PROCEEDINGS OF PARLIAMENT AND CHANCERY

161

1388   SC8/20/997   Petition of the Mercers of London

(1) (To)[1] the moost noble & Worthiest Lordes moost ryghtful & wysest conseille to owre lige (2) Lorde the kyng Compleynen if it lyke to yow. the folk of the mercerye of London: (as)[1] a (3) membre of the same Citee of many wronges subtiles & also open oppressions ydo to hem: by longe tyme here (4) bifore passed.

Of which: oon was where the eleccion of Mairaltee (5) is to be to the fre men of the Citee. bi gode & paisible auys of the wysest & trewest. at o day (6) in the yere frelich: there nought withstondyng the same fredam or (7) fraunchise: Nichol Brembre wyth his vpberers purposed hym the yere next after Iohn Northampton mair (8) of the same Citee: with stronge honde as it is ful knowen. & though debate & strenger partye. ayeins the pees: bifore (9) purueyde. was chosen mair. in destruccion of many ryght:

ffor in the same yere. the forsaid Nichol with outen nede ayein (10) the pees. made dyuerse enarmynges bi day & eke bi nyght: & destruyd the kynges trewe lyges. som with open slaughtre. (11) some bi false emprisonementʒ. & some: fledde the Citee for feere. as it is openlich knowen.

(12) And so ferthermore for to susteyne thise wronges & many othere. the next y(er)e[1] after the same Nichol ayeins (13) the forsaide fredam & trewe comunes did crye openlich. that no man sholde come to chese her mair. but such as were (14) sompned & tho that were sompned: were of his ordynaunce & after his auys. / And in the nyght next after folwynge. he did carye (15) grete quantitee of Armure to the Guyldehalle with which as wel straungers of the contree. as othere of with Inne were (16) armed on the morwe. ayeins his owne proclamacion. that was such: that no man shulde be armed & certein busshmentʒ (17) were laide. that when free men of the Citee. come to chese her mair. breken vp armed. cryinge with loude voice sle. sle. (18) folwing hem wherthourgh the peple for feere fledde to houses & other (hidi)nges.[1] as in londe of werre: adradde to be ded in comune.

(19) And thus yet hiderward hath the mairaltee. ben holden as it were of Conquest or maistrye: & many othere offices als. So (20) that what man pryue or apert in special that he myght wyte. grocchyng pleyned or helde ayeins any of his wronges: or bi (21) puttyng forth of whom so it were. were it neuer so vnpreuable. were apeched. & it were displesyng to hym Nichol. anon was (22) emprisoned. And though it were ayeins falshede of the leest officer. that hym lust meynteigne: was

holden vntrewe lige (23) man to owre kyng. for who reproued such an officer maynteigned bi hym of wronge or elles. he forfaited ayeins hym Nichol. & (24) he vnworthy as he saide: represented the kynges estat. / Also if any man. bi cause of seruyce or other leueful comaundement: (25) approched a lorde. to which lord he Nichol dradde his falshede to be knowe to. anon was apeched. that he was false to (26) the conseille of the Citee: & so to the kyng

And yif in general his falsenesse were ayeinsaide. as (27) of vs togydre of the mercerye. or othere craftes. or ony conseille wolde haue taken. to ayeinstande it: or as out of (28) mynde hath be vsed. wolden companye togydre how lawful so it were. for owre nede or profite: were anon apeched for arrysers (29) ayeins the pees. (&)[1] falsly many of vs: that yet stonden : endited. And we ben openlich disclaundred. holden vntrewe (30) & traitours: to owre kyng / for the same Nichol sayd bifor mair. Aldermen. & owre craft bifor hem gadred in place of (31) recorde. that xx. or xxx. of vs. were worthy to be drawen & hanged / the which thyng lyke to yowre worthy lordship. (32) by an even Iuge: to be proued or disproued. the whether that trowthe may shewe. for trouthe amonges vs. of fewe or elles (33) no man many day dorst be shewed. And nought oonlich vnshewed or hidde. it hath be by man now: but also. of bifore tyme. (34) the moost profitable poyntes of trewe gouernaunce of the Citee. compiled togidre. bi longe labour of discrete & Wyse (35) men: wyth out conseille of trewe men. for thei sholde nought be knowen ne contynued: in the tyme of Nichol Exton mair: outerliche were brent

(36) And so ferforth falsehede hath be vsed. that oft tyme he Nichol Brembre saide in sustenaunce (37) of his falshede: owre lige lordes wille was such. that neuer was such: as we suppose. He saide also whan he hadde disclaundred (38) vs. which of vs wolde yelde hym false to his kyng: the kyng sholde do hym grace cherise hym. & be good lorde to hym. And if (39) any of vs alle that wyth goddes help haue & shulle be founden trewe. was so hardy to profre prouyng of hym self trewe: (40) anon was comaunded to prisone. as wel bi the mair that now is: as of hym Nichol Brembre bifore

(Also)[1] we haue (41) be comaunded. oft tyme vp owre ligeaunce. to vnnedeful & vnleueful dyuerse doynges. And also to wythdrawe vs. (42) bi the same comaundement (fro)[1] thynges nedeful & lefful. as was shewed whan a companye of gode women. there (43) men dorst nought trauailleden barfote to owre lige lorde. to seche (gra)ce[1] of hym for trewe men as they supposed (44) for thanne were such proclamacions made. that no man ne woman sholde approche owre lige lorde for sechyng of grace & (45) ouermany othere comaundementʒ also. bifore

& sithen. bi suggestion & informacion of suche that wolde nought her (46) falsnesse had be knowen: to owre lige lorde. And lordes by yowre leue. owre lyge lordes comaundement to symple & (47) vnkonnyng men. is a gret thyng to ben vsed. so famulerlich: with outen nede. for they vnwyse to saue it mowe lyghtly ther ayeins forfait

(48) ffor thy graciouse lordes lyke it to yow to take hede. in what manere & where owre lige (49) lordes power hath ben mysused. by the forsaid Nichol: & hi(s vp)[1] berers for sithen (50) thise wronges bifore saide han ben vsed as accidental. or comune braunches outward: it sheweth wel. the rote (51) of hem is a ragged subi(ect)[1]. / or stok inward. that is: the forsaid Brere or brembre./ the whiche comune (52) wronge vses. & many other. if it lyke to yow: mowe be shewed & wel knowen bi an indifferent Iuge & mair (53) of owre Citee / the which wyth yowre ryghtful lordeship. ygraunted: for moost pryncipal remedye: as goddes lawe & (54) al resoun wole: that no domesman stonde togidre Iuge & partye: wronges sholle more openlich be knowe. & trouth (55) dor apere. And ellis. as amonge vs. we konne nought wyte in what manere. with(out a moch gretter)[2] (56) disese. sith the gouernaunce of this Citee standeth: as it is bifor saide/. / & wole stande whil vittaillers (57) bi suffraunce. presumen thilke states vpon hem. the which gouernaunce of bifor this tyme to moche folke yhidde: (58) sheweth hym self now open. whether it hath be a cause. or bygynnyng of dyuysion in the Citee & after in the Rewme: or no.

(59) Wherfore for grettest nede as to yow moost worthy. moost ryghtful & wysest lordes & conseille (60) to owre lige lorde the kyng. we biseche mekelich of yowre g(race coreccion)[3] of alle the wronges (61) bifore sayde & that it lyke to yowre lordeship. to be gracious menes to owre lyge lorde the kyng: that suche (62) wronges be knowen to hym. & that we mowe shewe vs & sith ben holden. suche trewe to hym: as we ben. & owe to ben.

(63) Also we biseche vnto yowre gracious lordeship. that if any of vs in (64) special or general. be apeched to owre lige lorde or to his worthy conseille bi comunyng (65) with othere. or approchyng to owre kyng. as wyth Brembre or his abettours with any wronge wytnesse beryng as that (66) it stode other wyse amonges vs here. than as it is now proued it hath ystonde / or any other wronge suggestion. by (67) which owre lige lorde hath ybe vnleeffullich enfourmed: that thanne. yowre worshipful lordship be such: that we (68) mowe come in answer to excuse vs / ffor we knowe wel as for by moche the more partye of vs. And as we hope for (69) alle: alle suche wronges han ben vnwytyng. to vs. or elles outerlich ayeins owre wille.

Proceedings of Parliament 197

And ryghtful (70) lordes. for oon the grettest remedye with othere. forto ayeinstonde many of thilke diseses afore saide (71) amonges vs: we prayen wyth mekenesse this specialich. that the Statut ordeigned & made bi parlement (72) holden at Westmystre in the sexte yere of owre kyng now regnynge: mowe stonde in strengthe & be excecut as wel (73) here in london as elles where in the rewme. the which is this Item ordinat(um)⁴ est (etc)⁴
(Three lines in Latin follow.)
Hand Textura / Chancery
Printed *RP*, III.225; CD, pp.33-37; Morsbach, *Neuenglischen Schriftsprache*, pp. 171-77; Emerson, *Middle English Reader*, p. 252; Kluge, *Mittelenglisches Lesebuch*, p. 42.
¹ torn   ² over erasure   ³ rubbed   ⁴ expanded

162

Before 1413   E28/29/69   Petition of Cecily Tikell of London

(1) Worschipfull Sires and my dere maistres In whom is my souereigne treste Bifore alle Creatures of my knoweleche (2) I comand me vnto ȝowr worthinesse with alle manere obeianse and mekenesse (3) Thokynge [ȝor]¹ ȝou with alle myn herte for þe grete godenesse and noble maisterschipe yat (4) ȝe hauen shewede to me Bifore þis tyme withouten eny cause of deserte in me Bishechynge ȝou þat ȝe (5) wol ben my helpe and cause of eacynge of myn Importable payne of longe enprisononement As I shal eueremor and with (6) oute fayuour do ȝou seruyce and plesance to my symple power Also speciali I praye ȝou þat In ese of me and (7) fortherynge of my simple persone ȝe wolde labor and trauaile for me to I myȝte Be brouȝte In to þe (8) kyngesbenche and so I meinprised to go at large vnderstandynge Gracious sires þat as touchyng . . .²costes þat ȝe (9) spenden in þis nede I shal so do to ȝou þat ȝe shul holde welapaide as sone þat I may speke with (10) my frende . . .² euermor deytyned woll þat I stonde destitute of alle manere helpe and frendschipe saue (11) only of goddes poruoiaunce In grete hynderance and destrucion of my powre astate And In þis manere I Bisechȝe (12) ȝou of helpe and þis to be done as hasteli as ȝe may to sende me a answer what ht plese ȝou to done In. (13) þis mater I write in grete haste in þe prisone of Neugate In þe feste of seynte luke þe iij day of (14) Nouembre

Le vre pour seruant Cecily Tikell þat dwellede . . .³ poules gate
Chancery hand
¹ cancelled   ² torn   ³ rubbed

163

1414   SC8/23/1143A   Petition of Thomas Paunfeld of Cambridgeshire

(1) To the worshipful and wyse syres and wyse Co*mm*u*n*es that to this p*re*sent p*ar*lement ben assembled

(2) Besecheth mekely ȝoure pore Bedeman Thom*a*s Paunfeld oon of the fre tenentȝ of oure liege (3) lord the kyng of his maner and tounshipe of Chestreton in the Shyre of Cambrigg: that ȝe wole considere how (4) that I pursuede diu*er*se billes by fore oure liege lord kyng henry the four the fader to oure liege lord the (5) kyng that now is and hise worchepeful lordes and co*mun*es in his p*ar*lement holden at West*m*i*nstre* (6) that x day of ffeuer the xiiij ȝer of his regne:

To the whiche billes myne adu*er*saries replieden by mouthe (7) and enformeden the kyng and the worshepeful lordes sprituelx and temporelx in that p*ar*lement: how (8) that I was outelawed by heye record of trespace wherethurgh that I ne oughte not to ben herd nor answered of no man*er* (9) compleynt in my billes writen but ȝif (it)[1] so were that I hadde brought my Chartre in myn hond wherby that (10) I myghte haue answered in lawe to alle man*er* of p*er*sones that ony replicacions wolden haue maked aȝeyns (11) ony article of my billes:

And worchepeful and discrete sires that myghte I not done that tyme: for (I wi)ste[1] not how I (12) was edited and outelawed of what man*er* trespace: but as Iohan Cokayn the Iustice recordede byfore (13) the kyng and made mencion at that tyme. whiche I trustede to god to haue proued by lawe by fore the kyng and the (14) worchepeful lordes and co*mun*es in that p*ar*lement that the p*ro*cesse of myn outelawerye was vnlawefully (15) made and al that longeth ther to: ȝif Iohan Cokayn the Iustice wolde haue brought in that record by fore the kyng (16) in the p*ar*lement and there to haue ben det*er*myned byfore hym and hise lordes and Co*mun*es afore seyde (17) (ȝo)r[1] they hadde dep*ar*ted thennes

ffor byfore hene of the p*er*sones that weren and ben (18) Commissioners vp on myn enditement wherby that I was outelawed: I myghte not haue ben remedied ne myne (19) neyghebores nother so sone at that tyme lyk as we oughten to haue ben of right and as me thoughte we shulde ben here: (20) and that was for cause of meyntenance that was aȝeyns vs and ȝit is. and that made me cause to come to that (21) heye Court of rightwisnesse: (þ)heder[1] to pleyne for to han declared thilke record aȝeyns my neighboures and me (22) vnlawefully mad and there sounere to han ben remedied of the wronges that we haue had by the Priour and Chanons (23) of Bernewelle and her meyntenors these .x.

ʒer (and)¹ more vnduely and vngoodly:

And now thanked be god (24) and the rightwisnesse of the discrete and trewe Iuges Sire william hankford and hise felawes: han after the laws of (25) the lond made me able for to ʒeue myne answeres in lawe as my symple wittes wole seruen me to alle maner (26) personnes that ony replicacions wolde maken aʒeyns ony of the articles of my billes after the (27) forme that sueth ʒif it like to the kyng: with swich conseil as he hath a(ss)igned¹ to (28) me and shal by the grace of god: for to declaren the entente of my billes for the kynges auantage and for (29) fortherynge of his trewe lieges better than I can in this heye Court of rightwisnesse:

And by cause that I am (30) of no power to pursue these materes in any other Court saue in this heye Court of rightwisnesse where as (31) most truste and hope to haue rightwisnesse and lawe rather than I shulde in ony other Court byfore ony of tho (32) personnes that weren and aren Commissioneres vp on myn enditement: for the heye meyntenance that I (33) knowe wel shuld be made aʒeyns me:

Also worchepeful sires: we beseche ʒow at the (34) reuerence of god: that ʒe wole praye to oure liege lord the kyng: that he wole fouche saf (35) of his special grace and his Ryal prerogatyf in this heye Court: to graunte me durynge my (36) pursuyte by the auctorite of his parlement to walken at large to pursue these materes that (37) ben folwynge in my bille: lyk as his gracious graunt was by the autorite of his parlement (38) and of his Rial prerogatif on good fryday at langeley the ferste ʒer of his regne at the (39) reuerence of oure lord god that deyede for vs alle as that day fil not withstondynge the (40) statut made vp on bonde bore men: which was holy pursued aʒeyns me whan I (41) was byfore the kyng the second day of march whan I was remitted to the prison of flete at the instance of (42) some of the Iuges til I hadde founde surete to pursue myn erroures and to reuerse myn outelawerye byfore (43) seyde:

And sithe the tyme that I was resseyued to meynprise by cause that I was endited of trespace (44) as an accessorie and not endited as a principal and delyuered out of prison at large by the (45) kynges commaundement in strengthyng and enhaunsyng of his Rial prerogatif that he grauntede to me by (46) the auctorite of his parlement:

ʒit myne aduersaries han pursued (47) me nowe and holden me in prison sithen seynt katerynes day twelve monthes last passed in to this (48) tyme. aʒeyns (the kynges graunt &)¹ ordinaunce no consideracion ne tendernesse hauynge in (49) my pore persone that am goddes cristene creature of my longe contynuance in prison (for these materes that ben)¹ (50) folwynge vij. ʒer and more to destroye me to the uttereste that

I shulde (51) no more haue come to the kynges presence to pursue my right but for to kepe (me stille in prison til I hadde)¹ (52) deyed for defaute of socour and helpe. and as it semeth to my (53) symple wittes there is litel charite of priestes whiche shulden cherice goddes christene (54) crature as the kynges trewe liege man:

And therfore I beseche ȝow that ȝe wole prayen to oure liege (55) lord the kyng of his special grace that swich remedie may be mad at this present parlement by the (56) auys of hise wise lordes spirituelx and temporelx in sauynge and encresynge of the kynges prerogatif in (57) tyme comynge and in fertherynge of hise trewe lieges after that he hath graunted hise graciouse (58) grauntes to ony of hise lieges: that fro hennes forward no persone of his Rewme deferre ony of hise (59) lieges fro hise graciouse grauntes that he hath graunted in esement and in fortheryng of hise (60) trewe lieges: and that vp on a suff(is)ant¹ peyne payinge to the kyng and a nother peyne payinge to (61) the partie so defferred fro the kynges graunt:

And also that ȝe wole praye the kyng (62) to ȝeue in charge to myne aduersaries whanne they comen to his worchopful presence to asken a (63) copie of my bille: that they wryten her replicacions aȝens the articles of myne billes by a day (64) assigned by oure liege lord the kyng vp on forfeture of her ferme: wherby that I may haue a copie ther of to my conseill (65) which that the kyng hath assigned me and shal by the grace of god to make trewe relacion vnto the kyng (66) of her replicacions

And than to prayen oure graciouse liege lord by the auys of hise lordes (67) spirituelx and temporelx ȝif it lyke hym by a day assigned that ȝe discrete and wyse comons mowen (68) comen to his heye presence: whan that he is avised vp on her replicacions makyng and thanne after his (69) heye discrecion to ȝeue rightful Iugement vp on these same materes in sauynge of his owne right and in fortherynge (70) of hise trewe lieges for the loue of god and of seynt charite:

And also to praye oure liege lord of (71) his special grace that the peticions afore rehersed and alle othere peticions that ben folwynge after hise (72) graciouse (grauntes)¹ mowe ben enacted in the parlement rolle: and also to ȝeue in charge to (73) the Clerk of the parlement: that I may haue (a copye)¹ of the same for the loue of god and of (74) seynt Charite:

Also to ȝow worechepeful and wyse Comunes greuouseliche compleynen alle the kynges (75) tenentȝ of the Ryal lordshipe and tounshipe of Chestreton in the Shyre of Cambrigge: the (76) whiche holden of the tenure of anxien demeyn of the Rial Coroune longynge to oure souereyn lord the kyng as it (77) sheweth by oure euydence of old record in the book called Domesday thus begynnynge. Dominica villa regis E &c (78) in the kynges eschekker at Westminstre:

Also we greuouseliche (79) compleyne vs vp on the Priour and Chanons of Bernewell in the Shyre of Cambrigg byfore seyd and vp (80) her predecessour that was the kynges fermour how that they han (81) cleymed and ʒit cleymen the regalite and the frehold of the kynges lordshype and tounshipe of Chestreton in (82) the Shyre byfore seyd as for her owne with oute ony excepcion wher it is wel knowen by alle manere of (83) euydences that the konne shewen for hem self or ony man for hem. that they were but fermours to (84) the kyng: and now they are not as it sheweth by her chartres of king henry the thridde:

And vnder (85) colour of the regalite and of the frehold whiche they presumen wilfully to haue: they haue cleymed and (86) ʒit cleymen the kynges trewe lieges that ben hise fre tenentʒ annexed to his coroune: as for her (87) bonde bore men and her bonde lond holderes: wher it is wel knowen by alle manere of euydences that (88) they konne shewe for hem self or any man for hem that they ben fre tenentʒ and fre holderes to the (89) kyng in chief and the chiefte resert and principalite of the same lordshipe and tounshipe shal retourne to (90) the kyng and to his forseide Coroune as for oure chief and perpetuel lord of the fee:

And ʒit algates (91) the forseide Priour and Chanons han seid and ʒit seyn that they ben chief lordes of the fee and that the kyng (92) ne none of hise heires han nought to entremete of hem for no trespace ne for no forfait that euere they (93) diden or is possible by hem to be done: which is an heye preiudice to the kyng as vs semeth and and heye (94) destruction to hise trewe lieges that ben hise fre tenentʒ annexed to his worthy coroune:

(95) And also the forseid Priour and Chanons han cleymed and ʒit cleymen of hem vnduely and vntrewely (96) bonde seruages and customes for her singuler profyt and non auantage to the kyng ne to hise heires in (97) tyme comynge but in perpetuel destruction of the kynges fre tenentʒ afore seid and othere (98) seruages and customes than euere we or oure auncestres diden to any kyng. whan the same lordshipe and (99) tounshipe was in other kynges handes by old tyme and sithe tyme of mynde:

And for cause that we haue pursued (100) to oure liege lord the kyng / as for oure chief lord of the fee for to haue remedie and socour of the grete wronges mischiefs (101) and diseses the whiche we haue suffred these .x. ʒer and more vnduely and vngoodly: The forseide Priour (102) and Chanons han pursued aʒeyns vs a Commission of oyer and termyner after the forme of a (103) statut mad vp on bond bore men and bond lond holderes: which statut was made the ferste ʒer of kyng

(104) Richard the seconde in his tendre age with oute mencion excepcion or declaracion made of the same fre (105) tenentȝ of the fre tenure of the ryal coroune byfore seid:

And by strengthe and colour of the forseide (106) statut so generaly mad vp on bonde bore men and bonde londe holderes: the forseide Priour and Chanons (107) han vs endited by men of her owne clothyng and also by enquestes enbraced as for her bonde bore men: (108) to the which statut we fre tenentȝ of the coroune owe not obeye: for we be not in the cas of the (109) statut and ne oughte not to answere lyk as bonde men of byrthe shulde: for the whiche the forseide statut was made:

(110) ffor we be fre tenentȝ and fre lond holderes annexed to the worthy coroune of oure most souereyn lord. (111) the kyng and that we wele proue and declare by oure euydence wreten in the kynges eschekker at Westminstre: wherfore (112) we wole answere as fre men oughte to done and proue that the suyte of the commission byfore seide which is mad vp on bonde (113) bore men and bonde lond holderes: was wrongfully taken aȝeyns vs and al the proces that longeth ther to with (114) oute auctorite and power and that shal we proue by the grace of god:

Neuertheles the (115) forsaide Priour and Chanons of Bernewell han vs enprisoned as for her bonde bore men and oppressed vs by (116) duresce of prison to be bounde to hem and to othere persones in singuler obligacions in .ml.ml. li (117) that we shulde not pursue oure right ne the kynges right aȝeyns hem: but onely to ȝolden vs to ben (118) her bonde cherles and oure heires for euermore to oure vttereste perpetuel destruction and disheritance (119) to the kyng and to his heires for euere but we haue the sounere remedie by ȝouer most gracious socour (120) and helpe at this present parlement

And thus worchepeful sires ȝif this be suff(red)[1]: the (121) freest knyght or Squyre of the Rewme ȝif they be dwellynge tenentȝ vnder ony of the (122) religious that haue swiche lordshipes of the kynges to ferme may be put in prison by swych cohercion and (123) compulsse as (ye)[2] mischeuouse statut byfore seid sheweth and declareth: for to ben the moste bonde tenentȝ (124) of al the Rewme: also in the contre they shullen ben endited by enquestes enbraced by these dede religiouse (125) fermours: and that for cause of the grete profites and the grete extorcions that the Sherreues of the Shyres (126) resceyuen and done: they mowe haue no remedie of the lawe but onely enprisonned manaced and oppressed: (127) and ȝif ony consaill of the lawe hem wolde helpe after the cours and fourme of lawe: they shulle ben (128) put in prison as her conseilloures fa(c)tours[1] and abettouers and as they were bonde men to these (129) religious byfore seide in so moche that they shulle non other mercy haue ne non other remedie but only for (130) to ȝolden hem to ben her bond cherles for euere more and her heyres (alle the dayes)² of her lyues to these (131) dede religious fermours:

Wherfore we beseche ȝow mekely discrete and wyse Comunes of this (132) present parlement: that ȝe praye for (vs to ouer liege lord)¹ the kyng and to hise worchepeful (133) lordes of (this present)¹ parlement in sauynge of the right of the coroune of yngelond and of the fredam (134) (and the fraunchise that was)¹ endowed ther to in the tyme of oure worthy kynges progenitour (135) seint edward: that he wole haue compassion and pite of these grete mischiefs and (falsetes so done)¹ to hise (136) [to hise]³ fre tenentȝ of his coroune byfore seyd: and to ordeyne at ȝoure (137) prayere resonable and intierie remedie in this partie for (goddes)¹ loue and for seynt charite after (138) the (forme)¹ that sueth ȝif it be lykynge to ȝow:

That is to seyn that he wole (139) at ȝoure instance and prayer in sauynge of his owne right and in fortherynge of (his)² trewe lieges: ordeyne (140) at this tyme or ȝe departen hennes fro this present parlement with auys of hise wise (141) lordes and also by the assent of (ȝow wyse)¹ and worchepeful comons: such remedie that fro hennes forward (142) none swiche commissions be take nor pursued aȝeyns the kynges fre tenentȝ annexed (143) to his worthy coroune by no religious fermours that (han such manors)¹ and tounshipes (144) of the kynges to ferme: til that it be pleynly determyned byfore hise Iustices of that on benche or of that (145) other by comon lawe: whether the forseid tenentȝ ben fre or bonde and whether they (146) ben worthy to ben punysshed by that forseide statut or non and that vp on a suffisant peyne payinge to the kyng (147) and a nother peyne payinge to the partie pursued and greued for such sute:

Also we (148) beseche ȝow that ȝe prayen to oure liege lord the kyng in fortheryng of (his trewe lieges)¹ (149) that alle other commissions brought or pursued aȝeyns any of hise fre tenentȝ in (150) manere byfore seide by the strengthe and colour of the forseide statut at this present parlement: (151) that they with alle the (processe circumstance)¹ and dependance mowen alle (152) vtterly ben (repeled)¹ and adnulled for honor and profyt of the kyng and for ese and (153) remedie to hise forseid fre tenentȝ: ȝif ony so be (in this cas of mesch)ief¹ at this tyme (154) withinne the Reme:

And also worchopeful sires: (that)² they ne cleyme ne haue none othere seruages (155) ne custumes of the kynges fre tenentȝ for her owne singuler profyt and none (156) auntage to the (kyng ne to)¹ none of hise heires othor than the kyng chief lord hadde in his tyme whanne

(157) the same lordshipes weren in his owne hondes withoute another (suffisant peyne payinge to)¹ the (158) kyng: a nother peyne to paie to the partyes that ben pursued and greued for swiche wrongful (159) cleymes and also vpon peyne of forfaiture of the same maneres (for euere)¹ for eschewynge of grete (160) meschiefs that mighten by swiche wrongful cleymes: falle and turne to gret preiudice to the kyng and (161) noiancie to al the Reume:

ffor manye of tho Religious that han swiche fermes of the kynges in gouernaunce: (162) by strengthe of the forseide statut disesen and destreyen manye of the kynges tenentʒ of the (163) same lordshipes and maken hem to voyde and gon out of hise lordshipes. by cause that they wolde hise lordshipes so destroyen that the kyng (164) nor none of hise heires (shulden)¹ neuer haue lust ne wille to cleyme tho lord-shipes in to her (165) owne handes aʒeyn: ne that non other lord of his rewme shulde desire to ferme tho lordshipes of the (166) kyng ne (of)¹ his tresorer to the kynges encres ʒerly: and that is the cause that they ben so (167) abated: so desolat of housyng and so destroyed and voyde of peple which is gret doel to alle the (168) kynges trewe lieges to knowe and to weten of swiche meschiefs done and vsed (169) with jnne the Rewme:

Besechinge also (to)¹ oure liege lord that he wole haue compassion and pyte (170) vp on vs that euere haue ben trewe lieges and trewe fre tenentʒ to his worthy coroune of his worthi (171) maner and tounshipe of Chestreton byfore seide that these greuouse meschiefs that ben done to vs mowen (172) ben amended now at this tyme or ʒe departen hennes and this commission mowe be (173) repeled and the obligacions to ben adnulled and to ben delyuered to ech man his owne obligacion (174) for (the loue)¹ of god and of seynt charite:

(End of first parchment. There is a second in the same hand and language.)
Non-Chancery hand
Printed *RP* IV.57-61.
¹ rubbed ² superior insert ³ to his cancelled

164

1416-21 C1/1/21 Petition of Rauf atte Ree of Lancashire (right end water damaged and torn)

(1) To my most gracyouse lord the kyng

These ben the desesis and wrongys I doon to Rauf atte Ree tenant (2) of our lord the kyng In the Ducherye of lancastre And fermor of ȝoure Maner of Ramesden Hall in (3) Essex by mayntenance of Iohn Tyrell in disheredacon of the heryta . . . as water atte Re fader of the forseyd (4) Rauf made enfeffement to certeyn persones to enfeffe Margaret his wyf. in the tenement I Clepid Danyell tenement (5) with al the apportenance longyng ther to the whych tenement stondith in . . . of the forseyd Margrete Scholde (6) descende to Thomas atte Ree and to his Eyres And be Cause the same Thomas deyde and al his Issew lyvyng the same (7) Margeret Sche stood in hool possessyon of the forseyd tenement duryng her . . . The same tenement scholde. turne to the (8) forseyd Rauf atte Ree Sone of the forseyd water and Margaret as Ryght heyr As by a Chartor In tayll more playnly hit schewyth. (9) Thus the forseyd Rauf be wey of Ryght. entryd and took p . . . tenement. affter decesse of his modor. the which possessyon of (10) Ryht herytage he kept. vn to the tyme that Iohn wethy of Essex thorwgh meyntenance of the forseyd Iohn Tyrell. and othor (11) mo of her Covey (that es to say Iohn Canon william Perham Iohn Folw. . .)[1] with strong hand. dryven hym . . . And malycyouslych ymagenyd (12) hym to Slee. So for drede of deth. he lefft his heritage Pursewyng to my gracyous lady of herforde. to help him and (13) Sokor hym in this greet myscheff. standyng in dowte of his lyf. and lesyng of his . . . gracyous lady of (14) herford. took the forseyd Rauf in to her howshald there abydyng vn to the tyme my lady with her wyse Consell had ful (15) examinacion. as wel by gode and trewe men of the same Contre And by Evydence of his dedys . . . that the forseyd (16) Rauf was wrongfully put from his Ryght Beyng present at that tyme in my ladyes presence. The forseyd Iohn Tyrell mayntenor (17) of this wrong. And at that tyme my lady reprevid him as for maynte . . . her vpon my gracyous lady (18) set the same Rauf in to playn possessyon of his forseyd heritage by vertu of examynacion a boven seyd in presence of (19) sir Gerard Braybrook Iohn Doreward Robert Darcy Robert Rykedon and other m . . . present. And vp on (20) this. the same Iohn wethy with othor foure persones. in presence of Robert Darcy Iustise of the pees (21) weren bownden Ech of hem. In a .C. li. for sewrte of the pees And anoon as my gracyouse lady was p . . . wethy with (22) mayntenance of Iohn Tyrell and othor of her Covey with strong hand and with owte process of lawe. drovyn (23) and expellyd the Same Rauf from his forseyd herytage. And Robbeden the same Rauf of all his . . . the berne. and othor (24) goodes and catell. the valew of a .C. li and more. Wher of the kynges ferme. schold haf been raysyd and paijd And affter that (25) my lady was goo to god. Thise forseyd partyes tok fro me . . . herytage which forseyd land. my fader ȝaf to me. and was in (26) possessyon the terme of .xvj. ȝeer and more. with owte lawe. and with oute any processe of the lawe. And tho (27) the same Tyrell made a vow that the forsey(d) . . . pleyne hym to lord ne lady more. And tho affterward. he sent to Iour maner of (28) Ramesdenhall twey Baylyes for to take the forseyd Rauf. lyves. or dethes. with Swerdes I drawe ȝef they myht hym (29) hafe . . . a slayn. but ȝef he wolde haue I ȝolde him. And ȝef hit had be so that he had I ȝolde hym. (30) he for to haue been Cast in prison. than scholde not he haue lyvid. iij. daijs But ȝef he wolde haue I seled hem (31) a Relees of all the wrong is . . . And than for dowte of his deeth he was fayn to fle that Cuntre. thenkyng in his Conseyt that (32) he wolde in to Normandy to our lyge lorde the kyng. that tyme beyng at the Castel of Monterell. Complaynyng to (33) our lyge lord the kyng . . . her vpon our lyge lord the kyng sent his gracyouse lettres dyrecte to the (34) Chaunceller of Ingelond to se vn to the forseyd Rauf. that al Ryht and Reson scholde haue be doon vn to hym. And affter that (35) the Chaunceller had a provision of the . . . vpon to go and to Come as his ful trust was in Saffte and in pees As the (36) kyngis tenant of his Maner of Ramesdon hall in Essex her vppon malicyously the same Iohn wethy with strong (37) mayntenance of the forseyd Iohn Tyrel and . . . In wayte a ȝens the pees and sewrte maad for the pees. to fore the (38) Iustyce Maymed the same Rauf as hit Schewyth at the syghte his Enemyes wenyng to haue slayn him and for to make an (39) Ende of the same Rauf him to slee . . . of Iohn Tyrell and othor mo. all these wronges han doon to the forseyd Rauf. (40) And ȝet standith in dowte of his lyff. ȝef he go to large Of the whyche wronges my ful gracyouse lord (41) the kyng. I besechy(e)[2] ȝow of ȝour specyall grace that I may . . . And that I myght haue in pees my Ryghtful (42) herytage. As I schal be Ioure trewe bedeman. all the dayes of my lyve. And ther to I beseche ȝow of grace. (43) and sokore. for his loue that deyde on the Rode tree a goode fryday.

Chancery hand
Printed PC I.xvi-ii.
[1] superior insert   [2] blotted

165

After 1417   C1/1/14   Petition of William Dodde, royal retainer
(1) To my worthy and gracious lord Bisshope of wynchestre Chaunceller of yngelond
Beseching (2) mekely youre pouere bedeman William Dodde

charyoter. wheche passed ouere the see in seruice with our (3) liege lorde & was oon of his charioterys in his viages / & of hyȝe treste ffefed in my land Iohan Brownyng & Iohan (atte)¹ hull (4) of Chekewell with my wyfe. wheche Iohan & Iohan after a ȝenste my wyll & wetynge pot my land to fferme / (5) & delyuered my mevable good the valewe of xx marke where hem leste & thus they kepe my dede & (the denture with)² (6) my mevable good vnto myne vndoynge lasse than y haue youre excylent & gracious helpe & lordship besechinge yow at reuerence (7) of þat worthy prince ys Sowle youre ffader whoos bedeman y am euere that ye woll sende for Iohan & Iohan (8) affor seide þat the cause may be knowe why they with holde my good / to myne vndoynge / also wheche am vndo for brusinge in (9) seruyce of our liege lorde / & in seruice of þat worthy Princesse my lady of clarence / & euere wolde yef my lemys (10) myght serve worthy Prince sone at reuere(n)ce³ of god & of that pereles princes his moder take this mater at hert of almes & charite:

Non-Chancery hand
Printed *PC* I.xiii.
¹ rubbed   ² marginal insert   ³ tear

166

Before 1421   C1/1/18   Petition of Roger Wodehill of Strete, Devon
(1) To oure liege lord the kyng
Bysechith mekely ȝoure poure prest Roger Wodehill person of Strete som tyme Clerc (2) of ȝoure fadris Spicerie whos soule god assoille that for as moche as the Abbot and the (Co)nuent¹ of Glastonbury ymaginith (3) a foe ȝenst the forseid person and wrongfully feynyth a ȝenst him & his men actions of trespas that be vntrewe (4) in ȝo(ur)e¹ Courtys and prisonyth his men at Glastonbury and ledyth a wey fro his personage his ploghyren and his plogh (5) and his plogh gere that his men mowe (not)¹ sowe his londe and othir wrongys doth to him and to his men that he dar not duelle vp on his (6) personage for to serue god nethir his men to do him eny seruise there in distruction of the forseid person (7) his men & his chirche but ȝif they haue ȝoure gracieux help and all this wronges they do be cause that (8) the person sewith a ȝenst hem in Court spirituell for dismes of his chirche that they haue wrongfully by nome (9) the forseid person and his chirche. notwithstondyng that the forseide person hath had a sentence for him in the (10) Courte of Cauntirbury by mestre Iohn kemp and an othir sentence in

the Courte of Rome by the popis Auditors. That it like (11) to ȝoure gracieuse astate considere the grete power and rychesse of the forsaid Abbot and the Conuent and the mene (12) power of the said person. and commande to write to ȝoure Chaunceler of yngelond to do clepe the parties (13) a for him and examine hem and make an ende by twene hem of all that hangith bitwene hem in ȝoure Courtys and so that the (14) forseid person haue riȝth for the mercy of crist

Non-Chancery hand
Printed *PC* I.xvi.
[1] torn

167

1421   SC8/24/1168   Petition of the soldiers in Calais

(1) To the worthy wise and discrete persones Speker of this present parlement and to alle the (2) knyghts of the Shires

Prayen and requiren on goddes behalue the pore liege men and Soudeours in the (3) Tovn of Caleys that hit like to ȝoure wise and gode discrecions tenderly to considere how that (4) the pore Soudeours be the space of V ȝeer a quarter except (. . . bodies)[1] and here (5) godes han truly serued the saufgarde of the forsaid Tovn with oute any plein paiement sauyng apprest (6) and vitaille the whiche vitaille hath be so high supportacion to the Soudeours that ellis here continuaunce (7) myȝt not haue be born So (that there is)[1] due to the forseid Soudeours in especial of the retenu (8) of oure worthy and gracious lord oure Capitaign the Erle of warrewyk be iuste rekenyng betuene the officers of oure (9) soueraign lord the king And the officers of oure forsaide Capitaign vnto the (iij day)[1] of (10) ffeuerer last passed Atte whiche day be the comaundement of oure soueraign lord there was abitted xxvj (11) Soudeours on horsback vnpaid so atte that day there was due to the forsaid Capitaign and Soudeours the (12) somme of xxvj ml. Dccxliij (l. xiij s. x d q.)[1] wherefore like vnto ȝoure high discrecions to (13) haue recomaunded amonge alle ȝoure other peticions the forseid Tovn and for to be gode menes to oure (14) most douty lord oure naturell soueraign lege lord the king (to that conclusion that þurgh)[1] (15) ȝoure gode and graciouse mediacion so to be proferred that the pore Soudeours may haue in (16) partie of paiement the somme that is receiued of the assignement last apointed be oure forsaid soueraign (17) lord as fer as hit wold strecche and for the remenaunt that is due vnto hem to ordeigne as best (18) liketh to ȝoure gode and graciouse lordship in releuyng of the grettest necessite that euere ȝour (19) forseid

Soudeours stode ynne saue hope of ȝoure habundant grace and mercy atte reuerence of god (and)[1] yn wey of charitee
Chancery hand
Printed *RP* IV.159.5.
[1] rubbed

168

1423   E28/41/76   Petition of Thomas Rokeby, royal retainer
(1) To the hyghe & myghty Prince the Duk of Gloucester protectour of ynglond & the right wyse & discrete counseyl of our (2) lord the kyng
Besecheth your humble seruant Thomas Rokeby Knyght that ther he has ben with holde & of retenue (3) for a yere wyt the full worthy & noble Kyng henry fader to our soueraigne liege lord that nowe ys in his viage in to hys (4) realme of ffrance & Normandie the yer of hys regne de iiij als it be hys endenture made be twix the forsayd noble kyng & the (5) forsayd Thomas Rokeby pleinli appiers & his forsayd retenue for the yer forsayd pleinly execute & fulfellid & so forth be comandement (6) of the forsayde ful noble kyng his seruice & demure continued fro yere to yer vn to four yer was nere spendid & passid (7) als it be certeins endenturs made also be twix the forsayd kyng & the forsayd Thomas Rokeby pleinly appiers for the (8) whilk time a gret part of the wageȝ of the forsayd Thomas is be hynde & nowth payd hym to gret hynderyng & annentisyng (9) bot if your graciouse lordshippis & help in this matere to him be shewyd lyke it to ȝour wyseȝ discrecions (10) & graciouses lordshippis to comaunde the Tresorer & Barons of the Cheker of our lord kyng to here his a compt in this matere (11) & certifie yow of the end of the forsayd acompt & aftre that to ordeigne that the forsayd Thomas myght be agreed of the (12) arerageȝ of his forsaid wageȝ als reson & Concience askys in discharging of the forsayd ful noble kyng & for the dede of Charite
(Another hand) D a Westminstre le .xviij. jour de may lan v &c primier
Chancery hand

169

1423   E28/41/103   Letter accompanying payment to the soldiers (draft)
(1) Right trusty and welbeloved / Albehit þat (wee)[1] be þaduys of

oure grete Counsseil / consideringe þe grete (2) disese. þat yee and ech of yow suffre dayly / and haue suffred of lang time / alswel in oure fadres daies. whom god assoille (3) / as in oures / for defaute of paiement of youre wages / hadde now late / assigned / and maad prouision of þe somme of .VMl. li./ (4) to be distrebued and. departed / amanges yow for to say. iiij Ml. li. vn to yow of þe said tovn and Castel / and. a. Ml. li. vn (5) to [yow]² (þaim)¹ of þe marches / And ouer þat of þe subside of wolles / xiij. s iiij d / of euery (6) sak wheigte / and of þe wollefell after þafferant / liche as certain oure lettres / þervpon vn to yow / (7) directed / plainly. maken mencion Naught withstandinge / wee / Consideringe þe saide somme. and assignement nought suffeceant ynow / (8) to þe hastife and Redy paiement of youre saide wages (owynge of tyme passed as wel of tyme comyng)¹ / Seynge youre grete pouert (9) and duresse / wolen (and)¹ graunte [and promette]² be þaduis [of oure s]² and consent of oure said grete (coun)sseil³/ þat (10) [what tyme and]² alssone / as any good. encreses and growes / vn to vs / be hit be graunt of Subside / or / (in any ot)her³ wyse [or manere]² (11) þat thanne þassignement for youre said paiement / shal bee notablely. enlargissed . . .³essed. Soo to stande and endure / withouten (12) Reuokinge or adnullinge in any wyse / vn to þe time þat yee of þe . . . ³marches / and ech of yow / been (13) fully content and paied / of al þat vn to yow ys. owynge and verailly . . .³ dorso.

Chancery hand
¹ superior insert   ² cancelled   ³ corner torn off

170

1424   E28/43/58(35)   Petition of Thomas Burton concerning prisoners in France

(1) To the kyng our souerayn lord & to my lordes of his counseil.

Besechet humebely your most obeisant subget Thomas (2) Burton knyght how that the saide Thomas hath accompted in your Escheqer for the kepyng of the Erle of Ewe. Arture of Britayne (3) & Bursegand that was Marchal of ffraunce And ouer CCC li relesed & lv li xvj s viij d disalowed ther ys clerely founden due to (4) the saide Thomas for the saide kepyng Clxxviij li x s x d as in the certificat made be your Tresorer & Barons in to your (5) saide counseil more pleynely ys declared of whiche somme ys due for the kepyng of the saide Erle of Ewe lix li x s iiij d & (6) for the said Arture & Bursegand Cxix li vj d That hit like to your benigne grace be auise of my said lordes of your said (7) counseil to consider the long labour and heuy and dredeful charge of

the said Thomas & the seide sommes above relesel and disalowed (8) and in discharge of the soule of the kyng your noble fader that was. whom god assoil ordaigne swyche paiement or (9) agrement for the said Thomas of the sommes aforsaid as thinketh to your saide benigne grace be auis of my (10) said lordes of your counseil for the love of god and dede of charitee.
Chancery hand

171

1424-26   C1/1/25   Petition of John Staverne of Canterbury
(1) To his gracious lord the Bysshopp of Wyncestre Chaunceller of Englond
Besechith mekely your pouere (2) bedeman Iohn Stauerne of Cantirbury that as myche as in a suete wyche the foresaide suppliant had before yowe ayens on Iohn (3) Bonyngton of Cantirbury foresaide be vertu of a wirtt sub pena forto awenswer before yowe to certeins matiers (4) and debates mouyd be twyn thame two: ȝee accordyd and Aiournyd the same matiers and debates to tyme that on Dauid (5) Marrys of the same Towen Notarie had shewed the treweth of the said matiers and debates And nowe it is so that same dauyd (6) will gladly knawelygge the treweth of the same matiers: bot he wald haue a maundement fro yowe for the cause (7) that he shuld noght be haldyn parciall in the same matier That it lik to your gracious lordship to graunte a (8) wirtte sub pena direct to the saide Dauid to apere be fore yow att a certein day forto declare the treweth in the matiers (9) foresaide fore loue of gode And in wey of charitee
  pleg' de prosequendo Iohannes Shirburn   Thomas Pettysworth
Non-Chancery hand
Printed PC I.xix.

172

1424-26   C1/1/26   Petition of Johan Kymburley of Derby (right end rubbed; matter in parentheses supplied from PC)
(1) To the high and mighty prince ryght dredd and gracieux lord of Wynchestre Chanceller of Englond
Consideryng if it (2) like youre highnes. howe youre poer beedman Iohan Kymburley of derby kynnesman to somtyme youre seruant sir (3) william hikeling bargayned in derby in lenten was twelf (mon)eth

(with oon) Iohan Goldsmyth the elder of Melton in leycestreshire (4) Marchant. And the said parties fully accorded bitwix hem as it appereth by an euidence seled ther vpon and (writen of the said) (5) Iohan Goldsmyth owen hand that he sholde by a moneth aftir the said Ester haue deliuered hym a tonn of wood price of (6) xiij li xs. for the which soume the said Iohan (Goldsmyth receyued) the verray value marchantlich in wolles of the same (7) Iohan kymburleys. and the said wood that he boughte yet never deliuered hym to his importable losse and hindryng (which (8) nys but a) poer man and . . .¹ of sufficeant remedie for lack of other laweful seuerte / like it youre noble grace thorugh (9) consideracion of rightwisnes and Iustice. the which re(leeveth many a) poer man. Vppon this mater by writt sub pena to sende (10) for the seid Iohan Goldsmyth to appere a fore yowe in the Chauncellerie att such day as yow list com(aund and heruppon) (11) right to be doon vn to the said beedman which euermor shal prai god for youre high and noble estat

(Signatures) Pleg' de persequendo Iohannes Stodley de london   Rogerus Wolley de derby
Non-Chancery hand
Printed *PC* I.xx.
¹ torn

173

1424-26   C1/1/27   Petition of Willyam Midylton of Holderness, Yorkshire

(1) To my graciouse Lorde of Wynchestre the Chauncellor of Engeland

Compleines Willyam Midylton of Waughen (2) in holdernesse in als mykill als Iohn of Cotyngham gentylman of Waughen forsayde a with certeigne men of (3) his. wapynd & armed. yat es to say. Iohn of Waughen husbandman. Thomas warde husbandman (Robert of Bate)¹ wryght. (4) & Iohn west wryght. wyth yair force of ye same Toune forsayde. maliciously agayne ye kyngis pece & (rebelliously)¹ agayne ye (5) gouernours of ye deuyne seruyce of ye kyrk of Wanghen forsayde in seruyce tyme opon seint Steuyn (6) day ye last in ye (same)¹ kyrke woulde haf slayn me with ane polle axe & all ye pepyll & ye preste so affrayde at ye (7) leuacion tyme clappyd saume ye buke for ferid. & I for drede of my dede habade still in ye same kyrk of seint peter (8) ffraunchiss .x. houreʒ lange & ye forsayde Iohan of Cotyng ham Iohn. Thomas Robert. & Iohn with yair force (9) en armed & wapened lygand still in ane awayte in ye kyngis way & aboute ye same kyrke to haf slayne me if I had comyn oute (10) of ye kyrk. & no man durst him arest to ye pece. & yat same Iohn of Cotyngham proferd openly to ye (11) qwhylk of yam forsayde yat myght haf kylled me. soulde haf had xx. noblis for my dede als (it is)¹ opynly knawen to (12) all yat toune & ye contreth. for ane worde I spak in ye kyrk. yat it wer better bell vnrogne at ye sauntes (13) tyme yan ye messe vnsogne. & I neuer sen yat day hidirward durst yer habyde in ye contree for drede of (14) my dede for yat Iohn of Cotyngham & his force forsayde. in harmyng & in costes of me & myne. xx li. Qwharfore lyke it to (15) yhour graciouse lordeschip in saueyng of my lyfe & ye kyngis pece & ye state of yat kyrke of seint peter (16) ffraunchess & my harmeʒ graunte a writ sub pena for yis for(sayd)¹ Iohn of Cotyngham & his iiij. felaughes (17) in propir personeʒ to com by for yhour self. for ye luf of god & by way of charite

(Another hand) Pleg' de persequendo Iohanes de Wayhen de Suggestan in Com' Ebor'   Iohanes hakyns de london

Non-Chancery hand
Printed *PC* I.xx.
¹ faded

174

1425   SC8/24/1197   Petition by Commons for speedy trial of Lollards

(1) Vn to the most excellent most worthy & gracious lordes of this present parlement

Shewyn & declaryn to (2) your hygh discrecion the Communes of this present parlement for as mych as divers persones that (3) here to for havyn bene arettyd & acusyd of treson felonye lollardrie & other such poyntes bene commyttyd (4) alday by the kynges comaundement & his counceyll some to the Tour of London & some to othir castels & holdes in (5) the rewme wher as they lye long tyme other while a yeer or two with out eny processe or execucion done a yens (6) hem to grete costes of our lord the kyng & grete perill & fere of her kepers & also emboldishing to other of her (7) covyne & assent / Plesith it vn to your moste excellent & worthy lordshipes so to ordeyne by your (8) most hye discrecions that all such prisoners that shul in tyme to come be commyttid to eny such place for (9) treson felony lollardrie or eny such other high poynt mowe in short tyme be sent & apere by for (10) her Iuges temporall or spirituell as the (caas)¹ askith. to the entent to be

quyt & delyverd or ellis to (11) have the iewys they have deservid in eschewyng of excessiue costes of our lord the kyng done about the (12) long kepyng of such prisoners & the grete perill fere & labour of her kepers for goddis sake & in wey of charite.
Non-Chancery hand
Printed *RP* IV.292.46.
[1] superior insert

175

1426   E28/47/83   Petition of Baltazar Vivald of Genoa
(1) To my lord of Bedford and oþer lordys of þe worþy counsel of England
Besekeþ mekely Baltaʒar vivald (2) marchant of Iene of yowr special grace to commaunde þe Tresorer and Barons of þe Chekker to restore (3) and delyuer to þe seid Baltaʒar þe Cloþis longyng to þe same Baltaʒar. þe whych þe (4) Awner of london arestid and haþ browʒth in to þe Chekker Receyuyng of þe seid Baltaʒar xxv. mark. (5) þe which somme he is acordit with þe seid Tresorer to paye to owr souereyn lord as for fyne of þe Cloþis aforeseyd
(Signatures) H. gloucestre   H Cantuar.   I Ebor Cant   T dunelm   P Elien   I Bathon   Cromwell   Typtot
Non-Chancery hand

176

1427   E28/48/19(4)   Petition of the mayor and citizens of Southampton
(1) To owre souerayne lord the kyng & to hys ryʒt worthy wyse & discrete Counsell bysechyth well humblely hys powre trewe (2) liege men the Mayr Aldremen & Burgeysys of Suthampton / that hyt dysplese nat vn to owre sayd souerayne lord / þe Kyng (3) ne to hys sayde worthy Counsell / that the sayd Mayr Aldremen & Burgeysys buth nat of power / for grete nede and pouerte (4) of ham selfe to make eny appreste of money / vn to owre sayd souerayne lord the Kyng at thys tyme / for trewly þe sayd towne (5) of Suthampton ys at thys tyme ryʒt powre & all moste desolate / for to that place ryʒt nowe comyth all most no maner of (6) peple neythere by water ne by londe / for the wheche cause grete partye of the dwellerys of that towne buth sodeynly departyd (7)

& ago (&)¹ meny howsys ben yshutte vppe & grene gras grewyth at hare dorys and in diuerse placys of euery strete of the (8) towne / Whar for / for / the grete nede & pouerte of ham selfe / the sayd Mayr & burgeysys now in all haste moste make agrete Tallage by (9) thynne ham selfe / to gadery money to paye to Quene Iohane hare fee ferme of the towne / The wheche grete & greuouse fee ferme / þe (10) sayd Mayr & burgeysys ne may but alytyll whyle here after bere ne paye / by thowte þat / that they have helpe socowr & pardon (11) of hare sayde fee ferme of hare sayd souerayne lord þe kyng & of the sayde Quene / thorwe helpe & prayer of þe sayd worthy Counsell:

Non-Chancery hand
¹ rubbed

177

1427-28 SC8/25/1222 Petition on behalf of the Archbishop of Canterbury

(1) Souuerain Lord We youre Humble Liegis han late vnderstande to oure greet heuynesse / that oure good fader the Archebisshop (2) of Canterbury (and Primat)¹ of al this land / shulde haue be detecte and noysed vngoodly and vnskilfully to oure (3) holy fader the pope / that he sholde haue been and pro(cured)¹ ayens the libertees of the Courte of Rome in this (4) lond and other wyse haue gouerned hym in his cure / thanne hit longeth to a good prelat for to doo be cause whereof oure (5) holy fader was meuyd to make certain proces a yens hym in preiudice of hym and oure aller moder þe cherche of (6) Canterbury w(hi)ch¹ we been alle holden to worship and susteyne in as muche as in vs is. / Wherfor (7) we beseche youre hieghnesse as humblely as we can for to haue (th)e¹ saide oure aller good fader recommissed (8) and yeue in special commandement to youre Ambassatours that shul goo to the Courte of Rome / or ellis (9) write to oure saide hooly fader þe pope / to haue þe saide Archebisshop and oure moder his cherche of Canterbury (19) specially recommissed withowte any credence yeuyng to any swich informacions or deteccions now maad / or (20) to be maad in tyme to commyng ayens faith and conscience / And yif any swich processe be maad / to cassen hem and annullen (21) hem / as swich that proceded of an vndewe and vnskilful suggestion / and þe trouthe not knowen

Chancery hand
Printed *RP* IV.322.18.
¹ torn

178

1429   E28/51/A6   Petition of the residents of Uchayron Percell, Wales

(1) To owr souereign lord the kyng

Besechyn mekely al tho poure tenantʒ and Comunes of Vchayron (2) percell of the Shyre of Cardygan There as the seid besechers suyn to yow owr souereign (lord)[1] & to yowre wyse . . .[2] a yenst (3) the abbot of Stratflere for diuers maters as yn the seid bille more playnly apperyth where hit lykyd to yowr hynesse (4) to comytte the seid bille to the Bishop of Ely the Bishop of Bath Cromewell and to the lord Scrope lordys of yowr seid councell. yevyng hem yn (5) comaundement to here & finally to determine the seid mater By autorite of the wheche comaundement . . .[2] lordys ruledyn (6) the seid Abbot to putte his answhere suche as he wold stonde to ayenst the mater yn the seid bille conteyned yn wrytyng. by forse of the whych rule (7) the seid Abbot put his seid answher yn wrytyng. the whych answer as hit apperyth yn the seid wrytyng lyeth muche on a record of a Cession (8) yhold on the monday next after seynt Iames day yn the ix yere of the reign of yowr late souereign lord yowr fader (9) on hose sowle god have mercy afore Iohn Merbury at that tyme beyng yowr Iustice of Southwales & on other recordes (10) ymade seth the seid Cession yn yowr Esker of Cardyngan. Wherefore like hit vn to yowr hynesse to send yowr priue seales to the seid Iohn (11) Merbury and to on Dauid ap Thomas liwtenant of yowr Shyre of Cardygan to the lord of Audeley now yowr Iustice of (12) Southwales the whech Dauid hath the gouernance vndur the seid lord ther of yowr lawe comaundyng by yowr seid priue (13) (seals)[1] the seide Iohn Merbury and the seid Dauid to be here afore yow graciouse (lord)[1] & yowr wyse councell on the (14) viij day next aftur seynt hillarie now next comyng so that they mowen be afore yow & yowr seid councell examined yn provyng of (15) the truthe of the seid mater and yn spede of the sute of the aforseid besechers. Aftur the whyche examinacioun so to procede (16) yn the seid matere aftur gode consience and lawe. And also anothir Priue seal to yowr Chamberlein of Southwales (17) comaundyng hym to respite the leve of the comunes yn the forseid bille rehersed of the seide besechers vn tille thys (18) matere be twene the seide besechers & the seid Abbot be determynd ffor the love of god & wey of charite

(Action recorded in French)
Non-Chancery hand
[1] superior insert   [2] torn

179

1430-31   C49/20/1   Conditions of payment of a Parliamentary subsidy

(1) To the wurship of god and for the grete love and entier affeccion the whiche we your poure (2) Communes of this your noble roialme haue to yow our most soueraigne lord (kyng henry)[1] the sixte (3) be thassent of alle the lordes spirituel and temporelx beyng in this present parlement (4) holden atte Westminstre the friday next afore the fest of Seynt hillar the yere of your regne the ixe (5) graunte to yow our saide soueraigne lorde for the defence of this your saide roialme in especiall (6) an hole quinsʒisme and an hole disme and the thridde parte of an hole quinsʒisme and of an hole disme (7) to be paied and arered of the moeble godes of the laye poeple of this your saide roialme in maner accustumed: (8) that is to say that one hole quinsʒisme and hole disme beforesaide to been arered and paied be the fest of (9) Seynt martyn in wynter next after the saide graunte (10) and that other thridde parte of that other hole quinsʒisme and disme beforesaide to been arered and paied be (11) the fest of Ester come tuelfemonethe next after the saide graunte. Purueied alwey that the laye poeple of the (12) Citee of lincoln ne none of hem be arted or compelled be force of the saide graunte of the thridde parte of (13) the saide quinsʒisme and disme to make paieme(nt)[2] or any thyng to paye of the same thridde parte (14) of quinsʒisme and disme to be paied atte the saide fest of Ester come tuelfmoneth but that the saide lay (15) poeple of the saide Citee and ichone of hem of the saide paiement of the saide thridde part of quinʒisme and (16) disme and of euery parte therof be alle vttirly acquite and dischargett

(Latin note follows in correcting hand.)
Non-Chancery hand
Printed *RP* IV.368.13.
[1] superior insert   [2] rubbed

180

1430-31   C49/20/2   Conditions of payment of a Parliamentary subsidy

(1) To the worship of god and for the grete loue and entier affeccion the whiche we your pouere (2) Comunes of this your noble roialme haue to (ʒou)[1] our . . .[2] soueraigne lord kyng henry the .vjte. be assent (3)

of your lordes sp*iri*tuell and temporell in this your present parlement
beyng holden atte Westm*inst*re (4) the friday next afore the fest of seint
hillar the yere of your regne the ixe be auctorite of the same (5) parlement graunte to yow our saide soueraigne lord the kyng for the defence
of this your saide (6) roialme and in especiall for the safe kepyng of
the see a subsidie to be paied in the forme þat (7) foloweth þat is to
say of euery tonne of wyne. of euery marchant denisʒein comyng into
(8) þis saide roialme be wey of marchandise fro the saide friday next
afore the fest of seint hillar (9) the forsaide yere of the saide regne vnto
the fest of seint Martyn in wynter þanne next suyng and so fro (10)
þe same fest of seint Martyn vnto the fest of seint Martyn in wynter
thenne next folowyng iij s. and of euery (11) other maner of marchandise of any marchant denisʒein passyng out of this saide roialme or
(12) comyng into þis saide (Roume)¹ be wey of marchandise duryng
the tyme aforesaide of the value of .xx. s x.j. d (13) wolle wollenclothe
hides and wollefell goyng oute of this saide roialme whete and rye and
flour of þe same and (14) all maner ffresshfisshe (comyng)¹ into þis
saide roialme oute of this graunte and auctorite except (15) and if any
marchandise of any marchaunt denisʒein oute of this saide roialme
passyng wherof the saide (16) subsidie is paied or agreed or surete made
therfore. be perisshed or lost be infortune of the see. or be take with
(17) enemys withouten covyne or fraude and þat founden and preued
before the Tresorer of England or afore (18) the chief Baron of the
Cheker for þe tyme beyng be resonable preues of the saide marchandises (19) so lost or perisshed þat thanne the saide marchauntʒ
denisʒeins. Awners of the saide marchandises. (20) so perisshed and
lost whenne hem liketh may ship as muche marchandises in value be
force and virtue of (21) the said auctorite in the same port (in ye)¹ whiche
the saide marchandises were shipped Inne as was so perisshed (22) lost
or taken withouten any subsidie therof to be had And ouer þat we your
saide pouere Comunes (23) graunte to yow our saide soueraigne lord
be þe auctorite aforesaide a subsidie to be paied in (24) the manere
folowyng / that is to say of euery tonne of swete wyne of euery marchaunt alien (25) comyng into this saide roialme be wey of marchandise fro þe saide friday vnto þe saide latter fest of (26) saint Martyn
.iij.s ouere the subsidie of .iij.s þe whiche euery marchaunt alien for
euery (27) tonne wyne atte þe tyme of this graunte custumably paied
to yow / And also of euery other (28) manere of marchandise of any
of the saide marchantʒ aliens passyng oute of this saide roialme or (29)
comyng into this saide roialme (be wey of merchandise¹)³ duryng þe
saide tyme. of the value of .xx. s. vj. d (30) ouere the subsidie of .xij.
d the whiche euery marchaunt alien for euery marchandise (31) to the

value of .xx s paied to yow custumably atte the tyme of this graunte and afore and that all the saide (32) graunte of all the saide subsidies with the fourme and all the circumstaunce therof be conteyned and expressed (33) in euery patent or commission of the Customers of euery port of this saide roialme and be force and (34) virtue of the auctorite aforesaide / And ouere þat (we)[1] your saide Comunes graunte to yow our saide (35) soueraigne lord be assent of your saide lordes spirituell and temporell for the defence aforesaide a (36) subsidie of .v. nobles of euery sak wolle and wollefelle to be hadde paied and rered fro the fest of seynt Martyn in (37) wynter þat shall be the yere of our lord a .Ml.CCCCXXXiiij vnto the fest of seint Martyn in wynter þenne next folowyng to (38) be hadde paied and rered in manere and fourme as it is hadde and paied and arered to yow our saide soueraigne (39) lord atte the tyme of this graunte

(The rest of the indenture, 21 lines, follows in French.)
Non-Chancery hand
Printed RP IV.369.14.
[1] superior insert in another hand   [2] 5-letter cancel   [3] over erasure

181

1430-31   SC8/25/1235   Petition concerning payments to Newgate prisoners

(1) To the kyng our soueraign lord and al the lordes spirituel & temporell in this present parlement

(2) Sheweth your most humble liege man Iohn Carpenter þexecutor of Richard Whityngton þat where (3) on sir Iohn Pulteney knyght somtyme Mair of London be his testament enrolled in the Hustenge of the said Cite the (4) monday next afore seint Luce (þeuangelist the)[1] xxiij yeer of kyng Edward the thridde amonges other thinges (5) bequath and deuised to the Master and prestes of the Chapell of Corpus Christi beside the Chirche of seint laurence of Candelwikstrete (6) alle the Londes and (tenementʒ tat he hadde)[1] in the Cite and Suburbes of London outake certein (7) tenementʒ þat ben excepted in the said testament On condicion and to þat entent that the said (8) Maister shuld amonges other thinges paie and deliuere in almesse euery yeer to theym (þat were)[1] (9) prisoners withynne a prison of the said Cite called Neugate iiij marc of sterlinges in (10) this fourme and atte the termes vnderwriten / þat is to sey on Cristemasse even x s on Goodfriday (11) xiij s iiij d on Midsomer even x s and on oure lady even þassumpcion x s and on alle (12) halewyn even x s And moreouer he wolde and bequath be þe said testa-

ment þat yef eny of the said (13) sommes were vnpaid at eny tyme before limited þat the forsaid Mastre shuld paie the double be way of (payne)[1] (14) wherof o part shuld be applied to the werk of Poules and the tother part to the Chambre of the Gildhalle of the (15) said Cite as it appereth be the said testament which sommes syn the deth of the said Sire Iohn haue alwey (16) ben (wel and treuly)[1] paid to the said prisoners til now late þat the said prison be cause þat it (17) was feble ouerlitel and so contagious of Eyr þat hit caused the deth of many men was throwen doun / and of (18) almesse with the goodes and after (the will of the)[1] said Richard renoueld and made agayn in a better maner (19) blessed be god / And now be cause þat ther nis no mencion made in the said testament who shuld distreigne for the said (20) rente in caas it were behinde and the said (prisoners be)[1] insufficeant þerto / the same rente is (21) deneied and vnpaid ayens the wil of the (said sir Iohn)[2] and greuouse hurt to the poore prisoners / Wherfore (22) plese it to the kyng our soueraign Lord be aduise and consent of alle the Lordes spirituel (23) and Temporell and Comunes assembled in this parlement / to ordeign be auctorite of the same parlement þat (24) the said rent be paid hens forward as it hath ben of olde / And þat the Mair or Chamberleyn of London now (25) beyng and (her)[1] successours haue ful power to destreigne (in the said mastres landes)[3] as well for þe said rent (26) of iiij marc and euery parcell þeroffe / as for the said payne yef it be behinde (27) at eny tyme as is rehersed in the said testament for goddis love and in the wey of charite

Chancery hand
Printed *RP* IV.370.16.
[1] rubbed   [2] over erasure   [3] superior insert

182

1430-31   C49/19/27   Parliamentary assent to peace negotiations with France

(1) ffor asmoche as in þe tretee of þe pees maade noȝt longe agoo. bytwyx þe kynges of noble (2) memoir. h. þe vte late our souerain lord & his fadre Charles of ffraunce it is (3) contiened þat noon of þe partyes shal entre / or make any tretee of pees or of accord with Charles (4) þe Daufyn / with oute þassent of þe þre estates of bothe Reumys þat is to say of England (5) & of ffraunce. And it is hold for certain. þat our holy ffader þe Pope sendeth nowe downe into ffraunce (6) þe moost Reuerent ffader in god the Cardinal of seint Crois / to trete þe pees. bytwyx þe kyng (7) and þe said Daufyn And also þe kyng of Spayn

sent hider but late agoo. (8) his Ambassadeurs which entred tretee of pees þe which tretee is yit hangyng. bytwyx þe kyng our (9) souerain lord & him / for þeim þeir Reumes. lordeshipes and subgittʒ And semblably (10) þe kyng of Scottes hath send now hider. his solempne Ambassadeurs. to trete a pees finale. bytwyx þe (11) kyng & him & her two Reumes / and as euery man endowed with reson may wel consider / it nys noʒt (12) couenable ne fittyng. ne lyke to be to þe plesir of god ne of þe world a crysten Prince to refuse pees (13) offred with menes resonable ne þe tretee þerof yf it be Desired of hym. þe which by þe lawe of god (14) him owed to pursue and folowe / and also consideryng þe birdon of þe werr / and how greuous. and heuy. it is (15) to þis land / and how behofful þerfor þe pees wer to hit: Plese it to þe comunes (16) of þis land beyng in þis present parlement to yeue her assentes to þat: (17) that my lordes of Bedford & Gloucester & my lord Cardinal & oþer of þe kynges blood & of his (18) Counsail may trete þe pees. on þe kynges behalf. with þe said partyes. or any oþer / (19) and yf þeim þynke þe meenys of pees offred by þat oþer partyes couenable. and good. (20) to þe kyng and his subgittʒ. þenne to Receyue hem / And semblably. to offre for þe kynges (21) partie menis þat shal be þought to hem couenable and expedient and by swych menys to conclude (22) & accorde þe pees to goddes plesire:

Savyng[1] to þe saide roialme of Englond and to (23) alle the kynges lieges and subiettes therof: their heires and their successores alle their libertees (24) fredoms lawes custumes and priueleges þat thei their auncestres and preddessours haueth had afore this (25) tyme (in þe saide Roialme)[2] and þat þei an iche of theym be demened and gouerned after the lawes vsages and (26) custumes of the saide roialme of Englond and in none other wise this act not withstandyng

Text non-Chancery, codicil Chancery hand
Printed *RP* IV.371.18.

[1] codicil on an attached strip in a different hand   [2] superior insert

183

1430-31   SC8/25/1238   Petition of Levin le Clerc of Ghent
(1) To the kyng oure soueraigne lord
Besechuth mekely leuin le Clerc Burgeois of Gand to Consider by (2) encheson of the trewe acquitaille that the seid towne hath doon and doth dayly in diuerse Maners vnto yow (3) oure soueraigne lord howe þat but late ago he boght of Robert Brampton of Caleys attourney (4) to his brother william Brampton of Chestreville in derby shire certain

wolles to the value of xijc & xv nobles (5) the whiche monoie the same leuin paied in hand to the said Robert noght havyng liuerey of the seid wolles (6) But the seid Robert bonde his seid Brother and hym self in the aboue seid somme to the same leuin to the entent (7) þat at a certain day he shuld have had lyuerey of the wolles aboue seid Notwythstondyng the whiche boonde the (8) seid leuin hath not as yet hadd noþer lyuerey of the seid wolles ne of the seid Monay at the aboue seid (9) day the whuche is nowe passed to his vndoyng wythoute youre gracious help and remede in this partie and ther opon (10) like hit yowe to consider how þat by youre auctorite a writt sub pena vndyr your gret seal was direct to the (11) seid william comaundyng hym by the same to haue be afore your Counseill at westminstre at a certain (12) day passed there to haue onswered in the matier aboue seid the which writt was by tyme deliuered to the same (13) william and by Cause he come not at that day a writt of attachement is passed by þe seid auctorite ayenst (14) the seid william the whuche for this (cause)[1] absentuth hym in place prieleged and wolle not appere so (15) that the same leuin is not like to haue the seid wolles noþer his seid money wythoute youre gracious help (16) (and remedie)[1] in this partie wher opon like it yow soueraigne lord of youre grace especiall (17) by auctorite of this present parlement to ordeigne þat the Chaunceler of Inglond for the tyme (beyng have)[1] (18) powair to graunte a writt of proclamacion direct to the Shirref of the seid Shire yevyng hym in Comaundement (19) by the same writt to make proclamacion in opo(n place wythynne)[1] the seid (20) Shire that þe seid william Brampton appere a fore yow in youre Chauncerye at a certain day to be conteigned in (21) the same writt by the discres(ion of the seid)[1] Chaunceler to onswere to the seid Suppliant of (22) the matier conteignode in þis supplicacion And yf the seid william appere at that day that thenne the seid (23) Chaunceler have power and auctorite to examyne here and determyne the seid matier aftur his discrescion (24) And to procede to Iuggement as well of the principall as of damage and Costage resonabull and to awarde execucion (25) for the seid besecher in þat partie . . .[2] be fieri fac elegit and Capias ad satisfaciend and theropon an exigent yf he be (26) not founde and thowe the seid william appere not at suche day as he shall have by the seid proclamacion (27) the seid Chaunceler have power to procede to Iuggement for the seid suppliant ayenst the seid william by (28) his defaute as well of the Principall as of damageʒ and ther vpon to awarde execucion in the fourme (29) afore rehersode And that the seid Suppliant may have as well the goodus of the seid william as þe goodus þat eny other (30) persone hath to his use in execucion for the seid Summe vnto the tyme that the seid (somme)[3] wyth (31) damages and

Costages in that partie resonabull be pleynly arerode or payode to the seid Suppliant And þat (32) semblable processe be made agayn þe seide Robert Brampton be þe cause aforseide

Chancery hand
Printed *RP* IV.372.21.
¹ torn, rubbed   ² cancelled   ³ superior insert

184

1430-31   SC8/25/1245   Petition of the residents of Marblethorp, Lincolnshire

(1) To the ful wyse and discret syrys the comynes of this present parlement

The pore tenauntes (2) and londholders of the toun of Malberthorp in the shire of lincoln whiche has ben and ȝit are vtterly destroyd (3) and waastid be ouer flowyng and gret distres of the water of the see and . . .¹ wyth oute gret and (4) contynuel help of mannys labur. whiche toun is and of olde tyme has bee charged at euery graunt of (5) ony hole taxe to oure souerayn lord to the somme of vj li xiiij s v d ob q for the whiche (charche)¹ (6) als wele grauntyd to oure saide souereyn lord at hys parlement holden at Westminstre xxij day of September (7) the yere of his reigne the viijte as for taxe and charche nowe grauntyd or to be grauntyd in this present (8) parlement the . . .² saide tenauntȝ and lond holders dar not inhabitt maynour nor occupye the saide toun (9) to the fynal destruccion as Wele of the saide toun for euer as for a gret contre vnder the same daunger to the (10) valu(e)¹ ȝerly of ij*ml* mark Please to ȝoure Wyse discressions consideryng the causes a fore (11) rehersyd and also howe at this day the londes and tenementȝ in the saide toun are of no value nor profit: to pray (12) oure souer(aigne)¹ lorde that the saide tenauntȝ londholdres and inhabitauntes in (13) the saide toun nowe and here aftyr be autorite of this present parlement be respitid as wele of the taxe and (14) charge grauntid to oure saide soueraigne lord in his parlement holden at Westminstre the xxij (15) day of September a for said the saide yere as of the taxe and charge grauntid or to be grauntid in this (16) present parlement on to the terme of x ȝere here aftyr. that then hit may be demenyd aftyr the hygh and (17) ful gracious discrecion of oure soueraigne lord

Chancery hand
Printed *RP* IV.385.5.
¹ rubbed   ² cancelled

185

1432   SC1/43/166   Petition of the Bishop of Bath (left top damaged; right top washed)

(1) (Worship)ful¹ fadre in god and my gracious lorde I recomaunde me in als humble maner as i (c)an² or may in any wyse to . . . lorshupes Bisechyng humblie to youre (2) noble & gracious lordshupes (yow lyk to vnderstande þat þe)² lord (D)reux¹ sir humferie Stafford & I Stounton tooke in Wilteshire certain (for)³ Risers (3) & broughte hem to (Wells)² in Somerset & þare putte hem in my prison withoute assent of me or of my officers (4) bi my (knawlech)² which prison is ordeyned to kepe clerkes conuict & to noon oþir entent And þare I fande þaim withowte any (5) maner of kepyng saaf of my seruauntez / And hir vpon I sent worde to R. hill Shreef of Somerset þat he (6) sholde ordeyne for þair kepyng / And he come to me in is owen persone þis daie & seies he wole noȝt intermete (7) hym of þe kepyng of þaim. Wherfore I biseche youre gracious lordshupes to considre how me owȝt noȝt (8) to have kepyng of þaim for þaim owghte to be keped in þe kynggys comene gaiole & noȝt in my poer prison (9) for it is agayne þe libertees & franchisez of holycherche and þe forsaid R. hill wole noȝt resseyve (10) þaim And þerfor I biseche yow þat ye wole consider þis matier & comaunde bi your highe discrecions (11) what ye wole bedoo in þis matier for sikerlie i dar kepe þaim no lenggre consideryng þe condicions (12) of men at þis daies And I biseche yow þat ye wole considre þees matiers effectuellie and þat I (13) myght have an answere bi þe berer of þis lettre Almyghty god sende yow as good lyf & prosperitee as (14) your noble hertez can best desire Writ at Banewell þe .xix. daie of Maij.

your preest & oratour N Bisshop of Baath⁴

(Another hand) The xxij day of (15) May þe x yere of þe k hit was accorded by þe consail þat a writ shulde be sent to þe shiref of (16) somerset to Receyue þees Rysers abouesaid and to doo kepe surely in þe kynges prison

Chancery hand

¹ torn   ² washed   ³ interlinear insert   ⁴ The initial "N" and the PRO date are in conflict.

186

1431   E28/51/53   Petition of Jeynkyn Stanlay, royal retainer (damaged)

(1) To the kyng our souerain lord and to his ful wyse Counsaill Sheweth and besecheth mekely your pouere (2) humble seruitor Ieynkyn Stanlay Squyer: howh that now late as the said suppliant was rydyng in the kynges high (3) wey in the hundred of wyrall withynne the Counte of chestre / there were certayn persones arraied in manere (4) of werre ayens the kyngs pees lieng in dyuers busshementes / of the which persones come xvj men with bowes and other wepen (5) makyng grete shotte and assaute to the said suppliant and his men And there purposed to haue slayn and murdred the said (6) Suppliant withoute cause or offence of hym which hath ben knowleged sethen of Summe of the said perso(ns)¹ Of the which (7) mysdoers the names of certain gentilmen and yemen principall gouernors of the said affray ben conteyned in (the bille)¹ (8) annexed herto / Besechyng to your graciouse lordshipes consi(dering)¹ thees premysses of your grace especial to (9) graunte your graciouses lettres of priue seal seuerally directe / that is to say . . . the said gentilmen (10) whos names ben conteyne . . . said bille a nother to alle the yemen whos names ben conteyned in the same bille / Charching hem vppon (11) their . . . to ben at their answere afore you and your . . . at a certain day by you to be lymytte And the thridde priue (12) seal directe to william Troutbek Chamberlain of Chestre . . . for the said gentilmen and yeme. . . and to se that the (13) two priue seals a foresaid to hem be serued and directe in general And this in sauacion of the pees at . . . of charite

Chancery hand
¹ torn

187

1432 SC8/26/1271 Petition of the citizens of Lymington and Newport, Hampshire

(1) To oure souerayn Lorde the Kyng and to his right wise Counseill Lowelly and humbly bisechen (2) all the Marchauntʒ and pouere inhabitauntʒ of the Hauene of Lymyngton lying withyn the Hundredes of (3) Neweforest & of Crischurche & of the Hauene of Neweport lying withyn the Isle of Wight yn the Shire of Southampton & of (4) oþer Hauenes yn the same Shire that hough of tyme oute of mynde to þe grete and notable availle of oure liege (5) lorde and grete profit of the saide hauenes there were wont many diuerse Shippes & vesselx with grete substaunce of (6) merchaundises nat staple ware but other as wele with wynde dryven as of purpos to come and arryve yn to the (7) saide hauenes and oure liege lordes Custumes therof trewly y paied there they

haue atte all tymes be discharged & (8) recharged. Nowe late by diuerse yeres yt is fallen so that yn defaute that no Custumers ne noon here (9) deputees be attendaunt to eny of the saide hauenes. many grete Shippes and vesselx dryven and also comyng (10) oute of ferre contreyes yn to þe saide hauenes with grete goodes & merchaundiȝes willyng (11) the Marchauntȝ of hem & gretely desiryng there to haue be discharged & recharged. for lakkyng of Custumers (12) haue passed fro the saide hauenes & sailled yn to other straunge londes to grete losse and disavaille yerly (13) of right grete notable sommes to oure liege lorde grete & hidous losse abatyng and hyndryng of þe saide (14) hauenes & grete discomfort of the saide Marchauntȝ of the Shippes & vesselx atte here comyng Wherfore yt lyketh (15) vn to youre high & worthy discreciouns graciously & tendrely to considere the premisses & yn especial the grete disavaille (16) aforsaide of oure liege lorde And thervpon atte this tyme after youre right noble and wise avys yt pleseth youre (17) myghti lordshippes to ordeyne remedie atte the reuerence of god and yn way of charite Consideryng (18) also youre right high discreccions yif yt be to youre plesir hough the hauene of Wynchilse & oþer (19) hauenes vnder þe port of Chichestre yn þe Shire of Sussex the hauenes of pool & of waymouth & oþer (20) hauenes vnder the port of Melcombe yn Dorset Shire & all the hauenes yn þe same Shires & yn þe shires of (21) Devenshire Kent Cornewaill & all other shires yn þe Reame except Southampton shire aforesaide euer hiderto (22) haue hadde & yit haue deputees vnder the Custumers of þe portȝ for the grete availl & commodite of (23) oure liege lorde & of all his Reame:

Chancery hand
Printed *RP* IV.417.8.

188

1432-39   SC1/57/121   Petition of Robert Coker of Somerset

(1) Bisecheth you Robert Coker Esquyer that where the kyng oure Souereigne lord his antecessours and his progenitours (2) of tyme that no mynde ys haue be sesid of certigne rente of dyuers persons freholders . . .[1] of the Castell of (3) Dunster in the Shire of Somerset to be hadde and leuyed bi the seid freholders the whiche be to the numbir of .xl. and moo. (4) and so to be paiyd to the lord of the seid Castell for the tyme beyng and he to be chargyd of the seid rente and to pay (5) hit to the Sherrif of the seid Shire for the tyme beyng yerli at the feste. of Candelmasse. And now hit ys so that the too (6) parties of the seid Castell and the too parties of all the remanent of the londes and

tenementes that late (7) were of sir Iohn lutrell knyght lord of the seid Castell ben grauntyd bi the kyng to you my lord and y nemnyd bi . . .¹ (8) lordship in the seid Commission and stonde chargyd vndir you my lord of the fee ferme as in the seid Commission is conteignyd (9) the whiche free holders of tyme abouesaid haue contynued to paye the seid rente in youre tyme tille now late Edward SeintIon (10) beyng (on)² of the freholders aboueseid and tenaunt of malice and euyll wille to the kyng oure souereigne lord his disheritaunce (11) and also the disheritaunce of Iames lutrell son to the seid sir Iohn now beyng in the kynges warde and also in disauaile (12) and Surcharge of you my lord and me vndir you beyng the kynges patenteer duryng the noun age of the said Iames hath withdrawe (13) the payment of his rente of v s afferyng yerli to his charge that amounteth to the Summe of .xvij s. & vj d. And also manesseth and (14) wylnouʒt Suffre . . .¹ vppon hym to be hadde. with oute that rumour ther vppon were like to rise and nouʒt oonli (15) this doth bi hym selfe but exciteth and Stureth othir dyuers of freholders and tenauntes that they sholde withdrawe ther (16) rentes And also impriseth the mater vppon hym Selfe. And at dyuers lawe dayes stureth Tathing men and also the xij men that they shold no (17) thyng presente and aftir his power of grete malice and euyll will wolde lette all the auantage that Sholde come (18) of all the Courtes that ther ben holde the whiche Sowneth to the kynges grete disauaile disheritaunce of the seid childe. and (19) surcharge to you my lord and me beyng vndir you Plese youre lordship thes maters throu youre wysdome to concider and to puruey (20) soche remedy that the kyng oure souereign lord and the seid heir be nouʒt disherityd ne the lyuelode in (21) youre tyme amenusyd ne apeiryd but that du remedy and correccion be hadde in thes seid maters so that non othir person (22) haue cause of inboldesshyng her aftir bi the seid Coward SeintIon

Chancery hand
Printed Somerset Record Soc. 33, p. 205.
¹ rubbed   ² superior insert

189

After 1432   C1/1/41   Petition of Thomas Appelton of Dartford, Kent (right side rubbed; matter in parentheses supplied from PC)

(1) To my most reuerent fadir in god and most gracious and rightwose lord the Bisshop of Bathe Chaunceler of Englond

(2) Besechith in the most humble wise your povir seruant Thomas Appelton That where as william Aleyn clerk (3) of the countynghous

with ynne the housold of the kyng our soueraigne lord. Roberd Aleyn
fadir to the seid william (4) and Thomas Cotes ymagenyng of grete
malice before thoght extorcionesli to oppresse and fynalli to distroye
your seid (5) Suppliaunt ayens concience and lawe / On seynt Stephenes
day at nyght be twene xj and xij of the Clokke at mydde nyght (6) the
vijthe. yer of the kyng our soueraigne lord with force and armes on
(7) horsbak in maner of werre riot and rowte araied. with bowys and
arowys swerdis and bokelers in maner of rebellion and Insurreccion
(8) a yens the dygnyte of our soueraigne lord the kynge and his crowne.
kome to the hous of your seid Suppliaunt. (9) at Derteford in the Shire
of kent. at mydde nyght. And took awey Anne the doghter and on of
the heyres of your seid (10) besecher beynge with ynne the age of xij.
yere. and in his warde whos mariage of right to hym perteyned. and
to non othir / And (11) that same doghter the seid william Aleyn
ravisshid be force vileynously . . .[1] and here enforced be the supportacion (12) and helpe of the seid Roberd. and Thomas Cotes. and weddid here ayens the wille of here said fadir. and alle here frendis (13)
expressely ayens lawe And ayens the forme of all maner Statutes in such
cas made before this tyme / And in lettynge (14) your besecher to take
the profit and avayle of here seid mariage. ffor the which mariage your
seid besecher (15) myght haue had CC mark of money. & she to haue
bene maryed to such dyuerse notable persones as myght exspende (16)
an C li of enheritaunce be yer of yerly lyflode / where as the seid william
Aleyn at that tyme hadde nor ʒit hath (17) no fote lond of his owne
in Englond. And aftir the seid william Aleyn took an accion of wast
in the comyn place vnIustly (18) withoute concience ayens your besecher
(and)[2] with grete mayntenaunce be color of his seid office broggid (19)
hyred and enbrasid to hym the Iorores the which Iorores were kept iiij.
dayes in london at the cost of the seid william (20) Aleyn (Thretyng
and manasyng your seid besecher) oppressiouesly that the seid Iorores
were redy to haue condempnyd your (21) seid Suppliaunt in a M li And
the seid william Aleyn Roberd Aleyn and Thomas Cotes thorow grete
manace and meyntenaunce of (22) dyuerse peple be cause of the office
of the seid william Aleyn put your seid besecher in fere of. his lyf and
compellid (23) hym vntrewly. be oppression to make a feffement of
all his londis and. his. tenementes to the value of iiij mark (24) be yere
with ynne the Shires of Essex and Middlesex (to certeyn persones at
the denomynaccion of (25) the seide william Aleyn) vpon condicion that
your seid suppliaunte sholde haue suffisaunt and (26) sure astate. noght
defesable of xxiiijti li be yere to be paied. to hym at iiij termes yerly
duryng his lyf of the issues and (27) profites of the seid londis and

tenementes with a sarteyn payne and reentre for defaute of payment (in maner and forme) (28) like as in certeyn dedis endentid. there of made be twene the seid parties pleynly aperith The (29) which xxiiijti li be yere the seid william Aleyn be covyne and confederacie hadde be twene hym and the seid Roberd (30) Aleyn and Thomas Cotes with (all maner of) profites comynge of the seid londis and tenementes withholdith (31) vntrewly ayens all reson and concience in his owne hand and paieth your seid. suppliaunt no peny nor no peny wolde paye (32) this ij. yere and an half. (last pased) and more And (also hath felde downe) all the tymbre of the seid lyflode to the (33) value of an C li and more and makith wast fro day to day. And latith the housyng of the seid lyflode falle doune and go to (34) noght for lakke of reparacion in his defaute (Please hit) to your highne(sse to considere thes premisses) (35) and be your most noble and high discrecion to ordeyne that your seid Suppliaunt myght haue Writtes direct (36) to the seid william Aleyn (Robert Aleyn and Thomas Cotes)[2] to appere before you in the Chauncerie. with ynne xl. dayes aftir the (37) date of the seid writts at Westminster (And that the seid tresspasours be ponysshid for the seid riottes oppressions (38) and offences aftir their deserte)[2] and yf the seid william Aleyn apere to the writ aforeseide. that thanne (39) be your discrecion restore the seid Suppliaunt to the seid londis and tementz yf hit be founde be due (40) examinacion that the seid rente of xxiij li be yere was be hy(nd) noght paied to your seid (Suppliaunt at) eny (41) terme with ynne the seide dedis endentid. comprised. with the damages that the seid besecher hath hadde in this partie. (42) And in cas the seid william Aleyne a pere noght in the Chauncerie to the seid writ. that thanne lyke you to ordeyne that (43) your seid supplaiunt be restorid to the seid londis and tenementes in maner and forme afore seid. with all (44) maner of damages that he hath hadde in this partie . . .[3] Considering of your rightwosenesse that your seid (45) Suppliaunt hath no more lyflode to lyve vpon / nor dar nethir ride nor go late nor rathe in to Essex nor Middlesex where the (46) seid londis and tenementis lieth for to distreyne nor for to make non entre (in the seid londis and) tenementis (47) nor dar not nor ys noght of power in no maner of wise pursue be lawe. ayen the seid william for his damages nor can haue (48) non officer to execute no writ ayens the seid william Aleyn whiles he s(tondith) in his office aforeseid And that for (49) the love of god and in the weye of Charite.

Non-Chancery hand
Printed *PC* I.xxxi-ii.
[1] cancel [2] superior insert [3] erasure

190

After 1432   C1/1/42   Petition of Gieffrey Qwyncy of Norwich (right side damaged; matter in parentheses supplied from PC)

(1) To my right worthy and gracious Lorde the Bisshop of Bathe Chaunceler of Ingelond

Besecheth lowly youre pouere seruaunt (2) Gieffrey Qwyncy Citeseyn and Chaundeler of Norwich that where he trewly vseth and hath vsed to bye and selle suche marchaundises (3) as lo(ngeth to his crafte by the wightes accordyng) to the estandarde of the kynges escheker / And also atte excitacion (4) of the pouer poeple / hath made candell of talghe with weyke of flex / to serve hem aswell / and as longe to endure as candell (5) (made with weyke of cotoun / sellyng ther of) contynuelly to þem þat verraily knowe the seid weyke made of flax / (6) a pounde lesse by a ferthyng thanne of candell. made with weyke of Cotoun / to gret refresshyng of (the seid pouer poeple / There Robert (7) Landasdale and William) Hempstede Shirreves of the seid Citee this last yeer for as moche as Cotoun was lyke to be at lasse (8) price in the seid Citee / if candell were vsuelly made there with weyke (of flex / And for the seide Gieffrey wolde not selle suche) (9) Marchaundise as longeth to his crafte by wightes by the seide late Shirreves ordeyned / not accordyng to the seid estandarde / wher of (10) every pounde weighte is half an (vnce hevier thanne the pounde of the seide estandarde whiche) wighte þe seid Gieffrey hath (11) redy to shewe by colour of heer office / brak & entrid þe hows of þe seid Gieffrey & CCxx li of candell / & a pece (12) of bras of hefe of a pound weighte ensealed & acordyng to þe (seide estandarde whar by þe seid Gieffry vsed to (13) bye and selle took . . .) body arested & imprisoned & notwithstondyng þe seid Gieffrey profered to hem sufficeant (14) suertee of a Ml marc to appere in his owen persone beforn þem / whanne and where they wolde desire / they (hym withhelden (15) in prison vnto the tyme the seide . . .) the seide late Shirreves xx s for his delyveraunce / and made his frendes (16) william Love and Iohn ffitʒ be bounden to the seide late Shirreves in xl li wherfor and by(cause þe seide late Shirreves (17) ne wolde not . . .) werkyng ageyn the seide Gieffry / ne in his owen persone sued to your good Lordship / and of (youre) grace hadde (18) too writtes sub pena directe to the same late Shirreves / the which (writtes the seide Gieffrey delivered to . . .) by (19) cause of which writtes thus delyvered the same late Shirreves forthwith vpon the seide lyvere of the seide writtes / wrongfully (20) arested the seide Gieffrey and hym inprison(ed and hym so beyng prisoner ledde . . .) bisily intreted hym to receyve (21) a geyn the seide writtes / and for the worship of heer estates to fynde hem suerete of C li by obligac*i*on symple to profre & (22) leye beforn hem xl li / affermyng and (be hestyng to the seid Gieffry . . .) he shuld treuly forthwith have his monye (23) ageyn and livere of the seide obligac*i*ons / by which trete the seide Gieffrey trostyng verrily to heer seide behestes receyved (24) ageyn the seide writtes and made Edmund Ripon (& þe seide Iohn ffitz be bounde by . . .) seide late Shirreves in (25) C li and by full harde menes chevised and leyed / beforn þe seide late Shirreves the seide xl li as they desired / whervpon the (26) seide late Shirreves delyvred to þe seid Gieffrey the (seide obligac*i*ons and xxli . . .) of þe (27) seide xl. li wrongfully by extorc*i*on ageyne heer seid behestes took & kepe to heer owen vse to þe verray distrucion (28) & aneyntisyng of þe poer degre of þe seid (Gieffrey) Please it to youre (graciouse Lordship . . .) Chauncerie the seide late (29) Shirreves in suche fourme and tyme as pleseth to yow / to be examined of these matiers and to abide your rightfull reule and ordinaunce (30) of the (same Bryngyng with hem the . . .) takyn of the seide Gieffrey & a pounde weyghte suche as they have compelled the seide Gieffrey and other (31) Chaundeleres in the seide Citee to selle by heer Marchaundises (Consideryng of your gret grace the poverte . . .) and that he in this case hath no remedeye atte co*mune* lawe

Chancery hand
Printed *PC* I.xxxii-iii.
[1] superior insert

191

1433   E28/54/42   Petition of Thomas Walton, Chamberlain of North Wales

(1) To the kyng oure sou*er*aigne lorde.

Besecheth mekely Thomas Walton late Chamberlayn of Northwales þ*at* where as (2) a subsidie of CCCC marc was granted to oure souʉeraigne lord youre fadir whos saule god assoile by the comyns of the (3) Counte of Caernarvan paiable at certain dayes comp*re*hendet in the said graunt the whech CCCC marc the said besecher hathe (4) knawlaget in his acompte And vnswared to youe sou*er*aigne lord of CCCl marc þ*er* of as hit apperyth by his accomptʒ (5) in youre Escheker of recorde & the Barons of youre said Escheker hath put him to vnsware why hit schuld not be demyd an concelement (6) for asmeche as omission was made of paiement of .l. marc p*ar*cell of the forsaid CCCC marc in the said acomptʒ. the wheche (7) l. marc the said besecher neu*er* recevuyd ne no parcell ther of but hit remaynes in the colloctours hondes of the saide (8) Counte. the which in the said Escheker the said besecher hath pretendet to auerre as the Court wold a ward. Neuer the (9) lesse the said besecher hath made gree & payet the forsaid. l. marc in youre seid Escheker to youe soueraigne lord as hit apperyth (10) in youre said Escheker of recorde / Please hit vnto youre high & graciouse lordship be the avise of youre full wise Consell (11) to consider the longe seruice þat the said besecher hath don a fore þis tyme Als well to oure said soueraigne lorde (12) youre fadir as to youe soueraigne lorde & the greuouse vexacion þat the said besecher hathe hade. (13) hath & most have continuelly to þis mater be determynet if hit schulde falle in triall in the Contre & non avauntage to (14) youe souerayn lord þeropon to graunt a priue seall dirett vnto youre Tresorer & to youre Barons of youre said (15) Escheker to discharge finally the said besecher of the maters afore saide receyuyng of the saide besecher .x. (marc)¹ li² for a fyn (16) in eschewyn of the cost labour & trauaill þat the said besecher schuld have aboute the triall of the said mater (17) for goddes love & in way of charite:

(Signatures in different hands) H gloucestre .I. Ebor I. Bathon Canc W lincoln Suffolk Scrop hungerford

Chancery hand

¹ cancelled ² interlinear insertion

192

1433 SC8/277/13830 Petition of Commons concerning the stews of Southwark

(1) Please Hit to the wysdome and high dyscrecion of the worschipfull Comunes in this present parlement (2) assemblid to consyder a gret myschief in late dayes begonne Among vntrwe lyvers and peple withe oute conscience and (3) yet duellyng in a Suspect and wycked place called the Stwys in the Burgh of Southewerke in the Shire (4) of Surrey That ys to wete how that withe In fewe dayes diuerse persones of ryght gret poverte and ryght (5) disolute governaunce withe in a fewe yeres dwellynge in the sayd suspecte place as well by recettyng (6) of comon women thefes mansleers and avoutoures as by murdererys and prive Roberyes done ther by hem selff (7) and other many withe oute pitye trowthe and good conscience ther pryvile logyd haue sodenly comyn to gret Rychesse (8) and ther withe purchasyd gret lyvelode of londes and tenementys to ryght grete value yerly and by (9) cause of sufficyaunt of freholde so purchased haue bene ofte returned by the shereve of the

shire and other (10) Bayllefs and sworen in enquestes as well for felonyes and trespases be twene the kyng and partie / and partie (11) (& partie)¹ as in assises and othere pleys of londe afore diuerse Iuges of oure liege lorde in hys (12) courtes And afore the Stward and marchall of hys houshold thorugh whiche causes many and dyuerse dysherytaunces and wrongfull (13) condempnacions of many true lyege men of oure souerayne lorde haue ben hadde and many murderyrys of (14) men and notarye theves have ben sauyd and gret morderyes and robberyes conseled and passed vnponischyd and how the (15) sayd suspecte peple enhabyte hem in Comune hostryes and tauernys in the high strete of the sayd burgh ther (16) Recettyng theves comune women and other mysdoers in lyk wyse as they deden atte the sayd suspecte place (17) of the stwys / like hit to youre high dyscrecions these premisses consydered and that suche peple (18) withe oute consience mowe not of reson be vnderstonden worthi of trouthe nor to bere witnesse of trouthe in (19) any cause wher ryght ys to be enquered to praye the kyng oure souerayne lorde that by the assent of the lordes (20) espirituele and temporele and by auctorite of this present parlement to ordeyne (that yef)² any suche (21) persone be retorned by any shereff bayllef or other mynisterys of oure souerayne lorde the kyng in the sayd (22) Shire of Surrey or by ony mynister afore the stuarde and marchall of the kynges houshold that as well for the (23) kyng as for any partye he (maye in)² all tymes here after be chalenged and the chalenge in this partye (24) allowed for the cause aforesayd And also that non suche that haue so duellyd atte the sayd Stwys be (25) sufferyd to holde any comune hostrie nor taverne in any other place withe in the sayd Sutwerk sauf (26) only atte the sayd Stwys in estcheuyng of mur(dere)ris³ robberyes and avoutries that ellys ben lykly to ben (27) hadde And that the Iusticeʒ of the pees in the sayd Shire of Surrey haue (power to enquere)¹ of all such (28) holders of hostries and tauernis and to punysche hem that suche ben by f(yn and raunson and)¹ enprisonyng of her (29) bodyes after the dyscrecion of the sayd Iusticeʒ for the love of god and in waye of Charitee

Chancery hand
Printed *RP* IV.447.1.
¹ superior insert   ² rubbed   ³ torn

193

1436   SC8/27/1309   Petition of Commons concerning the stews of Southwark

(1) Please hit to the Wisedomes and hye discrecions of the Worshipfull Comunes in this present parlement (2) assembled to consider two grete meschiefs nowe in late dayes bygonnen by vntrywe lyvers and people with owte consciens (3) and yet dwellyng in the Burgh of Suthwerk in the Shire of Surrey / Oon is that howe nowe late by Auctorite of (4) parlement was ordeyned and stablet that no person that had dwelled at the comune Stywes shulde hald any comune (5) hostryes ne comune Tavernes with yn the saide B(urg)h[1] ne thay shulde not passe in no maner enquestes with yn (6) the saide Shire safe only at the saide comune Stywes the whiche ordenaunce hath been to grete weel of alle the honest (7) people of the saide Burgh and Shire and put awey mony and grete periuries robberyes and other inconueniences (8) And nowe syn that tyme ther be comyn other strange persones and have set vp Stywehouses and houses of bordell and vnclene (9) lyvers with yn the hye stretes and among the honest dwellers of the saide Burgh and there they herber and refet alle maner of (10) myslyvers and avowterers theefs robbers mansleers and other myslyvers wherthurgh meny wemen ben ravysshed and brought (11) to evil levyng neightbores and strangers ofte tymes robbed and murdred that vnnethese any persone dar passe thair (12) house fro nyght come And also nowe late tyme ther been certeyn Alienes callid fflemmynges that have set vp comune (13) hostryes and comune Tavernes with yn the saide Burgh where ynne thay refet and herber alle maner Alienes and (14) strangers as wel ffrensshmen and Picardes as flemmynges and alle other nacions aswel Aduersaries to oure souuerayn (15) lord the kyng as frendes and there thay han thair comenycacions and metynges by thaym self nought sufferyng any englisshman (16) to be herbered or come among hem / by the whiche Alienes and strangers by liklynesse the Counseill ordenaunce and purveaunce (17) of oure saide souuerayn lord and his trywe liege people is discovered to his Aduersaries his custumes and (18) dywtees embesiled and conceiled to hym grete preiudice and alle his liege people / Thees premisses considered (19) like hit to youre high discrecions to pray the kyng oure souuerayn lord by the Assent of the lordes spirituels (20) and temporels and by Auctorite of this present parlement to graunte and ordeyne that no maner of persone (21) in eny tyme to come be hardy to take vppon hym to holde ne kepe any maner Stywes ne houses of bordell and vnclene lyvers in any place with yn (22) the saide Burgh safe only atte place called the comune Stywes on peyne of enprisonement of their bodyes by xl dayes (23) and makyng fyne and raunsom atte kynges will / And that no maner persone Aliene holde ne kepe comune hostrye ne (24) comune Taverne in any place with yn the saide Burgh after the fest of Estire next comyng on peyne of en-

prisonement (25) and makyng fyne and raunsom in the fourme abovesaide / And that the Iustices of pees in the saide Shire and the kynges baillif (26) of the saide Burgh for the tyme beyng and every of hem have power at alle tymes that thaym shal seme nedeful and expedient (27) to enquere in the saide Burgh of thees premisses And opon alle suche persones as thay or any of thaym fynde gilty (28) and dywly convycte afore thaym to do execucion and punysshement in the maner and fourme byforseide for Charite
Non-Chancery hand
Printed *RP* IV.511.1.
[1] torn

194

1433   SC8/26/1281   Petition concerning the murder of Isabell by her husband John Carpenter of Sussex (right side torn)

(1) A Roy nostre souerain seigneur

Besechen humbly youre Comunes of this present (2) parliament. that where one Iohn Carpenter of Brydham in the Shire of Sussex husbundman (the vii daye of (3) Fevever the yere of youre noble reigne the viiite)[1] saying to Isabell his wijff that was of the Age. of xvje. (4) yere and had be maried to him but xv dayes. that they wolde go to gedre on Pilgre(mage and made to arraye hir in (5) hir best arraie and toke hir with)[1] hym fro the said Toun of Brydham to the Toun of Stoghton in the (6) said Shire. And there in a woode he smote the said Isabell his wijff (on the hede that the brayne wende oute (7) and with his knyff)[1] yaf hire many other dedly woundes. And streped hir naked out of hir clothes (8) and toke his knyff and slitte hir bely fro the breste doun & (toke hir bowels oute of hir body and)[1] (9) loked if she were with Childe And thus the said Iohn mourdered horrebely his wijff. of the which horryble (10) mourdure the thoursday (next after the Fest of Seint Ambrose the Bishop the)[1] yere of your Reigne bi for said the (11) said Iohn was endyteth bi for Sire Iohn Bohun. knyght henri husee knyght and william (12) (Sydney youre Commissioners of youre pees withinne)[1] the Shire forsaid and proces made oute (13) vpon the same endytement according to youre lawe. til the same Iohn Carpenter was oute(lawed of the said (14) mourdure and nowe graciously for the same)[1] cause Arest. and in youre Prisone called the kynges benche. (15) Please hit to your hie Rightwysnesse to considre the horrible mourdur (fore said)[1] . . .[2] And by auctorite (16) of this your hie Court of Parliament to ordeine that this said Iohn Carpenter may be Iuged as a Traytour (and

(17) yat youre Iugges have power to yeve Iugement)¹ vpon him to be draw. and hanged as a Traytour . . .² in (18) Eschewyng of such horrible (mourdurs in tyme comyng Savyng allwey to the)¹ lordes of the ffee. Eschetez (19) of his landes aftire yere. day and wast

Chancery hand
Printed *RP* IV.447.43.
¹ torn off; supplied from *RP*   ² cancelled

195

1433   Fragment joined to C49/21/14   Proclamations and Petition concerning the safety of members of Parliament (damaged)

(1) the kyng woll þat if any assaute or affray be. made. to eny lord . . . parlement. (or elles to þe kynges counseille by)¹ (2) his comaund . . . conseill þat thenne proclamacion be made thre sondry dayes in þe . . . made. þat þe. (3) partie. so offendyng appere. byfore. þe. kyng in his . . . if it be. in terme. tyme. or elles atte. þe. next day (4) in terme. tyme folo . . . desired

1433   RP IV.453.60 (Conclusion)

Le Roy voet, que si ascun assaut ou affraye soit fait a ascun Seigneur Espirituel ou Temporell, Chivaler de Countee, Citezein ou Burgeis, venuz au Parlement, ou au Counseil du Roy par son commandement, & la esteant & entendant au Parlement, ou au Counseil; q'adonques soit Proclamation fait par trois jours severalx, en la pluis overt lieu de la Ville ou l'assaut ou affraye fuist enty fait, que la partie qi face tiel l'assaut ou affraie, soy rende devaunt le Roy en son Bank, deinz un quarter d'un an apres la Proclamation fait, s'il soit el temps du terme, ou autrement all prochein jour en temps de terme, ensuant le dit quarter, a faire & receivere en manere come il este desire par la Petition.

1444 C49/26/4 Ancient Petition (damaged; material in parentheses supplied from *RP*)

(5) P(ra)yen the comune (in this) present parliament assembled that it please vnto the kyng our souerain lord by þavis (6) of his lordes spirituell and temporell in þe said parliament beyng (to ordeine estable) and auctorise in the said (7) parliament and by auctorite of the same that if any persone or persones make any assault or affray vpon the said lordes (8) or comunes or vpon any of hem (beyng in the seid) parliament or from thens retournyng homeward or vpon any lord knyght of the Shire (9) Citezein or burgeis at any tyme here after by the kynges comandement comyng to (high court of) parliament þere (10) abidyng

or from thens retournyng to his dwellyng place. þat þen the seid lord knyght of the Shire Citeʒein (11) or burgeys vpon whom suche assault or affray is (made have such writte or writtes of proclama)cion as by an Act of þe said present (12) parliament for sire Thomas Parr knyghte is in like cas ordeined to be hade. to be directed (to such) Sherif or Sherifs (13) (where the trespas is supposed to be done) retournable or retournables at eny day to be desired by þe same partie compleignant (14) aforne the kyng in his benche. the same partie compleignant to haue þere(upon such apperance) or els upon þe (15) default of apperance of the person or persones vpon whom it is in þat partie compleigned suche (16) execucion as is ordeined also in the seid Acte for the seid sir Tho(mas)

Chancery hands
Printed *RP* V.111.41.
[1] over erasure in a different hand

196

1433   SC8/27/1303   Petition of Wylliam Warwyk of Salisbury
(1) To the ryght wise & discrete Comunes of thys Present parlement
Shewith lowely wylliam warwyk of Salesbery (2) marchant how that late he sende in to Bretayn water Trenchevile hys seruant factour and attournay to marchandise ther wyth (3) wollen cloth of diuers colours which cost hym here in Englond CC. li. at the ferst byeng by sidis custumis subsidijs (4) and other costis for the shippyng and saue hauyng ouer of the same cloth which seruant with the same cloth in the (5) monthe of October þe ixe yer of the reigne of oure souerayne lorde þat now ys arived / at (6) Gildo in Bretayn forsayd and there hade eschangid þe same cloth for canevas Tressecloth and other marchandise (7) of þat contray Ther the lord of Mountassi lond lord of the same port of Gildo nat consideryng þe (8) (pees)[1] and trewys þoo had by twene oure souerayn lord and the duk of Brytayn and soworne by the same duk (9) nor consideryng the lettres of the saue condut and saue(gard the)[2] which þe said seruant (10) þoo had and shewid as wel vnder the seal of the sayd Duk as vnder the seal of same lord whiche lettres (11) the sayd william warwyk hath yet to shewe toke the said seruant and hys (cloth and)[2] marchandise (12) and brought ham in to hys Castel of Gildo and imprisoned þe same seruant and Ingyned hym so þat he (13) was in point of deth and after ward made hym fast iij days wyth out mete and (drynke)[2] and thanne putte (14) hym to fynance

to pay .l. li. for hys deliuerance wher of the sayde lord by the hondys of hys pourtour of (15) the said Castell and other of hys minystres þere toke and was (payd at seynt malwis)² (16) of the sayde william warwyk of .xxviij. li. iij s.iiij d. in marchaundyse in party of payment of the saide l. li. and (17) afterward þe same lord of muntassiland for as moche as the said william war(wike)² as wel by (18) priue seals oute of thys lond as by supplicac*i*ons made ther in the name of hys said seruant suwyd to the (19) saide Duk for the deliuerance of hys sayde seruant and of hys said godys and (marchaundises)² lete (20) take þe sayd seruant and cast hym oute ouer hys castell wall to the see and drowened hym and kepyth styll (21) al the forsaid canvas Tressecloth and marchandises to hys owne use ayen þe forme (of the)² (22) Trewys saue condutis and save gardys by for seid to the harmys of the sayd william warwyk of CCCC. li. in anientesing (23) of the pover degree of the sayd bysecher (but due remedie be hastylych)² ordeyned and purueyd for hym (24) in thys p*a*rtie Plese hyt to yowre wyse discrecions to considere al thys for seyd mat*er*s and there apon to (25) pray the kyng oure souerayne lord to ordeyne by autoritee (of thys)² p*r*esent p*a*rlement (26) þat hyt be lawfull to the sayd besecher to sese and take such godys and marchandyses of the sayd lord of mountassilant (27) and of hys tenantys and s*er*uantȝ to (þe walwe of CCC. li. as)² he shal mowe fynde here after in (28) eny p*a*rtys of the lond geresey or garnesey in ful re(com)pense³ of hys lose and harme by foresayd (29) with oute inpechement of oure said souerayn (lord and of his heires)² in tyme comyng for the loue of god and in the way of Charitee

Chancery hand
Printed *RP* IV.475.23 See *CPR 1429-36*, p. 457.
¹ superior insert ² rubbed ³ com superior insert

197

1433-50   C1/2/18(21)   Petition of John Bredhill, retainer of John Bate, Clerk of Chancery

(1) To the worshipfull ffado*r* in god Iohn Bisshop of Bathe Chauncellere of Engelond

Compleyneth your pore (2) orato*r* Iohn Bredhill p*a*rson of the chirche of kyngesswynford oon of the s*er*uantes of Iohn Bate Clerk (3) of the Chauncery of our souereyn lord the kyng that Iohn Sutton knyght Iohn Sheldon Iohn Clerk Thomas yonge & Thomas (4) Bradley the tewseday in whitson wike the yere of the regne of our souereyn lord the kyng xvj wronfully entred in to the (5) parsonage of your seid suppliant at kyngessynford in the Counte of Stafford and ther breke vp iiij Cofors & bere away (6) alle his godes. that is to sey j Bibull (historia scholastica)[1] the maistor of stories / j legend aurea. j pupille. the (7) euangelistes glosed ij gloses vppon Iob. Alquyn vppon sentence. Alquyn de veritatibus. viij Bokes of Philosophie. (8) j Bok de regimine principum nobilium. iij Bokes of Bonauenture iiij. Bokes of sermons. the (9) maistor of sentence Augustyn de caritate. a doctor vppon luke. j myssal ij portuose. xl volumes of Gramare logik (10) Rethorik & othor science with stuffe of Parchyment & papire whiche godes were worth: l. li.

Also they toke away x li in money. xiij. spon(es of)[2] siluer. j maser. iij paire (11) bedes of corall. j paire bedes of aumbor. j paire bedes of gete vj broches vj rynges. ij Beddes of bokerham hangyng. (12) j silor with a testor. ij Couerlettes of Tapsery j Couerlette of wostede xvj couerlettes vj blankettes (13) iiij matrace iiij Bolsters xviij shetes viij Bordclothes xx sanappes. iij gownes furred ij hodes v hures.j Dowbelette (14) iij Chistes iiij Cofors. v bassyns. iij lavors ij paire trostell. iij tabull iiij Chaiers j bras potte of xvj galons (15) vj pannes vij pottes iij brandardes. iij yron broches iij frying pannes ij gredyrons iiij kichon knyves vj Chandellers. v salors (16) iiijxx peces of peautor vessell vij quarters of Boef v Bakons vj turnell viij Barell for ale. j bras morter (17) with a pestell of yron. A Chymney of yron ij wyn botell ij pottes of lethor. j. dorser iij Bankers x quysshons. j herneysed (18) girdill. xx lb wex. v yerdes of Blanket viij ellon of lynnon cloth x lb of lynnon yorn. ij paire wightes for gold. j. dial (19) a bowe. xxiiij arowes j haboryon & j sweyrd whiche godes were worth: xlviij. li.

Also they toke a way. x bushelʒ of (20) rie iij quarts of malt. j mowe of rie j wayn j payre wheles. j dongewayn CC thraves of stre iiij shoveles iiij spades j plough (21) iiij yockes. v kyn ij Calves iij Bores j Mere ij Coltes xvj hogges x pigges x Capons x hennes & vj mavlers whiche godes were worth (22) xvj li. x. s.

Also they toke vp the profites of the chirche that is to sey xxx teithe lambes xij ston of teithe (23) wolle. the teithe hay the offerynges the profites of the glebe the gardyn the chirche yerd and also they hewen doun (24) & brende his wodes & destroied his houses hegges & diches in harmes & valoue of : xj. li.

And also they putte away (25) his seruantes that is to sey sir Iohn Mere prest Richard Bredhill Thomas Morley & Iohn webbe by whiche your (26) seid suppliant myssed the seruice of his seid seruantes by the space of xij wekes to the harmes of .x.li vnto the vtterest (27) vndoyng

of your seid suppliant Wherfore the seid suppliant bisecheth your gracious ffadorhode of remedie aftor (28) reson & conscience at the high reuerence of the holy Trinite.
Chancery hand
Printed *PC* I.xvii.
¹ superior insert   ² torn

198

1434   E28/54/43   Petition of the mayor and citizens of Limerick
(1) To the kyng our souerayne lord and to his Ri3te wise counseill
Besichith mekely the Mair and the cominalte (2) of your Cite of Lymerik / in the parties of Irland That wher Harrie late kyng of Ingland fader of our soueraigne (3) lord kyng that nowe is by his lettres patente3 grauntyd to the Mair and cominalte of the saide (4) Cite thair heires and successours among other thynges foreuermore that they scholde haue alle manere proffites of (5) alle manere plees with in the saide Cite fines Amerciamentes forfaitures and other diuerce proffites (6) and commoditees to take by thair owne officers to thair owne vse / as in the same lettres patente3 playnely (7) apperith in resistens of thair enemyes your rebellious in the saide lande And that Thomas Comyn and Phelipp Russell sufficeant (8) Cite3eins of the same Cite my3te take and resseyuen alle the fines Amerciamentes and alle other proffites (9) and commoditees after the fourme and affecte of the same lettres patente3 / And the same proffites (10) and commoditees to dispende and besette in reparacions of the wallis and other diffences of the same Cite / (11) the whiche stonden now in grete dispair and drede by cause that diewe reparacion is not made And over that the saide (12) Thomas Comyn and Phelipp Russell my3te ben accomptable yerelye vnto the Mair and Bailiffes of the saide Cite for (13) the tyme beyng of alle the proffites and commoditees so by ham at eny tyme taken and resseuyd in the manere and (14) fourme as in the saide lettres patente3 it is conteignd like it vn to your gracious lordeschipp by Auys of your counseill (15) to considery the meschieff that the saide Cite stondith in and like is for to stonde by cause aforsaid / by your lettres patente3 (16) vnder your grete seal to ordeyne and assigne the saide Thomas Comyn and Phelipp Russell to take and resseyue alle the (17) saide proffites and commoditees and ham to dispende and bysette on the comune proffites of the saide Cite (18) And yerelye therof for to accompte in manere and fourme afore ywrete in saluacion of alle the kynges lieges (19) con-

uersaunt and diwellyng with in the saide Cite / for the loue of god and in waye of charitee.

(Signatures in different hands) H gloucestre   H Cantuar   .I. Ebor   .I. Bathon Canc   Richard   I huntington   Suffolk
Non-Chancery hand

199

1435   SC8/27/1307   Petition of Thomas Norton of Bristol
(1) To the wyse and discrete Comunes of this present parliament Beseketh yowe mekely Thomas Norton of Bristowe that there he (2) hath a bille hongyng before the lordes of the kynges Counsaill ayenst Thomas Stamford of the same tovne which comprehendyth (3) twayn maters: On is of the brekyng and the rasyng of the seales of a dede ymade by by Cristian Nele vndir her seal (4) and the Maires seal of Bristowe to on william Combe In fee simple of certeyne londes and tenementȝ in (5) the (burgh)[1] [tovne][2] of Bristowe before sayd: And bonde her and her heres to the (6) warante: The which william enfeffed Ths Spelly of Poroell of thes londes and tenementȝ in fee: the which Ths (7) deuysed this londe to Thomas Norton in his testament aftir the olde custom in the tovne be fore sayd in fee for euer more And (8) the othir mater is (that)[1] the sayd Thomas Stamford feyned a fals action of dette in the name of Iohn Mavyoll (9) in a foreyn Counte that is to say in the shire of Surrey proces contynewed in to the tyme that the said suppliant (10) was outlawed. where ther neuer was no contracte be twene the said Iohn Mavyoll and the said suppliant in the said shire nor (11) in no nother shire: the which bille was endosed to the lordes of the counsaill of kynge herry the fyfte that dede is on (12) whos soule god have mercy vnder the fourme that folwyth: that the lordes of the said counsaill for the tyme (13) beyng shuld haue power be auctorite of parlement to here and determyn all materes contenyd whith in the same (14) petycion by suche wey and processe as it semyth best to her discrecions: by force of whiche autorite the said (15) lordes sende out a wrytte lyke as the bille required to Robert Russell late Maire of Bristowe and Rogir . . .[3] (16) and Walter Mylton late baillifs of the said tovne to certifie vnto hem whether that this said Thomas (17) Stamford knovlegged the rasyng and the brekyng of the seales of the said dede or no. lyke as hit was surmy(se)d (18) in . . .[3] the which late Maire and baillifs haue certified vnto the lordes of the said counsell vndir her seales and the (19) Maires seal of office of the said tovne fro worde

to worde lyke as it is in a cedule annexed her to: the which is afore
(20) th(e lordes[3] in the counsell oforeseyd: Also for asmych that the
l)ordes of the counsaill wold be assertid of the verrey (21) trevthe of
this matere they commaundyd to come afore hem Sir Iohn Iuyn Chief
Baron of the Escheker at that tyme beyng (22) (re)corder[3] of Bristowe
and Robert longe at that time beyng of Counsaill of the said Thomas
Stamford the (23) which forsoke hym for his vntreuth and made hem
to swere vpon a boke to enforme hem trewely what they knewe of the
brekyng (24) of the said dede and rasyng of the seales of the same: the
which sir Iohn Iuyn and Robert longe hath affermed the (25) same cer-
tificate lyke as the Maire and baillifs certified: the which examinacion
is of record afore (26) the lordes of the counsaill So hangyng this mater
vn . . .[1] by the decesse of the said kynge herry the fyfte the said bille
(27) exspired: And aftir ward the said bille and the Actes ther vpon
made were autorysed and affermed in the parlement (28) of oure liege
lorde that nowe is yholde the monday next be fore the feste of seynt
Martyn the yere of his reigne the (29) ferste wyth the same power and
more yeue to the lordes of the kynges counsaill that nowe is wyth all
autorites (30) certificacions examinacions wyth all the munyeles and
circumstances of the same the which is afore the said (31) lordes of
record: Which power was committed by the lordes a bove said to sir
william Babyngton chief Iustice (32) of the comyn place and Iohn Cotayne another Iustice of the same place to here and determyn these
materes (33) a bove said: the which Iugges dyd come afore them the
sayd Thomas Stamford and made hym to wryte his answer to the (34)
said materes and the sayd Thomas Norton replid in writyng And
dyuerses days yafe to the (said)[1] Thomas (35) Stamford to remue: So
that he had a day peremtorely atte last to remue and to come in and
to abyde the revle (36) of the said Iustices: At the which day he was
called solemp(ly)[4] and appered not and so made defaut as hit apperith
a fore the (37) lordes of record be relacion of the same Iugges: And
so for lakkyng of power they myght not procede to the ende and (38)
determinacion of the materes above said That hit please vnto yowe to
pray oure soueraigne lord the (39) kynge and all the lordes espirituell
and temporelx of this present parlement seth that this matere is thus
(40) y certified and examynyd to ordeigne (by auctoryte of parlement)[1]
that this said dede may be also stronge and effectuell in lawe as hit
was any tyme afore (41) the brekyng ther of (sauyng euery person here
answer there to suche as they scholde haue hadde a fore that the (42)
seide dede was broke whenne he was yn streyngth thys peticion not
wythstondyng)[1] And þat the said suppliant may haue (43) his costes
and damages aftir the discrecion of the sayd Iugges (or els westship

& Iuyn)¹ And as touchyng (44) to the vntrewe sute that was taken in a foren shire by the said Thomas Stamford that the said Iugges (45) (or els westship & Iuyne)¹ mowe haue pleyn power by autorite of this present parlement to send for the said (46) Thomas Stamford and duely examine hym and other aftir her discrecions and if hit may be founde by her discrecions that he sewed the sute a bove said and toke out (47) the writtes that thenne the said Thomas Stamford may haue punysshement accordyng to the statut y made the ferthe (48) yere of kynge herry the ferthe a yenst attourneys that suyth fals sutes in foren shires and that the sayd Iugges (49) (or else westship & Iuyne)¹ may gif iuggement ayenst hym and to award to the said supplia(nt damages)⁴ aftir their discrecions and (50) accordyng to the losse that the suppliant hath take by the said outlawery And ouer that yf the said Thomas Stamford (51) duely warnyd make defaute afore theym that the said Iugges (or els westship or Iuyne)¹ by autorite of this present (52) parlement mowe haue power to procede to iuggement vpon his defaut and mor ouer yef eny of the said Iugges be (53) absent that he that ys present may haue power by auctorite of this parlement to procede vpon these matteres (54) and after the entent (and desyre)¹ a boue said in the worship of god and in weye of charyte

(Dorse, in another hand) As (55) tochynge þe brekyng and rasyng of þe seales of a dede ymade by Cristian Nele vnder here sele and þe (56) maires seal of Bristowe to on william Combe in fee simple of certein landes & tenementȝ in (57) þe subarbes of Bristowe with a clause of warante as þe peticion maketh mencion Atte þe (58) especiale request of þe Comunes and for diuerse causes conteined in þe (59) same peticion hit is ordeined by auctorite of þe seide parlement þat þe seyde dede be (60) . . .⁴ and effectuel in lawe as it was eny tyme afore þe brekyng þer of of Sauyng (61) to euery person her next . . .⁴ ner to such as þer shuld haue hadde afore þat þe seide dede was (62) broken wherinne it was in . . .⁴ and as tochyng þe remenant of þe seide peticion the plaintif may haue (63) his accion atte þe comune lawe

Chancery hand
Printed *RP* IV.509.
¹ superior insert ² cancelled ³ torn ⁴ rubbed

200

1436 E28/58/56 Petition of William Norton of Wales
(1) To þe kyng our souuerein lord
Besecheth lowely your poure seruaunt William Norton Squier. þat

þere as ye (2) of your speciale grace haue graunted to your seide besecher þe office of a mobre in þe shires of (3) Kermerdyn and Cardigan as in your lettres patentes þerevpon maade more plainely it apperethe: The whiche office dauyd ap (4) Morgan (vychan)¹ occupieth and þe prouffitȝ þerof takethe ayenst þeffecte of your seid graunte: Plese it to (5) your gracious lordship to considre þe premisses and þeruppon to graunte a priue seal direct to þe seid dauyd to appier (6) befor your discrete counsail at Westmynstre at a day and vpon a peyne by your hieghnesse to be limited. for goddys loue and in wey (7) of charitee:

(Another hand) le xxiij Iour doctober. lan xv. lettre ont feust faite au dit Dauid destre deugnt le consail. la ou il serra &c en lendemain de la Purificacion de nostre dame sur la peine de xl. li
    Chancery hand
    ¹ superior insert

201

1437   SC8/27/1305   Petition concerning rape of Isabell, wife of John Boteler of Lancashire

(1) To the right sage and full wise Comunes of this present parlement
    Besecheth mekely your (2) right sage and wyse discrecions Isabell that was the wife of Iohn Boteler of Beausey in the Shire of Lancaster (3) Knyght to consider that where one william Pulle late of wyrall in the Shire of Chestre Gentilman the moneday next (4) afore the fest of Seynt Iame the Appostell last passed the seid Isabell beyng atte Beausey aforeseid with force and (5) armes in riotouse manere with grete numbre of other mysdoers the house of the seid Besecher atte Beausey (6) aforeseid breke ageynst the peas of our soueraigne lorde the kyng And there the seid Besecher felonousely and (7) moste horribely rauysshed and her naked except hir kirtyll and hir smokke ledde with hym into the wilde and desolate (8) places of wales of the whiche rape he tofore the kynges Iustices atte lancastre is endited And in wales aforeseid and (9) in other secrete places her kept till nowe late that itt liked the kyng oure soueraigne lorde of his special (10) grace atte the besechyng of diuers of the ffrendes of the seid Besecher shewyng to hym the seid grete and horrible (11) felonye and offences to giff in commaundement aswell by his commission vndir his grete seal as by his (12) lettres of his priuey seal. aswell to diuers lordes as to other to take and bryng the seid william Pulle and other (13) of the seid mysdoers into the presence of oure seid soueraigne lorde. And also to take the seid

Besecher and her (14) to putte into safe warde into the tyme that itt liked the kyng in other wise for her to ordeigne wheruppon the seid william (15) Pulle perceyuyng the seid commaundement hym withdrewe and absented into desert and other secrete (16) places in wales and other Countrees where the kynges writt renneth noght: so that he in no wise by the seid Commissioners (17) as yitt may be take notwithstondyng that the seid Commissioners haue done thair diligence hym to haue (18) take in alle that thay in any wise godely myght doo. And so itt is that Thomas Stanley knyght one of the seide (19) Commissioners nowe late atte Birkhede in the seid Shire of Chestre the seid Besecher fonde and her brought (20) to Chestre and putte in warde. Please itt to your seid wise discrecions consideryng these premisses to pray (21) the kyng our soueraigne lorde to ordeigne by auctorite of this present parlement a writt of proclamacion (22) oute of his Chauncellarie of lancastre direct to the Shirref of the same Shire to do proclayme in the (23) tovne of lancastre atte euery marketday within two wekes next folowyng aftir the date of the seid writt that (24) the seid william Pulle Rauysshour appier afore the Iustices of our seid soueraigne lorde of his Countee (25) palentine the next Session there to be holden next aftir the seid proclamacion made to answer of the seid felonyes (26) wherof he afore the seid Iustices is endited by what so euer name the seid william be called or endited the (27) seid writt to be retourned atte the seid Session before the seid Iustices And if he appier not atte the seid Session: (28) that than he stand atteint of high Tresoun by the same auctorite. consideryng that the seid rauysshyng is done (29) in more horrible wise and with more heynouse violence than any hath be sene or knawen before this tyme And that the (30) seid william Rauysshour is and of long tyme hath be outelawed of felonye for mannes dethe by him foule murdred (31) and slayn not chargyng the execucion therof And that for the love of god and in werk of charitee.

Chancery hand
Printed *RP* IV.497.14. See *CPR 1436-41*, p. 83.

202

1437   SC8/27/1308   Petition concerning the estate of Thomas Norton of Bristol
(1) To the right wise and discreet Comons of this present parlement
Besechen mekely Thomas Norton Water Norton (2) of Bristowe Gentilmen Sonnes and executors of the testament of Thomas Norton late

of Bristowe Gentilman Thomas (3) Halewey Nicholas Deuenyssh and Iohn Papenham and Iohn Shepward of Bristowe Marchantȝ that it please you (4) to considre how that oon Thomas Stamford before our souerain lord the kyng at westminstre for certein (5) trespasses falshedes and disceites doon vnto the same Thomas Norton the fader atte the suyte of the same Thomas by bylle (6) was found gylty by verdite of xij notable men of the seid Toun of Bristowe to the harmes of the seid Thomas (7) Norton of iiijc marc wherupon it was awarded that the same Thomas Norton shuld recouere the seid somme of iiijc (8) marc ayens the seid Thomas Stamford. And that the seid (Thomas)[1] Stamford shulde be take to satisfie (9) our seid souerain lord of his redempcion by cause of the seid trespaces falshedes and deceites of whiche he was (10) conuicted. And after that the seid Thomas Stamford beyng atte barre at westminstre by fore our lord the (11) kyng at the peticion of the same Thomas Norton was comytted to the Marchall in prison to abide vnto tyme that he hadde (12) aswell satisfied the same Thomas Norton of his seid damages as our souerain lord of his seid redempcion. After (13) whiche the same Thomas Stamford pretendyng a fals othe to be made by the seid xij men in the seid suyte sued (14) atteynt therupon in due fourme of lawe. in whiche it was founden be xxiiij notable men of the seid Toun that the seid (15) xij men in the premisses hadde made good and true othe Wherupon the seid Thomas Stamford was by Iuggement barrid (16) of his seid atteynt and awarded ouere by the Court. that he shulde abide in prison vnto the tyme he hadde made (17) an other greet fyn with our lord the kyng for the same. After whiche tyme Thomas Stamford so beyng in prison (18) encresyng his greet vntrouthe and malice by favour supportacion and help of his keper there and by comfort of other vntrue (19) persones by sotill and malicious menes purposing to hurt vexe and vndoo your seid suppliantȝ and to make (20) hem waste and lese her godds and her bodyes to her greet hyndryng ymagined (contrevyd)[1] & feyned diuers (21) vntrue accions of trespases and fals enprisonementȝ in foreyn shires. that is to wite in london tweyn ayens the (22) seid Thomas Norton water Norton Thomas halewey & Iohn Papenham iiij of the seid bisechers by the names of (23) Thomas Norton and water Norton of Bristowe Gentilmen and Thomas Halewey and Iohn Papenham of Bristowe (24) marchauntȝ. And in Southrey oon ayens the same Thomas Norton water Norton and Iohn Papenham (25) by the same names and Nicholas Deuenyssh and Iohn Shipward (of Bristowe marchauntȝ supposyng)[2] (26) that thei shulde haue beten and enprisoned hym. where in trouthe thei were neuere gilty þerof ne som of (27) hem com not in suche places

ther the trespaces ys supposid to be doon by x yere before the trespaces supposid and somm of (28) hem neuere. and in this fourme before seid the seid suppliantȝ (ben grevousely vexed and labored (29) dailly)² and so ben likly by longe tyme to endure. by cause that if þe seid Thomas Stamford perceyue (30) that eny enquest woll not passe with his entent he woll be nonsuyd and þerupon he will begynn a newe feyned sute (32) ayen. so supposyng to labore the seid suppliantȝ infenytly by vntrue sutes withoute your good help and (33) socour. And now late our seid souerain lord enformed of the greet mysgouernaunce of the seid (34) Thomas Stamford hadde ayen hym and his liege peple for dyuers causes that meved him and his rightwys Counseill (35) the seid Thomas Stamford from the prison callid the kynges benche was remeved vnto his prison in london (36) y callid the fflete be his (lettres vnder his priue seale)¹ the whiche Thomas Stamford sueth now to our seid (37) souerain lord to be remeued and remyttid ayen to the seid prison of kynges benche to that entent that he myght be (38) there at large as he was before and there to enbrace the Iurours ayenst the seid suppliantȝ and also to be an (39) enfourmour a techer and a Counceillour as well be his writyng as otherwise to alle the prisoners (40) and mysdoers beyng in the seid prison of the kynges benche As he was before to the gret hurt and derogacion of oure (41) souerain lord and of his liege peple as it is openly knowen. Please it to your wise discrecions to consider these (42) premisses. and that diuers of the seid suppliantȝ for greet age ben impotent to laboure. (43) And therupon to praye our souerain lord the king by the assent of his (lordes espirituelx)¹ and (44) temporell in this present parlement assembled and by aucorite of the same parlement to ordeyne and (45) establie that the seid Thomas Stamford may abide and remayne still in the seid prison of fflete and in the kepyng and (46) warde of the wardeine of the same prison for the tyme beyng withoute eny remevement to be hadde of hym (47) into the seid prison called the kynges benche or into eny oþer prison out of the kepyng. and warde of the seid (48) wardeyn of fflete for the tyme beyng till the seid fynes and alle other thynges of the whiche the seid (Thomas Stamford (49) standeth charged ayens oure souerain)² lord be satisfied and (determyned)². And the seid (50) executors fully agreed and satisfied of the seid iiijc marc as lawe woll and requireth. and that for the (51) loue of god and in wey of charitee
(31 more lines in *RP*)

Chancery hand
Printed *RP* IV.509.38.
¹ rubbed, stained   ² creased

203

1438   E28/62/36   Petition of the weavers of Oxford
(Initialed) R h
(1) To the Kyng ooure soueragne Lord
Besechit mekely youre poure liege men of the crafte of weuers and of ffulleres of youre (2) Towne of Oxenford that whan Kyng Edward the furste yooure noble progenitour by his le*tt*res patentes grauntyd vnto yooure (3) said poure men of the craft of weuers of the said Towne that they shold haue here Gylde and alle there libertees and frauncheses (4) that they hadde in the tyme of kyng Harry Aiel of kyng Iohn and in the tyme of the noble kyng ffader of the said kyng Edward (5) so that euere yere they shold paye to the said kyng Iohn on marke of golde and that no man shold werk the said craft of weuers (6) w*i*thynne fyfe myle a boute the said towne but onely w*i*thynne the saide Towne and by men of the said craft of weuers of the (7) saide Towne And aftirward the said kyng Edward hauyng consideracion that where the numbre of the said craft of weuers in the said (8) Towne were wonede to be of lx p*er*sones and more in the tyme (of þe Aiel)[1] of the said kyng Iohn. and how they (9) were but xv p*er*sones in his tyme and than they were so poure and nedy that they myght noght paie to the same kyng Edward the said (10) mark of gold the wheche amountyth to vj li of sterlinges of his special grace by his le*tt*res patentes pardoned to the said (11) weuers of the said towne the said rent of a mark of gold yerely and the Arrerages of the same And furthermore grauntyde by hys (12) le*tt*res patentes that the said weuers fro that tyme furth shuld paye yerly by the haundes of the meire and Bailees of the (13) said Towne the wheche for the tyme shold be xlij s half atte mighelmasse and half atte the feste of Estur in the same manere (14) as they were wonede and accustomed to paie the said mark of gold as in the le*tt*res patentes of confirmacione of kyng Richard (15) the secunde after the conquest made vpon that is conteyned more pleynely And now hit is so souerayne lord that ther ben in the (16) said Town atte this tyme but ij p*er*sones of the said craft of weuers and they ben so poure and nedi that they han noght for to (17) paye the said xlij s. yerly by cause that othure that ben of the same craft dwelling wyth out the said Towne comyth dayly wythynne (18) the said towne and (.v.)[2] mile abowte and there they purchace and taken the matere apperteynyng to the same craffte and cariene (19) hit a way out of the said towne and werkythe hit in to grete hindryng of the payement of the said .xlij s. yerely and also into (20) grete damage and destruccione of the said p*er*sones of the said

Craft of weuers in the said Towne but they be by yoou souerayne (21) lord socoured in this partie That hit please vnto yooure noble grace and roial maieste to considere graciousely the symple numbre (22) of folke of the said Craft of weuers that ben present dwellyng in the said Towne and that they ben so poure of here goodes that they (23) may noght paye to yow the said yerly rent of .xlij s. And vpon that to graunte to the said folk of the Crafte of weuers and ffulleres of (24) the saide towne to them and to theire successours for euer more to haue a Gilde entier to gedere in the said Towne wyth alle theire (25) libertees and fraunchises to entierely and frely as the said folk of the craft of weuers and here predecessours of the (26) said Towne euer han hadde in the tyme of yooure noble progenitours a forsaide. and that the said folke of the craft of weuers and (27) fulleres of the said Towne that now ben and theire successores the wheche for the tyme shall be. shal paie the said xlij s. (28) yerly by the handes of the said Mair and Bayllees of the said Towne at the festes aforesaid wythought beryng or supportyng (29) (for þabouesaid cause)[1] ony othur charge And that the said folke of the craft of weuers and fullers and their (30) successoures among othur fraunchises and libertees fro this tyme furth haue suche libertees and fraunchises that they yerly in the (31) fest of the holy crosse in Septembre mow assemble their .ij. craftes in on place at theyre pleasire in the said Towne and there (32) chese ij persones of the moste wyse and discrete men of the said craftes that on of that on craft and that othur of that othur (33) craft the wheche ij maistres shall haue the gouernance of the said craftes wythinne the said Towne by the yere and that no persoone (34) worke ne ocupie by hem self ne be othur. the said craftes ne ony of the said craftes ne take any maner (mat)ier[3] apperteignyng (35) vnto the said craftes othur to ony of hem withynne the said Towne and .v. mile a boute but only the folke of the said (36) craftes (and of the said towne)[3] vpon the payne of forfeture to yow souerayne lord such matere be them so taken And that (37) the said .ij. maistres of the said craftes shull make theyre serches fro tyme in to tyme for the said forfeture when hit shall lyke hem (38) for suche matere so taken withynne the said Towne and .v. mile aboute or to be caried out of the said Towne and .v. mi(le)[3] (39) aboute as hit is forsaid. [that yo souerayn lord haue that on halfe and the said craftes that othur half of such maner (40) of forfeture][4] And also that the said maistres. of the said craftes the whyche for the tyme shall be. haue sufficiente (41) auctorite and pouere to make and ordeyne among the said Craftes alle goode constitucions and ordinances for the gode conseruacion (42) of the said Craftes as oftyn tymes as hem lyke wyth (oute)[1] ony pechement of yoow souerayn lord othur of yooure (43) heires or

Officers what euyr they ben payyng yerly to yoow souerayne lord and to yooure heirs .xlij s. by the handes of the (44) Maire and Baillees of the said Towne for the tyme beyng. att the termes of Estur and Mighelmasse be euen porciones. [ony (45) statutes or ordinaunces ymad in the contrare noght wythstondyng]⁴

Chancery hand
¹superior insert ²over erasure ³torn and rubbed ⁴cancelled

204

1438 E28/62/35 Privy Seal: Warrant transmitting petition of the weavers of Oxford

(1) HENRY by þe grace of (god)¹ Kyng of Englande and of ffraunce and Lorde of Irlande: To þe worshipfull fadre in (2) god þe Bisshop of Bath oure Chaunceller gretyng: Nowe late hathe shewed vnto vs þe weuers and fullers of oure (3) toune of Oxonford þat when kyng Edward þe furst oure progenitour by his lettres patentes graunted vnto þe (4) weuers and fullers of oure saide Toune þat þey sholde haue here Gilde and all þeire libertees and franchesies þat (5) þey had in þe tyme of kyng henry Aieul of kyng Iohan and in þe tyme of þe noble kyng fadre of þe saide kyng (6) Edward so þat euery yere þey shoulde paye to þe saide kyng Iohan a marc of golde and þat no man shoulde (7) werke þe saide crafte of weuers. withynne fyue myle aboute þe saide toune but oonly withynne þe saide toune & by (8) men of þe saide crafte of weuers of þe saide toune / And aftirward þe saide kyng Edward hauyng consideracion þat (9) where þe nombre of þe saide craft of weuers in þe saide toune were wont to be of .lx. persones and more in þe (10) tyme of þe Aieul of þe saide kyng Iohan and howe þey were but .xv. persones in his tyme and þan þey (11) were so poeuere and nedy þat þey myght noght paye to þe same kyng Edward þe saide marc of golde. þe which amounteth (12) to vj. li. of sterlinges: of his speciale grace by his lettres patentes pardoned to þe saide weuers of (13) oure saide toune. þe saide Rent of a marc of golde yerely and þarrerages of þe same: and forthermore graunted by his lettres patentes: þat þe (14) saide weuers fro þat tyme forthe shoulde paie yerely by þe handes of þe (15) Maire and Bailliefs of þe saide toune þat for þe tyme shoulde be .xlijs. halfe at michelmesse and half at þe feste (16) of Pasque in þe same maniere as þey were wont and accustumed to paie þe saide marc of golde: as in þe lettres (17) patentes of þe confirmacion of kyng Richard þe seconde after þe conquest made vpon þat / is conteyned

more plainely / (18) And nowe it is so. þat þer been in þe saide toune at þis tyme but .ije. persones of þe saide (19) crafte of weuers and þey be soo poeuere and nedy as it is saide þat þey haue noȝt for to paye þe saide .xlijs. (20) yerely by cause þat oþer þat been of þe same crafte duellyng withoute þe saide toune cometh (21) dayly within þe saide Toune and .v. myle aboute and þer þey purchace and take þe mater appertiegnyng (22) to þe same crafte and carie it awaye oute of þe saide toune and wirkith it into grete hinderyng of þe paiement of (23) þe saide .xlijs. yerely and also into grete damage and destruccion of þe saide persones of þe (saide)[2] crafte of (24) weuers in þe saide toune. but yf þey by vs be socored in þis partie. We þees premisses consideryng and (25) also þe symple nombre of folke of þe saide craft of weuers þat been present duellyng in þe saide toune and (26) þat þey bee soo poeuere of her goodes þat þey may noght paye to vs þe saide yerely rent of (27) xlijs. haue of oure grace especiale graunted vnto þe saide folke of þe craft of weuers and ffullers of (28) þe saide toune to þayme and to þeire successours for euer more to haue a Gilde entiere to gedre in þe (29) saide toune with all þeire libertees and fraunchises soo entierely and frely as þe saide folke of þe crafte of (30) weuers and her predecessours of þe saide toune euere haue had in þe tyme of oure noble progenitour aforsaide (31) and þat þe saide folk of þe craft of weuers and ffullers of þe saide toune þat nowe er and þeire (32) successours þat for þe tyme shall be. shall paye þe saide xlij s yerely by þe handes of þe saide maire and (33) bailliefs of þe saide toune at þe festes aforsaide withoute beryng or supportyng for þe abouesaide cause (34) any oþere charge And þat þe saide folke of þe craft of weuers and ffullers and þere successours (35) among oþere franchises and libertees fro þis tyme furth haue suche libertees and franchises þat þey yerely (36) in þe feste of þe holy cros in September may assemble þeire two craftes in o place at þeire pleasure in þe (37) saide toune and þere chese two persones of þe moost wyse and discrete men of þe saide craftes þat oon (38) of þat oon craft and þat oþere of þat oþere crafte þe which ije maistres shall haue þe gouuernance of (39) þe saide craftes within oure saide towne by þe yere and þat noo persone werke ne occupie by hym selfe (40) ne by oother þe saide craftes ne any of þe saide craftes ne take any manere matier appertiegnyng vnto þe (41) saide craftes. other to any of hem withynne þe saide toune and fyue myle aboute. but oonly þe folk of þe (42) saide craftes & of the saide toune vpon þe payne of forfaiture to vs suche matere by þayme so taken. And þat þe (43) saide two maistres of þe saide craftes shall make þeire serches fro tyme to tyme for þe saide forfaiture (44) when it shall like hem for suche matere so taken within

þe saide toune and .v. myle aboute or to be caried oute of (45) þe saide toune and .v. myle aboute as it is aforsaide. And also þat þe saide Maistres of þe saide craftes (46) þe which for þe tyme shall be haue souficeante autoritee and poaire to make and ordeigne amonges þe saide craftes all (47) gode constitucions and ordinances for þe gode conseruacion of þe saide craftes as oft tymes as hem like withouten eny (48) empeschement of vs other of oure heirs or officers what euere þey bee paiyng yerely to vs and to oure heirs xlij s by (49) þe handes of þe Maire and Bailliefs of þe saide toune for þe tyme beyng at þe (50) termes of Pasque and michelmesse by euen porcions. We woll and charge you þat herevpon ye doo make oure lettres (51) patentes vndre oure grete seal en deue forme. Yeuen vnder oure priue seal at oure Manoir of Sheene þe .xiij.e day (52) of Iuyll. The yere of oure regne xvije.
  Chancery hand
  [1] torn [2] superior insert

205

1438   E28/61/11   Petition of John Loveyn of Normandy
(1) To þe most Reuerend fader and right gracious lord Henry Cardinall of England
  Most loweli be sechithe (2) vn to youre most gracious and heigh lordship. youre pooure Horatour Iohn Loueyn Natyff in Normandie / wiche Iohn is þe kyng is (3) truwe liege man of England. and haþ been his Soldiour atte Gurnay in Normandie / bi þe termes of x. yere now (4) passide / as þe maister of þe said / youre suppliaunt sir Thomas kiryell knyght & late Capitayn of þe (5) said Gurnay euidenceth can report vn to youre said lordship / wiche suppliaunt now a hole ȝere passide was bi force of þe (6) Inimyes taken prisoner. and so hider too haþ contynued in duras of pryson yn Beuoys / in þe wiche þer be leide (7) plegges for þe finance / of youre said suppliaunt .C. li now to be paide. or els his body to pryson aȝen. wiche were (8) soroufull atte þis tyme / Please hit vn to youre heighnesse. consideryng þe truwe & diligent seruice al so þe (9) duras of prison of youre pooure suppliaunt. þat bi þe most gracious socour of youre said lordship and by (10) þe ordynance & helpe of þe Chaunceler of England. ȝe wuld graciousli graunte to þe same youre suppliaunt a (11) Saff Conducte in Duwe fourme / he wiþ xxti. persones to come from Brytayne in a Shippe lade wiþ Salt and oþer (12) merchandise saffeli yn to England / and so to haue saff passage aȝen in to Britayne as hit hath been vsed (13) bi oþer merchantes in like maner bi fore þis. The name of þe said Shippe call-

ed is .Seynt (14) ffyacre. of þe wiche þe maister is. maister Nicholas Issaunt of Garand. for þe loue of god and yn weye of Charitee:
(Notation by Moleyns that petition was granted.)
Non-Chancery hand

206

1439   C49/23/14   Royal proclamation appointing tax collectors
(1) The Kyng will that no man dwellyng within any Citee or Burgh of this roialme of the which Citee or Burgh it hath (2) ben vsed her afore and yit is (the names of certein men)[1] by the (persones for)[1] the saide Citee or Burgh (3) commyng to the parlement to be deliuered into the kynges Chauncerie (to be Collectours of the Xme (4) in the same Cite or Burgh)[2] And wheruppon the kyng hath sent his lettres patentes to the same persones (5) so named and deliuered into (his saide)[1] Chauncerie to be Collectours of the (xme or)[1] (parcell therof)[2] within (6) the saide Citee or Burgh And the which Collectours hath accounted and er boundyn to accompte of thaire receit in this (7) partie immediatly in the kynges Escheker be (in any)[1] wyse depute nor assigned to be Collectour of any xvme (8) (or any parcell therof to the kinge or his heires)[1] (graunted or)[2] to be graunted within any Shire of this roialme (9) o les than he mowe spende in the: shire oute of the saide Citee or Burgh in londes or tenementes to the value of (10) C.s by yere ouer the charges and reprises
Chancery hand
Printed RP V.25.39.
[1] correction over erasure in another hand   [2] superior insert in second hand

207

1439   SC8/27/1327   Petition of Commons to be excused from kissing the king because of the plague (right end damaged; material in parenthesis supplied from RP)
(1) To The Kyng oure Soueraigne Lord
Shewen mekely youre trewe liege people here (by youre Auc)torite riaill in this (2) present parlement for the Comuns of this youre noble Roialme assembled. Howe that a Sekenesse (called the pestilence (3) vniuerselly through this youre Roialme more comunely reyneth than hath bien usuell bifore this tyme the) whiche (4) is an infirmite most infectif. and the presence of suche soonfect most to be eschewed as

by noble ffisisseanes and wise Philosofors (5) bifore this tyme pleynly it hath (bene determyned And as experience dayly sheweth. Wherfore we youre pore true (6) liege people above all erthly thyng) tenderyng and desiryng the helth and welfare of youre most noble persone. the whiche is to (7) oure most grettest erthly comfort. byseche youre most noble grace in conseruyng of youre (most noble persone And in comfort of (8) vs all and of alle tho that we ben comen hider fore in) eschewyng of eny suche infeccion to you to fall whiche god defende (9) graciousely to conceyve howe where that eny of youre said Comunes holdyng of you by knyghtes service (oweth in doyng to (10) you homage by youre graciouse sufferance to kysse you to ordeine and graunte) by the auctorite of this (11) present parlement that eueriche of youre said lieges in the doyng of thair said homage may omitte the said kissyng of (12) you (and be excused therof at youre will þe homage beyng of the same force as though they kissed (13) you and have thair lettres at doyng of thair homage the kyssyng of you . . .) not withstondyng

Chancery hand
Printed *RP* V.31.58.

208

1439   SC8/27/1328   Petition of Commons concerning the spice trade

(1) To the right wyse and discrete Comunes of thys present parlement assembled

Plese hit your wyse discrecions (2) to considre the grete disceyte yat (is)¹ vsed by lumbardes Itaylions and by other merchauntes aliens with other (3) merchaunt3 of this Roialme in sellyng of all maner of Spyceres . . .² to lordes knyghtes Esquiers and to all other (4) kynges liegemen that byth stuff of Spyceryes for there houshold of sych merchaundises that beth not clene clensyd ne (5) clene garbaled in grete hurte and hynderyng of all the kynges liege poeple And to praye the kyng oure (6) souerain lord and all the lordes espirituelx and temporeles in this present parlement assembled and by auctoritee (7) of the same parlement to ordeign that in euery Port of this noble Roialme where eny espiceries be to sell or (8) profored to sale that the sayd spiceries . . .³ be trewly and duely garbelyd and clensyd in gode maner and trewe (9) fourme as hit is vsed in the porte and Citee of london vppon peyne of forfaiture of the sayd spiceries (be trewly so yfound)³ (10) vngarbelyd and vnclensyd And that euery liege man that kan or may fynde or preve eny such espiceries (11) vngarbeled and vnclensyd in fourme and manere abouesayde in euery place of this Roialme have full (12) powere by Auctoritee of the sayd parlement to seise and take the sayd spiceries . . .² for a forfaiture to the (13) kyng oure souerain lord. the kyng to haue the two parties therof and the fynder the thryd parte for his labore (14) and costys and that in weye of charitee

Chancery hand
Printed *RP* V.32.60.
¹ torn ² cancelled ³ rubbed

209

1441 SC1/44/11 Assignment of power of attorney by Richard Wydevyll

(1) Reuerent fader in god and my right worshipfull lord humble I recomande me to your gode lordshipp. And for (2) asmuche as hit is wele knowen to your seid lordshipp that I am disposed in hast with goddes mercy to passe the (3) see. my frendes haue auysed me to make my Generall Attorneys by the kynges letters Patentes vnder his Seall. (4) And by cause that my leyser asketh not now to come in propre persone to your presence (5) to certifie yow the names of suche persones as I haue ordeyned therto. I beseche yow lowely that hit like yow to (6) receyue lowes Iohn knyght my ffader Richard wydevyll Squyer william Tresham and william Garnetʒ. And that I (7) may haue the said letters Patentes therof made in due forme: And This my writyng signed with my Signe manuell. and Seald (8) with my Seall. vnder whiche I haue endented with the kyng oure soueraigne lord. I will holde ferme and stable: (9) Writen at the Abbey of Batayll the iiij day of Iuyll
(Signed) Richard Wydevyll
Non-Chancery hand

210

1442 C49/25/7 Petition concerning the administration of royal holdings (damaged; unless otherwise noted, material in parentheses is supplied from *RP*)

(1) To the kyng oure souerain lord

Besechethe youre Comunies of this youre present parlement (2) assembled that it plese youre highnesse to considre how that the Right Excellent most famouse and victoriouse Prince Harry (3) sumtyme kyng of Englond youre right noble fadir whome god assoyle by his letteres patentȝ enfeffid Harry Bisshop (4) of wynchestre now Cardinal of Englond Harry Archebisshop of Caunturbury waulter lord hungerford and other for the grete (5) truste that he hadde in hem of dyuers Castelleȝ manereȝ Towneȝ lordschippeȝ honureȝ londeȝ (6) tenementeȝ rentes reuersions seruiceȝ Iurisdictions libertees fraunchiseȝ fees avousons and other possessions (7) as well in Englond as in Waleȝ as of his enheritaunce (parcell)¹ of his Duchie of lancastre of the yerely value of (8) vi M*l* li and more by estimacion to haue to theym and to theire heireȝ to the entent and effecte to execute and perfourme (9) his wille vpon the seide feffement to hem by hym made and declarid in writyng the value of wiche Castelleȝ manerȝ (10) Towneȝ lordschippeȝ honureȝ londeȝ rentes tementeȝ reuersions Iurisdictions liberteȝ (11) fraunchiseȝ avousons and possessions aftur the seide extente fro the dethe of youre seid noble fadir in to the (12) fest of Seinte Michell last passed by the seide feffeeȝ resceiued and to be resceiued amounteth to the somme of (13) Cxiiij M*l* li and more be estimacion And how it is to suppose and conceyue that þe seide wille of youre seide (14) noble fadir by the seide feffeeȝ of so grete and notable sommes by hem resceiued of the issueȝ profiteȝ (15) and revenuȝ comyng of the seid Castelleȝ manereȝ Towneȝ lordschippeȝ honoureȝ londes tenementis (16) rentes reuersions seruices Iurisdictiones liberteeȝ fraunchyseȝ feeȝ and possessions by so long tyme beyng (17) in theire hondeȝ might afore this tyme dieuly haue ben fully executed and perfourmed aboue all other chargieȝ that (18) are knowyn wiche wille perfourmed it is to vndirstond by all reson good feith and consciens that alle the seid (19) Castelleȝ lordschippeȝ Manours londeȝ tenementȝ and all the other seid possessions as the olde (20) right and enheritaunce of youre seide noble fadir belongeth vn to yow souerain lord as heire to hym Consideryng that (21) the seid feffees haue no title ner interesse therynne but only vpon trust and to his vse to execute his wille as it is a fore (22) rehersid And that the seid feffeeȝ be but fewe in noumbre whereby of liklyhode the possession ther of by casuel(t)e² (23) of dethe myght reste in oon of theyme And so descende vn to his heireȝ that ouer lyved in wiche case and it fortune (24) vpon a temporall man thenne his wyfe were therof endowable And by suche menys your right and interesse therof by your lawe (25) the further fro yowe thenne thei now be to youre grete hurte and to youre likly disheritaunce therof Considered also that in (26) youre counceill the xv day of Iuyn the xij*the* yere of your Reigne beyng thenne there my lord of Bedford youre vncle whome (27) god assoile the seid feffeeȝ desired that by yow certeyne lordeȝ of youre councell myht be depute to see the bokes (28) of receyte and of the ministracion of th(e revenueȝ in all goodly) haste of thoo landeȝ that thei were so (29) enfeffid ynne And that done thei agreed that ye myght haue and resceyue alle that shulde growe of the seide feffement aftur (30) Michelmesse day thenne next comyng by the hondeȝ of the officereȝ and deputeeȝ of the seide feffeeȝ so (31) that proclamacion schulde be made be fore the parlement thenne next sewyng (that every man that wolde aske) (32) dette for housholde Chaumbre warderobe kynges werkes or for money borowed brynge ynne to the seide feffeeȝ the growndeȝ (33) that thei aske it by And if it myght apper that the sommeȝ of the assignementȝ or of the revenuȝ of þat (34) yere wolde not suffise for paiement for the kyngeȝ detteȝ afore rehersid and for perfourmyng of his Chaunterye and (35) (of his Toumbe thenne ye to make) to the seid feffeeȝ for the rest that schulde so be founde dieu assignement (36) and agrement And if (so were that the somme) of the assignement made to the seide feffeeȝ and the revenueȝ (37) of that yere wolde amounte to a gretter somme thenne the somme of the detteȝ And makyng of the seid Chauntrye (38) and Tombe thenne the residue ther(of to be paied up to yowe) And ouer that the seid feffeeȝ this done (39) willed and agreed to make astate to yowe souerain (lord of all the seide londes and tenementȝ) that thei stode (40) enfeffed ynne that is to sey of that / that was fee taille in fee taill And of that / that was fee symple in fee symple how be it and ye (41) toke astate therof of your seide feffeeȝ in suche (wise or that they enfeffe yowe) therynne ye might (42) not haue holde ner enjoye³ the seide possessions in enherit(aunce to youre availle and suerte in suche maner) And (43) fourme of enheritaunce and as parcell of youre seid Duchie as youre seide noble fadir hem hadde and helde at the tyme of the (44) seid feffement and be fore vpon whoos desireȝ writteȝ of proclamacion procedut acc(ordyng to theise premisseȝ Considered) (45) also that in the parlement at Redyng the xviij*the* yere of youre reigne the seid (feffeeȝ (46) among other grauntid to yow so)uerain lord that aftur the dette that thenne was owyng vn to the seide Cardinall (47) and to the seid Archebisshop of Caunturbury paied for the wiche assignement was made by the seid feffeeȝ vpon the (48) (seid Castelleȝ manereȝ Towneȝ lordschippe) honureȝ londeȝ tenementeȝ rentes reuersions seruiceȝ (49) Iurisdictions liberteeȝ (fraunchiseȝ feeȝ avousons and other possessions) (50) comprised by the seide feffement by certeyne personeȝ by your commaundement to the vse of the seid Cardinall (51) and Archebisshop Reseruyng to the seid feffeeȝ ij *ml* li yerely vn to the tyme thei hadde (perfourmed the seid kyngis wille their feffour) (52) that thenne all the surplusage therof schulde be delyuerid to the Tresor(er of youre householde for the tyme beyng for) (53) the expenseȝ of the same householde of wiche surplusage so resceiued the seid Tresorer (54) schulde accompte in your eschequer wiche dette long tyme be fore the first day of this present parleme(nt was paied to the seid Cardinall and Archebisshop) (55) And ouer that grete and notable sommes haue ben resceyued sithyn the (56) said (Parlement so beyng at Redyng And therupon of youre noble grace) theise premisseȝ considered and for (57) the comfort and ease of youre peple that it plese your high nesse by auctorite of this present parlement to (58) ordeigne and assigne certein persones suche (as may like to your highnesse to here the declaration) of the (59) seide feffeeȝ or of other persones by hem suche as thei will depu(te and name in writyng . . .)

(This is about one third of the total.)
Chancery hand
Printed *RP* V.56.29.
[1] superior insert   [2] crease   [3] enjoye *sic*

211

1443   SC1/57/89(65)   Petition concerning Fernand Dalueys and his ship Seynt Auton

(1) Ryght Reuerent fadir in god and Ryght Reuerent and Ryght worshipfulle Lord. we Recommaund vs vn to your (2) lordship please it vn to youre grace to aduertice that howe oure souerain lord by his gracious lettres (3) patentes made vndir his grete seal of Englond the .xix. day of ffeuerer the yere of his noble Reigne the .xxe. (4) tooke in his gracious saufe and soeure condut and in protecioune tuicioune and defence especiale fore two yere þen (5) nexst suyng ffernand dalueys de Vernico in Spayne Maister and marchaunt of a Shipp called Seynt Auton in Spayne of þe (6) borden of .CCC. tonne oþir within and what soo euyr oþir marchaunts the same ffernand othir ways occupied othir (7) froo þis light withdrawe maister Gouuernour or possessour of the same shipp. too geddir with oþir (8) marchaunts what soo euer þay bee and harre dowers and attourneys and .lx. persouns armed oþir not armed for (9) þe defence and (saufe)[1] kepyng of the same shipp in to þe Reaume of Englond or oþir lordshippes oþir his power with (10) the said shipp charged with wyne Irne oile wex and othir marchandises what (soeuyr)[1] þay bee and with competent nombre of (11) maryners fore the gouernaunce of the same shipp comyng there abydyng by daies and by nyghtes marchaundisyng. the (12) said shipp dischargyng and it agayne in partie oþir in alle wiþe oþir godes and marchaundises (13) lawefulles agayne chargyng and wiþe the same soo charged fro the same Reaume lordship oþir power agayne goyn and agayne (14) with þe same

shipp or oþir like godes and marchaundises charged in to þe same Reaume oþir lordshippes (15) and power foresaid agayne commyng and froo þense too harre propre parties a gayne goyng and soo as oft tymes as it shuld please vn to hame duryng (16) the said saufe condut agayne commyng withoute eny empechement impediment trouble oþir greuaunce what so euyr it be eny mark (17) countermark oþir reprisale graunted oþir to be graunted notwithstondyng as by þe said saufe condut (18) shewed vn to vs more playnely apperith. which ffernand by force of þe said saufe condut the .xij. day of Maij. the yere of þe (19) Reigne of oure souuerain lord the .xxj. came in too þe port of dalkey in Irland wiþe þe said shipp charged with (20) wyne and salt with xxxvj men onely on the said shipp. which wyne and salt was sold to þe marchaunts of the Citee of dyuelyn (21) and delyuered vn to þe said marchaunts. except .xl. tonne of wyne and .CCC. quarteres of salt which shipp with alle þe (22) apparaille of the same shipp and the said .xl. tonne of wyne and .CCC. quarteres with diuers othir godes. and herneys in the said shipp (23) beyng. soone aftir the said .xij day of Maij. at dalkey foresaid. was take by one Iohn Colwelle of Comoch in Engiond with a shipp (24) of the which shipp. oone Thomas Cradok of Brygewatir is owner and by william Cooke wiþe a spynnace wiþe diuers men (25) of armes in þe said shipp and spynnac in manere of werre. and vppon this atte praier and grete desire of the said (26) ffernand we send and lete shewe the said saufe condut vn to þe said Iohn Colwelle and william Cooke. and hame requyed on oure (27) souuerain lord is be halfe. and by autorite of the said saufe condut to delyuere the said shipp of þe said ffernand. with (28) alle þe apparaille of the same and the said .xl tonne of wyne and .CCC. quarteres of salt with alle the oþir godes (29) and herneys foresaid and willed hame to see and rede the said saufe condut. and þat to doo þay wold not but (30) þe said shipp of the said ffernand and the said .xl. tonne of wyne and .CCC. quarteres of salt wiþe þe said oþir (31) godes and herneys þay take with hame and yitt it holden in contempt of oure said souuerain lorde and hurt of the said saufe (32) condut and alsoo grete hurt as welle of þe trewe liege poeple of the said land as vn too þe said ffernand. and alsoo a grete (33) hurt like to be too alle saufe conduts of oure said souuerain lord in tyme to come. and also grete ensample vn to þe said (34) Iohn Colwelle and william Cooke and to alle oþirs to offende a gayns the saufe conduts of oure said souuerain lord in tyme to (35) comme las þen this be hastiefly remedyed / fore þe said Iohn Colwelle and william. Cooke as Rebelles and pirates on þe (36) see Romyng haþe take by fore þis tyme diuers shippes aliens with diuers marchaundises and godes in the said (37) shippes commyng in too þe said land. and alsoo beyng in diuers portes of the said land / some of hame beyng at peas and some vndir (38) þe saufe condut of oure said souuerain lord. to þe grete hurt of þe trewe liege poeple of þe said land. wherefore (39) we besechyn youre lordship þat it like vn too youe to resceyue this oure lettre send vn too youe by the said (40) ffernand. and in as moche as ye been oure souuerain lord is Chaunceller. by fore whome þe said saufe condut is of (41) recorde enroulled. þat it please vn too youre gracious lordshipp too move oure said souuerain lord þat he by (42) providence of his most sadd and discrete Counseille too ordeine that þe said ffernand myght be restored vn too the saiden (43) shipp of Seynt Auton with alle þe apparaille of the said shipp and too þe saiden .xl. tonne of wyne and .CCC. (44) quarteres of Salt and too alle þe said othire godes and herneys to geddir with alle the costes and (45) damages whiche the said ffernand haþe soeuffred and shalle soeuffre in the poursuyt thereof vn too oure said souuerain lord and to (46) his said Counseille. and also that þe saiden Iohn Coolwelle and william Cooke myght be chastised of harre said rebellioune and (47) Ryght Reuerent fadir in god and Ryght Reuerent and Ryght worshipfulle Lord (the holy gost)[1] preserue youre worshipfulle estate too his (48) most souuerain pleasir. Written atte Citte of Dyuelyn vndir the Comune seale of the said Citee the second day of Iuyle.

(49) Yo(ure)[2] fulle humble seruaunts Maire and Communes of the Citee of Dyuelyn.

Chancery hand
See *CPR 1441-46,* pp. 201, 247, 287.
[1] superior insert   [2] rubbed

212

1444   C49/26/5   Petition concerning the murder of Isabell, wife of Roger Bakeler, by John Bolton

(1) Prayen the Comunes of this present parlement that hit please the kyng oure soueraigne lord of his benygne (2) grace to consider how that now late Iohn Bolton nowe beynge in prison And in the Marschall ward of the kynges (3) benche the tiuesday next a fore the feste of Saynt lauerens the yere of youre reigne the xxije at Pekham in the (4) Counte of Surrey wold haue rauesshed Isabell late the wife of Roger Bakeler and for as muche as sche (5) wold not assent vn to him he vilanisly toke of here all the Atire of her hede And al so her clothes of her body otake her (6) smokke. And yet sche wolde neuer assent vn to his vnlefull desir but at all tymes kepte her a goode womman. (7) And at the last

be cause he cowde noghte haue his desir of her. he ther at the same tyme felonesly sleeth and murdred her (8) and kutte her throte twyes. and twyes stikked her thurgh her pappes and sides *with* a dagger wher vppon sche died. (9) And all so at the same tyme and plase after the said murdre noght repentyng hym of his said horible dede as hit semed. a (10) gowne. a kirtell. a hode. two kerchieffes and two keyes vppon her ther founde of the goods and catells of the said (11) Rog(er)[1] husbond to the said Isabell the whiche wer the weryng clothes of the said Isabell beyng vppon her (12) *p*erson felonesly toke and bare a way of the whiche forsaide murdre and roborie the said Iohn Bolton ys endited (13) wher of the recordes remayneth a for yowe of Recorde in your benche of the whiche Recorde the tenur ther of ys Annexed vn (14) to this bille. And the said Iohn Bolton of his sotell ymaginacion be cause he wold not answer to the saide enditement nether to (15) other diu*er*se horible felonies of the whiche he was endited he knowleched diu*er*se felonies and . . .[2] tresons and be cam a (16) prouowr and ther of appeled diu*er*se other men and vnder colour of that Appelle so hongyng he gate hym a Chartre of (17) *p*ardon of yow of all man*er* tresons and felonies ye beyng not lerned of the forsaid horible felonies and treson (18) the whiche Chartre ys allowed of Recorde. And ther vppon to ordeigne And g*r*aunte by the Au(ctorite of)[3] (19) this p*r*esent parlement that the saide Iohn Bolton so beyng in prison as hit ys forsaid by what name so eu*er* he (20) be named be putte to Answer vn to the said felonies comprehend(id in the)[3] said enditement3 And in (21) especiall to the murd*r*e of the said Isabell *with* out any p*r*ocesse to be made Ayenst hym considering that he ys (22) in the (Marschall warde of yo*ur* benche)[4] the said (Chartre)[3] or allowance ther of or any other chartre made (23) or to be made to the said Iohn a contrarie noght *with*stonding And all so that he be came a p*r*ouowr (24) or for any other cause as a fore (rehersed)[1] And yf he be founden gilty in the saide murdre he to be iuged (25) and demed as a traitour and suche execucion to be don vppon his body as schuld be don vppon a traitour (atteint of hie)[1] (26) treson not*with*stondyng the saide (chartre And he to forfete)[4] his goodes and Catels londes And ten*e*m*en*tes as the lawe (27) requireth of hym that ys atteint of ffelonie And that the (said chartre be)[1] not as for the saide murdre and Roborie (28) to hym in no wise auaillable but vtterly voide and noght in lawe. And all so that by the said Autorite A speciall co*m*mission (29) be (made to the)[1] Chief iustice of youre . . .[2] benche and other iustices nowe beyng p*r*esent to p*r*ocede (30) to the Areignment of the said Iohn in all goodly hast vppon the said murdr*e* (and Roberie)[1] accordinge to this (31) said Acte not*with*standinge the Aio*ur*nement of your Courtes in exsample and drede

to all other that wold offende (32) in like wise And that the saide (Chief Justice)¹ haue power by this saide Autorite to bringe thes saide recordes of (33) the saide enditementes by fore hym selue and the saide Comissioners at the day that they (shalle sitte uppon the said)³ (34) comission And ther vppon to procede in hast as hit ys forsaid (And yf any man desire here after to Rauisshe Any woman)⁴ (35) and for cause that sche wolle noghte assente (vnto hym sle and)¹ murdre her that any chartre to be made (36) to any suche person for any suche murdre (be)⁵ voide and noght auaillable in lawe for the loue of ihesu and yn way of charite
    Chancery hand
    Printed *RP* V.111.42.
    ¹ rubbed   ² cancelled   ³ torn, supplied from *RP*   ⁴ over erasure   ⁵ crease

213

1449   C49/27/14   Petition of Commons that priests be pardoned for accusations of rape

(1) Also preyen the Communes for asmoche as in diuerseʒ partieʒ of this Realme many prestes aswell seculer (2) as religiouse bene grevously vexud and troubled wrongwesly by diuerseʒ inditementes of felonie to their (3) full grete hurt a yeynst feyth and conciens for synguler lucre of other personeʒ and not for youre availle / (4) þat it please youre highnesse of youre influent grace by the auctorite of þis youre parliament to pardon (5) and acquite all and euery prest aswell religiouse as seculer of all maner felonieʒ. of rape done by fore the first (6) day of Iune next comynge And also to pardon and relese by the auctorite of the same parliament to all and euerich (7) prest Seculer stipendiar anuell all yat longeth or apperteineth to youe by wey of forfature of euerich of theim. by fore (8) the said first day of Iune by cause of takyng excessious selarie contrarie to the statutes theruppon made / And þat euerich of theim (9) may haue writtes here vppon suffisantʒ for theire discharge withouten eny Chartre suynte ffor the which we youre trewe liege (10) men to the helpe and relieff of youre necessite by the assent of the lordes spirituelles and temporelles (11) of this youre Realme graunten to youe oure soueraigne Lorde a subsidie to be take and rerud of all maner prestes (12) Seculers stipendiaries and Chauntre prestes within this youre Realme þat is to sey of euery prest vj s viij d to be (13) payed to youe at the ffest of Seynt Martyn in wynter next comyng

(Response on dorse) At the (14) reuerence of god and for the loue and tendernesse þat þe kyng hath to þe Chirche and to þe Ministres (15) of þe same he woll þat this bille. as to þe imposicion þat shuld be to the seculer preestes of this (16) Roialme not beneficed. as Stipendiaries and chaunterie preestes. be committid to þe Archebisshoppes and (17) Bisshoppes in þe Conuocacions of þe Clergies of this Roialme. by cause it touchith þe Immunite and (18) liberte of þe Chirch. the which þe kyng intendith to kepe withoute hurt or preiudice in alle (19) wyse. And as touchyng the pardon conteyned in this bille. in cas þe nobles of þe saide preestes be grauntid (20) to hym in þe said Conuocacions. then þe kyng woll þat the saide pardon stonde in his vertu (21) and strenght. with oute fyne or fee payng þerfore by auctorite of þis present parlement.

Chancery hand
Printed *RP* V.152.25.

214

1449   C49/27/17   Bill seeking to regularize the collection of customs

(1) That euery Marchaunt alien or estraunger of what Countre þat he be. that bringith into þis land. Corne. Vitail. (2) or any oder maner of marchandise: shall at the tyme of his entre. present hym self to the Custumer of the Poort. Creke (3) or oder place that he comyth to. or to his Clerk. and make declaracioun of the Corne. Vitail. or oder maner of (4) marchaundise that he hath brought / And furth with be sworne vpon þe boke. that all þe golde. siluer. in masse. (5) plate. and money. that he shall resceyve. for the seide Corne. vitail. or oder marchaundise. he shall employe hit (6) into marchaundise of þis lond. his resonable expenses and costes of intendaunce vpon the same exceptid And after the (7) seide employment before his departyng out of þis lond. he shall resort ayene to þe seide Custumer. or his Clerk. (8) and make vnto him a trwe declaracioun in generall of the seide employment so made by him. And to þentent þat the seide (9) Marchaunt3 repairyng into þis lond be not vnresonably greved by any of the seide Custumers in obseruance of þis (10) ordinaunce. nor any occasion yeuyn to þe seide Marchaunt3 ter by to forbere her resorte or comyng into þis lond. hit (11) is also ordeined þat non of hem shall resceive priuely nor apert. directly or indirectly of any of the seide Marchaunt3. (12) for þe takyng of his seide ougth ne for the enteryng þerof or of the declaracioun aboueseid. any maner of (13) gode. or gode worth. but freely and withoute any wilfull taryng or delaiyng of þe seide Marchaunt3 execute (14) þis seide ordinaunce. And þat for þe more euident and souner knolach of the deuoir and diligence doon by hym (15) in execucion of

þis ordinaunce. shall at þe lest before þe ende of euery terme in þe yere (16) brynge or make to be brought into the kynges Eschequer a plein and clere knolach of all þat shall be don by him in þis (17) behalue. And þat for the more surete of due execucioun to be don by the seide Custumers of þis ordinaunce. ych of (18) hem at the tyme of his admission to his office. shall be sworne in especial þat he shall trewly obserue and kepe þis (19) ordinaunce so þat and he be founde faillyng þerInne. he shall not oonly renne into the crime of periurie: but be put (29) oute of his office. and forfeite the summe of. xx. li. of the which he þat detectith him and conuictith hym þerof (30) shall haue þat oon half And oure souerain lorde þe kyng the oder half for expensis of his houshold. This ordinaunce to (31) endure for terme of foure yere next folowyng.[1]

(Note in the second hand) as to all the mater comprisid in this cedule not comprehendid (32) in the bille to the whiche this cedule is annexed the Comunes be not assented

Chancery hand
Printed *RP* V.156.
[1] Last sentence in a different hand.

215

1449   SC8/27/1345A   Petition of John Talbot to be named Chancellor of Ireland

(1) To the Kyng our Souereigne Lorde

Besecheth . . .[1] mekely your highnesse Iohn Talbot knight Sone and heir of Iohn Erle (2) of Shrewesbury that where it hath liked your highnesse of your most noble (grace by your lettres)[2] patentȝ beryng (3) date at Westminstre the ijde day of Septembre the yere of your blessed reigne xxvth to graunte (4) to your seid besecher thoffice of your Chaunceller of your lond of Irelond To haue and to occupy by hym self or by his (5) sufficiant depute as long as he bare hym well in the seid office. takyng in the seid office feeȝ wageȝ and rewardeȝ (6) to the seid office due and of olde tyme accustumed. the tenur of which lettres patentȝ to this bill is annexed. By (7) virtue of which lettres patentȝ your seid besecher was therof peasebly possessed fro the date of the (8) seid lettres patentȝ vnto now late that he by oon Thomas ffitȝ Gerot by colour of your lettres patentȝ (9) to hym made of the seid office long tyme sith the seid lettres patentȝ to your seid besecher made by the name comprehended (10) in the same lettres patentȝ. To haue to hym after the deth or decesse of your seid besecher which had the (seid)² (11) office of your graunte or immediatly after eny othir manne the same office of your graunte or of eny othir (12) whosoeuer thei were or othir wise in eny maner havyng or occupyng or as sone as þat office to your hand or (13) graunte of you or of eny othir by deth cessioun ammocioun resumpcioun dimissioun remocioun (14) permutacioun reddicioun or surrendre or elles in eny othir maner it be next then to come or elles happe to (15) ffall was putte oute. No defaute at eny tyme proved ne founde by no maner of meane in your Said Suppliant ne (16) that he mys bare hym in the seid office Please it your highnesse of your speciall grace the premisses (17) graciously considred by thassent of the lordʒ spirituell and temporell and the comunes of this (18) your noble Roialme in this present parlament assemblyd and by auctorite of the same to ratify afferme and approve the seid (19) lettres patentʒ to your seid besecher made. to haue to hym after theffecte of the same And that al othir lettres (20) patentʒ of the seid office to eny othir man made and in exicucion putte in derogacion or hurte of your seid besecher (21) concernyng the seid office be voide and of no force ne effecte And that your seid besecher may haue seueraly als (22) mony writtes and prive seals as shalbe behouefull and necessary to hym to be had (to)² be directid aswell to your (23) leutenant in or of your lond of Irelond as to othir of your counseill there: Comaundyng theim oppon their ligeaunce to do (24) restore your seid besecher vnto the seid office And hym there in In peasebly possession to putte To haue to hym and to (25) occupy after theffecte and fourme of the seid lettres patentʒ to your seid besecher made And (26) by the same auctorite that he may haue als mony writtes and prive seals as shalbe behoueful and necessary to (27) hym to be had to be directid vnto the seid Thomas ffitʒ Gerot chargyng hym oppon his ligeaunce for to restore and (28) deliuer withoute delay your grete Seal of your lond of Irelond beyng in his kepyng by colour of The seid lettres (29) patentʒ to hym made. To your seid besecher or to his sufficiant depute havyng sufficiant power of your seid besecher to (30) resceyve the seid seall And this atte reuerence of god and way of charite

(Response) The kyng by þaduise (31) and assent of the lordes spirituell and temporell beyng in this present parlement woll and grauntith þat (32) þe saide Sir Iohn Talbot haue and occupie the saide office of Chaunceller of Irelond by hym self or by his (33) sufficient depute there after the fourme of the kynges lettres patentes to hym made þerof. the (34) whiche lettres patentes byn thought gode and effectuell and to be approved after the tenure of (35) the same Also þat þe grete seal of þe saide lond belongyng to þe saide office. which þe (36) said Thomas hath geton vn to hym be delyuered to þe said Sir Iohn Talbot. or to his sufficiante depute hauyng power (37) of hym to resceiue hit. And þat þe said Sir Iohn Talbot. haue bothe writtes and priue seals. such and als many as byn (38) behovefull and necessarie for hym. als well to þe lieutenant of Irlond or his depute. and þe Counseill (39) þere to do restore the said Sir Iohn Talbot vn to þe said office. and hym to putte in pesible possession of þe (40) same: To haue and to occupie after the tenure of his said le*tt*res patentes. as to the said Thomas chargyng hym vppon (41) his ligeaunce for to restore and delyuere þe said seall to þe said Sir Iohn Talbot after þe tenure (42) of his said supplicacion any lettres patentes made to the said Thomas of þe said office in that partie notte withstondyng. (43) And as touchyng the remenaunt that ys desired by this peticion the kyng will be aduysed.

Text in non-Chancery, response in Chancery hand
Printed *RP* V.166.13.
[1] cancelled   [2] rubbed

216

1449   SC8/27/1347   Petition of Thomas Parr of Cumberland

(1) Besecheth *sir* Thomas Parr knyght one of the knyghts of þe shire in this *pre*sent Court of parlement for the (2) Shire of Cumbreland that where he þe .xiiij. day of marche þe yeer of our lorde king þat now is þe xxiiij (3) was comyng toward þis saide (court)[1] of parliament Robe*r*t Belyngeham late of Burnelshede in þe Countee (4) of Westmorland þe yonger Gentilman Thomas Belingeham late of the same in the same Countee Gentilman Robe*r*t (5) Dykonson late of the same in the same Countee yoman (Thomas Strykland)[1] late of Brendrigge in þe said Countee yoman and Iohn Selyngier late of (6) Shoote in the Countee of Deuon yoman þe day and yere aforsaid Vpon a ce*r*tain (7) ground called Cornewalesse ground beside the Crane in þe warde of the (vyntrye in london wher by the (8) heygh)[1] way of þe said *sir* Thomas lay to go to þe water of Thamyse from his loogyng place and from (9) thens to this said heigh Court of Parliament beyng at westmynstre. felonsly lay in awaite of þe same *sir* Thomas to (10) thentent to haue (murdred)[1] or slayn hym and þer þen to suche entent an assaulte made vpon (11) hym and vpon Robert Duket Thomas Wright and Mathewe Pierson his se*r*uantes to his grete affraying and ther (12) at þe same tyme greuously hurt and sore wounded þe said (seruantes þe comons of þis present)[1] (13) parliament to pray þe king our soue*r*ain lord by þavys of his lordes sp*iri*tual and tempo*r*all (14) beyng in þis *pre*sent p*ar*liament to ordeine estable and enacte in þis said parliament and by

auctoritee (15) of þe same parliament þat a writte of proclamacion be made in þe kinges Chauncerie direct and sent vnto (16) þe Shirifes of þe Citee of london for þe tyme beyng to proclayme within þe said Citee within two (17) dayes after þe liueree of þat writte to þeym or to one of þeim. þat þe seid (18) Robert Belyngeham Thomas Belyngham Thomas Strykland Iohan and Robert Dykonson and echone of hem in (19) their propre persones or propre persone appiere afore þe king in his benche at the mois of (20) Pasche (that shal be in the)[1] yeer of our lorde Ml.ccccxlvj. The said writte retorneable afore þe king (in his)[1] said (21) benche at þe said mois of Pasche And if they þen so appiere. þat from þe tyme of suche apperance vnto (22) tyme þat þe matere of þe seid assaute lying in awaite and greuouse hurtes and þe seid (23) woundyng bitwene þe seid sire Thomas and his said seruantʒ and eueryche of hem and þe (24) seid Robert Thomas Belyngeham Robert Thomas Strykland Iohan and echone of þeym after þe (25) cours of þe comen lawe of þis lande be fully discussed and determyned afore oure lord king in his (26) said benche. The same Robert Thomas Belyngeham Robert Thomas Strykland and Iohan to abide in þe kinges (27) prison in þe kepyng of þe mareschall of þe said benche. withoute þat þei or any of þeym (28) be hade in baille or put to mainprise afore þende of suche determynacion hade. So þat þe seid sire (29) Thomas and his said seruantes at the said moys in þe said benche appiere in propre persones (30) or propre persone or by attourney to sue with effect ayenst þe said Robert Thomas Belingeham (31) Robert Thomas Stryckland and Iohan and echone of hem as lawe woll from tyme to tyme in the premisses. And if (32) þe said Shirifes make nat þe said proclamacion within þe said two dayes by virtue of þe said (33) writ if it be to hem or to þat one of hem at any tyme afore. viij. dayes next afore þe said day of Retourne (34) deliuered. And also retourne afore þe kyng in his said benche at þe said mois þe seid proclamacion (35) by þeym made þat þen the said Shirifes forfette .c (li)[1] þat one half þerof to þe king (36) and þat oþer half to þe seid sire Thomas and his said seruantes. And if þe (37) same Robert Thomas Belingham Robert Thomas Strykland and Iohan or any of hem plede any plee or plees in barr (38) of þe Accion (or in abatemente of the bille billes)[2] or writte of the said sire Thomas or his said seruantʒ (39) in þe materes abouesaid triable or triableʒ in eny other place (þen within þe said Citee)[1] (40) þat all suche plee or plees stonde and be as voide and as no plee And if þe seid Robert (41) Thomas Belyngeham Robert Thomas Strykland and Iohan ne none of hem appiere nat afore our seid lord king in his said (42) benche at the seid mois. þat þen þei and echone of hem nat so appieryng be and stond as atteingted of (43) felonye. And þat in

þis cas neither þe kynges proteccion ne his Chartre of Pardon ne esson of (44) the kinges seruice stonde or be to þeym or to any of þeym in any avaylle or effect ne þat þei (45) ne none of þeym take by suche proteccion or pardon or esson any avauntage or availe in restreyng or delaying (46) of þis Acte. And if þe seid Robert Thomas Belyngeham Robert Thomas Strykland and Iohan for (47) defaute of the seid apperance be atteignted in the fourme aforseid þat þen after þat atteyndre (48) þei ne none of hem so atteygnted haue ne take any avauntage or benefice by writ of Errour assignyng in þat writte for (49) Errour þat þei or any of hem were or was in þe kinges seruice oute of þis Reawme (50) or in (pryson)¹ at the tyme of þe said proclamacion made
   Chancery hand
   Printed *RP* V.168.15.
 ¹ rubbed   ² rubbed or erased

217

   1450   SC8/2/52   Petition of Commons concerning trade with Braband, Holland (left margin torn; material in parentheses supplied from *RP*)

   (1) (Prayen) the Comeyns in this (your)¹ present parlement assembled to consider howe that atte your parlement (2) holden atte Westminstre the xxvij yere of your noble reigne for cause of a certeyn ordinaunce hadde (proclai)med (3) puplished and streytely kepte in the parties of Braband holland and ȝeland that no manere of cloth made in this Reame of (4) Englond shulde not come in to the said parties þer (to be sold) in eny wise vppon peyne of forfetur of the (5) same cloth wherefore ye our souerain lord by cause it ys expressely ageinis the trieux and appointement made & take (6) betwix (youre Rea)mes landes and subgiettes of the oon parties and the landes whiche the Duke of Burgoigne holdeth and (7) occupieth on þe oþer partie haue often her bifore this tyme do write your (8) (lettres requi)sitore and send your messages for due reformacion to haue be hadde in this behalfe whereof as yet (9) no due redresse is hadde vnto þe right intollerable hurt of all the Comeyns of this (Reame by) cause þat (10) many cloth makers þat is to wete men weuvers fullers diers and women kempers Carders & spynners & oþer biers (11) & sellers þerof such as can noon oþer occupacions (by verrey necessite be) compelled for their (12) levyng to do the occupacions And such of theym as can nat do noon oþer occupacions be come as ydell pepull (13) whiche prouoketh hem to (synne and myschevous lyvyng and) vppon this consideracion that it please you souerain (14) lord by

the aduyce and assent of your lordes spirituelx and temporelx assembled in your said parlement and (15) by auctorite (of the same par)lement it was ordeyned that but yf so were þat due continuell reformacion wer (16) made in the seid parties of Braband holland and ʒeland of the seid (ordenaunce betwi)x that tyme and the fest of seint (17) Michell þan next comyng so that all maner of cloth of woll made in this Reame myghte come and be accepted into (18) (the same par)ties of Braband holland and ʒeland ther to be vttred and sold as frely as eny oþer merchandises (19) þat than for defaute of such reformacion in (that behalve no manere of) merchandises ne goodes of the (20) growyng nor wurkyng of the landes and parties that the said Duke helde and occupied schuld not come in to the seid (21) (Reame after the seid Fest uppon) peyne of forfeitur of the merchandises þat is for to sey the one halfe (22) þerof to the kyng and oþer halfe þerof to hym that firste seiseth the seid merchandises (23) (in whos handes that ever) they wer founde and that ther vppon open proclamacion shuld be made betwyx þat tyme (24) and the xv day of Iuyll than next comyng withinne (the Citee of london and other) places necessarie & conuenient þerto (25) And yif eny suyt wer commenced aftere that tyme hadd for cause of eny such seisyng in which eny issue (26) (concernyng þat acte sh)uld be taken þat the seid issue shuld be tried in the shire wher the seid seisyn shulde be (27) hadde and in noon oþer place The whiche ordenaunce (shuld endure unto the) next parlement And for asmoch as be the (28) summyns and commensyng of this your present parlement the seid acte is fully expired & determyned (29) no (due reformation) of the parte of the seid Duke of the premysses yut hade that it please your highnesse (30) be the avise of your (lordes spirituelx and temporell in this your present parlement assembled) (31) and be the auctorite of the same to ordeyne and estable that open proclamacion be hadde in the Citee (32) of london and oþer places necessarie (and convenient) þerto betwyx this and the fest of Pentecost next (33) comeyng þat but yf so be dewe contenuell reformacion be made and hadde in the seid parties (of Braband) holland and (34) ʒeland betwyxte this tyme and the fest of Natiuite of Seynt Iohn Baptist next comeyng so that all maner cloth of woll (35) (made in) this your Reame mowe come & be accepted into the same parties of Braband holland and ʒeland þer (36) to be vttered and sold as frely as eny oþer merchandises (that than) for defaute of such reformacion (37) in that be halue no maner of merchandises ne goodes of the growyng nor wurkyng of the landes and parties that (38) þe (seid Duke) holde and occupieth shulle come in to the seid Reame after the seid fest vppon peyn of forfaitur (39) of the merchandises that is for to sey the (one halfe) þerof to þe kyng & þe oþer (40) halfe þerof to hym that first seiseth the seid merchandises in whos handes that ever they wer (41) founde and if eny suyt be (commenced) her after for cause of eny such seysyng in whiche eny issue concernyng (42) this acte shall be taken that the seid issue be tried in þe shire wher (the seid) seisyng is hadde and in (43) noon oþer place and that this acte indur in perpetuete

Non-Chancery hand
Printed *RP* V.201.57.
[1] superior insert

218

1450 SC8/28/1352 Petition of the inhabitants of the Isle of Wight
(1) Vn to the wise and discrete Comens of this parlement assembled
Prayn the poure peple inhabitant with in (2) þe (Ile)[1] of Wyght in þe Counte o Hampshire on to al the comons assembled in this present parlement (3) to considere the gret noyse þat dayli goth vppon þe Se bi oure Enemyes and þe aduersite þat (4) þei shewen daili on to þe said Ile The whiche Ile is vndirtake by a certayn of wariours of oure enemyes of ffraunce (5) to be conquerid in to here hondis bi shorte time the whiche god defende: vppon þe whiche the pure peple of þe (6) Ile ben discomforted and a mayd: Seyng þe febelnysse with in ham Self: Certefyeng your wysdoms þat (7) wher as þe said Ile hath be her a fore at þe Nombre of gret pepul sensabul hit hath be so pelyd and opressid (8) now late bi on Iohn Newport Steward of the said Ile made bi þe Duke of york for the whiche mysgouernaunce wos (9) (by hym)[1] discharged And put oute of hus office: And then aftur hus discharge the said Iohn Newport and oþur of hus secte (10) þe last Somer vppon þe See So thretenyng þe kinggis pepil of þe Ile and distressing (11) hem ther bodies her harneis and her godis bothe bi lond and bi See that þe pepul is forsake þe Ile so (12) at þis dai is not xvC pepul sensabul the whiche is on to vs al enhabitantes in þe Ile (13) grete heuynysse: Seyng no more Stuf of men nor no stuf of arterie sensabul left with in þe Ile (nor with)[2] (14) in þe Castell of þe same Ile hit hath cawsid vs alle to make supplicacion on to þe Duke of yorke and hus Consail for Supportacion (15) and aide of þe said Castel and Ile bothe for men and arterie in sauacion of þe Ilond and of þe kingges peple (16) ther: Certefyyng on to your aller wisdoms of (no relef)[2] (by cause of dobȝthe of Resumpcion)[1] and þat hit is noised (17) her þat bi þe resompcion þe Ile shal stond in þe kingges hand And þat þe (18) forsaid Iohn Newport sewith dailli to þe king our souerayne lord to be lewtenant Steward

Resseyuou*r* and Baylly w*i*th*i*n (19) þe said Ile the whiche god defend considering þe gret opression bi fore rehersid: And also hit is ope(n)li³ (20) Spoken and noysed þat þe said Iohn Newport hath Sold þe said Ile and desirith to haue þe hed offices ther to (21) þe entent to (hurt the poure peple to ther otteraunce ondoyng & distruccion of þe said Ile)⁴ the whiche god of (22) hus hie m*er*cy defende: Moreou*er* certefyyng your wisdoms (th*at*)² þe said Ioh(n)³ Newport hath at þis (23) day ne lyvelode to mentayne hus gret Countenaunce but bi þe opressing of þe peple in þe Contray þat (24) he Sitte in thorw þe whiche he hath gretli enpoured & hurt þe pure Ilond redy: ffor what time he was Steward of (25) þe Ile he had but x ma*r*c of fee (and)² kepte an h(ou)shold³ and a Countenaunce like a lord w*i*th as riche (26) wynys as couthe be ymagened Namyng him Silf Newport þe Galaunt oþer wise called Newport þe the Riche. wham (27) þe Contray Courson Daylay that evir he com ther: And afturtime þe said Iohn Newport was so discharged (28) bi þe Duke of yorke þe said Duke ordayned and made on harri Bruyn Squyer to be lewtenaunt and Steward of (29) þe said Ile whas rule hath be hono*u*rable ther bothe to god. þe lord and to þe peple of þe (30) Ile as lawe and ryth at al times hath required & w(el)² y rulyd in hus litil time þe Contray and were like to (31) bring hit in to hus furst astate if he were like to contynew. and abide w*i*th*i*n þe Ile for he hath bi Stowed a gret (32) good of hus owyn bothe in gonnys and in arterie lyyng w*i*th in him Silf w*i*th in þe said Ile þe whiche (33) is (at this)² day a gret strenthe riches Socour and comfort to al þe Ile Prayng Specialli to your aller wisdoms (34) in sauacion of þe said Ile and in sauacion of þe king*ges* pepil þ*er* That for as moche as þe (35) said harri Bruyn is þe king*ges* houshold man and borne to gret reputacion and wel anherited. and at no time (36) corrupte but egalli rulith þe said Ilond aftur Iustice w*i*th oute complaynt and enriched þe contray w*i*th (37) hus gret Stuf if nede of þe warre required that he mygh contenew stille in hus good rule keping (38) þe Countrei vndir þe forme as he hath bi gonne to þe most Savacion of þe said (39) Ilond and of þe king*ges* peple þ*er*: for whos good rule. we al wul ondurtake to þe king our (40) souerayne lord. And also þat al oþur officer of þe Ile þat is to say harri (41) Trenchard constabul & Porter may haue straytely in comaundement bi þe kyng to abide resident w*i*th (42) in þe said Ile Duryng þe time of . . .⁵ werr Certefyyng at al times þe kinggis hinesse that and (43) Iohn Newport shold com to. gouerne þe said Ile hit wul be cause of distruccion of þe Contray to wham no (44) man wul obeye excepte the king oure Souerayne lordis plesur for⁶ he and hus hath do so meny gret offencis in þe (45) see aboute þe Ilond in morthering þe kinggis peple and hus frendis castyng þem owte of har vessellis (46) in to þe See as (þei haue be comyng)² to þe port of Hampton bi þe whiche þe (47) kinggis costumes of hus port of Suthampton hath be lost bi hus riot kept vppon þe See of v or vj m mark in a yer (48) and also þe (said)¹ Newport hath . . .⁷ te king oure souerayne lord and defraudid him in grauntyng (49) x marc worth liflode . . .² gret hurt and trobul her aftur . . .⁷ for the said liflode is entailid the whiche (50) is hud fro þe kinggis hynesse bi þe whiche mene he disirith to be recompensid bi þe offices of the Ilond (51) aforesaid and also þe said Newport hath take þe same yere extorciousli (in Hampshire gret multitude)² of (52) diuerse graynes of Corne in þe kinggis name of þe pure peple of him þat had but iiij (quarters corne)¹ (53) toke on and made ham carie hit to hampton som man x mile & som man xx mile at har owin cost and þer as was plente (54) of corne he toke money to hus Owyn Vse to þe sum with in (þe shire of an c marc)² þe whiche þe (55) peple of þe Contrai curse him daily ther for And to þe witnysse her of for þe more credance we haue Set to oure Selis

Chancery hand
Printed *RP* V.204.2
[1] superior insert [2] rubbed [3] torn [4] over erasure [5] cancelled [6] from here on writing grows smaller and lighter [7] erasure

219

1450-54 C1/19/491 Petition of Thomas Bodyn (original version)
(1) To the most reuerent ffader yn god the Cardinall of yorke Chaunceler of Englond

Besechyth mekely yowre powre and (2) contynuall orator Thomas Bodyn of that as where accorde and couenaunt was made bitwene hym and on Robert Chirche Citezeyn (3) and haburdassher of London the .xv. day of ffeuerer the yere of the regne of kyng harry the .vj. after the conquest the .xx. by (4) the mediacion of ther. ffrendez beyng then yowre seyd suppliaunt wythyn the age of .xiiij. yer that he shuld be prentice with (5) the seid Robert yn and of the crafte of haburdassher fro the feste of all halowen then last past vnto the yende of .xij. yer (6) thenne nexte sewyng (in)¹ allway that the seid Robert shuld fynde to scole att his owne Costis and charge the seid Thomas (7) duryng twoo the ferst yeres of the seid terme that is to sey a yere and (halfe)¹ therof to lerne gramere and the residue of the (8) seid twoo yer whych amounteth to halfe a yer to lerne to wryte And theruppon the seid Thomas by the aduise of his (9) (fr)endis¹ trustyng to haue be found to scole yn forme afore seid graunted the same .xv. day by dede endentid thenne made bitwene (10) hym and the seid Robert to be trewe aprentice to the (seid)² same Robert duryng the seid terme of .xij. yer of whych (11) terme of .xij. yer he hath contenued yn the seruice of the seid Robert as his prentice yn the seid crafte fro the seid (12) ffest of all halowen vn to the ende of .viij. yere thenne nexte sewyng And more and often tymes yn the bigynnyng of the same terme (13) and mony tymes sethen the seid Thomas wyth hys frendis hath preyed and required the seid Robert to putt and to fynde hym (14) to scole yn forme afore seid after the effecte of the seid couenaunt & accorde which to do the seid Robert woll not but that to do (15) at all tymes vtturly hath refused to the grete hurte harme & losse of the seid Thomas. Plese it yowr goode and gracious (16) lordshipp to consider the premisses and that / the seid Thomas therof may haue no remedy bi the course of the comine (17) lawe of thys land And ther vppon to graunte a wryte sub pene to be directe to the seid Robert to apper bifore the kyng (18) yn hys Chauncery at a certyn day vppon a certeyn peyn bi yowre gracious lordshipp to be lymyted ther to answer and to (19) do and resceyve of & In these premisses as bi the Court of the same Chauncery then shall be ordeigned & he shall pray to god for yow &c

Non-Chancery hand
¹ torn   ² blotted

220

1450-54   C1/19/492   Petition of Thomas Bodyn (Chancery copy)
(1) To the most reuerend ffader in god the Archibisshop of york Cardynall and Chaunceller of England

Sheweth mekely to (2) youre gracious lordship Thomas Bodyn of london that where accord and covenaunt was made betwene hym and one Robert Chirche (3) Citeʒin and haburdassher of london the xv*th* day of ffeuerere the yere of the reigne of kyng henry the vj*the* (4) after the conquest the xx*th* be the medeacion of the frendeʒ . beyng thenne your said suppliant w*ith* in age of xiiij yere (5) that he shuld be prentice to the said Robert in and of the crafte of haburdassher fro the ffeste of Alhalowen then last passed vnto (6) the yend of xij yere thenne next comyng So alwey that the said Robert shuld fynd to scole at hys awen costes and charge the (7) (sa)id¹ Thomas duryng two the furst yeres (of the said terme that is to say a yere and half therof to lerne gramer and the (8) resydue of the said two yeres)² which amounteth to half-a-yere to scole for to lerne to write And ther uppon the said Thomas by the (9) aduise of his frendeʒ trustyng to haue be founde to scole in fourme aforsaid graunted the same xvth day by dede (10) indented thenne made betwene hym and the said Robert to be true Apprentice to the same Robert duryng the said terme of (11) xij yere of which terme of xij yere he hath contynued in the seruice of the said Robert as his prentice in the said (12) crafte from the said ffeste of Alhalowen vnto the yende of viij yere and more And often tymes in the bigynnyng of the same (13) terme and mony tymes sithon: the said Thomas with his frendes hath (prayed)² and required the said Robert to (14) putt and fynd hym to scole in fourme aforsaid after the effecte of the said covenaunt and accorde. the which to doo the said (15) Robert wolnot. but that to doo at all tymes vtturly hath refused to the grete hurte harme and losse of the said Thomas Please hit (16) your good and graciouce lordship to consider the premisses and that the said Thomas therof may haue no remedy by the course (17) of the comen lawe of this land / And theruppon to graunt a write to be direct to the said Robert to appere by fore the (18) kyng in his Chauncerie at a certeyn day and vppon a notable payne by your gracious lordship to be lymyted there to answere and (19) to doo and resceyve of and in thise premisses as by the Courte of the same Chauncerye thenne shall be ordeigned and he (20) shall pray to god for you

Chancery hand
¹ torn   ² superior insert

221

1450-54   C1/19/493   Answer of Robert Chirch to petition of Thomas Bodyn

(1) This is the Answer of Robert Chirch aʒeinst the bill of Thomas Bodyn

ffirst the seid Robert by protestacion (2) yat the mater in ye seid bill conteynyd is not sufficient to put hym to answer to in yis courte saith (3) yat ye seid Endentur of Apprentice by ye which the seid Thomas was bounde to ye seid Robert with (4) all ye circumstaunce yerof was made & had with in the Cite of london wher by ye custom (5) of the same Cite ane accion of couenaunt ys mayntenable as well withoute Especialte as with Especialte so yat (6) yf eny sich couenaunt of fyndyng at scole of the seid Thomas had be made & broken like as the seid Thomas hath (7) surmittyd he myght yer of haue had & ʒit may haue couenable remydy by pleynt within ye seid Cite after (8) the forme & cours of the Comine lawe yer and foryermor for þe mor declaracion (9) in yis mater ye seid Robert seith yat nygh aboute the fest of all halowen the ʒer of the reign (10) of our souereign lord the kyng yat no(w is)¹ xixth ye seid Thomas & Robert by ye mene (11) of one henri wakefeld wer agrede & Endentures yervpon made yat the same Thomas shuld be apprentice with (12) ye seid Robert for ye terme of xiij. ʒer yen next folowyng so yat sufficient suerte wer founde for (13) the seid Thomas to be trewe apprentice with ye seid Robert duryng ye terme aforsayd wherupon ye seid (14) Thomas abode with ye seid Robert fro yat tyme vnto ye terme of hillar ye xxth ʒer (15) of ye seid kyng yen next cummyng & no suerte for the parte of ye seid Thomas by all yat tyme (16) was founde wherfor ye seid Robert at yat tyme was in full purpose no mor to haue had to do with (17) ye seid Thomas in so mych yat ye seid Endenturis on euery parte afor yat tyme made wer broken & noght (18) enrollyd & so both parties at yer large so yat ye seid Thomas myght then haue departyd if hym had (19) list but ʒit ye seid henry eftsones entretyd ye seid Robert to take ye seid Thomas apprentice for (20) ye terme of xij. ʒer next folowyng ye fest of halowen yen last passyd promettyng to gete suerte for (21) ye seid Thomas to be true apprentice duryng ye same terme so yat ye seid Thomas in ye seid (22) terme shuld haue couenable lernyng & doctrine as reasonably for ye profite of sich apprentice shuld belong the which (23) he had withoute yat at ye seid Robert at yat tyme or eny tyme beth made couenaunt with the seid Thomas (24) to fynd hym at scole in (sich)² maner & forme as ye seid Thomas hath surmittyd wherupon ye seid (25) Endentures of Apprenteshode wer made like as ye seid Thomas hath declaryd the seid Thomas beyng at yat (26) tyme in (ye)² xiiij ʒer of his age or nygh vpon by vertue of which Endentures ye seid Thomas & by the enrolmente (27) yerof was admitte as A lauful apprentice after ye custom of the seid Cite ye xxx day of Octobr (28) ye ʒer of the reign of ye kyng aforsaid (xxj)² the which terme ye seid Thomas on his parte hath (29) not truly kept but by hys owne knowlage in hys seid bill nygh ye iij parte yerof yat is to witte all most (30) .iiij. ʒer wrongfully of hys obstinate willfulness hath broken & disobeyd which not withstondyng ye seid Robert (31) seith yat ye seid Thomas is & afor his departur was sufficiently lernyd & instruct both in redyng & also (32) in wrytyng as vnto sich apprentice resonably may suffice and ouer all yis ye seid Robert seith yat he & (33) ye (seid)² Thomas ye vij day of ffevurer nowe last passyd at ye grete instaunce of ye seid Thomas (34) wer put in award of iiij notable & thrifty persones then wardenʒ of ye Craft of haberdasshers of ye (35) seid Cite Arbitorʒ bytwix hem both indeferently chosen of all maner causes accions quereleʒ debates & (36) demaundes betwix hem afor yat tyme in eny maner of wise had meuyd (or)³ hangyng The which arbitorʒ with (37) in ye day to hem yerof limitte demyd awardyd & finally determynyd betwix ye seid Robert & Thomas (The)² which (38) award dome & determinacion ye seid Robert is & at all tymes hath bene redy on hys parte to kepe & performe (39) notwithstondyng yat ye seid Thomas yat al to hym yerof belongith fulfill will in no wise nor obey (40) The which maters & ich of hem ye seid Robert is redy to preue like as this Courte will award wherfor he prath (41) to be dismist oute of thys Courte & to be restoryd to hys Costes & Damages for hys gret & wrongfull vexacion after (42) the forme of the Statute.:

Chancery hand
¹ torn   ² superior insert   ³ over erasure

222

1453   C1/1/70   Petition of Thomas Fitz Harry and his wife (right side damaged; matter in parentheses supplied from *PC*)

(1) To the honorable lord the Erle of Salesbury Chaunceller of Englond

Humbly besechen youre Oratoures Thomas ffitʒ (2) harry and Iohanne his wif late the wyf of Rauf lyngen that where the seide Rauf by his testament and last wille ordeyne and made (3) the seide Iohanne his wif and Iohn his Sonne with other his executors (to have) the administracione of his goodes and (4) to execute his wille the whiche Iohanne and Iohn his sonne provid the seide testament and were Sworen by fore the ordinarie (5) to execute & performe the seide wille accordynge to the seid testament and aftir that the seide (Iohanne and) Iohn hur (6) sonne by mediacione of ther frendes in the presence of Iohn Barre knyght Thomas Bromewyche and other by ther writing (7) endented and ensealid acordid and concludid that the seid Iohanne shuld haue all the goodes that were hur seid late husbondes (8) (excepte) suche goodes as were in the maners of Aileminstre and lyngen and she to paie the dettes of hur seid late husbondes (9) by force of whiche accorde she hadde and occupied the seid goodes except the goodes a fore exceptid And paied of the dettes of hur (10) seid late (husbondes) the summe of .xliiij. li and more and entendid to haue content the remenaunt not content And (11) aftir this acorde the seid Iohn not dredyng god the kyng nor his lawes with the nombre of xl. misrulid persones with hym (12) arraied in manere of werre with (Iakes salats) habergeones bowis speres Gleives and other wepyns of werre the .vj. day of (13) September the xxxij*te* yere of the reigne of oure soueraigne lord nowe come into the manere of Sutton where the seid (14) Iohanne his moder dwellid and ther entrid and shette the (yate) of the place and as cruell and euille disposid child contrarie (15) to godes lawe & nature toke the seide Iohanne his moder and hur seruauntez and kept theim in warde And when (16) the seid Iohanne wolde haue departid for to (haue)[1] hadde socoure hur seid sonne vnkyndely (toke and) huld hur faste (17) in violence and in vngoodely wise that she might nat depart and so kept hur and hur seruantez ther in prison by the (18) space of vj. owres and more And in that tyme the seid misrulid persones by his commaunde-ment with Gleivis and (other wepyns) (19) hewe downe the beddes costeres and hongynges of hall and Chaumbres ther beyng and brake coffres and all manere fastenes (20) in the seid Manere and of the goodes ther founden chargid twoo waynes and cariet hit a waye And all so where the seide (Rauf) (21) of trust to performe his wille hadde enffef-fid the seid sire Iohn Barre and other in the seid Manere of (22) Sutton with other Maneres londez and tenementez of which Manere of Sut-ton the seid Rauf declarid his wille And (23) ordeine by his testament that (the) seid feoffes of the seid Manere with other londez and tenementez comprisid (24) in the seid wille as it apperith in the same shuld immediatly aftir his decesse enfeffe the seide Iohanne terme of hur lyff accordyng (25) whiche will the seid Ioh(anne by the) suffraunce of the seid feoffes after the deth of hur seid late husbond occupied and with (26) hur grete cost and laboure gaynyd and enblaied the seid Manere londez and tenementez and in the seid Maner housid the (27) enblaymentez And also (other profitez) therof growyng by hur laboure opteinyd to the value of .CC. marc (28) and more hur sonne a forseide with a grete multitude of people arraied in manere of werre the xxvij*th* day of September (29) the same yere come with force and entrid (into the seid) manere londez and tenementez And hit [to][2] kepith (30) with force and ther occupied wastid and destruid the seid enblaimentez and profitez to the value aboue rehersid (31) with other goodes of the seid Thomas ffitz harry to the value of (xl.li. And also) where that Iohn Vynter and William Pauers (32) hadde yeven to the seid Rauf and Iohanne the Manere of kenchestre to haue to theim and to theire heires of ther bodies (33) bygeten And thei therof by force of the seid gefte seis(ed and contenued) ther possessione in to the tyme the seid Rauf died And (34) aftir that the seid Iohanne contenued hur possessione in to nowe late the seid Iohn hur sonne entrid in to the seid Manere and put (35) hur out with force and so kepith hit And ouer this the seid Iohn (will) nat suffre his seid moder to ben endowid in (36) eny possessione that was hur seid late husbondez to the grete hurt of youre seid besechers That hit please youre lordeshippes (37) to consider thes premisses And that a privey seall apon peyne of his alligeaunce may be directe to the (38) seid Iohn commaundyng hym to appere afore you at a certayne day by you to ben limite to aunswere of this riotes misrule vngoodely (39) and vnlaufull demenyng And then therapon to procede as lawe feith and conscience requiren.

Chancery hand
Printed *PC* I.xlviii-ix.
[1] superior insert   [2] erased

223

1453-54   SC8/29/1446   Petition of Thomas de la More, Sheriff of Cumberland

(1) To þe kyng oure souerain lord

Sheweth vnto youre highnes Thomas De la More Squyer late Shiref of þe (2) Counte of Cumberland howe þat yn þe yere last passed þe said Thomas beyng Shiref of þe said Counte (3) grete discensions riotes and debates were moved and stired betwene certein persones so ferforth þat þe toon (4) half of þe Shire was diuided from þe tother and where þe said late Shiref sent his vndirshiref and (5) baillyfs to make leve of youre dettes yn diuerse parties of þe said Shire thei were by certein riotous peple (6) longyng to þe lord Egremond grevously wounded and bette so þat after þat the said late Shiref myght haue (7) noon Officers forto leve youre dettes for dreede of their deth And also howe þe said lord Egremond long before þe (8) said betyng saide yn þe presens of notable persones þat he wold haue þe said late Shiref hede and forthe (9) with þe foresaid late Shiref sent word of þe said manasse to þe Erle of Salesbury by his lettre and his (10) seal to thentent þat his good lordshipp shuld shewe it to yowe and your counseill / Besecheth also youre said highnes (11) þe said late Shiref to be aduertised howe þat þe olde extent of þe said Counte by cause of grete (12) importable and many fold ruynes and decayes myght not yn grete parte of long tyme be reysed by þe Sherefs þerof (13) to their right grete charges and likly oftetymes of their vndoyng þe which importable charges arn demaunded of (14) þe said Thomas late Shiref by þe sommones of þe pipe comyng oute of þe Eschequyer þat is (15) forto say. De perficuo Com xl. li where yn dede þer can not be arered vj li And also of xxij*ti* (16) oþer fermes asked of þe said late Shiref sub nomine vic xxxvj li wherof he can not rere viij. li. (17) ne wote not where viij of thise fermes lye with yn þe said Counte And also where ther is asked of hym for (18) youre demaynes yn þe said Counte xliij li xj li therof lyth wast and distroied by þe Scottes and þe watyr (19) of Eden: which charges amountes to þe somme of xxiiij xiiij li for which causes in especiall all such persones (20) as hath of late tyme be named to be Shirefs there haue enstraunged them from þe said Office and yet doon. so þat (21) throgh defaute of such Officers grete hurtes and inconueniences haue late growen and dayly groweth to yowe soueraigne (22) lord and to youre subgettes therefor noun execucion of þe lawe yn þat partie. And howe þe said late Shiref (23) also for þe same causes enstraunged hym and wold not take vppon hym þe said Office. vnto þe tyme he was putte (24) yn coumforth and trust to be vtterly and clerely discharged of all such sommes as he couthe make no leve of (25) wherfore please it to youre said highnes tendrely to considre þe premisses and howe yf þe (26) said late Shiref shuld be charged yn his accompte with þe said somme of xxiiij xiiij li which he can make (27) noo leve of, it shuld be to his vtter vndoyng of youre speciall grace to graunte to þe aforesaid late (28) Shiref a priue seal to be direct to þe Tresourer and Barones of youre Eschequyer commaundyng hem þat (29) yn thaccompte which þe said Thomas is to yelde to yowe before youre said Tresorer and Barons by cause (30) of his said office þat they charge hym not with þe hole extent of the said Shire. þat is to say (31) of þis ferme called firma per perspicuo Com. nor of þe other xxiiti fermes above rehersed asked (32) of þe said late Shiref sub nomine vic nor of þe ferme asked of hym for youre demayns landes (33) ner of noon other sommes of money by hym to be reysed by vertue of his said office yn þe said Shire: save (34) only of such parcelles as he with his trewe diligence myght or may arere. and gadre And also þat þe (35) said Thomas late Shiref be not vexed by any astate or person for any annuite or charge by yowe grauntet to be resceyved (36) of þe issues and profites of þe said Counte ferther þan he may arere or gadre as it is abouesaid And þat (37) of all þe remnaunt þat shuld growe vnto yowe with yn þe said Shire they vtterly and clerely (38) discharge the said Thomas late Shiref and therof acquiete hym his heires and his executours ayenst yowe and youre heires (39) for euermore by his othe or by þe othe of his depute sufficeant accomptyng for hym withouten any issue triall (40) or verrement to be takyn betwene yowe and hym thervppon for þe love of god. and yn wey of charite.

Chancery hand
Printed *RP* VI.63.3.

224

1454   SC8/28/1358   Petition of James, Earl of Wiltshire
(1) To the full wyse and discrete Comons of this present parlement
Sheweth vnto your notable discrecions and (2) wisdoms Iames Erle of Wiltshire and of Ormond That where he is seised in his demesne as in fee of þe Maner of Hukcote (3) with the Auowson of þe Chirche of Hukcote to þe seid Maner appertenyng and of a Croft called þe (4) litill mylne hamme with theire appurtenaunces in þe Countee of Bukingham of þe yift and (5) feffement of Iames late Erle of Ormond fader of þe seid Erle of wiltshire and Iohn Neell Clerk And þat þe seid (6) Erle of wiltshire at þe reuerence of our blissed lord Crist jhesus and of his blissed moder our lady Seint Marie (7) and in worship of that glorious Martir Seint Thomas somtyme Archebisshop of Caunterbury of whos blode the seid Erle (8) of wiltshire his fader and many of his Auncestres are lyneally descended And the which glorious martir was borne of his moder (9) within þe ground where nowe is sette þe hous or hospitall of þe seid martir called Seint Thomas of (10) Acres within þe Citee of london / And also for þe grete tenderance trust and loue þat þe seid Iames (11) late Erle of Ormond on whom god haue mercy when he was on lyve hade vnto þat devout and holy place / and also for asmoche (12) as þe moder of þe seid Erle of wiltshire is beryed within þat holy place / is disposed agreed and fully (13) sette for hym and his heirs in consideracion of þe premisses and by þe agrement comfort supportacion (14) and assent of your full grete and notable wisdomes / that Iohn Neell nowe Maistre of the seid hous or hospitall (15) shall haue þe seid Maner of hukcote with the Auowson therto appertenyng and the seid Croft with their appertenaunces (16) to hym and to his successors for euermore to þentent that he and his successors shall fynde twey (17) prestes within þe seid hous or hospitall perpetuelly and dayly to pray for þe gode estate of our souerain (18) lord the kyng and of our souerain lady the Queene and of the seid Erle of wiltshire / And for the soules of our souerain (19) lord þe kyng and þe Queene when þey ben passed out of þis world / And for þe soules of the fader of (20) þe seid Erle of wiltshire and of his moder / And for þe soule of þe gode lady Dame Iohane Beauchamp late lady of (21) Bergeuenny grauntdame to þe seid Erle of wiltshire and for þe soules of all oþer his Auncestres þat ben (22) dede And for þe soules of þe seid Erle of wiltshire and of his wyfe and theire heires after þeir discece / (23) and for all Cristen Soules which entent and disposicion þe seid Erle of wiltshire may nat performe ne fulfille (24) without your speciall fauour help and socour be to hym shewed in þis behalfe Wherfore please it

your full (25) grete and notable wisdomes to considre þe premisses and to pray þe kyng our souerain lord þat he by (26) þassent of his lordes spirituell and temporell in þis present parlement assembled and by þe auctoritee (27) of þe same will ordeyne and establissh that þe seid Iohn Neell nowe maistre of þe seid hous or hospitall (28) or his successours may entre in to þe seid maner of hukcote with the Auowson aforseid and Croft with (29) þeire appurtenaunces / And to haue and to holde þe seid maner and Auowson þerto appertenyng and Croft (30) with þeire Appurtenaunces to þe seid maistre and his succesours foreuermore (31) without Interrupcion impediment or empechement of þe seid Erle of wiltshire or of his heirs or of any oþer (32) persone or persones pretendyng title by theyme or to þeire vse / in perfourmyng of þe gode entent and disposicion (33) aboue rehersid / Prouided alwey þat þis Acte statute or ordenaunce shall not exclude ne forbarre none oþer persone (34) or persones of þeire title or right þat þey haue to þe seid maner with þauowson þerto (35) appertenyng and Croft with þeire appurtenaunces but onely to exclude and forbarre þe seid Erle of wiltshire (36) and his heirs and all oþer persone and persones claymyng or hauyng title or right to þe seid maner with (37) thouowson aforseid and Croft with þeire appurtenaunces to þe vse of þe seid Erle of wiltshire or (38) of his heires for þe love of god and in wey of charitee

Chancery hand
Printed *RP* V.257.57.

225

1454 C1/2/36/(53) Petition of John Frebarn of London, lighterman

(1) Vnto the full noble and gracious lord. my lord the Erle of Salesbury Chaunceller of Engeland

Mekely besecheth your (2) poure Oratour Iohn ffrebarn of london lighterman pitously complaynyng. how that the vije day of Septembre now last (3) passed in the xxxiije yer of the Regne of our souerain lord the kyng that now is. as his seruantʒ (4) called Iohn Scotte william Spencer Nicholas Essex Mathewe white Iohn Ducheman and Morice Argill were comyng (5) from seint Katerines by the Tour wharf hom(ewa)rd[1] toward the house of your seid besecher in Pety wales. ther cam vpon them (6) on the seid Tour wharf oon John Davy Squyer marchall of the Admiralte and Atte sute of partie. arrested the (seid)[1] (7) seruantʒ of your seid besecher. aswell vpon accion of trespas. as of surete of peas. and thervpon had them (8) in to the Tour of London.

and there were in prison by iij dayes in grete duresse. And your seid
besecher coude not haue them out (9) of prison there. but as he was
fayn for to take them to baile vnder surete for to brynge them to their
answer there atte Court (10) day whiche shall be on Monday next comyng / that is to sey. the xxje day of this present moneth of Octobre
/ And besides that. your (11) seid besecher paid for their fees xvij s.
that is to wite. to the seid Iohn Davy x s. to the maister porter iij s
iiij d. to the (12) vnder porter viij d. to the Iayler xvj d. to the Clerk
of the Court þere xiiij d. and for continuaunce of the Court there in
(13) to Monday next comyng vj d / And right gracious lord your seid
besecher is enformed for certein. that neither the seid Iohn Davy (14)
ner non other Officer ner minister of the Tour ner of the Admiralte.
oweth not to entremet hym. ner hath no power auctorite ner Iurisdiccion (15) for to arrest emprison ner vexe eny persone (in)² to the Tour
of london ner in eny other Court of the Admiralte. (16) for eny mater
meved or don betwene partie and partie withynne the body of this
Reaume. neither on water ner on (17) londe / As by diuerse statutȝ þervpon made by auctorite of parlementȝ in the tymes of the moost excellent Princes (18) kyng Richard the ijde and kyng harry the iiije. whos
soules god (assoile)¹ more plainly it appereth. These premisses (19)
tenderly considered / Please hit your noble lordship in asmoche as the
day of apperaunce of the seid seruantȝ in (20) the seid Tour approcheth
(nygh)¹ for to sende for the seid Iohn Davy by a sergeant of armes.
commaundyng the same Iohn (21) to appere before you at suche tyme
on this half the seid day. as may like vnto your good lordship. And
to charge hym for to (22) deliuer the seid seruantȝ clerely out of the
seid Tour. as for eny maters dependyng there ageyns them (23) by reson
of the accions aforesaid. and also . . .¹ discharge and dismisse out of
the Court there. the suretees that haue taken (24) them to baille for
to brynge them to answer. and also to restore ageyn vnto your (seid
besecher the seid xvij s)¹ that he was constrayned (25) wrongefully for
to pay for the fees of the seid seruantȝ Vpon the peyne comprised in
the seid Statutȝ. atte reuerence . . .¹ and for charite

Chancery hand
Printed PC I.xxxvi-vii.
¹ torn   ² rubbed

226

1455   SC8/28/1363   Petition of the abbot and convent of Seynt Germayne, Yorkshire

(1) To the kyng oure souerain Lorde
Moost humbly besechen youre poure Chappeleyns and continuell Oratoures thabbot and (2) Convent of the monastery of Seynt Germayne of Selby in the diocise of york þat where it lyked your highnes (3) because þat the more part of spirritueltees and temporaltees of the seid monastery lying and adioynyng (4) to the Rivers of humbre Owse Trent Aire doune derwent and the dyke which weren the grete relyef and sustenance of (5) your seid Oratoures werne of long tyme and yit ben by the Invndacions of the seid waters and brekyng in of the (6) bankes of hem there / so amynused dyscresed depauparte and anyentysed and also taxed and surcharged to the paying (7) of the dysmeʒ and su(bs)idies[1] þat diuers yeres the proufites and reuenues of them wolde vnneth suffice to (8) paie the hole dismes aftre the taxe of theim which hole dismeʒ of her possessions spirituelx and (9) temporelx amounten to the some of iiij xx. iiij. li. and more in the provinces of Caunterbury and yorke and for other (10) grete charges and pitevous causes and consideracons than shewed vnto youre highnes It lyked youre most benigne grace (11) of grete tendernes and ʒele to youre seid monastery and merite to youre soule and to thencresing of dyuine seruice (12) there by youre lettres patentes the seid special causes and other meritory causes rehersing for to graunte (13) vnto youre seid Oratours and to their successours and to the monastery Aforeseid to be quyte and discharged for euere (14) of alle dismeʒ to be grauntid in the seid provinces ouer the somme of .xl. li. so þat your (15) seid Oratours shulde paie after the graunte of euery hole disme in those provinces .xl li. oonly that is to seye .xv. li. (16) after an hole disme within the province of Caunterbury And so after the rate vpon euere graunt vpon eny part or quote of (17) any disme within the same prouince And .xxv. li. after an hole disme within the province of york And so after the rate (18) there in semblable wise as it more pleynly appiereth in youre seid lettres patentes. Please it (your most habundant)[2] (19) grace the premisses tenderly to considre at this tyme. And in releuacion of your seid continuel Oratours and Monastery (20) of youre patronage being for to prouide for your seid Oratours vpon this Act of resumpcion by thassent of your lordes (21) spirituelx and temporelx now in this youre present parlemet assembled in the wise and in þe maner and (22) fourme as folowith / At the Reuerence of god and in wey of Charite And they shal continuelly prey for youre Royal estate (23) and prosperite.

Prouided alwey that this Act or ordinance of Resumpcion extende not ne be preiudicial (24) to thabbot and Conuent of the monastery of seynt Germayne of Selby in the diocise of york (25) (duryng þe lif of thabbot þat now is)[3] [ne to her successours][4] of or for Any graunte or le*tt*res patentes of exoneracion or Acquitaill (26) vnto hem made of any dismeʒ or subsidieʒ aboue the so*m*me of .xv. li. after the taxe or quantite of an hole (27) disme graunted or to be graunted in the province of Caunterbury And aboue the so*m*me of .xxv. li after the (28) taxe or quantite of an hole disme graunted or to be graunted in the province of york and so after the Rate and quantite of hcm (29) more or lesse but þat the (grauntes)⁵ or le*tt*res patentes made to hem of or for the premisseʒ mowe stonde (30) in her force and so be vtterly except and forprised owte of this Act of Resumpcion

(Memorandum of action on dorse, in a third hand) The kyng by thavice (31) of the lordes sp*iri*tuelx and tempo*r*elx aggreed this p*ro*vysyon as it is desyred duryng the liffe of the Abbot that (32) nowe is and after his discesse the kyng taketh and resumeth in to his handes all the grauntes conteyned in þe p*ro*vysyon to be at his pleasure

Chancery hand
Printed *RP* V.308.

¹ torn ² over erasure ³ superior insert in a second hand ⁴ bracketed for excision ⁵ rubbed

227

1455   SC8/28/1369   Petition of William Neel and William Laweshull that their grants not be resumed

(1) To the King oure soue*r*ain Lorde

Besechen mekely youre humble and pou*r*e seru*a*nt*es* William Neel (2) yoman of youre Hon*n*o*u*rable Chambre and William Laweshull Grome of the same That where as in conside*r*ac*i*on aswel (3) of the long and continual seru*i*ce that they haue do vnto you as for the grete cost*es* charges and expenses by theym (4) born and doon in the same seruice in riding diu*er*se tymes at youre high comaundement*es* and other wise manyfold. (5) hit hath liked vnto youre highnesse forto Rewarde youre seid besechers as hit shall appere in the tenour here folwing (6) And for asmuche as they haue no thinge ellis to leve vppon in any wise but oonly the seid Rewardes and dred theym sore (7) forto forgo the same by force of an Acte of Resumpc*i*on whiche is made in this youre p*re*sent p*a*rlement vnto their (8) importable hurt but if hit be Remediyd by your (highnesse vnto whiche please hit þe*r*fore of your most (9) noble & benigne grace by thavis)¹ and assent of the lords sp*i*ritu*e*lx and tempo*r*elx assembled in this p*re*sent (10) p*a*rlement for to execute and p*r*ouide for youre seid besechers in the seid Acte according vnto the tenour here (11) folwing And they shall spec*i*ally pray to god for you

Prouided also that this Acte of Resump*ci*on or adnullac*i*on (12) extende nor in any Wise be pre*i*udicial vnto William Neel by the name of william Neel oon of oure Gromes of (13) oure Chaumbre in or of a gr*a*unte made by vs vnto him of thoo vj li vj s viij d whiche Geffrey Lescrop and his heires (14) to vs yerely owe for to yelde of the Residue of the Manoirs of Bowedon and haverebergh in the Countee of Leyc*estre* for . . . ² (15) terme of viij yeres [Nor vnto William Laweshull in or of a gr*a*unte by vs made vnto him of the landes and tenement*es* (16) Rent and seruice in the Tovn of wrotthyng made vnto him for the term of xxx yeres yelding vnto vs therof by yere iiij (17) li as hugh atte ffenne to vs therof before tyme yelded and xx s ou*er* of encresce by yere.]³ but that [alle]³ and eu*er*y (18) of our seid gr*a*unt*es* seuerally made vnto the seid william and william And oure le*tt*res patent*es* (19) seuerally theruppon made be good and effectual vnto theym and eich of theym. the seid Acte notwistanding.

(Dorse in a different hand) (20) As to Nele it is aggreed and as to William lawshull it is aggreed þ*a*t that he hath be resumed to þe kynges advayle

Chancery hand
Printed *RP* V.313b.
¹ over erasure   ² cancel   ³ cancelled

228

1455   SC8/28/1373   Petition of Thomas Scargill that his grant not be resumed

(1) To the kyng our sou*er*ain lord

Besecheth mekely your humble s*er*uaunt Thomas Scargill Squier late vssher (2) of your honorable Chambre that where as in consideracion of the long and continuall s*er*uice that he hath doon vnto you (3) in your honorable houshold about your gracious p*er*sone by the space of xx yeres and more it hath liked vnto your highnesse (4) for to make hym Squier and to susteyne that degre the xxx yere of your noble and gracious Regne forto gr*a*unt vnto him (5) by the name of Thomas Scargill Squier vj d by day to be take for t*er*me of his lif of the issues and profites (6) comyng of þe Counte of york by the handes of þe Shiref of the same Counte for the tyme beyng Please it vnto your (7) most noble and benigne gr*a*ce forto gr*a*unte by thaduise and assent of the lordes spiritualx and temporalx (8) assembled in this pr*e*sent parlement that in the acte of resumpc*ion* made in this said parlement a p*r*ouision (9) be made for your said besecher in the fourme folwyng and he shall spec*i*ally pray to god for you

(10) Prouided also that this acte of resumpsion extende not nor be preiudiciall vnto Thomas (11) Scargill Squier in or of a g*r*aunt made by vs vnto him by the same name of vj d by day to be take for terme (12) of his lif of the issues ser*u*ices reuenues p*r*ofites and other commodites comyng of the Counte of york by the (13) handes of the Shiref of the same Counte for the tyme beyng but that our said g*r*aunte and le*tt*res patentes (14) therupon made beryng date þe xvj day of Marche the xxxthe yere of our regne be good and effectuall vnto hym (15) aftir the tenour and p*ur*port of the same the said acte not withstandyng

(Dorse in another hand) The lordes spirituelx and (16) temp*o*relx consideryng that Thomas Scargyll hathe no thyng of the kynges yeft but vj d by the day save oonly (17) the parkership of þe park of haveryng of the Bour by the which he hath but lytle avayle obov his charges agree w*i*th this p*r*ovysyen

Chancery hand
Printed *RP* V.314b.

229

1455   SC8/28/1380A   Petition of John Heron to be made Constable of the Castel of Bameburgh

(1) To the kyng oure soueraigne lord

Mekely beseketh your humble ser*u*ant Iohn Heron Squyer that wher (2) it liked y*our* highnesse to g*r*aunt to y*our* said ser*u*ant thoffice of Constable of yo*ur* Castell (3) of Bameburgh. to haue and occupie for terme of his lif by him or by his depute sufficient / for whom he woll aunswere with (4) all maner fees wages and p*r*ofites to þe same office of olde tyme due and accustumed and also the kepyng of (5) your said Castell and ouersight of the lordship of the same Castell. and also .xl. li to be take of thissues fermes profites (6) and reuenues of the said Castell and lordship of Bameburgh comyng. by the handes of all maner Receyuours ffermers (7) and Occupiers of the same Castell and lordship for the tyme beyng / at the termes of Ester and of Seynt Michell by (8) euen porcions for the saufgarde of your said Castell. And in your last parlement holden before this present parlement. (9) it liked you by thauys and assent of y*our* lordes sp*i*rituelx and temporelx and your Comens in (10) þe same parlement assembled / and by auctorite of the same to ordeyne that your said besecher was restored and preferred (11) yerely to þe said fees wages and .xl. li specified in your said lettres of graunte to him made (12) accordyng to the purporte and tenour of the same lettres patentʒ of the said issues fermes profites (13) and reuenues afore all other assignementʒ and grauntes to eny persone or persones therof had or made. (14) eny other graunte or assignement by you made to eny other persone or persones not withstondyng. That it please (15) you of your moost habundaunt grace considered that þe said Castell stondith in þe fronter of your marches (16) toward Scotland and þat the same Castell is right ruinous and diuerse partes of the walles of the same Castell and (17) also the Dungeon forteresses and Toures therin likely to falle doun withoute þat the soner remedy of reparacion (18) be had in theym And also the see with dryftes of weder hath dryven the sandes to the walles of þe said Castell. so (19) that all people may haue cours to the same walles . . .[1] wherfore your said seruant ys put to þe more coste and charge (20) and because therof fyndeth .xl. persones dayely abydyng in the said Castell for the saufgarde of the same (21) and that he yeueth yerely to his lieutenant continuelly abydyng vpon the saufgarde of the same Castell .xx. marc and to (22) .ij. men watching there both wynter tyme and Somertyme to either of theym vj. marc yerely and mete and drynke and that (23) your said seruant hath nomore of you to supporte the said charges but the said .xl. li. that it like your (24) highnesse to graunte that a purven may be had for your said seruant in forme here vnder writen And if it like (25) your highnesse that your said seruant shall not be prouided for in this behalue that it may be (26) enacted in this high Courte of parlement that he be not empeched in tyme to come neither by you your heires ne successours (27) for eny losse or hurt þat might falle to the said Castell as godde for bede by your ennemys for lacke or defaute (28) of kepyng of the said Castell

(Similar hand but smaller script) Prouided also that this acte or peticion of resumpsion extende not nor in eny wise be (29) preiudiciall to oure graunte made by vs by oure lettres patentes to Iohn Heron Squyer in to for or of thoffice of Constable (30) and ouersight of oure Castell and lordship of Bameburgh ne to the wages fees and rewardes to the same of olde tyme due and (31) accustumed ne to oure graunte made by the same lettres patentes to the same Iohn of .xl. li yerely to be take of thissues (32) rentes profites and reuenues of the said Castell and lordship comyng for the kepyng and charges of the said Castell aswell in tyme (33) of werre as tyme of pease Considered that oure progenitours and we haue be chargeʒ for the kepyng of the said Castell with (34)

DC. marc yerly and nowe be charged but with the said xl. li And that oure said le*tt*res patentʒ be gode and (35) effe*c*tuell to the said Iohn this acte notwithstondyng

SC8/28/1380B (draft; cancels not recorded)

So alwey þat if þe seid (36) wages fees and rewardes atteigne to the somme of xl. li by yere. þat þen þe seid (graunte of xl li)² (38) yerely be not comprised within þis p*r*ouision and if þe seid fees wages & rewardes atteigne not (39) to the so*m*me of xl. li by yere. then þe seid graunte (of xl li yerely)² & le*tt*res patentes (40) þerof. to and for asmoche as so shal atteigne (to the sume of xl li with the wages fees and rewardes)² be & stond (41) (goode)² effe*c*tuell and availlable for the kepyng and charge of the said Castell as wel in tyme of werre as in tyme of pease

Text in Chancery, response in non-Chancery hand
Printed *RP* V.316b.
[1] cancel   [2] superior insert in a different hand

230

1455   SC8/28/1387   Petition of Thomas Yong for restitution after his arrest for speaking out in Parliament

(1) To the right wise and discret Comons in this present parlement assembled

Bese(cheth)[1] humbly Thomas yong that where (2) as he late beyng oon of the knyghtes for the shire and towne of Bristowe in dyue*rs* parlementes holden afore this demened (3) him in his saiyng in the same as wele faithfully and with alle suche trewe diligent labour as his symplenesse couthe or might (4) for the wele of the kyng oure soue*r*ain lorde and this his noble Realme and notwithstonding that by the olde liberte (5) and fredom of the Comy*ns* of this londe had enIoyed and p*r*escribed fro the tyme that no mynde is alle suche p*er*sones (6) as for the tyme been assembled / in eny parlement for the same Comy*ns* ought to haue theire fredom to speke and sey in the (7) hous of there assemble as to theym (is)² thought conuenyent or resonable withoute eny mane*r* chalange charge or punycion (8) therefore to be leyde to theym in eny wise Neue*r*thelesse by vntrewe sinistre reportes made to the kinges highnesse of (9) your said bisecher for matiers by him shewed in the hous accustumed for the Comyns in the said p*ar*lementes He was (10) therefore taken arrested and rigorously in open wise led to the Toure of London and there greuously in grete duresse long (11) tyme emprisoned (ayenst)² the said fredom and liberte and was there put in grete fere of ymportable punycion of his body and (12) drede of losse of his lif withoute eny enditement presentement appele due originall accusement or cause laufull had or sued (13) ayenst him as it is openly knowen: the not mowyng come to eny answere or declaracion in that partie whereby he not oonly suffered (14) grete hurt payn and disese in his body (but)² was by the occasion therof put to ouer grete excessyue losses and expenses of his (15) good amountyng to the somme of M*l*. mark and muche more Please hit your grete wisedoms tenderly to consider the premisses And (16) thervpon to pray the kyng our souerain lorde that hit like his (highness)² of his moost noble grace to graunte and prouide(17) by thavice of the lordes spirituell and temporell in this present parlement assembled that for the said losses costes damages (18) and imprisonment your said bi(secher)² haue sufficient and resonable recompense as good feith trouthe and conscience requiren

Chancery hand
Printed *RP* V.337.15.
¹ torn   ² rubbed

231

1455   SC8/28/1388   Petition of the citizens of Oxford
(1) To the right wise and discret Comuns of this present parlement
Besechen (mekely)¹ your contynuell Oratours the (2) Mair and Burgeises of the towne of Oxenford that where þe said towne is charged to þe kyng our souerayn lorde (3) yerely of a fee ferme of xl li beside and other charge of xxiij li v d And ouer that at euery xv*me* & xe of xxiiij. li (4) And howe þat the said towne in þe dais what tyme the same towne was thus charged with þe said (5) sommes was full enhabited with marchauntes artificers and grete multitude of lay people And now is desolate for the (6) more parte be cause of diuerse statutȝ in diuerse parlementȝ made that noo man shulde take noon apprentices (7) but if the fadres or þe modres of þe apprentices myght spende yerely xx s of free hold So that the said lay people (8) nowe in þe said towne of dyuers craftes may not bere þe charges aforsaid ne serue and plese the Clergie (9) beyng in þe vniuersyte that is there Wherfore many scolers withdrawe theym and voide the said vniuersyte seyng þat (10) they may not haue artificers to serue theym at their nede to þe perpetuell anyentesyng of þe said towne and grete (11) hyndryng of the said Clergie / Please it vnto your wisdoms the premysses tendrely considred to pray the kyng our souerayn (12) lord that it lyke his highnesse by þaduise

and assent of his lordes sp*iri*tuell and temporell in this p*re*sent p*ar*lement (13) assembled to ordeyne by auctoryte of þe same þat it be liefull to eu*er*y Burgeys of the said towne of (14) Oxenford to take apprentece or apprentices such as to hem semeth behofull in semblable maner as þe Citeȝens of the Citee (15) of london doo and vse how be it that þe fadre or fadres of the said apprentice or app*re*ntices haue not ne (16) neu*er* had eny free holde in londes te*ne*mentes rentes seruices or eny other possessions within þis (17) Roialme and þat (noon)² of the said Burgeyses of the said towne for takyng of eny such apprentice cont*r*arie to the (18) said statuȝ by our said souerain lord ne his heires nor noon other p*er*sone be disturbed inquieted greved vexed (19) or empeched eny statute afore þis tyme made to þe cont*r*arie not withstondyng Savyng allwey to the Chaunceller of (20) þe vniu*er*syte of Oxenford and to his successours ther custumes and priueleges of old tyme hadde and vsed. Prouyded (21) alwey that noon of the said Burgeises ne dwellers within the said toun shall take to apprentice eny scoler withoute þassent (22) and avise of þe fader and moder or þe speciall frendes of þe same scoler And this atte reu*er*ence of god and in way of Charitee:

Chancery hand
Printed *RP* V.337.16.
¹ torn   ² rubbed

232

1455   SC8/28/1393   Petition to Commons of Richard Ford, Clerk of the Exchequer

(1) To the right wyse notable and discrete Comons of this p*re*sent parlement assembled

(Humbly bisechith)¹ and (2) prayeth Richard fforde Remembrauncer of the kynges Eschequier on the part of the Tresorer of Englond that where the Tresorer (3) of Englond for the tyme beyng by the tyme that no mynd is as Tresorer and by vertu of (his offi)ce¹ hath yevyn and grauntid (4) the office of the Clerk of the pipe and remembrauncer on his part amonge othir offices whenne they voyde to suche p*er*sones (5) as by his discrecion semyd to be able and expedient to ocupie the seid office and now late (Marmaduke Lumley bishop of)² Karliell (6) late Tresorer of Englond by the agrement and consent of on Robart Cawode thenne Clerk of the office of the pipe yaff and graunted to (7) your seid besecher the seid office of the pipe by force of the which graunte he was therof possessed and ocupied and Thomas Thorp (8) thenne beyng remembrauncer of the seid Tresorers part for diuerse causes resonable mevyng Iohn Erle of Worcestre (9) thenne beyng Tresorer was ammoued and put oute of the seid office and the seid Erle beyng Tresorer yaff and graunted the seid office (10) of remembrauncer vn to your seid besecher by vertu of the which he was therof possessed and oon Iohn Gloucestre by the (11) graunte of the same Tresorer ocupyed and yit is possessed of the seid office of the pipe and your seid besecher (12) the seid office of Remembrauncer ocupied and enioyed vn to the tyme that the seid Thomas Thorp by colour of the kynges (13) lettres patentes made vn to him of the seid office of Remembrauncer for the terme of his lyfe contrary to the (14) liberte and the custume of the office of the seid Tresorer (by the)² tyme afore rehersed hadde and vsyd was put and kept (15) oute by grete fauour and supportacion and your seid besecher the which of tendre age was brought vp in the seid (16) Eschequier was destitute and vnpurveide of any office or occupacion there and how be hit that the seid Thomas (17) Thorp hadde no title to the seid office of Rembrauncer but it ocupyed by grete supportacion contrarye to the custume a boue rehersed and (18) also ayeinst the wylle of the said Erle beyng Tresorer wuld not be ammoved on lesse the(nne)² he myght bene preferred (19) to be third Baron of the seid Eschequier and theroppon by grete meanes made by (þe)² officers of the seid Eschequier and by othir welle disposed persones it was entredid (20) labored and concluded with sir willm ffallan Clerk thenne beyng third Baron of the seid Eschequier that he . . .³ shuld cese and (21) leue his ocupacion of Baron of the seid Eschequier and the seid Thomas Thorp to haue the seid ocupacion for the which conclusion (22) your seid besecher was reuled to be bounden by his obligacion to the seid william ffallan in a certeyne summe of money to (23) pay him yerely duryng his lyfe xl marc of lawfull money on lesse thenne by the kyng oure seid souerayne lord or by (24) the seide Erle or by any other persone atte the instaunce of the seid Erle or of your seid besecher were purveied (25) fore and recompensed (to the valewe of xl marc)² and more yerely duryng his lyfe so that no recompense be made to the (26) seid willyam of any benefice hauyng cure of Soule the which charge of xl marc your seid besecher seth that (27) tyme yerely hath boryn and payde vnto the seid willm ffallan to his grete enpouerisshing and importable charge / Please it (28) your grete wysdoms and discressions to considre these (premisses and)² also othir grete costis and charges (29) that your seid besecher hath dayly in occupacion of the seid office and to pray the kyng oure souerayn lord by (39) the assent of the Lordes spirituell and temporelx in this present parlement assembled and by (auctorite of)² (40) the seid parlement to ordeigne and establysshe that the obligac*i*on and suerte made to the seid willyam (41) ffallan by the seid Richard fforde for the yerly payement of the seid xl ma*r*c be voide and of none effect (nor)² strength

Chancery hand
Printed *RP* V.342.25.
¹ torn   ² rubbed   ³ cancel

INDENTURES

233

1384 E40/A1779 London indenture

(1) Memorandum that Iohn Chirteseye of the Schyr of hertford Gentilman made (astat)¹ bi dede Endentid vn to Richard willysdon And (2) to Anneys hys wyf of all hys w(h)arf¹ Callyd Pakemannys wharf with all the land And tenementys And portinaunce in the (3) parsch of seynt dunstonys in the Este in london And to holde vn to the seyd Richard wyllysdon And Anneys hys wyf to ther eyrys (4) And ther Assynes ffrom the date of seyd Endentur vn to the Ende of C. ʒer the wych dat of the seyd Endentur was in the (5) feste of seynt Archunwolde the ʒer of kyng Richard the ijd the vije Beryng vn to the seyd Iohn Chirtheseyd hys (6) eyres And to hys Assygnes xij li of lawfull money duryng the seyd terme Also bryng to seynt Mari overey And to Socage All the (7) Charge that to thethm ʒerli of of the seyd soyle by longyth Also beryng Almaner of certeyn And Casuell Chargis (8) As Aʒen holy chyrch. And to the kyng that ys or schall long vn(to)¹ the seyd land And tenement duryng the seyd terme (9) Also Richard wyllysdon s(h)all² vp on hys owne proper Cost wyth yn x ʒer next folovyng Affter (10) the dat of the seyde Endentur Enlarg Strecchyng in tho themesward the seyd wharfe xxiij fote of A sise And wall (11) All only of maydenston ston Also the seyd Richard wyllesdon Schall with yn the terme of the seyd x. ʒer to (12) take don All maner of hosyng. At the tyme of the seyd lese beryng [beryng]³ vp on all the seyd soyl And byld All the Soyle All (13) only wyth new tymbre puttyng to no thyng to of the olde tymbr And that to (be)¹ performyd yn the forme After wrytten That (14) ys to wyten wytten All the ffrountte of the seyde soyle Aʒenst the hye Strete And xl fote ynward of Storyes of heygh the fyrst (15) story of xij fote of heygh te ij of x fote te thryd of vij fote purposseuyd of sufficient tymbr All only of herte of oke (16) As Sufficienttyly longyth to Sych maner of Byldyng wyth All maner of [divyn]³ dividyng Garnysshyng And Coueryng (17) that schuld long to the seyd Bildyng [wyth All maner]³ Also the seyd Richard wyllesdon schall wythynne the seyd terme Of (18) x ʒer do byld vp on the seyd Soyle in warde A Chef dwellyng place A bove Stag [tat]³ that ys to wyte A hall of xl fote (19) of lengyth And xxiiij fote of brede A (parlour)⁴ kychyn And boterye As to Sych A hall Schulde long And the remenant of the soyle (20) Accept the Cartway And the seyd wharf of xxiiij fote to do bylde Chambrys And hovses for the marchaundyse sufficiently (21) forseyng that As well vndyr the seyd hall parlour And kechyn botery And All the seyd Chambr beselered vndurnethe the Grunde xij (22) fote in heygh And All the seyd Byldyng To be donn

Be [the of]³ the seyd Ihon Chirtheseye or hys Assign And ʒyf Caas be that the (23) seyd byldyng or Eny part ther of be not holly performyd in the maner A fore seyd by the Ende of the seyde x ʒer then (24) schall hit be lefull vn to the seyd Iohn Chirtheseye hys executoriis And hys Assygnes And to the seyde soyle with All portinaunces (25) to reentr And the seyd Richard wyllysdon hys executorijs And hys Assignis holli to put owte for Euer mor (26) thys Endentur noʒth withstandyng Also in the Same Endentur A Clause of destresse ʒyf the Rent be by hynde A (27) moneth of Eny [vsuall da]³ vusuall day of payment And ʒyf that be bi hynde iij Monethys to (r)eentr² &c (28) Also ʒyf dew Reperacion be noʒth don with lefull [warnyg]³ warnyng had be seyd lessour or his Assygnes (29) with yn xl dayes After warnyng to holly reentre &c

Non-Chancery hand
¹ h superior insert ² crease ³ cancelled ⁴ torn

234

1426   C146/C1223   Stonor indenture, London

(1) This bille endentid made atte london the xxiiij day of Nouembre the yere of kyng henri the sext after the conquest the fourthe (2) bitwene Thomas Stonore Squier of the Shire of Oxonford and william Rothewell of the Shire of lyncoln Squyer witnessith that the said (3) william hath boght the Maner of Repyngale with alle the londes and tenementes of the seid Thomas in the seid Shire of lyncoln with the (4) douson of the thirde parte of the Churche of Rypyngale vnder the fourme and condicione that folowen. that is to seyn the sad (5) william shall paye vnto the same Thomas for the seid Maner and tenementes at Stonore CC.xxiiij. xvj li xiij s. iiij d of (6) good lavfull money of Inglond the oon half þerof atte fest of Annunciacion of oure lady next comyng after the date aboueseid and (7) the other half atte fest of Seynt michell Archangle than next folowyng And that the seid Thomas vpon the seid payement atte fest of Annunciacion (8) of oure lady shall make a feffement of the Maner and tenementes aboueseid vnto the seid william and to his heirs and assignees (9) with a warantye for euermore vpon condicion that if the same william faill of his forseyd seconde payement of half CCxxiiij. (10) xvj li xiij s iiij d atte seid fest of Seynt Michell that than the seid Thomas the forseid Maner and tenementes (11) may reentre the. seysyne therof delyuered nat withstandyng And if the seid william well and trewely paye all the sume aboueseid (12) of CCxxiiij xvj li xiij s iiij d atte festes aboueseid thanne the forseid Thomas shall make vnto the same william as good (13) sufficient and sure estat of

the Maner and tenementes aboueseid and euery parcell therof as the counceles of the (13) seid Thomas and william will deuyse In witnesse wherof the said parties to this endentures entrechangeably haue put her (14) seals y yove at london the day and yere aboueseid.

Chancery hand

235

1427   E28/48/18   Winchester indenture

(1) Thys endenture (y)¹ made by Walter hore mair of þe Cite of Wynchestre & Cyteʒyns of the same Cyte þe (2) þrydde. day of September þe ʒer of þe regne of kyng (henry)² þe .vj. þe .v. wytennssuth þat (3) oure worshupful. & holy. fadur in god henry by þe grace of god Bysshup of Wynchestre & þe worthy Clerk / Abbot of (4) Beaulieu Walter Sandes knyght & Iohn Vuedale Squyer Commissioners of oure sayde liege lorde by. hys lettres of (5) priue seal. lat were. y.sende to þe sayde Mayr & Cyteʒins to trete wyth hem to haue en. apprest of hem. a. notable (6) somme in (helpyng of þe w)erres³ of oure sayde liege lord by twext whyche Commissioners. Mayr & Cyteʒins (7) diuerseʒ comunicacions .y.hadde to fore þe. day bwesaid & also diuerseʒ comunicacions & (8) dayes. y. hadde by. þe sayde Mayr & . Citeʒins by. twext hem self / to fore þat day / (& so)² (the day A)³ forsayde (9) the Mair & Cyteʒins answered & sayde þat wyth. diuerse late pestylenceʒ te þryftyust men &. so grete. a. multitude (10) of peple ys dede in oure cyte þat. þe þrydde man ys nat. y.left. a lyue þer ynne & þe kyngus (11) ferme of þat Cyte & oþer many diuerseʒ chargeʒ fallyng vpon þat Cyte fro day to day buþ now(12) as grete as euur þey were (as)² whan þe Cyte of peple & goud stovde most in prosperite & so for grete charges (13) fallyng vpon hem. day by day þey mowe vnneþe lyve but buþ. so pore. þat aprest. hy buþ nat in power (14) to make but and. hyt were in. here power to make. aprest or (of power to)² do plesance to oure (liege)² lord wyth here goud. hy (15) wolde do hyt as tendurly & with. as goude hert &. wyll as eny man þat lyuuth.

Non-Chancery hand

¹ crease   ² superior insert   ³ over erasure

236

c 1428   C49/22/19   Bristol deposition

(1) The certyficate of the Meyr and Baillyffes of Brystowe

Remembrance that the fryday next after þe fest of the (2) Exaltac*ion* of the holy Croyce the sexte yer of the kyng that nowe ys: Iohn Baylly late the Clerk of Phelip Excestre: come (3) a fore Robert Russell that tyme Meyr Roger lyuedon and Water Milton the yonger Baillifs. And many other worthy men syttyng yn open (4) Court And seyd openly yn heryng of alle men: that ther were that serteyn day and yere: he shewed to Thomas Stamford a dede (5) ensealed that Crystyan Nele somtyme of Brystowe made vnder her seal. And also vnder the Meyres seale: to Willyam Combe somtyme (6) Burgeis of Bristowe: of certeyn londes And tenementes: yn the towne: and þe subarbes of Bristowe: And whan he had (7) shewed the same dede: vn to the same Thomas: the same Thomas toke the seales yn his honde: and desyred the foresaid dede: And (8) for the same Iohn Bailly. wolde not delyuer hit hym: he pulled of the seales. that he helde yn his honde: and putte hem yn his (9) sleue: And whan the same Thomas hed harde these wordes: he said. that sothe hit was: that þe said Iohn Baylly shewed hym (10) suche a dede: And. yn struglyng be twene hem bothe: he brake of the seales: and so he knoweleched the brekyng ther of: openly (11) a fore alle the Court / and said these wordes: I didde hit. what wolle ye sey ther to: take youre auauntage:

Chancery hand

237

1445 C146/C3584   London indenture

(1) This bille endentid made be twyn Robert Clopton Ceteseyn and Alderman of london on the on party And Iohn Gerveys of (2) Bury Seynt Edmunde on the other party witnessith that where as the seid Robert hath certeyn londes and tenementes (3) in Bury afor seid And in the feldes of the same Toun And in the tounes of ffornham Alhalwyn ffornham (4) Martyn Berton And in other Tounes there with here appertenances the seid Robert hath solde alle the (5) seid londes and tenementes with the appertenances to the seid Iohn for CCCC marc for to be payd (6) at the ffestes vnderwrete / that is to sey At the feste of halumesse next comyng: xl marc and at the seid feste of (7) Candelmesse that shall be in the yer of our lord M*l*CCCCxlvj. xx. marc and so yerly at the seid feste of Candelmesse (8) xx marc into the tyme that þe seid sume of CCCC marc be fully content and paid to the seid Robert (9) or his certeyn Attorney And the seid Robert shall make or do make to the seid Iohn and to othere sweche as the seid Iohn (10) will name A sufficiaunt estate in all þe seid londes and tenementes with

the appertenances at (11) the seid feste of halumesse / at wheche tyme the seid Iohn shal fynde to the seid Robert And to sweche as he wil haue sufficiaunt (12) suerte for the seid paiementes be a vis of Counsel of þe seid Robert And for the more suerte of the seid (13) Iohn that he hys heires and assignes shulen haue the seid londes and tenementes withowte ony (14) recouere of the seid Robert or his heires The seid Robert shal make or do make to the seid Iohn and his heires (15) a. resonable suerte of An Annuyte in his Maner of wyndey in the Counte of Caumbregge or ellys in othere fee symple londes (16) to the value of xx marc yerly be a vis of Counseyll of þe seid Robert and Iohn that the seid Iohn shal haue (17) the seid londes and tenementes in Bury and in the other Tounes aforseid to hym hys heires and assignes pesybly (18) for the forseid Robert hys heires and assignes withowtyn ende And also Iohn harpour fermour of the seid londes (19) shal haue fre entre and issu to thresshyn fannyn and caryen all his Cornes straw and chaf howsyd in the Bernes there in to the feste (20) of Estryn nest commynge And also it shal be leful to the seid Robert And his Attorney for to distreyne in all the (21) forseid londes and tenementes for ony rente or ferme be hynde for the terme of Mighelmesse nest comyng or ellys (22) before / into the feste of Estryn aforeseid In witnesse where of either of the seid parties to other chaungeably haue put to these (23) present bill endentyd her seales: at the xx day of Iull In the yere of kyng herry the vjt the xx iij.

per copia sigillat
Non-Chancery hand

238

1445 E101/504/19 Lincoln indenture

(1) This is the Acorde made the xijte day of Septembre the xxiiijt ȝere of our souereyn lord kyng henry (2) the vjte. betwix Iohn ffox of wisbeche in ye counte of Cambrige on that one partie and william Boydell othirwise called (3) wright of (beche)¹ Saifterton in ye Counte of lincoln on that othir partie / that is to say that ye seid william shall (4) take doune all the timbre of the chapetre hous atte ye Nonnes of Staunford And make a low flore in ye same hous contenyng (5) vij somers & lx trasons. And make A new Rofe for ye same (hous)² contenyng vj bemes vj wyndbemeȝ vj principals. (6) xxvj cople sparres. with walplates & side trees. with braseȝ fro ye principals to ye seid Sidetrees whiche Rofe shall (7) conteyne in length .xxj ȝerdis & in brede viij. ȝerdes of assise ffor whiche werkmanship truly to be made. with

takyng (8) doune of ye olde Rofe / the seid Iohn shall pey to ye seid william xlvj s viij d acordyng to his wirkyng / And Agenne / (9) And also ordein timbre to ye seid werkes brought in to conuenable place with in ye ȝerde of ye seid Nonnes (10) This flore & Rofe to be made & sette vp. with in viij monethes next folowyng after ye Date herof

Also ye seid Iohn (11) & william be acordid yat ye seid william shall take doune ye Rofe of the Dortour of ye seid Nonneȝ And make a new Rofe for (12) ye seid Dortour contenyng. xlvj ȝerdis in length & viiij ȝerdis of assise in brede. with xij grete bemes. (13) xij principals xij wyndbemes lxvj cople sperreȝ (with)² walplates & syde trees acording to ye seid Rofe & xxte (14) braseȝ fro ye principals to ye side treeȝ ffor werkmanship of whiche Rofe & taking doune of the olde Rofe ye seid Iohn (15) shall pey to ye seid william vij marc as ye (seid)² werk pro-sedith and agenne. Also ye seid Iohn shall ordein (16) timbre for ye seid Rofe & do bryng hit to couenable place with in the ȝerde of ye seid Nonneȝ. And (17) ye seid william shal take asmuche of ye olde timbre as wille in eny wise serve to ye seid werkes And he shal make (18) & sette vp the seid Rofe withine xxte monethes next folowyng after ye date herof In wittenes where of the (19) seid Iohn & william has putte yeir seles to this Indentures. atte Staunford the day and ȝere forseid

Non-Chancery hand
¹ over erasure   ² superior insert

239

1453   E40/A2495   London indenture

(1) This indenture made bitwene Sire Iohn Burcestre knyght and Thomas hoo of þe Countee of Sussex Squier on þat one (2) partie and william lemyng Citeȝein and Grocer of london on þat other partie witnesseth þat þe seid Sire (3) Iohn and Thomas han graunted bargayned and solde vnto the seid william þe day of makyng of þis indenture all þe (4) tenementes with þe appertenances of þe seid sire Iohn liggyng beside þe grete Condite in westchepe (5) in þe paroche of Seint Marie Colchirche in london þat were somtyme Sysors of london Of all þe which tenementes (6) with þe appertenances the seid sire Iohn and Thomas graunten by þis indenture to make or do to make (7) to þe seid william or to his assignes as sure and as sufficient estate as kan be thought most sure and sufficient by þe (8) aduyse of þe Counseill of þe seid william with a sufficient warantis accordyng to þe same estate (in)¹ as (hasty (9) time as it)¹ kan be thought by þe counseill of þe seid william / And þe seid sire Iohn and Thomas graunten by (10) þis in-

denture to deliuer or do to be deliuered vnto þe seid william or to his assignes before þe (11) fest of þe natiuitee of seint Iohn Baptist next forto come after þe date of þis indenture all þe (12) Chartres euidences and munimentes þat þe seid sire Iohn and Thomas han or may haue touchyng or concernyng (13) þe same tenementes or any parcell þerof / Prouided alweys þat yf þere be more land or mo (14) tenementes conteyned in þe same euidences / þat þe seid william shall haue of all suche chartres euidences (15) and munimentes a copie in suche wise as kan be þought most seure by þe aduise of þe Counceill of þe (16) seid william / Also þat þe seid sire Iohn shall fynde to þe seid william sufficient seurtee þat dame Eliʒabeth (17) wyfe of þe seid sire Iohn after þe decece of þe same sire Iohn shall clayme no dower of (18) nor in þe seid tenementes nor any parcell þerof / yf god fortune hir to ouerlive þe (19) seid sire Iohn hir husbond To the which couenantʒ all aboueseid and euerych of þeym on þe partie of (20) þe seid sire Iohn and Thomas and of either of þeym wele and truly to be hold performed and kept in all þinges in (21) þe manere and fourme aforseid / þe seid Sire Iohn and Thomas bynden þeym and either of þeym by him self for all and in (22) þe hole her heirs her executors and all her goodes to þe forseid william (23) in an hundred pound sterlinges by þise present lettres In witnesse wherof þe parties aforseid to (24) þise indentures chaungeably han sette her seals þe xiijth day of Iuyn þe yer of þe reigne of (25) king henry þe sixt after þe conquest .xxxjth

Stodeley I
Chancery hand
[1] superior insert

240

1456   E40/A7651   Northampton indenture

(1) This endenture made bitwene hugh wyche Citeʒein and Mercer of london Arthure Ormesby Gentilman and william Sewster Citeʒein (2) and Mercer of london on that oon partye And henry Baldeswell of Northampton Mercer on that othir partie witnessith / that the said (3) hugh Arthure and william haue dymysed and leten to ferme to the said henry a Shop with Chambres and houses aboue bielded and alle their (4) appurtenances set in the olde Drapery of the towne of Northampton forsaid bitwix the tenement of the Abbot seynt (5) Iames biside Northampton abouesaid on that oon partie and the tenement late of Thomas Bibyng on that othir partie To haue and to (6) holde the said Shop with Chambres and houses aboue bielded and alle their

appurtenances to the said henry from the fest of (7) Cristemas next commyng aftir the date of these presentes vnto the ende and terme of twenty yeres than next suyng and fully to be (8) fulfilled yeldyng therefore yerely duryng the said terme to the said hugh Arthure and william to their heirs or assignees. fyve (9) markes sterlinges atte the festes of the Anunciacion of oure lady Virgyn Natiuite of seynt Iohn Baptist seynt Michell tharchaungell (10) and Natiuite of oure lorde by even porcions And in case be that the said Rent of fyve mark be behynde in part or in alle aftir eny of the (11) said festes by viij dayes vnpaid than hit shall be lefull to the said hugh Arthure and william in the said Shop with Chambers and houses (12) aboue bielded and their appurtenances to entre and distreyn And the distresses so taken lefully to bere away and towardes theym to (13) kepe and withholde vnto the tyme that of the said rent and of the arrereges of the same if any be to theym be made satisfaccion and payment And if (14) hit happen the said Rent of fyve mark to be behinde in part or in alle aftir any of the termes abouesaid by .xv. dayes not paid / or if the (15) said henry the said Shop with Chambers & (houses aboue bielded)¹ & all þeir appertenaunces or eny parcell (16) of hem let to serue to any persone or persones within the said terme withoute the speciall licence of the said hugh Arthure (17) and william Than hit shall be lefull to the said hugh Arthure and william and to their heirs and assignees in to the said shop with (18) Chambers and houses aboue bielded / and alle their appurtenances to reentre / And the said henry and all othir therof to put oute and (19) amoeve this endenture not withstonding And the said henry ouer the said yerely ferme of fyve mark shall pay yerely duryng the said (20) terme of twenty yeres to the wardeyns of the ffraternite & gilde of the holy Trinite and of oure lady virgyn in the Chirche (21) of Alhalowen in Northampton forsaid for the tyme beyng xx s sterlinges aftir the fourme of an endenture made bitwene the wardeyns and the (22) Brithirn and sustern of the said ffraternite on that oon partie and Richard wemmys late of Northampton forsaid Mercer and Iohan his (23) wif on that othir partie / of whiche endenture the date is xxviij day of the Moneth of Septembre In the yere of the reigne of kyng henry (24) the fifte after the conquest the vx*th* And the said henry shall sufficiently repaire the said Shop with Chambres and houses (25) aboue bielded and their appurtenance and theym ayens wynde and reyne defensible shall make atte his propre costes duryng (26) the terme abouesaid / and atte the ende of the said terme shall leve the said Shop with the Chambres and houses aboue bielded and their (27) appurtenances in as gode estate. as he receyued theym in the begynnyng of the said terme / Resonable vse excepte / And to alle these (28) couenantes and paymentes abouesaid on the partye

of the said henry wele and truly to be holde performed and paid the same (29) henry byndith him his heirs and executours / to the said hugh Arthure and william their heirs and executours by thes endentures In (30) witnesse wherof the parties forsaid to these endentures / chaungeably haue put and set their sealles yeuen the .iiij. day of Decembre (31) In the xxxiiij*th* yere of the reigne of kyng henry the sext.
(Signed) Plumer
Chancery hand
[1] over erasure

241

1462   C146/C273   Devonshire indenture

(1) Be hit y knowe to all maner mene that wher. aʒ Iohn Cheyne. Esquyer. haue by my dede. beringe date ate Pynhoe the latyste day of (2) Auerell the yeer of the regne of kyng harrey the Syxth after the conquest the fourtieth haue enfeoffid in fee with owte condici*o*n (3) walter lord hungerford Philipp Courtenay. knyghte Iohn ffortescu walter Sargeaunt Iohn longe preste & Iohn Mayne in all my (4) Maner of Nortonhautevile with all my londis and tenements and all the appertenancis in the Schere of Somerset. (5) And al soe in the haluyndell of the Maner of hulpryngton all my londis and tenements with all the appertenance (6) in the sshere of wiltshire [And longe tyme afore by a nothire dede berynge date ate Excestre in the feste of (7) seint mathew the apostell the yeer of the regne of kynge herry the Syxth after the conqueste the twelf haue feoffed william Palain (8) knyght James Chideleoh william Chideleogh . . . in all my landis & tenements withinne the paryssh of Pynhoe in the Schere (9) of Deuonsshire in the forme as hit apperith in the sayde dede][1] & rentholds for as moche as I am in dette to diuers (10) persons as well for my owne dywte as for my modir is dywte. And al soe my goodis mevabel suffisith note to performe my (11) entent that is to sey to doe some soth to the church wherby as well my fader my moder & tho that I am in especiall bounde to doe for as (12) my wyfe and I myghte the more tenderly be hadde in memoir of the churche with oute subsidi of the sayde londis vre as well tho (13) seruantes that the moste parte of hir dayis haue despendyd on my fader & my sayde modir is seruys al tho that haue dispendid tharre (14) dayis in my seruys buth no thinge rewardid wherfore my wyll and my entent is that my sayd feffeis aftir my disses doe leue and (15) divise all the reuenus and profits of the sayde Maners londis & tenements. And tho to take & deliuere to my Executors (16) soe that

they ther with mowe pay all my sayd detts and all so performe and execute my diuise and bequestis comprehendid (17) in my laste wille which apperith in my testament. And all this acomplisid and performyd. I woll that all the (18) sayde feffeis reles to the said Philip knyghte all the ryghte that they have in the sayde. Manerys. haluyndele of the sayde Maner (19) londis and tenements. So that the sayd sir Philip may. soulye performe. certein condicionis comprehendid. (20) in certain endenturis. made and endentid. by twyxte the sayd sir Philip and me In witnisse of the which to this (21) present endentur. I putte my seale. Wryten ate Pynhoe the furst day of the Monith of May. the yeer of the regne of kynge herry (22) the syxth. after the conquest. the fourtieth

Non-Chancery hand
[1] cancelled

Glossary of Forms

This glossary is compiled from a concordance of the 70,000 words of text which is available on computer tape. The glossary lists every spelling and grammatical form in the concordance except for the names of persons and places, which are listed in the Index of Names. The figures in parentheses indicate the number of occurrences for each form. The forms are identified by office and period: S for the Signet letters (items 1-109 in the anthology), P for Privy Seal (items 110-160), C for Chancery (items 161-232), and N for the Indentures (items 233-241). Periods are indicated by decade: 0, 1400-1409; 1, 1410-1419; 2, 1420-1429; 3, 1430-1439; 4, 1440-1449; 5, 1450-1459; 8 indicates items 161 (1388) and 233 (1384). Thus (2) S1 means that a form occurs twice in Signet documents between 1410 and 1419; (12) P3, twelve times in Privy Seal documents between 1430 and 1439; etc.

Only two provenances are listed for any one form, e.g., S1, P2. If only one provenance is given, the form is unique to that office and decade; if two are given the form may be found in still other offices and decades. More specific citations are included for items of special interest.

Definitions are included for words whose spellings are ambiguous or whose meanings have changed. Less common forms and usages have been checked against the *MED* and *OED* and their correspondences noted in the glossary.

a *art.* (407), an (46) all dates and offices. See discussion. ane (4) C3 (D. 173), C5 (D. 221.5).
aacompaned *vb. past part.* associated (1) P5.
abate *vb. pl. subj.* (1) S1; *ger.* abatyng (1) C3.
abatement *n.* (1) C4.
abbey *n.* (1) C3; abbeye (1) S2; abbaye (2) S1; *pl.* abbeyes (1) P5.
abbot *n.* (17) S1, C1; abot (1) S2; *pl.* abbottes (1) S1; abbotis (1) P4.
abide *inf.* (8) P3, C3; habyde (1) C2; *1 past sing.* habade (1) C2 (D. 173.7); *3 past sing.* abode (1) C5 (D. 221.14); *pr. part.* abiding (1) S2; abydynge

(3) S1, C3; *past part.* abiden (1) S2.

abitted *vb. past part.* (1) C1 (D.167.10). Not in *OED;* this is the only *MED* citation, with the tentative definition of "to pay a bit, pay (sb.) in part."

able *inf.* (3) C1, S2.

abode *n.* residence. (2) P3.

abondant *adj.* (1) P5; habundant(e) (3) C2, P3; habundaunt (1) C5; haboundant (1) P3.

abouesaid(e) *adj.* (29) S1, P2; abouesayde (1) C3; aboueseid (10) N2, C3.

about(e) *adv.* (15) C3, C5; abowte (3) S1, P3.

above *adv.* (4) C2, C3; aboue (15) C3, P3; aboven (1) P2; obove (1) C5 (D.228.17).

absence *n.* (9) S1, S2; absense (2) P5; absens (2) P3.

absent *adj.* (1) P3.

absentuth *vb. 3 sing.* (1) C3 (D. 183.14); *past sing.* absented (1) C3.

accept *adj.* acceptable. (1) P2.

accepted *vb. past part.* (3) S1, C4.

accessorie *n.* accessory, in the legal sense. (1) C1.

accidental *adj.* incidental (1) C8 (161.50). This instance cited in *MED,* defined as "growing out of something else,? outward, external."

accomplisshment *n.* (1) P5.

accompt *n.* (1) P2; accompte (2) P2, C3; *pl.* acomptʒ (1) C3; accomptes (1) S1. accomptʒ (1) C3.

accompt *inf.* (1) P2; accompte (4) P2, C3; *3 sing. subj.* accompte (1) P2; *past part.* accompted (2) C3, P4; accompt (1) P3; *ger.* accomptyng (1) C5. See accounted.

accomptable *adj.* accountable. (1) C3.

accord(e) *n.* a formal agreement, such as a treaty, legal settlement. (12) S1, S2; acorde (2) C5, N4.

accordyd *vb. past.* (1) C2; *pr. part.* accordyng(e) (11) C3, P3; according(e) (3) C3, C4; acordyng (2) C3, N4; acording (1) N4; *past Part.* accorded (6) S1, C2; acordid (2) C5, N4; acordit (1) C2.

accounted *vb. past. part.* (2) P3, C3.

accusacions *n.* (1) S1.

accusement *n.* (1) C5 (D.230.12). *OED* obs. 1715.

accuseth *vb. 3 sing.* (1) S1; *past part.* acusyd (1) C2 (D.174.3).

accustomed *vb. past part.* (2) C3, P3; accustumed (13) S1, P3; accustumd (1) S2 (D.101.6); accoustumed (1) S2 (D.105.2); acustumed (1) S1.

acertained *vb. past part.* (2) P2.

acomplisid *vb. past part.* (1) N5; *ger.* acomplishing (1) P2.

acquitaill(e) *n.* (3) C3, C5.

acquite *inf.* (1) C4; *3 pl.* acquiete (1) C5 (D.223.38); *past part.* acquite (1) C3.

acte *n.* a formal, legal document recording a decision. (18) C3, C4; act (7) P2,

C3; *pl.* actes (1) C3.
action *n.* (3) C3, P4; accion (4) C3, C4; *pl.* actions (1) C1; accions (3) C3, C4.
added *vb. past part.* (1) S1.
adioynyng *vb. pr. part.* adjoining. (1) C5.
administracione *n.* legal control, as of a minor's estate. (1) C5.
admiral *n.* (3) P3.
admiraltee *n.* (2) P3; admiralte (3) C5.
admission *n.* appointment to a post. (1) C4.
admitte *vb. past part.* he " was admitte as a lauful apprentice." (2) P3 (D.128.4), C5 (D.221.27).
adnullacion *n.* a law voiding specified grants of a previous reign. (1) C5 (D.227.11). *MED* gives *ad* as a variant for *an; no tion* form. *OED* obs. 1670.
adnullinge *ger.* See adnullacion. (1) C5.
adoo *n.* dealings with, as "materes and þinges as I shal haue adoo" (1) P3 (D.129.4).
adradde *vb. past part.* afraid. (1) C8 (D.161.18). *OED* arch. 1870 (William Morris).
aduenture *n.* (1) P4.
aduersaries *n.* (4) C1, C3; aduersairs (1) P4.
aduersite *n.* (1) C5.
aduertise *inf.* to inform or notify officially. (1) P4; aduertice (1) C4; *past part.* aduertised (1) C5.
aduis(e) *n.* (17) S1, P2; auis(e) (10) S1, P2; auys (7) C8, C1; avis(e) (6) S1, P3; S1, C2; avys(e) (4) S1, C3; auice (1) C5; aduyce (1) C4; aduyse (1) N5. See auise.
affeccion *n.* (3) C3, S5.
afferant *n.* fair or just proportion. (1) C3 (D.169.6). *OED* obs. 1475.
afferme *inf.* (1) C4; *pr. part.* affermyng (2) P3, C3; affirmyng (1) P3; *past part.* affermed (2) C3.
afferyng *vb. pr. part.* accruing (1) C3 (D.188.13). Not in *OED*. This meaning not in *MED*.
affiance *n.* trust. (1) PO (D.110.3). *OED* obs. 1753.
affinitee *n.* relatives. (1) P4; *pl.* affinitees (2) P4. All of the instances in D. 154.
affray(e) *n.* public attack or disturbance. (5) C3 (D.186.7 etc.). *OED* obs. 1810 except in Scotch dialect.
affrayde *vb. past part.* of affraien, to frighten. (1) C2; *ger.* affraying (1) C4.
afore *adv.* (94) C1, S1; afor (7) S1, C5; affor (1) C1. Frequently spelled as two words. See before.
aforesaid(e) *adj.* (13) S1, C3; aforsaid(e) (17) S1, C3; aforseid(e) (10) C3, C4; aforeseid(e) (8) C3, N4; afoersaide (1) P2 (D.115.4); aforesayd (1) c3; aforsayd (1) C5; aforeseyd (1) C2; oforeseyd (1) C3 (D.199.20).
aforne *prep.* before. (1) C3; a forn (1) P3.

after *prep.* (126) C8, N8; aftir(e) (31) S1, P2; aftur (10) C3, C4; aftre (9) S1, C2; affter (4) N8, C1; aftyr (3) C3; aftere (11) C4; aftire (1) C3; aftor (1) C3.
afterward *adv.* (3) C3; aftirward (3) C3; affterward (1) C1.
afturtime *adv.* (1) C5.
again *adv.* (1) P4; agayne (9) C2, C3; ageyn(e) (8) C3, P3; ayen(e) (5) S1, C3; ayein (3) C8, S1; agayn (2) C3; agenne (2) N4; aȝen (2) C3.
age *n.* (11) S1, P3.
aȝeynst See ayenst.
ago *adv.* (2) C2; agoo (2) C3.
agreable *adj.* (1) S2.
agree *inf.* (1) P3; *pl.* agree (1) C5; *3 sing. subj.* agree (1) S1; *past pl.* agreed (1) C4; *past part.* agreed (9) S1, C2; agrede (1) C5; aggreed (2) C5..
agreement *n.* (1) P4; agrement (5) C3, C4.
agreggeable *adj.* burdensome. (1) P3 (D.127.6). *OED* obs. 1500.
aide *n.* (1) C5; ayde (1) S4.
aiel(l) *n.* grandfather. (3) P3, C3; aieul (2) C3 (D.203.4). *OED* obs. 1809.
aiournement *n.* (1) C4. This passage (D.212.31) cited in *MED*.
aiournyd *vb. past* postponed to a set time. (1) C2.
albiet (3) S1, S5; albehit (2) C2, S2.
alday *adv.* daily. (1) C2 (D.174.4).
alderman *n.* (1) N4; *pl.* aldermen (3) C8, S1; aldremen (2) C2.
ale *n.* (1) C3.
algates *adv.* in any event. (2) S2 (D.89.8). *OED* obs. 1605 except in Northern dialect.
alien *adj.* foreign. (6) P3, C3; aliene (1) C3; *pl.* aliens (4) C3, C4.
alienes *n. pl.* foreigners. (3) C3; alientȝ (1) P3 (D.146.6).
all *adj.* (207) N8, C1; alle (120) C8, C1; al (94) S1, C1; *gen.* aller (4) C2 (D.177), C5 (D.218); althir (1) P4 (D.153.1).
alliaunces *n. pl.* (1) P4 (D.154.4).
alligeaunce *n.* loyalty. (1) C5 (D.222.37).
allocate *n.* only used when mentioning writs of Liberate and Allocate (i.e., payment). (13) S1, S2.
allowance *n.* (1) C4; allouance (1) P2; allowans (1) P5.
allowe *vb. subj. pr.* (1) S3; *past part.* allowed (3) P2, C3.
almes *n.* (1) C1; almous (1) P2 (D.120.8); almouse (1) P2 (D.119.8).
almighty *adj.* (1) S1; almyghty (4) S2, C3.
almost *adv.* (1) P3 (D.146.3).
als *adv.* as, q.v. *OED* obs.
also *adv.* (163) N8, C8; alsoo (4) P3, C4; all so (5) C4, C5 (3 in D.212); al soe (2) N6 (D.241).
alssone *adv.* as soon. (1) C2 (D.169.10). *OED* obs. 1420.
altymes *n. pl.* all times. (1) S1.

always *adv.* (1) P2; alwey (9) S1, P2; alweys (2) S1, N5; allway (2) P3, C5; allwey (2) C3, C5.

alyue *adj.* alive. (1) N2.

amayd *vb. past part.* amazed. (1) C5 (D.218.6).

ambassadeurs *n.* (2) C3; ambassiatours (5) S1; ambassatours (3) C2, P3; embassiatours (1) S1 (D.69.9).

ambassiat *n.* the services of an ambassador. (4 all in D.14 and 43) S1. *OED* obs. 1580; *MED* as a variant of *ambassade*.

amended *vb. past part.* changed. (1) S2.

amenusyd *vb. past part.* of amenusen, to diminish or reduce. (1) C3 (D.188.21); amynused (1) C5. *OED* obs. 1554.

amerciamentes *n.* amercements, court-directed fines. (2) C3 (D.198.5,8).

ammocioun *n.* removal from office. (1) C4 (D.215.13). *OED* arch.

amobre *n.* technical term in Welsh law for a fee paid to a lord on marriage of a girl in his manor. (1) C3 (D.200.2). *OED* citation 1727.

amoeve *inf.* remove. (1) N5 (D.240.19). *past part.* ammoved (1) C5; ammoued (1) C5. *OED* general use obs. 1613; technical term in law to 1832.

among *prep.* (10) S1, C3; amonges (7) C8, P3; amonge (3) C2, P3; amanges (1) C2 (D.169.4).

amounteth *vb. 3 sing.* (5) C3, C4; amountyth (1) C3; amountes (1) C5 (D.223.19), "which changes amountes to þe somme" etc. *pl.* amounten (1) C5; *pr. part.* amountyng (2) C5, P5.

amountes *n.* (1) C5.

and *conj.* (3826) all decades and offices; an (1) C3 (D.182.25).

anenst *adv.* towards (as behavior towards). (2) S1 (D.43.5, 10). *OED* prep. obs. 1525 except in Scottish law.

anherited *vb. past part.* inherited. (1) C5 (D.218.35).

anientisched *vb. past part.* diminished, lessened, weakened. (1) P2 (D.116.4); anyentysed (1) C5; *ger.* aneyntisyng (1) C3; anientesing (1) C3; annentisyng (1) C2; anyentesyng (1) C5. *OED* obs. 1530. See anyentisment.

annexed *vb. past part.* attached to, invariably referring to a second document included as supporting evidence. (10) S1, P3.

annoye *n.* annoyance, damage. (1) S1 (D.51.5).

annuel *adj.* yearly. (1) P3 (D.143.3); anuell referring to a priest assigned to say memorial masses for the dead (1) C4 (D.213.7).

annuels *n.* memorial religious services held yearly, usually on the anniversary of a person's death. (1) P3.

annuitee *n.* (7) S1; annuite (3) S1, C5; annuyte (1) N4; *pl.* annuitees (6) S1.

anullen *inf.* to annul. (1) C2.

annunciacion *n.* (2) N2; anunciation (1) C5.

anon *conj. & adv.* soon, next. (4) C8 (D.161); anoon (1) C1 (D.164.21).

another *adj.* (1) C3; a noþer (5) S1, P3; anothir (1) C2; a nothire (1) N6.

answer *n.* (1) C1, C3; answere (3) C3, C5; answher(e) (3) P4, C2 (D.178); answar (2) S1; ansuer (1) P2; *pl.* answeres (3) C1, S1; ansueres (1) P2.

answer *inf.* (6) C3, C4; answere (4) P3, P4; aunswere (3) P4, C5; ansuere (1) S5; awenswer (1) C2 (D.171.3); onswere (1) C3 (D.183.21); vnsware (1) C3 (D.191.5); *pl. subj.* answere (1) P4; *past.* answered (12) N2, P3; aunswered (2) P3; answerd (1) P1; *past part.* answered (3) C1, P5; vnswared (1) C3 (D.191.4); onswered (1) C3 (D.183.12).

antecessours *n.* ancestors. (1) C3 (D.188.1).

anxien *adj.* ancient. (1) C1 (D.163.76).

any *adj.* (130) all decades and offices; eny (104) only once in S1 (D.6.1), once in S5 (D.108.8), occasionally in P, more frequently in C; ony (16) C8; enny (5) P4. See discussion.

anyentisment *n.* harm, loss. (1) P3 (D.146.2). See anientisched.

anywise *adv.* in any way. (1) P4 (D.152.5).

apaide *vb. past part.* satisfied. (1) S1; appaide (1) S2 (D.104.2). *OED* arch. since 1700.

apeched *vb. past part.* formally accused. (3) C8 (D.161.25 etc.). Not in *OED*.

apeiryd *vb. past part.* harmed, injured. (1) C3 (D.188.21). *OED* obs. 1611.

apelle *n.* appeal. (1) S1.

apert *adj.* openly or publically, in contrast to priuely. (2) C8 (D.161.20), C4 (D.214.11). *OED* arch.

apostell *n.* (1) C5; appostell (1) C3.

apparaille *n.* (3) C4 (D.211).

apparteyne *inf.* belong, be applicable to. (1) S2; *3 sing.* apperteineþ (1) P3; apperteineth (1) C4; apperteneth (1) P1; appertenith (1) P5; *pr. part.* apperteignyng (1) C3; appertenyng (4) C5 (D.224); apperteynyng (1) C3; apperteignyng (2) C3.

appechements *n.* accusations. (1) S1.

appele *n.* legal appeal. (1) C5; appelle (2) S1, C4.

appeled *vb. 3 sing. past.* appealed, informed on, accused. (1) C4 (D.212.16).

apperance *n.* (4) C3, C4; apperaunce (1) C5.

appere *inf.* appear. (10) C3, C4; apper (3) P3, C4; apere (2) C2; appier (1) C3; appiere (4) C4 (D.216); *3 sing.* appereth (4) C2, C3; apperethe (1) C3; apperith (7) P3; appiers (2) C2 (D.168.5 & 7); appiereth (1) C5; *sing. subj.* appere (4) C3; apere (2) C3; appier (2) C3; *pl. subj.* appiere (4) C4 (D.216); *past* appered (1) C3; *pr. part.* appieryng (1) C4.

appertenance *n.* an additional right or possession which comes with property or office. (1) N5; apportenance (2) C1, P3; appurtenance (1) C5; *pl.* appertenances (6) S1, N4, N5; appertenancis (1) N5; appertenaunces (8) C5, N5; appurtenances (6) P2, N5; appurtenantʒ (2) P2; appurtenannces (1) S1; appourtenances (1) S2.

applied *vb. past part.* (1) C3.

Glossary of Forms 311

appointe *inf.* (1) P2; appointe (2) P2; *past* appointed (1) P5; *past part.* appointed (5) S1, P3; apointed (1) C2.
appointement *n.* (5) C5, P5.
apportes *n.* donations to a religious house. (1) P4 (D.151.5). OED obs. 1530.
apprenteshode *n.* apprenticehood. (1) C5.
apprentice *n.* (12) C5 (cf.231.15, 17); apprentece (1) (cf.231.14); aprentice (1) C5 (cf.219.10); *pl.* apprentices (4) C5 (D.231.6, 7). See D.220, 221, 231.
apprest(e) *n.* credit, loan. (3) S2, C2; aprest (2) N2. OED obs. 1443.
approche *inf.* approach. (1) C8; *pr. pl.* approcheth (1) C5 (D.225.20); *past.* approached (1) C8.
appropre *inf.* annex, incorporate. (1) S1.
appropriacion *n.* (1) S1.
approve *inf.* (1) C4; *past part.* approved (1) P4.
appunctuament *n.* appointment. (1) P3 (D.126.4). Form not recorded in *MED*. *OED* obs. 1600.
arained *vb. past part.* arraigned. (1) C3 (D.108.3).
arbitorȝ *n.* arbitors, arbitrators. (2) C5.
archangle (1) N2.
archbishop *n.* (1) P2; archebisshop (6) C2, C4; archebusshop (2) P4 (D.151.2, 11); archibisshop (1) C5; archebishop (2) S1; archebisshop (1) S1; archebischopp (1) P3; *pl.* archebisshoppes (1) C4.
archedeaknee *n.* archdeacon. (2) S2; *pl.* archediacones (1) S1 (D.1.11).
archiers *n.* (4) P4 (D.156).
areignment *n.* (1) C4.
arere *inf.* raise, as with taxes or levies. (2) C5 (D.223.34); *past part.* arered (5) C3, C5; arerode (1) C3 (D.183.31). OED obs. 1621.
arest *n.* (1) P3.
armed *vb. past part.* (8) C8, C3.
armee *n.* (3) S1, P3; arme (1) P3.
armerers *n.* (1) S2.
armes *n.* (9) C3, P4.
armure *n.* (1) C8.
arowes *n.* (1) C3; arowys (1) C3.
array(e) *n.* (A) order, arrangement, method (2) P3; (B) equipment, formal or military clothing (6) P3, C3; arraie (1) C3.
arraye *inf.* to dress, equip with proper clothing, esp. "arraid in manere of werre." Note D.194.4, "made to array hir in hir best arraie." (1) C3; *past part.* arraied (4) P3, C3; araied (1) C3.
arrerages *n.* unpaid wages. (2) P3, C3; arrereges (1) N5; areragez (1) C2.
arrest *inf.* (1) C5; arreste (1) P3; arest (1) C2; areste (1) P5; *past.* arested (3) C3, P5; arrested (2) P3, C5; arestid (1) C2; *past part.* arrested (1) C5; arrestid (1) P3; arrest (1) P2 (D.124.4); arest (1) C3 (D.194.14); arested (1)

C3; arestid (1) P3; arettyd (1) C2 (D.174.3).
arryve *inf.* (1) C3; *past.* arriued (1) S2; aryved (1) P1; *past part.* arived (1) C3.
arrysers *n.* rebels, "arrysers ayeins the pees." (1) C8 (D.161.28). This meaning not in *OED. See* risers.
arted *vb. past part.* forced. (1) C3 (D.179.12). *OED* no. 2 obs. 1553.
arterie *n.* archers. (3) C5 (all in D.218). Usual form *archerie*; this form not in *OED* or *MED*.
article *n.* an individual item in a document. (1) C1; *pl.* articles (7) C2, S2.
artificers *n.* craftsmen. (2) C5 (D.231.5, 10).
artitulerly *adv.* articularly, point-by-point. (1) P5 (D.158.45). *OED* obs. 1744.
as *conj.* (811) all decades and offices; als (17) mostly in non-Chancery items; D.6.4 the only Signet entry; aʒ (1) N6 (D.241.1).
asferforth *adv.* as far as. (1) P5 (D.158.5). Form not in *OED* or *MED*.
aske *inf.* (1) C4; *3 sing.* asketh (5) S1, P3; axeth (2) S2, P3; askith (1) C2; askyth (1) S4; askys (1) C2 (D.168.12); *3 sing. subj.* aske (2) S1, C4; *pl.* asken (1) S1 (D.69.10); *past part.* asked (19) P3, C5 (D.142, D.223 only); *ger.* axing (1) P5 (D.159.23).
asmuch (43) S1, S2; asmoche (15) S1, P2; asmeche (1) C3 (D.191.6); asmych (1) C3 (D.199.20).
aspye *inf.* (1) P2; *past part.* aspied (1) P3, P5.
assault(e) *n.* (3) C3, C4 (D.195.7, 11); assaut(e) (6) C3, C4 (D.195.1 etc.).
assemble *n.* assembly. (1) C5 (D.230.7).
assemble *inf.* (2) C3; *past part.* assembled (28, usually in the phrase "in this present Parlement assembled") C1, C3; assemblid (1) C3; assemblyd (1) C4.
assent *n.* (25) S1, P2; *pl.* assentes (1) C3.
assente *inf.* (1) C4; *pr. part.* assentyng (1) S2; *past part.* assented(e) (4) P2, C4.
assenteurs *n.* those who assent. (1) P2 (D.122.16).
assertid *vb. past part.* (1) C3 (D.199.20).
assign *inf.* (4) N8, P3; assigne (3) P2, P3; *pr. part.* assignyng (1) C4; *past part.* assigned (8) S1, C2.
assignes *n.* (7) N4, P4; assignees (3) N2, N5; assygnes (3) N8; assynes (1) N8; assignis (1) N8.
assignement *n.* (9) P2, C2; *pl.* assignementʒ (6) C4, P5; assignementes (2) P4.
assise *n.* standard size. (2) N4 (D.238.7, 12). *OED* meaning no. 6; this meaning obs. 1624.
assises *n.* courts of assize. (1) C3 (D.192.11).
assiste *inf.* (1) P2.
assistence *n.* (1) P2; assistens (1) S4.
assoil(e) *inf.* absolve, invariably in phrases like "whome god assoile." (7) P2, C3 (D.139.3 etc.); assoille (4) S1, C2; assoil (2) C2, P3; assoyle (1) C4. *OED* meaning arch.
assure *vb. pl. subj.* (1) P2; *past* assured (3) P2; *past part.* assured (2) P2. All

citations are in D.122.

aswel(l) *adv.* also (22) S1, S2.

at *prep.* (352) all dates and offices. atte (86) S1, P1; att (7) P1, P2; ate (36) N5 (D.241.1 etc.).

atire *n.* (1) C4.

attachement *n.* as part of "a writ of attachement." (1) C3 (D.183.13).

atteigne *inf.* reach, as in the phrase "atteigne to the somme of xl L." (1) C5; *pl.* atteigne (2) C5. All in D. 229.

atteint *vb. past part.* convicted by law. (5) C3, C4 (D.108.3 etc.); atteynt (2) C3; atteigntd (2) C4 (D.216.47); atteygnted (1) C4 (D.216.48); atteingted (1) C4 (D.216.42).

attemptates *n.* violations of laws or treaties. (3) S1 (D.46). *OED* obs. 1721.

attempted *vb. past part.* (1) P4.

attendaunt *n.* (1) C3.

atteyndre *n.* conviction. (1) C4 (D.216.47).

attorney *n.* (2) N4; attourney (2) C3, C4; attourne (2) S2 (D.89); attornay (1) C3; *pl.* attorneys (3) P3, C3; attournees (2) P3; attornes (1) S1; attourneys (1) C4.

auctorise *inf.* authorize by law. (1) C3 (D.195.6).

auctorite *n.* (35) C1, P3; autorite (8) C2, C3; auctoritee (6) P2, C3; auctoryte (2) C3, C5; aucorite (1) C3 (D.202.44); *pl.* autorites (1) C3.

audience *n.* (1) S1 (D.40.22).

auditors *n.* official examiners, the Pope's in this case. (1) C1 (D.166.10).

auerre *inf.* aver, declare. (1) C3.

auise *inf.* advise. (1) P2; *past part.* aduised (5) S1, P2; auised (2) P3; aduysed (1) C5; auysed (1) S1, C4; avysed (1) S1. See aduise.

aulmosner *n.* almoner; Fr. *almosnere.* (1) S2 (D.101.5).

aulnage *n.* var. of aunage, revenue from cloth inspection. (1) S1 (D.38.2).

aumber *n.* amber. (1) C3.

auncestres *n.* (3) C3, C5; ancecessours (1) C3 (D.188.1).

auiodance *n.* vacancy. (1) S2 (D.78.8).

auowson *n.* the right to determine who will receive a benefice. (4) C5 (D.224); *pl.* avousons (3) C4 (D.210); ouowson (1) C5 (D.224.37).

autorysed *vb. past part.* authorized. (1) C3 (D.199.27).

avail *n.* (1) P1; availle (4) C3, C4; avayle (2) C3, C5; availl (1) C3; advayle (1) C5; avaylle (1) C4.

availlable *adj.* (1) C5; auaillable (2) C4.

avaled *vb. past.* remove a hat as a sign of respect. (1) P3 (D.142.23). *OED* meaning no. 6; this meaning obs. 1557.

avauntage *n.* (3) C3, C5; auantage (4) S1, C1.

avoutoures *n.* adulterers (1) C3 (D.192.6); avowterers (1) C3 (D.193.10). *OED* has v forms to 1600.

avoutries *n*. adulteries. (1) C3 (D.192.26).
avowed *vb. past part*. (1) P3.
awaite *n*. waiting, ambush. (2) C4 (D.216.9, 22); awayte (1) C2. *OED* obs. 1691. See awayte.
award *n*. (2) C5.
award *inf*. (2) C3, C5; awarde (3) P3, C3; *past part*. awarded (2) C3; awardyd (1) C5.
away(e) *adv*. (6) P3, C3; awey (4) S1, C3.
awayte *inf*. wait. (3) P3; *pr. part*. awaytyng (1) S1.
awen own, q.v.
awner(s) owner(s), q.v.
awowe *n*. pledge. (1) P2 (D.113.18).
axe *n*. (1) C2.
ayeinsaide *vb. past part*. contradicted. (1) C8 (D.161.26).
ayeinstande *inf*. oppose, withstand. (1) C8 (D.161.27); *pr. part*. aȝeinstonding (1) S1.
ayeinward *adv*. back, again. (1) S1 (D.69.6); ayenward (1) P3.
ayenst *prep*. (18) PO, S1; ayens (18) C2, C3; ayeins (9) C8 (8), S1; aȝeyns (8) C1; ayeinst (6) S1, N2; ayen (3) C3; aȝenst (3) N8, P3; ayein (2) C8, S1; ayeinste (1) P3; ayeines (1) S1; aȝeinst (1) C5; ayeynst (1) C4; aȝen (1) N8; ageynst (1) C3; ageinis (1) C4; ageyns (1) C5.

bad *vb. past*. (2) P3 (D.142.29, 145.13).
bagge *n*. bag, in "clerc of our petit bagge." (1) S1 (D.17.2).
baile *n*. temporary release from legal custody. (2) C5; baille (1) C4; *pl.* bailles (1) P3.
baillif *n*. (1) C3; bayllef (1) C3; baylly (1) C5; *pl*. bailifs (7) S1, P2; bailees (1) C3; bailiffes (1) C3; bailliefs (2) C3; baillieȝ (1) P2; baillifes (1) P3; bailyffes (1) N2; bailyfs (1) C5; bayllees (1) C3; bayllefs (1) C3.
bailliwyk *n*. (2) P3; baillywyk (1) P3.
bakons *n*. bacon. (1) C3.
balyngers *n*. small naval vessels. (1) S1 (D.2.2). *OED* obs. 1622.
bankers *n*. either ornamental wall hangings or seat covers. (1) C3 (D.197.17).
bankes *n*. of a river. (1) C5.
barbour *n*. barber. (1) S1.
barell *n*. (1) C3.
barfote *adj*. barefoot. (1) C8 (D.161.43).
bargayne *n*. (1) S2.
bargayned *vb. past part*. (2) C2, N5.
barge *n*. (1) S1; *pl*. barges (1) S1.
baron *n*. (6) C3, P4; *pl*. barons (11) C2, C3; barouns (1) P3; barones (1) C5.
barr(e) *n*. fig., the court of law, "plees in barr." (3) P3, C3.

Glossary of Forms 315

barrid *vb. past part.* prevented from bringing suit. (1) C3.

be *vb.* (814); bee (23): *1 sing.* am (12) S1, P1; *3 sing.* is (347) C8, S1; es (4) C1, P2; ys (42) N8, S1; *neg.* nis (1) C3 (D181.19); nys (2) C3 (D.172.8, 182.11); beeth (1) S1; beth (1) C5; *pl.* beth (3) P3, C3; buth (2) C2, N6; are (4) C3, C4; ar (2) S2, P3; er (2) C3 (D.204.31, 206.6); aren (1) C1; arn (1) C5; *pr. part.* beeng (1) P3; beeyng (1) P3; being (3) P4, C5; beyng (91) S1, C1; beynge (9) S1, C3; *past part.* been (37) S1, C1; ben (77) C8, C1; bien (1) C3 (D.207.3); byn (2) C4; bene (12) P1, C2. See also was.

beal(l) *adj.* Fr. *bel*, "good', in the English phrase "our beal vncle." (3) P3 (D.132, 133, 134); bel (1) P2.

became *vb. past.* (1) C4 (D.212.23).

because *conj.* (15) S1, C1; bycause (25) S1, C1; bicause (1) C8.

beddes *n.* (2) C3, C5.

bedeman *n.* one who prays for another, invariably found in phrases like "your continuel bedeman," etc. (8) C1, C2; beedman (2) C2.

bedes *n.* beads. (3) C3 (D.197.11).

before *adv. and prep.* (55) S1, S2; befor (2) P3, C3; befoer (1) P2; bifore (16) C8, C1; byfore (21) P2, C1; bifor (2) C8; beforn (3) C3 (D.190). See afore.

beforesaid *adj.* (2) C3; byforeseide (1) P3; byforseide (1) C3.

begynn *inf.* (1) C3; *past part.* begonne (1) C3; bigonne (1) C5; bygonnen (1) C3 (D.193.2); ; *ger.* beginnyng (1) P4; begynnyng(e) (2) S1, N5; bigynnyng (2) C5; bygynnyng (1) S1.

behalf *n.* (3) S1, C3; behalfe (2) C3, C4; behalue (8) S1, P1; behalve (1) C4; bihalf (1) S1.

behestes *n.* (2) C3.

behestyng *ger.* (1) C3 (D.190.22).

behinde *adv.* (5) S1, C3; behynd(e) (5) S1, C1; bihynde (1) N4; byhynde (1) N4.

behoof *n.* advantage, best interest. (1) P2 (D.117.15).

behoueful(l) *adv.* advantageous. (3) P3, C4; behouful (1) S4; behovefull (1) C4; behofful (1) C3; behoful(l) (2) P3, C4.

bell(e) *n.* (2) S1, C2; *pl.* belles (1) S1.

belong *inf.* (1) C5; *3 sing.* belongeth (1) C4; belongith (1) C5; *pl.* bylongyth (1) N8; *pr. part.* belongyng(e) (3) S1, C4. See also long(e).

beloued *adj. (past part.)* (16) Usually in the phrase "trusty and wel beloued." S1, S2; belouyd (1) P3.

bely *n.* belly. (1) C3.

bemes *n.* beams. (2) N4.

benche *n.* figurative, law court. (20) S1, C3.

benefice *n.* (6) S2, P2.

beneficed *vb. past part.* (1) C4.

benigne *adj.* (8) C2, C3; benygne (1) C4; *adv.* benyngly (1) P2.

beniuolence *n.* (2) S1, P4.

bequath *vb. past.* bequeathed. (2) C3 (D.181.5, 12).

bequestis *n.* (1) N5 (D.241.16).

bere *inf.* bear, behave. (8) S1, P2; beer (1) S2; *sing. subj.* bere (4) P3, C3; bare (1) C4; *past.* bare (1) C4; bere (1) C3; *pr. part.* beryng (2) C3; *past part.* born(e) (3) C2, C5; boryn (1) C5; *ger.* beringe (2) S1, N5; beryng(e) (7) S1, C3.

berer *n.* carrier, usually the person delivering a document. (4) S2, P2; *pl.* berers (2) C8, S1.

berne *n.* barn. (1) C1 (D.164.23); *pl.* bernes (1) N4.

beryed *vb. past part.* buried. (1) C5.

beseche *vb. 1 sing.* (5) P2, C1; bisech(e) (5) P5, C3; besechye (1) C1; *3 sing.* besecheth (15) C1, C3; besecheþ (1) C2; besechiþ (1) C3; besechith (6) P3, C3; besechyth (1) C5; besechuth (1) C3; bischeth (5) P2, C3; bisechith (1) C3; bysechith (1) C1; bysechyth (1) C2; biseches (1) P3 (D.123.1); beseketh (2) C3, C5; besekeþ (1) C2; *pl.* beseche (3) S1, P2; biseche (2) S1; byseche (1) C3; besechethe (1) C4 (D.210.1); besechith (1) C3 (D.145.31); besichith (1) C3 (D.198.1); besechiþ (1) C3 (D.203.1); besechen (6) C3, C5; besechyn (2) C2, C4; bisechen (1) C3; *pr. part.* beseching(e) (2) C1; besechyng (4) P2, C3; bisechyng (1) C3; bishechynge (1) C1.

besecher *n.* (63) P3, C3; bisecher (3) P2, C5; bysecher (5) P3, C3; beseker (3) P3; *pl.* besechers (7) C3, C5; bisechers (1) C3.

beselered *vb. past part.* placed beneath a house, like a cellar. (1) N1 (D.233.21). Not recorded in *MED* or *OED*.

besette See set, bysette.

beside *adv. and prep.* (20) S1, S2; biside (2) S1, N5.

besides *adv.* additionally, in the phrase "besides that." (1) C5; by sidis (1) C3 (D.196.3).

best(e) *adj.* (19) S1, P1.

bestbeloued *adj.* (1) P4.

besy *adj.* busy. (1) S1 (D.65.7).

betake *inf.* (1) P2 (D.123.5).

betaught *vb. past part* of bitechen. 'Commended to" in the phrase "þat is God betaught." (1) S2; betaght (2) S1.

beten *vb. past part.* beaten. (1) C3; bette (1) C5 (D.223.6); *ger.* betyng (1) C5.

bethought *vb past part.* consider, deem. (1) P5 (D.158.47).

betrowthed *vb. past part.* (1) S2.

better *adj.* (11) S1, C1; bettre (1) S1.

between *prep.* (1) S2; bitwene (8) C1, N2; betwene (6) S1, C5; bytwene (2) C1, C3; betwyn (4) C2, C3; betwen (1) S1; betuene (1) C2. See betwyxte.

betwyxte *prep.* (1) C4 (D.217.34); betwix (16) S1, S2; bitwix (7) S1, P2; betwyx (2) C4; bytwix (2) P4, C5; bitwyx (1) P2; bytwyx (4) C3 (D.182); bytwyxte (1) N6; bytwext (2) N2. See also between.

beware *inf.* (1) P3.
beyonde *prep.* (1) P3 (D.139.5).
bibull *n.* Bible. (1) C3 (D.197.6).
biers *n.* buyers. (1) C5 (D.217.10).
bill(e) *n.* term covering pleas, petitions, agreements, laws, etc. (35) S1, C1; bylle (1) C3; *pl.* billes (11) C1, P2.
birdon *n.* burden. (1) C3.
birth *n.* (1) P2; berth(e) (2) P3.
biset *vb. past part.* beset. (1) S1.
bisie *inf.* busy. (1) S1.
bisily *adv.* busily. (1) C3.
bisiness *n.* (1) S1.
bishop *n.* (4) C3, C5; bisshop(e) (29) S1, P2; bysshop (5) S1, S2; bischop (1) P2; bysshup (1) N2; bysshopp (1) C2; *pl.* bisshopes (3) S1, P2; bischoppes (1) P3; bisshoppes (1) C4.
bishopriche *n.* (1) S1; bisshoprich(e) (10) S1, S2; bysshopriche (6) S1, S2; *pl.* bisshopriches (1) P5.
bistowed *vb. past part.* bestowed. (1) C5 (D.218.31).
blame *n.* (1) P5.
blanket *n.* (1) C3; *pl.* blankettes (1) C3. Both in D.197.
blessed *adj. (past part.)* (6) P3, C3; blissed (3) P4, C5; blissid (3) P2 (D.113); blessid (2) P2; blessyd (1) P2.
blood *n.* (1) C3; blode (1) C5.
bodily *adv.* (1) P2; bodyly (2) P4.
body *n.* (11) S1, P2; *pl.* bodies (3) C2, C5; bodyes (3) C3.
boef *n.* beef. (1) C3 (D.197.16).
bok *n.* book. (2) P3, C3; boke (2) C3, C4; buke (here, the Bible) (1) C2 (D.173.7); *pl.* bokes (4) C3, C4.
bokelers *n.* (2, in the phrase "swerdis and bokelers") P3, C3.
bokerham *n.* buckram. (1) C3 (D.197.11).
bolsters *n. pl.* (1) C3.
bonchef *n.* prosperity, luck. (1) P4 (D.153.19). *OED* obs. 1563.
bonde *n.* (1) C1; boonde (1) C3 (D.183.7).
bonde *vb. past.* of binden. (1) C3; *past part.* bounde (7) S1, P3; bounden (6) S1, P3; boundyn (1) C3; bownden (1) C1.
bordell *n.*, in the phrase "houses of bordell." (2) C3 (D.193.8, 21). *OED* obs. 1620, but *OED* also lists bordello as obs.
borden *n.* burden, the carrying capacity of a ship. (1) C4 (D.211.6).
bore See borne.
bores *n. pl.* boars. (1) C3.
borne *vb. past part.* as in childbirth. (1) C5; bore (1) C1 (D.163.40). See bere.
borowed *vb. past part.* (1) C4.

botell *n.* bottle. (1) C3.
botery(e) *n.* buttery. (2) N8.
both *adj.* (7) S1, P2; bothe (22) S1, P2; booth (1) S1; booþe (1) S1; boþe (4) S1, S2.
bounde See bonde.
bounteuous *adj.* in the phrase "roiale largesse and bounteuous grace." (1) P5 (D.159.23).
bowe *n.* (1) C3; *pl.* bowes (2) C3, P4; bowis (1) C5; bowys (1) C3.
bowels *n.* (1) C3.
brake *vb. past.* broke. (2) N2, C5; brak (2) C3, P5; breke (3); C3 *pl.* breken (1) N8; *past part.* broken (5) P4, C5; broke (1) C3; *ger.* brekyng (6) C3, C5.
brandards *n.* gridirons, trivets. (1) C3 (D.197.15). *MED brandire(n); OED brander* obs. 1708.
bras *n.* and *adj.* brass. (3) C3; *pl.* braseʒ (2) N4.
braunches *n.* (1) C8.
brayne *n.* brain. (1) C3 (D.194.6).
breche *n.* breach. (1) P4.
brede *n.* breadth. (3) N8, N4.
breste *n.* breast. (1) C3 (D.194.8).
bring *inf.* (2) P4, C5; bryng (6) S1, P3; brynge (5) S1, C4; bringe (1) C4; *3 sing.* bringeth (1) S2; bringith (1) C4; *past.* brought (2) C3; *past part.* brought(e) (10) C1, C3; browgth (1) C2; brawt (1) S1; brougte (1) C1; *ger.* bryngyng (1) C3.
bringer *n.* (3) S1; *pl.* bringers (1) S1.
brocage *n.* brokerage. (1) S2 (D.87.6). *OED* obs. 1755.
broches *n.* (2) C3.
broggid *vb. past.* suborned. (1) C3 (D.189.18). *MED* cites the *PC* version of this as its sole example. *OED* has *brogger,* variant of *broker.*
brother *n.* (8) S1, S2; broþer (17) S1, S2; brothre (3) S1, P3; broþir (3) S1; brothr (2) P3 (D.127.7, 10); brothir (1) S1; *pl.* bretheryn (1) P4; brethern (1) P3; brithirn (1) N5.
brusinge *ger.* bruising. (1) C1 (D.165.8). *PC* version cited in *MED.*
brynne *inf.* burn. (1) S1; *past* brende (1) C3; *past part.* brent (1) C8.
bulle *n.* official document. (2) S1; *pl.* bulles (6) S1, S2.
burgeis *n.* (3) N2, C3; burgeys (3) C3, P4; *pl.* burgeysys (4) C2 (D.176); burgeises (2) C5; burgeyses (1) C5.
burgh *n.* (17) S1, C3 (16); burg (1) C3.
bushelʒ *n.* (1) C3.
busshementes *n.* ambushes. (1) C3; busshmentʒ (1) C8 (D.161.16). *OED* arch. 1550.
but *conj.* (121) C8, S1; bot (3) C2, P4; buth (1) N5 (D.241.14).
by *prep.* (792) N8, C8; bi (11) C8, S1.

Glossary of Forms 319

bye *inf.* buy. (2) C3 (D.190.2, 13); *pl.* byth (1) C3 (D.208.4); *past* boght (1) C3; *past part.* boght (1) N2; boughte (1) C2; buʒt (1) P3 (D126.6); *ger.* byeng (1) C3.

bygeten *vb. past part.* begotten. (1) C5.

byld *inf.* (3) N8; *past part.* bielded (7) N5 (D.240); *ger.* byldyng(e) (4) S1, N8.

byndith *vb. 3 sing.* (1) N5; *pl.* bynden (1) N5.

bynethe *prep.* (1) P3.

by nome *vb. past.* seized. (1) C1 (D.166.8). *OED* obs. 1494.

bysette *inf.* (1) C3; *past part.* biset (1) S1.

by sidis *adv.* (1) C3 (D.196. 3).

calle *inf.* (1) S1; *3 sing. subj.* calleth (4) S1, P3; *pl. subj.* calle (3) S1; *pr. part.* callyng (6) P3 (D.132, etc.); *past part.* called (29) P1, S2; callid (7) P2, C3; callidde (1) P2 (D.123.6); callyd (1) N8; ycallid (1) C3 (D.202.36); ycalled (1) P3 (D.146.15).

calves *n.* (1) C3.

can *vb.* (25) S1, C1; kan (10) P2, C3 (D.208.10), all but one instance are in P2 or N5; *past.* couthe (4) S1, C5; coude (2) C5, P5; cowde (1) C4.

candell *n.* 1(4) C3 (D.190).

canvas *n.* (1) C3.

capons *n.* (1) C3.

captaine *n.* (1) S1; capitaign (3) C2 (D.167); capitayn (2) C3, P3; captayne (1) P3; *pl.* capitaines (1) P2.

carders *n.* of the weaving trade. (1) C4.

cardinal(l) *n.* (16) P3, C3; cardynall (1) C5; *gen* cardinales (1) P3.

carrakes *n.* merchant ships. (1) S1 (D.2.2). *OED* obs. 1703.

carye *inf.* carry. (1) C8; caryen (1) N4; *pl.* carie (1) C3; cariene (1) C3 (D.203.18); *past.* cariet (1) C5 (D.222.20); *past part.* caried (2) C3.

case *n.* (8) P3, C3; cas (30) S1, S2; caas (9) S1, S2.

cassen *inf.* to void, cancel. (1) C2 (D.177.20). *OED* obs. 1700.

castel(l) *n.* (62) S1, C1; castil (1) S1; chastel (1) S1 (D.8.4); *pl.* castelleʒ (5) C4 (D.210); castels (1) C2.

castlewarde *n.* (1) P3.

castyng *pr. part.* (1) C5.

casuell *adj.* incidental. (1) N8.

casuelte *n.* contingency. (1) C4; *pl.* casueltees (1) P5.

catell *n.* chattels. (1) C1; katell (1) S2; *pl.* catèlls (1) C4; catels (2) S1, C4.

caterye *n.* purchasing office of the royal household. (1) S1 (D.97.3). *OED* obs. 1531.

cathedral(e) *n.* (6) S1, S2.

cause *n.* (38) S1, P1; ceuse (1) C3; *pl.* causes (19) S1, S2.

caused *vb. past.* (1) C3; *past part.* cawsid (1) C5 (D.218.14).

cedule See sedule.
certain(e) *adj.* (37) S1, S2; certein(e) (25) S1, P1; certeyne (18) C1, C3; certayn(e) (5) C3, C5; serteyn (2) N2, P3; certyn (1) C5; sarteyn (1) C3 (D.189.27); certaigne (1) P3; certeigne (1) C2; certigne (1) C3; *pl.* certeins (2) C2 (D.168.7, 171.3).
certificacions *n.* (1) C3.
certificat(e) *n.* (3) C2, P3; certificatt (1) P3; certyficate (1) N2.
certifie *inf.* (3) C2, C3; *pl. subj.* certiffie (1) S1; *pr. part.* ceritfieng (1) S1; certefyeng (1) C5; certefyyng (3) C5 (D.218); *past part.* certified 5) S1, C3; ycertified ()) C3 (D.199.40).
cese *inf.* cease. (1) C5; cesse (1) P3; *pl. subj.* cesse (3) S1, P4; *past part.* cessed (1) P4; *ger.* cessing(e) (2) P3; ceesing (1) P4.
chaf *n.* chaff. (1) N4 (D.237.19).
chaiers *n.* chairs. (1) C3.
chalenge *n.* (1) C3; chalange (1) C5.
chalenge *vb. pl. subj.* (1) S2; *past part.* chalenged (2) S2, C3.
chamberlain *n.* (3) S1, S2; chamberleyn (3) P3, C3; chamberlein (2) C3, P3; chamberlayn (1) C3; *pl.* chamberlains (1) P3; chamberlayns (1) P3; chaumberleins (1) P3.
chambre *n.* (8) S1, P3; chaumbre (2) C4, C5; chambr (1) N8; *pl.* chambres (4) N5 (D.240); chambers (3) N5 (D.240); chambrys (1) N8; chaumbres (1) C5.
chambrer *n.* attendant. (2) P2.
chancellor *n.* (1) S1 (D.57.8); chauncel(l)er (36) S1, C1; chanceller (8) S1, S2.
chancerye *n.* (1) P3; chauncerie (8) C3, C4; chancellerie (4) S1; chauncery (2) C5; chauncerye (2) C3, C5; chauncellerie (2) C2, P4; chauncellarie (2) C3, P4; chauncellere (1) C3; chauncellarye (1) P4.
chanons *n.* canons. (1) C1.
chapell *n.* (1) C3; chapelle (8) S1, P2; chapele (1) S1.
chapellain *n.* (2) S1; chapeleyn (3) P4 (D.153); chapelyn (1) P3; chaplein (1) S1; *pl.* chapeleynes (2) P4; chappeleyns (1) C5.
charge *n.* responsibility. (22) P2, C2; charg (1) P2; *pl.* charges (21) S1, P2; chargeiȝ (1) C4 (D.210.17); chargis (1) N8; chargeȝ (1) N2.
charge *inf.* (2) P2; *pl.* charge (40) S1, S2 (invariably in the formulaic "we wol and charge yow"); *past.* charged (1) P3; *pr. part.* chargyng (6) S2, P2; chargeyng (1) S2; *past part.* charget (1) S2; chargid (1) C5; chargyd (1) C3; charged (19) S1, P2.
charitee *n.* (19) P2, C2; charite (14) C2, C3; charte (1) P3; chierte (1) S1.
chartre *n.* (11) C1, P1; chartor (1) C1; chatre (1) C4; *pl.* chartres (3) P4, N5; chartris (1) P4.
charyoter *n.* driver, coachman. (1) C1 (D.165.2); *pl.* charioterys (1) C1.
chastised *vb. past part.* (1) C4.

Glossary of Forms 321

chaundeler *n.* one who deals in candles. (1) C3; *pl.* chaundeleres (1) C3. Both in D.190.
chaunge *n.* (1) S2.
chaunge *vb. pl. subj.* (1) P4.
chaungeably *adv.* (3) N4, N5.
chaunterie *n.* (1) C4; chaunterye (1) C4; chauntre (1) C4; chauntrye (1) C4.
cheker *n.* Exchequer. (3) P3, C3 (D.142.36). *OED* obs.1691. See also escheker, esker.
chere *n.* cheer, encouragement. (1) S1.
cherise *inf.* cherish. (1) C8; cherice (1) C1.
cheryng *pr. part.* cheering. (1) P3.
chese *inf.* choose. (4) N8, S1; *sing. subj.* chese (2) C3; *past part.* chosen (5) C8, C5; "that þey be chose" (1) S1 (D.87.5).
chevised *vb. past.* contributed, paid. (1) C3 (D.190.25). *OED* obs. 1487.
chief *n.* (1) *adj.* (8) S1, C3; chef *adj.* (1) N8.
child(e) *n.* (3) P3, C5; *pl.* children (1) P3.
chistes *n. pl.* chests. (1) C3.
chose See chese.
christene *adj.* Christian. (1) C1; cristen(e) (5) C8, S1; cristian (1) C3; crystyan (1) N2.
church(e) *n.* (5) P1, N2; chirch(e) (63) S1, P1; chriche (1) S2; chyrch (1) N8; kyrk(e) (7) C2 (D.173); kirk (1) P1 (D.112.7).
chymney *n.* (1) C3.
circumstances *n.* (3) S1, P2; circumstaunce (2) C3, C5; *pl.* circumstaunces (1) P5.
cite *n.* (28) S1, S2; citee (31) C8, S1; cyte (5) N2 (D.235); *pl.* citees (3) S1, P2.
citeʒin *n.* (1) C5; citeʒein (5) C3, N5; citeʒeyn (1) C5; citeseyn (1) C3; *pl.* cyteʒins (3) N2 (D.235); citeʒins (1) N2; citeʒeins (1) C3; citeʒens (1) C5; cyteʒyns (1) N2.
clappyd *vb. past.* shut. (1) C2 (D.173.7).
clause *n.* (6) N8, S1.
clayme. *inf.* claim. (1) N4; *pr. part.* claymyng (1) C5.
clene *adj.* (2) C3.
clensyd *vb. past part.* (2) C3.
clepe *inf.* summon. (1) C1 (D.166.12); *past part.* cleped, named (6) P3; clepet (1) P1; i clepid (1) C1.
clerely *adv.* (13) S1, S2; clerly (3) S1, P4; cleerly (2) S1.
clergie *n.* (5) S1, P3; *pl.* clergies (1) C4.
clerk(e) *n.* (19) N2, P2; clerc (35) S1, C1; *pl.* clerkes (3) S1, C3; clerkis (1) P3.
clokke *n.* (1) C3.
closed *vb. past part.* (38, usually in the phrase "sende to yow closed within") S1, S2 (D.2.1 etc.). *OED* arch.
cloth *n.* material. (12) C3, C4; *pl.* cloþes (1) S1; cloþis (2) C2.

clothes *n.* wearing apparel. (3) C3, C5.
coffres *n.* (1) C5; coffors (2) C3.
collacion *n.* assignment of a benefice. (10) S1, S2.
collectour *n.* (1) C3; *gen.* colloctours (1) C3 (D.191.7); *pl.* collectours (3) C3 (D.206).
college *n.* (2) S1.
colour *n.* (7) P2, P3; color (1) C3; *pl.* colours (1) C3.
coltes *n.* (1) C3 (D.197.21).
combrous *adj.* (2) P3 (D.139.2, 14)
come *inf.* (31) C8, S1; com (3) C3, C5; comen (1) S1; *imp.* come (1) P3; *3 sing.* comeþ (1) S1; commeth (1) S2; comyth (1) C4; comyht (1) P2; *pl.* come (1) S1; comen (1) S2; *3 sing. subj.* come (1) P3; com (1) S1; *pl. subj.* come (1) S2; *past* come (13) C8, S1; cam (5) P3, C4; com (1) C4; kome (1) C3 (D.189.8); kam (1) P2 (D.113.16); *pr. part.* comyng(e) (30) P3, C3; commyng(e) (17) P3, C3; comeyng (2) C4; coming (1) S1 (D.36.2); cummyng (1) C5; commynde (1) P5 (D.158.25); *past part.* come (8) S1, C1; comen (3) S1, S2; comyn (3) C2, C3; *ger.* comyng(e) (29) P1, S1; commyng(e) (5) S1, S2.
comenceour *n.* one who has taken a university degree. (1) S1 (D.25.2). OED obs. 1733.
comend *vb. pl. subj.* (1) S1.
comense *inf.* to begin, to graduate from a university. (1) P3 (D.146.17); commenced (2) C4; *ger.* commensyng (1) C4.
comfort *n.* (7) S1, P3; confort (1) S1; coumforth (1) C5 (D.223.24); *pl.* comfortes (2) P1.
cominalte *n.* the people of a town or state. (3) S1, C3; *pl.* cominaltees (1) S1 (D.1.8). OED obs. 1631.
commande *inf.* (2) S1, C1; commaunde (1) C2; comaund (1) C2; comaunde (1) C2; *1 sing.* comand (1) C1; *3 sing.* commandeth (1) P3; *pl.* comaunde (1) C2; *past.* commaunded (1) P5; commaundyd (1) C3; *past part.* comaunded (2) C8; commaunded (1) P4; comanddid (1) P2; comanded (1) S1; *part.* comaundyng (6) P3, C3; commaundyng (3) C5.
commaunde *n.* (1) P5; comaund (1) C3.
com(m)andement *n.* (11) S1, C1; com(m)aundement (30) S1, C1; *pl.* comandementes (1) C5; comaundentȝ (1) C8.
com(m)issaries *n.* commissioners. (5, all in Signet Office documents) S1, S2.
com(m)ission *n.* (9) S1, P3.
com(m)issioners (9) S1, C1; commissioneres (1) C1. See com(m)issaries.
comitte *inf.* (1) C2; *pl.* committe (1) S1; *past part.* commit(t)ed (7) S2, C3; comytted (1) C3; committid (1) C4; commyttid (1) C2; commyttyd (1) C2.
com(m)odite *n.* (2) C3; *pl.* com(m)oditees (7) S1, P2; commodites (1) C5; commoditeȝ (1) P2.

Glossary of Forms

commoned *vb. past pl.* gathered, met, grouped. (1) P3; comuned (1) PO; *past part.* commynde (1) P5.

communicacion *n.* (2) P3; *pl.* comunicacions (2) N2; comenycacions (1) C3 (D.193.15).

companye *n.* (1) C8; compaigne (1) S1.

companye *inf.* congregate. (1) C8; *past part.* compaigned, accompanied. (2) P3.

compelle *inf.* (1) S1; *past.* compellid (1) C3; *past part.* compelled (3) C3, C4.

competent *adj.* adequate. (1) C4.

compiled *vb. past part.* (1) C8.

complaine *inf.* (1) P3; compleine (2) S1; compleyne (1) S1; *imp.* complaine (1) P3; *3 sing.* compleineth (2) S2; compleyneth (1) C3; compleines (1) C2 (D.173); *pl.* compleynen (1) C8; *pr. part.* complaynyng (2) C1, C5; compleyning (1) S2; *past part.* compleined (1) S1.

complaint *n.* (1) P2; compleinte (2) S1; complaynt (1) C5; compleynt (1) S1, S2; *pl.* complaintes (1) S1; compleintes (1) S1.

compleignant *n.* (3) S2, C3.

comprehende *vb. pl.* (1) P2; *3 sing.* comprehendyth (1) C3; *past part.* comprehendid (4) C4, N5; comprehended (2) S1, C4; comprehendet (1) C3.

comprised *vb. past part.* (4) S2, C3; comprisid (2) C4, C5.

comune *adj.* (19) C8, C3; comyn (8) C3; comen (2) C4, C5; comine (2) C5; commoun (1) S1; commune (1) P2.

comunely *adv.* (1) C3.

com(m)unes *n.* invariably refers to the House of Commons. (27) C8, C1; comons (6) C3, C4; comuns (2) C3, C5; comens (2) C5; comeyns (2) C5; comunnes (1) C3; comynes (1) C3; comunies (1) C4.

conceiled *past part.* stolen, kept illegally. (1) C3 (D.193.18).

conceit *n.* (1) P1; conseyt (1) C1; *pl.* conceites (1) P5.

conceive See conceyue.

concelement *n.* (1) C3.

concernen *vb. pr. pl.* (1) S1; *pr. part.* concernyng (5) P3, C4.

conceyve *inf.* (2) P3, C3; conceyue (1) C4; *pl.* conceive (1) S1. (D.69.2).

conclude *inf.* (4) S1, C3; *past part.* concluded (3) S1, C5; concludid (1) C5.

conclusion *n.* (7) S1, C1.

condempnacions *n.* (1) C3.

condempnyd *vb. past part.* (1) C3.

condescended *vb. past part.* (1) P2.

condicion(e) *n.* (8) S1, C3; *pl.* condicions (1) C3; condicionis (1) N5.

condite *n.* conduit. (1) N5 (D.239.4); *past part.* conduyed (1) S2 (D.96.4).

conducte *n.* usually in the phrase "saufe condut." (1) C3; condut (11) C3, C4 (10 instances in D.211); condit (1) P1; conduyt (1) S2; *pl.* conduts (2) C4; condutis (1) C3 (D.196.22).

conduit *inf.* conduct. (1) S2; *past part.* conduyed (1) S2 (D.96.4).

confederacie n. (1) C3.
confermed vb. past part. (3) S1, P2; confermyd (1) P4.
confessed vb. past. (1) P5.
confessour n. (5) S1.
confirmacion(e) n. (8) S1, S2; confermacon (1) P2.
conforme vb. pl. subj. (1) S1.
conquerid vb. past part. (1) C5.
conquest(e) n. (12) C8, C3.
conscience n. (15) S1, S2; concience (6) C2, P3; consciens (2) C3, C4; consience (2) C3; conciens (1) C4.
consecracion n. (2) S1.
consent n. (3) S1, S2.
conseruacion n. (5) S1.
conseruyng ger. (2) C3, P4.
consider(e) inf. (25) S1, C1; considre (12) P3, C3; concider (1) C3; consyder (1) C3; considery (1) C3 (D.198.15); pr. part. consideryng (28) S1, S2; considering(e) (12) S1, P2; concideryng (2) P3; past part. considered (11) S1, S2; considred (2) C4, C5; consydered (1) C3.
consideracion n. (8) C1, C2; consideracions (1) P4; consideracons (1) C5.
consolation n. (1) P2; consolacion (2) S2, P3.
constable n. (3) P3, C5; conestable (1) S1; constabul (1) C5.
constitucions n. (2) C3.
constrayned vb. past part. (1) C5.
contagious adj. (1) C3.
contemplatif adj. (1) P4.
contempt n. (1) C4.
contendentes n. contenders. (1) S1 (D.64.2). Not in *MED;* *OED* obs. 1694.
content inf. (1) P3; contente (2) S1, P2; pl. subj. contente (1) S2; past part. content(e) (6) PO, S1, contented (2) S1, P3; ger. contenting (1) P5.
content n. contents. (2) C5, N5; contenn(e) (3) S1, S2.
contentacion n. satisfaction. (1) P5 (D.158.14). *OED* obs. 1603.
conteyne inf. (1) N4; 3 sing. conteneth (1) S2; past part. conteined (1) C3; contiened (1) C3; conteyned (13) C3, P3; contened (24) S1, S2; contenyd (1) C3; content (1) P3 (D.142.10); conteyne (1) C3 (D.186.10); conteigned (2) C3; conteignyd (1) P5; conteignode (1) C3 (D.183.22); pr. part. contenyng (5) S1, S2. See cotene.
continual(l) (1) C5; continuel(l) (6) P3, C4; contynuel(l) (3) P3, C3; contynuall (1) C5; contenuell (1) C4.
continuance n. (2) S1, P3; continuaunce (2) C1, C5; continance (1) P3.
continue inf. (4) S1, P2; contenew (1) C5; contynew (1) C5; 3 sing. continueth (1) S1; past. contynewed (1) C3; past part. contynued (4) C8, C3; contenued (3) C5; continued (2) S1, C2.

Glossary of Forms 325

continuelly *adv.* (9) S1, S2; continuely (1) S1; contynuelly (1) C3.
contracte *n.* (1) C3.
contrary(e) *n., adj., adv.* no distinction in forms. (4) S1, C5; contrarie (12) P2, C3.
contre(e) *n.* (12) P1, C1; cuntre(e) (7) S1, S2; contray (6) C3, C5; countre (1) C4; countrei (1) C5; contreth (1) C2 (D.173.12); *pl.* countrees (3) P3, C3; contrees (3) S1, P3; countres (1) P3; cuntrees (1) P3; contreyes (1) C3.
contrevyd *vb. past part.* contrived. (1) C3.
controuersie *n.* (3) S1, S2; contrauersie (1) S1.
conuenable *adj.* convenient. (1) N4.
conuencion *n.* meeting of two or three people. (2) S2.
conuersaunt *adj.* (2) P3, C3.
conuictith *vb. 3 sing.* (1) C4; *past part.* conuicted (1) C3; conuict (1) C3; convycte (1) C3.
conuocacions *n.* (2) C4.
convenient *adj.* (1) C4; conuenient (2) C4, P5; conuenyent (1) C5.
convent *n.* (1) C5 (D.226.2); couent (7, all Signet Office documents) S1; conuent (6) C1, S1.
coost *n.* coast. (1) S1.
copie *n.* (12, 11 of them in Signet Office documents) S1, S2.
cople *n.* couple, in the technical sense of a pair of rafters, (2) N4 (D.238.6, 13).
corage *n.* (1) P2 (D.117.14).
corall *n.* coral. (1) C3 (D.197.11).
corne *n.* (3) C4 (D.214); *pl.* cornes (1) N4.
coroners *n.* (1) S2.
correccion *n.* (1) C3; coreccion (1) C8.
correcte *inf.* (1) P4.
corrodie *n.* annuity for living expenses. (4) S2, P3 (D.94.2 etc.).
corrupte *adj.* (1) C5.
cost *inf.* (1) P3; *past.* cost (1) C3.
costage *n.* (1) C3; *pl.* costages (1) C3. Both in D.183. *OED* obs. 1670.
cost(e) *n.* (8) N8, C3; *pl.* costes (16) C2, C3; costis (3) C3, C5; costys (1) C3.
costeres *n.* hangings for the sides of a bed. (1) C5 (D.222.19). *OED* obs. 1482.
costumes *n.* (1) C5.
cosynage *n.* helpful behavior toward a relative. (1) P3 (D.126.2). *OED* obs. 1579.
cotene *inf.* contain. (1) P1 (D.112.9). A variant unrecorded in the *MED*.
cotoun *n.* cotton. (3) C3 (D.190).
coude See can.
couenable *adj.* suitable. (9) S1, S2; *pl.* couenables in the phrase "in vitailles couenables." (1) P4 (D.156.10).
couenant *n.* (1) P3; covenaunt (2) C5; couenaunt (5) C5; *pl.* couenantes (1) N5; couenantȝ (1) N5.

couerlette *n.* (1) C3; *pl.* couerlettes (2) C3. All in D. 197.
counceillour *n.* (1) C3; conseilour (1) P5; *pl.* councellours (2) P3; counsaillours (1) P3.
counsail(l)(e) *n.* (39) P2, C3; counseil(l)(e) (38) S1, P2; councell (21) P3, C5; conseil (18) S1, S2; counsel(l) (13) P3, C3; consail (6) P2, P3; consell (2) C1, C3; conceil (2) C4, C5; counsey(l) (2) C2, N4; counceyll (1) C2; counsale (1) P3; counsseill (1) C2; *pl.* counseles (1) N2. See discussion.
counseilled *vb. past part.* (1) S1; conseled (1) C3.
counte(e) *n.* (34) P3, C3; conte(e) (3) S1, S2; contie (1) S1; countye (1) P3.
countenance *n.* (1) P3; countenaunce (3) P3, C5.
countermark *n.* in the phrase "mark countermark," i.e. reprisal. (1) C4. (D.211.17). Not in *MED; OED* obs. 1755.
countrollours *n.* (1) P2.
countynghous *n.* (1) C3 (D.189.3).
cours *n.* practice, custom. (6) S1, C4; course (2) C5.
courson *vb. pr. pl.* curse. (1) C5 (D.218.27).
court(e) (40) S1, C1; *pl.* courtes (5) P3, C3; courtys (2) C1.
cousin *n.* (7) S1, S2; cosin (8) S1, P2; cosyn (2) P3; cousyn (1) P4.
couthe See can.
coverying *ger.* (1) P4. coueryng (1) N8.
covey *n.* group. (2) C1 (D.164,11, 22).
covyne *n.* confederacy, collusion. (3) C2, C3 (D.174.7 etc.). *OED* obs. 1513.
coward *n.* (1) C3.
coyned *vb. past part.* coined. (1) P3.
craft(e) *n.* (37) C8, C3; craffte (1) C3; *pl.* craftes (23) C8, C3.
creacion *n.* (1) S2.
creature *n.* (2) C1, P2; crature (1) C1; *pl.* creatures (1) C1.
credence *n.* trust, document attesting trustworthiness. (8) S1, P2.
credibly *adv.* (1) P3; credebly (2) P3, P4.
creke *n.* creek. (1) C4.
crime *n.* (1) C4; *pl.* crimes (2) S5.
cristian *adj.* (1) C3; cristen(e) (5) S1, P3; crysten (1) C3.
croft *n.* an enclosed area, esp. for farming. (5) C5 (D.224).
cross(e) *n.* (2) C3; croyce (1) N2.
crowne *n.* (1) C3; corowne (1) S1; corone (1) P5.
cruell *adj.* (1) C5.
crye *inf.* (1) C8; *pr. part.* cryinge (1) C8.
cure *n.* (3) S2, P3.
cured *vb. past part.* (1) S5.
custum *n.* tradition (3) C3, C5; custum(e) (5) S1, P1 (D.5.5, 111.4); *pl.* custumes (3) C3, C5; coustumes (1) S2; custum(e), customary payment (2) S1, P5 (D.4.3, 159.37); *pl.* custumes, (6) P3, C3; custumis (1) C3 (196.3).

custumably *adv.* (2) C3 (D.180.27). *OED* obs. 1697.
custumer *n.* collector of customs. (2) C4; *pl.* custumers (7) C3, C4 (D.214.2); coustumers (1) P2. *OED* obs. 1748.

dagger *n.* 1(4) P3 (D.142).
damage *n.* (3) C3; *pl.* damages (9) C3, C4; damageʒ (1) C3.
dame *n.* (2) C5, N5.
dar *vb. 3 sing, pl, 3 sing. subj.* dare. (6) C1, C3; *past* dorst (2) 8; durst (2) C2.
date *n.* (18) N8, N2; dat (2) N8.
daufyn *n.* dauphin. (2) C3 (D.182.4, 7).
daunger *n.* danger. (2) S1, C3.
day *n.* (292) C8, PO; daie (6) P2, C3; daye (2) P3, C3; dai (1) C5; *pl.* dayes (20) C1, P2; daies (4) C2, C3; days (2) P3, C3; dayis (2) N5; daijs (1) C1; dais (1) C5.
dayly *adv.* (16) S2, C2; dayli (1) C5; daylay (1) C5; dailli (1) C5; dailly (1) C3; daili (1) C5; dayely (1) C5.
deanee *n.* deanery. (6) S1; deannee (1) S1 (D.62.5 etc.). Form not in *OED* or *MED*.
debate *n.* (1) C8; debat (2) S2, P3; *pl.* debates (5) C2, C5.
decayes *n. pl.* (1) C5 (D.223.12).
deceites *n.* (1) C3; disceites (1) C3; *sing.* disceyte (1) C3.
decese *n.* (6) S1, S2; decesse (5) C1, C3; decece (1) N5; discece (1) C5; disses (1) N5.
decided *vb. past part.* (1) P2.
declaracion *n.* (3) S1, C5; declaracioun (3) C4 (D.214).
declare *inf.* (5) S1, C2; declaren (1) C1; *pl.* declaryn (1) C2 (D.174.1); *pl. subj.* declare (1) S2; *past.* declared (3) PO, P2; *past part.* declared (5) S1, C1; declarid (2) C4, C5; declaryd (1) C5.
ded *adj.* dead. (2) P1, C8; dede (2) C3, P5; deed (1) S1.
dede *n.* (A) an act, deed. (9) C1, C3; *pl.* dedys (1) C1; (B) a legal document (9) C1, C3; *pl.* dedis (2) C3.
dedly *adv.* (1) C3.
deen *n.* dean. (2) S1; dean (1) S1; *pl.* denes (1) S1.
default(e) *n.* failure to perform specified acts. (2) S1, C1; defaut(e) (21) S1, C1; *pl.* defaultes (1) S1.
defence *n.* (7) C3, C4; defense (1) P3; *pl.* diffences (1) C3.
defend(e) *inf.* (2) S1, P3; *3 sing. subj.* defend(e) (8) S1, P3 (usually in the formulaic "þat God defende").
defensible *adj.* (1) N5; defensable (2) P3.
deferret See dyffer.
defesable *adj.* capable of being annulled. (1) C3 (D.189.26).
defiance *adj.* challenge. (1) P3 (D.142.34).

defie *vb. 1 sing.* challenge. (1) P3 (D.142.34).
defraudid *vb. past part.* (1) C5.
degree *n.* (1) C3; degre (2) C3, C5.
delaied *vb. past part.* (1) P4; *ger.* delaying (1) C4.
delay(e) *n.* (5) S2, P3.
deliberacion *n.* (1) S1.
deliuer(e) *inf.* (7) S1, C3; delyuer (6) S2, P2; *past* deliuered (3) C2, P3; delyuered (2) C1, P5; delivered (1) C3 (D.190.18); delyvered (1) C3; delyvred (1) C3; *past part.* deliuered (9) S1, C2; delyueret (4) C1; deliured (2) P2 (D.115.10); delyueret (1) P1 (D.112.8); delyuerid (1) C4; delyverd (1) C2; delyvered (1) C3; *ger.* deliueryng (2) P3, P4.
deliuerance *n.* (8) S1, S2; deliueraunce (1) P3; delyveraunce (1) C3.
demaunded *vb. past part.* (4) P3, C5.
demaundes *n. pl.* (1) C5.
demed *vb. past part.* judged, deemed. (1) C4; demyd (1) C3.
demened *vb. past.* demeaned. (2) P3, C5; *past part.* demened (1) C3; demenid (1) P2; demenyd (1) C3; *ger.* demenyng (1) C5.
demesne *n.* (3) C5, P5; demene (2) P2, P5; *pl.* demayns (1) C5; demaynes (1) C5 (both in D.223).
demure *n.* sojourn. (1) C2 (D. 168.6). *MED* different sense; *OED* obs. 1550.
deneied *vb. past part.* (1) C3.
denerye *n.* (1) P3. See also deanee.
denisʒein *n.* denizen, inhabitant. (3) C3; *pl.* denisʒeins (1) C3. All in D.180.
denominacion *n.* selection, nomination. (1) P2; denomynaccion (1) C3 (D.189.24).
denture *n.* an indenture, q.v. (1) C1 (D.165.5). *OED* obs. 1541.
depart *inf.* (1) C5; *3 sing. subj.* departe (2) S1, P3; *past.* departed (1) P5; departid (1) P2; departyd (1) C2; *past part.* departed (3) C1, C2; departid (1) C5; departyd (1) C5; *ger.* departyng (4) S1, S2.
departur *n.* (1) C5.
depauparte *past part.* impoverished. (1) C5 (D.226.6).
dependyng *vb. pr. part.* (1) C5.
depute *n.* deputy. (13) P3, C3; *pl.* deputees (3) P2, C3; deputeeʒ (1) C4.
depute *vb. 1 sing.* (1) P3; *past part.* deputed (1) S1; depute (1) C4.
dere *adj.* dear. (3) S1, C1; dier (1) P2.
derogacion *n.* harm caused by the infringement on a legal right. (2) C3, C4.
descende *inf.* (2) C1, C4; *past part.* descended (2) S2, C5.
desclaunderouse *adj.* given to slander, libelous. (1) S2 (D.93.5). Form not in *OED* or *MED*. See disclaundred.
desert *adj.* deserted. (1) C3.
deserte *n.* merit, desert. (2) C1, C3.
deserue *vb. 1 sing.* (1) PO (D.110.4); *past part.* deservid (1) C1.

Glossary of Forms 329

desir(e) n. (14) S1, S2; pl. desireʒ (1) C4.

desire inf. (4) S1, C3; 1 sing. desyre (1) P2; 3 sing. desireth (4) S1, P2; desireþ (1) S1; desirith (1) C5; pl. desire (10) S1, P2; desiren (1) S1; desireth (1) P2 (D.116.5); 3 sing. subj. desire (1) C4; pl. subj. desire (7) S1, C1; past. desired (2) P2, C3; desyred (1) C5; pr. part. desiryng (4) P3, C3; past part. desired (11) S1, P2; desirid (2) P2, P3; desyred (1) N2.

desolat(e) adj. (4) C2, P3.

despenses n. expenses. (1) S2, P3. See dispende.

destitute adj. (2) C1, C5.

destroye inf. (1) C1; destrue (1) S1; past. destruid (1) C5; destruyd (1) C8; destroied (1) C3; past part. distroied (1) C5; destroyd (1) C3.

destruc(c)ion(e) n. (7) C8, C1; distru(c)cion (3) C3, C5; distruction (1) C1.

det n. (1) S1; dette (4) C3, C4; pl. dettes (7) S2, C3; detts (1) N5; detteʒ (2) C4.

deteccions n. (1) C2 (D.177.19).

detectith vb. 3 sing. (1) C4; past part. detecte (1) C2 (D.177.2).

determinacion n. (3) P2, C3; determynacion (1) C4.

determine inf. (1) C3; determyn (2) C3; past part. determined (1) P2; determynd (1) C3; determyned (5) C1, C3; determynyd (1) C5; determynet (1) C3 (D.191.13).

deth(e) n. death. (14) C1, P2; ded(e) (4) C2, P5; deþ (1) S1; deeth (1) C1; deeþ (1) S1; pl. dethes (1) C1.

deuise inf. (2) P2; deuyse (1) N2; divise (1) N5; past. deuysed (1) C3; past part. deuised (1) C3; devysed (1) P3.

deuocion n. (2) S1, P3.

deuoir(e) n. duty, diligence. (2) S1, C4 (D.214.14); pl. devoirs (1) P5; deuairs (1) P3. OED obs. 1671.

devout(e) adj. (2) P3, C5; deuout (2) S1, P4.

deuoutly adv. (1) P4; deuoutely (1) S1.

deytyned vb. past part. detained. (1) C1 (D.162.10).

dial n. an instrument for telling time (see MED). (1) C3 (D.197.18).

diches n. ditches. (1) C3.

died past part. (2) C4, C5; past. deyde (2) C1; deyed (2) C1; deyede (1) C1 (D.163.39).

diers n. dyers. (1) C4 (D.217.10).

different adj. (8) P2, P3.

differre inf. defer. (1) P5; 3 sing. subj. dyffer (1) P5; pl. subj. differ (1) P5.

diligence n. persistence; in law, contractual obligations. (6) S1, P2; diligentʒ (1) P5; pl. diligenceʒ (1) P3.

diligent adj. (2) C3, C5.

diligently adv. (2) P2, P3.

dimes See disme.

dimmissioun n. relinquishment of office. (1) C4 (D.215.13). OED obs. 1568.

diner *n.* dinner. (1) P3 (D.145.10).
diocise *n.* (2) C5 (D.226); dyose (1) P3 (D.141.3).
directed See dyrecte.
directly *adv.* (1) C4.
disalowed *vb. past part.* (2) C2.
disapoint *inf.* (1) P5.
disassent *n.* dissent. (1) P2 (D.122.12). *OED* obs. 1643.
disavaille *n.* harm, loss. (2) C3; disauaile (2) C3.
discensions *n.* (1) C5.
disceyte *n.* (1) C3; *pl.* deceites (1) C3; disceites (1) C3.
disceyued *vb. past part.* (1) S1.
discharge *n.* (6) S1, P2.
discharge *inf.* (4) S1, P3; *imp.* dischargeþ (1) C3 (D.179.16); *pl. subj.* discharge (1) C5; *pr. part.* dischargyng (1) C4; *past part.* discharged (12) S1, P3; *ger.* discharging (1) C2.
disclaundred *vb. past part.* slandered. (2) C8 (D.161.29, 37). See desclanderouse.
discomfort *n.* (2) S1, C3.
discomforted *vb. past part.* (1) C5.
discord *n.* (1) P2.
discovered *vb. past part.* (1) C3.
discrec(c)ion *n.* (21) S1, P2; dyscrecion (2) C3; discresion (1) C3; discrescion (1) C3 (D.183.21); *pl.* discrec(c)ions (19) S1, C2; discressions (2) C3, C5; dyscreciouns (1) C3; dyscrecions (1) C3; discreciouns (1) C3.
discret(e) *adj.* wise, prudent, etc., esp. in phrases like "discrete Comons," "discrete Councell." (27) C8, C1; descrete (2) P2; discreet (1) C3.
discretly *adv.* (1) S2.
discussed *vb. past part.* (1) C4.
disese *n.* usually in the sense of "unease," "discomfort." (3) S1, C2; *pl.* diseses (1) S1; desesis (1) C2.
disheredacon *n.* deprivation of inheritance. (1) C8 (D.164.3). This is the sole *MED* citation; *OED disherit* obs. 1700.
disheritaunce *n.* deprivation of inheritance. (4) C3, C4; *Pl.* dysheritaunces (1) C3.
disherityd *vb. past part.* (1) C3 (D.188.20).
disme *n.* subsidy of one tenth of profit. (13) C3, C5; dysm (1) P3 (D.131.11); *pl.* dymes (3) S1 (D.26); dismeʒ (3) C5 (D.226); dismes (2) C1, C5; dimes (1) S1; dysmes (1) P3; dysmeʒ (1) C5.
dismisse *inf.* (1) C5; *past part.* dismist (1) C5.
disobeyd *vb. past part.* (1) C5.
disolute *adj.* (1) C3.
dispair *n.* (1) C3.
dispende *inf.* spend, give out. (3) C3; *3 sing. subj.* dispende (1) S1; *past part.* dispendid (1) P5; despendyd (1) N5.

Glossary of Forms 331

displeasire *n.* (1) P4.
displeaunsse *n.* displeasure. (1) P2.
displesyng *vb. pr. part.*(1) C8.
disport *n.* amusement. (2) S1.
dispose *vb. pr. pl.* (3) P3; *3 sing.* disposeth (1) P3; *pr. part.* disposyng (3) P3; *past part.* disposed (1) S1, C4; disposid (1) C5.
disposicion *n.* (4) S2, P5.
disproued *vb. past part.* (1) N8.
dissesed *vb. past part.* deprived of seizen. (1) S2.
distrebued *vb. past part.* distributed. (1) C2.
distres *n.* (1) C3; destresse (1) N8 (D.233.26) referring to legal repossession for arrearage); *pl.* distresses (1) N5.
distressing *ger.* (1) C5.
distreyn(e) *inf.* to enforce payment. (3) C3, N4; destreigne (1) C3.
disturbeth *vb. 3 sing.* (1) S2; *past part.* disturbed (1) C5.
divers *adj.* (1) N5; diuers(e) (39) S1, P2; dyuers(e) (16) C8, C3; diuerce (1) C3; *pl.* diuerseʒ (5) N2, C4; diuerses (1) S1; dyuerses (1) C3.
diuided *vb. past part.* (1) C5; *ger.* dividyng (1) N8.
diuin(e) *adj.* always modifying "service." (3) S1, P3; dyuine (1) C5; deuyne (1) C2.
diuinitee *n.* (1) S1.
diuise *n.* command, device. (1) N5 (D.241.16).
divise *vb. 3 pl. subj.* bequeath. (1) N6 (D.241.15).
do *inf.* (2) S1, P2; doo (6) S1, S2; doe (2) N5; *imp.* dothe (1) S1 (D.70.9); *1 sing.* do (2) C1, P1; *pl.* do (2) S1, S2; doo (1) S1; *3 sing.* do (10) S1, S2; doo (1) P2; doe (1) N5; doth (4) C1, C3; dooþ (2) S1, S2; *pl.* do (1) C1; doo (1) P2; *pl. subj.* do (34) S1, S2; doo (30) S1, S2, usually expressing volition, "we wol þat ye do write hit ayein." *past.* did (5) S1, S2; did(d)e (4) S1, P2; dyd (1) C3; dede (1) P3; deden (1) C3 (D.192.16); doon (1) C1 (D.164.1); *pr. part* doing (1) S5 (idiomatic, D.108.8); *past part.* done (12) C1, P3; don (16) P2, P3; donn (1) N8; do (2) S1, S4; doo (8) S2, P2; doon (36) S1, S2; doen (1) P2; ydo (1) C8; *ger.* doyng (5) S1, P3; *pl.* doynges (1) C8 (D.161.41).
doctor *n.* (1) C3.
doctrine *n.* (1) C5.
doers *n.* agents. (1) S1; dowers (1) C4.
doghter *n.* (3) S2, C3.
dome *n.* doom, i.e., sentence. (1) C5 (D.221.38).
domesman *n.* chief magistrate. (1) C8 (D.161.54).
dongewayn *n.* dungcart. (1) C3 (D.197.20).
dores *n.* (1) P3; dorys (1) C2.
dormant *used as adv.* a type or writ which always remained in effect. (1) S1

(D.18.4).

dorser *n.* either an ornamental cloth or a basket, probably the latter. (1) C3 (D.197.17). *OED dosser* obs. 1516.

dortour *n.* the dormitory of a convent. (1) N4 (D.238.11). OED obs. 1592.

double *adj.* (1) C3.

douson *n.* a variant or perhaps mistake for advowson. (1) N8 (D.234.4). This variant not in *MED*. See auowson.

doute *n.* doubt. (1) P2; dowte (4) S1 (1), C1 (3); dobȝthe (1) C5 (D.218.16).

douty *adj.* doughty. (1) C2.

dowblette *n.* doublet. (1) C3; *pl.* doublettis (1) P3.

dower *n.* A) an endowment. (1) P4; B) marriage property (1) N5.

down(e) *adv.* (10) P3, C3; doun(e) (11) C3, P3.

downefallen *vb. past part.* (1) P3 (D.149.16).

downward *adv.* (1) P3.

dowtyng *vb. pr. part.* (1) P3. See doute.

drank *vb. past.* (1) P3.

drapery *n.* the cloth market and surrounding area. (1) N5.

drawe *inf.* (1) S1; *imp.* drawe (3) P3; *past part.* draw (1) C3, in the phrase "to be draw and hanged" (D.194.17); drawen (2) C8, P3; *ger.* drawyng (1) P3.

dred *vb. pr. pl.* dread. (1) C5 (D.227.6); *past.* dradde (1) C8 (D.161.25); *ger.* dredyng (1) C5.

dredd(e) *adj.* dreaded. (2) P2, C2.

drede *n.* dread, fear. (5) C1, C2; dreede (1) C5 (D.223.7).

dredeful *adj.* (1) C2.

droitȝ *n. pl.* customary fines and duties. (2) P4 (D.156.26, 27). *OED* a law term.

drowened *vb. past.* drowned. (1) C3.

dryftes *n. pl.* (1) C5.

drynke *n.* (2) C3, C5. Only in the phrase "mete and drynke."

drynorysse *n.* dry-nurse. (2) P2.

dryven *vb. past pl.* (1) C1 (D.164.11); *past part.* dryven (3) C3, C5; drovyn (1) C1 (D.164.22).

duchie *n.* (15) S1, P2; duchery(e) (3) P3, C1; duchee (1) P3.

due *adj.* proper, customary, expected, authorized, almost always in the phrase, "in due forme." (59, over half in Signet Office letters) S1, S2; dew (2) S2, N8; dewe (2) S1, C5; deue (1) P3; deuhe (1) P2 (D.115.21); diewe (1) C3; dieu (1) C4; duwe (1) C3; du (1) C3.

duelle *inf.* dwell. (1) C1; *3 sing.* dwelleth (1) P3; *past* dwellid (1) C5; dwellede (1) C1; *pr. part.* dwellyng(e) (7) C3, P4; duellyng (5) P3, C3; dwelling (1) C3; diwellyng (1) C3 (D.198.19); *past part.* dwelled(e) (2) C1, P3; duellyd (1) C3 (D.192.24).

duely *adv.* (6) S1 (3), P3; deuhly (1) P2 (D.115.21); dywly (1) C3 (D.193.28);

Glossary of Forms 333

dieuly (1) C4 (D.210.17).
duke *n.* (9) S1, C5 (8); duc (33) S1 (16), S2 (2); *pl.* ducs (1) S1.
dungeon *n.* (3) P3, C5.
duresse *n.* (4) S1, C2; duras (2) C3.
during *adv.* (4) S1, P3; duringe (1) S1; durynge (44) N8, S1.
dwellers *n. pl.* (2) C3, C5; dwellerys (1) C2 (D.176.6).
dwelleth See duelle.
dwellyng *n.* place of residence. (2) N8, C3.
dyffer *vb. 3 sing. subj.* (1) P5; *past part.* deferret (1) S1 (D.24.7).
dygnyte *n.* dignity. (1) C3.
dymysed *vb. past part.* transferred goods or property. (1) N5 (D.240.3).
dyrecte *inf.* (1) P2; *past part.* direct(e) (24) S1, C2; directed (3) C2, P2; directid (3) P3, C4; dirett (2) S1, C3; dyrecte (2) C1.
dyscresed *vb. past part.* decreased. (1) C5 (D.226.6).
dysplese *vb. 3 sing. subj.* (1) C2.
dywte *n.* duty. (2) N6; *pl.* dywtees (1) C3 (D.193.18).

eacynge *ger.* easing. (1) C1 (D.162.5).
ech(e) *adj.* (11) C1, S1; iche (3) P3 (D.128.10), C3 (D.182.25); eich (1) C5 (D.227.19); euch (1) P3 (D.148.3); ich (1) C5 (D.221.40); ych (1) C4 (D.214.17).
echone *pronoun.* each one. (4, all in D.216) C4; ichone (1) C3 (D.179.15).
edifyng *ger.* (1) P3.
effect *n.* (10) S1, P2 (D.2.6, 49.5, etc.); effecte (7) P2, C4 (D.117.4, 200.4, etc.); affecte (1) C3 (D.198.9).
effectuel(l) *adj.* (5) PO, C3; effectual(l) (2) C5.
effectuelly *adv.* (5) S1, P2; effectuellie (1) C3.
eftsones *adv.* soon, later. (1) C5 (D.221.19). *OED* arch.
egalli *adv.* equally, fairly. (1) C5 (D.218.36).
egle *n.* eagle, referring to Henry V's signet of "þegle" (3) S2 (D.91, 93, 94); þeegle (1) S2 (D.90).
either *pronoun.* (5) P3, C5.
eke *adv.* also. (1) C8 (D.161.10).
elbowe *n.* (1) P3.
elder *adj.* (1) C2.
eleccion *n.* (2) C8, S1.
elit *n.* one elected or chosen for an ecclesiastical position, especially as bishop. (10) S1, S2; eslit (1) S1 (D.24.13).
elite *vb. past part.* elected. (1) S2 (D.101.2). See also elit.
elleswhere *adv.* (1) S1.
ellon *n. pl.* ells. (1) C3 (D.197.18).
els *adv.* else. (5) S1, C3; elles (14) C8, S1; ellis (7) S1, P3; ellys (4) P2, C3;

ellus (1) P3; *adj.* ellis (1) C5 (D.227.6).
embesiled *vb. past part.* (1) C3 (D.193.18).
emboldishing *ger.* making bold. (1) C2 (D.174.6); inboldesshyng (1) C3. This ref. cited in *MED; OED* obs. 1512.
empeched *vb. past part.* called to account before the law. (2) C5; empesched (1) P5.
empechement *n.* (2) C4, C5; empeschement (2) C3, P4; inpechement (1) C3.
empension *n.* pension. (4) S1, S2.
empleted *vb. past part.* sued. (1) S1. *OED* arch. 1559.
employe *inf.* (1) C4; *past part.* emploied (1) P3.
employment *n.* (2) C4; enploiement (1) P5 (D.158.41).
empored *vb. past part.* impoverished. (1) S1 (D.40.5); enpoured (1) C5 (D.218.24).
enacte *inf.* to make legally binding. (1) C4 (D.216.14); *past part.* enact (1) P2 (D.122.14); enacted (2) P2, C5; to record *past part.* enact (1) P2 (D.122.12).
enarmynges *n.* attacks. (1) C8.
enblaied *vb. past.* harvested. (1) C5 (D.222.26). Form not in *OED.*
enblaimentʒ *n.* normally "em-," grain crops. (2) C5.
enbrace *inf.* normally "em-." to bribe or otherwise prejudice a jury. (1) C3; *past part.* enbrasid (1) C3.
encheson *n.* reason, basis. (1) C3 (D.183.2). *OED* obs. 1642.
encloosed *vb. past part.* (1) P3. See closed.
encombrous *adj.* (1) S2.
encresce *n.* (1) C5 (D.227.17).
encreses *vb. 3 sing.* (1) C2 (D.169.10); *pr. part.* encresyng (2) C3, C5; *past part.* encresced (1) P2.
end(e) *n.* (30) S1, S2; eende (1) S1 (D.19.3).
endaungered *vb. past part.* (1) S1.
endented *vb. past part.* contracted. (2) C4, C5; endentid (7) C3, C5; endentyd (1) N4; indented (1) C5.
edited *vb. past part* charged with a crime. (12) C8, C1; endyteth (1) C3 (D.194.11).
enditement *n.* (6) C1, S1; endytement (1) C3; *pl.* enditementes (1) C4, enditementʒ (1) C4 (same document, D. 212); inditementes (1) C4.
endorsement *n.* (1) P3; endocement (1) P3.
endosed *vb. past part.* indorsed. (1) C3; endoced (1) P2 (D.122.6). *OED* obs. 1613.
endowable *adj.* (1) C4.
endowed *vb. past part.* (3) S1, P3; endowid (1) C5.
endur(e) *inf.* (8) S1, C2; *3 sing. subj.* indur (1) C5 (D.217.43).
enemye *n.* (1) P3; *pl.* enemyes (5) C1, P3; ennemys (3) S1, C5; enemys (2) P3, C3; enemis (1) S1; inimyes (1) C3.

Glossary of Forms 335

enfeffe *inf.* (3) S1, C1; *pl. subj.* enfeffe (1) C4; *past.* enfeffed (1) C4; enfeffid (1) C4; *past part.* enfeffed (2) C4; enfeffid (1) P4; enfeoffed (1) P3; enfeoffid (1) N5; enffeffid (2) C5.

enfeffement *n.* (1) C1.

enfeffeours *n.* (1) S2.

enforced *vb. past.* (1) C3.

enforme *inf.* (2) P3; *past part.* enfourmed (17) S1, P1; enformed (6) S1, P1; enformid (1) P2; informed (1) P3; enformeden (1) C1 (D.163.7).

enfourmer *n.*(1) C3.

engaged *vb. past part.* (1) P3.

England *n.* (35) S1, S2; Englande (10) S1, S2; Engeland (7) P0, S1; Englond (28) S1, P2, etc.; Englonde (3) P3, P5 (2 in D.158); Engelond (1) C3; Inglond (6) P3, P5; Ingelond (3) C1, P3; Ingland (1) C3 (D.198.2); Yngelond (2) C1 (D.165.1, 166.12); Ynglond (1) C2 (D.168.1).

Englissh *adj.* (1) P3 (D.145.12); Englyssh (1) S2 (D.81.14).

Englisshman *n.* (1) C3 (D.193.15).

enhaunsyng *ger.* (1) C1.

enjoye *inf.* (1) C4; *past part.* enioyed (2) C5.

enlarg *inf.* (1) N8. See enlargissed.

enlargissed *vb. past. part.* enlarged. (1) C2 (D.169.11).

enpouerisshing *ger.* (1) C5.

enprowe *inf.* improve. (1) P2 (D.115.3).

enquere *inf.* inquire. (2) C3; *past part.* enquered (1) C3 (all entries D.192, 193).

enquest *n.* (1) C3; *pl.* enquestes (2) C3.

enriched *vb. past.* (1) C5.

enrolled *vb. past part.* (3) S1, C3; enrollyd (1) C5; enroulled (1) C4.

enrolmente *n.* (1) C5.

ensample *n.* example. (1) C4.

enseal(l)ed *vb. past part.* document authenticated by attaching a seal. (3) S1, P3; enseled (1) S2; ensealid (1) C5; weight authenticated by attaching a seal (1) C3 (D.190.12).

enstraunged *vb. past part.* estranged. (2) C5. Entry cited in *MED*.

entencion *n.* (1) S1.

entendance *n.* attendance, service. (1) S5; *pl.* entendaunt3 (2) P2; entendant3 (2) P2. Usually in the phrase "for þe good service and entendaunt3."

entende *inf.* attend. (3) S1, S2; *subj. pl.* entende (1) S5.

entendid *vb. past* intended. (1) C5.

entent See intent.

enterprise *n.* (1) P3 (D.136.6).

entier *adj.* (3) P1, C3; *adv.* entier (1) C3 (D.203.24); entiere (1) C3 (D.204.28).

entierly *adv.* (5) S1, P3; entierely (2) C3.

entre *inf.* enter. (3) C3, C5; *past* entrid (4) C3, C5; entred (1) C3; entryd (1)

C1; *past part.* entred (3) S1, P2; *ger.* enteryng (1) C4.
entrechangeably *adv.* (1) N2.
entree *n.* entry. (1) P3; entre (3) C3, C4; *pl.* entres (1) P2.
entremet *in.* interfere, intervene. (1) C5 (D.225.14); intermete (1) C3 (D.225.14). *OED* obs. 1583.
entretyd *vb. past part.* entreated. (1) C5; intreted (1) C3; entredid (1) C5.
equite *n.* (1) S1 (D.58.5).
erl *n.* earl. (13) S1, P3; erle (31) S1, P3; *gen. sing.* erilles (1) P3 (D.124.5); *pl.* erles (1) S1; erlis (1) P3.
errour *n.* (2) C4; *pl.* errours (1) C1.
erthly *adj.* (2) C3.
eschangid *vb. past part.* (1) C3.
eschaped *vb. past part.* escaped. (1) P5.
escheker *n.* (12) P3, C3; eschequer (8) S1 (5), S2; eschequier (7) P4, C5 (6, D.232); eschequyer (3) P3, C5; eschequir (2) S3; eschequer (1) C2; eschequyr (1) P3. See esker, checker.
eschete3 *n.* (1) C3 (D.194.18).
eschetours *n.* (2) S2, P2.
eschewe *inf.* (1) S1; *past part.* eschewed (1) C3; *ger.* eschewyng (3) C2, C3; eschuyng (1) P3; eschewyn (1) C3; estcheuyng (1) C3 (D.192.26). Usually "in eschewyng."
escourt *n.* (1) S1.
ese *n.* ease. (6) S1, S2.
esker *n.* exchequer. (1) C2 (D.178.10). Form not in *OED* or *MED*. See cheker.
especial(e) *adj.* (14) S1, C1; especiall (6) P3, C3.
especially *adv.* (1) C4.
especialte *n.* detailed provision in a contract. (2) C5 (D.221.5).
espiall *n.* spying. (1) P4 (D.156.14).
espiceries *n.* spiceries. (2) C3.
espirituel(e) *adj.* ecclesiastical, especially in the phrase "Lordes Espirituel." (2) C3; espirituell (1) C3; esperituel (2) S1; *pl.* espirituelx (2) C3.
esquier *n.* (1) S1; esquyer (2) C3, C5; escuier (1) S1; *pl.* esquiers (1) C3.
esson *n.* essoin, excuse. (2) C4 (D.216.43).
est(e) *n., adj.* east. (2) N8, P3.
estable *inf.* establish, always in phrase like "to ordein, estable," etc. (3) C3, C4; establie (1) C3. See establissh.
establissh *inf.* (1) C5. establysshe (1) C5. Found only in the phrase "ordeine and establissh." See estable.
estandarde *n.* standard. (4, all in D. 190) C3.
estate *n.* (8) S1, P3; astate (10) C1, C3; astat (1) N8; estat (6) S1, P2; a state (1) P5 (D.160.5); esstate (1) P5; *pl.* estates (3) P3, C3; estats (1) P3; estat3

(1) S1; estatys (1) P3 (D.122.29); estatys (1) P3.
ester *n.* Easter. (7) S1, S2; estire (1) C3; estur (1) C3; estryn (2) N4 (D.237.20, 22).
estimacion *n.* (4) S1, C4.
estraunger *n.* stranger. (1) C4.
et *Fr./Lat.* and, used in the phrase "oure goode grace et beniuolence." (1) S1 (D.69.12).
ete *vb. past.* ate. (1) P3 (D.145.9).
euangelist *n.* (1) C3 (D.181.4); *pl.* euangelistes (1) C3.
even *n.* evening. (5) P3, C3.
even *adj.* (1) C8 (D.161.32); euen (2) S1, C5.
ever *adv.* (2) C5 (D.217.23, 40); euer (18) S1, P2; euere (12) P2, P3; euyr (3) P2, C4; euir (1) P5; evir (1) C5; euur (1) N2; eure (1) S1.
euermore *adv.* (5) S1, C5; euermor (2) C1, C2; eueremor (1) C1.
every *adj.* (3) C3, C4; euery (39) P2, C2; euerich (7) P3, P4; eueriche (3) S1 (2), C3; euerych (2) S2, N5; eueri (1) P3. The Chancery preference is euery, which appears 34 times in Chancery documents.
euidence *n.* (2) P2, C2; evydence (1) C1; *pl.* euidences (4) P3, N5 (3).
euidenceth *vb. 3 sing.* (1) C3 (D.205.5).
euident *adj.* (1) C4.
evil *n., adj.* (1) C3; euel (3) S1, P3; euyll (2) C3 (D.188.10, 17); euille (1) C5.
exaltacion *n.* (1) N2.
examinacion *n.* (3) C1, C3; examinacioun (1) C3; examynacion (1) C1; *pl.* examinacions (2) C3.
examine *inf.* (2) C1, C3; examyne (1) C3; *subj. pl.* examineth (1) S1; *past.* examined (1) P3; *past part.* examined (7) S1, P3; examyned (1) P5; examynyd (1) C3.
example *n.* (2) S1, P3.
excellence *n.* In the address "your excellence." (1) S1.
excellent *adj.* Always used in courtesy phrases like "moste excellent worthy Lordships." (8) S1, C2. excylent (1) C1.
excepcion *n.* (1) S1.
except(e) *prep.* (9) S1 (D.1.7), the rest P4, C3, etc.; accept (1) N8 (D.233.20).
excepted *vb. past part.* (1) C3; exceptid (2) C4, C5; except(e) (4) C2, C3.
excessious *adj.* excessive. (1) C4 (D.213.8). Cited in *MED*.
excessiue *adj.* (1) C2; excessyue (1) C5.
excitacion *n.* arousing. (1) C3.
exciteth *vb. 3 sing.* (1) C3.
exclude *inf.* (2) C5.
excoutories *pl. adj.* "writtes excoutories" (1) P5 (D.158.9).
excusacions *n.* excuses. (2) P3, P4; excusaions (1) P4 (D.152.3).
excused *vb. past part.* (2) P3, C3.

excuses *n.* (1) P5.
execucion *n.* (18) S1, C2; exicucion (2) C3, C4; execucioun (1) C4; *pl.* execucions (1) P3.
execute *inf.* (7) C3, C4; *pl. subj.* execute (2) S1, N5; *past part.* execute (1) C2; executed (1) C4; executyd (1) P4.
executor *n.* (1) C3; executour (1) P4; *pl.* executors (5) C3, C5; executours (5) S4, P4; executoriis, executorijs (2) N8; executories (1) P5; exeketeurs (1) P2.
exemplified *vb. past part.* (1) P5.
exigent *n.* a writ requiring a defendent to appear on pain of outlawry. (1) C3 (D.183.25). Cited in *MED*.
exoneracion *n.* (1) C5.
expedicion *n.* (2) P4.
expedient *adj.* (5) P3, C3.
expellyd *vb. past part.* (1) C1.
expenses *n.* (5) P5, C4; expensis (3) C4, P5.
experience *n.* (1) C3.
expert *adj.* (1) S5.
expired *vb. past.* (2) S1; *past part.* expired (1) C5.
exploit *n.* (1) P5.
expresse *adj.* (1) S1 (D.63.1).
expresse *inf.* communicate. (1) P5; *past part.* expressed (3) S1, P5.
expressely *adv.* (3) S1, C3; expresly (1) S2.
example *n.* (1) C4. See also ensample.
exspende *inf.* (1) C3.
exspired *vb. past. p.* (1) C3.
extende *vb. 3 sing. subj.*, always in a phrase indicating that a bill, act, etc. should "extend not" to a person or office. (4) C5.
extent(e) *n.* (3) C4, C5.
extorcion *n.* (1) C5; *pl.* extorcions (1) S2.
extorcionesli *adv.* extortionately. (1) C3 (D.189.4).
eyr *n.* air. (1) C3.
eyres See heir.

factour *n.* agent. (1) C5.
faculte *n.* university staff. (1) P3; *pl.* facultees (1) P3. Both in D.146.
fader *n.* father. (123) S1, S2; fadir (13) C3, C4; fadre (11) P3, C3; fadur (1) N2; ffader (13) P3, C3; ffador (1) C3; *gen.* fadres (1) C2; fadris (1) C1; *pl.* faders (3) S1, S2; fadres (3) P4, C5. fader is the overwhelming preference in Signet Office letters, where it appears in virtually every case in the address ('Worshipful fader in God"). Fadir appears chiefly in D.189 and D.210, C3, C4.
ffadorhode *n.* fatherhood. (1) C3.

faile *inf.* (1) P3; *imp.* faileth (1) P3 (D.134.11); faylleth (1) P3 (D.132.11); *sing. subj.* faill (1) N2; *pl. subj.* faille (4) P3, S5; faile (2) S1, S5; *pr. part.* faillyng (1) C4.

faintly *adv.* (1) P3.

faith *n.* (2) P3, C2; feith (4) S1, C4; faiþ (2) P2; feithe (1) P3; feyth (1) C4.

faithfully *adv.* (1) C5.

fall(e) *inf.* (9) C3, C5; fallen (1) P3; ffall (1) C4; *3 sing.* fallen (1) P3 (D.136.6); *sing. subj.* falle (2) P2; fal (1) P3; *past* fel (1) S2; fil (1) C1; fill (1) P3; *pr. part.* fallyng (2) N2; *past part.* fallen (4) P3, C3; falle (1) S2.

false *adj.* (3) C8; fals (3) P3, C3.

falseness (1) C8; falsnesse (1) C8 (both in D.161).

falshede *n.* (3), falsehede (1) C8 (all in D.161); *pl.* falshedes (2) C3.

falsly *adv.* (1) C8 (D.161.29).

famouse *adj.* (1) C4.

famulerlich *adv.* freely. (1) C8 (D.161.47).

fannyn *inf.* to winnow. (1) N4 (D.237.19).

farthest *adj.* (1) P3; fartherst (1) P3.

fast *adv.* near. (1) P3; faste, securely. (1) C3.

fast *inf.* (1) C3 (D.196.13).

fastenes *n.* strong boxes. (1) C3 (D.222.29). Not recorded in *OED* or *MED*.

fauorable *adj.* (1) S1.

fauorably *adv.* (2) S2, P2.

fauour *n.* (12) S1, P2; favour (1) C3; fauore (1) P3; fayuor (1) C1; fauor (1) S1; faueur (1) P4 (D.157.7); fayuour (1) C1.

fayn *adv.* fain, gladly. (2) C1, C5.

feaultee *n.* fealty. (1) S2; feaulte (1) S1; feawte (1) S1; fewte (1) S1. Found exclusively in Henry V's Signet letters.

febelnysse *n.* (1) C5.

feble *adj.* (1) C3; febyll (1) P3.

fee *n.* (28) S1, C2; ffee (1) C3; *pl.* feeȝ (3) C4; fees (11) P2, C4.

feele *vb. 3 sing. subj.* perceive, imagine. (1) P2.

feere *n.* fear. (2) C8; fere (4) C2, C3.

feest *n.* feast, holy day. (1) S3; fest (34) P4, C3; feste (19) S1, P3; ffest (2) C4, C5; ffeste (2) C5; *pl.* festes (5) C3, N2; ffestes (1) N4.

feffees *n.* holders of fiefs. (1) C4; feffeeȝ (14) C4 (all the preceding citations from D.210); feoffes (3) P4, C5; feffeis (2) N5.

feffement *n.* enfeoffment. (8) C3, C4; feoffement (1) P2. See feoffed.

feffour *n.* fiefer, one who invests another with a fief. (1) C4.

felawes *n.* companions. (1) C1 (D.163.24); felaws (1) P3 (D.142.21,22); felaughes (1) C2 (D.173.16).

feld *n.* field of battle. (4) P3; *pl.* feldes, agricultural fields. (1) N4.

felde *vb. past part.* felled (trees). (1) C3 (D.189.32).

felonousely *adv.* (2) P3, C3; felonesly (2) C4 (D.212); felonsly (1) C4.
felony *n.* (1) C2 (D.174.9); felonye (4) C2, C3; felonie (4) P3, C4; ffelonie (1) C4; *pl.* felonies (5) C4; felonieȝ (1) C4; felonyes (2) C3.
feloweship *n.* (1) P3; feleship (1) P2; felship (1) S4.
feod *adj.* enfeoffed, feed, always "oure feod man/men." (7) P3 (D.132-D.134); foed (1) P3 (D.133.5).
feoffed *vb. past part.* enfeoffed. (1) N5; ffefed (1) C1. See feffement.
fer *adv.* far. (2) S2, C2; ferr (1) P2; ferre (1) C3.
ferforth *adv.* far. (2) C8, C5; ferfoorth (1) S2.
ferid *n.* fear: "clappyd saume ye Buke for ferid." (1) C2 (D.173.7).
ferme *n.* farm. (20) S1, C1; *pl.* fermes (8) P4, C5; fermys (1) P3. See fferme.
fferme *inf.* farm. (2) P2, C1.
fermor *n.* usually tax farmer. (1) C1 (D.164.2); fermour (1) N4 (D.237.18); *pl.* fermours (2) S1, P3; fermers (1) P3; ffermers (1) C5; ffermours (1) P2.
ferther *adv.* (4) S1, P2; ferþer (1) S1; further (1) C4; furder (1) P3.
ferthermore *adv.* (1) C8; ferþermore (3) S1, S2; fferthermore (4) S1; fferþermore (1) S2; ffurthermore (1) S2; furthermore (1) C3; ffurthermore (1) S2; furthremore (1) S1; forthermore (1) C3; forthyrmor (1) C5; foryermor (1) C5. Frequent ff forms because the word begins a new clause.
ferthest *adj.* (1) P3; ferþest (1) P3.
ferthyng *n.* farthing. (1) C3.
ferveure *n.* fervor. (1) P3.
festiuall *n.* (1) P2.
fewe *adj.* (4) C8, C5; *comp.* fewer (1) S1.
feyn *vb. 1 sing.* dissemble, feign. (1) P2; *3 sing.* feynth (1) C1; *past.* feyned (1) C3; *past part.* feyned (4) P2, P3.
fifte *adj.* fifth. (2) P3, N5; fyfte (2) C3.
fight *inf.* (1) P3; fyght (1) P3.
filacer *n.* one who files, esp. writs and other official records. (1) P3 (D.140.2).
fin *n.* fine. (1) P3; fyn (4) P3, C3; fyne (5) P5 C2; ffyne (1) P5; *pl.* fines (2) C3; fynes (1) C3.
finall *adj.* (1) P3; finale (1) C3; fynal (1) C3.
finally *adv.* (3) C3, C5; fynalli (1) C3.
finance *n.* borrowing money. (1) C3 (D.205.7); fynance (1) C3 (D.196.14).
finisshed *vb. past part.* (1) C3.
first *adj.* (9), *adv.* (7) S1, P2; firste (1) C5; furst (9) S1, S2; ffirst (2) P2; ferst (2) C3, C5; ferste (2) C1, C3; fyrst (1) N8; furste (1) C3. There are no distinctions between adj. and adv. usage.
fisshe *n.* (1) C3 (D.180.14).
fittyng *adj.* suitable. (1) C3.
fixed *vb. past part.* (1) P3.
flax *n.* (1) C3; flex (2) C3 (D.190).

Glossary of Forms 341

fle *inf.* flee. (1) C1. *past.* fledde (2) C8 (D.161).
flore *n.* floor. (2) N8.
flour *n.* ground grain. (1) C3.
folk(e) *n.* (14) C8, P3. Most citations in D.203 and D.204.
folowe *inf.* (1) P3; *3 sing.* foloweth (2) C3, P3; folweth (1) S1; folwyth (1) C3 (D.199.12); folowith (1) C5; *3 pl.* folow (1) P3; folowen (1) N2; *pr. part.* folowyng (12) P3, C3; folwing (3) C8, C5; folwyng (2) P3, C5; folwynge (2) C1; filowyng (2) P3; folowing (1) P4; folewinge (1) P2; folovyng (1) N8; folwynge (1) C8. Usually in the phrase "[a date] next followynge."
foote *n.* (2) P4; fote (11) P4 N8 (9).
footemen *n.* (1) S1.
for *prep.* (821), ffor (33) all dates and offices. fore (8) S1, S2; fo (1) P3 (D.137.5).
forasmuche *conj.* (1) S1; forasmoch(e) (2) P3.
forbere *inf.* exclude. (1) C4; forbarre (2) C5.
force *n.* strength, military forces. (22) C2, C3; forse (1) C3. Found only in Chancery documents.
foreuermore *adv.* (as one word) (2) C3, C5.
foreyn *adj.* foreign. (3) C3; foren (1) C3.
forfaite *inf.* (1) P4; forfete (1) C4; *3 sing. subj.* forfeite (1) C4; *pl. subj.* forfette (1) C4; *past part.* forfaited (2) P5; forfait (2) C8, S1.
forfaiture *n.* (4) C3; forfetur(e) (3) C3, C4; forfature (1) C4; forfeitur (1) C4; *pl.* forfaitures (2) P5, C3.
forged *vb. past part.* (1) P3.
forgo *inf.* (1) C5.
forme *n.* (29) S1 (17), C3; fourme (63) P2.
forprised *vb. past part.* exempt. (1) C5.
forsaid *adj.* (39) S1, C8; forseyde (20, all but 2 in D. 164), C1; forsaide (19) C8, C1; forseid (18) C1, C2; forsayd (12, all but 2 in D.168); forsayde (8, all but 2 in D.173); forseide (3) S1, C1.
forsake *vb. past part.* (1) C5 (D.218.11); *past.* forsoke (1) C3.
forseyng *ger.* foreseeing, maintaining. (1) N8 (D.233.21).
fortalice *n.* a fortified place. (2) P3 (D.132.13, D.134.13); fortalys (1) P3 (D.133.6). *OED* arch.
forteresses *n.* (1) C5.
forth(e) *adv.* (11) C8, P3; forþe (1) S1; furth (4) C3, C4.
fortheryng(e) *ger.* furthering. (3) C1, P3.
forth riȝt *adv.* (1) P3 (D.142.39).
forthward See forward.
forthwith *adv.* (4) P3, C3; forwiþ (1) S1 (D.81.8).
ffor thy *adv.* forthy, therefore. (1) C8 (D.161.48).
forto *conj.* (as one word) (18) S1, P2.
fortune *n.* (3) P4, C4.

forward *adv.* (2) P3, C3; forthward (1) P4 (D.151.16).
foryeue *inf.* forgive. (1) S1.
foule *adv.* foully. (1) C1 (D.201.30).
found See fynd(e).
founded *vb. past part.* established (of religious houses, etc.) (1) S1.
foundoures *n.* (1) P4.
four(e) *adj.* (3) C1, C2.
fourthe *ordinal adj.* (2) P3, N2 (D.144.9, 234.1); four (1) C1 (D.163.4).
fourtieth *adj.* (2) N6.
foynyng *ger.* thrusting. (1) P3 (D.142.39).
ffraternite *n.* (2) N5.
frauncise *n.* (7) P4, C4; ffraunchise (1) P4; ffraunchess (1) C3; ffraunchiss (1) C2; *pl.* franchises (4) S1, C3; fraunchises (4) C3, C4; frauchiseȝ (3) C4; franchesies (1) C3; frauncheses (1) C3; ffraunchess (1) C3; ffraunchieȝ (1) P3; franchiseȝ (1) C3; fraunchyseȝ (1) C4.
frankplegge *n.* court held for production of members of a tithing. (1) P3.
fraude *n.* (1) C3.
free *adj.* (7) S1, P3; fre (5) S1, C8.
fredom *n.* (3) C5 (D.230); fredam (2) C8; *pl.* fredoms (1) C5.
freehold(e) *n.* (2) C5 (D.231.7, 16).
freeholders *n.* (4) C5 (D.188).
freely *adv.* (1) C4; frely (4) C3, C5; frelich (1) C8 (D.161.6).
frend(e) *n.* (9) PO, P3; *pl.* frendes (7) P3, C3; frendis (3) C3, C5; frendeȝ (2) C5; ffrendes (1) C3; ffrendeȝ (1) C5.
frendschipe *n.* (1) C1; frensship (1) S1.
ffressh *adj.* (1) C3.
fretted *vb. past part.* (1) loaded. (1) P5.
from *prep.* (29) S1, C1; fro (70) S1, C8; froo (2) C4 (D.211); ffrom (1) N8.
fronter *n.* frontier. (1) C5.
ffrountte *n.* front. (1) N8.
frying *adj.* (1) C3 (D.197.15).
fuage *n.* feuage, or fumage, a hearth-tax. (1) S1 (D.71.6, 8). Not in *MED; OED* obs. 1706.
fulfill(e) *inf.* (2) C5; *past part.* fulfilled (1) N5; fulfellid (1) C2.
full *adj., adv.* (21) S1, P2; ful (28) C8, C1.
fullers *n. pl.* cloth workers. (4) C3, C5; fulleres (1) C3; ffulleres (2) C3; ffullers (3) C3 (D.203, 204).
fully *adv.* (16) S1, C2.
fundaccion *n.* (2) S1, P4.
furred *adj.* (1) C3.
further. See ferther.
furthermore. See ferthermore.

Glossary of Forms 343

fynd(e) *inf.* discover, provide for. (11) S1, P3; *3 sing.* fynde (1) C3; fyndeth (1) C5; *3 sing. subj.* fynde (2) S1; *past.* founde (1) P5; fonde (1) C5 (D.201.19); fande (1) C3 (D.185.4); *past part.* found(e) (19) S1, C1; founden (8) C8, S1; yfound (1) C3 (D.208.9); *ger.* fyndyng (1) C5 (D.221.6).
ffysshynges *n.* fish preserves. (1) P3 (D.144.12).
fyve *adj.* (16) C3, N5; fyfe (1) C3.

gaderers *n.* tax-gatherers. (1) P2.
gadre *inf.* gather. (2) C5 (D.223.34, 36); gadery (1) C2 (D.176.9); *past part.* gadred (1) C8.
gage *n.* a pledge, security. (1) P3 (D.148.8).
gaiole *n.* jail. (1) C3.
galaunt *adj.* gallant. (1) C5.
galons *n.* (1) C5.
garbaled *vb. past part.* cleaned (1) C3; garblyd (1) C3. Both in D. 208. *OED* obs. 1812.
gardyn *n.* (1) C3.
garnisons *n.* garrisons, armed troops. (1) S2 (D.96.7). *OED.* obs. 1600.
garnysshyng *ger.* decorated covering. (1) N8.
gartier *n.* here, the Order of the Garter. (1) P2 (D.123.3).
gate *n.* (1) C1; yate (1) C5.
gaynyd *vb. past part.* gained. (1) C5.
general(l) *n.* "in general" (3) S1, S2.
general(l) *adj.* (5) C8, S1; *pl.* generalx (2) P4 (D.156).
gentilesse *n.* (1) P3 (D.129.2).
gentilman *n.* (8) S1, C3; gentylman (1) C2; *pl.* gentilmen (7) S1, C3.
gere *n.* gear. (1) C1.
gete *inf.* (6) P3, C5; geten (1) S1; *past.* gate (2) P3, C5; *past part.* geten (2) S1, P5; geton (1) C4.
geve See yeue.
gide *n.* ? guide. (1) P3 (D.144.13).
gifte See yift(e).
gilde *n.* (4) C3, C5; gylde (1) C3.
gildhalle *n.* (1) C3.
gilty *adj.* (5) P3, C3; gylty (2) P3, C3.
girdill *n.* (1) C3.
gladde *adj.* (2) P2, P3.
gladly *adv.* (1) C2.
gladnesse *n.* (1) P2.
glebe *n.* land forming part of a benefice. (1) C3 (D.197.23). *OED* arch.
gleives *n.* glaives, spear-like weapons. (1) C5 (D.222.12); gleivis (1) C5 (D.222.18).

glorious *adj.* (2) C5 (D.224.7, 8).
glosed *vb. past part.* glossed. (1) C3.
gloses *n.* glosses. (1) C3.
go *inf.* (13) S2, C1; goo (4) S1, S2; goon (1) P2; *3 sing.* goth (1) C5 (D.218.3); *3 sing. subj.* go (1) C1 (D.164.40); *past.* went (1) P3; wende (1) C3 (D.194.6); wentte (1) P2 (D.113.21); *pr. part.* goyng (3) S1, P3; goyn (1) C4 (D.211.3); *past part.* goon (2) P3, P5; goone (1) P2; goen (1) P1 (D.112.7); goo (1) C1 (D.164.25); *ger.* goyng (3) S1, S2.
god *n.* (241) S1, S2; godde (6) P2 (D.113); gode (1) C2 (D.171.9); *gen.* goddes (17) S1, C8; goddis (6) P2, C2; goddys (1) C3; (usually in a phrase like "with Goddes grace.").
gold(e) *n.* (16) P1, C1.
goldsmyth *n.* (4) C2 (D.172).
good *adj.* (59) C8, S1; gode (26) C8, S1; goode (20) S1, C1; goud(e) (3) N2 (D.235); gude (1) P1. See goods.
goodly *adv.* (9) S1, P2; goodely (3) S1, S2; godely (2) P2, C3.
goodnesse *n.* (1) S1; godenesse (1) C1.
goods *n.* merchandise, property. (1) C4 (D.212.10); goodes (24) S1, C1; goodis (2) S1, N5; goodus (2) C3 (D.183); goodys (1) S1; godes (16) S1, P3; godis (1) C5; godys (2) C3 (D.196); godds (1) C3; good(e) (8) P2, C1.
gost *n.* spirit, "holy ghost." (2) S1, P1 (D.10.4, 112.12); goost (1) S1 (D.9.4).
gouernaille *n.* authority. (1) P3 (D.136.2). *OED* obs. 1597.
gouernance *n.* (8) S1, C8; gouernaunce (3) C8, P3; gouuernance (3) P2, C3; gouuernaunce (1) P2; governaunce (1) C3; *pl.* gouernaunces (1) P4.
gouernour *n.* (1) S1; gouuernour (1) C4; *pl.* gouernors (1) C5; gouernours (1) C2.
gouerne *inf.* (6) S1, S2; *3 sing.* gouerneþ (2) S1 (D.43.5, 7); *pl.* gouerne (1) S1; *past part.* gouerned (2) C2, C3.
gowne *n.* (1) C4; *pl.* gownes (1) C3.
grace *n.* (78) C8, S1.
gracious *adj.* (53) P2, C1; graciouse (19) P3, C1; gracieux (13, 15 in D.40) S1, P5; gracyous(e) (7, all in D.164) C1; gratious (2) P2; gracieuse (1) C1; graciouce (1) C5; gracioux (1) P3; gratiouse (1) P2; *pl.* graciouses (2) C1 (D.168.10), C3 (D.186.9).
graciously *adv.* (7) P3, C3; graciousely (2) C3; graciousli (1) C3.
gramer *n.* (11, all but 1 in D. 146) P3, C5; gramere (1) C5; gramare (1) C3.
gras *n.* (1) C2.
graunde *adj.* grand(father). (1) P5 (D.159.45).
graunt(e) *n.* (46) S2, P2; grant(e) (11) S1, S2; *pl.* grauntes (5) P5, C5; grantes (4) S1, S2; grantʒ (1) P3.
graunt *inf.* (41) S2, C1; grante (1) S1; *3 sing.* graunt (1) S1; graunteth (1) P3; grauntith (1) C4; *pl.* graunten (3) N5 (D.239.6, 9), C4 (D.213.11); graunt

(1) P3; grante (1) S1; *past.* grauntede (1) C1; *past part.* graunted (34) S1 (3), P3; granted (30) S1, S2 (in 28 cases); grauntyd (7) C3; grauntid (6) C3, C4; grauntede (1) P2; grantid (1) P3; grauntyde (1) C3; *pr. part.* grauntyng (1) C5.

grauntdame *n.* (1) C5.

gredyrons *n.* gridirons. (1) C3.

gree *n.* agreement to pay. (1) C3 (D.191.9). *OED* examples after 1606 dial.

grete *vb. 1 sing.* greet. (2) P3; *1 pl.* grete (48) S1, S2; greet (1) S5 (D.109.1). Almost always found in varients of the formulaic "We grete yow well." *ger.* gretyng (2) S3, C3 (as a salutation).

grete *adj.* great. (211) C1, S1; greet (37) S1, C1; gret (19) C8, S1; greete (4) P2, P4; grette (1) P2. The signet office clearly preferred greet, particularly to refer to the Great Seal, thereby avoiding confusion with grete, which is used in the formulaic salutation "We grete yow wel." *comp.* greter (1) P4; gretter (2) S1; *supl.* grettest (2) C2, C3.

grene *adj.* green. (1) C3.

gretly *adv.* (2) S1, P2; gretely (4) S1, S2; gretli (1) C5.

greuaunce *n.* (1) C4.

greue *n.* grief. (1) P2; *pl.* griefs (1) S2.

greuous *adj.* (4) S1, S2; greuouse (5) S1, C2.

grevousely *adv.* (1) C3; grevously (2) C4, C5; greuously (2) C4, C5.

greved *vb. past part.* grieved. (2) C4, C5.

grocer *n.* (1) N5; grocier (1) S2.

grome *n.* groom. (1) C5; *pl.* gromes (1) C5.

ground *n.* (3) C4, C5; grounde (2) S2, P3; grond (4) S2 (D.105); grunde (1) N8; *pl.* grondeʒ (1) C4.

growe *inf.* (3) C4, C5; *3 sing.* groweth (1) P3; grewyth (1) C3; growes (1) C2 (D.169.10); *3 pl.* groweth (1) C5 (D.223.21); *pr. pl.* growyng (1) C5; *past part.* growen (1) C5; *ger.* growyng (3) C4, C5.

grucching *ger.* complaining, grumbling. (1) P2; grocchyng (1) C8 (D.117.12). *OED* obs. 1679.

guarde See safeguarde.

gunnys *n.* guns. (1) P3. gonnys (1) C3.

haburdassher *n.* (4) C5 (D.219, 220); *pl.* haberdasshers (1) C5 (D.221.34).

haboryon *n.* habergeon, a mail coat. (1) C5; *pl.* habergeons (1) C5.

half(e) *n.* (29) P3, C3.

hall(e) *n.* (10) P3, C5.

haluyndele, haluyndell *n.* half. (2) N6 (D.241).

hanaper *n.* office of Chancery to which fees were paid. (1) S1 (D.11.3). This office abolished 1832.

hand *n.* (16), hande (3) S1, C1; honde (3) C8, N2; hond (1) C1; *pl.* handes (31) S1, P2; haundes (1) C3; hondes (2) S1, C3; hondeȝ (2) C4; hondis (1) C5; hondys (1) C3.
hangith *vb. 3 sing.* (1) C1; *pr. part.* hangyng (5) S1, C3; hongyng (2) C3, C4; hanging (1) P4; *past part.* hanged (2) C8, C3. See hongynges.
happen *3 sing. subj.*, usually in a phrase beginning "if it happen" etc. (4) S1, P3; happe (1) C4 (D.215.14); *past.* happed (2) P3; *past part.* hapned (1) S1(D.46.3).
harde *adj.* severe. (1) C3 (D.190.25).
hardy *adv.* bold, audacious. (2) C8, C3 (D.161.39, 193.21).
harme *n.* (5) S1, P3; *pl.* harmes (4) S2, C3; harmeȝ (1) C2; harmys (1) C3.
harmed *past part.* (1) S2; *ger.* harmyng (2) S1, C2.
harmeful *adj.* (1) S2.
harneis *n.* equipment. (1) C5; herneys (4) C4 (D.211); hernois (1) S2.
haste *n.* (21) S1, C1; hast (11) S1, P1; haast (1) S1. A formulaic word in phrases like "in al haste," etc.
hasted *vb. past part.* (3) S1, S2.
hastely *adv.* (1) P2; hasteli (1) C1; hastylych (1) C3 (D.196.23); hastiefly (1) C4 (D.211.35).
hasty *adj.* quick, prompt. (6) S1, S2; hastie (1) S1; hastife (1) C2 (D.169.8).
hate *n.* (1) P3.
have *vb.* (30); haue (428) (totals); *inf.* have; haue; haf(e) (6) C1, C2; han (2) C1; *1 sing.* have; haue; *3 sing.* have; haue; haþ (18, 14 in S1, S2); haath (3) S1; haaþ (2) S1; haþe (1) C4; haht (2) P2 (D.113.13, 17); has (5) P1, C2; *pl.* have; haue; han (19) C8, C1; haan (1) S1 (D.69.25); hauen (1) C1 (D.162.4); havyn (1) C2 (D.174.3); has (1) N4 (D.238.19); *1 sing. subj.* haue; *3 sing. subj.* have; haue; *pl. subj.* have; *past sing. & pl.* hadd(e) (59); had(e) (48); hed (1) N2 (D.236.9); *past pl.* hadden (1) S1 (D.5.4); haddeyn (1) S2 (D.81.5); *pr. part.* hauyng(e) (12) S1, P3; havyng (4) S1, C3; *past part.* had(e) (18); hadd(e) (15) haad(e) (4) S1 (D.69); yhadde (2) N2 (D.235.7, 8); *ger.* hauyng (10); havyng (3); hauynge (2) S1, C1; havyn (1) C2 (D.174.3).
hauene *n.* haven. (3) C3; *pl.* hauenes (11) C3 (all in D.187).
hay *n.* fodder. (1) C3.
he *sing. masc. pron.* (382) C8, PO; *gen.* his (553); hise (3) C1 (D.163 only); hus (15, all in D. 218) C5; hys (5) S2, C2; is (1) C3 (D.185.6); *obj.* him (113), hym (287) C8, S1. See also himself.
hed *n.* head. (1) C5; hede (2) C3, C4.
heed *n.* notice, attention, as in "take heed." (1) S2; hede (2) C8, S1.
hefe *n.* heft, weight. (1) C3 (D.190.12).
hegges *n.* hedges. (1) C3.
heir (2) C3, C4; heire (3) S1, S2; heyr (1) C1; *pl.* heirs (12) C3, C4; heires (16) P2, C3; heireȝ (2) C4 (D.210); heres (2) P3, C3; herys (1) P3; heyres (1)

Glossary of Forms 347

C3; heyrys (2) P2; eyres (2) N8, C1 (D.164.6, 233.6); eyrys (1) N8 (D.233.2).
help *inf.* (2) C1; helpe (1) S1; *pr. part and ger.* helpyng (3) S1, S4.
help *n.* (8), helpe (15) C8, C1; heelp (2) S1.
helth *n.* health. (2) P3, S5; hele (3) S1, P2.
hens forth *sub.* "fro hens forth." (1) P5 (D.158.41).
hensforward *adv.* (1) P4 (D.154.4).
herbergage *n.* lodging. (1) P3 (D.146.16).
here *inf.* to hear. (5) S2, P3; heer (1) C3; hier (1) P2 (D.117.18); *3 sing. subj.*
  heer (1) P5; *past.* harde (1) N2 (D.236.9); *past part.* herd (2) C1, S1; *ger.*
  heryng (1) N2.
here *adv.* (57) C8, S1; her (15) S1, C1; heer (3) S1; heere (4) S1, S2; hier (2) P2.
hereafter (as one word) *adv.* (5) S1, P2; hereaftre (1) S1; herafter (1) P1.
herebefore *adv.* (2) P3, S4.
herein (as one word) *adv.* (1) P4; herinne (1) P3.
hereto (as one word) *adv.* (1) P3; herto (1) C3.
hereupon *adv.* (1) P3; heruppon (1) P2; hervpon (1) P3.
herewiþynne (as one word) *adv.* (1) S1.
heritage *n.* inheritance. (6) C1, S1; herytage (4) C1 (D.164).
herneys See harneis.
herneysed *vb. past part.* adorned. (1) C3 (D.197.17).
herof (as one word) *adv.* here of. (4) S1, N4.
hert(e) *n.* heart. (10) C1, S1; *gen.* herttis (1) P2; *pl.* herteȝ (1) C4.
hertily *adv.* (2) P2, P3; hertly (9) P3, P4; hertely (3) S1, P3; hertlye (1) P3;
  herttyly (1) P2.
heuynesse *n.* (3) S1, P3; heuynysse (1) C5.
hevy *adj.* (1) P3; heuy (2) C2, C3; *comp.* hevier (1) C3.
hewe *vb. past pl.* (1) C5 (D.222.19); hewen (1) C3.
heynouse *adj.* heinous. (1) C3 (D.201.29).
hidde *vb. past part.* hidden. (1) C8.
hider *adv.* hither. (5) S2, C3; hedir (1) S1.
hiderto *adv.* (2) P4, C3.
hiderward *adv.* (1) C8; hidirward (1) C2.
hides *n.* leather. (1) C3.
hidings *n.* hiding places. (1) C8.
hidous *adj.* hideous. (1) C3.
high *adj.* (30) S1, C2; hygh(e) (8) P2, C3; heygh (4) C4, N8; heigh (3) C3, P4;
  highe (1) C3; hiegh (1) P3; hye (9) P2, PC3; heye (5) C1 (D.163); hie (4)
  C3, C4.
highness *n.* (1) C5; highnesse (18) C3, C4; highnes (8) P2, C5; hieghness (4)
  P3, C3; heighnesse (3) C3, P4; hignes (1) P2 (D.115.23); hynesse (8) P2,
  P3; hinesse (1) C5 (D.218.42).
himself *pro. reflexive and intensive.* (2) P4, N5 (D.156.4, 239.21); hymself(e)

(10) C8, S1; himsilf (2) C5 (D.218); hymselue (1) C4.
hindre *inf.* hinder. (1) P5; *past part.* hyndred (1) S1; *ger.* hindryng(e) (4) S1, C3; hyndryng ((3) C3, C5; hynderyng (2) C2, C3. See hynderance.
hode *n.* head cover. (2) P3, C4; *pl.* hodes (1) C3.
hogges *n.* hogs. (1) C3.
holde *inf.* (7) S1, C1; hald (1) C3; halde (1) S1; *3 sing.* holde (1) C4; holdeth (1) C5 (D.217.6); holdith (1) P4; *pl.* hald(e) (6) S1 (5), S2; holde (1) S1; *past* huld (1) C5 (D.222.16); *pr. part.* holdyng (1) C3; *past part.* holden (20) C8, C1; hold(e) (6) S2, C3; halden (2) S1, P3; haldyn (1) C2; yhold (1) C2 (D.178.8); yholde (1) C3 (D.199.28). Phrases like "to holden at Westminster" seem to have been largely formulaic.
holders *n.* owners. (3) C3.
holdes *n.* fortified places. (1) C2.
hole *adj.* whole. (18) C3, C4; hool (3) C1, P3.
holly *adv.* wholly. (2) N8; holli (1) N8; hooly (2) S1, P3 (D.62.12, 149.16).
holy *adj.* (23) S1, C1; holi (1) S1; hooly (1) C3 (D.177.9).
homage *n.* (5) S2, C4; hommage (1) S2.
home *n.* (1) S1; hom (1) S1; hoom (9, all S1, S2).
homeward *adv.* (2) C3, C5.
hongynges *n. pl.* wall hangings. (1) C5 (D.222.19). See hangith.
honorable *adj.* (3) C5; honourable (1) C5; honnourable (1) C5.
honour *n.* (3) P3, P4; *pl.* feudal holdings, honureʒ (3), honoureʒ (1) all in D.210.
hoost *n.* (28), oost (5), ost (1), all in S1 and S2, referring to Henry V's army in France.
hope *n.* (2) C1, C2.
horrible *adj.* (4) C3; horryble (1) C3; horible (3) C4.
horribely *adv.* (1) C3; horrebely (1) C3.
hors *n. sing.* (1) P3; *pl.* hors (3) S2, P3.
horsback *n.* (1) C2; horsbak (2) C3, P4.
horsmen *n.* (1) S1.
hospital(l) *n.* (10) S1, P3; ospital (5) S1.
hostrie *n.* inn. All entries in D. 192 and D.193. (1) C3; hostrye (1) C3; *pl.* hostryes (3) C3; hostries (1) C3.
hosyng *n.* hosing. (1) N8 (D.233.12).
houreʒ *n.* (1) C3; owres (1) C5.
house *n.* (7) S1, P4; hous (16) S1, S2; hows (6) S1 (5), C3; howse (1) S1; *pl.* houses (11) C8, C3; hovses (1) N8; howsys (1) C3.
household *n.* (10) P5 (all in D. 158); houshold (7) P3, C3; housholde (1) C4; housold (1) C3 (D.189.3); howshald (1) C1; howshold(e) (2) S1.
housid *vb. past part.* housed. (1) C5 (D.222.26); howsyd (1) N4.
housyng *ger.* (1) C3.
how *adv., conj.* (36) S1, C8; howe (20) P2, C3; hou (4) P3, C4; howh (1) C3;

hough (2) C3 (D.187.4, 18).
huissher See vssher.
humble *adj.* (21) S1, P1.
humbly *adv.* (10) P3, C3; humblely (2) C3; humblie (1) P2; humebely (1) C2.
humblesse *n.* deference. (2) P2 (D.113.7, 22).
hundred *numeral* (2) P3, N5; hundreth (1) P3 (D.143.3); hundred *n.* subdivision of a county. (1) C3; *pl.* hundredes (2) P3. C3.
hures *n.* head coverings. (1) C3 (D.197.13) *OED* obs. 1482.
hurt *n.* (18) p1, S2; hurte (9) P2, P3; *pl.* hurtes (2) C4, C5.
hurt *inf.* (2) C3, C4; *past* (2) C4, C5; *past part.* hurt (2) P1, P5; hurte (1) P2.
husbandman *n.* (2) C3; husbundman (1) C3.
husbond *n.* (3) C4, C5; howsbond (1) S2; *pl.* husbondes (3) C5; husbondeʒ (1) C5.
hustenge *n.* a city court. (1) C3 (D.181.3).
hyght *vb. past part.* called. (1) S1 (D.28.2). *OED* arch.
hynderance *n.* (1) C1. See hindre.
hyred *vb. past.* hired or bribed. (2) P3, C3.

I *sing. pron.* (154) PO, C1; Y (5) PO, C1; *gen.* my (158) PO, C1; myn (14) C1, P3; myne (8) C1, C2; *obj.* me (55) PO, C1.
iakes *n.* stuffed or plated jackets for protection in fighting. (1) C5 (D.222.12). Form not in *OED*.
iayler *n.* jailer. (1) C5 (D.225.12).
ich, iche See ech; ichone see echone.
iewelx See iuel.
iewys *n.* juise, judicial sentence. (1) C2 (D.174.11). *OED* obs. 1626.
if *conj.* (77) C8, S1; yf (26) S1, P2; yif (18) C8, S1; ʒif (5) C1 (4), P5; ʒef (5) C1 (D.164); yef (4) C1, C3.
ile See isle.
ilond *n.* island. (5) C5. (D.218, see isle).
immediatly *adv.* (6) P3, C3.
immunite (1) C4 (D.213.17).
impediment *n.* (2) C4, C5 (D.211.16, 224.31).
importable *adj.* heavy severe, unendurable. (6) C1, C3; ymportable (1) C5.
importune *adj.* persistent. (1) P5 (D.158.22).
importunite *n.* persistence. (1) P5 (D.158.30).
imposicion *n.* tax or levy. (1) C4 (D.213.15).
impotent *adj.* feeble, weak. (1) C3 (D.202.42).
impriseth *vb. 3 sing.* undertakes. (1) C3 (D.188.16).
imprisoned *vb. past part.* (2) C3; enprisoned (1) C3; emprisoned (2) C8, C5; inprisoned (1) C3; *ger.* enprisonyng (1) C3.
imprisonment *n.* (1) C5; enprisonement (3) P3, C3; enprisononement (error?)

(1) C1 (D.162.5); *pl.* emprisonmentʒ (1) C8; enprisonementʒ (1) C3.
in *prep.* (1683) C8, etc.; yn (199) N8, S1; ynne (27) S1, C1; inne (9) C8, S1, P1; en (2) S1 (D.2.6, D.8.2): "en due forme."
incidentʒ *n. pl.* (1) P5.
inconuenyence *n.* (1) P4; *pl.* inconueniences (3) C3, C5.
inconueniently *adv.* (1) P3.
incorrupte *adj.* not decayed. (1) P4 (D.153.4).
indenture *n.* (5) N5 (D.239); endenture (9) P2, P4; endentur (7) N8 (5 times, D.233), C5, N6; *pl.* endentures (8) S1, N2; indentures (3) P3, N4; endenturis (2) C5, N5; endenturs (1) C2. See also denture.
indifferently *adv.* (1) P2; indefferently (1) C5.
indingnacion *n.* (1) P4 (D.154.4).
indirectly *adv.* (1) C4.
inducte *vb. past part.* inducted. (1) P3.
infeccion *n.* (1) C3 (D.207.8).
infectif *adj.* infectious. (1) C3 (D.207.4).
infenytly *adv.* infinitely. (1) C3 (D.202.32).
infirmite *n.* (2) S1, C3.
influent *adj.* effective, influential. (1) C4 (D.213.4).
informacion *n.* (3) C8, S2; enformacion (1) P1; *pl.* informacions (1) C2.
informed See enforme.
infortune *n.* misfortune. (1) C3 (D.180.16).
ingyned *vb. past part.* tortured, engined. (1) C3 (D.196.12).
inhabitant *n.* (1) C5; *pl.* inhabitauntʒ (1) C3; inhabitauncs (1) C3; enhabitantes (1) C5.
inhabitt *inf.* (1) C3; *3 pl.* enhabyte (1) C3; *past part.* enhabited (1) C5.
inheritaunce *n.* (1) P4; enheritaunce (5) C3, C4.
iniuries *n.* (1) S1 (D.44.3).
inoght *n., adv.* enough. (1) P1 (D.112.10); anogh (1) S1 (D.43.10); ynogh (1) S2; ynow (1) C2 (D.169.7).
inquiete *inf.* disturb, disquiet. (1) S1; *past part.* inquieted (1) C5.
instance *n.* (1) C1; instaunce (2) C5.
institute *vb. past part.* put in possession of a benefice. (2) P3 (D.128.4, 12).
instruccion *n.* (3) S1, P3.
instruct *vb. past part.* instructed. (1) C5.
instrument *n.* (1) P1 (D.112.9).
insufficeant *adj.* incompetent, unable to act. (1) C3 (D.181.20).
insurreccion *n.* (1) C3 (D.189.7).
intendaunce *n.* management, attention. (1) C5 (D.214.6). *OED* obs. 1611.
intendith *vb. 3 sing.* intends, plans. (1) C4 (D.213.18).
intent *n.* (1) P4; entent (29) S1, S2; entente (4) C1, S2.
interesse *n.* legal claim. (2) C4 (D.210.21, 24).

interrupcion *n*. (2) P4, C5.
interrupte *vb. pl.* (1) P4 (D.153.10).
into *prep*. (43) S1, P3; ynto (2) S1, P3.
intollerable *adj*. (1) C4 (D.217.9).
invndacions *n*. (1) C5.
inward *adv*. (1) P1; ynward (1) N8.
ioialx See iuel.
ioye *n*. joy. (1) P2.
ioyfull *adj*. (2) S2, P2.
ioyned *vb. past part*. joined. (1) P3.
irland *n*. (8) S1, P3; irlande (4) S2, P3; irelond (4) C4 (D.215); irlond (1) S2.
irne *n*. iron. (1) C5.
isle *n*. (1) C3 (D.187.3); ile (26, all in D.218 referring to the Isle of Wight) C5.
issue *n*. (5) C5; issew (1) C1; issu (1) N4; *pl*. issues (12) S1, P2; issueȝ (1) C4; issuȝ (1) P3.
it *neuter pron*. (213) S1, C8, etc.; hit (161) N8, PO; yt (8) P3, C3; hyt (6) P2, C2; itt (4) C3 (D.201); ht (1) C1 (D.162.12). Nearly half of the instances of hit are in Signet documents.
item *adv*. adapted from Latin official documents; next, in addition. (19) S1, P2. Appears mainly in informal Privy Seal Minutes.
iuel *n*. jewel. (1) P1; iuillo (1) P1 (cancelled). (Both in D.112.9); *pl*. iewelx (1) P3 (D.148.8); ioialx (2) P3 (D.131.22, 23).
iuge *n*. judge. (1) C8; *pl*. iuges (5) C1, P2; iugges (5) C3.
iuged *vb. past part*. judged. (2) C3, C4.
iugement *n*. judgement (4) S5, C3; iuggement (4) P4, C3.
jupardie *n*. jeopardy. (1) P3; iooardie (1) P3. (Both are in D.136.5).
iurisdiccion *n*. (2) P3, C5; *pl*. iurisdictions (3) C4 (D.210); iurisdictiones (1) C4 (D.210).
iurours *n*. jurors. (1) C3; iorores (3) C3 (D.189).
iust *adj*. true. (1) P5; iuste (2) S1, C2.
iustice *n*. (12) S1, C1; iustyce (1) C1; iustise (1) C1 (D.164.20); *pl*. iustices (13) S1, P2; iusticeȝ (12) C3 (D.192.27, 29).
iustified *vb. past part*. (1) P3.
iustly *adv*. honestly, fairly. (1) S1 (D.32.9).

keepe *inf*. (1) S2; kepe (16) S1, C1; *3 sing*. kepith (2) C5; kepyth (1) C3, kepeth (1) P5; *pl*. kepe (3) C1, S2; *subj. sing*. kepe (5) S1, C1; *subj. pl*. kepe (1) P2; *past* kept (1) C1; kepe (1) C3 (D.190.27); *past part*. kept (17) S1, C1; kepte (3) C4, C5; keped (1) C3; *ger*. keeping (46) S1, S2; kepyng(e) (36) S1, P1; keepinge (1) S2; keepynge (1) S2. Usually in the phrase "and God haue yow in his keping."
kempers *n*. cloth combers. (1) C5 (D.217.10).

keper *n.* keeper, usually of the Privy Seal. (14) P3, P4; *pl.* kepers (2) C3.
kerchieffes *n.* (1) C4.
keyes *n.* (1) C4 (D.212.10).
king *n.* (66) S1, C2; kyng (298) C8, C1; kynge (9) P1, P2; kinge (2) C3, P5; *gen.* kynges (60) P2, C1; kinges (16) P2, P3; kyngis (7) C1, P3; kingges (5) C5 (D.218); kinggis (4) C5 (D.218); kyngeʒ (2) P2, C4; kingis (1) P5; kynggys (1) C3 (D.185.8); kyngus (1) N2 (D.235.10); kyngs (1) C3 (D.186.4) *pl.* kynges (3) C3, P5.
kirk, kyrk, etc. See church(e).
kirtell *n.* gown. (1) C3; kirtyll (1) C3.
kist *n.* chest. (1) P1 (D.112.8).
knight *n.* (9) S1, S2; knyght (26) S1, C2; knyghte (3) C3, N5; knyʒt (2) S2 (D.76); *pl.* knyghtes (3) C3, C5; knyghts (2) C2, C4.
knowe *inf.* (1) S1; knawe (2) S1; *imp.* knoweþ (1) S1; *1 sing.* knowe (1) C1; *3 sing.* knoweth (2) P3; knowyht (1) P2 (D.113.4); knowht (1) P2 (D.113.24); *pl.* knowe (14) S1, C8 (usually in the phrase "as ye knowe"); knawe (1) S1; knowe (1) C3; knowin (1) P2 (D.117.22); *past* knewe (3) P3, C3; *past part.* knowen (10) C8, S1; knowe (3) C8, C1; knawen (2) C2 (D.173.11), C3 (D.201.29); knowyn (1) C4 (D.210.18) yknowe (1) N5 (D.241.1).
knowlege *n.* (3) S2; knowlage (3) P1, C5; knowlech(e) (3) S1, S2; knoweleche (3) C1, S1; knowelache (2) S1; knawlech(e) (2) S1, C3 (D.185.4); knolach (2) C4; knawelygge (1) C2 (D.171.6); knowlache (1) S2; knaweleche (1) S1; knowlich (1) P2; knowloche (1) S1 (D.5.10).
knowleged *vb. past part.* (1) C3; knowleched (1) C4; knoweleched (1) N2; knovlegged (1) C3 (D.199.17); knawlaget (1) C3 (D.191.4).
knyff *n.* knife. (2) C3; *pl.* knyves (1) C3.
kutte *vb. past sing.* (1) C4 (D.212.8).
kychyn *n.* kitchen. (1), kechyn (1), both in N8 (D.233.19, 21); kichon (1) C3 (D.197.15).
kylled *vb. past part.* (1) C2.
kyn *n. pl.* kine, cattle. (1) C3 (D.197.21).
kyndenesse *n.* (1) P3; *pl.* kyndenesses (1) P3.
kynnesman *n.* (1) C2.
kysse *inf.* (1) C3; *past.* kissed (1) C3; *ger.* kyssyng (1) C3; kissyng (1) C3. All citations from D.207.

labour *n.* (10) C8, S1; laboure (4) P2, C5; labor (1) P2; labore (2) P3, C3; labur (1) C3 (D.184.4); *pl.* labours (2) P3; laboures (1) P3.
laboure *inf.* (1) C3; labor (1) C3; labore (1) C3; *subj. pl.* laboure (1) S1; *past.* labored (4) P3 (D.142); *past part.* labored (5) P3, C3; laboured (1) P5.
laborenis *n.* laborers. (1) S4 (D.107.5). Form not recorded in *OED; MED* meaning no. 6, *labour, laboras.*

Glossary of Forms

laborious *adj.* (1) P2 (D.117.6).
lack *n.* (1) C2; lak (3) S2, P4; lacke (2) S1, C5; lakke (1) C3. See lak .
lade *vb. past part.* laden, loaded. (3) P3, C3.
lady *n.* (19) PO, C1; *gen.* ladyes (1) C1.
lak *inf.* lack. (1) P4; *3 subj.* lak (2) S1, P4; *ger.* lakking (2) C3.
lambes *n.* (1) C3.
land *n.* (29) S1, C1; lond (20) C1, S1 (8 in D.214, D.215, D.218); londe (7) C8, C1; lande (6) S1, C3; *pl.* londes (21) S1, C3 (9 in N documents); landes (18) S1, P2; londis (12) C3, N5 (D.189, 241); londeʒ (8) C4, C5 (D.210, 222); londys (2) P3 (D.144); landis (1) N5; landeʒ (1) C4.
langage *n.* (1) P3 (D.142.28).
large *adj.* (9) C1, P3.
largesse *n.* (1) P5: "his oune roiale largesse" (D.159.23).
las *conj.* unless. (1) C4 (D.211.35) *OED* obs. 1762.
last *adj., adv.* (48) S1, C1; laste (5) P2, P3.
late *adj.* former, deceased. (37) all decades and offices, *adv.* lately (70) all decades and offices; lat *adv.* (1) N2 (D.235.5); *supl.* latyste (1) N5 (D.241.1).
later *adv.* (1) error for less(e)? in the phrase "neuer þe later." S1 (D.69.26).
Latine *n.* (1) S2 (D.81.13); Latyn (1) P3 (D.146.5).
latter *adj.* (1) C3.
lavors *n.* pitchers, water jugs. (1) C3 (D.197.14).
lawe *n.* (50) C1, S1; *pl.* lawes (6) S2, C3; laws (1) C1.
lawful *adj.* (1) C8; lawfull (3) C3, C5; laweful (1) C2; lauful(l) (2) C5; lavfull (1) N2; *pl.* lawefulles (1) C4 (D.211.13). See lefull.
lawfully *adv.* (3) S1, P4; lawefully (1) S1.
lay(e) *adj.* non-clerical. (5) C3, C4.
ledyth *vb. 3 sing.* leads. (1) C1; *past.* ledde (1) C3 (D.201.7); *past part.* led (1) C5; ledde (1) C3.
leful(l) *adj.* lawful, permissable, etc. (5) N8, N5; liefull (1) C5 (D.231.13). See lawful.
lefully *adv.* justifiably. (1) N5.
lemys *n.* limbs. (1) C1 (D.165.9).
lene *inf.* lend. (3) P3 (D.131); *past part.* lent (6) P3 (D.131).
length *n.* (2) N4; lengyth (1) N8 (D.233.19).
lerne *inf.* (4) C5; *past part.* lerned (3) P2, C4; lernyd (1) C5 (D.221.31).
lernyng *n.* learning. (1) C5.
lese *inf.* lose. (1) C3 (D.202.20); leese (1) S1 (D.31.5); *ger.* lesyng (1) C1. See lost.
lese *n.* lease. (1) N8 (D.233.12).
less *adv.* (3) C3, C4; lasse (2) C1, C3.
lessour *n.* lessor. (1) N8.
let *inf.* allow. (1) P1 (D.112.2); lete (1) P2; lette (1) S2; *3 sing.* latith (1) C3; *pl.* lete (4) S1, P2 (D.57.1 etc. "we lete yow wite"); *past* lete (2) P3, C3

(D.145.18 "(he) lete theym walke"); *pr. part.* latyng (1) S1 (D43.9); *ger.* lettynge (1) C3 (D.189.13).

let *inf.* rent. (1) N5 (D.240.16); *past part.* leten (1) N5 (D.240.3); *ger.* letyng (1) P2 (D.115.13).

lethor *n.* leather. (1) C3.

lette *inf.* hinder, prevent. (3) P3, P5 (D.145.15, 188.17); *3 sing.* letteth (1) S2 (D.89.3); *past.* letted (1) P2 (D.122.32).

lettre *n.* (14) S1, P3, invariably refers to Signet or Privy Seal missives; *pl.* lettres (175) S1, C1; letters (5) P2, P3; letteres (1) C4 (D.210.3); lettris (2) P2.

letys *n. pl.* lete courts, local courts with minor powers. (1) P3 (D.144.13).

leuacion *n.* in the Mass, the elevation of the Host and Chalice. (1) C3. *OED* obs. 1559.

leeve *n.* permission. (4) C3, C5; leue (2) C8, S1.

leve *n.* leave. (4) C3, C5.

leve *inf.* leave. (4) P3, C5; leue (3) C5; *subj. pl.* leue (3) S1, P4; *past* left (1) N2; lefft (1) C1; *pr. part.* levyng (3) P3, C3; leuyng (1) S1; *past part.* left (3) S1, P1; lefte (1) P3; yleft (1) N2 (D.235.10); *ger.* levyng (1) C5.

leuer *adv. comp.* of lef, rather, more agreeable. (2) S1; *supl.* leuest (1) S1 (D.43.19).

leuyed *vb. past part.* levied. (1) C3 (D.188.3).

leye *inf.* lay. (1) C3 (D.190.22); *past pl.* leyn (1) P3; leyed (1) C3; *past part.* laide (1) C8; leide (1) C5; leyd (1) S1; leyde (1) C5.

liberall *adj.* "scholars of all other liberall sciences . . . savyng onely for Scolers of Gramer." (1) P3 (D.146.24).

liberate *n.* used only in referring to writs of liberate and allocate, which ordered official agencies to pay the party named in the writ. (14) S1, S2.

liberte *n.* legal privilege. (4) C4, C5; *pl.* libertees (13) S1, C3; libertes (2) S1, P3; liberteeʒ (2) C4; liberteʒ (1) C4.

licence *n.* official authorization. (7) S1, P3; licens (1) P5 (D.158.35); *pl.* licences (1) P3.

liege *adj.* (42) C1, S1; lige (7) C8 (D.161); lyge (5) C8, P2; lege (1) C2; lyege (1) C3.

lieges *n. pl.* (7) S1, C1; liegis (1) C3; lyges (1) C8.

lieth See lyeth.

lieutenancie *n.* (2) P3, P4.

lieutenant *n.* deputy ruler. (8) P3, C4; leutenant (1) C4 (D.215.23); lewtenant (1) C5, lewtenaunt (1) C5 (D.218); liwtenant (1) C3; *pl.* lieutenantʒ (3) P2, P4.

life *n.* (1) P2 (D.118.5); lif (8) S2, P4; lyfe (7) P3, C5; lyf (7) S1, C1; lyve (3) P2, C1; lyff (2) C1, C5; liffe (1) C5; *gen.* lyuys (1) P2; *pl.* lyues (1) S2; lyves (1) C1.

ligeaunce *n.* (4) C8, C4.

ligeman *n.* (1) S1 (D.65.2).

Glossary of Forms 355

light *n*. point of view. (1) C4 (D.211.7).
lighterman *n*. (1) C5.
lignie *n*. line of descent. (1) P2.
like *adv.* and *prep.* (29) S1, C1; lyke (16) S2, P2; lyk (5) S1, P2; liche (3) P1, P3 (D.111.5, 149.16, 169.6).
like *inf.* (2) C3, C5; lyke (1) S1 (e.g., "as may like vnto your good lordship," D.225.21); *3 pres.* liketh (2) C2, C3; lyketh (1) C3; likeþ (1) S1; lykis (1) P2 (D.119.3); lykys (1) P2 (D.120.4); *3 pres. impersonal subj.* like (17), lyke (13) all offices and periods (e.g., "ȝif it like to the kyng," D.163.27); *past* liked (4) C3, C5; lyked (2) C5 (D.226.5, 10); *past part.* liked (4) P3, C4; lykyd (2) P2, C3; liket (1) P1 (D.112.2) (e.g., "it hath liked your highnesse," D.215.2).
likely *adv.* (2) P3, C5; likly (4) P3, C3; lykly (2) P3, C3; like (2) C5 (D.218.30, 31).
liklinesse *n*. (1) P4; liklynesse (2) P3, C3; lyklynesse (1) P2.
liklyhode *n*. (1) C4.
limit *inf.* (1) S2; *past part.* limited (3) S2, P3; lymyted (2) C5; lemytedd (1) P3; limite (1) C5; limitte (1) C5; lymytte (1) C3.
list *vb.* please *3 sing.* (1) P2 (D.115.22); *pl.* list (1) C2 (D.172.10); *past part.* list (1) C5 (D.221.19).
litel *adj.* (2) C1, S2; litil (3) S1, P3; litill (1) C5; lytle (1) C5; lytyll (1) C2; *comp.* lesse (3) C3, C5; lasse (2) C1, C3; *supl.* lest(e) (4) S2, P2; leest(e) (2) C8, P2.
livere *n*. delivery of legal rights. (1) C3; liueree (6) S1, C4; lyuere (2) S1; lyuerey (2) C3; liuerey (1) C3; lyueree (1) S1; lyvere (1) C3.
loggyng *n*. lodging. (1) P3; loogyng (1) C4 (D.216.8); *pl.* loggynges (1) P5.
logik *n*. (1) C3 (D.197.9).
logyd *vb. past part.* lodged. (1) C3.
loked *vb. past* looked. (1) C3.
lollardrie *n*. (2) C2 (D.174.3, 9).
londholders *n. pl.* (1) C3; londholdres (1) C3 (D.184.2, 12).
long *adj.* (22) S1, P2; longe (17) C8, S1; lang (1) C2 (D.169.2); lange (1) C2 (D.173.8); *comp.* lenger (2) P3; lenggre (1) C3 (D.185.11).
long(e) *inf.* belong. (4) S1, N8; *3 sing.* longeth (14) S1, C1; longeþ (9) S1, S2; loongeth (2) P2; longyth (1) N8; *3 pl.* langeth (1) P3; longen (4) S1, S2; *past.* longed (1) S1; *pr. part.* longyng (8) S1, C1; longing (3) P2; longgyng (1) P3; longyn (1) P4.
lord *n*. (301) C8. PO, etc. lorde (72) C8, S1; *gen.* lordes (4) C8, P3; lordis (2) P3, C5; *pl.* lordes (67) C8, S1; lordys (9) P2, C2; lords (1) C5; lordeȝ (1) C4; lordȝ (1) C4.
lordship *n*. (33) C8, S1; lordshipp (7) P3, C4; lordeschip(p) (2) C2, C3; lordshippe (1) P2; lordchipe (1) P4; *pl.* lordshippes (4) S1, C3; lordshipes (2) C2, C3; lordeship(p)es (2) C3, C5; lordshippis (2) C2; lordshupes (2) C3

(D.185.2, 7); lordships (1) S1 (D.1.2); lorshupes (1) C3 (D.185.1).
losse n. (9) P2, C3; lose (1) C3 (D.196.28); pl. losses (2) C5.
lost vb. past part. lost. (6) S1, C3; loste (1) P2. See lese.
loude adj. (1) C8 (D.161.17).
love n. (1) C2, C3; loue (18) C1, P3; luf (1) C3 (D.173.17).
lowe adj. (1) N4.
lowlinesse n. (1) P2.
lowly adj. (2) P2, C3; lowely (4) P3, C3; lowelly (1) C3; loweli (1) C3; lowelich (1) P2 (D.123.1).
lucre n. monetary gain, advantage. (1) C4 (D.213.3).
lust vb. 3 sing. (impers.) pleases. (1) C8; pl. (impers.) lust (2) S1.
luste n. pleasure. (1) P2 (D.113.2).
lychwyse adv. (1) S1 (D.32.13).
lyeth vb. 3 sing. (2) P3, C2; lyth (1) C5; pl. lieth (1) C3 (D.189.46), lye (2) C2, C5; past lay (3) C4, P5; pr. part. lying (3) C3, C4; lyyng (1) C5 (D.218.32); lieng (1) C3 (D.186.4); liggyng (1) N5 (D.239.4); lygand (1) C2 (D.173.9).
lyghtly adv. easily. (1) C8.
lyneally adv. (1) C5.
lynnencloth n. (1) P3 (D.145.12).
lynnon n. linen. (2) C3 (D.197.18).
lyve inf. live. (2) C3, N2; 3 sing. lyuuth (1) N5 (D.235.15); past part. lyved (1) C4; lyvid (1) C1.
lyued vb. past part. ? believed. (1) P3 (D.142.30).
lyvelode n. income, livelihood. (20) C3, C5; lyflode (5) P3, P4; lyuelode (2) S1, C3; liflode (2) P3, C5; lifloode (1) P3.
lyvyng ger. (2) C1, C5.
lyvers n. those who live. (4) C3 (D.192.2, 193).

maieste n. majesty. (3) P1, C3; mageste (2) P2, P5.
mainprise n. surety. (1) C4 (D.216.28); meynprise (1) C1 (D.163.43). OED legal usage to 1845. See meinprised.
maintenance n. wrongful interference in a lawsuit. (1) S2 (D.82.7); mayntenance (3) C1 (D.164); mayntenaunce (1) C3 (D.189.18); meyntenance (3) C1 (D.163, 164); meyntenaunce (1) C3 (D.189.21). support, performance, mayntenance (1) P3 (D.146.2). See mayntenor, mentayne, maynteigne.
mair n. mayor. (19) C8, C3; maire (7) S1, S2; mayr (7) C3, N2; maier (2) P3; meyr (2) N2; mare (1) P1; meire (1) C3; pl. maires (2) C3; meyres (1) N8.
mairaltee n. (2) C8.
maister See master.
maisterschipe n. (1) C1.
maistrye n. control by force. (1) C8 (D.161.19).

Glossary of Forms 357

make *inf.* (47) C1, S1; (in the phrase "do make") (38) S1, S2; maken (1) C1 (D.163.26); maake (in "do maake") (6) S1, S2 only; *1 sing.* make (1) P3; *3 sing.* maketh (2) S1, S2; *pl.* make (2) C3, P4; maken (1) S1, C2; *3 sing. subj.* make (3) P3; *pl. subj.* make (3) C3, C4; maake (1) S1 (D.20.4); *past* made (6) C1, P2; *pr. part.* makyng (3) S1, P4; *past part.* made (168) N8, C8; maad (31) S1, C1; maade (10) S1, P2; mad (1) C1; maked (1) C1 (D.163.10); ymade (3) N2 (D.235.1), C3 (D.178.10, 199.3); *ger.* making (1) S2; makyng (6) S1, P3.
makers *n.* (1) C5.
malice *n.* (7) P3, C3.
malicious *adj.* (1) C3 (D.202.19).
maliciously *adv.* (1) C2; malicyously (1) C1 (D.164.36); maliciousely (1) P3; malycyouslych (1) C1 (D.164.11).
malt *n.* (1) C3.
man *n.* (49) C8, P1; manne (1) C4; *gen.* mannes (1) C3; mannys (1) C3; *pl.* men (65) C8, S1; mene (1) N6 (D.241.1); *gen. pl.* mennys (1) P5 (D.158.13).
maner *n.* way, kind, type of, etc. (70) C1, S1; manere (46) C8, S1; maniere (3) C3, P4.
manesseth *vb. 3 sing.* menaces. (1) C3 (D.188.13); *pr. part.* manasyng (1) C3 (D.189.20); *ger.* menasing (1) P3 (D.142.34).
manly *adj.* (1) P3.
manoir *n.* manor. (7) S1, P2; maner (20) C1, N2; manere (5) C5 (D.222); *pl.* manoirs (3) S1, P3; manoyrs (1) S3; manours (1) C3; maners (3) C3, C4; maneres (3) P4, C5; manereȝ (3) C4; manerȝ (1) C4; manerys (1) N5.
mansion *n.* (4) P2, P3.
mansleers *n.* man-slayers, murderers. (2) C3.
manuell *adj.* (1) C3 (D.209.7).
many *adj.* (32) C8, S1. meny (3) C3, C4; mony (5) C4, C5.
manyfold *adv.* (1) C5 (D.227.4).
marc *n.* monetary unit. (51) all dates and offices; *pl.* marcȝ (1) P3 (D.145.15).
march *n.* a district under military or legal jurisdiction. (4) P3; marche (1) P2. *pl.* marches (17) S1, C2; marcheȝ (1) P2.
marchandise See merchandise.
marchant See merchant.
marchantlich *adv.* in the manner of fair trade and commerce: "the verray value merchantlich." (1) C2 (D.172.6). marchaundisyng *vb. pr. part.* (1) C4 (D.211.11).
marchaundisyng, *pr. part.* (1) C4 (D.211.11).
marches *n.* boundaries (17) S1, S2; marcheȝ (1) P2. Frequently in the phrase "towne and marches" (D.132.15 etc.).
mare *n.* female horse. (1) P2 (D.111.2); mere (1) C3 (D.197.21).
mariage *n.* (9) S2, P2; *pl.* mariages (1) P5.

maried *vb. past part.* (1) C3; maryed (1) C3.

mark(e) *n.* a monetary unit equalling two-thirds of a pound. (19) S1, C1; marc (51) S1, P3; *pl.* markes (1) N5.

marketday *n.* (1) C3 (D.201.23).

marschal(l) *n.* marshall. (2) P2, C4; marchal(l) (6) P2, C2; mareschal(l) (3) S2, P2; *pl.* mareschalx (2) P4 (D.156.30, 31).

martir *n.* martyr. (5) P3, C5.

maryners *n.* (1) C4.

maser *n.* a maple drinking bowl. (1) C3 (D.197.10).

mason *n.* (2) S1 (D.28.2).

masse *n.* (2) P3, C4; messe (1) C3.

master *n.* master, often a title. (1) C3 (D.181.5); maistre (40) S1, S5; maister (21) S1, P3; mastre (1) C3; mayster (1) P2; mestre (1) C1; authority, maistor (2) C3 (D.197.6, 9); *pl.* maistres (12) S1, P3; mastres (1) C3; maysters (1) P3.

mater *n.* matter. (19) C1, P3; matere (42) S1 (22), C2; matier (10) P3; matire (9) P1 (6), P0; matiere (1) S1; *pl.* materes (25) S1, P2; matiers (15) P3, C3; maters (9) S1, C3; matieres (1) P4; matires (1) P2; matteres (1) P3.

matrace *n.* mattress. (1) C3 (D.197.13).

maumet *n.* a puppet or false idol. (1) S1 (D.70.5). *OED* obs. 1630.

maundement *n.* commandment, a written order. (1) C2 (D.171.6). *OED* obs. 1597.

mavlers *n.* mallards, ducks. (1) C3 (D.197.21). *OED mavelard* obs. 1500.

may *vb. 1, 3 sing., pl.* (152) C8, C1; maye (3) P3, C3; *past.* myght (42) C8, S1; might (12) S1, P2; myghte (6) S1, C1; myȝt(e) (5) S1, C1; myht (4) P1, C1; mighte (2) S1, P2; miȝt (2) S1; mygh (1) C5 (D.218.37). See mow.

maymed *vb. past.* (1) C1; *past part.* maymed (1) P2.

maynour *inf.* control, manage. (1) C3 (D.184.8). *MED* uses this citation; this meaning not in *OED*.

maynteigne *inf.* maintain, provide with support. (1) P3; mentayne (1) C5; meynteigne (1) C8; *pl.* mayntene (1) S1; *past part.* maintened (1) S1; maynteigned (1) C8.

mayntenable *adj.* (1) C5.

mayntenance See maintenance.

mayntenor *n.* maintainer. (1) C1; *pl.* meyntenors (1) C1.

meane *n.* method, way. (1) C4; meene (1) P3; mene (2) C5, N5; *pl.* menes (4) C1, C3; meanes (2) P5, C5; menys (2) C3, C4; meenes (1) S1; meenys (1) C3 (D.182.19); menis (1) C3; mennys (1) P5.

meane *adj.* "in þe meane tyme." (1) P5 (158.16).

mediacion *n.* (2) C2, C5; mediacione (1) C5; medeacion (1) C5.

medicines *n.* (1) P5.

medis *n.* meads, meadows. (1) P3.

meekly *adv.* (1) P3 (D.128.2); mekely (27) C1, S1; mekelich (1) P2 (D.123.1,

Glossary of Forms 359

"lowelich and mekelich").
meete *inf.* (1) P3; mete (1) P3; *past part.* met (1) P3; mete (1) P3. See metynges.
meinprised *vb. past part.* released from custody by surety. (1) C1 (D.162.8). See mainprise.
mekenesse *n.* (1) C1.
membre *n.* (1) C8 (D.161.3); *pl.* membres (3) S1 (D.57).
memoir *n.* memory. (2) C3, N5.
memorandum *n.* (3) P5, C5.
mencion *n.* mention. (8) C1, S1.
mene *n.* mean, intercession. (1) C5 (D.221.10).
mene *adj.* normally main, large and strong: "the mene power." (1) C1 (D.166.11).
mene *inf.* mix, var. of "mengen." (1) P3 (D.142.6). *OED* meng obs. except dial.
menes *n.* means, money, instrument by which effect may be secured. (3) C3; menys (2) C3, C4; menis (1) C3 (D.182.21); menes (1) C2 (D.167.13 either "means" or "men."
mentayne *inf.* maintain. (1) C5 (D.218.23). See maynteigne
mercer *n.* (4) N5 (D.240).
mercerye *n.* Mercers Guild of London. (2) C8 (D.161.2, 27).
merchandise *n.* (2) C3; marchandise (14) S1, C2; marchaundise (4) C3, C4; marchaundyse (2) C3, N8; merchaundise (1) P5; *pl.* merchandises (8) C5 (D.217); marchandises (7) C3; marchaundises (6) C3, C4; merchaundiseʒ (3) P3; merchaundises (3) P3, C3; marchandyses (1) C3; merchandiʒes (1) P3.
merchant *n.* (1) S1; marchant (8) S1, C3; marchaunt (6) C3, C4; merchaunt (4) P3 (D.145); *pl.* marchauntʒ (10) C3, C4; merchauntʒ (6) P3(5), C3; marchaunts (4) C4 (D.211); merchauntes (3) P3; marchantes (3) S2; merchantes (2) S1, C3; marchantʒ (2) C3; merchandes (1) S1; marchandes (1) S1; marchauntes (1) C5; merchantʒ (1) P3.
merciable *adj.* merciful. (1) P3 (D.147.8).
mercy *n.* (16) S1, P2.
mere See mare.
merite *n.* merit. (1) C5.
meritorious *adj.* (1) P3.
meritory *adj.* meritorious. (1) C5 (D.226.12).
merque *n.* seizure of the property of a foreign state or of foreign citizens as a reprisal for unpaid debts, injuries, etc. (2) S1 (D.69.14, 15). *OED* obs. 1473. *MED* cites a Privy Council version of this Signet letter.
message *n.* (1) P1; *pl.* messages (1) C5.
mete *n.* meat. (2) C3, C5.
metynges *n.* (1) C3 (D.193.15). See meete.
mevable *adj.* moveable. (2) C1; mevabel (1) N5; moeble (1) C3.
meyne *n.* retainers. (1) S1 (D.6.5).

midsomer *adj.* (1) C3; mydsomer (1) P3.
might *n.* (1) P2 (D.122.9).
might *vb.* See may, mow(e).
mighty *adj.* (1) C2; myghti (2) P3, C3; myghty (5) P2, C2.
mile *n.* (4) C3 (D.203); myle (6) C3.
milnes See mylne.
minister *n.* officer, servant. (1) C5; mynister (1) C3; *pl.* ministres (1) C4; minystres (1) C3; mynisterys (1) C3.
ministracion *n.* administration, management. (1) C4 (D.210.28).
ministred *vb. past part.* administered. (1) P3; *ger.* ministring (1) P4.
mischief *n.* (2) P2, P3; meschieff (1) C3; myscheff (1) C1; myschief (1) C3; *pl.* meschiefs (1) C3.
misdoers *n.* (1) P3; mysdoers (12) P3, C3; mysdoerys (2) P4.
misrule *n.* (1) C5.
misrulid *vb. past part.* misruled, misbehaved. (2) C5.
mocion *n.* (2) P5, S5.
moder *n.* (14) S1, C1; modir (2) N5; modor (1) C1; *gen.* modir is (2) N5 (D.241.10, 13); *pl.* modres (1) C5 (D.231.7).
mois *n.* in law, a month (from OF). (4) C4 (D.216); moys (1) C4 (D.216.19). *OED* obs. 1491.
monday *n.* (10) S2, P1; Moneday (2) S2, C3.
monastery(e) *n.* (11) P4, C5.
money *n.* (17) S1, P3; mony (5) C3, C4; monay (1) C3; moneye (1) S1; monoie (1) C3 (D.183.5); monoye (1) P4; monye (1) C3.
monk *n.* (1) S1; *pl.* monkes (1) P1.
monthe *n.* (1) C3 (D.196.5); moneth (7) P3, C3; moneþ (3) S1; monith (1) N5; *pl.* monethes (2) N4; monethys (1) N8; monthes (1) C1.
more *adj.* (90) S1, C1; mor (4) P3, C5; mo (4) C1, P3; moo (3) P3, C3; moore (2) S2; mare (1) P2 (D.123.11); mowe (1) C3 (D.196.27). See muche, most.
moreouer *adv.* (3) S1, C3.
morning *n.* (2) P1 (D.112.6, 12).
mortisment *n.* amortizement. (1) P3 (D.146.22). *OED* obs. 1465.
moro *n.* morrow. (1) S1 (D.81.4); morwe (1) C8 (D.161.16). In both cases in the phrase "on the . . . " See to morwe.
most *adj.* (60) S1, C1; moste (15) P2, C3; moost (15) C8, S1. See muche, more.
mote *vb. 3 sing. subj.* may. (2) P2 (D.113.12, 117.16)
mouthe *n.* (3) S1, C1.
move *inf.* (1) C4 (D.211.41); moeue (1) P2; *pr. part.* moeuyng (3) P4 S3; mevyng (2) S2, C5. *past part.* meved (2) C3, C5; meuyd (2) C3, C5; moved (1) C5 (C.223.3); mouyd (1) C2; moued (1) P3; mouyed (1) P3. See mevable.
mow *vb. pr. part. of* mouen, may. (3) S1, P1 (D.64.5 etc); mowe *2 sing.* (3) C8, C2 (D.161.47, etc.); *pl.* (9) S1, P2 (D.43.10, etc.); mowen (1) C2

Glossary of Forms 361

(D.178.14). *OED* obs. 1533. See may.
mowe *n.* stack. (1) C3 (D.197.20).
mowyng *ger. of* mouen, having the power, being able. (1) C5 (D.230.13).
muche *n.* (16) S1, S2; moche (19) S1, P1; mych (3) P3, C3; myche (2) P2, C3. See more, most.
multitude *n.* (3) N2, C5.
muniment *n.* (1) P1; *pl.* munimentes (2) N5.
munyeles *n.* ? reminders, from "monen." (1) C3 (D.199.30). Form not recorded in *MED* or *OED*.
murdre *n.* (7) C4 (D.212); mourdure (2) C3; mourdur (1) C3; *pl.* murdererys, murderyrys, morderyes, murdereris C3 (D.192.6, 13, 14, 26); mourdures (1) C3 (D.194.18).
murdre *vb. 3 sing. subj.* (1) C4; *past* mourdered (1) C3; murdred (1) C4; *past part.* murdred (5) C3, C4; *ger.* morthering (1) C5 (D.218.45).
must *vb. pl. of* moten. (1) S1 (D.81.12); *3 sing.* most (1) C3 (D.191.13); *pl.* moste (1) C2 (D.176.8). See mote.
mydnyght *n.* (1) P5; mydde nyght (2) C3.
mykill *n.* much. (1) C2 (D.173.2).
mylles *n.* mills. (1) P3. See mylne.
mylne *n.* mill. (1) C5; *pl.* milnes (1) P3.
mynd *n.* mind. (1) C5; mynde (5) C8, S1; mende (1) P4 (D.153.7). Usually in the phrase "tyme oute of mynde," D.187.4, 230.5, etc.
mys bare *vb. 3 sing. subj.* misbehave. (1) C4 (D.215.16).
myschevous *adj.* (1) C5. See mischief.
mysdede *n.* (1) P3.
mysgouernaunce *n.* (2) C3, C5.
myslyvers *n.* mis-livers, wrong-doers. (2) C3.
myssal *n.* (1) C3.
myssed *vb. past part.* (1) C3; myssette (1) S1 (D.53.5).
mysused *vb. past part.* (1) C8.

nacions *n.* (1) C3.
naked *adj.* (2) C3.
name *n.* (21) S1, P2; nam (1) S1 (D.22.2); *pl.* names (12) S1, P2; namys (2) P2; namis (1) P3.
name *inf.* (1) N4; *pr. part.* namyng (2) P3, C5; *past part.* named (3) C3, C4; nempned (1) S1 (D.66.4); ynemnyd (1) C3 (D.188.7).
namely *adv.* especially. (1) S1.
natheles *adv.* nevertheless. (1) S5.
natiuite *n.* (3) C5, N5; natiuitee (1) N5 (D.239.11).
nature *n.* (1) C5.
naturell *adj.* (1) C2.

natyff *n.* native. (1) C3 (D.205.2).
nauie *n.* navy. (1) S1 (D.51.4).
nay *adv.* negative response, used only in indirect quotations: "he answered nay." (4) P3 (D.142).
ne *conj.* nor. (77) C8, S1; as proclitic negative. (13) S1, P2. *OED* arch.
necessary *adv.* (2) C4 (D.215); necessarie (8) S1, P3; necessaire (1) S2; *pl.* necessaires (1) S1 (D.29.5).
necessite *n.* (5) C1, S2; necessitee (1) P3; *pl.* necessitees (4) P3 (D.131).
nede *n.* need. (14) C8, S1.
nede *inf.* require, be necessary. (1) S1 (D.41.5); *impersonal.* nedeth (1) S5 (D.109.2, "vs nedeth"); *past part.* neded (1) S1.
nedeful *adj.* (4) C8, P3; nedefull (1) P3.
nedes *adv.* necessarily: "those þat most nedes teche." (1) P3 (D.146.4).
nedy *adj.* needy. (3) C3; nedi (1) C3.
neer *adj.* (1) S1 (D.69.15); nere *adv.* nearly. (1) C2 (D.168.6).
neighboures *n.* (1) C8; neightbores (1) C3 (D.193.11); neyghebores (1) C1.
neither *adj.* (8) S1, C4; noþer (4) P2, C3; nouther (3) S1; nethir (2) C1, C3; neyther(e) (2) P2, C3; neiþer (2) P2, P3; neithr (1) P2; nether (1) C4; neyþer (1) P3; nother (1) C1. See discussion.
never *adv.* (1) C2 (D.172.7); neuer (16) C8, S1; neuere (5) P3, C3.
neuertheles *adv.* (1) P4; neueretheles (1) S2; neuerthelees (1) P4; neuerthelesse (1) C5.
new *adj.* (4) N8, N4; newe *adj.* (4) S1, S2; newe *n.* (1) S2 (D.86.7 "or elles of newe"); newe *adv.* (1) S1 (D.57.7).
next *adj. and adv.* (85) C8, P1; nexte (3) C5, P5; nexst (1) C4; nest (2) N4 (D.237.20, 21).
nigh *adv.* (1) S1 (D.69.26); nygh (4) C5 (D.221, 225.20).
night *n.* (2) S1; nyght (8) C8, P1; nyht (1) P1; *pl.* nyghtes (2) C4, P5.
no *neg. particle.* (118) C8, P1; noo (6) S1, P2.
noble *adj.* (61) C8, S1; nobill (3) P3 (D.144).
nobles *n. pl.* gold coins. (3) C3, C4; noblis (1) C3.
noiancie, *n.* annoyance. (1) C1 (D.163.161). *NED* obs. 1670.
noised *vb. past part.* rumored, told (1) C5; noysed (2) C3, C5. See noyse.
nominacion *n.* (2) S2.
no more *n.* (1) S1 (D.44.7); *adj.* (1) C5 (D.218.13); *adv.* (1) C1 (D.163.51).
non age *n.* minority. (1) S1 (D.63.4); noun age (1) C3.
none *pron.* (8) P3, C3; noon (25) S1, P2; non (17) S1, P2; noun (1) C5; nane (1) P1 (D.111.6).
nonnes *n.* nuns. (2) N4; nonneʒ (2). All D.238.
nonsuyd *past part.* nonsuited, cessation of a suit. (1) C3 CD.202.30). Vb. *OED* obs. 1487.

Glossary of Forms

nor *conj.* (43) S1, C1; ner (21) S1, P3. See ne.
north *adj.* (3) S1, P3.
norysse *n.* nurse. (2) P2 (D.121).
not *neg. particle.* (158) S1, P2; nat (28) S1, P3; noght (19) C3, C4; nought (10) C8, P2; noȝt (8) P3, C3; nouȝt (4) P3, C3; notte (2) P2, C4; noghte (2) C4; nogth (2) N8; nowht (2) P2, C2; note (1) N5 (D.241.10); noht (1) P3 (D.136.8).
notable *adj.* (22) S1, P2.
notablely *adv.* (1) C2 (D.169.11).
notarie *n.* official scribe. (1) C2; notarye (1) S2; *adj.* notorious (1) C3 (D.192.14).
noted *vb. past part.* (1) S1 (D.65.6).
notwithstanding *conj. and prep.* (3) S1, C4; notwithstondyng(e) (16) S1, C1; natwiþstandyng (6) S1, S2; notwiþstandyng(e) (3) S1; notwiþstanding (2) S1; notwithstonding (1) C5; notwyþstandyng (1) S1; notwythstondyng (1) C3; notwistanding (1) C5; natwithstandyng (1) P5; naughtwithstandinge (1) S2; nogthwithstondyng (1) C4; nottewithstondyng (1) C4; notwythstondyng (1) C3. Frequently written as two words.
now *adv.* (85) C8, PO; nowe (39) C1, C3.
nowht *n.* naught, nothing. (1) S1 (D.16.6); noght (1) C3 (D.189.34).
noyse *n.* (5) P3, C5. See noised.
numbre *n.* (3) C3; numbir (1) C3; nombre (9) S1, P2; nombr (1) P3.
nyght come *n.* nightfall. (1) C3 (D.193.12).

o reduced form of on (3) P2 (D.122.24, 25; 137.5); *OED* obs. 1450. Reduced form of one (3) C8, C3 (D.161.5, 181.14); *OED* obs. 1489. Reduced form of un- (2) S1, C3. Reduced form of of (1) C5 (D.218.2). See also oo, one.
oo reduced form of on (1) P2 (D.122.9); reduced form of one (2) P2 (D.122.11, 24); reduced form of un- (2) P2 (D.122.10, 14). See o, one, on lasse.
obeianse *n.* (1) C1 (D.162.2).
obeisant *adj.* (1) C2 (D.170.1).
obey *inf.* (1) C5; obeye (1) C5; obeie (1) P2.
obligacion *n.* (3) C3, C5; *pl.* obligacions (4) C3, P3.
obseruance *n.* (1) C4 (D.214.9).
obserue *inf.* (2) C4, P5; *subj.* obserue (1) P3; *ger.* obseruynge (1) S1.
obstinate *adj.* (1) C5 (D.221.30).
occasion *n.* (5) P2, C3.
occupacion *n.* (5) S1, C5; ocupacion (2) C5; *pl.* occupacions (5) P3, C4.
occupiers *n.* (1) C5.
occupy *inf.* (2) C4 (D.215); occupie (7) S1, P2; ocupie (1); C5 occupye (1) C5; *3 sing.* occupieth (4) C3, P4; ocupieth (1) P4; *3 sing. subj.* occupie (3) S1, C3; ocupie (1) C3; *past.* occupied (7) C4, C5; occupyed (2) C5; *pr. part.*

ocupyng (1) C4; *past part.* occupied (4) S2, P3; ocupied (2) C5; occupiede (1) P2.

ocludid *vb. past part.* concluded. cf. Lat. occludere. (1) P2 (D.113.3). Not recorded in *OED* or *MED.*

octaues *n.* the eighth day after a feast day. (1) P3 (D.137.4).

odieux *adj.* odious. (1) P3 (D.127.6).

oeps *n.* benefit. (1) P3 (D.140.6). *OED* obs. 1436.

of *prep.* (4416) C8, N8, etc.; o (1) C5 (D.218.2).

offence *n.* (1) C3; *pl.* offences (2) C3; offencis (1) C5; offenses (1) P5.

offende *inf.* (3) C4, P5; *pr. part.* offendyng (1) C3.

office *n.* always "position." (54) S1, P2; *pl.* offices (5) C8, P2.

officer *n.* (5) C8, C3; *pl.* officers (14) S1, C1; officereʒ (1) C4 (D.210.30); officiers (1) P2 (D.122.15).

offre *inf.* offer. (1) C3; *past part.* offred (2) C3 (D.182); *ger.* offerynges (1) C3.

oft tyme *adv.* often. (2) C8 (D.161); oft tymes (2) C4 (D.204.47, 211.15); ofte tymes (2) S1, C3 (D.9.1, 193.11).

ofte *adv.* (2) S1, C3 (D.46.2, 192.9). See often.

oile *n.* (1) C3; oyle (1) P3.

oke *n.* oak. (1) N8.

old *adj.* (1) C5; olde (17) P3, C3.

omission *n.* (1) C3 (D.191.6).

omitte *inf.* (1) C3 (D.207.11).

on *prep.* (147) C8, N8. See also o, oo.

oncle See vncle.

oncurteise *adj.* uncourteous. (1) P3 (D.142.28).

one *n.* and *adj.* (17) P3, C3; on (9) P3, C3; oon (4) C8, S1; oone (1) C4; oo (5) P2 (D.122); o (3) C8, S1. See also o, oo.

ones *n.* once. "all at ones." (1) P3 (D.146.11); onys (2) P2.

on lasse *conj.* unless. (1) S1 (D.62.4); o lasse (1) S1 (D.69.20); oo lesse (2) P2 (D.122.10, 14); o les (1) C3 (D.206.9).

only *adv.* (11) C1, P2; oonly (7) C3, C4; onely (5) P3, C3; oonli (1) C3; oonlich (1) C8 (D.161.33).

open *inf.* (1) P2; *past part.* opened (1) P2.

open *adj.* unconcealed, public. (8) C8, P3.

openly *adv.* (7) C3, C5; opynly (1) C2; openlich (3) C8 (D.161).

opinions *n.* (1) P2.

opon See upon.

oppresse *inf.* (1) C3; *past part.* opressid (1) C5; *ger.* opressing (1) C5.

oppresseres *n.* (1) P3.

oppression *n.* (1) C3; oppressioun (1) P4; opression (1) C5; *pl.* oppressions (2) C8, C3.

oppressiouesly *adv.* oppresively. (1) C3 (D.189.20). *MED* citation of this entry is based on the printed version and differs in spelling.

opteinyd *vb. past.* obtained. (1) C5 (D.222.27).

or *conj.* (376) C8, N8; vre (1) N5 (D.241.1).

orator *n.* one who prays religiously, (2) C3, C5, or a petitioner (1) C5; oratour (4) P3, C3; oratoure (1) C5; horatour (1) C3; *pl.* oratours (5) C5; oratoures (3) C5. (All plurals but one in D.226).

ordein *inf.* (2) N4 (D.238.9, 15); ordeyne (19) S1, S2; ordeigne (10) P3, C2; ordeine (9) S1, P2; ordeign (2) C3; ordaigne (1) C2 (D.170.8); *1 sing.* ordeigne (1) P3 (D.126.8); *pl.* ordeyne (1) S1 (D.39.5); *subj. pl.* ordeine (12) S1, S2; ordeyne (7) S1, S2; ordenne (2) S1, S2; ordeineth (2) S1, S2; ordeyneth (2) S2, P2; *past.* ordayned (1) C5; ordeine (1) C5 (D.222.23); ordeyne (1) C5 (D.222.2); *past part.* ordeined (14) S1, P5; ordeyned (12) S1, S4; ordeigned (3) P4, C5; ordeynned (1) P2; ordened (1) S1; ordenned (1) S2; ordeynet (1) P1 (D.112.6).

ordinance *n.* (4) S1, P5; ordinaunce (12) C1, C3; ordenaunce (6) P2, C3; ordenance (2) P2, P5; ordounance (2) P2; ordynance (1) C3; ordynaunce (1) C8; *pl.* ordinances (2) C3; ordennances (1) S1.

ordinarie *n.* justice. (1) C5.

ordre *n.* religious order. (1) S1.

originall *adj.* (1) C5.

ost, oost See hoost.

ostiarshippe *n.* the office of doorkeeper. (1) P2 (D.123.3).

otake. See outake.

othe *n.* oath. (6) P4. C4; oothe (1) S1; ougth (1) C4 (D.214.12).

other *pron., adj.* (155) C1, S1; oþer (59) S1, P2; othir (33) S1, P1; oþir (20) S1 , C4 (15, D.211); othere (8) C8, C3; oþere (8) S1, P2; oder (7) P3, C4 (5, D.214); othur (7) C3 (D.203); othre (6) P5 (D.159); othor (6) C1, C3; othr (4) P2, P4; oþur (2) C5 (D.218); oothir (2) S2; othire (1) C4; othure (1) C3; oother (1) C3; (as part of a double negative) nother (1) C3; nothir (1) P2; *gen.* others (2) P3; *pl.* oþirs (1) C4.

otherwise *adv.* (1) C3; otherwyse (1) S1; oþerwise (2) P2, P3; oþerwyse (1) S2; othirwise (1) N4.

otteraunce *n.* extreme, outermost. (1) C5 (D.218.21). *OED outrance* obs. 1609.

ouer(e) *adv.* (29) P2, C3; over (1) C3 (D.198.11).

ouerflowyng *pr. part.* (1) C3.

ouerlad *past part.* overburdened. (1) S2.

ouerlitel *adj.* too small. (1) C3.

ouerlive *inf.* outlive. (1) N5.

ouermany *adj.* too many. (1) C8.

ouerpluse *n.* surplus. (1) P3 (D.144.21).

ouer ruled *vb. past part.* (1) P5.

ouersee *inf.* (1) S2.

ouersight(e) *n. supervision. (3)* S2, C5.
oughte *vb. 1 sing.* (1) C1; *3 sing.* ought (1) P5; oughte (2) S1, S2; aught (1) S2 (D.82.5); owȝt (1) C3 (D.185.7); *pl.* ought (1) C5; oughten (1) C1 (D.163.19); owghte (1) C3; aught (1) S1 (D.67.7).
oureself *pron.* (1) S2 (D.89.9).
out *adv.* (31) C8, S1; oute (49) S1, C9; outen (5) C8, P2 (in the phrase "with outen" only); owt (3) S1, S2; owte (11) C1, S1; ought (1) P3 (D.128.17).
outake *prep.* except. (1) C3 (D.181.6); otake (1) C4 (D.212.5).
outerliche *adv.* utterly. (1) C8 (D.161.35). See otteraunce.
outlawed *vb. past part.* (1) C3; outelawed (5) C1, C3.
outelawerye *n.* (2) C1 (D.163.14, 42).
outward *adv.* (1) C8; outeward (1) P1.
owe *inf.* (1) S2; *3 sing.* oweth (4) P3, C3; *3 pl.* owe (1) C5; *pr. part.* owyng(e) (3) C2, C4; *past part.* owed (1) C3. See ought.
own *adj.* (1) S5; owne (15) C8, S1; owen (7) S2, P2; oune (3) P5 (D.159); owyn (1) C4 (D.218.32); awen (1) C5 (D.220.6).
owner *n.* (1) C4; awner (1) C2 (D.175.4); *pl.* awners (1) C3 (D.180.19).

paiable *adj.* (3) P3, C3.
paire *n.* (5) C3 (D.197); payre (1) C3.
paisable *adj.* peaceable. (1) C8.
paix *n.* peace (Fr.): "breche of oure saide paix." (2) P4 (D.154.2, 6). See pease.
pale *n.* enclosed or defined area. (2) P3.
paleis *n.* palace. (2) P3; paloys (1) P4 (D.154.6).
palentine *adj.* palatine, possessing royal powers. (1) C3 (D.201.25).
pannes *n.* pans. (2) C3.
papire *n.* paper. (1) C3 (D.197.10).
pappes *n.* breasts. (1) C4.
parceiue *inf.* (1) S2; *3 sing. subj.* perceyue (1) C3; *ger.* perceyuyng (1) C3.
parcell *n.* piece. (15) C3, C4; *pl.* parcelles (1) C5.
parchyment *n.* (1) C3 (D.197.10).
parciall *adj.* partial. (1) C2.
parcialtee *n.* (1) P2.
pardon *inf.* (2) C5; *past.* pardoned (2) C3; *past part.* pardonned (1) S5.
pardon *n.* (9) S1, P3.
park *n.* (1) C5 (D.228.17); *pl.* parcs (1) S2 (D.104.6).
parkership *n.* the office of park keeper. (1) C5.
parliament *n.* (18) C3, C4 (D.194, 195, 199, 213, 216 only); parlement (104) C1, S1; parlament (1) C4; parlemet (1) C5 (D.226.21 error?); *pl.* parlementes (2) C5; parlementȝ (2) C5.
parlour *n.* (2) N8.
paroche *n.* parish. (2) P5, N5 (D.239.5); *OED* learned form, obs. 1600. parsch

Glossary of Forms 367

(1) N8 (D.233.3). See also paryssh.
parochiele *adj.* (1) S1.
parson See person.
parsonage See personage.
part *n.* (17) C2, C3; parte (15) C3, C4; *pl.* partes (2) P2, C5. See also party.
partiegnyng *vb. pres. part.* (1) P3 (D.136.13).
party *n.* used interchangeably with part(e). (4) C3, N4; partee (1) P3; partie (62) S1, C1; partye (8) C8, S1; *pl.* parties (37) S1, C1; partyes (4) C1, C3; partieʒ (1) C4; partys (1) C3.
paryssh *n.* parish. (1) N8; parych (1) P5. See paroche.
passage *n.* (8) S2, P3.
passe *inf.* (9) C3, P4; *pl.* passeþ (1) S2 (D.81.14); *3 sing. subj.* passe (1) P5; *pr. part.* passyng (3) C3 (D.180); *past part.* passed (37) C8, S1; passid (4) P3, C3; passyd (3) P2, C5; passide (2) C3 (D.205); pased (1) C3; passet (1) P1 (D.112.2); past (2) S4, C5. Normally used in dating phrases: "a feast day late passed," "now passed," etc.
pastures *n.* (1) C3.
patent *adj. and n.* official document (6) S1, P2; patente (3) S1; *pl.* patentes (67) S1, S2; patentʒ (23) P2, P3; patenteʒ (5) C3; patententʒ (1) P3 (D.139.10); patentis (1) P3. With two exceptions, all plural forms are in the phrase "letters patentes" etc.
patenteer *n.* patenter, one who has received a patent. (1) C3 (D.188.12).
patron *n.* (3) P3 (D.128).
patronage *n.* (2) S2, C5.
pay *inf.* (5) C3, C5; paye (19) S1, C3; paie (11) C3, C5; pey (1) N8 (D.238.8, 15); *3 sing.* paieth (1) C3 (D.189.31); *3 sing. subj.* paye (2) S1, N2; *past.* paid (1) C5; *pr. part.* paiyng (3) P3, C3; payng (1) C4; *past part.* paied (22) C2, C3; paid (8) S1, P2; paide (4) S2, C3; payd(e) (4) C2, C3; payed (1) C4; paiyd (1) C3; paijd (1) C1 (D.164.24); payode (1) C3 (D.183.31); payet (1) C3 (D.191.9); ypaied (1) C3 (D.187.7); *ger.* paying (1) C5.
payment *n.* (6) S3, C3; paiment (21) S1, P2; payement (6) C3, C5; *pl.* paiementʒ (2) P3, P5; payementes (1) N5; paimentes (1) N4; paiments (1) P2.
payn *n.* (1) C5; payne (7) C1, C3; peyn (2) C5; peyne (12) P2, P3.
pease *n.* peace. (2) C5; pees (39) C8, S1; peas (4) P3, C3; pece (3) C2, C3. See paix, peasibly.
peasebly *adv.* (2) C4; pesibly (1) S2; pesybly (1) N4. See pesible.
peautor *n.* pewter. (1) C3.
pece *n.* piece (1) C3 (D.190.11); *pl.* peces (1) C3 (D.197.16).
pelyd *vb. past part. of* pelen, beaten down. (1) C5 ("so pelyd and opressid," D.218.7). *OED* obs. 1606.
pension *n.* (5) S1, P3; *pl.* pensions (1) P4.
peny *n.* (5) C3, P4.

people n. (12) C3, P3; peple (20) C8, C3; poeple (12) P3, C3; pepil (5) S1, P3; pepul (3) C5 (D.218); pepyll (2) S1, C3; pepull (1) C5; pueple (1) S2; pleople (1) C3 (D.146.7, ?error).
perauanture adv. (2) S1, P3.
perceyue See parceiue.
pereies adj. peerless. (1) C1.
peremtorely adv. compulsorily. (1) C3 (D.199.35).
pereth vb. 3 sing. appears. (1) P2 (D.115.10). See appere.
perfite adj. perfect. (2) P2; parfit (1) PO (D.110.3).
performe inf. (5) C5, N5; perfourme (2) C4, C5; past part. perfourmed (5) C4, P5; performyd (2) N8, N5; performed (1) N5; ger. perfourmyng (2) C4, C5.
peril n. (1) S1; perill (3) C3, P4; perell (1) P5; pl. periles (1) P3.
perisshed vb. past part. (4) C3 (D.180).
periurie n. perjury. (1) C4; pl. periuries (1) C3.
permutacioun n. exchange of office or benefice. (1) C5 (D.215.14).
perpetuel adj. (1) S1; perpetuell (3) P3, C5; perpetuelle (2) S1, P3.
perpetuelly adv. (2) C3, C5.
persone n. person. (49) S1, S5; person (15) S1, C1; personne (4) S1, P4; persoone (1) C3 (D.203.33); pl. persones (64) C1, S1; persons (5) P3, C3; personnes (5) S1, P3; personeʒ (3) C3, C4; persouns (1) C4; personys (2) P4.
person n. parson. (8) S1, P3; parson (1) C3 (D.197.2).
personage n. parsonage. (2) C1 (D.166.4, 6); parsonage (1) C3.
personneles adj. personal. (1) S1 (D.31.4).
perteyned vb. past part. (1) C3; ger. perteynyng (2) P3; pertenyng(e) (2) P2 (D.123.4, 13); partieignyng (1) P3 (D.136.13).
pesible adj. peaceable. (1) C4. See peasebly.
pestell n. pestle. (1) C3.
pestilence n. (1) C3; pl. pestylenceʒ (1) N2.
petit adj. petty (Fr.): "clerc of our petit bagge." (1) S1 (D.17.2).
petition n. (2) C3; peticion (5)   C3, P3; petycion (1) C3; pl. peticions (1) C1.
pety adj. lesser. (1) C5.
philosofors n. (1) C3 (D.207.4).
philosophie n. (1) C3 (D.197.7).
phisicien n. (1) S2 (D.98.2); pl. ffisisseanes (1) C3 (D.207.4).
pigges n. (1) C3.
pight vb. past part. pitched. (1) P3; pighte (1) P3 (D.132.2, 134.3). OED past part. obs. 1700.
pikk n. pike. (1) P3 (D.142.12).
pilgrimage n. (3) P2, P3; pilgrymage (1) P3; pilgremage (1) C3; pl. pilgrymages (2) P3.
pipe n. dept of the Exchequer that handled the "pipe roll" accounts. (5) C5

(D.223.14, 232.4, etc.).

pirates *n.* (1) C4.

pitee *n.* pity. (2) S1; pite (1) S5; pitye (1) C3.

pitevous *adj.* piteous. (1) C5 (D.226.10).

pitously *adv.* (1) C5.

place *n.* (45) N8, S1; plaise (1) P1; plase (1) C4 (D.212.9); plasse (1) P2 (D.112.7); pleys (1) C3; *pl.* places (12) S1, C3; placys (1) C3.

plainly *adv.* (7) S1, P2; pleinly (7) S1, C2; pleynly (4) C3, C5; plainely (2) C3; playnely (2) C3, C4; playnly (2) C1, C2; pleynely (2) C2, C3; pleinely (1) S2; pleinli (1) C2.

plate *n.* precious metal. (2) P3, C4.

playn *adj.* (2) C1, P3; plein (3) S1, C2; pleine (3) S1, S2; pleyne (2) C1; pleyn (1) C3.

pleasance *n.* (1) P4; plesance (2) C1, N2.

please *vb. 3 sing. impers.* with (h)it. (45) P1, C3; plese (14) S1, P1; pleseth (2) C3; pleese (1) P3; plesith (1) C2; *past part. not impers.* plesed (1) S2 (D.89.5); plesid (1) P5; plesit (1) P2.

pleasure *n.* (1) C3; pleasire (2) C3, C5; plesir (2) C3; plesire (1) C3; plesur (1) C5; *pl.* plesirs (1) P5.

plede *vb. 3 pl. subj.* (1) C4 (D.216.37).

plee *n.* (7) S1, C4; *pl.* plees (3) C3, C4; pleys (1) C3 (D.192.11).

plegges *n.* (1) C3.

plesament *n.* pleasure. (1) S1 (D.40.3). Form not in *OED* or *MED*.

pleyned *vb. past.* complained. (1) C8 (D.161.20).

pleynt *n.* complaint. (1) C5.

plogh *n.* (2) C1 (D.166); plough (1) C3 (D.197.20).

ploghyren *n.* the iron part of a plough, colter. (1) C1 (D.166.4).

poentot *n.* suffering, cf. Lat. "poenetentia." (1) P2 (D.115.15). Form not recorded in *OED* or *MED*.

point *n.* (4) P3, C3; poynt (2) S1, C2; *pl.* poyntes (2) C8, C3.

polle *n.* "poll axe." (1) C3 (D.173.6).

poor *adj.* (1) P2 (D.113.4); poure (21) C1, C3; pore (14) C1, S1; pouere (9) C1, C3; powre (6) C1, P1; poer (6) P3, C3; poeuere (5) P3 (D.127), C3 (D.204); poore (2) P2, C3; pouer (2) C3; pure (2) C5 (D.218.5,24); pooure (2) C3 (D.205); pover (1) C3; povir (1) C3 (D.189.2); *comp.* porer (19) S1 (D.58.5); *supl.* porest (1) P2 (D.122.21).

pope *n.* (6) S1, P2; *gen.* popes (1) S2; popis (1) C1.

porcions *n.* (4) S1, P4.

porsours *n.* pursers, account-keepers. (1) P2.

port *n.* (12) S1, C3; porte (2) P1, C3; poort (1) C4; *pl.* portes (9) S1, C4; portʒ (4) P3, C3.

porter *n.* (4) P3, C5; pourtour (1) C3.

portinaunce *n. pl.* appurtenances (q.v.), that which comes with a piece of property. (1) N8; portinaunces (1) N8 (D.233.24). *OED pertinence* obs. 1525..

portuose *n. pl.* portases, portable breviaries. (1) C3 (D.197.9). *OED* obs. 1528.

possessed *vb. past part.* (4) C4, C5.

possession *n.* (6) S1, S2; possessyon (4) C1 (D.164); possessione (3) C5 (D.222); *pl.* possessions (18) S1, P3.

possessour *n.* (1) C4 (D.211.7).

possible *adj.* (4) S1, P3.

potte *n.* (1) C3; *pl.* pottes (2) C3. All in D.197.

poverte *n.* (2) C3; pouerte (2) C3; pourete (1) S2; pouert (1) C2 (D.169.8).

pound *n.* monetary unit. (2) S1, N5 (D.50.5, 239.23); weight, pound (1), pounde (4) C3. All in D.190.

power *n.* (35) C8, C1; powere (2) P3, C3; powair (1) C3; powaire (1) S1; poaire (1) C3 (D.204, 46); poiar (3) P3, P5.

pray *inf.* (17) C3, P3; praye (5) C1, P2; prey (3) P3, C5; prai (1) C2; praie (1) P2; *1 sing.* pray (5) P1, C3; praye (1) C1; praie (1) PO; *3 sing.* prath (1) C5 (D.221.40); prayeth (1) C5; preieth (1) P5; *1 pl.* pray (11) S1, S2; praye (4) P3, P4; prey (1) S1; *3 pl.* prayen (3) C1, P3; prayn (1) C5 (D.218.1); preyen (1) C4, usually in the standard phrase "Prayen the Communes"; *pr. part.* prayng (2) P3, C5; prayeng (2) P3; prayenge (1) P2; praing (1) P2; preying (1) S1; prayend (1) P4 (D.153.9); *past part.* prayed (1) C5; preyed (1) C5.

prayer *n.* (1) C3; praier (1) C4.

prebende *n.* (16) S1, S2.

preceptis *n.* precepts, written orders. (1) P3 (D.144.14).

predecessour *n.* (2) S1; *pl.* predecessours (4) S1, C3; preddessours (1) C3 (D.182.24).

preferred *vb. past part.* (2) C5.

preferrement *n.* advancement, but normally indicating priority in receiving taxes or subsidies. (13) S1, S2; *pl.* preferrementȝ (2) P3.

preiudice *n.* prejudice. (4) S1, C3.

preiudicial(l) *adj.* (5) P5, C5; preiudiciel (1) S1.

prelat *n.* (1) C3.

premises *n.* the aforementioned. See *OED* definition 2. (3) P5; premisses (26) P3, C3; premisseȝ (3) P3, C4; premysses (3) C3, C5.

prentice *n.* apprentice. (4) C5.

prerogatif *n.* (2) C1; prerogatyf (1) C1 (All in D.163); *pl.* prerogatifs (1) P2; prerogatifes (1) P2. (Both in D.122).

prescribed *vb. past.* held by legal prescription. (1) C5 (D.230.5). *OED* 5 cites this idiom.

prese *n.* prise, the right of seizure. (1) P3 (D.124.4).

presence *n.* (12) C1, P2; presens (1) C5.

present *adj.* (76) C1, P2 (generally found in the phrase "this present parlement"); as *adv.* (2) C3: "that ben present dwelling" (D.203.22).
presentacion *n.* (8) S1, P3 (7).
presente *inf.* (1) C3; *past.* presented (1) S1; *past part.* presented (1) S1.
presentement *n.* the presenting of legal documents before an authority which can act upon them. (1) C5 (D.230.12).
presenter *n.* (2) C3.
presentes *n.* these present documents. (1) N5.
preserue *vb. 1 pl.* (1) S1.
prest *n.* priest. (7) C1, P3; preest (6) S1, P1; preste (4) S1, C2; *pl.* priestes (1) C1; preestes (4) P3, C4; prestes (7) S1, C3; prestys (2) P4.
prest *adj.* ready, at hand. (1) C3 (D.131.19).
presume *vb. 3 sing. subj.* (1) P2.
pretendet *vb. past part.* (1) C3 (D.191.8); *pr.part.* pretendyng (2) C3, C5.
preue *inf.* prove. (1) C5 (D.221.40); preve (1) C3 (D.208.10); *past part.* proued (2) C8, C1; proved (1) C4; preued (1) C3 (D.180.17); provid (1) C5 (D.222.4); *ger.* provyng (1) C3.
preuves *n.* proofs. (1) C3.
preyse *vb. 3 sing. subj.* praise. (2) P4; prayes (1) P4.
price *n.* (4) P3, C3.
primat *n.* (1) C3.
primerment *adv.* first (Fr.). (1) P2 (D.115.1).
prince *n.* (17) C1, S1; prynce (5) P2, P3; pince (1) P5 (error); *pl.* princes (5) S1, P3.
princesse *n.* (1) C1; princes (1) C1. Both in D.165.
principal *n.* primary culprit. (1) C1 (D.163.44); principall, money. (2) C3 (D.183.24, 28); principall *adj.* (1) C3 (D.186.7); *pl.* principals *n. pl.* the main rafters and support beams. (3) N4 (D.238).
priory *n.* (1) P1 (D.112.8); priorie (6) S1, P3 (5); priourie (1) S2; *pl.* priouries (7) P4 (D.151); priories (1) P5.
priour *n.* (18) C1, P1; pryour (2) C3; prieur (1) S1 (D.37.3); *pl.* prioures (1) S1.
prison *n.* (30) C1, S1; prisone (3) C8, C1; pryson (3) C3, C4; *pl.* prisons (1) P3.
prisoned *vb. past part.* (1) P3 (D.145.16); *3 sing.* prisonyth (1) C1 (D.166.4).
prisoner *n.* (3) C3, C4; *pl.* prisoners (11) S1, C3; prisonners (1) S2; prysoners (1) S1.
priuat *adj.* here part of the unusual phrase "letters of Priuat [i.e. privy] seale." (1) C3 (D.145.32).
priueleged *vb. past part.* (1) C3.
priueleges *n.* (2) C3, C5; priuileges (2) S1; pruilegijs (1) P4 (D.153.5).
priuely *adv.* (2) P3, C4.
privey *adj.* always in reference to the Privy Seal. (1) C5; priue (40) S1, P2; prive (5) P3, C3; priuay (5) P3; pryvy (1) P3; priuey (1) C3; priue (1) P5;

priuee (1) P4. See pryue.
procede *inf.* (10) P2, C3; *3 sing.* prosedith (1) N4 (D.238.15); procedut (1) C4 (D.210.44); *past.* proceded (1) P3; *past part.* proceded (1) C3.
process *n.* usually legal proceeding. (1) C1; processe (8) C1, C3; proces (3) C3.
procession *n.* (1) P2.
proclamacion *n.* (21) C8, S1; *pl.* proclamacions (2) C8, S2.
proclame *inf.* (1) S1; proclayme (2) C3, C4; *past part.* proclamed (1) S2.
proctour *n.* (2) S2; *pl.* proctours (4) S2, P4.
procured *vb. past part.* (1) C3.
proef *n.* proof. (1) P5 (D.159.12).
profession *n.* religious vows. (2) S1 (D.53.7, 8).
profit *n.* (3) C3; prouffit (4) S1, P2; proffit (3) S1, S2; profite (3) C8, C5; profffyt (1) S2; proufit (2) P3, P4; *pl.* profites (12) C3, C5; proffites (7) C3 (D.198); profiteȝ (3) C4, C5; profitȝ (2) S2, P2; prouffitȝ (2) S1, C3; profits (1) N5; proufits (1) P2; proufites (1) C5; profitȝ (1) P3.
profitable *adj.* (1) C8 (D.161.34).
profre *inf.* (2) C8, C3; *3 pl.* profre (1) S1; *past.* proferd (1) C3; profered (1) C3; *past part.* proferred (1) C2; profored (1) C3.
progenitour *n.* (3) C3; *pl.* progenitours (6) S1, C3; progenitoures (2) P4.
prolonged *vb. past part.* (1) P1.
promette *vb. pl.* promise. (1) C2 (D.169.9); *ger.* promettyng (1) C5.
promise *n.* (1) P5; promisse (1) P3.
promised *vb. past part.* (1) P3; promysed (1) P3.
promocion *n.* (1) S1.
proper *adj.* personal, individual. (1) N8; propre (7) C3, C4; propir (1) C3.
prorogacion *n.* legal continuance. (2) S1 (D.48.4 etc.).
prorogue *inf.* (1) S1; *past part.* proroged (2) S1.
prosperite *n.* (6) S1, P1; prosperitee (2) P2, C3.
protection *n.* (1) S1, P3; proteccioun(e) (4) S1, C4; *pl.* protecciouns (1) S2.
protectour *n.* (1) C2.
protestacion *n.* legal demurral. (1) C5.
proued See preue.
prouide *inf.* (2) C5; *past part.* prouided (7) C5; prouyded (1) C5.
providence *n.* provision. (1) C4.
province *n.* (4) C5; prouince (1) C5; *pl.* provinces (3) C5. All citations in D.226.
provision *n.* (1) C1; provysyen (1) C5; provysyon (2) C5; prouision (7) S1, C2; *pl.* prouisions (6) S1 (5) P2.
prouoketh *vb. 3 sing.* (1) C5.
prouoste *n.* (1) S1; *pl.* prouostes (1) P2.
prouowr *n.* prover, one who becomes an informer to win amnesty or a lesser sentence. (2) C4 (D.212.16, 23). *OED prover;* this meaning obs. 1588.
pryue *adv.* prively, privately. (1) C8 (D.161.20).

pryvile *adv.* privily, privately. (1) C3 (D.192.7).
puissance *n.* strength, power. (1) P3; puissans (1) P3; puissaunce (2) P2, P3.
pulled *vb. past.* (1) N2.
punycion *n.* punishment. (2) C5 (D.230.7, 11).
punysche *inf.* punish. (1) C3; *past part.* ponysshid (1) C3.
punysshement *n.* (1) C3.
puplished *vb. past part.* published. (1) C5 (D.217.3).
purchace *vb. 3 pl.* (2) C3; *past part.* purchased (1) C3; pourchaced (1) P3; purchasyd (1) C3.
purpetuete *n.* perpetuity. (1) C5 (D.217.43).
purport *n.* (1) C5; purporte (1) C5; pourport (1) S1.
purpose *n.* (2) P2, C5; purpos (3) S1, P2.
purposeth *vb. 3 sing.* (1) P3; purposith (1) P3; *pl.* purposed (2) C8, C3; *pr. part.* purposing (1) C3; *past part.* purposid (1) P3; purposseuyd (1) N8 (D.233.15).
purs *n.* purse. (1) P5.
pursue *inf.* (8) C1, P3; poursue (2) S1, P3; *past.* pursuede (1) C1; *pr. part.* pursewyng (1) C1; *past part.* pursued (3) S1, C1; poursued (2) S1; poursuyd (1) S1.
pursute *n.* (1) P5; poursuyt (4) S1, C4 (D.64, 211.45); pursuyte (1) C1 (D.163.36); poursuite (1) S1; *pl.* poursuites (1) S2.
purveaunce *n.* (2) P3, C3; purueance (1) P3; poruoiaunce (1) C1.
purven *n.* a remedy, preparatory measure (Fr. purveien). (1) C5 (D.229.24). Form not recorded in *OED.*
puruey *inf.* (1) C3; purueye (1) P4; pourueye (1) P4; porveye (1) P3; *past part.* purueied (2) P3, C3; purueyd (1) C3; purueyde (1) C8; purveied (1) C5; pourveied (1) P3.
put *inf.* (9) S1, C3; putte (7) S1, C3; putt (2) P2, C5; *1 sing.* putte (1) N5; *3 sing.* put (14) S1, P3; putte (10) S1, C3; *pl.* putte (1) C3; *subj. pl.* put (1) S1; *past.* pot (1) C1 (D.165.4); *pr. part.* puttyng (2) C8, N8; *past part.* put (12) S1, P3; putte (8) S1, C3.

quantite *n.* (3) C5 (D.226); quantitee (1) C8.
quarter *n.* (8) P3, C2; *pl.* quarteres (5) C4 (D.211); quarters (1) C3.
quarts *n.* (1) C3.
queene *n.* (2) C5; quene (8) S2, P3; *gen.* quenes (1) S1.
quereleȝ *n.* quarrels. (1) C5.
quiete *n.* (1) S1.
quietly *adv.* (2) P4 (D.153).
quiknyng *ger.* bringing to life. (1) P3.
quinȝeme *n.* a tax of a fifteenth. (1) P4; quinsȝisme (6) C3 (D.179); quinȝisme (1) C3; quynȝisme (1) P3; *pl.* quinȝimes (4) S1 (D.26).

quote *n.* quota, a proper share of money owed. (1) C5 (D.226.16).
quysshons *n.* cushions (1) C3.
quyt *vb. past part.* acquitted, discharged. (1) C3; quyte (1) C5.

rape *n.* (2) C3 (D.201.8), C4 (D.213.5).
rased *vb. past part.* erased, removed. (2) S1 (D.53.3, 5); *ger.* rasyng (2) C3.
rate *n.* value. (3) C5 (D.226).
rathe *adv.* early. (1) C3 (D.189.45).
rather *adv.* (1) C1.
ratifficacion *n.* (1) C2.
ratify *inf.* (1) C4.
rauisshe *inf.* (1) C4; *past.* rauysshed (1) C3; ravisshid (1) C3 (D.189.11); *past part.* ravysshed (1) C3; *ger.* rauysshyng (1) C3.
raunsom *n.* (3) C3.
rauysshour *n.* ravisher. (2) C3.
raysyd *vb. past part.* raised. (1) C1 (D.164.24); reysed (2) C5.
realme *n.* (7) S1, C2; reaume (25) S1, P2; roialme (22) C3, P3; rewme (10) S1, S2; reame (8) C3, C5 (6); reamme (4) P3; reume (4) P3; royaume (4) S1, S2; roiaume (2) P2; roume (1) C3; reawme (1) C4; royavme (1) P4; (?) relem (1) S5 (D.109.3); *pl.* reumes (2) C3; reaumes (1) P2; reumys (1) C3; rewmes (1) S2.
reasonably *adv.* (1) C5; resonably (2) S1, C5; resounably (1) S2.
rebell *n.* (6) P3; *pl.* rebelles (1) C4.
rebellion *n.* (1) C3; rebellioune (1) C4.
rebellious *n.* rebels: "in resistens of thair enymes your rebellious." (1) C3 (D.198.7).
rebelliously *adv.* (1) C3.
receit *n.* act of receiving. (1) C3; receyte (1) C4 (D.210.28); *pl.* recepts (1) P2 (D.115.19).
receiue *inf.* (3) S1, P4; resceyve (6) P2 P3; receyue (3) C3, C4; resceyue (3) P3, C4; receve (1) P3; resceiue (1) C4; resceive (1) C4; resseyue (1) C3; resseyve (1) C3; resseyuen (1) C3 (D.198.8); *3 sing. subj.* receiue (1) S2; *pl. subj.* receyue (1) P2; *past.* receyued (2) C2, N5; *pr. part.* reccyuyng (1) C2 (D.175.4); resceyvyng (1) P3; *past part.* receiued (3) S1, C2; receyued (3) S1, S2; resceiued (3) C4 (D.210); receyuet (2) P1; receyved (1) C3; resceyued (1) S1; resseyued (1) C1; resceyved (1) C5; recevuyd (1) C3 (D.191.7); resseuyd (1) C3; *ger.* receyuing (1) S5; receyuyng (1) C3; resceyuyng (1) S1.
receivere *n.* one who receives taxes. (1) C3 (D.195.4); resseyuour (1) C5 (D.218.18); *pl.* resceiuours (1) P2 (D.123.7); receyuours (1) C5 (D.229.6).
recepcion *n.* (1) S2.
recettyng *ger.* receiving, harboring (a criminal). (2) C3 (D.192.5, 16).
recharged *vb. past part.* re-loaded (ships). (2) C3 (D.187.8, 11).

Glossary of Forms 375

recluse *n.* a solitary. (1) S1 (D.18.2).
recomande *vb. 1 sing.* (2) P1, C4; recomaunde (3) P1, P2; recomandde (1) P2; recommaund (1) P3; *pl.* recommande (1) S1; recommaund (1) C4; *past part.* recomaunded (1) C2; recommended (1) P3.
recommissed *vb. past part.* recommended. (2) C2 (D.177.7, 19).
recompensacion *n.* recompense. (1) P3 (D.140.13).
recompense *n.* (4) C5, P5; recompence (1) P3; recompens (1) P3.
recompensed *vb. past part.* (1) C5.
record *n.* (9) C1, P2; recorde (7) C8, C3; *pl.* recordes (4) C3, C4.
recordede *vb. past part.* (1) C1; *pr.part.* recordyng (1) P3.
recorder *n.* (1) C3 (D.199.22).
recouere *n.* recovery in law. (1) N4.
recouere *inf.* (1) C3; *past part.* rekiueryd (1) P2 (D.117.16).
recurs *n.* recourse. (2) P4.
reddicioun *n.* restoration. (1) C4 (D.215.14) *OED* obs. 1642.
rede *inf.* read. (1) C4 (D.211.29); *past part.* redd (2) P2 (D.122.6, 21); *ger.* redyng (1) C5 (D.221.31).
redely *adv.* (3) S1, P3; redyly (1) P3.
redempcion *n.* 1(2) C3.
redoubted *adj.* respected. (1) P2 (D.118.3).
redresse *n.* (1) C4.
redy *adj.* (22) S1, C2.
reentre *n.* re-entry, the right to re-enter or regain possession. (1) C3 (D.189.27).
reentre *inf.* to regain possession. (3) N8, N2; reentr (1) N8.
refet *vb. pl.* refreshed with food. (2) C3 (D.193.9, 13). *OED* obs. 1440.
reformation *n.* reform, redress. (1) C5; reformacion (5) C5 (all D.217).
refresshement *n.* refreshment. (1) P2.
refresshing *ger.* (1) S1; refresshyng (1) C3.
refuse *inf.* (1) C3; *past part.* refused (3) C5, P5.
regalie *n.* regality. (1) S1.
regard *n.* (1) P5.
regent *n.* (4) S2, P5 (D.81,159).
registre *n.* (1) S1.
rehersed *vb. past part.* mentioned, explained. (7) P2, C3; rehersid (7) P2, C4; rehersyd (1) C3; rehersode (1) C3 (D.183.29); *pr.part.* rehersing (1) C5.
reign *n.* (3) C3, C5; regne (20) C1, C3; reigne (16) P3, C3. See reyneth.
reioise *inf.* rejoice, have full possession. (1) P2; reiosse (2) S2.
rekene *inf.* reckon, account. (1) P2; *ger.* rekenyng (1) C2.
relacion *n.* narration. (1) C3 (D.199.37).
relees *n.* release, quit claim. (1) C1.
releeveth *vb. 3 sing.* (1) C3; *ger.* releuyung (1) C2 (D.167.18).
relese *inf.* (1) C4; *pl.subj.* reles (1) N5; *past part.* relesed (1) C2 (D.170.3); relesel

(1) C2 (170.7, ?error).
releuacion *n.* the act of relieving. (1) C5 (D.226.19).
relieff *n.* (1) C4; relyef (1) C5; relef (1) C5.
religious *adj.* (1) P4; religiouse (2) C4. See rligion.
remanant *n.* (3) S1; remenant (6) S1, P2; remenaunt (3) C2, C5; remanent (2) S2, C3; remanaunt (1) C5.
remayne *inf.* (2) C3, P4; *3 sing.* remaynes (1) C3 (D.191.7); *pl.* remayneth (1) C4 (D.212.13); *pl.subj.* remaigne (2) P3; *pr. part.* remaignyng (1) P4.
remedy *n.* (5) C3, C5; remedie (9) P3, C3; remede (4) S1, C3; remedye (1) C3; remydy (1) C5; *pl.* remedies (2) P3, P5.
remedied *vb. past part.* (2) C1; remediyd (1) C5 (D.227.8); remedyed (1) C4.
remembrance *n.* (2) S1, N2; remembrauncte (1) P2 (D.113.14).
remembrauncer *n.* an Exchequer office. (6) C5 (D.232); rembrauncer (1) C5 (D.232.17).
remembred *vb. past part.* (2) S1, P3.
remeved *vb. past part.* removed. (1) C3; remeued (1) C3 (both in D. 202); remwet (1) P2 (D.112.8). See remue.
remevement *n.* removement. (1) C3 (D.202.46).
remitte *vb. pl.* (1) S1; *past part.* remitted (2) P3; remited (1) P2; remyttid (1) C3.
remocioun *n.* remotion, the act of removing or being removed. (1) C4 (D.215.13). *OED* rare.
remue *inf.* remove. (2) C3 (D.199.35). See remeved.
ren *inf.* run. (1) P4 (D.154.3); renne (2) C3 (D.104.5), C4 (D.214.19); *3 sing.* renneth (2) P3, C3; *pr.part.* rennyng (1) S1.
rent *n.* (11) C3, C5; rente (7) C3; *pl.* rentes (14) S2, P2; rentis (2) P3.
rentholds *n.* (1) N6.
renunciacion *n.* (3) S1, S2.
repaiement *n.* (2) P3 (D.131.8, 16).
repair *inf.* (1) P3; repaire (1) N5; *pr. part.* repairyng (1) C4.
reparacion *n.* (14) S1, S2; reperacion (1) N8; *pl.* reparacions (1) C3.
repentyng *vb. pr. part.* (1) C4.
replicacions *n.* replies. (2) C1 (D.163.10, 26).
replid *vb. past sing.* replied. (1) C3; *past pl.* replieden (1) C1 (D.163.6).
report *inf.* (2) P3, C3.
reportes *n.* (2) P2, C5.
represented *vb. past.* (1) C8.
reprisale *n.* remedy. (1) C4 (D.211.17).
reprises *n.* yearly taxes on estates. (1) C3 (D.206.10).
reproef *n.* reproof. (1) P2 (D.122.19).
reproued *vb. past.* (1) C8 (D.161.23); reprevid (1) C1 (D.164.17).
reputacion *n.* (1) C5.
requir *inf.* (1) P3; requere (3) P3, P5; *3 sing.* requireth (7) S2, P2; requereth

Glossary of Forms

(1) S2; requerith (1) P5; requyreth (1) P3; *3 pl.* requireth (1) P3 (D.128.20); requiren (2) C5; *past.* required (2) C3, C5; requyed (1) C4 (D.211.26, ?error); *past part.* required (6) C5, P5.

requisitore *adj.* expressing a request. (1) C4 (D.217.8).

rere *inf.* raise (money). (1) C5; *past part.* rered (4) C3, P5; rerud (1) C4 (D.213.11). See arere.

rescous *n.* rescue. (6) P3 (D.132, D.134). See also reskewe.

reserued *vb. past part.* (1) P2; *pr. part.* reseruyng (1) C4.

resident *n.* (1) C5.

residue *n.* remainder. (3) C4, C5; resydue (1) C5.

resigne *inf.* (2) S1; *past.* resigned (1) P3.

resiste *inf.* (3) P3.

resistence *n.* (1) P4; resistens (1) C3.

reskewe *inf.* rescue. (1) P3.

reson *n.* (17) S1, C1. See reasonably.

resonable *adj.* (16) S1, P2; resounable (5) S1, S2; resonabull (2) C3; raisounable (1) S1 (D.32.10).

resort *inf.* (1) C4 (D.214.7).

resorte *n.* attendance. (1) C4 (D.214.10).

respit *n.* (1) S1.

respite *inf.* (1) C3; *past part.* respited (1) S2; respitid (1) C3.

responsiue *adj.* (1) S1 (D.57.5).

rest *n.* (3) S1, C4; reste (6) S1, P2; reest (1) P3 (D.131.21).

restitucion *n.* (9) S1 (8), S2.

restore *inf.* (7) C2, C3; *pl. subj.* restore (1) C3 (D.189.39); *past part.* restored (2) C4, C5 restorid (1) C3 (D.189.43); restoryd (1) C5.

restreyng *ger. for* restreynyng. (1) C4 (D.216.45 ? error).

restyng *pr. part.* (1) P4.

resume *inf.* (1) P4; *3 sing.* resumeth (1) C5; *past part.* resumed (1) C5.

resumpcion *n.* usually "act of . . . " (7) C5; resumpcioun (1) C4; resumpsion (2) C5; resompcion (1) C5.

retenue *n.* (12) S1, C2; retenu (2) P2, C2.

rethorik *n.* (1) C3 (D.197.10).

retournable *adj.* (1) C3; retourneable (1) C3; *pl.* retournables (1) C3 (D.195.13).

retourne *n.* act of returning. (1) C4; *pl.* financial gain, retornes (1) P3.

retourne *inf.* (2) S1, S2; *pl. subj.* retourne (1) C4; *pr. part.* retournyng (2) S1; *past part.* returned (1) C3; retorned (1) C3; retourned (1) C3; *ger.* retournyng (2) S1, C3.

reuenues *n.* income. (7) S1, P2; reuenuʒ (5) P2, P3; reuenus (2) P5, N5; revenueʒ (2) C4; revenuʒ (2) C4.

reverence *n.* (1) C5 (D.225.25); reuerence (16) C1, C2.

reuerend *adj.* (1) C3; reuerent (9) P3, C3.

reuerse *inf.* (1) C1.
reuersions *n.* rights of succession when the original grant expires. (5) C4 (D.210); reuercions (1) P2.
reviguryng *ger.* reinvigorating. (1) P3 (D.146.29). *OED* obs. 1447.
revoke *inf.* (1) S1; *ger.* reuokinge (1) C2.
reward *n.* (4) P2, P3; *pl.* rewardes (5) C5; rewardeʒ (1) C4.
rewarde *inf.* (1) C5; *past part.* rewardid (1) N5.
reyne *n.* rain. (1) C5.
reyneth *vb. 3 sing.* reigns. (1) C3. See reigne.
riche *adj.* (2) C5 (D.218.25, 26).
riches *n.* (1) C5.
ride *inf.* (1) C3; *past* rode (1) P3 (D.145.11); *pr. part.* rydyng (1) C3; *past part.* riden (1) P3 (D.146.8); *ger.* riding (1) C5.
right *n.* (16) S1, C1; ryght (3) C1, C3; riʒth (1) C1 (D.166.14); ryth (1) C5 (D.218.30); *pl.* rightes (1) P3; ryghtes (1) S1.
right *adj.* (124) S1, C1; ryght (18) C8, S1; ryht (16) C1, S1; riʒt (16) S1, S2; ryʒt (3) C2; ryghte (1) N5; riʒte (1) C3.
rightfull *adj.* (1) C3; ryghtful (2) C8, C1.
rightwisnesse *n.* righteousness (5) C1 (D.163); rightwisnes (1) C3; rightwosenesse (1) C3 (D.189.44); rightwysnesse (1) C3.
rightwyse *adj.* righteous. (1) S1; rightwys (2) C3, P5; rightwose (1) C3 (D.189.1).
rigorously *adv.* (1) C5.
riot *n.* (2) C3, C5; ryot (1) P3; *pl.* riotes (2) C5; riottes (2) C3, P4.
riotous *adj.* (2) P4, C5; riotouse (1) C3.
rise *inf.* (1) C3; *past pl.* rose (1) P3.
risers *n.* rebels. (1) C3 (D.185.2); rysers (1) C3. *OED* obs. 1655. See arrysers.
rligion *n.* religion. (1) P5 (D.158.39).
robbed *past part.* (1) C3; *past pl.* robbeden (1) C1 (D.164.23).
robbers *n.* (1) C3.
roberie *n.* (1) C4; roborie (2) C4; *pl.* robberyes (3) C3; roberyes (1) C3.
rodde *n.* rod, symbol of office. (1) P2 (D.123.4).
rode *n.* rood, or cross: "rode tree." (1) C1 (D.164.43).
rofe *n.* (11) N4 (D.238).
rolle *n.* a roll of parchment pages. (1) S2 (D.77.2); *pl.* rolles (1) P5 (D.159.31).
romyng *pr. part.* roaming. (1) C4.
rowte *n.* route, riot. (1) C3 (189.7).
royal *adj.* (3) S5, P5; roial (4) S1, P1; roiale (3) P2, P5; rial (2) C1; riall (1) C3; ryal (1) C1 (D.163.35); roile (1) P5 (D.159.42).
ruinous *adj.* (1) C5.
rule *n.* (5) P3, C3; reule (2) C3, P4; revle (1) C3 (D.199.35); *pl.* reules (1) P4; rules (1) P3.
rule *inf.* (2) S1, P3; *3 sing.* rulith (1) C5; *past pl.* ruledyn (1) C3 (D.178.5);

past part. reuled (4) P2, C3; yrulyd (1) C5 (D.218.30).
rumor *n.* uproar. (6) P3 (D.142); rumour (1) C3 (D.188.14).
ruynes *n.* ruins. (1) C5.
rychesse *n.* riches. (2) C1, C3.
rye *n.* (1) C3; rie (2) C3.
ryng *inf.* ring. (1) S1; *past part.* rong (2) S1 (D.5.4).
rynges *n. pl.* (1) C3.
ryver *n.* (1) P5; *pl.* rivers (1) C5.

saale cloþes *n.* sailcloths, cloth for making sails. (1) C1 (D.38.2).
sacrament *n.* (1) P2.
sacred *vb. past part.* consecrated. (1) S2 (D.80.3).
sadd *adj.* sad, serious. (1) C4 (D.211.42).
safe *adj.* (3) P3, C3; saufe (11) (D.211); saue (6) P1, P2; sauf (5) S1, S2; saff (2) C3 (D.205); saaf (2) S1, S2; saf (1) C1; save (1) C3; sauue (1) P3 (D.131.4). 15 times in combination with condut, conduit; 5 times in combination with gard, ward.
safeguarde *n.* (1) P3; saufgard(e) (6) P2, C2; sauegard(e) (4) P2, C3; sauue gard (1) P3; saufegard (2) P2; *pl.* savegardys (1) C3. Usually written as two words.
saffeli *adv.* safely. (1) C3; sauely (2) P3, P4; saufly (2) S2, P5.
saffte *n.* safety. (1) C1 (D.164.35).
sage *adj.* (3) P3, C3.
sailed *vb. past.* (3) P3 (D.145); *past part.* sailled (1) C3; seiled (1) P5 (D.159.37).
saint *adj.* (16) S1, C3; saynt (1) C4; seint (33) S1, P3; seinte (1) C4; seynt (36) P3, C3; seynte (1) C1; senct (1) P2 (D.113.19); *n. gen. pl.* sauntes (1) C2 (D.173.12).
sak *n.* sack. (2) C3; *pl.* sakes (1) P3.
sake *n.* (3) P2, C3.
salats *n. pl.* sallets, light headpieces for armor. (1) C5 (D.222.12).
sale *n.* act of selling. (2) P3 (D.131.23), C3 (D.208.8).
salors *n.* cellars, containers. (1) C3 (D.197.15).
salt *n.* (7) C3, C4 (6).
saluacion *n.* (1) C3.
same *adj.* (329) C8, S1.
sanappes *n. pl.* strips of cloth placed over the outer part of the table cloth to preserve it from being soiled. (1) C3 (D.197.13). *OED* obs. 1440.
sandes *n.* (1) C5 (D.229.18).
satisfaccion *n.* (1) N5.
satisfie *inf.* (1) C3; *past part.* satisfied (4) S1, C3.
savacion *n.* preservation. (1) C5; sauacion (3) C3 (D.186.13), C5 (D.218); sauuacion (1) S1.

saue *inf.* (2) C8, P2; *pr. part.* sauying (5) S2 P4; savyng (3) C3, C5; *past part.* saued (1) P2; sauyd (1) C3; *ger.* saueyng (1) C2 (D.173.15); sauying (1) P4 (D.153.6).

save *prep.* (2) C5; safe (2) C3; sauf (1) C3; saue (1) P2. Found only in the phrase "save only."

saufwarde *n.* safe-guarding. (1) S1 (D.51.6).

saume *adv.* together, "clappyd saume ye buke." (1) C2 (D.173.7).

savyng *prep.* (1) P3; sauyng (5) C2, C3.

say *inf.* (15) C1, C2; sey (17) S1, P3; saye (2) P2, P3; seye (2) P3, C5; *3 sing.* seith (4) P3, C5; sayeth (1) P3; sayth (1) S2 (D.75.3); seies (1) C3 (D.185.6); *pl.* sey (1) S1; *past.* seid (8) P3 (D.142.22, D.145.25 etc.); saide (4) C8, P3; sayd (1) C8; *past pl.* seiden (1) P3 (D.145.24); *pr. part.* saying (1) C3; sayng (1) P3; seieng (1) P3; seyng (1) C5; *past part.* seid (710) P2, C3; said (695) C1, P1; saide (408) C8, S1; seide (92) C3, C4; seyd (46) C1, S1; sayd (42) P1, P3; sayde (17) C3, N2; seyde (6) C1, N8; saiden (3) C4 (D.211); sayn (2) S1, N2; sad (1) N2; *ger.* saiyng (1) C5 (D.230.3).

science *n.* information. (2) S2 (D.90.1), C3 (D.197.10); *pl.* sciences (1) P3 (D.146.24).

scole *n.* school. (9) C5 (D.219, 220, 221; always in phrases "to" or "at scole"). *pl.* scoles (3) P3.

scolemaistres *n.* (1) P3 (D.146.3).

scoler *n.* scholar, student. (4) P3, C5; *pl.* scholers (7) P3, C5.

scripture *n.* style of writing, engraving. (2) S2 (D.81.16, 19).

scrupule *n.* legal uncertainty. (2) S1 (D.62.2, 7).

seal *n.* normally refers to one of the king's seals of state: the Great Seal, Privy Seal, or Signet Seal. (59) S1, S2; seel (39) S1, S2; seall (8) P3, C3; seale (5) P3, C3; seell (4) P2 (D.115); sealle (1) P3; seele (1) P3; *pl.* seales (9) C3, N2; seals (8) C3, C4; seeles (4) S2; sealx (2) P4 (D.156); sealles (1) N4; seles (1) N4.

seald *vb. past part* (1) C4; seled (3) C1, C2.

seche *inf. seek.* (1) C8; *ger.* sechyng (1) C8. Both in D.161.

second *adj.* (6) S1, C1; seconde (5) P3, C3; secund(e) (2) P3, C3.

secrely *adv.* secretly. (1) S1 (D.70.3).

secret *adj.* (3) P5; secrete (3) C3, P5. In D.158, "secret signet" refers to the Signet Seal.

secretarie *n.* (1) P3 (D.136.10).

secte *n.* a following. (1) C5 (D.218.9).

seculer *adj.* non-monastic. (4) C4; *pl.* seculers (1) C4. All in D.213.

sedule *n.* schedule, list. (1) P3; cedule (16) S1, S2.

see *n.* sea. (24) S1, C1; se (1) C5.

see *inf.* (6) S1, P1; se (7) S1, C1; *imp.* seeþ (1) S1 (D.52.5); seeth (1) S2 (D.84.5); *subj. pl.* see (8) S1, S2; se (5) S1, S2; *past.* sawe (3) P3 (D.142); sye (1) P3

Glossary of Forms 381

(D.142.37); *pr. part.* seyng (3) P3, C5; seynge (1) C2; *past part.* seen (10) S1, S2; seene (1) S1; sene 81) C3; sey (1) P3 (D.142.32); seyen (4) S1.

seise *inf.* seize, hold legally. (1) C4; sese (1) C3; *3 sing.* seiseth (2) C4; *pl.* sesed (1) P5 (D.160.2); *past part.* sesed (1) P5 (D.160.3); sesid (1) C3 (D.188.2); saised (1) S2; *ger.* seisyng (2) C5 (D.217.25, 42; see seisyn); seysyng (1) C4 (D.217.41).

seisyn *n.* legal possession. (1) C5 (D.217.26, variant of seisyng D.217.25, 42, seysyng D.217.42); seysyne (1) N2 (D.234.11).

seke *adj.* sick . (1) P2; seek (1) P3. See sikeness.

selarie *n.* salary. (1) C4 (D.213.8).

self *pro.* (15) S1 (D.18.3, 65.5), C2, P3, etc., 4 times with pl. (e.g., D.193.15, 203.34); selfe (6) C2, C3, 3 times with pl.; silf (2) C5 (D.218.26, 32, sing); selff (1) C3 (D.192.6 with pl); selue (1) C4 (D.212.33 sing.); selfes (1) P2 (D.122.36 with pl.).

sell *inf.* (1) C3; selle (4) C3; *past pl.* sold (5) C4, C5; solde (2) N4, N5; *pr.part.* sellyng (1) C3 (D.190.5); *ger.* sellyng (1) C3 (D.208.3).

sellers *n. pl.* (1) C5.

semblable *adj.* (10) S1, P2.

semblably *adv.* (8) S1, P3; semblablely (1) S1; sembly (1) P3 (D.132.10).

semble *n.* aphetic form of assembly. (1) P3 (D.130.9). *OED* obs. 1717.

seme *inf.* (1) C3; *impers.* semeth (7) S1, P2; semeþ (4) S1; semyth (1) C3; *3 pl.* semeth (1) P2 (D.122.8); *past.* semed (1) C4; semyd (1) C5.

send *inf.* (3) S1, C3; sende (5) C1, P3; *1 sing.* send (1) P1; sende (1) N2; *3 sing.* sendeth (2) P3, C3; *pl.* sende (51) S1, P2; send (8) S1, P1; sendde (1) P2; *past* sent (20) S1, C1; send (1) C4 (D.211.39); sende (1) C3; *past part.* sent (11) S1, S2; send (2) S1, C3; ysende (1) N2 (D.235.5).

seneschal *n.* (2) S2 (D.77.3, 5).

sensabul *adj.* perceptible. (3) C5 (D.218).

sentence *n.* judgment. (3) C1, P4 (D.157.5, 166.9, 10); wisdom (2) C3 (D.197.7, 9).

serchers *n.* officials who inspect for taxable items. (1) P2.

serches *n.* inspections. (2) C3 (D.203.37, 204.43).

sergeant *n.* (2) P3, C5; *pl.* sergeantes (1) P2.

sermons *n.* (1) C3.

seruant *n.* (40) S1, C1; seruaunt (4) C3, C5; *pl.* seruantes (9) C3, C4; seruantʒ (8) C4, C5; seruans (1) S2 (D.90.2); serauntes (?error) (1) P3 (D.150.4); seruantez (1) C5; seruauntez (1) C3; servantʒ (1) C5; suruentʒ (1) C5.

serue *inf.* (10) C1, S1; serve (3) C1, C3; sarue (1) P4; seruen (1) C1 (D.163.25); *past part.* serued (2) C2, C3.

seruice *n.* (49) C1, S1; seruyce (5) C8, C1; seruise (2) C1, P2; seruys (2) N5; seruyse (2) P2; service (1) C3 (D.207.9); ceruice (1) P3 (D.146.28); *pl.* seruices (7) P3, C4; seruicez (2) C4.

seruitor *n.* (1) C3; seruiteur (2) P5; seruitour (1) P5. The last two spellings are in D. 159.

sese See seise.

session *n.* (3) C3 (D.201); cession (3) P3, C3; cessioun (1) C4; *pl.* cessions (3) P3 (D.142).

sette *inf.* (3) S1, P2; *1 sing.* sette (1) P3; *3 sing.* set (2) C1, P3; *subj.* set (1) S1; *past.* set (1) S1; *past part.* set (4) C3, N5; sette (7) S1, P3; *ger.* settyng (2) P3 (D.131.3, 4).

seueral *adj.* separate. (1) S1; seuerall (2) P3, P5; *pl.* sauerales (1) S1 (D.2.6); seueralx (1) P3 (D.148.4).

seuerally *adv.* separately, individually. (3) C3, C5; seuerealy (1) C4.

seurkepyng *n.* (1) S1 (D.51.6).

sewed, sewith. See sue.

sext See sixt.

sexti *adj.* sixty. (1) P3 (D.142.12).

shall *vb. pr. sing. and pl.* (89) P2, C3; shal (79) S1, C1; shul (10) C1, S1; schul (1) S1; schall (7) N8, P2; shull (6) P3, C3; shalle (3) P2, C4; schal (3) C1, P2; *pl.* shullen (2) S1, C2; shulen (1) N4; shulleth (1) P1 (D.110.4); *past sing. and pl.* shuld (42) C1, S1; shulde (23) C8, C1; sholde (15) C8, P2; shold (7) C3, C5; shoulde (4) C4 (D.204); soulde (1) C2 (D.173.11); shulden (1) C1 (D.163.53).

shalbe *vb.* (as one word) (4) S2, C4.

shame *n.* (4) P2, P3; schame (1) P2.

sharp *adj.* (1) P5 (D.159.2).

sharpely *adv.* (1) S1 (D.69.25).

she (9) S1, C3; sche (5) C1, C4 (4 in D.212); scho (2) P2 (D.119.7, D.120.7); sheo (1) P2 (D.121.7). The last three citations are from different versions of the same document. *gen.* her (29) S1, C1; hir (18) S2, C3; hur (18) C5 (all in D.222). See also herself.

sherif *n.* (1) C3; shiref (18) C3, C5 (17, D.223); shirref (2) C3; sherrif (1) C3; sherief (1) P4; shirif (1) P3; shereff (1) C3; shreef (1) C3 (D.185.5) shereve (1) C3; *pl.* shirifes (3) C4 (D.216); sherifs (1) C3; shereues (1) S1; sherefs (1) C5; shirefs (1) C5; shirrefs (1) P2; shirreves (11) C3 (D.190).

shette *vb. past.* shut. (1) C5 (D.222.14); *past part.* shet (1) P3.

shetes *n.* sheets. (1) C3.

shewe *inf.* (7) C8, S1; *3 sing.* sheweth (3) C5; shewieth (1) P3 (D.140.1); shewith (1) C3; schewyth (2) C1 (D.164.8, 38); *pl.* shewe (3) S1, S2; sheweth (3) C3 (D.181.2, 220.1, 224.1); shewyn (1) C2 (D.174.1); shewen (2) C3, C5; *past.* shewed (3) N2, C5; shewid (1) C3; *pr. part.* shewing (1) P4; shewyng (1) C3; *past part.* shewed (14) C8, S1; shewede (1) C1; shewyd (2) C2, P3.

shillyngis *n.* shillings. (1) P3 (D.143.3).

ship *n.* (16) P1, P3; shipp (19) P1, C4 (18 in D.211); shippe (2) C3; *pl.* shippes

Glossary of Forms 383

(16) S1, P3; shyppes (1) P3.
shipped *vb. past part.* (1) C3; *ger.* shipping (3) S1, P5; shippyng (2) S1, C3.
shire *n.* (56) S1, P2; shir (4) S1, P3; shyre (3) C1, C3; schere (2) N5; schyr (1) N8; sshere (1) N5 (D.241.6); chyre (1) P4 (D.153.13); *pl.* shires (7) C2, C3.
shoo *n.* shoe. (1) P3.
shop *n.* (7) N5 (D.240).
short *adj.* (5) S1, P3; shorte (1) C5.
shotte *n.* shot, shooting. (1) C3 (D.186.5).
shoveles *n.* (1) C3 (D.197.20).
shryne *n.* (1) P4 (D.153.4).
side *n.* (9) S1, P3; syde (4) S1, P2; *pl.* sides (1) C4.
sidetrees *n.* architectural beam-supports. (2) N4; sidetreeȝ (1) N4 (both in D. 238).
siege *n.* (1) S2.
signe *n.* signature, in "signe manuell." (1) C4 (D.209.7).
signet *n.* the Signet seal. (113) S1, S2.
signifie *vb. pr. pl.* make known. (1) P2 (D.117.1); signiffie (4) S1, P2.
sikeness *n.* sickness. (1) S5; sikenesse (1) P5; sekenesse (3) S1, C3; seknesse (1) P2.
sikerlie *adv.* surely, certainly. (1) C3 (D.185.11); sekirly (1) S2 (D.105.4).
silor *n.* canopy. (1) C3 (D.197.12).
siluer *n.* (5) P3, C3; syluer (1) P1.
simple *adj.* (3) P1, C1; symple (11) C8, C1.
singuler *adj.* special. (5) P2, P3; singulier (2) P2, P3; synguler (1) C3.
sinistre *n.* threatening. (1) C5.
sir *adj. (address)* (46) S1, C1; sire (22), PO, N5 (12); *pl.* sires (4) C1; syres (1) C1; syrys (1) C3 (D.184.1).
sise *n.* size. (1) N8 (D.233.10).
sith *adv. and prep.* since. (6) S2, P2 (D.115.22 etc.); sithe (5) C1, S2; sithen (5) C8, C1; siþ (2) P2 (D.115.24, 26)); sithon (1) C5; syht (1) P2 (D.113.15); seth (3) C2, C3; sethen (2) C3, C5.
sitte *inf.* (1) P3, C4; *3 sing.* sitte (1) C5 (D.218.24); sitteth (1) P2; *past.* sat (3) (D.142); *pr.part.* sitting (1) P3; syttyng (1) N2.
sixt *adj.* (1) N5; syxth (3) N5 (D.241); sext (2) N2; sixte (1) C3; sexte (1) N2.
slaughtre *n.* (1) C1 (D.161.10).
slee *inf.* slay. (2) C1; *imp.* sle: "cryinge with loude voice sle, sle." (2) C8 (D.161.17); *3 sing. subj.* sle (1) C4 (D.212.35); *past.* sleeth (1) C4 (D.212.7); *past part.* slayn (9) C1, P2; slayne (1) C3.
sleue *n.* sleeve. (1) N2 (D.236.9).
slitte *vb. past.* (1) C3 (D.194.8).
smokke *n.* smock, the usual undergarment for women. (2) C3, C4.
smyte *inf.* (1) P3; *past.* smote (1) C3; smite (1) P3 (D.142.40).

so *adv., conj., etc.* (220) C8, S1; soo (18) S1, C2; soe (1) N6 (D.241.16).
socage *inf.* pay socage, land rent. (1) N8 (D.233.6). *OED* does not list verbal use.
socour *n.* assistance. (7) S1, C1; soccoure (1) C5; socowr (1) C3; sokor(e) (2) C1 (D.164).
socoured *vb. past part.* (1) C3; socored (1) C3.
sodeine *adj.* sudden. (1) P4.
sodenly *adv.* (1) C3; sodeynly (1) C2 (D.176.6).
soiourneth *vb. 3 sing.* (1) S1 (D.6.10).
soldiour *n.* (1) C5; *pl.* soudeours (10) C2 (D.167); soudiours (1) P3; sowdyours (1) P3; souldiours (1) P3.
solemply *adv.* (1) C3.
solempne *adj.* formal, ceremonious. (1) C3 (D.182.10).
some *adj.* (11) C8, C1; sum (5) S1, P1; som (5) C8, C1; somm (1) C3; somme (1) P5 (D.158.11); summe (1) C3.
somer *n.* summer. (1) C5 (D.218.10).
somers *n.* bearing beams. (1) N4 (D.238.5).
somertyme *n.* (1) C5 (D.229.22).
sommones *n.* sommons. (1) C5 (D.223.14); summyns (1) C4 (D.217.28).
sompned *vb. past part.* summoned. (2) C8 (D.161).
somtyme *adv.* (8) S1, C3; sumtyme (3) S1, C4.
son *n.* (1) C3; sonne (6) C5 (D.222); sone (2) C1, C4; soon (1) S2; *pl.* sones (1) C3; sonnes (1) C3.
sonday *n.* (2) P3 (D.145.9, 11).
sonderly *adv.* separately, individually. (1) P3.
sondry *adj.* separate. (1) C3.
soone *adv.* (3) S2, C4; sone (9) P1, S1; *comp.* sonner (3) S1, P3; soner (1) C5; sonnor (1) P3; souner (1) C4; sounere (1) C1.
soonfect *n.* ? infection. (1) C3 (D.207.4). Error? Form not recorded in *OED*.
sore *adv.* (2) C4, C5 (D.216.12, 227.6).
soroufull *adj.* (1) C3.
sotell *adj.* crafty. (1) C4; sotill (1) C3; see subtiles.
soth *n.* good deed: "to do some soth to the church." (1) N5 (D.241.11); sothe, truth. (1) N2 (D.236.9).
souereign *n.* (5) C3; souerain (55) S1, P2; soueraigne (41) C2, P2; souuerain (21) P2, P3; souerayne (18) C3, C5; souerayn (12) C3, P4; souereyne (10) P2 (D.213); soueraign (9) C2, C3; souueraign (8) P2; souereyn (6) P1, C3; souereigne (5) C1, C3; souuerayn (4) P3, C3; souueraigne (3) P2; souuerein (2) P3, C3; souuereigne (1) P2; souerainge (1) P1 (D.112.12); soueragne (1) C3; souerein (1) P1; *pl.* souueraines (1) S1.
soule *n.* soul. (9) C1, P2; sowle (4) C1, P2; saule (1) C3; *pl.* soules (8) P3, C5; soulys (1) P4.

Glossary of Forms 385

sowe *inf.* (1) C1 (D.166.5).
sowneth *vb. 3 sing.* sounds, i. e., tends towards: "which sowneth to the kynges grete disauaile," (1) C3 (D.188.18).
soyl(e) *n.* property. (7) N8 (D.233).
space *n.* interval of time. (6) C2, P3.
spades *n.* (1) C3.
sparing *vb. ger.* (1) P3.
sparres *n.* building timbers. (1) N4; sperreʒ (1) N4 (D.238.6, 13).
spech *n.* conversation. (1) P3 (D.142.18).
special *adj.* (15) C1, C2; speciall (7) P3, C4; speciale (5) S1, S2; specyall (1) C1.
specially *adv.* (6) P3, C3; specialy (4) S1, P1; specialli (1) C5; speciali (1) C1.
specified *vb. past part.* (7) S1, P4; specified (1) S1.
spede *vb. subj. pl.* speed, hurry. (1) S1; *past part.* sped (1) P5; spedd (1) P3.
spedy *adv.* (1) P3.
speed *n.* (1) P3; spede (7) S1, S2.
speke *inf.* (3) C1, P1; *imp.* spekeþ (2) S1 (D.16.9, D.26.10); *past.* spak (1) C3 (D.173.12); *past part.* spoke (1) S2 (D.98.2); spoken (1) C5 (D.218.20).
speker *n.* (1) C2 (D.167.1).
spende *inf.* (2) C3, C5; *pl.* spenden (1) C1 (D.162.9); *past part.* spendid (1) C2 (D.168.6).
speres *n.* spears. (1) C5 (D.222.12).
spicerie *n.* a storehouse for spices. (1) C1 (D.166.2); *pl.* spiceries (3) C3 (D.208); spyceryes (1) C3.
spiritual *adj.* (1) C4; spirituell (11) C1, C3; spirituel (6) S1, P3; *pl.* spirituelx (9) C4, C5; spiritualx (1) C5; spirituelles (1) C4; spirituels (1) C3.
spiritueltees *n.* estates belonging to a church office. (1) C5 (D.226.3).
spoilled *vb. past part.* (1) S1.
spones *n.* spoons. (1) C3.
spycers *n.* spicers, spice merchants. (1) C3.
spyannac *n.* pinnace. (1) C4 (D.211.25); spynnace (1) C4 (D.211.24).
spynners *n.* (1) C4.
squier *n.* (19) S1, S2; squyer (16) P2, C3; sqwyer (2) S1; *pl.* squiers (1) P4.
stable *adj.* unmovable. (1) C4 (D.209.8).
stablet *vb. past part.* established. (1) C3 (D.193.4).
stag *n.* floor of a building, "above stag," upper floor. (1) C5 (D.233.18).
stand *inf.* (1) S1; stonde (3) C3, C5; stande (2) P2, C2; stond (1) C5; *3 sing.* standeth (4) S1, S2; stondith (4) C1, C3; stondeth (2) P3; standith (1) C1; stont (1) P2 (D.122.28); *pl.* stande (3) S2, P3; standen (2) P3 (D.136.6, 8); stonden (2) C8, C3; stant (1) P2 (D.116.3); stonde (1) C4; *subj. sing.* stand(e) (3) S2, P5; stonde (2) C1, C4; stand (1) C3 (D.201.28); *subj. pl.* stond (2) C4, C5; stonde (2) C4; *past sing.* stode (3) P3 (D.142); stood (1) C1 (D.164.7);

past pl. stode (3) C2, P3; stande (1) S1 (D.14.4); stovde (1) N2 (D.235.12); *pr. part.* standyng (1) C1; *past part.* stande (1) S1 (D.14.4); stonde (1) P3 (D.139.2).

staple *n.* a place which has royal authority to monopolize trade in specified goods; usually refers to the Staple at Calais. (3) P3, C3.

state *n.* estate, condition. (1) C3; property (1) P5 (D.160.5).

statute *n.* law. (2) C5; statut (2) S2, C1; statuyt (1) P5 (D.159.40); *pl.* statutes (4) P3, C3; statuȝ (1) C5; statutȝ (3) C5.

statute *adj.* statutory, "acte statute." (1) C5 (D.224.33).

stede *n.* place. (1) S1.

stere *inf.* to guide. (1) S1 (D.53.8).

sterlinges *n.* English money. (6) C3, N4.

sterre *n.* star, "sterre chambre." (1) P3 (D.142.1).

steward *n.* (4) C5 (D.218); stuarde (1) C3; stward (1) C3 (D.192.12); styward (1) P4 (D.153).

stikked *vb. past.* stuck, stabbed. (1) C4 (D.212.8).

still *adv.* (4) C3, P5; stille (8) S1, P3; styll (1) C3; stylle (1) P3.

stipendiar *adj.* receiving a stipend. (1) C4 (D.213.7).

stipendiaries *n.* (2) C4 (D.213.12, 16).

stired See sturre.

stokfissh *n.* dried fish. (1) P3; stockfyssh (1) P3 (both D.145).

stolen *vb. past part.* (1) P3.

ston *n.* stone (2) N8, C3.

stories *n.* tales. (1) C3 (D.197.6).

story *n.* the floor-level of a building. (1) N8; *pl.* storyes (1) N8 (both in D.233).

straitely *adv.* directly, immediately. (2) P2, P4; straytely (1) C5; streytely (1) C4.

strange *adj.* foreign. (2) P2, C3; straunge (1) C3.

strangers *n.* aliens. (3) C3 (D.193); straungers (2) C8, P3.

strangly *adv.* strongly. (1) P4 (D.154.3).

straw *n.* (1) N4.

stre *n.* straw. (1) C3 (D.197.20). *OED* dial., last example 1422.

strecche *inf.* stretch. (1) C2; *pr. part.* strecchyng (1) N8.

streht *adv.* straight. (1) P2 (D.113.21).

strength *n.* (1) C5 (D.232.41); strenghth (1) P3 (D.145.18); strenght (1) C4; strenthe (1) C5; streyngth (1) C3 (D.199.42); *pl.* strengthes (2) P3.

strengthyng *ger.* strengthening. (2) S1, C1 (D.69.14, 163.45).

streped *vb. past.* stripped. (1) C3.

strete *n.* street. (3) N8, C3; *pl.* stretes (1) C3.

strong *adj.* (3) C1; stronge (2) C8, C3. *comp.* strenger (1) C8.

struglyng *ger.* (1) N2.

stuff *n.* supplies. (2) P3, C3; stuf (3) P5 (D.218); stuffe (2) P2, C3.

stuffed *vb. past part.* (1) P4.

Glossary of Forms

sturre *inf.* stir. (1) S1; *3 sing.* stureth (2) C3 (D.188.15, 16); *past part.* stured (2) P3, S5; stired (1) C5; *ger.* sturyng (1) P3.

stwys *n.* stews, brothels. (4) C3 (D.192); stywes (4) C3 (D.193).

style *n.* the formulaic phrase or phrases used in an official document. (2) S1 (D.1); stile (1), stille (2) S2 (all in D.81); *pl.* styles (1) S1.

stynte *inf.* cease. (1) P3 (D.142.44).

stywehouses *n.* brothels. (1) C3 (D.193.8).

subget *n.* subject. (1) C2; subgit (4) P2 (D.113); *pl.* subgettes (6) S1, P3; subgittȝ (5) P3, C3; sugettes (4) S1; suggettes (4) S1; sougettes (3) S1; subgettȝ (1) P3; subgiettes (1) C3 (D.217.6); subgitȝ (1) S1; subgittes (1) S1; subgitts (1) P3; subiettes (1) C3 (D.182.23); soubgettes (1) S1; sougetes (1) P3; sougittes (1) S1; sugites (1) P2.

subside *n.* (3) S1, C2; subsidie (9) C3, C4; subsidi (1) N6; *pl.* subsidies (3) C3, C5; subsidieȝ (1) C5; subsidijs (1) C3 (D.196.3).

substance *n.* portion. (1) S1; substaunce (1) C3.

substancial *adj.* (1) S1.

subtiles *adj.* "wronges subtiles." (1) C8 (D.161.3). See sotell.

suburbes *n.* (1) C3; subarbes (1) N2 (D.236.6).

succession *n.* (1) P2.

successors *n.* (2) C5 (D.224); succesours (1) C4; successores (2) C3; successoures (2) C3, P4; successours (11) C3, C5.

such *adj. and adv.* (72) C8, PO and throughout; suche (113) C8, P1; swich (5) C1, S1, C3 (D.177); sich (4) C5 (D.221); sych (3) N8, C3 (D.208.4); soche (1) C3 (D.188.20); sweche (2) N4 (D.237.9, 11); swiche (1) P2 (D.117.18); swych (1) C3 (D.182.21); suyche (1) P4 (D.153.18).

sue *inf.* undertake legal action. (2) P3, C4; *3 sing.* sewith (2) C1, C5; *pl.* suyn (1) C3 (D.178.2); *past* sued (3) C3, C5; suyd (1) P2 (D.122.10); suwyd (1) C3 (D.196.18); sewed (1) C3; *pr. part.* suyng (1) P2 (D.122.7); suynge (1) P2 (D.122.4); *past part.* suyd (1) P2 (D.122.22).

sueth *vb. 3 sing.* follows, pursues. (2) C1, P2; *pr. part.* sewyng (3) C4, C5 (D.210.31, 219.6, 12); suyng (3) C3, C4 (D.180.9, 211.5, 240.7).

sufferance *n.* permission. (1) C3; suffraunce (2) P3, C5.

suffice *inf.* (3) S1, C5; suffise (1) C4; *3 pl.* suffisith (1) N5 (D.241.10).

sufficient *adj.* (12) C5, N5; sufficeant (6) C3, P3; suffisaunt (4) P3, C3; soufficeant (4) S1, P2; sufficiant (3) C4; suffisant (3) P3, P4; suffeceant (1) C2; sufficiaunt (2) N4; sufficiaunte (1) P2; sufficeaunt (1) P2; sufficiante (1) C4; sufficiente (1) C3; suffissaunt (1) P2; soufficeante (1) S1; souffissante (1) S1; souficeante (1) C3; *pl.* souffisantȝ (1) C4 (D.213.9); suffisantȝ (1) C4.

sufficiently *adv.* (3) C5, N5; sufficienttyly (1) N8 (D.233.16).

sufficyaunt *n.* sufficiency. (1) C3 (D.192.9).

suffre *inf.* permit. (4) S1, C3; soeffre (1) P4; soeuffre (1) C4; *3 sing.* suffreth (1) S2; *pl.* suffre (2) S1, S2; *sing. subj.* suffre (1) P5; *past* suffered (1) C5;

soffred (1) P3; *pr. part.* sufferyng (1) C3; *past part.* suffred (1) C2; soeuffred (1) C4.
suggestion *n.* (4) C8, C3; sugestion (2) S1, P3; *pl.* suggestions (1) S1.
suite *n.* (law) suit, petition. (1) S1 (D.27.3); sute (6) C3, P5; suyt (3) P3, C4; suyte (3) P2, C3; suete (1) C3; *pl.* suytes (1) P2; sutes (1) C3.
sum *n.* total. (1) P1 (D.111.5); somme (42) S1, C2; summe (5) C3, C4; sume (3) C3, N2; soume (1) C3 (D.172.6); *pl.* sommes (12) S1, C3; someʒ (1) C4.
sumwhat *adv.* (2) S2, P3.
suppliant *n.* (27) C2, C3; suppliaunt (14) C3, C5; supplaiunt (1) C3 (D.189.43); supplaiunte (1) C3; *pl.* suppliantʒ (5) C3 (D.202).
supplicacion *n.* a petition or "bill." (19) S1, S2; supplicacon (2) S1; supplicaion (1) S1; *pl.* supplicacions (4) S1, C3.
supportacion *n.* support. (8) C2, C3.
supporte *inf.* (3) P2, P4; *ger.* supporting (2) C3.
suppose *inf.* (1) C4; *pl.* suppose (5) C8, S1; *past.* supposed (1) C8; *pr. part.* supposyng (2) C3; *past part.* supposed (3) P3, C3; supposid (2) C3.
surcesse *inf.* cease. (1) S1 (D.64.12).
surcharge *n.* over-charge, an unfair additional charge. (2) C3 (D.188.12, 19).
surcharged *vb. past part.* overcharged. (1) C5.
sure *adj.* (7) C3, P4; seur (2) S2 (D.96.3, 5); seure (1) N5; soeure (1) C4 (D.211.4).
surely *adv.* (1) C3; seurly (2) S1, S2; suerly (1) P3.
surete *n.* surety. (5) C1, C3; suerte (8) C5, N4; seurte (4) S1; seuretee (4) P3 (D.131); seurtee (3) S1, N5; sewrte (2) C1 (D.164.21, 37); seurete (1) S1; suerete (1) C3; suertee (1) C3; *pl.* seurtees (4) S1; surties (2) P3; suretees (1) C5; seuretees (1) P3.
surmittyd *vb. past part.* alleged. (2) C5 (D.221.7).
surmysed. *vb. past part.* alleged. (1) C3 (D.199.17).
surplusage *n.* excess. (1) C4 (D.210.52).
surrendre *n.* the surrendering or resignation of an office or position. (1) C4.
surueour *n.* surveyor. (1) S1.
suspect *adj.* suspicious. (1) C3; suspecte (4) C3. All in D.192.
suspence *n.* suspension. (1) P5.
sustenance *n.* support. (1) C5; sustenaunce (1) C8; sustinance (1) P3.
sustentacion *n.* sustaining. (1) P2 (D.114.5).
sustern *n. pl.* sisters. (1) N5 (D.240.22).
susteyn *inf.* sustain. (6) C8, S1; sustene (1) P3.
suynte *adj.* following, ensuing. (1) C4 (D.213.9). *OED* dial., last example 1422.
suyteurs *n. gen.sing.* suitor's. (1) P2 (D.122.21).
swerdes *n. pl.* swords. (1) C1; swerdis (2) P3, C3; swerdys (1) S1; *sing.* sweyrd (1) C3 (D.197.19).
swere *inf.* (3) S2, C3; *past part.* sworn (3) P2, P3; sworne (3) S1, C4; sworen

Glossary of Forms 389

(2) C3, C5; sworin (1) P2; soworne (1) C3.
swetnesse *n.* (1) P3 (D.146.32).
syghte *n.* (1) C1.
syht See sith.
symplenesse *n.* (1) C5. See simple.
syn *adv.* since. (2) C3; sen (1) C2 (D.173.13).
synne *n.* sin. (1) C3 (D.217.13).
sysors *n.* assizers, but here evidently meaning "legally joined to." (1) N5 D.239.5). *OED sizer* in this sense obs. 1614.

tabull *n.* table. (1) C3.
taile *n.* the bottom portion of a letter that would eventually be folded so that the "tail" would show the address on the outside. (1) S1 (D.1.9).
taill *adj.* in "fee taill," entailed. (1), taille (1) C4 (D.210.40); tayll (1) C1; *n. pl.* tailles, legal stipulations (5) P3, P5 (D.131.18).
take *inf.* (40) C8, N8 and throughout; *3 sing.* takeþ (2) S1; taketh (1) C5; takethe (1) C3 (D.200.4); *pl.* take (3) P2, C3; *subj. sing.* take (1) C1; taake (1) S1; *subj. pl.* take (5) S1, S2; *past* toke (21) S1, C3; took (6) S1, C3; tooke (2) C3, C4; tok (1) C1; *pr. part.* takyng (9) S1, S2; *past part.* taken (36) C8, P3; take (19) S1, P3; taaken (2) S1; takyn (2) C2, C5; taake (1) S2 (D.90.1); ?tweyn (1) C3 (D.202.21); *ger.* takyng (5) C4, C5; taking (2) S1, N4.
talghe *n.* tallow. (1) C3 (D.190.4).
tallage *n.* tax. (1) C2 (D.176.8).
tapsery *n.* tapestry. (1) C3 (D.197.12).
tarie *vb. pl.* tarry. (1) S1; taryen (1) S1 (D.30.6); *3 sing. subj.* tarye (1) S1; *past.* taried (1) P3; *past part.* taried (1) S2; taryed (1) P3; *ger.* taryinge (1) S2; taryeng (1) S1 (D.69.21); taryng (1) C4.
tathing *adj.* tithing. (1) C3 (D.188.16).
taverne *n.* (2) C3; *pl.* tavernes (1) C3; tauernis (1) C3; tauernys (1) C3. All in D.192 and D.193.
taxe *n.* (7) C3, C5.
taxed *vb. past part.* (1) C5.
taylour *n.* tailor. (1) S5 (D.108.2).
teche *inf.* teach. (2) P3 (D.146.4, 19); *past.* taught (1) P3 (D.146.13); tought (2) C3, N5.
techer *n.* teacher. (1) C3 (D.202.39).
teithe *adj.* tithe produce. (3) C3 (D.197).
telle *inf.* (1) S2 (D.93.8).
temporalitees *n.* material possessions of the church. (6) S1, S2; temporaltees (15) S1, S2; temporeltees (2) S1.
temporall *adj.* lay (possessions, jurisdiction, etc.). (4) C2, P3; temporell (12) C3, C4; temporel(e) (5) S1, P2; *pl.* temporelx (11) C1, C3 (formula:

"spirituelx and temporelx," D.163.7, 199.39, etc.); temporalx (1) C5 (D.228.7) temporeles (1) C3; temporelles (1) C4; temporels (1) C3.

tenant *n.* (4) C1, S2; tenaunt (1) C3; tennant (1) P3; *pl.* tennantʒ (2) C3; tenantʒ (1) C3; tenentʒ (1) C1; tenntʒ (1) C3 (D.184.8); tenauntes (1) C3; tenantys (1) C3 (D.196.27); tennantes (1) C3.

tenderance *n.* tenderness. (1) C5 (D.224.10).

tenderly *adv.* (6) S2, C3; tendrely (4) S1, C3; tendurly (1) N2.

tendernesse *n.* (3) C1, C4; tendernes (1) C5.

tendre *vb. pl.* be tender, considerate. (1) S5 (D.109.5); *pr. part.* tenderyng (1) C3 (D.207.6).

tendre *adj.* (1) C5.

tenement *n.* dwelling. (9) N8, C1; *pl.* tentementes (27) S1, N2; tementʒ (12) S1, P2; tenementeʒ (7) C4; tenements (5) N5 (D.241); tenementis (4) P3, C3; tenmentis (1) C3 (D.189.46); tenementys (1) N8, C3; tenenementes (1) C3 (D.206.9).

tenor *n.* meaning. (1) P2 (D.115.19); tenour (5) S1, C5; tenure (4) P1, C4; tenur (2) C4; teneur (2) S1; teneure (1) S1; tennour (1) S1.

tentes *n.* (2) P3.

tenthe *n.* (1) P5 (D.159.36).

term *n.* (1) C5 (D.227.16); terme (60) N8, S1; *pl.* termes (7) S1, C3.

terminable *adj.* determinable. (1) P2 (D.122.7).

testament *n.* (15) S1, C3.

testor *n.* tester, a canopy or its supports. (1) C3 (D.197.12).

tewseday *n.* (1) C3 (D.197.4); tysday (1) P1 (D.112.6).

than *conj.* (10) C1, P3; þan (4) S1, P5; thanne (3) C3, P5; þanne (3) S1, P5; yan (2) S1, C2; yanne (1) S1; thenne (1) C4 (D.210.37); yenne (1) S1 (D.69.20); þen (1) C4 (D.211.35). See also then.

thanke *inf.* (1) S4; thankke (1) P2; *1 sing.* thanke (1) P3; þankke (1) P2; *1 pl.* thank (1) P3; thanke (1) P4; þanke (1) P2; *3 sing. subj.* þankke (1) P2; *pr. part.* thankyng (1) P3; thokynge (1) C1 (D.162.3, ? error); *past part.* thanked (1) C1; þankid (2) P3 (D.117.2, 23).

that *pro.* (799) N8, C8; þat (842) S1, C1; yat (80) S1, P1; *pl.* those (2) P3, C5; thoo (2) C4, C5; tho (11) N8, C8; þoo (3) C3.

thaym self *pro.* (1) C3 (D.193.15); hemselfes (1) P2 (D.122.36); hemself(f) (3) C3, N2; hamself(e) (4) C2, C5.

the *art.* (3512) N8, C8; þe (1988) S1, C1; ye (156) S1, P1; te (2) N8 (D.233.15).

theefs *n.* thieves. (1) C3; theves (2) C3; thefes (1) C3.

then *adv.* (15) P3, C3; thenne (27) C3, C4; than (16) C1, S1; þen (14) P3, C3; þanne (7) S1, P3; þan (6) S1, C3; þenne (4) P3, P4; yen (3) C5. See also than.

þenkke *inf.* (2) P2 (D.113.2, 23); *3 sing. impersonal* thinketh (1) C2; þenkeþ (2) S1 (D.43.11, 55.4); yenkey (1) S1; þenke (1) S1; *pl.* þynke (1) C3; þenke

Glossary of Forms 391

(1) S1; *subj. pl.* þinke (1) S1; *past* þought (2) C3, N5; *pr. part.* thenkyng (1) C1.

thens *adv.* thence. (6) S2, C3; thennes (2) C1, P3; thennys (2) P2 (D.113.12, 21); þens (1) P3; þense (1) C4.

þerby *adv.* (1) P2 (D.102.2).

there (95) C8, S1; ther (93) N8, P1; þere (44) S1, S2; þer (29) S1, S2; yer (9) P1, P3; þare (2) C3; þaire (1) S1; yere (1) S1; theer (1) S1.

þereafter *adv.* (1) S1 (D.43.5); þerafter (1) S2 (D.81.16).

therefore *adv.* (4) P2, C5; therfor(e) (9) S1, C1; þerfore (14) S1, P2; þerfor (3) S1, C3; therefor (1) C5; yerfor (1) S1.

therein *adv.* (29 S2; þerinne (4) S1, S2; therin (3) P5, C5; þerin (2) S1; þerynne (2) S1, P3; therinne (1) P2.

thereof *adv.* (3) S2, C4; therof (42) P2, N2; þerof (36) S1, P2; yerof (5) S1, C5; þereof (1) S2; þeroffe (1) C3.

therevpon *adv.* (1) P2; þervpon (12) S1, C3; theruppon (5) P3, C4; therupon (4) C3, C5; thervpon (4) S1, C3; thervppon (2) C5; þeruppon (2) S1, C3; þerevpon (2) S1, C3; þerupon (1) C3; þervppon (1) S1; þereupon (1) C3; therapon (1) C5; theropon (1) C3; theroppon (1) C5; þeropon (1) C3; yervpon (1) C5; þerappon (1) P5.

therto *adv.* (6) S1, P2; þerto (13) S1, P2.

they *pro.* (91) C8, C1; þey (41) S1, P2; þei (34) S1, P2; thei (14) C8, P2; yay (14) S1; þay (12) S1, P2; thay (9) S2, P2; þai (7) S1; thai (1) S1; þiey (1) P2 (D.117.12); yai (1) S1; hy (2) N2 (D.235.13, 14); *gen.* their (45) S2, P2; þeire (19) S1, P3; theire (12) C3, C4; thair (11) S1, C3; þaire (10) S1, S2; ther (9) C3, C4; þair (7) P2, C3; yaire (7) S1; þeir (6) P2, S3; theyre (2) C3 (D.203.31, 37); þer(e) (3) S1, C3; yair (2) C2; thaire (1) C3; yeir (1) N4; yer (1) C5; yayre (1) S1; þare (1) S2; tharre (1) N5 (D.241.13); her (47) C1, S1; heer (5) S1, C3; har (1) C5; hare (4) C2; hure (3) P5 (D.160); harre (3) C4 (D.211 only); here (1) C3 (D.199.41); *gen. free form.* theirs (1) P2 (D.122.37); yaires (1) S1 (D.69.23); *obj.* theym(e) (32) P3, C4; them (21) P2, C3; þaim (13) S1, P2; þeym (11) C4, N5; theim (9) P3, C4; þeim (8) S1, P3; þeime (8) P3 (D.142); þayme (5) S1, S2; þaym (4) S1, S2; thaym (3) C3 (D.193); thame (1) C2 (D.171.4); thayme (1) P3; thethm (1) N8 (D.233.7); þam (1) P2 (D.119.3); yaim (1) S1; yaym (1) S1; yam (1) C2; hem (139) C8, S1; hame (6) C4 (D.211 only); ham (5) S1, C3. See also thaymself.

þi See þu.

thider *adv.* thither. (3) S2, P3; thedir (2) P3; þeder (1) P3; theder (1) P3; þiþer (1) P2.

thilke *dem.pro.* this. (1) C1 (D.163.21).

thing *pro.* (10) S1, S2; thyng (15) C8, S1; þing (4) S1, P3; þyng (3) S1, S2; thinge (2) C5, N5; ying (1) S1; *pl.* þinges (9) S1, P2; thynges (6) C8, C3;

thinges (3) P3, C3; þingis (1) P3; yinges (1) S1.
thinketh See þenkke.
third adj. (3) C5; thridde (9) C3, P4; thrid (3) P4; þrydde (2) N2; thirde (1) N2; thryd (1) N8, C3; þredde (1) P5 (D.159.33); pl. thriddes (3) P4 (D.156).
this pro. (251) S1, C2; þis (154) S1, C1; thys (19) N8, P2; yes (1) P1; yis (6) S1, P1; pl. þees (29) S1, S2; these (20) C1, C3; thes (10) P3, C3; thise (8) C8, C1; thees (8) S2, C3; þes (5) S1; þese (4) S2, P2; þise (2) N5.
though conj. (2) C8, C3; þow (2) S2; thowe (1) C3; thof (3) P5 (D.158).
thought n. (6) S1, C4; thoughte (1) C1; thoght (1) C3; thowte (1) C3 (D.176.10).
thraves n. measures for grain. (1) C3 (D.197.20). OED northern form.
three adj. and n. (1) P2; thre (3) P3, C3; þre (2) P3, C3.
thresshyn inf. thresh. (1) N4 (D.237.19).
thretenyng vb. pr. part. (1) C5 (D.218.10); thretyng (1) C3 (D.189.20).
thridly adv. thirdly. (1) S2 (D.78.7). See also third.
thrifty adj. respectable. (3) S1, C5; supl. þryftyust (1) N2 (D.235.9).
throte n. (1) C4.
through prep. (1) C3 (D.207.3); thurgh (4) S1, P3; þurgh (3) C2, P3; thorugh (2) C2, C3; thourgh (1) C8; throu (1) C3 (D.188.19); thorogh (1) S1; throgh (1) C5; thorwe (1) C3; thorwgh (1) C1; thorw (1) C5 (D.218.24); thorow (1) C3 (D.189.21); þorow (1) S1; þorowe (1) S2.
throwen vb. past part. thrown. (1) C3 (D. 181.17).
þu pro. nom. thou, you. (1) P3 (D.142.26); gen. þi (2) P3 (D.142.34); þine (1) P3 (D.142.34).
thus adv. (9) C8, C1; þus (1) P3.
thynne adv. thence. (1) C2 (D.176.9).
till conj. (2) C3; til (14) S1, P1; tylle (2) P2; tille (1) C3.
timbre n. timber. (4) N4 (D.238); tymbre (2) C3, N8; tymbr (2) N8.
time n. (19) S1, P2; tyme (301) N8, C8; pl. tymes (29) S1, P2; times (3) P4, C5.
tithinges n. (1) P3; tithynges (2) P1, P3.
title n. (8) S1, S2.
to prep. (2520); too (7) S1, C4.
tofore adv. before. (4) S2, P2.
togedir adv. (6) P2, P3 (D.145); togedre (2) C3; togydre (2) C8; togidre (1) C8; togeders (2) P3; togider (1) P2; togeddir (1) C4; too geddir (1) C4; togedrs (1) P3.
tombe n. (1) C4; toumbe (1) C4.
to morwe n. (3) S2, S5. See moro.
tonn n. ton. (1) C3 (D.172.5); tonne (1) C4 (D.211.6).
tonne n. tun, a large cask of wine. (8) C3, C4 (D.180, 211).
toon n. in the phrase "þe toon," indicates "the one." (2) P3, C5.
tother n. the other, usually used in the phrase "þe toon ...þe tother." (2) C3, C5; toþer (2) S1, P3.

touche *inf.* concern, be relevant to. (1) P3; *3 sing.* toucheth (4) P3 (D.122); touchith (1) C4; *pl.* touchen (2) S1, P3; *subj. pl.* touche (1) P3; *pr. part.* touching (22) S1, S2; touchyng (12) PO, C1; touchinge (1) S1.

tounshipe *n.* township. (1) C1; *pl.* tovneships (1) S1.

tournes *n.* sheriff's turns, semi-annual inquisitions into the hundreds. (1) P3 (D.144.13).

toward *prep.* (11) P3, C4; towardes (8) S1, P2.

town *n.* (33) S1, S2; towne (65) S1, P2; toune (31) S2, P3; toun (22) S1, S2; tovn (8) S1, C2; tovne (8) S1, P3; towen (1) C2; *pl.* tounes (3) N4; towneʒ (3) C4; towns (1) P3; townes (1) P4.

towre *n.* tower, esp. Tower of London. (1) S1; tour (10) C3, C5; toure (1) C5; *pl.* toures (2) S1, C5.

traitour *n.* (9) C4, P5; traytour (2) C3; *pl.* traitours (2) C8, P5.

translacion *n.* the transferring from one church office to another. (3) S1, S2.

trasons *n.* beams, transoms. (1) N4 (D.238.5). Not in *OED*.

trauaill *n.* work, effort. (1) C3 (D.191.16); trauaile (1) C1 (D.162.7).

trauailleden *inf.* travel. (1) C8 (D.161.43).

tree *n.* (1) C1; *pl.* trees (2) N4; treeʒ (1) N4. All plurals in D. 238.

treson *n.* (6) C3, C4; tresoun (1) C3 (D.201.28); *pl.* treasons (2) P5; tresons (2) C4; trasons (1) N4.

trespas *n.* (3) C1, C3; trespace (3) C1 (D.163); tresspasse (1) P3; *pl.* trespaces (4) C3, S5; trespases (2) C3; trespasses (1) C3.

tressecloth *n.* some sort of cloth. (2) C3 (D.196.6, 21). *OED* has *tress*, a braid of fibers, obs. 1550.

tresspasours *n.* (1) C3.

tresurer *n.* (1) P4; tresorer (30) P2, C2; tresorier (10) P5 (D.158); tresourer (4) P2, C3; tresourier (4) P2 (D.115); treseror (1) P2; *pl.* tresorers (1) C5; tresouriers (1) P2.

trete *inf.* negotiate. (4) S1, C3; *subj. pl.* trete (4) S1; *past part.* treted (1) P2; tretid (1) P2.

tretee *n.* treaty. (9) S1, C3; trete (1) C3.

tretyce *n.* treatise. (1) P3 (D.146.13).

trewes *n.* truce. (11) S1; trieux (1) C5 (D.217.5); trewys (2) C3 (D.196.8, 22); trieues (1) S1 (D.32.9).

triable *adj.* capable of being tried. (1) C4; *pl.* triableʒ (1) C4 (D.216.39).

triall *n.* (3) C3, C5.

tribulacions *n.* (1) S1.

tried *vb. past part.* brought to trial. (3) P3, C4.

trinitee *n.* (1) S1; trinite (6) S1, P2; trynite (1) P3; trynyte (1) P2.

trostell *n.* trestle. (1) C3 (D.197.14).

trouble *n.* (2) C4, P4; troble (1) P4; trobul (1) C5.

troubled *vb. past part.* (3) P2, C4; trobled (1) P4.

troublers n. (1) S2.
true adj. (6) P3, C3; trewe (32) C8, C1; trwe (4) P2, C4; truwe (2) C5 (D.205.3, 8); trew (1) P3; trywe (1) C3 (D.193.17); *supl.* trewest (1) C8.
truly adv. (6) C2, P2; trewely (4) S1, C3; treuly (2) C3; trwly (1) P2 (D.113.10).
trust n. (16) S1, C1; truste (7) S1, P2; treste (2) C1 (D.162.1, 165.3).
truste vb. *1 sing.* (2) P2, P3; *3 sing.* trusteth (1) P3; *pl.* trust (2) S1, P3; truste (1) S4; *past.* trustede (1) C1 (D.163.13); *pr. part.* trusting (2) P5, S5; trustyng (2) C5; tristing (1) P2 (D.117.3); trostyng (1) C3 (D.190.23).
trustely adv. (1) S1 (D.43.10).
trusty adv. (141) S1, S2; trusti (3) S1, P2.
truthe n. (1) C3 (D.178.15); trouthe (12) C8, S1; trouth (3) P3, P4; treweth (3) C2 (D.171); trowthe (2) C8, C3; trewthe (1) S1; trowþe (1) S1; trevthe (1) C3 (D.199.21).
tuelfemonethe n. (1) C3; tuelfmoneth (1) C3; twolfmonth (1) P2.
tuicion n. care, guarding. (1) P3; tuicioune (1) C4.
turne *inf.* (2) P1, C1; tourne (1) P2; *3 sing.* tourneth (1) S1.
turnell n. a turning device; see *OED, turnel,* for possibilities. (1) C3 (D.197.16).
twayn adj. two. (1) C3; tweyn (1) C3.
twelve n. and adj. (1) C1 (D.163.47); twelf (2) C2, N5.
twenty adj. (2) N5 (D.240).
twey See two.
tweyn See take.
two adj. (24) S1, P1; twoo (3) C5; too (5) P3, C3; twey (2) C1, C5; tweye (1) P5.
twyes adj. twice. (2) C4 (D.212.8).
tyde n. time. (1) S1 (D.69.3).
tydinges n. (1) S2; tythyngs (1) P1 (D.112.11).

vacacion n. vacancy, absence of a person filling a church office. (2) S2; *pl.* vacacions (1) P5.
vaillable adj. available, useful. (3) S1; vaylable (1) S1. *OED* obs. 1565.
value n. (28) S1, P3; valew (2) C1, P3; valewe (2) C1, C5; valoue (1) C3 (D.197.24); walwe (1) C3 (D.196.27).
verdite n. verdict. (1) C3 (D.202.6).
vergiershippe n. the office of the carrier of an official symbol in a procession. (1) P2 (D.123.3); viergerschup (1) P2 (D.118.2).
verrement n. proof. (1) C5 (D.223.40).
verrey adj. true, accurate. (2) C3, C4; verray (5) S1, P2; verraye (1) S1; verrai (1) S1; verraie (1) P3; uerraie (1) P3.
verrily adv. truly. (1) C3; verraily (1) C3; verailly (1) C2.
vessell n. ship. (1) S1 (D.69.25); container (1) C3 (D.197.16); *pl.* always ships. vesselx (4) S1, C3; vesslx (1) C3 (D.187.5); vessellis (1) C5 (D.218.45).
vetyllere n. victualler. (1) P2 (D.114.4). See vitail.

vexacion *n.* (2) C3, C5.
vexe *inf.* (3) S1, C3; *past part.* vexed (5) S1, C3; vexud (1) C4 (D.213.2); wexed (1) S2 (D.93.6).
viage *n.* voyage, journey, mission. (3) P1, C2; *pl.* viages (1) C2.
vicare *n.* (1) P3; vicaire (1) S2.
vicontee *n.* viscounty. (1) S2 (D.105.2). See visconte.
victoriouse *adj.* (1) C4; victorieux (1) P5 (D.159.2).
vierger *n.* verger. (1) P2 (D.118.4). See vergiershippe.
vieu *n.* view, inspection. (1) P3 (D.147.4).
vikary *n.* vicar. (1) P3.
vikerage *n.* the office of vicar. (1) P3.
vilanisly *adv.* villainously. (1) C4; vileynously (1) C3 (D.189.11).
villed *vb. past part.* degraded from its former status. (1) S1 (D.40.5).
vineres *n.* vineyards. (1) P3 (D.144.12). *OED* obs. 1513.
violence *n.* (2) C3, C5.
virgyn *n.* (2) N5 (D.240.9, 20).
virtue *n.* (3) C3, C4; vertue (9) S1, S2; vertu (8) C1, C2. Usually in the phrase "by virtue of."
visconte *n.* (1) S1 (D.61.4); viconte (1) 52 (D.105.2).
visitid *vb. past.* (1) P2 (D.117.16).
vitail *n.* victual, provisions. (3) C4 (D.214); vitaille (2) S2; vetaille (1) P2; *pl.* vitailles (4) S1, P4.
vnce *n.* ounce. (1) C3.
vncle *n.* (16) S1, P2; oncle (2) P3 (D.131.2, 13); *pl.* oncles (1) P3 (D.131.9).
vnclene *adj.* (2) C3.
vnclensyd *vb. past part.* (2) C3 (D.208.10, 11).
under *prep.* (1) S1 (D.26.12); vnder (183) S1, P2; vndir (12) P3, C3; vndre (9) S1, P2; vndyr (2) N8, C3; vndur (1) C2.
vnderstande *inf.* (3) S1, P3; vnderstand (1) S1; vndirstond (1) C4 (D.210.18); *1 sing.* vnderstand (3) S1; *pl.* vnderstond (1) S1 (D.69.17); vndrstonde (1) P3 (D.135.4); *pr. part.* vnderstandynge (1) C1; vnderstondyng (1) S1 (D.40.19); *past part.* vnderstande (16) S1, C3; vnderstanden (7) S1, P2; understanden (1) S2; vnderstonden (1) C3; *ger.* vnderstandyng (1) P3; vndrestondyng (1) P3.
vndertake *vb. past part.* (1) P4; vndirtake (1) C5; *inf.* ondurtake (1) C5 (D.218.39).
vnderwriten *vb. past part.* written below, following. (1) C3; vnderwrete (1) N4 (D.237.6).
vndewe *adj.* undue. (1) C3 (D.177.21). See vnduely.
vndirsheref *n.* (1) C5.
vndoo *inf.* undo, ruin. (1) C3; *past part.* vndo (1) C1 (D.165.8); *ger.* vndoyng (5) C3, C5; vndoynge (2) C1; ondoyng (1) C5 (D.218.21).

vnduely *adv.* (1) C1. See vndewe.
vndurnethe *adv.* (1) N8 (D.233.21).
vnese *n.* unease, discomfort. (1) S1.
vngarbeled *vb. past part.* not cleaned or ordered. (1), vngarbelyd (1), both in D.208. D.208.10 cited in *OED.*
vngoodly *adv.* (2) C1, C3 (D.163.23, 177.2); vngoodely *adj.* (2) C5 (D.222.17, 38).
vnhurt *adj.* (1) P5.
vniverselly *adv.* (1) C3.
vniuersite *n.* (1) P3; vniuersyte (3) C5 (D.231); vniuersitee (1) P3; *pl.* vniuersitees (1) P3.
vniustly *adv.* (1) C3.
vnknowen *vb. past part.* unknown. (1) P3.
vnkonnyng *adj.* uncunning, unsophisticated. (1) C8 (D.161.47).
vnkyndely *adv.* against the law of nature. (1) C5 (D.222.16).
vnlaufull *adj.* (1) C5. See also vnleeful.
vnlawefully *adv.* (2) C1 (D.163).
vnleeful *adj.* (1) S2 (D.87.6); vnlefull (1) C4; vnleueful (1) C8. See vnlaufull, leful(l).
vnmyght *n.* weakness, lack of sufficient support. (1) P2 (D.122.9).
vnnedeful *adj.* (1) C8.
vnneth *adv.* uneath, scarcely, with difficulty. (1) C5; vneþe (1) N2.
vnnethese *adv.* uneaths, scarcely. (1) C3 (D.193.11).
vnpaid *vb. past part.* (4) C2, C3; vnpaide (1) S1.
vnponischyd *vb. past part.* unpunished. (1) C3.
vnpreuable *adj.* unproveable. (1) C8 (D.161.21).
vnpurveide *vb. past part.* unprovided. (1) C5.
unquieted *vb. past part.* (1) S1 (D.40.7).
vnresonably *adv.* (1) C4.
vnrogne *vb. past part.* unrung. (1) C2 (D.173.12).
vnruliest *adj.* (1) P3.
vnshewed *vb. past part.* kept from view. (1) C8 (D.161.33).
vnskilful *adj.* unreasonable. (1) C2.
vnskilfully *adv.* (1) C2.
vnsogne *vb. past part.* unsung. (1) C2 (D.173.13).
vntil *prep.* (1) S1 (D.40.13); vntille (2) C2; vnto often found where ModE would use until.
unto *prep.* to, until. (1) C4 (D.217.27); vnto (338; in 109 cases spelled as two words) N8, C1; vntoo (6) C4 (D.211).
vntreuth *n.* (1) C3; ontrouth (1) P3 (D.142.6); vntrouthe (1) C3.
vntrewly *adv.* (2) C3.
vntrue *adj.* (4) P3, C3; vntrewe (5) C8, C1; vntrwe (1) C3; vntrywe (1) C3.

vnworthy *adj.* (1) C8.
vnwyse *adj.* (1) C8.
voice *n.* (1) C8.
void *adj.* (1) P5; voide (17) S1, S2; voyde (3) S1, S2.
voidance *n.* (2) S1, S2.
voided *vb. past.* (2) S1, S2; voyded (1) S1; *3 sing.* voydeth (1) S2.
volumes *n.* (1) C3 (D.197.9).
vouche *vb. imp.* "vouche ye saaf." (1) S1 (D.40.13); fouche (saf) (1) C1 (D.163.34).
vow *n.* (1) C1; vowe (1) P3.
up *adv.* (1) C4; vp (13) N8, C8 and throughout; vppe (1) C3.
vpberers *n.* supporters. (2) C8 (D.161.7. 49). *OED* obs. 1624.
upon *prep.* (4) PO, S1; uppon (4) P3, C4; vpon (94) S1, C1; vppon (45) S1, C1; vapon (1) P2 (D.114.8); opon (6) PO, C3; apon (4) P2, C3.
vrgent *adj.* (1) S4.
vsag *n.* usage. (1) S1 (D.5.5); *pl.* vsages (1) C3 (D.182.25).
use *n.* (1) C3 (D.196.21); vse (10) S1, C3; (D.24.12, 89.8, etc.).
vse *inf.* (2) S2 (D.81.12, 13); *3 sing.* vseth (1) C3; *pl.* use (1) C5; *past.* used (2) C3, P3; *past part.* vsed (18) C8, S1; vsyd (1) P5.
vssher *n.* usher. (1) C5 (D.228.1); huissher (1) S1 (D.73.2).
usuell *adj.* usual. (1) C3; vusuall (1) N8 (D.233.27).
vsuelly *adv.* (1) C3.
vtter *adj.* (1) C5; *supl.* utterest (1) C1; vtterest (1) C3; vttermast (1) S1 (D.69.10).
vttered *vb. past part.* spoke. (1) C4; vttred (1) C4.
vtterly *adv.* (6) C3, C4; vtturly (2) C5; vttirly (1) C3; outerliche (1) C8 (D.161.35).
vyntrye *n.* (1) C4 (D.216.7).

wach *n.* watch, supervision. (2) P2; wach(e) (1) P2 (D.119.6, 120.6, 121.6).
wages *n.* (15) C2, P3; wageʒ (3) C2, C4.
walke *inf.* (1) P3; walken (1) C1 (D.163.36). Both in the phrase "walk at large."
wall *n.* (2) N8, C3; *pl.* walles (3) C5 (D.229); wallis (1) C3.
walplates *n.* wallplates, in building construction. (2) N4 (D.238.6, 13).
Walsshman *n.* Welshman. (1) P5 (D.159.5).
wapened *vb. past part.* weaponed. (1) C2; wapynd (1) C2 (D.173.3, 9).
warantye *n.* warranty, an assurance. (1) N2 (D.234.9).
warde *n.* legal guardianship. (24) S1, S2; *pl.* wardes (3) S1, P5.
wardein *n.* warden. (2) S1, P3; wardiene (1) C3; wardeyn (1) C3; *pl.* wardeyns (2) N5; wardenʒ (1) C5.
warderobe *n.* (1) C4 (D.210.32).
warderober *n.* (2) S2, P3 (D.85.2, 142.4).
wariours *n. pl.* (1) C5.
warned *vb. past* (1) P3; *past part.* (1) S1; *ger.* warnyng (4) N8, P4.

warrant *n.* (6) P2, C3; warant (5) P2, C3; warent (1) P3; *pl.* warrentes (1) P3; warantis (1) N5; warrantʒ (1) P3; warantʒ (1) P2.

warre *n.* war. (1) C5; werre (15) C8, S1; werr (2) C3, C5; *pl.* werres (1) N2; werris (1) P5 (D.159.2); werrys (1) P2 (D.114.6).

was *vb. past sing.* (197) N8, C8; wos (1) C5 (D.218.8); *past pl.* were (106) S1, P2; wer (17) S1, P2; weren (7) S1, C1; werin (1) P2 (D.117.24); werne (1) C5 (D.226.5).

wast *n.* waste. (4) C3.

waste *inf.* (1) C3 (D.202.20); *past part.* wastid (1) C5; waastid (1) C3 (D.184.3).

watching *vb. past part.* (1) C5 (D.229.22).

water *n.* (9) S1, C1; watyr (1) C5; *pl.* waters (1) C5; wateres (1) P3; wateris (1) S4.

way *n.* (18) P2, P3; wey (28) C1, S1; waye (6) S1, S2; weye (4) S1, P2; *pl.* ways (1) C4; waies (1) P5; weys (1) S1.

wayn *n.* wain, a cart. (1) C3 (D.197.20); *pl.* waynes (1) C5 (222.20).

wayte *n.* ambush. (1) C1 (D.164.37).

we *pro.* (462) S1, C1; approximately 350 listings are in Signet letters; wee (3) S1, C3; *gen.* our (263); oure (893); owr (21, 7 in D.2, 10 in D.6, 2 in D.8, rest in D.175, 178); owre (16, 12 in D.161, 3 in D.176), C8, C3; ooure (1) C3 (D.203.1); *absolute* oures (5) S1, C2.

wedde *n.* security: "leyd to wedde;" i.e., seized as security. (1) S1 (D.14.3); *pl.* weddes (1) P3 (D.131.14).

weddid *vb. past.* (1) C3 (D.189.12).

weder *n.* weather. (1) C5 (D.229.18).

week *n.* (1) S1; wike (1) C3 (D.197.4); woke (1) P2 (D.122.5); *pl.* wekes (3) S1, P3; wokes (1) P3.

weel *n.* weal, prosperity. (3) P2, P3; weele (2) S1; wele (2) P5.

weighte *n.* weight. (2) C3 (D.190.10, 12); weght (1) P3; weyghte (1) C3; wheigte (1) C2; wighte (1) C3 (D.190.10); *pl.* wightes (3) C3 (D.190).

welapaide *vb. past part.* (1) C1 (D.162.9).

welbeloued *adj. and n.* (108) S1, S2; welbelouyd (4) P3; welbeloved (1) S2.

welfare *n.* (3) P3, C3; welfar (1) P2.

well *adv.* (22) N8, C3; wel (114) S1, S2; wele (16) S1, S2; welle (3) S1, C4; wlle (1) P2 (D.113.12).

wenyng *vb. pr. part.* weening, thinking, intending. (1) C1 (D.164.38).

wepen *n.* weapon. (1) C3; *pl.* wepyns (2) C5.

werk *inf.* (1) C3 (D.203.5); werke (1) C3; *pl.* werkythe (1) C3 (D.203.19); wirkith (1) C3 (D.204.22); *subj. sing.* werke (1) C3; worke (1) C3 (D.203.34); *pr. part.* werkyng (1) C3; *ger.* wirking (1) N4; wurkyng (2) C4. All citations to C3 are D.203 and 204. See also work.

werkmanship *n.* (2) N4. See work.

weryng *vb. pr. part.* wearing, those things being worn: "the weryng clothes." (1) C4 (D.212.11).

Glossary of Forms 399

wesher *n.* washer. (1) P2 (D.120.3).
wete *subj. pl.* be informed. (1) S1 (D.69.1, 4); *pr. part.* wetinge (1) P3; wetynge (1) C1.
weuers *n.* weavers. (28) C3 (D.203, 204); weuvers (1) C4.
wex *n.* wax. (2) C3, C4.
weyke *n.* wick, esp. candle-wick. (5) C3 (D.190).
wharf *n.* (4) N8, C5; wharfe (1) N8 (D.225, 233).
what *pro.* (46) C8, S1; whatt (1) P2 (D.119.4).
whatsom euir *pro.* (1) P5 (D.158.40).
wheles *n.* wheels. (1) C3.
when *adv.* (9) C8, P2; whan (12) C8, C1; whanne (7) S1, P2; whenne (3) C3, C5; wan (2) P3 (D.145.15, 24).
whens *adv.* whence. (1) S2 (D.96.7).
where *adv.* (65) C8, S1; wher (29) S1, C1;
whereby *conj.* (2) C4, C5; wherby (3) C1, N5; whar by (1) C3 (D.190.12).
wherefore *conj.* (12) S1, C2; wherfore (27) P3, C3; wherfor (17) S1, P2; werfore (1) P3 (D.145.30); wharfor(e) (3) S1, C2; qwharfore (1) C2 (D.173.14).
whereof *adv.* (6) C2, P3; wherof (10) S1, N2.
wheresoeuer *adv.* (1) P4 (D.152.3).
wherethurgh *adv.* wherethrough, through which means. (2) C1, P4; wherthurgh (1) C3; wherthourgh (1) C8; wherthrow (1) P5 (D.158.38).
whereupon *adv.* (1) P3; wherupon (4) C3, C5; whervpon (2) S1, C3; wheruppon (1) C3; whervppon (1) C3.
wherto *adv.* (1) S1 (D.53.8).
whete *n.* wheat. (1) C3 (D.180.13).
whether *conj.* (4) C8, S1; wheþer (3) S1, P3; wheder (2) P3.
which *pro.* (149) C8, S1; whiche (206) PO, C1; wiche (13) P3, C3; wheche (12) S1, C2; whyche (7) C1, P2; whych (6) C1, C2; wyche (5) C2, P3; whech (3) S2, C3; whuche (3) P3, C3; wich (2) P2, P3; wych (1) N8; whilk (1) C2; qwhylk (1) C2 (D.173.11).
while *adv.* (4) S1, C2; whyle (1) C2; whiles (4) S1, P3.
who *pro.* (2) C8, C3; *gen.* whos (14) C1, C3; whoos (3) C1, C3; whas (1) C5 (D.218.29); who (1) P3 (D.141.3); whoes (1) P2 (D.114.2); whois (1) P2 (D.122.13); hose (1) C2 (D.178.9); *obj.* whom (22) C8, C1; whome (5) S1, P3; whoom (2) P2; wham (2) C5 (D.218.26, 43); whoome (1) P3.
whosoeuer *pro.* (1) C4 (D.215.12).
why *pro.* (4) C1, S1.
wife *n.* (4) S1, C3; wyf (9) S1, C1; wyfe (5) C1, P3; wif (3) C5, P5; wijff (3) C3 (D.194).
wilde *adj.* (1) C3 (D.201.7).
wilfull *adj.* (1) C4; wilfulle (1) S1.
wilfully *adv.* (1) S1.

will *n*. (7) P3, C3; wille (14) C8, S1; wil (6) S1, P3; wyll (3) C1, C5; wylle (1) C5. All senses of will are here combined. As in MnE, there was no apparent spelling differentiation among them.

will *vb. 1 sing.* wol (1) P3 (D.142.32), wole (1) S1 (D.70.1); *2 sing.* will (1) P3 (D.142.27); *3 sing.* will (13) P2, C2, etc., wil (3) P5, N4, wul (1) C5 (D.218.43), wol (12) S1, P3 (6 in D.131), wole (3) C1, C3 (2 in D.185), wylnought (1) C3 (D.188.14), wolnot (1) C5 (D.220.25) but usually two words; *pl.* will (7) P2, S4, etc., wol (142) mostly in S, wolle (2) (D.152), wollen (3) S1; *past.* willed (4) P3, C4 (all expressing volition); wold (20) S1, P3; wolde (36) S1, P3; wuld (2) C3, C5; wolden (2) C8, C1; woulde (1) C2 (D.173.6); wald (1) C2 (D.171.6); nolde (1) P2 (D.113.12); *pr. part.* willyng (7) P3, C3; wolnyng (6) only in S1, S2; willing (3) P2, P5; wollyng (1) S2; *past part.* willed (1) S1 (D.1.2).

willfulness *n*. (1) C5.

wisdoms *n*. wisdom, persons of wisdom. (5) C5; wisdomes (2) C5; wisedomes (1) C3; wisedoms (1) C5; wysdoms (2) C5. See wysdome.

wise *n*. way, method. (53) S1, P2.

wise *adj.* (15) S1, C3; wyse (53) C8, C1; *pl.* wyseȝ (1) C2; *supl.* wysest (2) C8.

wite *inf.* wit, know, be informed. (13) S1, P1; wete (4) S1, C3 (D.69.1, 4), 192.4); witte (2) S1, C5; wite (2) C8, N8; wyten (1) N8; *imper.* witeth (1) S1 (D.51.1); witteth (1) S1 (D.69.14); witiþ (1) P2 (D.117.25); wytten (1) N8; *3 sing.* wote (1) C5 (D.223.17); *pl.* wot (1), wote (3) all in S1, S2; *subj. pl.* witt (1) S1 (D.49.4); *past* wist (1) P3 (D.142.39); wiste (1) C1 (D.163.11); *pr. part.* wittyng (1) S2; wityng (1) P1; wetinge (1) P3; wetynge (1) C1.

with *prep.* (346) N8, C8; wiþ (57) S1, S2; wyth (24) C8, N8; withe (8) C3 (D.192); wyht (7) P2 (D.113); wiþe (6) C4 (D.211); wiy (6) S1 (D.69); wyt (2) S1, C2; whith (1) C3 (D.199.13).

withdrawe *inf.* (1) C3; wythdrawe (1) C8; *pl.* withdrawe (1) C5 (D.231.9); *past.* withdrewe (1) C3 (D.201.15); *past part.* withdrawe (2) C3, C4.

witholde *inf.* (1) N5 (D.240.13); *3 sing.* withholdith (1) C3 (D.189.30); *pl.* withhold (1) C1; *past.* withhelden (1) C3 (D.190.14); *past part.* witholden (1) P4 (D.156.2); with holde (1) C2.

within *prep.* (29) P3, C3; wythynne (15) P2, C3; wiþin (13) S1, S2; wiþinne (5) S1; withinne (4) P3, C3; wythyn (3) S2, P3; wiþynne (3) S1; wythynne (3) C3, C5; wyþynne (2) S1; wyþinne (1) S1; wyþyn (1) S2; wythyn (1) C5; withine (1) N4; wythinne (1) C3; (?) wytten (1) N8 (D.233.14). As two words with in (17) S1, P3; with inne (4) P1, P3; wiþ ynne (8) S1, S2; with ynne (7) S2, C3; with yn (8, 6 in D.193) C3; wiþ yn (2) S1, S2; wyth in (1) N8 (D.233.9).

without *prep.* (4) S1, C5; withoute (23) S1, P2; withouten (12) C1, C2; wiþowte (4) S1, S2; wiþoute (3) S1, S2; wythoute (3) C3, P4; withowte (3) C3, N4; wythought (1) C3 (D.203.28); wythouten (1) P3 (D.140.17); withowtyn (1) N4. As two words with oute (5) C1, P2; wyth out (3) C8, C3; with out

Glossary of Forms 401

(2) C2, P3; with owte (2) C1; with outen (2) C8, P5 (D.136.8, 159.23); wiþ oute (1) P2; wyth oute (1) C3.
witnesse *n.* (5) N2, C3; witnisse (1) N5; wittenes (1) N4; wittnesse (1) P4.
witnesseth *vb. 3 sing.* (1) N5; witnessith (3) N2, N4; wittenesseth (1) P4; wytennssuth (1) N2 (D.235.2).
wittes *n.* (2) C1.
wodes *n.* woods. (1) C3 (D.197.24).
wolcome *inf.* (1) P3.
wolle *n.* wool. (4) P3, C3; wol *(2) C4; pl.* wolles (8) C2, C3.
wollefell *adj.* (2) S2, C3; wollefelle (1) C3; (both C3 in D.180).
wollen *adj.* woolen. (1) C3 (D.196.3).
wollenclothe *n.* (1) C3 (D.180.13).
woman *n.* (2) C8, C4; womman (2) S2, C3; *pl.* women (4) C8, C3; wemen (1) C3.
wonede *vb. past part.* accustomed, used to be. (2) C3 (D.203.8, 14); wont (4) P3, C3 (D.142.14, 187.5, etc.).
wood *n.* (2) C2; woode (1) C3.
word *n.* (3) P3, C5; worde (7) S1, P2; woord (2) S2; *pl.* wordes (3) S1, N2.
work *n.* (1) P3 (D.146.33); werk (3) C3, N4; *pl.* werkes (6) S1, P2. See werk.
workemen *n.* (1) S4. See werkmanship.
world *n.* (2) C3, C5; worlde (1) P2.
worship *n.* (10) S1, P2; wrshyp (2) P2 (D.113.11, 26); wurship (1) C3; worshyp (1) P2.
worschipped *vb. past part.* (1) S2.
worshipful *adj.* (94) S1, S2; worshipfull (8) P1, P3; worschipful(l) (6) S1, C1; worchepeful (4) C1 (D.163); worsshupfull (2) P0; worshupful (1) N2; worshepeful (1) C1; worshepful (1) S1; worshipfulle (1) C4; wurshipful (1) S2; worchopful (1) C1; worechepeful (1) C1.
worth *adj.* (6) C3, C5.
worthinesse *n.* (1) C1 (D.162.2).
worthy *adj.* (20) C8, C1; worthi (20) S1, C3; worþy (1) C2; *supl.* worthiest (19 C8.
wostede *n.* worsted. (1) C3.
wot(e) See wite.
wounded *vb. past.* (1) C4; *past part.* wounded (1) C5; *ger.* woundyng (1) C4 (D.216.23).
woundes *n.* (1) C3.
writ *n.* (10) S1, C3; writt (11) C2, C3; writte (8) P3, C3; wrytte (1) C3; write (1) C5; wirtt (1), wirtte (1) C2 (D.171.3, 8); wryte (1) C5; *pl.* writtes (38) S1, S2; writteȝ (1) C4; writtis (1) P5; wryttes (1) S1; writts (1) C3.
write *inf.* (9) S1, S2; wryte (4) P2, P3; *1 sing.* (3) P0, C1; *3 sing.* writeth (1) P2; *pl.* (5) S1, S2; *subj. pl.* (3) all S1; *past* wrote (3) S1, P3; wroote (1) S2 (D.78.4); *past part.* writen (13) S1, P1; written (1) S1; wreton (1) P2; wreten

(3) S1, P2; write (1) S1; writon (1) P3; wryten (1) N6; wrytten (1) N8; wrytyn (1) P2; ywrete (1) C3 (D.198.18); *ger. / noun forms, sing.* writyng (7) P3, C3; writing (4) P2, P5; wrytyng (4) C3, C5; wryting (2) P5; writiyng (1) C5 (D.222.6); *pl.* writinges (1) P2; wrytinges (1) P5.
wroght *vb. past part.* done, performed, accomplished. (1) S1 (D.69.20).
wrong *n.* (7) S1, C1; wronge (1) C8; wroong (1) P3 (D.127.6); *pl.* wronges (10) C8, C1; wrongys (1) C1.
wrongfull *adj.* (3) P3, C3.
wrongfully *adv.* (9) C1, S1; wrongefully (1) C5; wronfully (1) C3 (D.197.4).
wrongwesly *adv.* wrongfully. (1) C4 (D.213.2).
wryght *n.* (2) C2 (D.173.3, 4).
wycked *adj.* (1) C3 (D.192.3).
wyndbemes *n.* windbeams, beams that cross and tie together the rafters in a roof. (1) N4; windbemeʒ (1) N4. Both in D. 238.
wynde *n.* (2) C3, N5.
wyne *n.* (11) C3, C4; wyn (1) C3; *pl.* wynys (1) C5.
wynnynges *n.* winnings ("of werre"). (2) P4 (D.156.24, 25).
wynter *n.* (8) S1, C3.
wysdome *n.* (2) C3. See wisdoms.

ydell *adj.* idle. (1) C4.
ye *pro. nom.* (315) PO, S1; ʒe (13) C1 (9), P2 (3); yee (5) S2 C2; ʒee (1) C2; *obj.* yow(e) (302) PO, S1, etc.; you (156) S1, S2; ʒow (14) only in C1, P2; youe (9) C3, C4; ʒou (8) C1 (7 in D.162); yoou (1) C3 (D.203.20); *gen.* your(e) (649) P1, S1; yowr (32) C8, S1; ʒowr (25) P2 (24 in D.113); ʒoure (15) C1, C2; ʒowre (11) P2 (D.114); youre (4) C3 (D.203); ʒour (4) C1, C2; yooure (4) C3 (all in D.203); yhour (1) C2 (D.173.15); Iour (1) C1 (D.164.27); ioure (1) C1 (D.164.42); *absolute form* youres (5) S1, C2; ʒowrys (2) P2 (D.113); *intensive.* yhour self (1) C2 (D.173.17).
yelde *inf.* yield. (3) C8, P3; *pr. part.* yelding (1) C5; yeldyng (2) P3, N5; *past part.* yelded (1) C5; I ʒolde (2) C1.
yeman *n.* yeoman. (2) S1; yoman (2) C4, C5; *pl.* yemen (3) C3 (D.186).
yen *n.* eyes (eyen). (1) S1 (D.40.9).
yerd *n.* (church) yard. (1) C3; ʒerde (2) N4.
yerdes *n.* yards, measurements. (1) C3; ʒerdes (1) N4; ʒerdis (3) N4.
yere *n.* year. (99) C8, S1; yer (25) C8, C1; ʒer (18) N8, C1; yeer (15) S1, P3; ʒere (4) C1, C3; yeere (1) P5; *pl.* yeres (18) P3, C3; yerys (1) P3.
yerely *adv.* (32) S1, C3; yerly (20) S1, P3; yerelye (2) C3; yerli (2) C3; yeerly (2) S1; yerle (1) P3; ʒerli (1) N8; ʒerly (1) C3.
yet *adv.* (13) C8, P1; yit (17) S1, P1; ʒit (1) C1, C3; yitt (2) C3, C4; yitte (2) S1; yut (1) C5 (D.217.29); ʒet (1) C1.
yeue *inf.* (5) S1, P2; ʒeue (1) C1 (D.163.25); geve (1) P3 (D.143.4); *imp.* yeueth

(1) S2; *3 sing.* yeueth (1) C5; *pl.* yeue (2) S1; *3 sing. subj.* yeue (1) P3; *pl. subj.* yeue (3) S1, P2; *past.* yaf (4) S1, P3; yaff (2) C5; yafe (1) C3 (D.199.34) ʒaf (1) C1 (D.164.25); gaf (1) P4 (D.153.7); *pres. part.* yeuyng (3) S1, P3; yevyng (2) C3; *past part.* yeven (16) S1, P3; yeuen (112) S1, S2; yeue (4) S1, C3; yevyn (1) C5; yoven (1) P4; youyn (1) P4; yiuen (1) S2; y yove (1) N2; gyuen (1) P5 (D.159.21)

yhourself See ye.

yift(e) *n.* (15) S1, S2; yeft(e) (2) S1, S2; gifte (3) S1, P3; gefte (1) C5; *pl.* yiftes (3) S1, P3; giftes (1) P4.

ymaginacion *n.* (1) C4 (D.212.14).

ymagyn *inf.* imagine. (1) S1; *pl.* ymaginith (1) C1; *past* imagenyd (1) C1; ymagined (1) C3; *pr. part.* ymagenyng (1) C3; *past part.* ymagened (1) C5.

yockes *n.* yokes. (1) C3 (D.197.21).

yonge *adj.* young. (2) P3 (D.146.16); *comp.* yonger (2) N2, C4.

yorn *n.* yarn. (1) C3 (D.197.18).

you / yow See ye.

yron *n.* (3) C3 (D.197).

yshutte *vb. past part.* shut. (1) C2 (D.176.7).

ʒele *n.* zeal (1) C5.

Index of Names

The following index is of proper names and places found in the documents. It lists items by document and line number: a reference listing 227.4 can be translated as "document 227, line 4." Items with multiple references in a single document are indicated by *passim*. Names are listed under the usual spelling found in the documents. Thus *Butler* is listed under *Boteler*, *Oxford* under *Oxenford*, and so forth. No attempt has been made to identify similar names in separate documents as referring to the same person. William *Bowes* and William *Bowys* may indeed be the same person but each spelling has been listed separately. Similarly, *Lord* Tiptoft and *Iohn* Tiptoft have been kept separate, as well as *Windsor* and *Windsor Castle*, even though such pairs are in all likelihood identical.

Abbot, William, 145 *passim*; Iohn, 128.3; Willyam, 153.2.
Adam, Richard, 151.11.
Ady, Iohan, 127 *passim*.
Aileminstre, Manor (probably in Herefordshire), 222.8.
Aire (river), 226.4.
Ake, William, 19.4.
Albany, Duke of, 70.5.
Alencon (France), 8.5; 48.3.
Aleyn, William, and Roberd, his father, 189 *passim*.
Alkeryngton, Richard, 25.3.
Alquyn (Alcuin), 197.7.
Amsterdam, 145 *passim*.
Amyas (Amiens, France), 96.5.
Andrewe, Richard, 151.4.
Andrew, Andrieu, Thomas, Signet clerk, 78.7; signed 52, 80.
ap Morgan, Dauyd, 200.3.
ap Thomas, Dauid, 178 *passim*.

Appelton, Thomas, petition of, 189.
Ardern, John, 106 *passim*.
Argill, Morice, 225.4.
Armesby, John, 92.3.
Arras (France), 96.5.
Arthure, Hugh, 240 *passim*.
Arture of Britayne (Arthur, brother of John, Duke of Brittany), 170 *passim*.
Arundell, Earl of, 53.4.
Ascow, Iohan, 45 *passim*.
Asteley, Ioan, petition of, 121.
Aubiualle (Abbeyville, France), 96.6.
Audeley, Lord of, 178.11.
Augustyn (St.), 197.9.
Aullforth, John, 86.3.

Babyngton, William, 199.31.
Badburham (Babraham, Cambridgeshire), 144.11.
Baieux (Bayeux, France), Signet letters

Index of Names

signed in, 16-20.
Baire (Bavaria), Duke John of, 43 *passim*.
Bakeler, Roger, 212 *passim*; Isabell, his wife, 212 *passim*.
Baldeswell, Henry, indenture of, 240.
Bameburgh, Castle (Bamburgh, Northumberland) 229 *passim*.
Banelyngham, Castle (Balinghem, Picardy), 114 *passim*; 115.7.
Banewell (Somerset), 185.14.
Bangore, Bishop of, 16.3; 23.3; 147.10.
Barnay, see Bernay.
Barowe, William, 23.3.
Barre, John, 22 *passim*.
Bassyngbourn, Manor (Cambridgeshire), 144.11.
Bataille (Battle Abbey), Abbot of, 24.15; 209.9.
Bate, Robert of, 173.3; Iohn, 197.2.
Bath(e), Bishop of, 128.1; 142.2; 150.5; 151.2; 175.5; 178.4; 185 (petition of); 189.1; 190.1; 191.17; 197.1; 198.19; 204.2; Cathedral, 5.2; 37.3; City, 5.3.
Bayll, Iohn, 75.1.
Baylly, Iohn 236 *passim*.
Baynton, Manor (Yorkshire), 19.4.
Beauchamp, Walter, 116.1; Iohane, 224.20.
Beaufort, Henry (Bishop of Winchester, Cardinal), 131 *passim*; 144.24; 182 *passim*; 205.1; 210 *passim*; 219.1; 220.1; letter by, 113, 127. See also Wynchester.
Beaulieu, Abbot of, 235.4.
Beausey (Lancashire), 201 *passim*.
Beche Saifterton (? Lincolnshire), 238.3.
Becket, St. Thomas, 224.7.
Bed(e)ford, Duke of, 32.11; 51.5; 60.4; 116.7; 117.25; 159.4; 175.1; 182.17; 210.26; Town, 142 *passim*.
Beekhelwyn (Bec-Hellouin, France), Abbey of, Signet letters signed at, 30, 31.
Beggar, Priory of (Richmond, Yorkshire), 140 *passim*.
Bekynton, Thomas, 151 *passim*.
Beling(e)ham, Belyng(e)ham, Thomas, 216 *passim*; Robert, 216 *passim*.
Beneste, Thomas, 108.
Benet (Benedict Nicolls, Bishop of St. David's), 16 *passim*.
Bergeuenny (Abergavenny), 224.21.
Berkyng (Barking), Recluse of, 18.2.
Bernay (France), Signet letters signed at, 28-29.
Bernewell, Prior and Canons of, 163 *passim*; Iohanes, 128.20.
Berton (Great Barton, Suffolk), 237.4.
Beuerle (Beverley), 145.22.
Beuoys (Beauvais, France), 205.6.
Bibyng, Thomas, 240.5.
Birdsale, Manor (Yorkshire), 19.4.
Birkhede (Birkenhead, Cheshire), 201.19.
Bodyn, Thomas, petition of, 219, 220; answer to his petition, 221.
Bohun, Iohn, 194.11.
Bolton, Iohn, 212 *passim*; Thomas, 20.3.
Bona Villa, Laurence de, 155.3.
Bone, Iohan, 65.2.
Bonsergeant, Robert, 41.2.
Bonyngton, Iohn, 171.3.
Boteler, Isabell, wife of Iohn, 201 *passim*.
Botiller, James le, Earl of Ormond, 124.3. See also Ormond; Wiltshire.
Bourdeux, Constable of, 60.2; Seneschal and Mayor, 77.5.
Bourgoigne, etc. (Burgundy), Duke of, 43.13; 81.5; 96.6; 132.1; 133.1; 134 *passim*; 156.31; 217 *passim*; Burgundians, 132, 134.
Bowedon, Manor (Great Bowden, Leicestershire), 227.14.
Bowes, William, 157.3.
Bowys, William, 29.2.
Boydell, William, indenture of, 238.
Braband (Brabant), petition about the merchants of, 217 *passim*.
Bradley, Thomas, 197.4.
Bramham, Manor (Yorkshire), 19.5.

Brampton, Robert, 183 *passim*; William, 147.3; 183 *passim*.
Braybrook, Gerard, 164.19.
Bredhill, Iohn, 197; Richard, 197.25.
Brekstone, 104.2.
Brembre, Nichol, 161 *passim*.
Brendrigge (Westmoreland), 216.5.
Bretaigne, etc., Duke of, 32 *passim*; 36.2; 46.4; 48.2; Province of, 32.3; 196.2; 205.12.
Brewester, signature of, 152.
Bristow(e) (Bristol), 30.2; 44 *passim*; 199 *passim*; 202 *passim*; 230.2; deposition of the mayor and bailiffs of, 236.
Brithelmeston (Brighton, Sussex), 125.3.
Bromwwyche, Thomas, 222.6.
Brothnam, Morgrete, petiton of, 120.
Brounce, Thomas, 6.6.
Brounflet(e), Henry, 95.2; Thomas, 19.2.
Brount, Richard, 47.3.
Brownyng, Iohan, 165.3.
Bruges, etc. (City), 102.2; 135 *passim*.
Bruyn, Harri, 218 *passim*.
Brydham (Sussex), 194 *passim*.
Bryggewatir (Bridgwater, Somerset), 211.24.
Buckinghamshire, 47.2; 224.4.
Buktoft, William, 47.3.
Burcestre, Iohn, indenture of, 239; Elizabeth, his wife, 239.16.
Burgh, William, 44.4.
Burnelshede (Burneshead, Westmoreland), 216.3.
Bursegand (Marshal of France), 170.3.
Burton, Thomas, petition of, 170.
Bury St. Edmunde, etc., 237.2; monastery and abbot, 153 *passim*.
Bynden, Thomas, 239.21.
Byngham, William, 146.11.

Caen (France), Signet letters signed in, 3-7, 15, 21-26; Town, 4 *passim*.
Caernarvan (Wales), 191.3.
Calais, etc., 57.9; 69.22; 96.2; 107 *passim*; 113.20; 114.4; 115 *passim*; 132 *passim*; 133 *passim*; 134 *passim*; 135 *passim*; 139.13; 148 *passim*; 156 *passim*; 183.3; petition of the soldiers of, 167.
Calot, Laurence, 136.11.
Cambrigge, etc., County of, 144.12; 163.3; 237.15; 238.2; University of, 6.12; 146 *passim*.
Candelwikstrete, Church of St. Lawrence of, 181.5.
Canon, Iohn, 164.11.
Canterbury, Archbishop of, 16.9; 26.10; 116.1; 122.41; 123.14; 124.5; 150.4; 151.2; 175.5; 177 *passim*; 198.19; 210 *passim*; 224.7; Cathedral, 177 *passim*; City, 50.4; 134.6; 171.2; Court of, 166.10; Province(s) of, 226 *passim*.
Cappe, Iohn, petition of, 114.
Cardygan, etc. (shire of Wales), 178 *passim*.
Carlele, etc. (Carlisle), Bishop of, 74.4; 122.42; 149.3; 232.5; Castle, 149 *passim*.
Carpenter, Isabell and Iohn, petition concerning, 181, 194 *passim*.
Cassons, Iohn, 123 *passim*; Ianym, petition of, 118.
Castel (Castile), King of, 51.1.
Caud(-rey, Richard?), 63.12.
Cawode, Robart, 232.6.
Charles, King of France, 182.2.
Charles, the Daufyn, 182.3.
Charyngcrosse, 159.8.
Chaucer (Thomas), 113.17.
Chaundeler, Iohan, 10.2.
Chekewell (Chigwell, Essex), 165.4.
Chestre, County of, 186 *passim*; 201 *passim*; Bishopric and Diocese of, 78 *passim*; 80.2; Bishop of, 86.2.
Chestreton (Cambridgeshire), 163.3.
Chestreville (Chesterfield, Derbyshire), 183.4.
Cheyne, Iohn, 241.1.
Chicheley, Robert, 18.2; Henry or Harry, See Canterbury, Archbishop of.
Chichester, Bishopric and Diocese of,

Index of Names

8.4; 17 *passim*; 25.4; 35.2; 141.3; Cathedral, 7.2; 8.3; 17.3; 24.10; 25.4; Port, 187.19.
Chideleo(g)h, James, 241.8; William, 241.8.
Chirche, Robert, 219 *passim*; 220 *passim*.
Chirtesey, etc., Iohn, 233 *passim*.
Chrischurche, hundred of (Hampshire), 187.3.
Clarehall (Cambridge), petition of, 146.
Clarence, Duke of, 29.2; Duchess of, 165.9.
Claworth (Clayworth, Nottinghamshire), 89.3.
Clerk, Radnus, 128.20; Iohn, 197.3.
Clifford, Iohan, 118.2.
Clopton, Robert, indenture of, 237.
Clyfford, Lord, 154.8.
Cochare, Thomas, 50.2.
Cokayn, Iohan, 163 *passim*.
Coker, Robert, petition of, 188.
Cokeram, William, 145 *passim*.
Colchestre, etc., City, 127.3; person's name, 28.2, 3.
Coldkenyngton, Manor. See Kenyngton.
Cole, Iames, 103 *passim*.
Colland, Thomas, petition of, 147.
Co(o)lwelle, Iohn, 211 *passim*.
Combe, William, 199 *passim*; 236.5.
Comoch, 211.23.
Comyn, Thomas, 198 *passim*.
Cooke, Iohn, 68.3; William, 211 *passim*.
Copthorn, Iohn, 6.5.
Corff, William, 6.9.
Cornewaill(e) (Cornwall), 32.4; 187.21; Iohan, 99.2.
Cornewalesse Ground beside the Crane (Vintry, London), 216.7.
Cotayne, Iohn, 199.32.
Cotes, Thomas, 189 *passim*.
Cotyngham, Iohn of, 173 *passim*.
Couentree, 146.9.
Courrenays, ("cousin" to Henry V), 49.3.

Courtenay, Philipp, 241 *passim*.
Cradok, Thomas, 211.24.
Crakfarwes (Carrickfergus, N. Ireland), 145.7.
Crane (in London), 216.7.
Crathorn(e), Thomas, 145 *passim*.
Croke, Iohn, petition of, 143.
Croix, Thomas de la, 96.1.
Crom(e)well, 175.5; 178.4; Lord, 122.43; 142.3; Rauf, 116.1; William, 54.3.
Crotey (le Crotoy, in France), 104.2; 137.2.
Cruche, Iohan, 25.2.
Cumberland, etc., 149.14; 216.2; 223.2.
Curson, William, 42.2.

Daggevile, Thomas, 147.4.
Dalkesound (Ireland), 145.8.
Dalkey (Ireland), 211.19.
Dalueys, Ffernand, 211 *passim*.
Darcy, Robert, 164. *passim*.
Dariega, Petre de, 111.3.
Dartas(se), Ianico, 34.2; 55.3.
Davy, John, 225 *passim*.
Depeden (John), signature, 90, 94-96.
Derby, City, 172 *passim*; 183.4.
Derham, Richard, 6.12; 7.2; 8.2.
Derteford (Dartford, Kent), 189.9.
Derwent (river), 226.4.
Deuenyssh, Nicholas, 202 *passim*.
Deuonsshire, Devenshire, 187.21; 241.9.
Develyn, Dyuelyn (Dublin), 20.2; 145.9, 211 *passim*.
Deye, Margerye, 92 *passim*.
Dixon, Nicholl, 126.9.
Dodde, William, petition of, 165.
Doncastre, Manor (Yorkshire), 19.4.
Doreward, Iohn, 164.19.
Dorset (shire), 187.20.
Doudale, Robert, 129.8.
Doune (river Don), 226.4.
Douorre (Dover), 50.2; 94.5.
Dreux (France), 95.6; 96.9.
Dreux, Lord, 185.2.
Duchelond (Germany), 43.4.

Ducheman, Iohn, 225.4.
Duket, Robert, 216.11.
Dunelm See Duresme.
Dunster, Castle (Somerset), 188.3.
Duresme (Durham), Bishop of, 112; 122.42; 159.14; Signature, 175.5; Cathedral, 112.7. See Dunelm.
Dykonson, Robert, 216 passim.

Ebor. See York, Archbishop of.
Edward I, 203 passim; 204 passim; Edward III, 181.4.
Edynbourgh, 159.13.
Egremond, Lord, 223 passim.
Elien (Bishop of Ely), 123.14; 124.5; 175.5.
Ellerker, Iohn, 19.2.
Enderby, Iohn, 142 passim.
Essex, county, 164 passim; 189 passim; Nicholas, 225.4.
Etwell, Harry, 142 passim.
Ewe (Eu, France), Earl of, 170 passim.
Excester, etc. (Exeter), Duke of, 6.2; 63.2; 116.1; 117.16; Bishop of, 6.5; Bishopric of, 88.4; Cathedral, 78.3, 88.3; City, 241.6; Phelip, 236.2.
Exton, Nichol, 161.35.

Faleyse, Faloiʒe, etc. (Falaise, France), 17.4; Signet letters signed in, 9-14.
Ffallan, William, 232 passim.
Farnham (probably Farnham, Essex), 127.2.
(F)fastolf, Iohn, 125.3; Hugh, 15.2; 59.3.
Ffaunhop, Lord, 142 passim.
Ffeltewell, Thomas, 25.5.
Ffenys, Iames, 151.4.
(F)fitʒ, Iohn, 142 passim; 190.16.
Ffitʒ Geffray, Iohn, 142 passim.
Ffitʒ Gerot, Thomas, 215 passim.
Ffitʒ Harry, Thomas, and his wife Iohanne, petition of, 222.
Ffitʒ Hugh, Lord, 31.3; 86.3; Robert, 86.3.
(F)Flandres, 43.14; 57 passim; 69 passim.

Flemmynges, 132, 134, 193.
(F)flete (prison), 163.41; 202 passim.
Fford, Richard, petition of, 232.
Ffornham Alhalwyn Ffornham Martyn Berton (Fornham All Saints and St. Martin, Suffolk), 237.3.
Ffortescu, Iohn, 241.3.
Ffosbroke, Maud, petition of, 119.
Ffowler, William, 47.2.
Ffox, Iohn, indenture of, 238.
(F)France, 70.3; 81 passim; 117.6; 124.3; 126 passim; 131.3; 136 passim; 156.30; 159.3; 168.4; 170.3; 182 passim; 204.1; 218.4; King of, 81 passim; 99.3; 182 passim; Queen of, 81.5.
(F)Frank, Iohn, 129; 159.30; Thomas, petition of, 140; William, 140.3.
Ffrebarn, Iohn, petition of, 225.
Fronsac, Castle (France), 60.3.
Ffry(e), Robert, 72.5; 110.

Gand (Ghent), 183 passim.
Garand (Guerande, France), 205.14.
Garnesey (Guernsey), 196.28.
Garnetʒ, William, 209.6.
Gars(e)dale, Richard, 64 passim.
Garueys, Gerueys, etc., Piers, 15 passim; 59.2; Iohn, indenture of, 237.
Gene (Genoa), 69 passim; 175.2.
Gerard, Hug [sic], 147.6.
Geresey (Jersey), 196.28.
Gilbert, Master, of Salisbury, 109.6.
Gildo (Notre Dame du Guildo, Brittany), 196 passim.
Glamorganshire, 159.5.
Glastonbury, Abbot and Convent of, 166 passim.
Glatton (Huntingdonshire), 27.2.
Gloucester, etc., Duke of, 81.20; 89.10; 116 passim; 118.3; 119.1; 120.1; 121.1; 122 passim; 123.14; 124.5; 125 (treaty); 131.28; 132.15; 133.3; 134.15; 142.2; 144.24; 168.1; 175.5; 182.17; 191.17; 198.19; Abbot of, 83.2; Iohn, 232.10; City, 90.5; Shire, 33 passim.

Index of Names 409

Godard, William and Agneis, 66 *passim*.
Goddeshous (Grammar School, Cambridge), 146.
Gode, Thomas, 127.2.
Goldsmyth, Iohan, 172 *passim*.
Golclyff (Goldcliff, Monmouthshire), 155.3.
Graces (St. Mary Graces, London), 39 *passim*.
Gravelyng, Water of (Gravelines, France), 132.2; 133.1; 134.2.
Gray, Thomas, 84 *passim*.
Graystok, Baron of, 154.8.
Grenway, Roger, 40.19.
Guisnes, etc., Castle (Guines, France), 115.6; 156 *passim*.
Gurnay (Gournay, France), 205 *passim*.
Guyenne (France), 71.2; 77.3; 81.17.
Guyldehalle, etc. (London), 161.15; 181.14.
Gyles, Thomas, 68.2.

Haburgeham, Robert, 31 *passim*.
Hakyns, Iohanes, 173.17.
Haleway, Thomas, 202 *passim*.
Hall, William, 160 *passim*.
Hambury, Church, 6.9.
Hamelak (Helmsley, Yorkshire), 63.4.
Hamond, (signature), 1.12.
Hampshire, etc., 94.2; 218.2; Viscount of, 105.2.
Hampton, City, 51.4; 146.9; 218.46; Iohn, 151.4.
Hanham, Iohan, 97.2.
Hankford, William, 163.24.
Hansere (Hanse commercial league), 135.2.
Harowedon, Richard, 11.2.
Harpour, Iohn, 237.18.
Haseley, Thomas, petition of, 159.
Hastynges, Free Chapel, 68.3; Deanery of, 141.3; Town, 125.3.
Haukyn, Laurence, 24.10.
Haverebergh, Manor (Harborough Market, Leicestershire), 227.14.

Haveryng of the Bour Park (Essex), 228.17.
Hayton, Will., 6.13.
Hempstede, William, 190.7.
Henry, Harry, etc., King of England. Henry I, 203 *passim*; Henry II, 203,4; 204.5; Henry IV, 144.9; 163.4; 225.18; Henry V, 81.22; 144.9; 168.3; 198.2; 210.2; Henry VI, 168.3; 179.2; 180.2; 204.1; 219.3; 220.3; 234.1; 235.2; 238.1; 239.25; 240.31; 241 *passim*.
Herberfeld, William, 147.3.
Hereford, Bishop of, 88.3; 91.2; Cathedral, 78.9; Lady of, 164 *passim*.
Herlam (Haarlem, Netherlands), 145.4.
Heron, Iohn, petition of, 229.
Hertford (shire), 128.3; 233.1).
Hertishil, etc., Iohan and Robert, 89 *passim*.
Hethe, Iohn, 52 *passim*; signatures 87, 88.
Hikeling, William, 172.3.
Hohom, Iohn, 19.4.
Holand, William and Margerie, 27 *passim*.
Holdernesse (Yorkshire), 173 *passim*.
Holland, etc., 43.14; petition about the merchants of, 217.
Holme, Richard, 6.12.
Hondesacre (Hansacre), Prebend of (Lichfield), 86.2.
Hoo, Thomas, indenture of, 239.
Hore, Walter, indenture of, 235.
[H]Ospital of þe Trinite (Bristol), 44.3.
Hukcote, Manor and Church (Hulcott, Buckinghamshire), 224 *passim*.
Hull, ship of, 145 *passim*; Iohn, 14.1; Iohan atte, 165.3.
Hulpryngton, Manor (Wiltshire), 241.5.
Humbre (river), 226.4.
Hungerford, Lord, 122.43; 191.17; 210.4; 241.3; Walter, 116.1; 210.4.
Hunte, Iohan, 94.3.
Huntington, Earl of, 12.2; 40.6;

123.14; 124.5; 198.19.
Husee, Henry, 194.11.
Hyde, Abbey (Hampshire), 94.2.

Iarnemouthe (Yarmouth, Wiltshire), 52.4.
Iohane, Iehanne (Queen Joan), 140.4; 176.9.
Iohn, etc., King of England, 203, 204 *passim*.
Iohn, Copeman, 145.3.
Iohnsone, Sederyk, 145.30.
Irelond, etc., 30.2; 81 *passim*; 124 *passim*; 129.4; 145 *passim*; 198.2; 204.1; 211.19; 215 *passim*.
Iseland (Iceland), 145.2.
Iseldon (Islington, Middlesex), 128.5.
Issaunt, Nicholas, 205.14.
Itaylions (Italians), 208.2.
Iuyn, Iohn, 199 *passim*.

Kemp, Iohn, 166.10.
Kenchestre, Manor (Hertfordshire), 222.32.
Kendale, Richard, 146.13.
Kenelworth, Castle, Signet letter dated at, 108.9.
Kent (shire), 187.21; 189.9.
Kentwood, etc., William, 101 *passim*.
Kenyngton, etc., Manor (Middlesex), 123.6; 144.19.
Kermerdyn (Carmarthen, Wales), Priory of, 90 *passim*.
Kiryell, Thomas, 205.4.
Kylmaynan (Kilmainham, Ireland), Prior of, 30.3.
Kymburley, Iohan, petition of, 172.
Kyngesswynford (Staffordshire), 197 *passim*.
Kynwolmersh, etc., William, 62 *passim*; 159.15.

Laigny sur Marne (Lagny, France), Signet letter signed at, 97.
Lambehithe, etc. (Lambeth), Signet letter signed at, 92, 93.
Lancaster, etc., Shire, 85.2; 201.2; City, 201 *passim*; Duchy, 159.25;
164.2; 210.7; Chancery of, 201.22; County Palatine of, 201.25.
Landasale, Robert, 190.7.
Langeley (Kings Langley, Herefordshire), 163.38.
Lanthony (Gloucestershire), Prior of, 90.5.
Laweshull, William, petition of, 227.
Lemyng, William, indenture of, 239.
Lentwardyn, 64.6.
Lescrop, Geffrey, 227.13.
Leuin le Clerc Burgeois of Gand (Ghent), petition of, 183.
Leycestre, Lercestre (Leicester), 72.5; 92.3; 159.29; 172.3; 227.14.
Lichefeld, 86.3.
Lieges (Liège) "elit" of, 43.5.
Lincoln, Shire, 143.4; 184.2; 234 *passim*; 238.3; City, 179 *passim*; Bishop of, 6.6; 150.5; 191.17.
Lisieux (France), Signet letter signed at, 27.
Litill Mylne Hamme Croft (Buckinghamshire), 224.4.
Logge, Piers, 61.2.
Lollards, 159.7; petition against, 174.
London, City, 18.3; 24.2; 34.4; 62.6; 81.10; 161 *passim*; 202.21; 208.9; 216 *passim*; 217 *passim*; 221.4; 231.15; 239 *passim*; Tower of, 39.3; 159 *passim*; 174.4; 225 *passim*; 230.10; Bishop of, 97.2; 103.4; 116.1; 117.21; Mayor of, 161 *passim*; 181.3; Sisors of, 239.5; Archdeacon of, 101.3.
Longe, Iohn, 241.3.
Longuille, Earl of, 71.8.
Longley (Langley), Thomas, Bishop of Durham, 112.
Loueyn, Iohn, petition of, 205.
Louiers (Louviers, France), Signet letters signed in, 32-34.
Love, William, 190.16.
Lowyngbargh, Iohn, 150.3.
Lughtbourgh (Loughborough, Leicestershire), church of, 72.4.
Lumbardes (Lombards), 208.2.
Lumbardye, 139.3.

Index of Names 411

Lumley, Marmaduke, Bishop of Carlisle, 232.5.
Lurchon, Iohn, 160 *passim*.
Lutrell, Iohn, 188 *passim*; Iames, his son, 188 *passim*.
Luxemburgh, Iohan de, 96.6.
Lymerik (Ireland), petition of the mayor and citizens of, 198.
Lymyngton (Hampshire), petition of the citizens of, 187.2.
Lyndewode, William, 142.3.
Lyngen, Manor (Herefordshire), 222.8; Rauf and his son Iohn, 222 *passim*.
Lynne, 145.22.
Lyuedon, Roger, 236.3.

Malberthorp (Marblethorp, Lincolnshire), petition of the citizens of, 184.
Maluern, Iohn, 103.3.
Mante (Mantes, France), Signet letters signed in, 61-68, 71-72.
Mareschal des Rues, 99.2.
Marrys, Dauid, 171 *passim*.
Marshal, the Earl, 117.10; 122.42.
Martyn, Hamon, 32.3.
Mauley, Pierres, and his wife Maude, 19.6.
Mavyoll, Iohn, 199 *passim*.
Maydenston (Maidstone, Kent), 233.11.
Mayne, Iohn, 241.3.
Meaulx (Meaux, France), Signet letters signed at, 98-103.
Melcombe (Regis), port of (Dorset), 187.20.
Meleun (Melun, France), Signet letters signed in, 83-89.
Melton (Melton Mowbray, Leicestershire), 172.3.
Merbury, Iohn, 178 *passim*.
Mercer's Guild, petition of, 161.
Mere, Iohn, 197.25.
Merton (Surrey), 127.11.
Meweys, Thomas, 94.2.
Midylton, William, petition of, 173.
Milton, etc., Walter, 199.16; 236.3.

Moleyn(s), Adam, 151.4; deposition signed by, 142; notation by, 143, 144, 145, 153, 205; signature, 148, 150.
Monsirtan ou Sault Yonne (France), Signet letter signed at, 82.
Monterell, Castle (Montreuil, France), 164.32.
More, Thomas de la, petition of, 223.
Moreton, W., 107.2.
Morley, Thomas, 197.25.
Moronval by Dreux (France), Signet letters signed at, 95, 96.
Morton, church of, 49.2.
Mountassilant, Mountassi Lond, etc. Lord of, 196 *passim*.
Munke, Henri, 150.3.
Mydelton, "a man yat is clepet," 112.4.
Mynours, William, 73.2.
Mynstreworth (Gloucestershire), church of, 33.4.

Neel, Nele, etc., William, petition of, 227; Cristian, 199.55; John, 224 *passim*.
Neucastell (Newcastle), Sheriff of, 154.8; Mayor of, 154.8.
Neugate (Newgate Prison), 159.6; 162.13; 181 *passim*.
Neuil (Neville), Iohn, 154.8; Thomas, 154.8.
Neustede vpon Acolm (Newstead on Ancolm, Lincolnshire), Prior of, 143 *passim*.
Neweforest, hundred of (Southampton), 187.3.
Neweport, hundred of (Southampton), 187.3; Iohn, 218 *passim*.
Noreys, Henry, 145.24.
Norfolk, Shire, 128 *passim*.
Normandy, etc., 4.3; 28.5; 38.3; 69.8; 113.22; 117.7; 126 *passim*; 131.3; 136 *passim*; 148.9; 159 *passim*; 164.32; 168.4; 205 *passim*.
North, Iohn, 147.4.
Northampton, City, 240 *passim*; Iohn,

161.7; church of Alhalowen in, 240.21.
Northumberland, etc., Earl of, 70.1; 116.1; 131.28; 142.3.
North Wales, district of, 145.20; Chamberlain of, 145.29; 191.1.
Northwodebernyngham (NorthWold and Barningham, Norfolk), 128 *passim*.
Norton, Thomas, petition of, 199; 202 *passim*; Thomas and Walter, petition of, 202; William, petition of, 200.
Nortonhautevile, Manor (Somerset), 241.4.
Norwich, etc., 190 *passim*; Bishop of, 116.1; 122.42.
Notyngham, County of, 89.3.

Ogle, Robert, 154.8.
Oldecastle, Iohn, 159.6.
Oriell (Oriel College, Oxford), Provost of, 64 *passim*.
Orliens, etc., Duke of, 70 *passim*; 72.3.
Ormesby, Arthure, indenture of, 240.
Ormond, Earl of, 124.3; 224 *passim*; see also Wiltshire, Earl of.
Owse (river Ouse, Yorkshire), 226.4.
Oxenford, etc., Shire, 147 *passim*; 234.2; City, 203.2; 204.3; University, 146.4; 231.20; petition of the weavers of, 203, 204; petition of the citizens of, 231.
Oye (Oise, France), fortalice of, 132.13; 133.7; 134.13.

Pakemannys Wharf (London), 233.2.
Palain, William, 241.7.
Palton, Iohn, 128 *passim*.
Papenham, Iohn, 202 *passim*.
Paris, 96 *passim*; 102.2.
Parr(e), Thomas, 195.12; petition of, 216; Gilbert, 159.42.
Pauers, William, 222.31.
Paunfeld, Thomas, petition of, 163.
Payn, Thomas, 159 *passim*.
Pek, William, 142.24.

Pekham (Peckham, Surrey), 212.3.
Penelles, Richard, 49.3.
Percy, Rauf, 154.8; Thomas, 154.8.
Perham, William, 164.11.
Peterburgh, Abbey, 138.2.
Petresham, Manor, 106.2.
Pettysworth, Thomas, 171.9.
Picardes, 132.2; 134.2; 193.14.
Pierson, Mathewe, 216.11.
Plumer, signature, 240.
Pont de Larche (Pont de l'Arche, France), Signet letter signed in, 35.
Pontfret, Castle (Pontefract, Yorkshire), 70.8.
Pontfreu (probably Pontefract, Yorkshire), letter written at, 112.
Pool (Dorset), haven of, 187.19.
Pope, the, 35.3; 88.2; 177 *passim*; 182.5; Pope's court, 91.2; Pope's auditors, 166.10; William, petition of, 123. See Rome.
Poroell, 196.6.
Portesmouth, 3.2; 105.3.
Portile (? Portheitho or Port Eyron, North Wales), 145 *passim*.
Poules Gate (Paul's Gate, London), 162.14.
Prentys, Iohan, 13.2.
Prestewyke [William], Clerk of Parliament, 141.3.
Pulle, William, 201 *passim*.
Pulteney, Iohn, 181.3.
Pynhoe (Pinhoe, Devon), 241 *passim*.
Pryton, William, 156 *passim*.

Queene, of Henry IV, 18.5; 140 *passim*; 176 *passim*; of Henry V, 98.2; 141.2; of Henry VI, 157.1; 224 *passim*; of France, 81.5. See also Iohane.
Qwyncy, Gieffrey, petition of, 190.

Rachedale, William, 128 *passim*.
Radclif, Iohn of, 60.2.
Rademeld (Rodmell or Redmile, Leicestershire), parish church of, 25.6.
Ramesden Hall, etc., Manor (Essex), 164 *passim*.

Index of Names

Redyng (Reading, Berkshire), Parliament held at, 210 passim.
Ree, Rauf atte, 82.2; petition of, 164; Margaret, wife of Rauf, 164 passim; Thomas, 164.6.
Renoueld, Richard, 181.18.
Repyngale, see Rypyngale.
Reson, William, 19.3.
Richard II, 203.14; 204.17; 225.18; 233.5.
Richemond (Yorkshire), 140.3; Honour of, 144 passim.
Ripon, Edmund, 190.24.
Rodyngton, Robert, 3.1.
Rokeby, Thomas, petition of, 168.
Roklee, Robert, 100.2.
Rolleston, Robert, 85.2; 142.4.
Rome, Court of, 64 passim; 166.10; 177.8.
Roos, William, of Hamelak, 63.4; Iohn, 63 passim.
Rose, Iames, 145.30.
Rosen, Heyn, 145.4.
Rosyngton, Manor (Yorkshire); 19.4.
Rothewell, William, indenture of, 234.
Roucestre, Bishop of, 122.42.
Rouen, Roan, etc. (France), documents dated from, 36-39, 41-54, 60, 73-80, 126; merchants of, 102.2.
Rudby (Yorkshire), Church of, 19.3.
Ruggewey (Ridgeway), Manor, near Bristol, 44.4.
Russell, Phelipp, 198 passim; Robert, Mayor of Bristol, 44.4; 199.15; 236.3.
Ruthueil (beside Meaux, France), Signet letter signed at, 99.
Rykedon, Robert, 164.19.
Rypton (Ripton, Huntingdonshire), 146.10.
Rypyngale , Repyngale (Rippingale, Lincolnshire), Manor and Church of, 234 passim.

Saheny, Bawdewyn, 157.2.
St. Albons, Abbot of, 80.2; 128.3.
St. Antony, Hospital of (London), 62.2.
St. Asseph (Asaph), Bishop of, 151.3.
St. Bartholomew (Westsmithfield, London), 67 passim.
St. Crois, Cardinal of (Nicholas Albergati, Cardinal of Santa Croce), 182.6.
St. Dauid, Cathedral (Wales), 16 passim; Bishop of, 16 passim; 24 passim; 142.2.
St. Denys of Moronval beside Dreux, Signet letters signed at, 95, 96.
St. Dunstonys in the Este, Parish of (London), 233.3.
St. Edmund (the Confessor), Shrine of, 153.4.
St. Faron beside Meaulx (France), Signet letters signed at, 100, 101.
St. Germayne, Monastery (Selby, Yorkshire), petition of, 226.
St. Iames beside Northampton, Abbot of, 240.4.
St. Iames next Charyngcrosse (London), 159.8.
St. Iamys (of Compostella, Spain), 113.19.
St. Iohn, etc., Iohn, 76.2; Edward, 188 passim.
St. Iohn of Ierusalem, Hospital of (London), 144.2.
St. Iohn ȝacherie (London), Parson of, 146.12.
St. Katherines by the Tour (of London) Wharf, 225.5.
St. Laurence of Candelwikstrete (London), 181.5.
St. Liȝ (Senlis, France), Signet letter signed at, 105.
St. Malwis (St. Mawes, Cornwall), 196.15.
St. Mari Overey (Southwark), 233.6.
St. Marie of Colchirche, Parish of (London), 239.5.
St. Martin(es le) Grande (London), 62.5.
St. Omer (France), 96.5.
St. Osewoldes, Priory (Gloucester), 33.3.
St. Paul's, London, 101.2.

St. Peter Ffraunchiss, Church in Wawne (Holderness, Yorkshire), 173 *passim*.
St. Stephns, Church of (St. Albans), 128 *passim*.
St. Thomas of Acres, Hospital (London), 224.9.
Sale, William, 145 *passim*.
Salisbury, etc., 6.13; Citizens of, 109.6; 196.1; Dean of, 9.2; 10.2; Bishop of, 151.3; Earl of, 142.2; 145.40; 150.5; 160.1; 222.1; 223.9; 225.1; petition of, 149.
Salwyn, etc., Roger, 114.2; 115.16.
Sandes, Walter, 235.4.
Sandewych, etc., 125.9; 132.17; 134.18.
Sandford, Robert, 22.4.
Sargeaunt, Walter, 241.3.
Scargill, Thomas, petition of, 228.
Scotland, etc., 6.2; 70.4; 149.2; 159 *passim*; 229.16; King of, 70.3; 159.11; 182.10; "the maumet of," 70.5; inhabitants of, 223.18.
Scotte, Iohn, 225.4.
Scrope, Scroop, etc., Lord, 122.43; 178.4; 191.17.
Selby, Monastery of St. Germain, 226 *passim*; Richard, petition of, 128.
Selyngier, Iohn, 216 *passim*.
Sengelton, Thomas, 127 *passim*.
Sewster, William, indenture of, 240.
Sheldon, Iohn, 197.3.
Shene (Sheen, Surrey), House of Syon or of Jesus of Bethlehem, 18.6; 26 *passim*; 53 *passim*; 103.2; Manor, 106.2.
Shepward, Shipward, Iohn, 202 *passim*.
Shirburn, Iohannes, 171.9.
Shiryngton, Robert, 7.2; 8.1; signature, 55, 56, 57, 59, 60, 61, 62, 64, 68, 73, 75, 76, 83, 91, 92, 98, 99, 102, 104.
Shoote (Shute, Devon), 216.6.
Shrewesbury, etc., Signet letter signed in, 91.6; Earl of, 215.2.

Sicile (Sicily), King of, 157.10.
Skydmore, Iohn, 93.2.
Slake [Nicholas], 13.1.
Snell, Iohn, 101.5.
Solihille (Solihull, Warwickshire), 108.2.
Somerset, Shire of, 185 *passim*; 188.3; 241.4; Sheriff of, 185 *passim*.
Somerseth, Iohn, 151.4.
Soper, William, letter and petition, 111; 139.
Southampton, petition of the mayor and citizens of, 176; 187 *passim*; Town, 111.7; 218.47.
Southewerke, Borough (Surrey), 193.3; stews of, 192 *passim*.
Southrey (Lincolnshire), 202.24.
Southwales (administrative district), Justice of, 178 *passim*; Chamberlain of, 178.16.
Spaigne (Spain), 14.2; 111.2; 211.5; King of, 182.7.
Spelly, Thomas, 199.6.
Spencer, William, 225.4.
Spendeloue, Iohan, 74.2.
Spruce, Prussia, 135.2.
Spynall (Epinal, France), 157.2.
Stafford, County of, 197.5; Earl of, 122.42; 150.5; Humferie, 185.2.
Stamford, Thomas, 199 *passim*; 202 *passim*; 236 *passim*.
Stanhapp, Richard, 89 *passim*.
Stanlay, Jeynkyn, petition of, 186.
Stanley, Thomas, 201.18.
Staple, The (Calais), 107.9; 139.13.
Stauerne, Iohn, petition of, 171.
Staunford (Stamford, Lincolnshire), 238 *passim*.
Stodeley, I., signature, 239.25.
Stodley, Iohannes, 172.11.
Stoghton (Stoughton, Sussex), 194.5.
Stok, Iohn, petition of, 138.
Stokes, Iohn, instructions to, 135.
Stone, signature, 30.
Stonore (Oxfordshire), 234.5; Thomas, indenture of, 234.
Stopyndon, Iohn, 78.2.

Index of Names 415

Stounton, I., 185.2.
Stourton, Iohn, 158.2.
Stowemarkett (Suffolk), 127 passim.
Stratflere (Ystrad Fflur or Strata Florida, Wales), Abbot of, 178.3.
Strete (Devonshire), 166.1.
Stryckland, etc., Thomas, 216 passim.
Sturgeon, Richard, petition of, 160.
Suffolk, Earl of, 150.5; 151.3; 153.14; signature, 191, 198.
Suggestan (Sigston, Yorkshire), 173.17.
Surrey, Shire of, 192 passim; 193.3; 199.9; 212.4.
Sussex, Shire of, 187.19; 194.2; 239.1.
Suthwell, Thomas, 72.2.
Sutton, Manor (probably in Herefordshire), 222 passim; Iohn, 197.3.
Swan, Iohn, 138.3.
Swerdys (Swords, Ireland), Prebend of, 20.2.
Sydney, William, 194.12.
Syon, see Shene.

Talbot, Lord, 84.2; Iohn, petition of, 215.
Thamyse, etc. (river Thames), 159.36; 216.8; 233.10.
Thornton, Roger, 154.8.
Thorp, Thomas, 232 passim.
Tikell, Cecily, petition of, 162.
Tiptoft, Tiptot, etc., Lord, 122.43; 141 passim; 175.5; Iohn, 77.3; 116.1; petition of, 144.
Toky, Thomas, 38 passim.
Toly, William, 24.15; 78.6; 83.2; (signature) 47, 49, 50, 66, 67, 82, 84, 85, 86, 89, 93, 97, 101, 103, 105.
Touque, Castle (Touques, France), Signet letter signed at, 2.
Tottenham, "Sokettis Lond" in the parish of, 160.3.
Toure, etc. (Tower). See London, Tower of.
Trenchard, Harri, 218.41.
Trenchevile, Water [sic], 196.2.
Trent (river), 226.4.

Tresham, William, 151.5; 209.6.
Tretherf, Robert, 147.4.
Troutbek, William, 186.12.
Troyes (France), 81 passim; 102.2.
Tyrell, Iohn, 164 passim.

Van Ley, Petre, 145.2.
Vchayron Percell (Cardiganshire), petition of citizens of, 178.
Vernico (Guernica, Spain), 211.5.
Vernon (France), Signet letters signed in, 55-59.
Vivald, Baltazar, of Genoa, petition of, 175.
Vuedale, Iohn, 235.4.
Vynter, Iohn, 222.31.
Vyntrye(ward, London), 216.7.

Wakefield, Henri, 221.11.
Wales, 151.6; 155.3; 201 passim; 210.7; Pety Wales (London), 225.5; Henry, 145.14.
Walford, Robert, 147.4.
Waltham, letter written at, 113; Roger, 22.2.
Walton, Thomas, petition of, 191.
Walweyne, wife of Thomas, 93 passim.
Walysby, William, petition of, 141.
Ware, Henry, 24.13; 33.3; 35.2.
Warton (Lancashire), church of, 85.2.
Warwyk, Warrewik, etc., Town, 108.4; Earl of, 53.5; 116.1; 167.8; William, petition of, 196.
Water, Iames, 129.8.
Waterford (Ireland), 30.2.
Waterton, Robert of, 104.5.
Watyr of Eden (Eden Water, river), 223.18.
Waughen (Wanghen) in Holderness (Wawne, Yorkshire), 173 passim.
Wawton, Thomas, 142 passim.
Wayhen, Iohanes de, 173.17.
Waymouth (Weymouth, Dorset), 187.19.
Webbe, Iohn, 197.25.
Webley (Weobley, Herefordshire),

Signet letter signed at, 90.7.
Welles, City, 185.3; Bishop of Bath and, 128.1; 151.2.
Wemmys, Richard and Iohan his wife, 240.22.
West, Iohn, 173.4.
Westchepe (London), Great Conduit in, 239.4.
Westminster, etc., 1.5; 2.4; 26.3; 131.1; 142.1; 145 *passim*; 150.1; 159.33; 163.5; 179.4; 180.3; 183.11; 184 *passim*; 189.37; 200.6; 202 *passim*; 215.3; 216.9; 217.2; Palace of, 130.2; 154.6; Church of, 11.3; 28.3; Exchequer at, 2.4; 26.3; Master Mason of, 28.3; documents dated at, 106, 107, 117, 118, 129, 132, 133, 134, 135, 136, 141, 152, 154, 155, 156.
Westmorland, Earl of, 70.2; 116.1; 154.8 (Wesperlande); County of, 216.4.
Westsmythfeld (London), 67.2.
Wethy, Iohn, 164 *passim*.
Weuers, Craft of, 203; 204; 217.10.
Whelpdale, Roger, 74.4.
White, Mathewe, 225.4.
Whitingham, Robert, 148.6.
Whityngton, etc., Richard, 11.2; 181.2.
Wiclyff, Robert, 19.2.
Wilby, Lord, 117.10.
William, Marke, 44.2.
Williamsone, Clays, 145.4.
Willyam, Abbot of Bury St. Edmunds, petition by, 153.
Willysdon, Richard, and Anneys his wife, 233 *passim*.
Wilton, Viscount of, 61.4; Lady of, 110.2.
Wiltshire, 185.2; 241.6; Earl of, petition by, 224.

Windesore, etc., 6.11; 123.3; 148.10, 151.19; 159.13; Castle, 109.4; 157.12; 159.11; King's Chapel, 118.2.
Wisbeche (Wisbech, Cambridgeshire), 238.2.
Woborne, Iohn, 6.10.
Wodehill, Roger, 58.2; petition of, 166.
Wolley, Roger, 172.11.
Worcestre, etc., Bishop of, 79.2; 116.1; 122.42; Earl of, 232 *passim*.
Wortham (probably in Suffolk), parson of, 65.5.
Wright, Thomas, 216.11.
Wrotthyng, Town (probably Wrattin, Cambridgeshire, or Worthing, Sussex), 227.16.
Wyche, Hugh, indenture of, 240.
Wydevyll, Richard, petition of, 209.
Wyggemore, Iohan, 126.9.
Wyght, Isle of, petition of the citizens of, 218.
Wynbush (Wymbyssh), Nicol, 17.2.
Wynchestre, mayor and citizens of, 235 *passim*; Bishop of, 116 *passim*; 118.1; 122.41; 165.1; 171.1; 172.1; 173.1; 210.4; 235.3. See also Beaufort, Henry.
Wynchilse (Sussex), haven of, 187.18.
Wyndey, Manor (Cambridgeshire), 237.15.
Wyrall (Cheshire), 201.3; hundred of, 186.3.
Wythryng, West, prebend, 25.2.

Yonge, Thomas, 197.
York, Duke of, 218 *passim*; letters of, 126, 129; commission to, 136.

3eland (Zeeland, Netherlands), 217 *passim*.